Building a Peaceful Nation

Rochester Studies in African History and the Diaspora

Toyin Falola, Series Editor
The Jacob and Frances Sanger Mossiker Chair in the
Humanities and University Distinguished Teaching Professor
University of Texas at Austin

Recent Titles

Western Frontiers of African Art
Moyo Okediji

Women and Slavery in Nineteenth-Century Colonial Cuba
Sarah L. Franklin

*Ethnicity in Zimbabwe: Transformations
in Kalanga and Ndebele Societies, 1860–1990*
Enocent Msindo

Edward Wilmot Blyden and the Racial Nationalist Imagination
Teshale Tibebu

South Africa and the World Economy: Remaking Race, State, and Region
William G. Martin

*Enchanted Calvinism: Labor Migration, Afflicting Spirits,
and Christian Therapy in the Presbyterian Church of Ghana*
Adam Mohr

Ira Aldridge: Performing Shakespeare in Europe, 1852–1855
Bernth Lindfors

Blood on the Tides: "The Ozidi Saga" and Oral Epic Narratology
Isidore Okpewho

The Politics of Chieftaincy: Authority and Property in Colonial Ghana, 1920–1950
Naaborko Sackeyfio-Lenoch

Nigerian Pentecostalism
Nimi Wariboko

A complete list of titles in the Rochester Studies in African History and the Diaspora series may be found on our website, www.urpress.com.

Building a Peaceful Nation

Julius Nyerere and the Establishment of Sovereignty in Tanzania, 1960–1964

Paul Bjerk

UNIVERSITY OF ROCHESTER PRESS

Copyright © 2018 by Paul Bjerk

All Rights Reserved. Except as permitted under current legislation, no part of this work may be photocopied, stored in a retrieval system, published, performed in public, adapted, broadcast, transmitted, recorded, or reproduced in any form or by any means, without the prior permission of the copyright owner.

First published 2015
Reprinted in paperback and transferred to digital printing 2018

University of Rochester Press
668 Mt. Hope Avenue, Rochester, NY 14620, USA
www.urpress.com
and Boydell & Brewer Limited
PO Box 9, Woodbridge, Suffolk IP12 3DF, UK
www.boydellandbrewer.com

ISSN: 1092-5228
hardcover ISBN: 978-1-58046-505-2
paperback ISBN: 978-1-58046-935-7

Library of Congress Cataloging-in-Publication Data

Bjerk, Paul, author.
  Building a peaceful nation : Julius Nyerere and the establishment of sovereignty in Tanzania, 1960–1964 / Paul Bjerk.
    pages cm. — (Rochester studies in African history and the diaspora, ISSN 1092-5228 ; v. 63)
  "An earlier version of chapter 8 was published as 'Postcolonial Realism: Tanganyika's Foreign Policy under Nyerere, 1960–1963,' International Journal of African Historical Studies 44, no. 2 (2011): 215–46, and is reproduced with permission."
  Includes bibliographical references and index.
  ISBN 978-1-58046-505-2 (hardcover : alk. paper) 1. Nyerere, Julius K., 1922–1999. 2. TANU (Organization) 3. Self-determination, National—Tanzania. 4. Sovereignty. 5. Tanzania—Foreign relations—20th century. 6. Tanzania—History—1918–1964. 7. Postcolonialism—Tanzania. I. Title. II. Series: Rochester studies in African history and the diaspora ; v. 63.
  DT448.25.N9B54 2015
  320.1509678—dc23   2014040339

This publication is printed on acid-free paper.
Printed in the United States of America

A world seething with hatred is an intolerable place to live in. But we cannot reach the goal by hypocrisy or wishful thinking. We can only do it by honest thinking, honest talking and honest living.

—Julius K. Nyerere, 1952

I hope that in studying my "practices" people will be kind—but also honest. Tanzania can learn from my mistakes as well as from our aims and achievements.

—Julius K. Nyerere, 1997

Contents

	List of Illustrations	ix
	Acknowledgments	xi
	Abbreviations	xv
	Introduction	1
	Part 1: Searching for a Sovereign Discourse	
1	The Education of Julius Nyerere	23
2	Contemplating the Postcolony	34
	Part 2: Internal Sovereignty	
3	Independence and the Fear of Division	61
4	The Invention of Ujamaa	97
5	The Origins of Villagization	109
6	The 1964 Army Mutiny	131
7	The National Youth Service	155
	Part 3: External Sovereignty	
8	A Realist Foreign Policy	183
9	The Cold War and the Union Treaty	206
10	Contending with International Intrigue	228
	Conclusion	255
	Notes	271
	Bibliography	343
	Index	367

Illustrations

Figures

I.1	Map of East Africa	6
2.1	Julius Nyerere, Bibi Titi Mohamed, Sophia Kawawa, and Maria Nyerere	40
2.2	The Constitutional Conference, Dar es Salaam, March 1961	45
3.1	Julius Nyerere speaks at a political event, circa 1961	66
3.2	The independence cabinet, 1961	76
3.3	Rashidi Kawawa in his office	80
6.1	Oscar Kambona, Rashidi Kawawa, and Julius Nyerere with a military adviser	134
7.1	Julius Nyerere greets National Service (JKT) members	173
8.1	Julius Nyerere with Kwame Nkrumah, 1965	193
9.1	Julius Nyerere swears in Abeid Karume as first vice president, April 1964	226
10.1	National Service (JKT) demonstration against the "Western Plot" of November 1964	240
10.2	Julius Nyerere speaks at a TANU rally, 1964	244

Acknowledgments

A memory from November 1998, while chaperoning a group of Tanzanian journalism students on a trip to western Tanzania to visit camps for refugees fleeing neighboring countries at war: As we leave the town of Kigoma, on the shores of Lake Tanganyika, a pickup truck full of uniformed police comes barreling down the main street. The sight would be unusual in the United States, but not in many countries where budgets are tight and vehicles are in short supply. The pickup is clearly on a mission, not just fulfilling everyday tasks. It looks like news and I suggest the students go check it out. Several of them had some journalism experience, and it doesn't take them long to get some background: a Congolese fishing boat has landed on the Tanzanian shore, suspected of carrying armed men who are then taken in for questioning. There are dozens, probably hundreds, of fishing boats on the lake that day, not to mention the many refugees crossing into Tanzania from the Congo. I don't know how the police got word of this boat or its passengers, but clearly they quickly deciphered a minor transgression of Tanzania's boundaries.[1] This was the act of a sovereign state defending its borders. A banal sign to be sure, but nevertheless the sort of act that seems unexpected in Africa where the phrase "failed state" has been a disparaging epithet thrown about as a way of explaining away complex conflicts. Some states may be fairly labeled as having failed, but Tanzania is not one of them.

The publication of this book is a goal long awaited. My students and colleagues at Tumaini University in Iringa introduced me to Julius Nyerere, and I quickly came to understand what he meant for Africa, and also what he could mean to Americans. They brought me out to see "Mwalimu" Nyerere place a shield at the foot of Imani Changa's monument to Chief Mkwawa in the middle of the Iringa wilderness and then give a speech on education before a peasant crowd in the dusty village of Kalenga. Before I left Tanzania I made it my aim to write this book.

My parents deserve thanks for raising a young man both studious and adventurous. I also thank Arne and Mary Blomquist, Bishop Owdenburg Mdegella, Gary Langness, and the other folks at Augustana Lutheran Church in West Saint Paul who put me on the path to Tanzania in the first place, and Damian Ngandango, Albastino Mbembe, and all the great people at Ipogoro Lutheran Church. It was a life-changing journey that has blessed me a million times over. At the University of Wisconsin, I could not have asked for a better adviser than Thomas Spear, a profound scholar and a great guy. Florence Bernault, Michael Schatzberg, Harold Scheub, and Aili Tripp were likewise guides who opened my eyes in many ways. My fellow graduate students in Madison are too numerous to mention, but I probably spent the most time on topic (broadly defined) with Mukoma wa Ngugi, Daniel Magaziner, Lowell Brower, Ryan Ronnenberg, and Naaborko Sackeyfio. And I probably learned more from Robyn Autry than anyone else. Finally, the community at St. Mark's Lutheran Church in Madison kept me grounded through my PhD studies.

In Tanzania, Joseph Butiku, Johnson Rugoye, the Honorable Nimrod Mkono, and all the staff of the Mwalimu Nyerere Foundation took me in as one of their own and facilitated my research. Through them I was able to speak to dozens of participants in this history who had worked closely with Mwalimu Nyerere, and I wish to thank each one who was willing to speak to me. With Ron Aminzade and Kjell Bergh on this side of the Atlantic, it is my sincere hope that the foundation will be a cornerstone of civil society in East Africa. Likewise I wish to acknowledge the help of the staff at COSTECH in Dar es Salaam and the advice and guidance of Nestor Luanda, the late Haroub Othman, Gameliel Fimbo, Bertram Mapunda, Issa Shivji, and other scholars at the University of Dar es Salaam. And I extend sincere appreciation to Leander Schneider, James Brennan, Derek Peterson, Gregory Maddox, Gary Thomas Burgess, Kathryn DeLuna, Rhiannon Stephens, Jan Shetler, James Giblin and colleagues at Texas Tech University, Lynne Falwell, Karlos Hill, Sa'ad Abi-Hamad, Gretchen Adams, and Justin Hart all of whom commented crucially on the manuscript. I am thankful to Toyin Falola and the anonymous reviewers for the University of Rochester Press, as well as for the excellent work of the editorial staff. It goes without saying that any remaining shortcomings are mine.

In Tanzania, the Tanzania National Archives and the East Africana Collection at the University of Dar es Salaam; in the United Kingdom, Rhodes House, the Borthwick institute, the Edinburgh University Archives, and the magnificent Public Record Office; in Lisbon, the Arquivo Histórico Diplomatico and the Arquivo Histórico do Ultramar; in Ottawa, the Canadian Library and Archives; in the United States, the Hoover Institution at Stanford and the National Archives and Records Administration in College Park, Maryland—all were places where history has been preserved and is brought to life every day. I owe a debt of gratitude to their helpful staff members, such as TNA's idealistic Moshi Omari Mwinyimvua. I would also like to thank the myriad sources of financial support for this project: the Foreign Language Area Studies Program, the Fulbright Commission, the John F. Kennedy and Lyndon B. Johnson Libraries, the Worldwide University Network, the Scott Kloeck-Jenson Internship grant, the Blattberg

Writing Award, and the University of Wisconsin Departments of History and Latin American Studies. Texas Tech University has also been notably supportive of its junior faculty, underwriting two overseas research trips in my time here. Many thanks to Assah Mwembene at Tanzania Information Services, and Elikana Ngogo and Mercy Chang'a for their hospitality.

Finally, I thank my wife, Angella, for good ideas, good humor, and her love. For all those not mentioned, please know that I could go on like this forever. Thank you.

Abbreviations

AHD	Arquivo Histórico Diplomático, Lisbon
AHU	Arquivo Histórico Ultramarino, Lisbon
AMNUT	All-Muslim National Union of Tanganyika
ANC	African National Congress (separate parties in South Africa, Zambia, and Tanganyika)
ASP	Afro-Shirazi Party
BI	Borthwick Institute of Historical Research, York
BStU	Stasi Records Office, Berlin
CCM	Chama cha Mapinduzi
CIA	Central Intelligence Agency (United States)
CUF	Civic United Front
EASCO	East African Common Services Organization
EUA	Edinburgh University Archives, Edinburgh
FRELIMO	Frente de Liberação de Moçambique
HI	Hoover Institution and Russian Government Archive, Stanford University, Stanford, CA
ICFTU	International Confederation of Free Trade Unions
JFK	John F. Kennedy Library, Boston, MA
JKT	Jeshi la Kujenga Taifa (National Youth Service)
LAC	Library and Archives Canada, Ottawa
LBJ	Lyndon B. Johnson Library, Austin, TX
MANU	Mozambique African National Union
MNF	Mwalimu Nyerere Foundation, Dar es Salaam
NARA	National Archives and Records Administration, College Park, MD

NATO	North Atlantic Treaty Organization
NEC	National Executive Committee
OAU	Organization of African Unity
PAFMECA	Pan-African Freedom Movement of East and Central Africa
PAFMECSA	Pan-African Freedom Movement of East, Central, and Southern Africa
PRO	Public Record Office, National Archives, London
RH	Rhodes House, Oxford
SAPMO	Stiftung Archiv der Parteien und Massenorganisationen der Deutschen Demokratischen Republik, Bundesarchiv, Berlin
TAA	Tanganyika African Association
TANU	Tanganyika African National Union
TBC	Tanganyika Broadcasting Corporation
TFL	Tanganyika Federation of Labour
TNA	National Archives, Dar es Salaam
TNS	Tanganyika National Society
TYL	TANU Youth League
UDENAMO	União Democrática Nacional de Moçambique
UNAR	Union Nationale Rwandaise
UNIP	United National Independence Party (Zambia)
URTZ	United Republic of Tanganyika and Zanzibar
UTP	United Tanganyika Party
ZANU	Zimbabwean African National Union
ZAPU	Zimbabwean African People's Union
ZNP	Zanzibar National Party

Introduction

> The morning of Monday, January 20th, was grim and the hot heavy weather, without even a murmur of breeze, didn't help. It felt like the whole city was holding its breath waiting to hear what had happened. Nobody knew.
>
> —Lady Marion Chesham, 1964

A City of Rumors

On January 19, 1964, Tanganyika's president, Julius Nyerere, lingered at the statehouse, confident that the immediate crisis of the previous week's revolution in Zanzibar had passed. Most of his cabinet and several of the Zanzibari revolutionary leaders lounged on the terrace in the cool ocean breeze on this warm tropical evening. They drank beer, thinking big and making plans, the dream of revolution and the taste of freedom that it offered alive in their imaginations. "Nyerere seemed in no hurry to return to this pledge session and we talked for almost an hour." He relaxed with Ambassador William Leonhart in the living room at the former colonial governor's mansion, sizing up the situation. They gossiped. Leonhart motioned through the terrace doors to the silhouette of self-proclaimed "Field Marshal" John Okello, the clueless young hero of the island putsch, who had been recruited into action by the Youth League of the fractious Zanzibari nationalist party, the Afro-Shirazi Party (ASP).[1] In the clipped cadences of American diplomatic reporting, the ambassador narrated: "Asked Nyerere whether he was sane. Nyerere said yes. He quickly added that he had 'no depth.' He was 'common policeman' who had suddenly found himself in middle of Zanzibar situation and had no idea of what to do next. They would keep him in Tanganyika for a few days, cool him off, and try to give him some useful ideas."[2]

For all their fire and fearlessness, the Zanzibari revolutionaries, like new parents, suddenly had responsibilities. A little bewildered, they sought assurance from a trusted authority. They "kept turning to Tanganyika. Karume had been here once; Hanga, Babu and others several times during the week. They needed help, guidance, and emergency supplies." Tanganyika under Nyerere had established an orderly government comprising Europeans, Indians, and Africans, its grassroots political party woven into local society throughout the nation. It was a harbor of peace in a Cold War storm that threatened to blow the small "African Cuba" just off its shore into a torrential squall that could drown ideological disputes in a racialized class war between aristocratic landowners who claimed Arab descent and plantation workers whose mainland grandparents had been brought to the island as slaves.

"This is not a communist revolution," Nyerere assured the American diplomat, with a subtle note of warning. A "communist revolution may yet come to Zanzibar but it will be another revolution if it does." The Americans, keen to avoid such a course of events, sought to support a British lead to buttress East African governments and shore up a nationalist government in Zanzibar. Nyerere's concern was to maintain local African control over political developments in Zanzibar and ward off the American urge to intervene. In a hushed tone that would not carry to the terrace, Nyerere told Leonhart "that he did not think we should rely too much on British"; the ambassador further noted: "Zanzibar situation still in early phase and he was trying deal with most urgent problems. He had sent Tanganyika police to Zanzibar to help reestablish order."

That same night, with much of the Tanganyikan police force in Zanzibar, order in Dar es Salaam disintegrated. The army mutinied. They were frustrated with the presence of British officers two years after independence and demanded better pay and immediate Africanization of the officer corps. Locking up both British and African officers, they took over an unguarded capital city. They came knocking at Nyerere's door at midnight to find his wife and children and an irate mother who scolded them for their presumptuous indiscipline. The president, however, had already been sequestered, according to a prearranged emergency procedure, across the harbor in a Catholic mission.[3]

The mutineers, it was said, "had taken over Dar es Salaam lock, stock, and barrel," and the police did not know what was happening.[4] The postcolonial woes of the Tanganyikan state, so new and unformed, its people possessing a vivid array of imaginations, gave birth to a rumor mill of particular power and influence. "Word got round," reported a British resident, "that Julius had been arrested and that it served him right because he was no good as a President as he uses all the money for himself."

> My ayah [housemaid] told me this—that she had heard this going round in the staff quarters and she felt the same way too. I told her how Bloody stupid she and the rest were. J [Julius Nyerere] was not like that. All the money went on them and he was not the sort of person to squander money on himself and that she and the rest of Tanganyika were Jolly lucky to have such a man in power. There were many more similar comments made by Africans and it would appear that given the slightest change they too would have started to rebel.[5]

As the surreal day of the mutiny progressed, she continued, "the rumour got round that it was Kambona himself who was behind it all!!!" The writer was a friend of Lady Marion Chesham, a British-American widow who was a member of the Tanganyikan parliament. Like many expatriates, the writer was deeply suspicious of the clumsy ambitions of Nyerere's minister of foreign affairs, Oscar Kambona, whom they felt would steer the country into racial division and administrative collapse. The idea that Nyerere alone was the central figure binding Tanganyika's political class together engendered a vision of the nation. This vision, in the early years of independence, was for many people cognitively inseparable from his person. Thus, Lady Chesham's friend concluded, "if J had not broadcast on Tuesday night hell would have broken loose all over the country." A British diplomat voiced the same worry about possible chaos to his superiors in London: "Dar es Salaam is still a city of rumours," and if whispers of police cooperation in the mutiny were true, the "danger is that country might be without any security force whatsoever which can be relied upon."[6] For his part, Nyerere scolded the anxious inhabitants of the city, telling them that the rumors threatened to do more damage than the mutiny itself. "In addition to the incidents themselves," he said, "the rumours which spread have raised all sorts of doubts about the stability of our country and our Government."[7] He set up an undercover "rumour-busting squad" to apprehend the sources of false rumors.[8]

Where some Europeans sought someone "stronger" to wield the force of government for their protection and Americans saw Cold War forces at work, local residents took hold of rumors of a more immediate nature, debating Nyerere's personal morality and the shaky legitimacy of the new government. Rumors find traction where their logic presents a context of immediate concern to the hearer.[9] In seeking the reality behind a rumor, the hearer considers its context. With attention focused on the veracity of the rumor, the accuracy of its context goes easily unnoticed. Thus, a persistent rumor reverses its own empirical logic; the rumor effects a "proof" of its own context. A context—that is actually much broader, complex, and questionable than the contested "facts" of the rumor—seems objective in reference to even the most perfidious murmurings.[10] Knowledge in a time of rapid and bewildering change is therefore uncertain. Facts mean something different to everyone. In Uganda, Prime Minister Milton Obote, himself beset by ethnic intrigue undermining his nationalist efforts, told the American ambassador that he suspected prominent ethnic leaders had been the instigators of the mutiny. "Speculating about causes Obote said he had feeling for some time all was not well in Tanganyika. He referred to the Fundikira and Marealle cases and implied that this could have had influence on troops which were attached to these Chiefs, a theory I have heard expressed elsewhere."[11]

In reality, loyalties to these prominent colonial-era chiefs had little to do with it. Obote brought his own context to bear on the very different situation that Nyerere faced. Obote's thesis of chiefly rebellion resonated with others eager to blame "tribalism" for complex conflicts. Tribe, in the twentieth century, was largely a colonial construct, based loosely on older cultural identities; chiefs with colonial salaries were given authority over ethnically identified segments of the population. Some colonial chieftaincies were sheer invention; others built on preexisting offices. In both cases their employment in the colonial state fundamentally changed the nature of their status and authority.[12] In Tanganyika, chiefs were not a source of subversion. A strong contingent of the mutineers later arrested came from Iringa, where the local Hehe chief, Adam Sapi Mkwawa, was Nyerere's strongest supporter among the former colonial chiefs. Chagga Chief Thomas Marealle in Kilimanjaro, bitter but powerless when his position of authority was eliminated with the coming of independence, had just lost his lawsuit against Nyerere's government when retroactive legislation was passed denying compensation to chiefs who had formerly been in the pay of the colonial Native Authority.[13] Nyamwezi chief Abdallah Fundikira in Tabora, who had been a principled opponent, proclaimed his loyalty to the nation in a parliamentary session by echoing Nyerere's own most deeply held convictions: "If there is a lesson to be learnt here, Sir, it has been one big lesson that we have to come even closer together and strengthen our unity."[14]

Chief Fundikira took his cue from the fearful lack of unity among Tanganyika's recently independent neighbors. Tanganyikans were painfully aware of instability all around them. Independence had washed over much of the continent in less than a decade, leaving a remnant group of hostile states ruled by white-minority governments in southern Africa. This regional context was a constant point of reference for Tanganyika's leadership as they sought to discern their own future. Party stalwart Bibi Titi Mohamed echoed Chief Fundikira's point by making a comparison that preoccupied many Africans and Europeans—to the Congo, where troops mutinied in the days following independence in 1960, thereby inaugurating a rapid spiral of chaotic conflict and foreign intervention that was still ravaging the country nearly four years later. With her own country's stability restored after the mutiny, Bibi Titi patriotically proclaimed the sovereignty of the Tanganyikan state in Parliament, contrasting its authority to the situation in Congo:[15] "Our soldiers, who we entrusted with our weapons, should not think of Tanganyika as a country that can be played with ... a country to turn to their desires like they see in other places. They should not think like that. When they think like that one thinks of the danger that now reigns in Congo that has not ended, people are just dying. And this was the goal of that day."[16]

Crawford Young observed that the dilemmas fueling the Congo Crisis and undergirding the authoritarian state that arose "exemplify broader African patterns."[17] Despite the violence of the Zanzibari Revolution, which eventually led to its union with Tanganyika in April 1964 creating the new country of "Tanzania," Tanzania's story lacks Congo's convulsive ferocity. But its quest for sovereignty entailed the same underlying issues as those that Young laid out for Congo. Maintaining a perilously thin veil of sovereign authority during the mutiny, Nyerere's government remained intact and could credibly claim that the British intervention that ended the mutiny came at its sovereign invitation. The government's cautious response derived from observing neighboring countries and the perils they implied. Of these early years Nyerere recalled, "The general concern was to take over the instruments of political power and to consolidate political control of the country."[18]

The task at hand for the newly independent countries of Africa was to establish sovereignty, which meant a government empowered to be the ultimate authority within the country in place of the former colonial power, and recognized as the legitimate representative of that country in the international community. The possibility of democracy depended on the establishment of sovereignty. The tragic irony, in most countries, was that democracy was sacrificed for the sake of sovereignty; but it is hard to imagine any other course. All of the newly independent countries of sub-Saharan Africa went through a period of undemocratic state consolidation in the 1960s. For some, this became a violent process; for others, one of cynical patronage. Tanzania was one of the few states that maintained a modicum of democratic process with an enforced ideological unity rather than corrupt patronage or violent coercion. Nyerere put up with the personality cult that built up around him, but mocked it, tolerating merely "mwalimu" (teacher) as a humble title derived from his early career as an educator. He insisted that sovereignty properly resided in institutions run by representatives subject to elections, not individual leaders. He and his colleagues navigated the postcolonial landscape of the Cold War, creating new institutions and modifying old ones, in order to build a peaceful nation.

The Regional Context: Decolonization and the Cold War

In the early 1960s among Tanganyika's neighbors, a new regional order was under construction as the wave of decolonization gathered strength due to both increasing pressure in the colonies themselves and weakening support for empire among the metropolitan powers.[19] To the west, the Congo was the first to become independent, in June 1960, but was soon engulfed in violent chaos after the harried departure of the Belgian government gave way to ruthless Cold War competition and violent internal intrigue.[20]

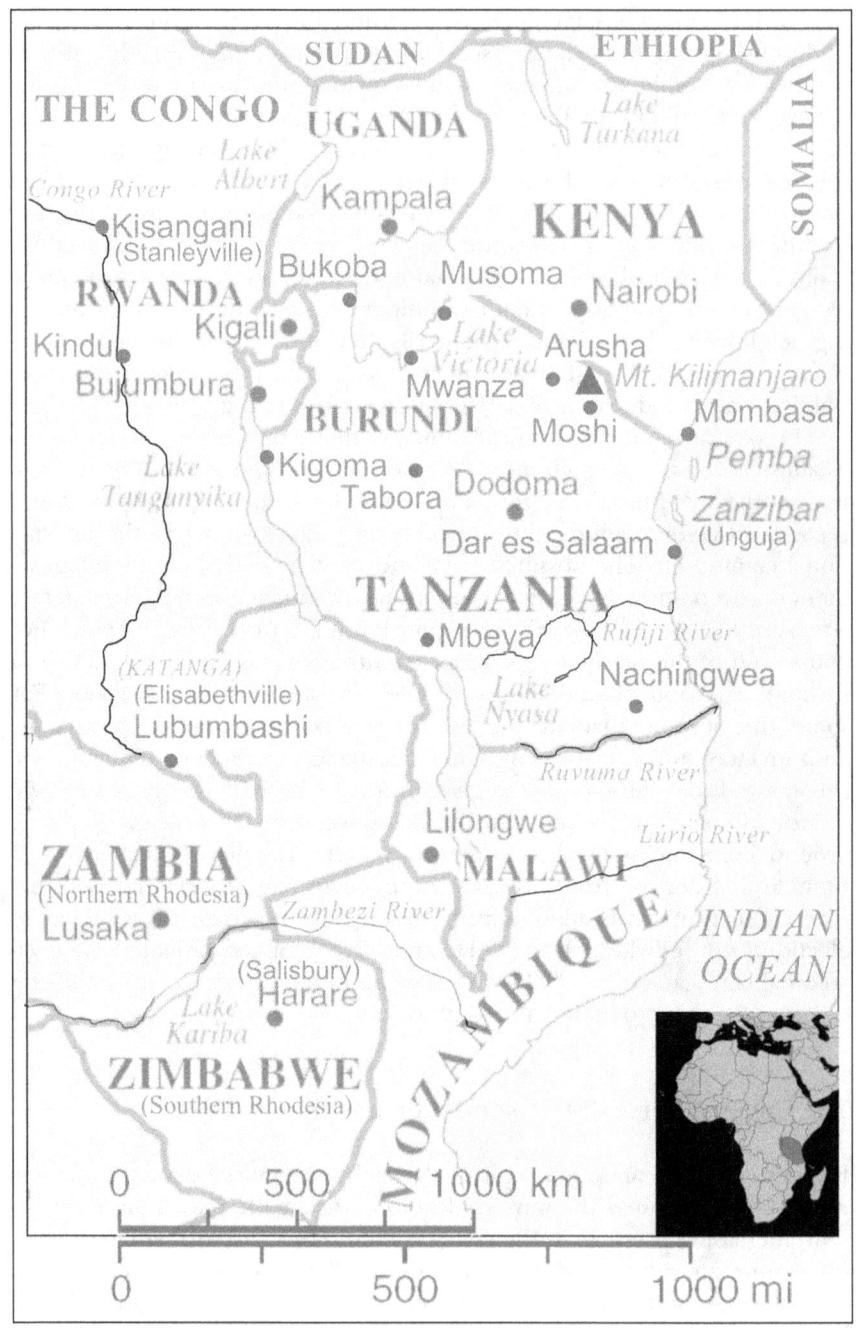

Figure I.1. Map of East Africa. Adapted from United Nations Department of Peacekeeping Operations. © United Nations.

To the south, white settler communities held on to vast territories and dug in their heels against decolonization or democratization, receiving quiet support from the United States because of their strategic utility in the Cold War. Fascist Portugal could not countenance the dissolution of its empire; its remaining colonies in Mozambique and Angola were emblems of long-vanished prestige.[21] Northern Rhodesia, with its small settler presence, steadily began a metamorphosis into independent Zambia with support from Tanganyika. Meanwhile, Southern Rhodesian whites began to see themselves as anticolonial rebels, ready to declare independence from Her Majesty's Government in Britain in order to defend their undemocratic control over the country.[22] All the white settler regimes had the moral and military support of South Africa as it tried to fortify a "cordon sanitaire" to block the tide of majority rule in Africa.[23] South Africa's relatively large white minority kept a firm grip on political and economic power through the policy of strict segregation known as apartheid, violently repressing the articulate and increasingly militant movement representing the black majority there.[24]

Closer to home, Ugandans took uncertain steps toward independence amid deep suspicions between various indigenous communities about what sort of power structure might replace the colonial state.[25] Kenya, to its north, featured prominently in Tanganyika's regional perspective. There, a well-connected settler community had built a nascent industrial economy atop a strong agricultural base while an independence movement of literate politicians like Jomo Kenyatta advocated for local cultural agency.[26] Politicians were taken aback by a violent peasant insurgency and the brutal colonial response that sought to cleanse "Mau Mau" from the Kenyan psyche.[27] The rebellion's violence had created deep rifts in Kenyan society, often marked by ethnic distinctions, but also dividing ethnically homogeneous communities.[28] Ethnicities were not so much groups of people related by blood or even language; rather, they were communities of belonging. Ethnic identity offered a sense of place, and therefore potential benefits and protection in the fluid social environment of East Africa where state boundaries had been only recently drawn by colonial powers. Ethnicities were preeminently political communities bound by an ideology of distant kinship.[29] Emerging from prison as a unifier, the charismatic Kenyatta cunningly shaped ethnic loyalties into a wary consensus that calmed the Kenyan political scene. Nyerere saw Kenyatta as a promising partner in regional integration.[30]

With more trepidation, Nyerere monitored the deteriorating situation in Ruanda-Urundi, the Belgian trusteeship. As in Kenya, the struggle for independence brought with it political violence along lines that blurred ethnicity and class in a colonial practice that had marked an educated Tutsi elite to govern a rural Hutu peasantry. This division was only heightened by Belgian interference as independence approached. In newly independent Rwanda, Gregoire Kayibanda's Hutu power movement violently persecuted Tutsi citizens while winning elections to form a Hutu-dominated government. In Burundi, the assassination of Tutsi Prince Louis Rwagasore, who had campaigned for ethnic harmony, allowed a military controlled by Michel Micombero to ensure Tutsi control of the postcolonial state. Thousands of refugees from both countries streamed into neighboring countries, with outbreaks of violence foreshadowing the subsequent deadly clashes. In the early 1970s, Burundi sent tens of thousands of Hutu refugees to Tanzania to escape persecution and worse at the hands of the Tutsi-controlled government. Two decades later, thousands of Rwandan refugees, both Hutu and Tutsi, fled to Tanzania to escape genocidal mobs and paramilitary forces encouraged and armed by the Hutu-controlled government in Rwanda, while a Tutsi-led rebel group advanced across the country.[31]

Despite their proximate adversaries, such local conflicts gained traction in the midst of pressures resulting from the global conflict known as the Cold War. The United States and the Soviet Union both considered a direct confrontation tantamount to suicide because of their nuclear arsenals. Instead, they competed for client nations to expand their spheres of influence. From an ideological standpoint both opposed colonialism, but in practice both sought dependencies under a thin veil of nominal sovereignty. Each perceived a zero-sum game in which every client of the other represented a loss of influence. For the newly independent nations of Africa and Southeast Asia, this competition led to intense pressures to identify themselves as loyal to one side or the other, while the superpowers attempted to manipulate their internal politics. Sometimes this meddling came in the form of political demands in exchange for foreign aid. Sometimes it came in the form of direct intervention in local politics—paying off particular politicians and military leaders, arming rebels, fomenting dissent, and occasionally instigating a coup d'état. Many newly independent countries proclaimed their refusal to align themselves exclusively with either side, but very few were able to refuse alliance with the Americans or the Soviets.[32]

China's ability to cut its own course, in addition to its consistent ideological support for postcolonial liberation, made it an attractive Cold War patron for Tanzania. But Chinese support offered no escape from Cold War pressures. The Soviets were threatened by China's independence, while Western policymakers saw Chinese communism as just as much a threat to their interests as Soviet expansion, even though China's relative poverty meant that it could not be a decisive player in the 1960s. In Africa as in Southeast Asia, the Cold War was an ever-present threat to the sovereignty of the postcolonial nations.

During this period, a paternalist "constellation of meanings, images, ideas, and values" inserted stereotypes of an unstable and irrational Third World into American policy, especially toward the resource-rich Congo.[33] The perception of Congo's turmoil found expression in rumors that its first prime minister, Patrice Lumumba, was emotionally unstable. These cultivated rumors offered a justification for intervention.[34] Lumumba was not so much "insane"—which is how some American diplomats described him—as inexplicable to outsiders who saw political competition in the country as a delusional "comic opera."[35] At stake was not Lumumba's emotional life. The real issue was more specific and political. Lumumba's independence represented uncertainty for US policy. The Western desire to "get rid of Lumumba" signaled not only a superpower struggle for influence in the Congo but also a struggle between Lumumba's seeking Congolese autonomy and outside powers' seeking a client state.[36] It was a struggle between sovereignty and neocolonialism. The end of this particular drama is well known. Lumumba was brutally killed at the hands of political enemies in the breakaway province of Katanga, with the quiet assent of outgoing American president Dwight Eisenhower, and Lumumba's body was dissolved in acid.[37]

Both the negative assessment of Lumumba's mental state and the image of the Congo as a "comic opera" were tropes of American diplomatic discourse that served as justification for intervention.[38] Echoing the "colonial knowledge" of "un-civilization, pre-history, and primitive knowledge" that justified imperial control elsewhere, rumors surrounding the Congo Crisis shaped European and American reactions to the events of 1964 in Tanganyika.[39] For Americans and Europeans, the Congo comparison hinted that Africa was a place of irrational violence. Lady Chesham's friend fretted, "Everyone is now wondering what sort of punishment the mutineers must have and nothing short of High Treason will do otherwise it would be only too easy to do such a thing again and it could turn into another Congo."[40]

References to "the old Congo flavour" became common during the mutiny, not only for Europeans but for Africans as well.[41] In Africa, the political disasters accompanying Congolese independence demonstrated the dangers of the Cold War and its neocolonial logic. In the midst of the mutiny in Dar es Salaam, the Congolese quagmire loomed as a fearful precedent for the Tanganyikan leadership. A barrage of headlines from the Congo conflict filled the *Tanganyika Standard* in the early 1960s, impending a similar bloody fate for Tanganyika.[42] Ethnic violence in Zanzibar was attributed to the influence of the Congolese war bleeding into coastal politics.[43] On the mainland, many questioned Nyerere's position that people of all races should be eligible for citizenship, and foreign intrigue in the Congo reinforced those doubts. It was the Congo, more than any other country, that represented the potential disaster of independence and its real and very personal dangers. Its fundamental weakness, in the eyes of Tanganyikan politicians, was its disorderly lack of unity that had made it vulnerable to the worst of Cold War intrigues and undermined its newly won sovereignty. A close friend and colleague of Nyerere, Vedastus Kyaruzi, who served as a key foreign policy adviser, recalled the seeds of self-doubt that the news coming from the Congo planted in a new generation of leaders in Tanganyika: "Is it possible that the Congo situation could happen here? It was terrifying. The Congo situation was really frightening for us, we each individually and collectively, we feared what was going to happen in this country and if we were going to make a mess of things like they did in the Congo."[44]

Kyaruzi tells of visiting Nyerere and finding him "extremely tense" as he contemplated the Congolese situation. A medical doctor by profession, Kyaruzi felt embarrassed and thought it better to leave. "I had never seen him so tense." Then Nyerere abruptly asked him before he could go, "Doctor, shall we succeed?" Kyaruzi told him that in the Congo there were many different leaders, and they were all fighting for power, but in Tanganyika Nyerere was alone and the whole country was behind him and his ideal of unity. Nyerere, in existential consideration of his uncertain fate, reflecting perhaps on the brutal end of Lumumba, sang a verse from the coastal bridal song: "Don't cry, baby, don't cry; you yourself chose, you yourself decided."[45]

In Tanganyika, as in the Congo, government was intensely identified with one person.[46] Kyaruzi reminded Nyerere that he was the legitimizing figure who symbolized the state's stability. Another friend of Nyerere, Marion Chesham, saw Nyerere's role much as Kyaruzi did: "You are the personification of the best in Tanganyika, its ideals and its hopes. . . . You (like it or not) are the cement that binds all this together and makes it possible."[47] Lady Chesham was an American who had married into British nobility and become an estate holder in colonial Tanganyika. She had been elected to the colonial legislative council as an advocate for the independence movement, and continued as a member of parliament in the new state. Chesham was a symbol and enthusiastic supporter of Nyerere's belief that race had no place in politics.

Nyerere's ability to exude a mature, sophisticated presence in the context of postcolonial Africa was a key aspect of his ability to uphold Tanganyika's autonomy in the face of foreign intervention. This myopic personalization of national politics became a feature of postcolonial Africa.[48] The reliance on personalistic rule related directly to the uncertain condition of the new nation-states. The ephemeral new nation contained in the old colonial boundaries was bound by loyalty, whether of fear or affection, to its founding president. At the moment of independence, the nation was little more than a colonial phantom. Government institutions were, in Nyerere words, "still tinged with colonialism" and bore no particular legitimacy beyond their efficacy. The state's administration rested in the hands of the president, upon whom legitimacy depended and in whom the citizenry trusted to reform the institutions of government. Outside powers were aware of this as well and understood that if a friendly agent occupied the seat of government, the country could be as acquiescent as a colonial dependency.

The 1964 mutiny of the Tanganyika Rifles, like the Congo Crisis of 1960, generated multiple discourses of African sovereignty. For Europeans, the chaotic events reinforced prejudices that Africans were incompetent at self-government, which justified foreign intervention. For Africans, such events demonstrated two specific dangers of independence: violent struggle for control of the postcolonial state and foreign interference undermining governmental authority. Both domestic and foreign pressures impeded the government's establishment of authority over the institutional geography of the state. The Congo's immediate explosion highlighted the constraints of postcolonial sovereignty. These found expression in the conversations of diplomats and politicians in Tanzania, but rarely as explicit statements about political theory. More often opinions about sovereignty hid in metaphors and assumptions that indicated the broader interpretive contexts influencing people's actions. Such manipulations of meaning constituted the political negotiations shaping postcolonial East Africa.

The Theoretical Argument

A journalist's recent portrayal of political turmoil in Mali contrasts the country's luminous medieval past with an impoverished and unstable present: "The proud home of an ancient civilization has never quite managed to maintain itself as a sovereign state."[49] The writer goes on to highlight the theme of the failed state, so prominent in policy and scholarly circles.[50] "With little effort, criminal and terrorist groups can seize countries, or parts of them—just as narcotraffickers have effectively taken over West African states like Guinea Bissau." Although recent years have seen the consolidation of power in postwar countries like Liberia or Rwanda and the expansion of democracy in more peaceful places like Ghana or Zambia, African nations have faced considerable instability since independence, and this general impression remains in place today. An influential scholarly voice on state power in Africa went so far as to claim that "no large African country can be said to have consolidated control over its entire territory."[51]

In the case of Tanzania, I disagree. Legitimate government institutions extend into every corner of Tanzanian territory, and its borders are well established and defended. It is a sovereign and functioning nation-state with a common language, a largely literate people, basic policing, the rule of law, a well-disciplined military, regular elections with real choices, a lively and critical press, and a growing economy with passable roads, health care, and educational facilities throughout the country. Most who have visited Tanzania would comment on the robust nature of its sovereignty, but such observers would be remiss to ignore the everyday (and occasionally violent) corruption at all levels of the state, the obvious judicial favoritism granted to one dominant political party, and the frustration of many citizens with governmental indifference. Notwithstanding such serious shortcomings, the Tanzanian government is stable and effective within its territory and has made a significant impact on regional issues despite its limited military and economic capacity. These internal and external capacities are the basic identifying features of sovereignty.

Decolonization implied the subsequent establishment of sovereignty, but this process was not automatic. As John Kelly and Martha Kaplan have noted, "Decolonization was also the superimposition of something, the reconfiguration of local civil hierarchies into the terms of a new, global plan for political order."[52] Kelly and Kaplan start from Benedict Anderson's insights, and credit him with "annihilating shared descent definitions of nation" and demonstrating that "the nation is first of all imagined, ideal, and realized in codependence with a state."[53] Leaving aside Anderson's specifics of print and Protestantism, a nation—in Anthony Smith's sense of a named human community identifying with a shared culture bound to a territory—is a product of historical forces provoking communal loyalties.[54] Conflict can contribute to this process, but national identity is generally the long-term legacy of enduring states. As James Brennan and Ronald Aminzade have recently shown, Tanzanian national identity emerged out of ongoing tensions between inclusive and exclusive means of defining postcolonial citizenship.[55] This tends to be a process fraught with conflict, but unlike many of the countries created from the decolonization process in the mid-twentieth century, Tanzania has been internally peaceful since independence with a robust and activist civilian government.

Achille Mbembe's observation that in modern states any "distinction between a state of war and a state of peace is increasingly illusory" is well taken.[56] Critics of the Tanzanian government point to its forceful repression of dissent justified largely by its persistent military mobilization in support of the liberation of southern Africa.[57] So my definition of peace is minimalist: it is the absence of organized violence affecting large segments of the population inside the country. The unexamined use of the ideal trajectories implied in terms like "peace," "democracy," or "development" as analytical reference points for African states gives rise to contradictory demands for both untrammeled local autonomy and undisputed central authority without the acknowledgment that every state is a

Introduction 13

compromise between the two. Mbembe suggests that an Orientalist construction of Africa as an "abject" continent representing "absolute otherness" is paired with analytical "presentism" that attempts to "measure the gap between what the continent is and what we are told it *should* be."[58] This "discourse of the gap and the lack" coincides with Susan Geiger's critique of a "theory of lacks and absences" that minimizes the active role played by Tanzanian nationalists in constituting the new state.[59] Mbembe and Geiger both highlight the gendered implications of these emasculating tendencies, in terms not only of neocolonial paternalism but also of the reified imaginary of violent resistance constituting the defining trope for African agency during decolonization.[60] Mbembe's thesis throws into sharp relief the contradiction between tropes of heroic rebellion and normative visions of political stability.

Regarding the postcolonial state, Mbembe goes on to assert that its coercive power "compels its subjects to rearticulate that power" by participating in it, and thereby ratifying it.[61] The irony of this "conviviality" between rulers and ruled is that "this very process of ratification becomes itself the site for a subtle de-legitimation of state power," and therefore the central analytical trope of "resistance" proves to be enmeshed in a cultural complex that is not easily dismantled into opposing forces of authoritarianism and democratization. Within these complex discourses, Mbembe sought instead to identify "the conditions of possibility for the African subject to exercise his or her own sovereignty."[62] The Tanzanian case suggests that political leaders can intervene productively in this cultural complex and thereby mitigate some of the more baleful conditions of excess, vulgarity, and impotence in Mbembe's postcolony.

This consideration results from two major arguments, with the presumption that both were inherently cross-cultural endeavors: (1) Nyerere's government established Tanzania as a credibly sovereign nation both internally and externally, and this was the essential pragmatic task for the leadership of a newly decolonized country; and (2) The fundamental tactic of the Tanzanian leadership in establishing this sovereignty was the manipulation of discourse, including its production, negotiation, and suppression. I propose that these two arguments provide an appropriate paradigm for analyzing the politics of postcolonial states marked by their scarce military and economic capacities. In Tanzania, the multifaceted establishment of sovereignty demarcated the range of legitimate political discourse and anchored a constrained democratic practice.[63] These provided the foundation of a stable state and the basis for a new nation.

The first argument is a relatively conventional accounting of sovereignty, which in its formal sense describes a bureaucratic government that is recognized and empowered as the ultimate authority within a defined territory and acknowledged as the legitimate representative of that territory and its people in the international community. These interlaced internal and external dimensions find echo in the indigenous and foreign cultural groundings of sovereignty in postcolonial African states.[64] The fundamental questions of decolonization address these interacting realms generated by the rapid European conquest of the territory, its equally rapid demise, and the extent of African agency in between. What followed was the need to conform the new nations to an international system built around a constitutive ideology of sovereignty.[65] While it is reasonable to argue that the fiction of the unitary state places too much emphasis on "order and authority over the less predictable qualities of democratic freedom," the sovereign state's need for security cannot be easily dismissed.[66] Siba Grovogui responds to such critiques by noting that the long history of conflict and oppression in human society can hardly be blamed on the modern system of sovereign states, and that the practical implications of abandoning sovereignty would only imply an alternative (and probably less democratic) global power structure.[67] From a pragmatic standpoint, sovereignty is the inescapable ideological foundation of political order in the world today.[68]

In Tanzania, politicians referred to "territorial integrity and sovereignty" as *mamlaka ya nchi*, literally "authority of the country."[69] This was a commonsense translation of a word rooted in a modern European notion of authority vested in a territorial representative (individual or institutional), but not necessarily one defined by democratic election or ideological legitimacy.[70] My focus is on the qualities of "empirical" sovereignty as a practice of power rather than the mere presence or absence of "juridical" sovereignty as a convention of the international order. While juridical sovereignty certainly serves as a tool for the broader purpose of establishing robust sovereign authority, it can just as easily present a conforming facade that masks a lack of internal or external authority. We also find that even empirical sovereignty is a more ambiguous status than it first appears, one rooted in the subtle manipulation of a public political discourse shared by elites and peasants alike. Sovereignty, Cynthia Weber proposes, refers to no "natural" state—a shared culture or popular consensus—that can be signified; rather, it is simulated through discursive practice. "What become important," she argues, "are the signs of sovereignty—the ability to access the code of sovereignty."[71]

This leads into the second argument: an underlying thesis concerning what Elizabeth Ermarth identified as "agency in the discursive condition."[72] It is a power that one of Nyerere's grade school teachers called *njia ya midomo tu*, "the way of just the lips"—the ability to shape perceptions of the world through words and rituals.[73] Actions, like words, are most powerful in what they communicate. Discursive agency is a limited and fragmentary power that undermines standard biographical portrayals of uniquely influential leaders like those populating heroic narratives of African independence. It is not merely the ability to persuade on any particular issue, but rather something closer to Mbembe's concept of the "conviviality" between rulers and subjects who share a common imaginary of power.[74] In Tanzania, this recalls Cranford Pratt's description of Nyerere's ability "to manipulate the circumstances of politics in order to lead his people to moral perceptions which as yet they only imperfectly comprehend."[75] Similarly, Chambi Chachage more recently noted that Nyerere's primary legacy lies not in a particular policy but "in generating passionate public debate aimed at bringing positive social and economic change."[76]

We must recall, however, that public figures articulate a language already shaped in institutional propaganda, political rhetoric, and countless private conversations. The core proposition in the idea of discourse is that meaning is created by the distinguishing of differences, such as happens in conversation, and structures of meanings define entire ways of thinking. A word's meaning has no permanent anchor, nor do discourses have any fixed structures.[77] Meanings and discourses emerge from interactions manipulated on multiple levels by multiple actors, and no one is fully in control of their use or effect.[78] Nor, as Mbembe's thesis suggests, are discursive debates the sole province of elite politicians. Ermarth argues that this fracturing of an individual's effect on history does not eliminate personal agency, but rather requires a more complex evaluation that necessitates a reevaluation of the philosophical underpinnings of modernity, including such articles of faith as democracy itself.[79] Given this context, Nyerere provides a case study of a politician's discursive agency.[80] But we must keep in mind that everyone, with varying degrees of impact, was seeking to exercise discursive agency. Numerous scholars have demonstrated that unlettered peasants and urban housewives fundamentally shaped the discourse of Tanzanian nationalism to which elites like Nyerere had to respond.[81] Collectively they created the context within which politicians had to operate.

In order to provide context, most chapters in this book include an extended digression on broad cultural discourses that left explicit traces in people's perceptions and interactions with the events covered by the chapter.[82] Whether the influence of Utilitarianism on Nyerere's education, the perceived functioning of ethnic organizations, or the constructed memories of the roles of youth, these are all mere sketches of multifarious attitudes and beliefs. They are not meant to be authoritative, but rather suggestive of what Mbembe called the "time of entanglement" that accompanied decolonization. This perspective concurs with "the cultural turn" in the social sciences.[83] The approach here derives from Peter Ekeh's paradigm of "civic" and "primordial" publics, building on Clifford Geertz's anthropological view of postcolonial societies.[84] The key to Ekeh's proposition is that these categories are not exclusive but integrated, overlapping, and constitutive. As they inevitably engaged these cultural discourses as the basis for political action, Nyerere and his colleagues, through their policies, introduced novel iterations of the "socially routinized" activities noted in theories of practice.[85]

Both sovereignty and discursive agency, with their robust theoretical literatures, serve as useful analytical categories for the postcolonial state. They are not deployed here as policy prescriptions, or as qualities that can be measured to evaluate "success" by any definition. The question is not the presence or absence of sovereignty per se, but its ongoing negotiation in the internal and external contexts of the state. It provides a point of observation into the challenges of establishing a mode of governance between a postcolonial state and the diverse people of its territory, and of conforming that state to an international regime defined by this constitutive concept.[86] Similarly, discursive agency provides a means of understanding a wide variety of communicative acts—from private speech to state ritual, from performance to protest—within a political landscape more expansive than the formal activities of political parties and governments. Although applied here in a limited study of a specific country, these analytical categories provide potential points of departure for comparative studies of politics in postcolonial states.

For this research, I interviewed more than a hundred people in Tanzania, Uganda, Kenya, and the United States, mostly former civil servants but also labor leaders, politicians, military officers, and grassroots activists. I conducted most of these unstructured interviews on video in an informal partnership with the Mwalimu Nyerere Foundation (MNF) in Dar es Salaam, which provided me with a letter of introduction stating that my interviews would eventually be stored in the MNF library and be made publicly available. Most of the interviews cited here are on DVD and are now available by request at the MNF offices in Dar es Salaam. I started with a list of names based on my own research and on advice given by people at the MNF and then traveled around the region, finding interviewees and arranging the interviews on my own accord. I conducted the interviews in Swahili and English using my own equipment. Despite inevitable gaps and the infiltration of "official" versions of events, these interviews brought much new insight. Just as important, the labor-intensive task of identifying, locating, and building relationships with interviewees lent another layer of subjective insight about the human geography of East African political classes.

In casting a wide net, I have tried to gain multiple perspectives on this history and to critically assess topics that lean heavily on particular archival sources. I consulted newspapers and tens of thousands of documents in multiple archives in Tanzania, the United States, the United Kingdom, Portugal, and Germany, taking notes on a small computer and photographing documents where allowed. In many instances official archival documents are still "sanitized" or unavailable to the public. I successfully requested declassification of numerous documents, but access to secret information will never be the key to postcolonial histories. At best they expose incriminating details of specific events, but they are usually as banal as the rest of the archive. The most useful material in the British and American archives are the records of conversations with various Tanzanian officials, but even these bear layers of filtering between the original conversation and its reporting.[87] American diplomats were wont to see Cold War concerns as prevalent, but different writers displayed varying levels of concern about communism as a uniquely pervasive political force. British observers bore aspects of both the intimate knowledge and the distorting prejudices of their colonial antecedants. Portuguese writers show signs of a distinctly complex effort to contain their resentment about the decolonization trend and repackage colonial analyses into the ideological terms favored by Cold War allies. The East German material that I saw was almost exclusively concerned with Cold War competition in Zanzibar.

What historians seek in the close examination of entire archives are cracks in the discursive facade. We find phrases and stray information that suggest deeper dynamics beyond the surface of the observers' reportage. Contradictions between official accounts and a historian's interpretation are to be expected in critical examinations of evidence, but there is no magic methodology by which we can extricate unbiased information from inevitably biased informants. By carefully comparing and corroborating information in various sources, we can render an accurate picture even when details remain murky. Explicit source critique, which has a rich literature in postcolonial studies, is a necessary task for historians of modern Africa but should not block attempts to recover histories embedded in these sources.[88]

The United States and the United Kingdom produced copious diplomatic reporting, and Tanzania produced sheaves of administrative documentation. All of this material bears a range of ethnocentric bias, not so much in the "facts" such as they are, but in their interpretation and the particular topics that ignited a writer's interest.[89] What I found is that the very areas that have the least documentation in declassified Tanzanian archives are the most documented in foreign archives; and issues to which foreign diplomats gave little attention are copiously represented in available Tanzanian archives. The issues of interest to foreigners were often those considered national security secrets for the Tanzanians, and therefore excluded from publicly accessioned archives. Conversely, topics considered mundane administrative matters that are readily available in Tanzanian archives often reveal aspects of upcountry politics that were beyond the gaze of foreign diplomats. The problem with archival collections is not the presence of false details and interpretations that are wrong; these are ripe for scholarly inquiry. The greater challenge is to divine what has been systematically ignored.[90]

This book gives an account of sovereignty in a postcolonial African state. It is not a biography or evaluation of Julius Nyerere. It is certainly evident that most who met him were impressed with his intelligence and good humor, and compared to many counterparts in "third world" countries he bore power with grace and humility.[91] Most scholars acknowledge that he was a defining figure in this story and played a central role in shaping Tanzania's national trajectory, but here he serves as but one representative of the young generation that took the reins of governance after independence.[92] I tend to believe Nyerere was honest in his intentions, and tend to dismiss inflammatory conspiracy theories such as Aboud Jumbe's unfounded allegation that he led a "systematic campaign to deny [Muslims] basic rights."[93] This resonant accusation has its roots in the bitter political campaigns of late colonial Zanzibar and remains a potent rhetorical strategy.[94] If anything, Jumbe was one of the most enthusiastic participants in the project of melding Tanganyika and Zanzibar into a single polity under a single secular political party in the 1970s. Much more research is needed before we can convincingly address such accusations or offer a broader critical evaluation of Nyerere himself. Even then, the utility of such an evaluation is limited, except perhaps as a contribution to the Vatican's self-regarding debate about whether Nyerere should be beatified or not.[95]

What is certain is that a political class under Nyerere's leadership chose policies intended to prevent internal conflict, and that these same policies tended to undermine popular participation in political and economic decision making. In his determination to turn questionable ideology into successful policy, Nyerere acted increasingly like a mere dictator. By the 1970s Tanzania was turning into a police state pursuing wildly ambitious economic plans hampered by corruption in the government and cynicism in the population at large. What remains notable, however, amid the dangers of postcolonial Africa, is how thoroughly Nyerere put an intellectual project into action as a deliberate set of policies.

Timothy Parsons has suggested that we need a historical perspective on the postcolonial African state that moves beyond the modernization paradigm with its focus on political parties and elite actors.[96] I agree, but we also need to revisit those elites and outdated state histories in order to accurately assess how high politics gave context to everyday lives and vice versa.[97] Revising both older scholarship and William Edgett Smith's lively reporting, this study is meant to complement the large literature on Tanzanian politics and social history that I reviewed in the journal *History in Africa* a few years ago.[98] While Nyerere is an inevitable focal point in this story, and an admirable man in many respects, I do not argue that he heroically shaped Tanzania. Rather, I argue that his efforts, together with those of colleagues and opponents, amount to an observable case of discursive agency. If we can see Nyerere amid the people and pressures of Tanzanian independence, we can bind Ermarth's thesis of "agency in the discursive condition" to a history of events.[99]

Tanzania's establishment of sovereignty in the middle of the Cold War engaged political values from African and European cultural settings, both local and global. Neither these values nor their cultural settings can be related hierarchically; they do not depend on each other in an evolutionary way. Although they differ, these epistemological settings are intertwined in Africa's modern history; they hide in the shadows of rumors, which bear the disputed facts that historians debate. The manner of their admixture in Tanzania took form according to the contingent demands of the early 1960s in East Africa. The discursive agency exemplified by Nyerere and practiced in Tanzanian politics offers a window into the construction of postcolonial sovereignty and the humble possibilities of individual influence. Using "the way of the lips," Tanzania's founding leaders established a sovereign nation in order to pursue their contested and imperfectly achieved aims of peaceful prosperity and social equality.

Part 1

Searching for a Sovereign Discourse

1

The Education of Julius Nyerere

In 1943 Julius Kambarage Nyerere joined Andrew Tibandebage in a student political group at Makerere University in Uganda, where they discussed how Tanganyika might gain its independence by making a claim to the United Nations Trusteeship Committee. After finishing studies at Makerere University in 1945, Nyerere took up a teaching post at St. Mary's Secondary School in Tabora, Tanganyika and threw himself happily into his duties. With Tibandebage, Nyerere coached a debating team at St. Mary's and made a deep impression on an upcoming generation at the neighboring Tabora Boys' School. Rashidi Kawawa, Job Lusinde, and Oscar Kambona all became leaders in the independence movement, in large measure inspired by this enthusiastic young teacher and his debating club.[1] Nyerere kept in close touch with friends back home, including James Irenge, his teacher from Mwisenge Native Authority School who saw his leadership potential and quietly nurtured Nyerere's political ambition during his former pupil's regular visits home.[2]

In 1949 Nyerere traveled to Edinburgh University in Scotland, as one of a small group of East Africans who were given scholarships to study in the United Kingdom. A university education abroad was the final step in a colonial educational track reserved for a small group of top students that would help transform African society into a more European one—or so officials hoped. They were trained as teachers, doctors, and social workers. Nyerere was a typical member of the independence generation described by Frederick Cooper: "Leaders—western educated, but rarely more than one generation removed from their milieux of origin—saw themselves as choosing the best of what Europe and Africa had to offer."[3] While local ideas nourished their hearts, the driving philosophy of the colonial education they imbibed was British Utilitarianism. Probing Nyerere's educational journey offers insight into the broader intellectual discourse that offered young African elites the means to pierce metropolitan prejudices and transform the justifications of colonial rule into a rationale for independence.

Nurturing a Political Vision

Born in 1922, Nyerere grew up in a small hilltop village called Butiama, some miles inland from the eastern shore of Lake Victoria, on the edge of what is now the Serengeti National Park. His father, Nyerere Burito, was one of the oldest of eight chiefs in the Zanaki Federation. British officials described him as "a gentleman of the old school . . . [who] dearly loves to chat about old times."[4] Although Burito was a minor chief, his children still had access to colonial schools, where chiefly sons were given free education. Burito favored his eldest son, Wanzagi, as his successor, but the second child of his fifth wife also began to show promise as a young boy working on the farm and herding cattle. Mugaya Nyang'ombe named her precocious son Kambarage, after an ancestral rain-making spirit.[5] When he turned twelve in 1934, he was sent off to Mwisenge Native Authority School in Musoma, where an iconoclastic young teacher named James Irenge took him under his wing. Irenge risked his supervisors' wrath to preach the virtues of self-determination and African nationalism to his maturing charges, inviting them for evening discussions in his cramped teacher's quarters. He told them stories of the tiny mother sparrow who drove off the crows stealing her eggs, and of the owl who simply opened his eyes and put all the other birds to flight. "So that owl, this way, chases them away."

> Kambarage would come with his friends and they would sit at the table, and I would sit on the bed. . . . I was teaching them a certain "special" subject of politics, of history, of things of the past and how they were, and how we would be able to govern for ourselves. . . . I was telling them we should remove the foreigners. . . . "Guns by themselves, and cannon, we can't use. We are not experts with them. . . . We'll use another way, of just the lips. 'We don't want them!' All of us, 'We don't want them!' They'll leave."[6]

When his pupils howled in protest at the seeming futility of their teacher's Gandhian strategy, he declared all the more emphatically: "Yes. So, let's do it that way, with the lips."[7] Young Kambarage took the lesson to heart and over the years influentially pursued "the way of the lips" as he shaped political debates and perceptions through rhetorical, and occasionally coercive, interventions in both the African and European conceptual realms of postcolonial politics. Irenge's truculent memories can be self-serving, but the phrase "the way of the lips" emerges nowhere else in Tanzanian political discourse, and so appears as Irenge's own long-held conviction that nonviolent protest could overthrow colonial rule.

Nyerere's educational journey took him from a small village on the edge of the Serengeti plains through mission boarding schools and the elite excitement of Makerere, the only university in the region, and finally to exotic Scotland. Along the way he was baptized as a Roman Catholic and took the name Julius just before setting off to university in 1943.[8] The journey to Uganda gave him a sense of fluency in multiple intellectual contexts, preparing him for the challenges that faced the postwar generation that brought on independence across much of sub-Saharan Africa. Under Irenge's mentorship, Nyerere's political interests were evident well before he left for Edinburgh. His ambition upon arrival at Makerere was to transform African society. The Tanganyika African Welfare Association that he founded with Andrew Tibandebage debated the complexities of the reestablishment of African sovereignty in East Africa, and the ideological choices before them.[9] A 1943 letter to the editor of the *Tanganyika Standard* signed by "JUKANYE," a student at Makerere University in Kampala, opined that people in East Africa were "mainly African and the African being naturally socialistic, economics in East Africa should be based on socialistic principles."[10] James Brennan proposed that JUKANYE was Julius Kambarage Nyerere, who, at the age of twenty-one, creatively envisioned a particular socialism arising not from Marxian theory but from African culture. This innovation was a key piece of imagining a sovereign African polity, both culturally rooted and internationally viable.

A sense of the restless scope of Makerere student debates can be found in a scathing condemnation of the limited role of women in colonial African society that Nyerere wrote 1944. Writing in Swahili, he clearly aimed for an African audience, fully intending to shape public opinion "in order to help [women] escape the condition of slavery that they are in today."[11] Citing John Stuart Mill's *The Subjection of Women*, the tract bore all the marks of his colonial education and religion, and not a little of its arrogance. But it also exemplified the rhetorical expertise that came to define his public persona as *Mwalimu* during his long political career. Skillfully setting up his straw men, targeting the pride and prejudices of the traditionalists he sought to influence, he struck with humor and barbed logic.[12]

In the essay, bluntly titled "Freedom of Women," it is the double-edge of Nyerere's sword that stands out, cutting as sharply into the conditions of colonialism as into unfair gender norms. In writing the pamphlet on women, he later explained, "I was moving towards the idea of freedom theoretically."[13] With cunning insight into African insecurities in the face of colonial prejudices, he used his brash critique of women's place in colonial African society to quietly question the logic of British rule and consider the implications of independence. In a section on "Women and Native Authorities," his repeated examples of colonial mistreatment of women served just as powerfully to demonstrate the contradictions of indirect rule with its dependence on local African agents. He pointed to the trivial impact of popular laws limiting chiefly powers of capital punishment: "The government makes laws to prohibit small issues and ignores the really big issues."[14]

Nyerere ended the pamphlet with a homely children's story much like those taught to him by his garrulous grade school teacher from Mwisenge. He told a comical tale of an eagle who thought he was a chicken and was afraid to fly; the misinformed eagle needed only to spread his wings and leap into the unknown. This was the situation of women in colonial African society, he argued, and equally that of Africans under British rule. "By your own efforts and with the help of your friends, pull yourselves out of this weak condition so that you can benefit from freedom and justice in the world of peace!"[15] Despite its naive veneer, the tract was a skillful discursive intervention, elaborating an implicit analysis of colonial oppression within an explicit defense of the rights of women. Each argument reinforced the other; each disguised the other's underlying radicalism.[16]

A political career continued to tug at Nyerere's ambitions. His former teacher James Irenge recalled the difficult dilemma that vexed Nyerere in 1948 when, through the efforts of another mentor, Father Richard Walsh, the colonial government offered him a scholarship to study biology in the United Kingdom.[17] The young man was torn between graduate studies and a a more immediate urge to respond to the changing circumstances of his people, the Zanaki in rural Musoma. He observed that the Zanaki people were divided into seven areas, each with its own chief, or *mtemi*. He thought that if they could be united under one ruler, his people would be better placed to lobby for their interests in the colonial state. In the midst of this deliberation, he embarked on a journey around Zanaki country, akin to the ritual walk his elders called *kukerera*. In Zanaki country, each new generation, or *rikora*, traditionally walked the boundaries of the land, defining the polity, or *ekyaro*. Through this ritual walk, the social institution of the *rikora*, rather than the more personal institution of the chief, took "responsibility for healing the land," by this enactment of the local genesis myth of the founding figure who first took possession of the land.[18] As Irenge recalled, "During his vacation, Mwl. Kambarage came home to Zanaki. During this time Mwl. Kambarage traveled all around Zanaki country by foot to meet with all the chiefs in those days in order to work with them to show them the value of uniting together under one leader, so that development in Zanaki country could be obtained."[19]

Whether Nyerere made such a journey is now difficult to know for sure. Perhaps more important, however, is the memory that he did, grounding his ascension to authority in a local idiom of walks laden with political portent.[20] His efforts among the chiefs paid off, and many of them were supportive of the election of a paramount chief, following the recent example of Thomas Marealle in Chagga country, and similar efforts in Buhaya on the other side of the lake.[21] So despite the rare opportunity to study abroad, Nyerere was pulled by a sense of obligation at home. Irenge recalled that Nyerere came to him with this dilemma: "If the problem is how to get an appropriate leader that all the chiefs can trust and accept to be the leader of all of Zanaki country. If this is the question, and they can't find another but think that I (Kambarage) would please them as the chief they want to lead them, then I am ready to postpone the trip to England to study for the opportunity I was given there."[22]

Irenge's counsel was that Nyerere should go for studies in the UK, "so that when he would return without doubt he would lead all of Musoma and not just Zanaki country which is but a small part of this district." Nyerere later recounted to an American reporter that "a number of educated people in the tribe had advocated amalgamation of the Zanaki. . . . If we had one chief, I argued, it would better for the tribe. . . . They asked me, 'Why don't you do it yourself?' I said, 'No, no, I can't be chief.'"[23] Instead, twenty-seven-year-old Nyerere took his teacher's advice and prepared to travel abroad.

In 1949 he arrived in the UK to study biology, the subject he had been teaching at St. Mary's. Upon reaching London in April, he told his supervising administrator that he wanted to study political science. She retorted "that this would hardly be countenanced, in view of the extension of his scholarship for prelim. science training."[24] He continued to lobby for political science, writing a letter to the administration explaining his reasons.

> I still feel, however, and say strongly, that if I can be useful to my country after my studies here, I will be more useful if I take an arts rather than a science degree. That, however, is not easy to prove. One thing is certain, that I am more capable of studying for an arts than a science degree. A teacher of mine who has known me for many years both as a pupil and as a teacher, said, after hearing that I was coming here to study science, that it was like doing sculpture with a pen. I am certain he did not mean to say that I am foolish but he knows me and he knows what he is talking about.[25]

It is not clear whether the teacher Nyerere refers to is Irenge or Father Walsh, but by June he had successfully redirected his studies to pursue an arts degree and enrolled at the University of Edinburgh, where he focused on history, political science, and economics.[26] Through these efforts, Nyerere embarked on a course of study to prepare himself to become a political leader for the Zanaki people, and perhaps all of Musoma. In conversation with Father Walsh, he may have nurtured an even broader ambition.[27] His education sharpened his rhetorical perspicacity, but more than one observer has noted that the art of argument was well established in Zanaki culture.[28] Nyerere's lifetime love of energetic debate was first nurtured at home.

An Evolving Political Philosophy

A. R. Radcliffe-Brown's 1940 volume on African political systems provided a concise analytical framework for thinking about the philosophical challenges of what statecraft might mean for Africa if decolonization got under way. The essays, edited by pioneering anthropologists of Africa, were windows into cutting-edge scholarship on the intersection of culture and power that gives rise to the infinite variety of politics in human society. The book was included in the reading list for a social anthropology course that Nyerere took as a part of his master of arts degree at Edinburgh from 1949 to 1952. The instructor for the course, a widely respected professor named Ralph Piddington, had studied under Radcliffe-Brown, and presumably urged his new African student to comment on the book. Much of Nyerere's later political thinking evolved to explain the process implied in Radcliffe-Brown's preface by which people in a nonstate system adapted to working within a state system.

> States are merely territorial groups within a larger political system in which their relations are defined by war or its possibility, treaties, and international law. A political system of this kind, such as now exists in Europe, of sovereign nations linked by international relations, is only one type of political system. Political theory and practice (including colonial administration) have often suffered by reason of this type of system being set up, consciously or unconsciously, as a norm.[29]

Radcliffe-Brown's work provided a critical counterpoint to a more linear theory of social development evident in Nyerere's notes from his survey course in British history at Edinburgh under the eminent Professor Richard Pares.[30] The notebook, now in the Borthwick Institute in York, is a series of short chapter summaries on British history.[31] The course anchored the history of modern Britain in the Roman conquest, with required readings that included Sir Walter Bagehot's classic history of the English Constitution and Harold Mattingly's brand-new translation of Tacitus on the Roman conquest of Germany and Britain.[32] Early Romanization in ancient Britain was "slavish and unintelligent," according to Nyerere's notes. "The introduction of towns as artificial political units which the Romans believed to be essential for human civilization was a new idea." When the Roman Empire began to lose influence, "even those who had been a little Romanized relaxed into barbarism." Projecting indirect rule backward two millennia, Nyerere noted the course's description of a Roman government that differed little from British rule in Africa: "The Romans did not do much to transform Britain. For instance, they did not mean to change British relations or the social structure of the natives. They wanted to rule Britain through existing chiefs, although they had to abandon this policy of indirect rule after the UC rebellion of Boadicea. In Roman Britain, therefore, many things went on very much as they had done before, particularly in the civilian zone."

In Nyerere's telescoped historical consciousness, as presented in these notes, Britain was itself a postcolony, its institutions shaped by indirect rule under the Romans. The kernel of his theory of villagization may have taken root when he learned that the Romans had imposed towns on rural areas "as a method of pushing ahead Roman civilization" and that "the existence of towns must have stimulated economic activity. They were artificial collections of consumers." But then, according to his notes, the Romans stopped building towns after AD 200 when "the Roman Government had ceased to be civilized" and began falling under attack by Teutonic tribes on the continent, at which point Britain's decentralized society protected it from the economic and social shocks of Roman collapse. The theory of history Nyerere encountered at Edinburgh was not the simple American faith in progress and modernization, but rather a more tragic European theory of human community that valued material development but measured it against a harsher view of political reality. "History gives a cruel experience of human nature," wrote John Stuart Mill in his essay on the inequalities facing nineteenth-century women, "in showing how ... [the] entire earthly happiness of any class of persons, was measured by what they had the power of enforcing."[33] It was a realist lesson that would give Nyerere pause more than once in his political career.

By all accounts, Nyerere enjoyed his years in Scotland immensely. In a 1960 letter to George Shepperson, a young professor and friend, Nyerere recalled of his years in Edinburgh: "I evolved the whole of my political philosophy while I was there."[34] Clearly Nyerere's praise of Edinburgh entailed a touch of flattery, because his intellectual foundation was rooted firmly in East Africa. His political philosophy had been in formation since he was a teenager under the wing of the cantankerous Irenge, and his interest in socialism seems to have begun at university in Uganda.

In Edinburgh, he returned to J. S. Mill for a top grade on a paper in moral philosophy titled "Is Happiness the Thing to Aim At?"[35] Evidently a critique of Utilitarianism in response to F. H. Bradley's *Ethical Studies*, which was one of the examination books for the course, the paper's title provides another hint of Nyerere's evolving philosophical orientation.[36] The other examination book was T. H. Green's *Principles of Political Obligation*, which addressed the issues raised in Radcliffe-Brown's preface on how to construct a new state in a stateless society, and how to regulate the mutual obligations between state and citizen. Green's influence can be seen in Nyerere's later approaches to village concepts of consensus, the minimal requirements of democratic choice, the duties of citizenship, and the coercive role of the state as sovereign to enforce democratically constituted policies.[37]

In the tutor for the moral philosophy course he found close friend, a Jamaican by the name of Sidney Collins who studied race relations in Britain. The professor, the illustrious John Macmurray, a strong adherent of pacifism and Christian socialism, along with radical philosopher Axel Stern, provided a stimulating course focused on the ethics of governance. Recommended books included a wide range of classic readings on ethics and the state, including texts by Plato, Hobbes, Locke, and Rousseau and nineteenth-century works by Mill and Kierkegaard, as well as clearly provocative modern works ranging from Freud to the radical intellectual and politician Harold Laski. These readings, together with Nyerere's professor in political economy, Alexander Grey, who studied the history of socialism "from Moses to Lenin," cultivated the inspiring possibilities that socialist ideals represented in postwar Scotland.[38] "As a result of my choice of subjects," Nyerere recalled, "I found I had ample time to read many other things outside my degree course, and I did. I also spent a great deal of time arguing with fellow students about everything under the sun except Marxism (which is above!). I did a great deal of thinking about politics in Africa."[39]

Nyerere's thinking on race and colonialism involved the task of locating African politics in a broader historical and philosophical map. His professor of constitutional law cited *The Federalist* "with its important commentary on the problems of combining different polities and cultures into an effective unity" as an influence on Nyerere's thinking on nation building and Pan-Africanism.[40] Inspired by America's ideals and its anticolonial struggle, Nyerere wanted to take a course on British imperial and American history, but the schedule clashed with his course in economic history "and he wanted, primarily, to get some knowledge of economic forces in history."[41] Edinburgh, like Makerere, provided a period for active intellectual searching, debating, and mulling over the challenges of a multicultural society. Nyerere spent his time at Edinburgh enjoying the intellectual adventure of studying in a foreign land. With a "reasonable application" he easily passed his subjects, leaving time for socializing and testing the political waters on the edges of the metropole. An acquaintance recalled the idealistic African student who had adjusted comfortably to an active student life at the University of Edinburgh, all except for the chilly Scottish winds:

> He [Nyerere] took a prominent and active part in opposing the proposed Central African Federation. An informal, international and inter-confessional group used to meet at Bill Cattanach's flat.... Very soon the Edinburgh World Church Group, which was the name which this rather loosely organised and mainly student group gave themselves, took to circularising petitions, running protest meetings, sending out speakers, lobbying M.P.s, writing to the press, etc.... I well remember crossing the Firth of Forth

with him one spring evening on the old Granton Ferry—now no longer running—to address a weeknight meeting in the old parish kirk of Burntisland. . . . Julius didn't like the cold and we were swept by a chill wind which was coming up the estuary. He talked with great interest and with his quiet conviction about the future of Tanganyika.[42]

With an eloquence that impressed many who knew him, he spoke to various groups around Scotland criticizing a proposal to federate Nyasaland with Northern and Southern Rhodesia, arguing that democratic constitutions were necessary before any such federation ensued.[43] The mother of a friend recalled Nyerere's "happy disposition" and his appetite for political debate as he formulated the ideas for a publication on racialism for the Fabian Society: "I liked to hear him say, as he said often when talking of the Africans, Asians and White People in Tanganyika, 'There is plenty of room for all of them in Tanganyika.' I wish the Congo, where I lived, could have had a leader like Julius Nyerere at this time."[44]

Both academic and social contacts led Nyerere to active involvement in the Fabian Society, a group of moderate socialists inspired by T. H. Green and the brand of British Utilitarianism that dominated the moral philosophy course at Edinburgh.[45] Nyerere submitted a pamphlet to a Fabian publication denouncing the European legacy of racism and articulating his utopian ambition for Africa as a point of ideological unity. The article went unpublished because of its length, was lost, and only recovered by George Shepperson, who saved a copy that was finally published in part later as the opening chapter of Nyerere's first book of speeches and writings.[46] In it he wrote, "I appeal to my fellow Africans to take the initiative in this building up of a harmonious society. The Europeans have had the initiative and all the opportunities for over 200 years and everywhere they have succeeded in producing inter-racial chaos."[47] He later told Shepperson that the article "expressed for myself what I have since been trying to put into practice."[48] In the essay, Nyerere distinguished democracy from efficiency, taking issue with Utilitarianism's "Greatest Happiness Principle" as the justification for government paternalism. Its foil was J. S. Mill's dismissive ethnocentrism that offered a high-minded justification for colonialism. Mill had argued: "Despotism is a legitimate mode of government in dealing with barbarians, provided the end be their improvement, and the means justified by actually effecting that end. Liberty, as a principle, has no application to any state of things anterior to the time when mankind have become capable of being improved by free and equal discussion. Until then, there is nothing for them but implicit obedience to an Akbar or a Charlemagne, if they are so fortunate as to find one."[49]

Nyerere countered that democratic theory made it impossible for the people's choice to be the "wrong" choice, even if it were shown to be the less beneficial one for them. Democracy was by definition what people chose for themselves, regardless of its wisdom. (It was a position that he regularly disregarded after independence as he found himself seduced by the utility of Mill's authoritarian rationale.) He also rejected proposals for racial "parity" in voting as opposed to universal suffrage on the same basis. The parity policy proposed that each race, regardless of population, should have the same number of representatives in the colonial legislature. Even if colonial rule, with its education and capital, could be shown to be most efficient for East Africa, it remained an insult to the African majority in an age of democracy. The key was the sovereignty of democratically elected government, Nyerere argued: "If 'freedom' and not 'efficiency' is the cardinal thing in democracy, then the government which they [the people] want, is the government which matters as far as they are concerned, and therefore, as far as they are concerned it is the right government. For the wrong government is a government which is imposed upon them by an external force or by the will of the minority. However efficient such a government may be it would be the wrong government."[50]

For all his consummate political skills, Nyerere retained an intense intellectuality in the practice and presentation of his policies. This tension between the authoritarian (and occasionally misguided) efficiency of technocratic choices and the self-interested (but often wise) compromises of democratic choice was one that would bedevil him for his entire career. Both approaches sought the Utilitarian ideal of the most good for the most people but diverged on the question of who was best to judge what was good. At stake was the nature of leadership; the postcolonial state was a delicately balanced creation perched between colonial rule, premised on Mill's self-justifying despotism, and an inchoate vision of popular sovereignty. What responsibility did a leader bear for the fate of the postcolony? Would the "inefficient" choices of a largely illiterate electorate be sufficient to safeguard their interests in a rapidly changing world where they wielded so little power? What if a democratic experiment should lead to division and paralysis? Could a unifying ideology guide democratic choices toward productive ends? This last possibility became Nyerere's hope, and also his rationale for overruling democratic principle.

In this orientation he found soul mates among the democratic socialists of the Fabian Society, with whom he retained an ongoing rapport through his personal assistant Joan Wicken, a Fabian stalwart who came to Tanganyika in the 1950s during a study tour of several British colonies in Africa. She also wrestled with the tension between "political power and the use of compulsion" in her report for Somerville College at Oxford upon her return. She noted that the nationalist movements were "coalitions of the most varied forms of opposition and discontent," and that while this was one of their strengths, it also produced an incoherent range of protests that occasionally left their educated leaders "embarrassed by the declarations of their local officials."[51] Moved by her upcountry journeys with the TANU leadership flocked by enthusiastic villagers, she returned to work with the nationalist movement. With remarkable devotion to Nyerere's vision and the cause of African freedom, Wicken became his personal assistant, speechwriter, and loyal critic, accompanying him for his whole career in public service.[52]

2

Contemplating the Postcolony

A former labor leader and politician, Peter Kisumo identified ethnic organizations, with their modernist and even democratic goals, as catalysts for nationalist organizations like Nyerere's party, the Tanganyika African National Union (TANU), or the Tanganyika Federation of Labour (TFL). He also noted their shortcomings. For Kisumo, the independence movement had to be a national one that took the colonial state as the basis for constructing postcolonial sovereignty:

> Before we got to the national organizations, like trade unions, there were tribal organizations.... Some wanted to remove the chief, others gathered the strength of the tribe; and where could they take it? If you gather the strength of a tribe, you can only ask for independence. Ultimately independence could not be demanded from the chief, it had to come from the colonial power.[1]

Local civil society associations offered models for organizational structures. But they also held the potential for divisive competition over what sorts of organizations would bear people's political aspirations, and over the nature of citizenship and authority that would guide the envisioned state. In reference to the ubiquitous efforts at ethnicity-based political mobilization in late colonial Tanganyika, John Iliffe concurred: "Nationalism not only grew up alongside other political tendencies; to a considerable extent it grew out of them." Despite TANU's relatively understated ideology in the preindependence period, we need to understand what this dynamic meant in policy and discourse because, in Iliffe's view, "it was in altering men's perception of their interests that ideology was crucial to Tanganyikan nationalism."[2]

The impact of Nyerere's thought on political perceptions, as Iliffe suggests, was real. But accounts from observers such as Pratt who had a front-row view of these events have uncritically presented Nyerere's developing political philosophy during this period without placing it in a historical chronology.[3] More recent historians like Brennan have begun to develop a more critical account of events and have made inroads into the cultural and intellectual currents shaping their discursive context, especially the racialist tropes of economic exploitation that fueled many postcolonial political debates.[4] A primary concern that emerged in the late 1950s was how to ensure that an independent government would be robust in the face of such potential divisions. Nyerere's main strategy for stability became the promotion of a one-party state. This orientation certainly built on models in China and the Soviet Union, but it also emerged from the consensus-driven logic of local institutions like the ethnic associations of the late colonial era.

In the late colonial period, Tanganyikans responded to the administrative importance placed on categorizing people by "tribe" (translated as "kabila") by creating ethnic organizations to provide social welfare and to raise their voice in a government. The ambitious, if limited, efforts of these organizations to provide social services threw the redundancy of colonial administration into sharp relief, even as they constructed new identities derived from administrative categories.[5] Long-standing guilds of traders and social leaders in western Tanganyika were formalized into mutual aid societies such as the Unity of Lake Tanganyika Nations Association, Ujiji. The newly registered mutual aid society listed as its subscribers the leaders of local ethnic groups, noted as the *Kabila ya Kikao*: "The Afore-said are the Lake Tanganyika Tribes with their members."[6]

New organizations sprouted up in imitation of successful organizations like the Meru Citizens' Union and the Chagga Democratic Party, often with their guidance.[7] Some found significant success. A well-organized protest against colonial reallocations of Meru land brought the voices of Meru farmers to the United Nations in the early 1950s.[8] The Tanganyika Citizens' Union, headed by Petro Njau, who had led the democratization effort in Chagga country, advised and encouraged similar regional organizations, helping them to overcome their own hesitance and sense of dependency on the colonial state.[9] Njau attended a meeting in Lushoto with over one thousand Shambaa representatives who sought his guidance to form a Shambaa Citizens' Union. They explained that they did not seek to create something that would challenge the colonial government; they simply wanted to be good citizens: "We want to be taught to know the issues of the country and to be able to contribute to the struggle with them using the strength of working with our own hands."[10] In the process, they subtly developed an argument for their right to be heard in a new local council system.

The difference between "ethnicity" and "tribe" is somewhat unclear in everyday usage.[11] Tanzanians use the everyday word *kabila*, loosely translated as "tribe," to talk about ethnicity, which refers to a mix of social and political identities bound by a shared language and domestic culture that gives a sense of common origin to its adherents.[12] But in English usage, the word *tribe* carries significant baggage that equates "tribal society" with primitivism. Ethnicity is a more accurate sociological concept that seeks to understand the way in which people identify themselves through ideologies of cultural and genealogical affinities, in part by enforcing normative morals and sources of authority.[13] Precolonial politics were a constantly rewoven tapestry of loyalties and social obligations in which ethnicity was but one component among many. The memory of those former political relations was distorted in the colonial period, but language differences and local practices ensured that ethnicity remained a powerful factor in the politics of independence. Regardless of the complex reality of ethnicity, the independence movement had to engage the distorted discourse of "tribe" as it existed in the late colonial period when ethnic organizations flowered across the territory.

Tanganyika had never existed as a sovereign state, and its past offered little guidance for the new nation. Neither of the competing Cold War ideologies represented Africa, and neither could those models of social organization be simply shoehorned into the Tanganyikan context. The prospect of self-government was at once full of robust possibility and littered with delicate tasks that could threaten the entire dream of independence if they were mishandled. In the drive to independence in the late 1950s, Nyerere traveled the country campaigning and talking with TANU activists, probing them for ideas on how extant models of political organization could be yoked to the nationalist cause without introducing ethnic or racial division. By 1960 Nyerere began to discourage ethnic political activity, refusing affiliation with the otherwise supportive associations like the Chagga Democratic Party, and urging the Meru Citizens' Union to close its doors. Somewhat indecisively, perhaps afraid of offending the still-influential holders of chiefly offices, Nyerere occasionally voiced support for a continued role for "native authorities."[14]

Grassroots TANU activist Edward Barongo went around the country preaching against the tribal organizations, occasionally meeting with stalwart defiance by elders and local notables.[15] Barongo convinced the Buhaya Council to give its full support to Nyerere after a nascent separatist campaign sprouted in this westerly province that bordered on culturally similar kingdoms in Burundi, Rwanda, and Uganda.[16] Well-organized local political initiatives in the Meru District near Arusha, and in Sukumaland around Mwanza, had paved the way for TANU's success, but by 1960 Nyerere pushed them to choose between incorporation and irrelevance.

In Mwanza, a burgeoning cooperative movement had become a powerful force in local agricultural marketing, while the colonially sponsored Sukumaland Council faced a challenge from an insurgent Sukuma Union, both of which provided models for African political organization.[17]

In 1958 a chiefly group organized around David Kidaha Makwaia and his brother Hussein proposed a number of measures to strengthen the Sukumaland Council. Kidaha Makwaia had been one of the first Africans to sit on the colonial Legislative Council in the 1940s, and he served as junior minister for lands, a powerful position in the African politics of Tanganyika. He had resigned his chiefly position to become a politician and cultivated a chummy relationship with Edward Twining, the colonial governor until 1958. Where the leaders of the Meru movement had committed their support to TANU, Makwaia remained aloof of the nationalist movement and supported Twining's incrementalism, possibly in a bid to build on his authority in Sukumaland. The colonial administrator in Mwanza rejected Makwaia's proposals because he sensed an "inner cabinet of chiefs aiming at being an entirely independent Central Government." Perhaps influenced by these British fears, Nyerere privately pressed the last colonial commissioner for the district to "break the Sukumaland Federal Council," adding, "We can't have another Katanga here."[18]

The anxious reference to the Congolese civil war sparked by Katanganese separatism signaled the worries that accompanied TANU's surprisingly easy drive for independence. *Uhuru* (freedom) came peacefully and far earlier than expected. This brought the possibility that governance would prove the more difficult task, as it had in the Congo. However, TANU's grassroots activists had created a robust nationalist movement that had no parallel in the Congo, and its moderation in its negotiations with an amenable colonial state created a cooperative approach to decolonization that augured well for a stable transition. Nevertheless, the interaction of regional separatism, ethnic loyalties, and Cold War politics in the Congolese disintegration only served to reinforce deep-seated fears of political division.

The Drive to Independence

Other authors, John Iliffe in particular, have more thoroughly documented the broad-based nationalist movement, but a brief sketch of Nyerere's role during this period provides a useful prelude to the creation of the sovereign state that followed.[19] When he returned from Edinburgh, Nyerere joined a few of his educated peers among the predominantly Muslim elders of the Tanganyikan African Association (TAA), an organization that had been pressing for greater African influence in the colonial government. Nyerere had helped found a TAA branch at Makerere University in the 1940s, and some of his colleagues there had been instrumental in rejuvenating the organization in the early 1950s. Emulating the activism of ambitious ethnic associations in Sukumaland near Lake Victoria and

Chagga country around Mount Kilimanjaro, a group of young members under the leadership of Vedastus Kyaruzi and Abdulwahid Sykes began to radicalize the TAA, proposing constitutional developments for the territory that would lead to "responsible government" by the early 1960s. The government reacted by ignoring their suggestions and transferring Kyaruzi and another Makerere-trained medical doctor to isolated rural hospitals.[20]

Upon arriving back home, Nyerere had returned briefly to his village, and then took a teaching post in at St. Francis Secondary School in Pugu, on the outskirts of Dar es Salaam. He worked on the TAA's new constitution, proposing to transform it into a nationalist movement.[21] Because of his support for nationalist goals, and because he was the only African in the country with a European master's degree, the TAA members thought Nyerere could best represent their new radical goals to the colonial government.[22] They selected Nyerere as president of the organization in April 1953. In keeping with the vision worked out by Kyaruzi and Sykes, the new constitution extended the TAA's territorial scope into a centralized decision-making body. The following July, at the organization's annual meeting in Dar es Salaam, Nyerere moved that the association be reorganized as the Tanganyika African National Union (TANU).[23] The new name emphasized its new goal of organizing for independence, a task arising from the knowledge of a visiting UN mission, due later that year, to consider the same issue.

Refuting repeated accusations that TANU supported a racialist, all-African vision of nationhood, TANU spokesmen Andrew Tibandebage, George Patrick Kunambi, and Kirilo Japhet promulgated a nonracialist "government of Tanganyikans for Tanganyikans by Tanganyikans." Tempering this vision with hesitance born of their upbringing in a paternal colonial state, they announced, "We feel that this should only come when the people of Tanganyika—particularly the Africans—are ready for it."[24] TANU's tactic put its aims within the ideological framework of colonial philosophy. They intended to prepare the Tanganyikan populace for self-government in an indefinite future. In January of the new year, the UN delegation came back with a positive report, recommending self-government within a quarter century. During the wedding of Kunambi, a young party member from a chiefly family in Morogoro, the gathered TANU members received news that the UN mission had recommended independence for Tanganyika by 1980 at the latest. Unfortunately for the wedding party, their celebrations were cut short as the overjoyed guests excitedly prepared to press their case for independence.[25] The report energized the nationalist movement and jump-started TANU's rapid growth as a self-sufficient organization largely funded through local memberships.

With funding from the families of Dossa Aziz and Abdulwahid Sykes, and major contributions from Dar es Salaam's Indian business community,

TANU organized Nyerere's first visit to UN headquarters in New York City in March 1955.[26] Nyerere told the UN Trusteeship Council that "with your help and with the help of the Administering Authority we would be governing ourselves long before twenty or twenty-five years."[27] It was a timetable that seemed ambitious to all at the time, not the least to Tanganyikan villagers. Village elders asked young party organizers whether they knew how to make sewing needles or matchsticks, mocking independence advocates as being incapable of producing even these smallest of industrial commodities, let alone the automobiles and airplanes that Europeans had brought to the country.[28]

After his return from New York, Nyerere's principal at St. Francis told him to choose either politics or teaching, knowing that to give up his teacher's salary would put the young family man in a difficult position. Nyerere spoke with supportive members of Dar es Salaam's business community who offered him a salary and the use of a car, allowing him to take up organizing on a full-time basis. Abdulwahid Sykes's younger brother, Abbas, encouraged another young teacher named Oscar Kambona to join the party, sending him to Nyerere with a letter of recommendation for the role of TANU's first general secretary.[29]

From the TAA network of urban clubs, Kambona recruited an impressive grassroots infrastructure of local TANU branches, a youth wing, an elders' council, and an enthusiastic women's auxiliary, whose most prominent voice was Bibi Titi Mohamed.[30] In Songea, where elders recalled the horrible defeat of the Maji Maji rebellion, youthful activists ignored their grandmothers and bought TANU cards.[31] Kambona and Bibi Titi signed up new members with astonishing speed. From just two thousand members countrywide in early 1955, TANU had issued forty thousand membership cards by the end of the year. By 1960 it had over a million members. With financial support from some sympathetic Catholic priests, the party arranged another visit to the United Nations in 1957, by which time TANU, with its enthusiastic women's and youth wings, had become a political juggernaut across the territory.[32]

In the wake of TANU's formation, lurid tales of Mau Mau atrocities in Kenya splashed across newspaper headlines in Tanganyika, feeding whites' anxieties. Trying to set a progressive course, the European settler members of the Tanganyika chapter of the Capricorn Africa Society recruited a few prominent Africans and transformed themselves into the Tanganyika National Society (TNS), a nonpolitical committee organized to debate issues of sovereign statehood for Tanganyika, with an eye toward tempering African nationalism and promoting "nonracialist" gradualism that would allow for the maintenance of white privilege.[33] Promoting "common patriotism" to stanch "racial tension from outside," the TNS argued that economic prosperity would be impossible without racial stability. In practice,

Figure 2.1. Chief Minister Julius Nyerere with Bibi Titi Mohamed (*center foreground*), Umoja wa Wanawake (UWT) chairperson Sophia Kawawa (*right*), and Maria Nyerere (*far right*). © Tanzania Information Services (MAELEZO).

the TNS sought to limit the franchise in a self-governing Tanganyika to "mutually agreed qualifications such as property or salary; education, character and evidence of responsibility; attested loyalty to Tanganyika." The TNS proposal, being intentionally vague as to who would be party to the "mutual agreement," would exclude the mass of the African population in favor of a limited franchise oriented toward the Crown of England as the "Protector of Spiritual Values." The TNS grounded Tanganyikan nationalism in the civilizing mission of British colonialism. "It is one of the objects of the Society to make effective the moral, cultural, and spiritual standards of civilisation and to help members of all races to attain these standards." In a line of reasoning rooted in J. S. Mill's distrust of "barbarians," TNS leaders deflected criticism of their discomfort with the racial equality implied in the limited vote recommended by the United Nations: "In Tanganyika it is at present difficult to impose the discipline and sanctions necessary in any well ordered democracy without the non-European tending to assume that the motive behind their application is based on racial discrimination."[34]

TANU struck a delicate balance between breaking down a racialized social order and reconstituting it as a national order. Aware of colonial fears, even their own fears, of a violent rebellion like the Mau Mau gaining ground in Tanganyika, the TANU leadership presented itself as a peaceful and reasonable alternative. It was an intimidating strategy for a group of political novices, according to Peter Kisumo: "You could either go with violence or negotiation, and when we go for negotiations we see that the British are better at it than us!"[35] In Rashidi Kawawa's recollection, the strategy entailed a bluff riding on British anxieties about events in Kenya: "The English knew that if we failed we would go into the forest and become a Mau Mau."[36] While the British were certainly monitoring the possible spread of a Mau Mau ideology in Tanganyika, the reference may have served more accurately as a heartening delusion for TANU's youthful and untested activists.[37]

With Mau Mau as a tacit reference in their public rhetoric, TANU politicians traveled the country citing the 1905 Maji Maji rebellion against the Germans as a powerful memory of anticolonial mobilization.[38] They emphasized that Maji Maji (like Mau Mau) failed because it did not unite the whole country, and that its military strategy was doomed against European weaponry. At meetings across the territory, Nyerere illustrated the futility of a violent battle with the colonial state, arguing with World War II veterans who ached to put their military experience to use as guerrilla warriors in rural forests. "What forest will you go to?" he bitingly asked. "There are Europeans on every side of us."[39] Taking his cue from James Irenge's evening lessons so long ago, Nyerere told TANU volunteers: "We'll use the strength of our lips."[40] Kawawa began to come around to Nyerere's view: "We understood that if we used weapons we would fail against the English, so our strength was to work together.... If we have one voice they will leave.... Nyerere detested the language of prejudice and hate."[41] With great effect, TANU offered a peaceful alternative, *Umoja ni Nguvu*, "Unity Is Strength." TANU flags decorated houses across the country.

From TANU's perspective, there were also dangers if popular rhetoric got ahead of nationalist politics. It was a time when "there were too many pied pipers," Kisumo recalled, noting the fractious demands of the labor movement. "When a dog is hunting it gets used to the whistle of one person." With advice from Kenyan labor leader Tom Mboya, Rashidi Kawawa took the lead in melding the trade unions into a united labor movement, under the umbrella of the TFL. Nyerere and Kawawa argued that labor's goals would be best served by the demand for independence, and TANU began to draw much of its grassroots strength, as well as its top leadership, from labor's ranks, working with the unions "shoulder to shoulder."[42] For Kisumo, "independence was a call accepted by all; when you explain that we are being stepped on, we are being exploited, we are not being treated right."

Labor unions were particularly responsive to this logic, but independence became a rallying cry that united a wider range of interest groups, including numerous ethnic organizations around the country. Groups like Nyerere's Zanaki sought to organize themselves for a greater political voice in selecting their own paramount chiefs, while nationalist forces in Chagga country around Mount Kilimanjaro opposed the chiefly paramountcy they had constructed only a few years before. A TANU activist in Mwanza echoed these priorities: "Independence could not come from the chief, but had to come from the colonial state."[43] Realizing their obsolescence, more ethnic organizations began to organize against their own chiefs, many of whom remained allied with the colonial government.[44]

Debates about the influence of race in public life continued and took on a more complex cast as discussions about "nonracialism" ceased to be merely philosophical and became political. Out of the TNS was born the United Tanganyika Party (UTP), the first national party registered in opposition to TANU, with strong financial backing from the white community and some supportive Africans.[45] It represented the idea of legislative "racial parity," which meant that each racial group—African, Asian, and European—should have the same number of representatives in the Legislative Council regardless of their actual numbers in the population. Nyerere had rejected this idea since his time in Edinburgh, and TANU opposed the UTP consistently. Because of this, TANU was accused of racialism, as in this letter to the editor in the *Tanganyika Standard*: "When TANU uses the word 'African' does it make a racial distinction?"[46] The concerns of the writer arose from an awareness of grassroots militancy and undeniably racialist African sentiment. A reply from Rodericks Simkoko defended the distinctly racial national vision, foreshadowing future political ruptures: "How can you nationalise three different races of which each has got her motherland? . . . TANU is a purely African organisation which means the union of the true inhabitants of Tanganyika. . . . The African in Tanganyika is the only person belonging to Tanganyika and is the only person called Tanganyikan and the rest are self-calling Tanganyikans to suit themselves."[47]

Nyerere's clever riposte to this letter came in the form of a response to earlier letters accusing TANU of agreeing too closely with the UTP, and the latter's promotion of unequal racial "parity." Appealing directly to Asians, but indirectly to Africans who doubted the possibility of Asian loyalty in a "postracial" Tanganyika, Nyerere invoked Indian prime minister Nehru's advice to Indians in Africa to identify their interests with Africans' interests. Nyerere implied, on the one hand, that Indians heeding Nehru's counsel might well be accepted as loyal Tanganyikans in an independent nation. On the other hand, he indirectly warned that "if Indians ignore [Nehru's] advice it is easy to see why Africans would regard them with suspicion." The heart of Nyerere's argument directly addressed the insidious logic deriving from Mill's Utilitarian tyrant in the age of Mau Mau. Professions of goodwill and desires to aid and educate, Nyerere argued, were both hypocritical and oppressive "when the 'unfortunate brethren' are viewed as an object of fear." Proclaiming TANU's ideology of "equal rights for all men" in contrast to the UTP position of equal rights only for "civilized" men, Nyerere anchored a far-reaching political position on nonracialism in TANU's devastating critique of the UTP. Nyerere's letter, which was just as damaging to pro-African racialists as to Europeans hoping to prevent an African-majority government, also condemned the arrogance based in colonial belief that authoritarian power was necessary to civilize and govern colonial peoples. He wrote: "I have said that I do not mind whether we have an Asian, European, or African Prime Minister in a self-governing Tanganyika. Both the UTP and the Tanganyika National Society would say the same. But the bases for saying that are different. Our friends of the UTP and the TNS start with the 'civilized man' willing to give concessions to the uncivilized. We start with the so-called uncivilized man demanding his rights as a man, that is the right to manage or mismanage his own affairs."[48]

Zuberi Mtemvu, a leading member of the TANU faction advocating racial favoritism for Africans, caustically dismissed the UTP and its rationale for white supremacy. He called the UTP a "paternalistic organization . . . which sees TANU as a danger to the Europeans and Asians in Tanganyika, and this makes its multi-racialism and even its paternalism a mockery." In an echo of Nyerere's letter, Mtemvu argued that TANU sought sovereignty, cognizant of its difficulties. "We do not regard the African as a child, we regard him as an adult who . . . should be free to manage or mismanage his own affairs."[49] Casting aside the veiled racism of paternalism, the acknowledgment by both Nyerere and Mtemvu that the newly enfranchised citizen might "mismanage his own affairs" hinted at a lingering anxiety about what democratic choice might mean for the colonial order under which they had always lived. With political responsibility would come the very real burden of consequences in formulating a postcolonial political order. For most people, that moment was still considered to be years in the future, but the outgoing British governor Edward Twining admitted in a private conversation with Nyerere that "the train might arrive ahead of schedule."[50]

In 1958, in accord with the UTP position, the government proposed a multiracial "tripartite" election based on racial parity. Many members of TANU, led by Bhoke Munanka and Mtemvu, demanded a boycott of the election, on the grounds that it was blatantly undemocratic.[51] At a party meeting in Tabora that year, Nyerere stepped down from his position as chair to oppose the boycott and unapologetically argue for participation, telling the meeting, "If we refuse, we are refusing independence."[52] Nyerere convinced the members that participation, even if unsavory, was a step in the right direction, leading strategically to the ultimate goal of universal suffrage for a single pool of candidates of all races. TANU did participate and engineered a stunning victory. Turning the British stratagem back on itself, TANU recruited candidates from each racial group that supported its nationalist policies.

In the election, TANU-endorsed candidates of every racial group won nearly every seat. The party newsletter *Sauti ya TANU* (The voice of TANU) proclaimed the victory with a biting Swahili aphorism, turning paternalist tables on colonial discourse: "If a child cries for a knife, let him cut himself."[53] Internally, TANU controlled the government, and progress toward independence quickened dramatically. Nyerere wrote a letter to colleagues in the Fabian Colonial Bureau saying that the "atmosphere has been suddenly revolutionised. . . . They know that TANU is invincible as long as there is no violence in the country." Fearing that combative colonial administrators would exercise the sort of cynical manipulation that was fueling violence in Rwanda, Nyerere pressed for their removal claiming "there is no likelihood of a break of violence in this country."[54]

With TANU's electoral dominance, the party of white moderation, the UTP, lost its leadership and began closing its doors within a month.[55] But almost immediately a new politics of exclusion emerged. In protest against TANU's participation in the tripartite election and its willingness to work closely with Europeans and Asians, Zuberi Mtemvu and his followers split with TANU and formed a rival political party, the African National Congress (ANC), which represented an ideology of racial exclusion directed toward Europeans and Asians with the slogan "Africa for Africans." Bhoke Munanka, Oscar Kambona, and others who sympathized with Mtemvu's position remained loyal to Nyerere and TANU, but quietly they pushed for racialist policies within the party. Another party formed around this time, the All-Muslim National Union of Tanganyika (AMNUT), representing coastal Muslim interests and working closely with the long-standing East African Muslim Welfare Society.[56] Each new party intimated rifts in the nationalist movement of unknowable consequence.[57]

With Harold Macmillan as the new prime minister in London supporting decolonization, former Kenyan administrator Richard Turnbull as a tough but forward-looking governor in Dar es Salaam, and TANU as a dominant force in Tanganyika, nationalist and colonial leaders agreed that "responsible government" would follow elections in September 1960. After an overwhelming TANU victory, Nyerere became chief minister in the legislature. TANU's election manifesto that year promised independence by the end of 1961, universal adult suffrage, Africanization of the civil service, integration and improvement in the educational system, the democratization of local government that was still under colonially appointed chiefs, fair terms for British expatriate civil servants willing to stay on after independence, and the waging of "a ruthless and relentless war against corruption everywhere."[58]

After a one-day constitutional conference in Dar es Salaam in March 1961, Nyerere officially became prime minister in May with the inauguration

Figure 2.2. The Constitutional Conference, March 1961. *From left:* Minister of Agriculture Derek Bryceson, Minister of Education Oscar Kambona, Legal Advisor Roland Brown, Chief Minister Julius Nyerere (*standing*), Minister of Commerce and Industry Nsilo Swai, Minister of Finance Ernest Vasey. © National Archives, UK.

of "internal self-government" as a prelude to independence. Formal independence came on December 9, 1961, with Tanganyika as a Commonwealth country still loyal to the Queen of England with Nyerere as prime minister and Richard Turnbull as governor-general. Six weeks later, to the bewilderment of both voters and European residents, Nyerere resigned, leaving the government to former labor leader Rashidi Kawawa, and took the year off to reshape TANU from a nationalist movement into an institution of governance. A year later Tanganyika became a republic, with Nyerere as the overwhelmingly popular elected president.

During this period the small opposition parties struggled against a political system dominated by TANU, with Nyerere at its head pushing for a one-party state. Mtemvu's ANC was banned repeatedly from holding public meetings, and ambitious rival politicians were by turns rusticated to remote parts of the country, given promotions out of the country, or absorbed ever more closely into Nyerere's fold. But their ideas did not disappear. The ANC motto of "Africa for Africans" gained traction among many

Tanganyikans who supported a racially exclusive logic of citizenship that echoed the divisive political rhetoric in Ruanda-Urundi.[59] The short-lived People's Democratic Party (PDP) that succeeded the ANC took up Mtemvu's cause as his party lost influence in the face of TANU successes and the active suppression of ANC activities. More worrisome was the percolation of racialist ideas within TANU itself, especially in the populist youth and women's wings. But, as Nyerere intended, a one-party state could contain those tensions within an internal debate while Nyerere controlled the terms of discussion. Africans looked with new eyes upon the task of governance, aware that government by a culturally African majority would reshape the entire of logic of authority, and that a truly sovereign state would necessarily represent and reflect African theories of social organization. Just what that would mean, however, was not yet clear to anyone.

The Legacy of Ethnic Politics

In the 1950s Tanganyikan society had become increasingly politicized as labor unions, political parties, and ethnic associations vied for influence. With independence, the government itself began to jockey for position in the new order, trying to contain internal threats to the nascent nation. There was no historical precedent to guide the young leaders of the new government, except the success that Ghana represented as an independent African state and, by 1961, the failure that the Congo exemplified with Katanga in secession. Nationalist leaders in Tanganyika endeavored "to grope forward," in Nyerere's phrasing, toward a new model of governance.[60] As the new prime minister said, "It may be that we shall create a new synthesis of individual liberty and the needs of man in society; freedom for each individual to develop the spark of divinity within himself at the same time as he contributes and benefits from his membership of a community. . . . If we can integrate these things into a new pattern of society then the world will have reason to be grateful that we have gained our independence."[61]

With independence came the need for a "new synthesis" in terms of administration, multicultural in both personnel and concept, that would confound the arrogant postures of the Cold War powers which both claimed "that they have evolved the perfect pattern of society." Nyerere perceived this task as a requirement for respectable membership in the international community. A sovereign Tanganyika would require a new concept of the relationship between citizen and state. The task obviously was a grandiose one, but given the circumstances there seemed to be little choice. The resonant organizational culture of self-conscious unity and mutual obligation articulated in late colonial ethnic associations provided seed material for a new nationalist conception of government.

Economic growth to keep pace with rising popular expectations was essential, and economic strategy grew from colonial precedent. The East Africa Royal Commission report of 1955 detailed a plan for economic growth in East Africa, reinforced in many ways by a World Bank report produced on the eve of independence.[62] The logic of the commission's report grew from the common wisdom of the era that in developing countries there existed a delicate balance between social stability and the demands of growing populations for a higher standard of living. Even as they promoted private economic interest, the commissioners proposed an interventionist state to "create conditions favourable to the exercise of those activities which make for progress," and to induce "modifications of traditional African society." They recommended a targeted plan for state-led development. Its broadest goal was to transform a colonial economy defined by a perceived conflict between "attitudes of clan, tribe and race" and "the impact of the modern world." Each of these impeded colonial governance, but both were inevitable by-products of Britain's mandate to modernize Tanganyikan society. "Human society stands buffeted between these two forces," the report stated, "and where the pressure is greatest there is a real breakdown."[63] To confront these trends, it recommended reforms that would expand Africans' access to private property and entrepreneurship with the hope of channeling these notionally destructive processes toward the creation of a nascent African middle class that would support a liberal state.

Nyerere's new government agreed that these trends were necessary and desired developments that harkened a new industrial economy and signaled TANU's task of marginalizing custom, ethnicity, and religion in order to forge a national identity.[64] But they were also disintegrative forces, as the British feared, that needed a national consciousness to replace them. Nyerere in particular absorbed the report's received wisdom that land tenure needed reform, that manufacturing could only grow incrementally, that foreign investment could not be avoided, that compulsion could occasionally yield popular benefits, and that all depended on transforming the rural economy. Pondering the report's assumption of a destructive dichotomy between custom and modernization, Nyerere sought a means to confront it. The new African state needed to risk disintegration for the sake of forming a national consciousness that could subsume the territory's myriad ethnic traditions.

Under British colonialism, ethnic identity and the political structures attached to it were harnessed to government under a theory of indirect rule, which saw Tanganyika's myriad ethnicities as so many delimited tribes, each a distinct political unit. Where there were chiefs, they were hired on and defended by the state. Such state support undermined the checks and balances that had once governed their relationship to their subjects. Where no chiefs existed, they were invented.[65] In both cases, local authority became more despotic, and "tribe" signaled a distinctly colonial discourse that implied political primitivism of the type for which J. S. Mill prescribed "an Akbar or a Charlemagne." This benevolent tyrant was the colonial state, and the newly hired chiefs were its agents. African residents of Tanganyika manipulated the colonial concept of tribe for their own purposes, and because of this TANU had to engage its logic for the larger national project.

As Nyerere prepared for the reality of governance, he sought a new relationship between state and citizen. His thinking recalled his reading of T. H. Green at Edinburgh, who contemplated the displacement of inherited obligations in the "clan-based system" with the contractual obligations of citizens. The independent government would have to reconstruct the social obligations once allocated to families, clans, and ethnic organizations. Nyerere gave notice to a crowd, "It is most probable taxes will be raised. We must put our hands in our pockets because we need more schools and hospitals."[66] With the burden of governance on the new leadership, ideals had to be quickly balanced with their coincident risks. At his first visit to the United Nations in 1955, Nyerere addressed his awareness of the implications of the nationalist movement—not simply independence, but also the subsequent need to establish a functioning nation: "Another objective of the Union [TANU] is to build up a national consciousness among the African peoples in Tanganyika. It has been said—and this is quite right—that Tanganyika is tribal, and we realize that we need to break up this tribal consciousness among the people and build up a national consciousness."[67]

During the transition to independence, Tanganyikans debated the still undefined hopes for national identity. Nyerere wanted to shape national consciousness into an inclusive and egalitarian vision of society, but in order to do so he needed to gain a dominant influence in public discourse. In particular, he sought to drive racialism from political debate in Tanganyika, and he was willing to sacrifice both democratic principle and his own career to achieve this. Nyerere's insistence on political and social unity arose from cultural habits of interaction between people and political authorities, and his own reflections on those habits and their implications in the formation of a constitutional state. Local cultural habits, rooted in provincial communities largely defined by ethnicity, were necessary for a sovereign African state. At the same time, the divisive potential of ethnic identity demanded that the specifics of local moral constructs be subsumed under national unity while their general principles were reified into a governing philosophy.[68] Nyerere's governing philosophy developed not as a philosophical ideal but as a strategy for the specific circumstances of Tanganyika at independence—especially the divisive issue of ethnic and racial politics, and their potential for subversive violence.[69]

By limiting social and political organization, the colonial government constrained the very ethnic groups defined by its own anthropologists, thus short-circuiting the transposition of these identities from dependent administrative agents to autonomous political units. For a half century, the colonial state had left the provision of social services to missionaries, clans, and village organizations. In the 1950s the government sought, somewhat impotently, to become the provider of the social services it had once left to the invented "tribes" that had been conveniently thought to serve these purposes.[70] TANU's victory in the 1958 tripartite election turned the question of colonial executive power relations on its head. The African nationalist party became the key to governmental power and not vice versa. The colonial government became a TANU government, with only the executive privileges of the governor-general and the state bureaucracy separating the party from total power in the territory. As with the colonial state, TANU's new hegemony left little room for competing political bodies. TANU's role resembled that of a colonial civil servant: administering unidirectional state action while articulating the needs of an illiterate populace whose desires were hard to discern in terms immediately amenable to a bureaucratic system. TANU had to absorb the moral obligations of the myriad ethnic associations and bind them into a new unified national vision, all the while fulfilling the paternalist role of the late colonial state.

Under colonial rule people had learned to express political demands through legally constituted ethnic organizations that came to reflect a colonial construct of "tribe."[71] Two fundamental motivations animated this invented ethnic ideology. The first was the felt need to create unity. Theories of genealogy rapidly faded into abstraction without the deliberate cultivation of a sense of ethnic unity. The second was obligation; the reproduction of ethnic structure and identity depended on the everyday practice of mutual obligation. The struggle to maintain this "moral economy" of ethnic identity was an ongoing conversation across British East Africa.[72] This ideal of unity, instituted in respect for local custom and lineage authorities, was fundamental to equitable management of patronage obligations. For example, in the decentralized villages of Zigua-speaking areas in Handeni District, British administrators had constructed a Zigua "tribe" with local representatives that had no basis in the local social structure, but were rather inheritors of the German system of appointed *akidas*.[73] Upon this imposed structure, British administrators and local authorities constructed a Zigua Tribal Council as an instrument of colonial rule.[74] By the late colonial period, community leaders working with an administrative system built around such tribal designations established mutual aid organizations like the *Chama cha Ukoo wa Wazigua* (Party of the Zigua Clan), built around these constructed tribal identities.[75] Ethnicity, articulated in the formal association of people identifying themselves as Zigua, was as much organizational strategy as a genealogical category. The unity it sought was not primordial but political.

Upcountry, the unity of community elders both established and checked the power of colonially appointed chiefs. In a homespun account of history and politics in Bukwimba country in the central part of the territory, Kadasson Mange illustrated the nature of this African social contract in a vision of protest against the chiefly hierarchy of colonial customary authority:[76]

> The chief will ask why [the villagers] have chased away their former headman to which [the villagers] will reply: "The former headman has been a fool, he never knew how to make rain; our food plantations are drying up due to lack of rain, so here we come to report to you that that man is no longer our headman. We have already chased him away from our village and we humbly ask you for another who knows how to make rain." The chief will then say that he will in due course send them another headman to which they all reply "*Wabeja Wanyama kutwingija ili buli lyenili*" (Thanks, your majesty, for removing from us this parasite). They will then leave happily homewards.[77]

Even in this scene of rural political conflict, we encounter the notional unity of the "villagers" who chase out their headman and present their case to the chief. They represent the sentiment that later gave rise to formally constituted tribal associations.[78] Their actions hinge on a previous consensus that unified the villagers. The institution of chief, where it existed, is seen as a centralizing, unifying institution. But we too easily ignore the deliberate cultivation of that unity in an ideology of ethnic or community cohesion. The office of chief in everyday life was not consciously taken to be one of unity, but of patronage, constituted by the submission of clients to a hierarchy of authorities, each bound by ties of mutual obligation.[79] Authority in many areas of the country was bound up in deliberative institutions of "imbalanced exchange" constructing what Roy Willis called a "consensual state."[80] The villagers in Mange's account demonstrated such a consensus articulated in the ideology of chieftainship. It was a power to oppose and control the chiefs appointed by the colonial state, who were often resented by their subjects. Mbuta Milando, a grandson of a colonial village headman from the Lake Victoria region, who briefly served as an area commissioner in western Tanganyika, also explained this ideology of interdependence of chief and subjects promoted in populist discourse.

> They are our chiefs after all, they are not their own chiefs. This is not their power irrespective of us. This is their power in respect of the fact they are our chiefs. . . . So it was not very easy for them to fight us as chiefs, because we were they, we were one among ourselves. . . . We were responsible for selecting and electing a chief, and for blessing him as the chief. We were part of the system of tribal leadership. Without us there is no chiefdom. So we were very powerful.[81]

Political activist and government minister Vedastus Kyaruzi further compared political decision making to long-standing norms of village government, illustrating how TANU's precursor, the Tanganyika African Association, reproduced the operation of colonial chiefly councils working toward consensus. "You take the chairman," Kyaruzi proposed, comparing the TAA chair to a local chief, "if he gets three people saying the same thing, nobody will raise a refutation. He fears to say the opposite."[82] Tanganyikans faced the challenge of building a democratic system in a culture oriented toward political consensus rather than competition. For Nyerere and the TANU leadership, this cultural background emerged in a strong preference for consensual decision making within the party and for organizing national politics as a single party system.[83] The political habits of ethnic organizations had to be absorbed without the divisive potential of their specific regional identities. This was a powerful approach to constructing a postcolonial government, but it brought with it a hostility toward division that regarded even legitimate democratic competition between opposing parties with abiding suspicion.

Debating the One-Party State

The colonial state had always depended on the administrative detour of indirect rule to communicate with its rural subjects, resulting in the constant misinterpretation of official directives. Likewise, rural residents could present pleas before a local chief without ever knowing whether or how their thoughts were subsequently communicated to the state.[84] Local "customary" authorities on the colonial payroll offered the state a claim on local order and at the same time used this position to manipulate and limit the state's overwhelming access to coercive force.[85] Nyerere's theory of governance at independence envisioned the inherited "machinery" of the colonial state in a new relationship to the people under its authority as members of an extended family. As independence approached, Nyerere wrote: "In his own traditional society the African has always been a free individual, very much a member of his community, but seeing no conflict between his own interests and those of his community. This is because the structure of his society was, in fact, a direct extension of the family."[86]

The nationalist movement, transformed into a governing political party, anchored Nyerere's institutionalization of a government that was still conceived by the public in personal terms. He was the personal face of the party, while its grassroots structure created a practice of personal interaction that contrasted with bureaucratic government administration. In preparation for independence, TANU reconstituted its Elders'

Committee, reinforcing the party's claim to authority.[87] Democracy, in the one-party system that Nyerere had begun to imagine, would be based on a model of authority aligned with a self-serving presentation of consensual practice in the region. The presence or absence of an organized opposition, in this conception, "makes little difference to free discussion and equality in freedom." This phrasing self-consciously echoed Mill, who equated the rights of liberty with adult responsibilities, and emphasized the ability to maintain open discussion as being prerequisite to maturity.[88] The echo of this ideal in Nyerere's version of village politics, where the maturity of community elders insured their right to participate in the discussion, served to anchor the question of liberty in Nyerere's rhetoric. In 1959, just prior to his announcement that the British had agreed to responsible self-government the following year, Nyerere publicly contemplated a one-party state for the first time in an interview with Russell Howe of the London *Sunday Times*. He said that he expected that Tanganyika would be a one-party state for fifteen years after independence. To reconcile a one-party state with democratic practice, he proposed: "The two essentials for 'representative' democracy are the freedom of the individual, and the regular opportunity for him to join with his fellows in replacing, or reinstating, the government of his country by means of the ballot-box and without recourse to assassination. An organized opposition is not an essential element."[89]

In response, Zuberi Mtemvu wrote an eloquent letter to the *Tanganyika Standard* to make the case for an opposition party. Mtemvu had left TANU together with several followers to protest Nyerere's compromise in participating in the racially rigged tripartite election, and formed the ANC to represent a racially defined model of politics for Tanganyika. The ANC designated Africans as the only legitimate holders of major public offices. As much as Mtemvu represented a confrontational racial policy, he also represented the legitimate reality of a competing political party. His letters on that topic sparked several months of robust debate by readers of the *Tanganyika Standard*. In a compelling defense of multiparty democracy, Mtemvu argued that in order for there to be real choice, "people must be free to criticize the government."

> Opposition must have a real chance to organise, to secure information, and to gain support in public opinions in order to be able to defeat the Government and to form the government in its turn.... In slightly different language, it means that political parties must not play "for keeps" to gain their way at the cost of abolishing the opposition or the rules of the game. That is why the essence of the democratic method is often described as sportsmanship. The method makes peaceful change possible and every election becomes, as it were, a lawful revolution.[90]

The debate that ensued pitted Mtemvu's democratic theory against his party's threat to upset the racial and political unity of the country, such as it was. T. K. Malaba responded to Mtemvu's letter, endorsing its democratic theory but worrying about the divisive politics of "Africa for Africans" as the country tried "to build up one nation of people of all races," amid the lingering race-based resentments of colonialism. "It is very premature" Malaba continued, "to talk of an opposition party now unless Mr. Mtemvu wants to break the solid foundation we have laid."[91] In response, Abdallah Stanslaus offered full support for Mtemvu's multiparty democracy, recognizing the need to assure "that our beloved country is ruled by democratic principles, without any muzzling of our so-called Opposition Party, as is happening in Ghana."[92]

Some writers continued to support Nyerere's position that political debate could best happen within a single party, while others insisted on Mtemvu's right to an independent party. One emphasized the trepidation with which many people approached the unknown consequences of independence, but aligned himself with Mtemvu's protest that fifteen years of one-party rule would pave the way to autocracy. Absorbed in habits of colonial tutelage, the writer opined that opposition politics should be established before the British left, "for we have always regarded them as our leaders and teachers. Whatever mistakes we are going to make about democracy in their presence can be easily corrected by them."[93] Joseph Kasella Bantu, a loyal TANU hand, responded by presenting TANU as the analogue of a village council of elders, both "keen critic as well as adviser of the people whom TANU itself elected to the Legislature." In performing its critical duties, TANU would encompass all opinions and thus be "working as an opposition" and as a vehicle for the final consensus. With a notable lack of skepticism, Bantu offered India and Ghana as countries where a similar configuration was taking root.[94]

With the inception of internal self-government, the TANU newsletter, *Sauti ya TANU*, printed a series of articles explaining the origins of democracy and the functions of government. Issue no. 76 specifically targeted those who argued that TANU's dominance meant that democracy did not exist in Tanganyika, and those who believed that a workers' party had to oppose the ruling party. Nyerere, writing as "a citizen governed by a TANU government," pointed out that if one of the main parties in Britain won all the seats in Parliament, no one would argue that Britain was not a democracy. "This shows clearly that if the majority happen to vote for one party, then this is indeed pure democracy."[95] In Nyerere's insistence on unity and determination to avoid planting the seeds of divisive violence, TANU sought to absorb conflict through its ability to forge consensus with resonant ideologies of unity and obligation. But as the nationalist movement took up its role as the administrator of the transitional colonial state, TANU fell subject to the particular theories of governance that adhered to it—of personal authority gradually giving way to bureaucratic authoritarianism.[96] Preparing for independence, Nyerere dramatized his own experience of political consciousness as a gradual realization that the institutions of government had a life separate from those who represented them:

> The affairs of the community, as I have shown, were conducted by free and equal discussion, but nevertheless the African's mental conception of "Government" was personal—not institutional. When the word "government" was mentioned, the African thought of the chief. . . . In colonial Africa this "personal" conception of government was unchanged, except that the average person hearing "government" mentioned now thought of the District Commissioner. . . . When, later, the idea of government as an institution began to take hold of some African "agitators" such as myself, who had been reading Abraham Lincoln and John Stuart Mill . . . it was the very people who had come to symbolize "Government" in their persons who resisted our demands—the District Commissioner, the Provincial Commissioners, and the Governors.[97]

As African political leaders looked toward independence, they became absorbed in broad theories of political economy. For Tanganyika in the 1950s, this included echoes of late colonial authoritarianism meant to bring about transformative social change. The increasingly active labor movement was a key point of debate, setting populist militancy against government expertise in guiding the economy. The debate over opposition parties in the newspapers was soon overtaken by debate about the labor movement. The challenge for TANU was how to maintain its ability to represent the familial virtues and communal sentiment that girded its legitimacy while at the same time credibly taking the reins of the state in its internal and external manifestations.

When Nyerere spoke of the future of the struggle for African independence, the strategic balance of unity and obligation formed the core of his thought. In the name of Pan-Africanism, he advocated for a decentralized unity formed through the cooperation of states in regional federations. He bound this logic to the existential troika of governmental enemies—"poverty, ignorance, and disease"—that he repeated constantly in his speeches across Tanganyika and abroad, such as at a conference of independent African nations in 1960. "In the struggle against colonialism the fundamental unity of the people of Africa is evident and deeply felt," Nyerere explained. "It is, however, a unity forged in adversity in battle against outside Government. If the triumph in this battle is to be followed by an equal triumph against the forces of neo-imperialism and also against poverty, ignorance, and disease, then this unity must be strengthened and maintained."[98]

In shaping national institutions, Nyerere drew on the habits of consensus cultivated in ethnic organizations to guide political decision making at all levels. As anyone who has participated in East African institutions is aware, the lengthy method of reaching a consensus through continuous discussion is a ubiquitous aspect of organizational behavior in the region.[99] Nyerere referred to this mode of decision making in an article published in 1961 in a book titled *Africa Speaks*. Declaring government by all people in free discussion to be the ideal of democracy, he cited a quote from a "delightful little book" by the missionary and political activist Guy Clutton-Brock: "The Elders sit under the big tree, and talk until they agree."[100] Hearkening in this way to Rousseau might work for small communities, he suggested, but in larger societies it had to be modified through systems of representation.[101]

Elaborating an argument he had been developing for several years, Nyerere explained the reasoning behind his one-party proposal: "The same nationalist movement, having united the people and led them to independence, must inevitably form the first Government of the new state." A multiparty system, built around interparty competition, demanded internal party discipline. In the situation of postcolonial Africa, where successful nationalist movements brought about independence and dominated national politics, such party loyalties would threaten the free discussion that he counted as the basis of democracy. So long as regular elections took place, he concluded, "an organized opposition is not an essential element."[102] When he later initiated the one-party state proposal at a TANU conference in January 1963, he built on this point: "The task of imposing party discipline, of limiting freedom of expression in Parliament, with no rival party to help, would sooner or later involve us in something far worse than the factionalism of which I have accused the two-party enthusiasts. It would become more and more necessary to limit freedom of discussion within the party itself, until eventually it was almost entirely suppressed."[103]

Nyerere presented a one-party state not only as a hedge against civil war, but also as a *more* democratic system for Africa than the multiparty systems of Europe, where feudal class differences had left the legacy of political parties representing their opposing socioeconomic perspectives. He proposed that any real divisions in the postcolonial era were those between patriots and traitors—those who supported decolonization and those who did not; any lesser divisions were superficial and could only lead to factionalism. In this Manichean presentation, Nyerere argued, the former was dangerous, leading to existential strife; the latter a waste of time, nothing more than a glorified "football match."

Nyerere's argument against opposition politics echoed those used by dictators around the world, but less obvious is its locally resonant logic of unity and its presumed virtue. Nyerere's rhetoric here, and his conception of democracy as simply a form of free and open discussion, derived both from a nostalgic vision of precolonial African society and from his Edinburgh education. Echoing T. H. Green's Utilitarian philosophy, Nyerere argued that democracy would mean little without a sovereign government able to carry out its mandates. "The maintenance of law and order in any society," Nyerere argued at the United Nations, "depends upon there being one supreme authority which is accepted by the majority and which, if need be, can assert its authority on a dissenting minority."[104]

Green's Utilitarianism had a foundational influence on Fabian socialism, which was an integral part of TANU's inheritance.[105] TANU's Kivukoni College took root in Dar es Salaam in late 1960 with help from the Fabian Colonial Bureau in London, which arranged teachers and shipments of books for the library, bringing Nyerere's Edinburgh education to TANU cadres.[106] Fabian stalwart Joan Wicken arrived in country to spearhead TANU's ideological education program, modeling Kivukoni on Ruskin College at Oxford, tied closely to Britain's Labour Party. Karimjee Trusts donated £60,000 in cash, while TANU and the Bukoba Native Cooperative Union pledged £50,000 each toward the construction of the college. Meanwhile, Wicken mobilized an international fund-raising drive, appealing to donors in country and abroad. As she recalled, "Sometimes we did as many as six meetings a day; sometimes we visited individual farmers and traders... and the response was incredible. People without cash gave maize meal, chickens, beans, eggs—anything they had. Wealthier people gave notes, traders (mostly Asian) cheques, and in one place a chief gave a cow, another a treasured silver watch."[107]

Upcountry the TANU Youth League embarked on a literacy drive in January 1960, and the TANU Women's Union attracted rural women to literacy classes with lessons in sewing and knitting.[108] Through its cadres TANU seeded a new nationalist sense of citizenship in the hearts and minds of the diverse peoples that lived in the territory of Tanganyika—not just by enumerating newly attained rights but also by promoting an emotional bond to the new national community.

Throughout his career, Nyerere sought to unify his African intellectual roots with his European ones. It is notable that the one-party politics introduced by Nyerere bore a distinct likeness to the ideology presented in Kadasson Mange's history of Bukwimba: through village consensus the headman was called into account for his obligations to his subjects and removed not through a competition, whether electoral or physical, but rather through the consensual opinion of the village that had reached a point of irreversible dissatisfaction. Consensus is a process of articulating the subtleties of a mutual understanding, and of arriving at a proposal to which all parties agree that can then guide cooperative action. The chief or president, in this understanding, is portrayed as a receptacle of local consensus.[109] This understanding allowed African communities to keep a rein on political authority in their areas during the colonial period. The supporters of powerful ethnic representatives like Thomas Marealle in Chagga country or Kidaha Makwaia in Sukuma country hoped that locally constructed authorities could likewise constrain the totalizing state that Nyerere imagined.

Racial affinity presented a powerful ideology of unity that echoed the politics of ethnicity. Nyerere's challenge was to marginalize the politics of race until a more inclusive political ideology could be inaugurated. Eliminating divisive racial discourse proved a far more stubborn task than progressives of the time could have expected, because, as Brennan has argued, racial invective provided a powerful populist tool for constructing a national identity.[110] The question was how much suppression could take place without destroying the democratic legitimacy of the state and its sovereignty.

Part 2

Internal Sovereignty

3

Independence and the Fear of Division

As they took the reins of independent government in Tanganyika, Nyerere and his colleagues feared that the divisive politics of the opposition would undermine the establishment of a peaceful nation. Although their fears bore some justification in the racialist tone of TANU's opponents, there was no existential threat to the government at independence as there had been in the Congo. Instead, the TANU-led government preemptively tried to dictate the ideological limitations of politics within the new nation by using selective political repression. TANU thereby sought to define the character of sovereignty in the new nation as nonracial.

With preparations for independence celebrations firmly under way, Nyerere's frustrations with the restive labor movement and the racialist views of its leaders poured out in speech after speech and pushed him toward tighter control of political opposition. He intimated a fear that foreigners were trying to manipulate the labor movement; he implied that the labor leadership would lead to dictatorship and that TANU represented the real democratic choice. With fears of instability uppermost in the minds of TANU's leadership, independence inaugurated a new state that valued security over democracy. Somewhat hypocritically, Nyerere justified TANU's suppression of the opposition by goading the voters to choose another party if they wished: "I am telling you, let not anyone get hexed even a little to threaten this government. Once we are governing ourselves we don't want another person to come and start a dictatorship here. We don't rule by dictatorship. If we are no good, then choose another and we'll see."[1]

Comparing the colonial state to an animal brought down by a group of hunters, Nyerere displayed a knack for the earthy metaphor that animated rural speech.[2] He lambasted labor leaders for encouraging strikes in protest of the slow pace of Africanization in government offices in the months just before independence. He alleged that labor's ongoing mobilization arose from a purely selfish ambition for power on the part of young leaders who neither understood nor respected the achievement that independence represented and the grave responsibilities of governance.

> Let me explain to you the state of the country under a Prime Minister. I didn't go to school until I was older. After raising goats and sheep and hunting I realized that there is a certain pattern. When hunting there is no problem, other than maybe someone gets wounded by an arrow, but that is not a big problem. Problems start when the animal has died, that's when fighting starts, because this one wants that piece and another cuts another piece, and that's when people start to get their fingers cut. This is the difficulty of having a Prime Minister in the country; the hunters, in this case, are you, the labor unions, TANU, cooperatives etc. We have cried for independence without difficulty. Now that this animal called Independence has fallen, conflicts begin. People are fighting each other for meat.[3]

Indeed, independence was a living thing, and much debated throughout the country. The TANU government was fully aware of the symbolic power of the independence celebrations for its standing as a new nation on the world stage, and just as aware of the violence that had undermined that new hope elsewhere. Newspaper headlines gave voice to foreign prejudices, painting African independence stereotypically as a step toward barbarism. One report described attacks on the symbols of colonial rule during independence celebrations in the Cameroons in January 1960; celebrations were cut short, foreign dignitaries sent home, and 40 people lay dead.[4] Closer to home, Congolese voters lined up while civil war broke out amid ineffectual UN peacekeepers, ruthless foreign mercenaries, and upcountry militias fighting with spears and poison-tipped arrows.[5] Meanwhile, hundreds of Belgians fled as antiwhite violence rose after independence in the Congo, arriving in secrecy by train in Dar es Salaam in July 1960, and thence transferred to a charter flight to Belgium.[6] In Ruanda-Urundi, violence broke out, leaving dozens dead and a fearful antagonism that undermined the quest for a unified nationalist vision. After elections there in 1959, American intelligence sources reported that "there appears to be no place whatsoever in the Ruanda political situation for a 'national reconciliation.'"[7] Inasmuch as these incidents functioned as a discourse justifying foreign prejudices, they were also fearful precedents for Tanganyikan politicians who approached independence with a good deal of trepidation.

With all the bad press in neighboring countries, Minister of Home Affairs George Kahama warned people explicitly not to "mar the brightest day in our history" because any incident would be "magnified out of all proportion" and thus sully Tanganyika's image. "Tanganyika has a reputation throughout the world as a peace-loving country," he said. Cautioning against acts of vengeance and words of intimidation, Kahama assured the public there would be no need to panic since the government would ensure law and order. "If I could," he pondered in bourgeois reverie, "I would certainly put a ban on drunkenness." He offered instead TANU's mantra of apolitical social improvement: "The challenge that lies ahead when everyone must vow to do all within his power to increase the health and prosperity of this country and actively to join in the fight against ignorance, poverty and disease. That is the real meaning of independence."[8]

The triumphant drive to independence had knit together a powerful nationalist vision of multiracial unity. Without violence and largely on his own terms, Nyerere led Tanganyika to independence two decades earlier than expected. The nascent forces opposing TANU's political dominance coalesced around the labor movement and the nativist rhetoric of Zuberi Mtemvu and his breakaway party, the African National Congress. Both the ANC and the labor movement built support with racial demagoguery under the banner of Africanization. Their message resonated among many in TANU and its constituencies and threatened to dissolve the nationalist consensus crystallized in Nyerere's party and its ideology. They represented a personal affront to Nyerere and his beliefs, but they also represented the sort of ethnic antagonism that threatened Ruanda-Urundi. The ANC threatened TANU's theme of intercultural cooperation with discordant notes of race-baiting amid their democratic ideals: "When is [Nyerere] going to give us the constitution that guarantees one man, one vote, one value, and which should bring to an end the participation of Indians and Europeans in the legislative and executive organs because they happen to be Indians and Europeans and richer than we are?"[9]

Nyerere was afraid that racial animosity could take root in Tanganyika if TANU did not vigilantly oppose it. Bad publicity arising from any incidents would multiply the crippling economic consequences of ongoing strikes, destroy any prospect of improving living standards, and animate racial hatred if it were not already in flames. It was a vicious circle already evident in Ruanda-Urundi and the Congo and threatening Uganda and Kenya. Nyerere realized that ethnic conflict often masked class conflict. He sought to define the nationalist movement waging the battle for independence so as to negate internal schisms: "The people who are waging this battle in Africa are not former feudal overlords who want to reestablish a lost authority. They are not a rich mercantile class whose freedom to exploit the masses is being limited by the colonial powers. They are the common people of Africa. The ordinary men and women of this continent are now demanding for themselves those rights of humanity."[10]

The prospect of a divisive opposition confronted Nyerere with an impossible choice between democratic principles and the necessary pursuit of nonracialism and economic growth if there were to be any hope for peace. The rise of ethnic nationalism in alliance with the labor movement threatened to undermine TANU's political capital in negotiations with the colonial state and spark divisive competition between internal political entities like labor unions representing particular groups of workers, ethnic leaders with specific local constituencies, and African racialists who wanted to exclude minorities. Nyerere viewed these opponents as representatives of certain segments of the whole population, and believed that their pursuit of their own interests threatened what he perceived as the fragile unity of the new nation. Emulating the Machiavellian tactics of Nkrumah in Ghana and Nehru in India, Nyerere chose to suppress racialist opposition within his own party and in the opposition parties, thereby bolstering the authority of a unitary Tanganyikan government. He hoped to seed an African nationalism defined not by populist xenophobia but by a loyalty to local cultural mores, TANU's developing Africanist philosophy, and an elected African majority.

Governing Labor in an African Context

Tanganyika had never been a simple capitalist economy, and labor had long been woven into ideas about citizenship and community. The colonial economy was a dependent one, and precolonial economies were built around very different socioeconomic relationships than the financial institutions and markets of twentieth-century capitalism.[11] Governance in East Africa historically was intimately linked to the control of labor, and this was a well-established theme in popular historical memory. In the 1950s, among Ndendeuli people in the southern districts of Songea and Tunduru, a regular and apparently long-standing part of village life was participation in communal work parties organized on a rotating basis by household heads to prepare ground for planting. Both the decentralized leadership of such parties and the obligation to participate in them were integral to Ndendeuli social organization. "We cannot live alone in small hamlets because we need the labour of other people," insisted one villager.[12]

Among Sukuma people just south of Lake Victoria, work parties were the province of unmarried youth, for whom communal work was both social and remunerative. Young people from a village were members of a Basumba labor society and would hire themselves out for agricultural work. But as a sort of community insurance, they also provided free labor for rebuilding a house destroyed by fire, maintaining community irrigation works, or providing for community defense and security.[13] Sukuma people had another system of more centralized labor allocation through chiefly tribute relations. Sukuma chief David Kidaha Makwaia, upon returning from school as a young man, was given a large field to plant, a task intended to teach the young noble "how to be a manager of people."[14]

Elders in the Iringa region likewise recalled labor tributes demanded by the old Hehe state. Prior to the European conquest, the Hehe *mtwa* (chief) existed above the law and administered his domain through officials in every village. In an interview in the early 1970s, one elder recalled the system: "The Mtwa was the father of the society.... When the Mtwa wanted certain work to be done he issued orders to his subordinates who would then make the necessary announcement. When the Mtwa wanted his fields to be cultivated, he could order the various Vasagila [state officials] to give him a certain number of people who would work on his fields in turn."[15]

It is not clear if this memory reflected precolonial practice, or colonial corvée labor projected into the past, but it was firmly entrenched in people's memory of precolonial times. Both German and British administrators demanded labor from colonial chiefs.[16] Colonial governance was built largely on the matter of mobilizing and managing labor, compulsions that refracted through local narratives of labor and community.[17] These ideas of moral expectation remained cogent, reinterpreted into song and story well into the independence era.[18] This cultural context may have shaped workers' perceptions, during the last years of colonial rule, that leaders in the increasingly active unions were too dictatorial.[19]

In Nyamwezi areas in the dry central part of the country, key to the precolonial caravan trade, chiefs had commanded large retinues of slaves and could demand labor of their subjects much as Hehe leaders were remembered to do. After the German conquest, administrators drew on chiefly custom to demand labor for colonial projects, and many chiefs sought the government's favor by enthusiastically and sometimes coercively calling out villagers for service. The effect of this colonial abuse of local custom, with its echo of slavery, was to send men to the coast to seek wage work, while their families retreated to scattered homesteads in hopes of avoiding chiefly predations.[20] But as these traditional chiefs in government service lost their legitimacy, a localized institution of "millet chiefs," chosen and appointed by community members, took hold to organize work parties. Their popularity was much resented by both government officials and customary chiefs, who were aware that their authority over labor had been co-opted at the community level. As TANU came to prominence in the mid-1950s, Nyamwezi millet chiefs became unofficial party representatives, passing on campaign information and organizing political rallies. With their involvement, TANU rallies opened with the cry "People of the Threshing Stick! People of the Fork! People of the Broom!" The tools of work parties, and the elected millet chiefs that managed them, became symbols of TANU's vision of democratic independence.[21]

Figure 3.1. Chief Minister Julius Nyerere speaks at a political event, circa 1961. Minister of Commerce and Industry Nsilo Swai and Minister of Education Oscar Kambona sit at far left; Minister of Legal Affairs Abdallah Fundikira sits at far right (*foreground*). © Tanzania Information Services (MAELEZO).

Publicly envisioning self-rule in the approach to independence, Nyerere updated the paternalist sentiment of a late colonial motto *Uhuru na Jasho* (Freedom and Sweat) coined by TANU supporter Randal Sadleir.[22] Nyerere's *Uhuru na Kazi* (Freedom and Work) deliberately equated self-governance with work to address the high expectations of immediate material benefit from independence, as well as his concern that TANU's populist energy would dissipate into the more complex requirements of governance.[23] This concern is evident in a party pronouncement the following year that all should work hard because "laziness is the main enemy of the nation."[24] The slogan permeated TANU's grass roots where politically aware people greeted each other by calling out, "Uhuru!" and responding "Kazi ya TANU!"[25] Before a crowd of fifteen thousand on a hot afternoon in January 1960, Nyerere compared the country to a football team, by pointing out that although the one who scores is celebrated, the goal is an accomplishment of the whole team: "We want our responsible government to be modeled on that." From this, he proposed that because every person was created in God's image, all were worthy of respect regardless of their occupation. All were implicated in the work of nation building, which Nyerere presented as literally physical: "If we want to build a bridge we shall tell European youths, Asian youths, and African youths that they must go out and build it."[26] Subtly paraphrasing a Bible passage, he told the crowd that if someone doesn't want to work, then they should just leave the country because there was much work to be done.[27] But he also invoked local habits of labor organization through long-standing obligations enforced by precolonial and colonial-era chiefs.

Confronting Christopher Tumbo

In addition to Mtemvu's ANC and its racialist fellow travelers in TANU, the labor movement represented a powerful independent force in Tanganyika in the late 1950s. By far the strongest union was the Plantation Workers Union with a hundred thousand members in 1957 working in the sisal fields. Another sixty thousand union members were scattered among a handful of national unions in the export economy and government service.[28] The late 1950s were a time of spiraling strikes led by ambitious leaders as eager to make a statement about African independence as to secure wage gains. Initially they could do both. Between 1958 and 1960, sisal cutters saw their wages double as a result of union pressure.[29] TANU actively backed the unions in the mid-1950s, urging the public to support the strikers. Even local chiefs occasionally threw their support behind strikers. But by 1959, there were 205 strikes adding up to 400,000 workdays lost, and in 1960, even more determined stoppages caused a loss of nearly 1.5 million days of labor. As independence approached, this drain on the economy began to worry TANU leaders, not least because some among the movement's radical leadership called for a racially distinct black African nation. They articulated this vision using "Africanization" as a code word.[30] Ostensibly referring to the gradual replacement of expatriate workers with local ones, in common usage it denoted a policy of favoring racially African people and treating non-Africans as second-class citizens.[31] On Christmas Day 1959, African postal workers went on strike against the advice of the TFL and without informing their distrusted Asian counterparts.[32]

The new year brought a flood of wildcat strikes on the docks in Dar es Salaam Harbor and in the sisal industry upcountry. Building on this momentum, labor leaders wanted to shut down the entire transportation and communication infrastructure of the country—on the docks, the posts, and the railways.[33] Their ambitions found much support, but were also met with dissension.[34] As the Dockworkers' and Stevedores' Union mulled whether to strike, a letter writer told *Tanganyika Standard* readers that threats of a strike on the docks "are the foolish utterances of a Union official who is not a dockworker and who does not represent the dockworkers."[35] The letter writer may have been referring to the ambitious young leader of the Tanganyika Railway Workers' Union, Christopher Kasanga Tumbo.

Tumbo had conferred with his East African colleagues over the New Year's holiday, and when he returned he announced that a strike was "almost inevitable." He then maintained steady pressure on management for a seven-and-three-quarter-shilling daily wage increase through repeated threats to strike.[36] Calculating that the wage increase would cost £2 million a year, the railway manager personally wrote his most valuable employees enjoining them to "stay loyal," and then used the newspapers to accuse Tumbo of holding the country "ransom."[37] The charismatic Tumbo was a rising star in the Tanganyikan political arena. Leading the Railway Workers' Union gave the precocious twenty-five-year-old tremendous political influence that translated into economic power when a strike threatened. The Tanganyika African Government Workers' Union condemned Tumbo's plans, and the Kenya Railway Workers' Union was not ready to cooperate in a joint action in both countries. Tumbo launched tirades against both organizations, demanding an apology from the government workers and dismissing the Kenyan labor leaders as colonial stooges.[38] On February 10, 1960, ten thousand members of the Railway Union began a bitter strike that lasted nearly three months, testing Nyerere's patience and eventually losing TANU support, marking the first break between TANU and the labor movement radicals.[39]

The strike gave rise to an intense publicity battle. Railway management claimed the strike was ineffectual, with no disruption to schedules, and accused the union of enforcing the walkout with threats of mob justice. Within three days of the walkout, Tumbo met with the railway manager to discuss an end to the strike. Nyerere was out of the country and TANU inconspicuously kept its distance at first while its allied union, the TFL, limited its support of the strike to calls for racial solidarity. Calling on the Asian Harbour Workers' Union for support, Rashidi Kawawa, as TFL president, expressed "great shock that Europeans and Asians are volunteering as strike-breakers in the railway labor dispute." Kawawa admonished both sides not to turn the strike into a racial battle that would upset the political culture envisioned by TANU's leadership, "in which people of all origins and creeds shall live together in peace and as members of one nation."[40]

Public support for the strike soon began to drop off. By the end of the first week, the Iringa Trades Council, which had supported Tumbo's call for a boycott of Indian shops to protest strikebreakers, called for an end to the boycott.[41] As the strike entered its third week, TANU finally entered the fray, calling on "all leaders concerned with the railway strike to make some effort to come to an agreement and end the strike as soon as possible."[42] Nevertheless, a brief strike on the docks finally took hold in support of the railway workers, and wildcat sisal workers struck in the Morogoro region even after an agreement was reached throughout the sisal industry to raise wages.[43] Meanwhile, under Tumbo's obstinate leadership, the railway strike dragged on for another two months, with rallies of support from local supporters and promises of support garnered abroad.[44] Finally, while traveling with Tom Mboya to Brussels, Tumbo failed to find support from the International Confederation of Free Trade Unions (ICFTU).[45] With this disappointment, Tumbo agreed to international arbitration, and publicly acceded to the idea of a permanent commission for industrial disputes.[46] The Railway Union accepted an underwhelming settlement with the Railway Administration, but it was not the end of Tumbo's popularity or his ambition.

In July the Railway Union met to celebrate the strike and plan future steps. Tumbo made Africanization his central target, stirring up resentments about colonial inequalities. In an opening speech, he recalled the great European revolutions, and warned "this can also happen here. As long as some people get 6,000 [shillings] while others get 40, what do you expect?" His taste of power had left a distinct impression on him. Of his recent travels, he raved that wherever he went, "a white man served me." Despite moderating speeches by TFL president Kawawa and TANU general secretary Oscar Kambona, who both pointed out the multiracial character of the crowd gathered for the meeting, Tumbo carried the rank and file with denunciations of European and Asian strikebreakers. On the third day of the conference, Tumbo's stand against a race-blind union register won the day, "because Asians and Europeans," according to the meeting's minutes, "do not have the proper spirit to be called Tanganyikans."[47]

In the Legislative Council in October, Nyerere excoriated the policy of rapid Africanization pushed by Tumbo and others, "citing figures to show that in none of the areas in question was there available even a fraction of the qualified African personnel needed to 'Africanize.'" Mocking past speeches by individual members, Nyerere finished each critique with suggestions like "the Honorable Member should have his head examined by a doctor."[48] Speaking for over an hour, Nyerere explained that Africanization was only one aspect of the broader policy of "localization" that entailed filling civil service posts with permanent residents and future citizens, regardless of their race. Africanization, he continued, was a manner of focusing on the training and placement of racially African citizens who had been excluded from education during the colonial period. In this sense, such favoritism was comparable to the favoritism granted to whites and Asians in the 1960 "responsible government" constitution; it was a temporary strategy to ensure a full representation of the various groups that made up the country despite their demographic or educational inequalities. He emphasized that non-Africans could have the same love for the country and its people as Africans, and that in any case, the task of fighting for independence was over. It had all been agreed on, and what remained was simply a complex process of transition that could not happen overnight. "I have spoken at such length to show that this issue of our independence is no longer a matter of demanding it, rather it is a matter of making plans."[49]

In the new government constituted in September 1960, Rashidi Kawawa was made minister for local government and housing, and TANU fought hard to ensure that its candidate, Michael Kamaliza, prevailed over Tumbo for leadership of the TFL.[50] With Kawawa in the government and TANU ally Kamaliza at the head of the TFL, the two organizations were joined at the hip.[51] This was clearly the intention of the top TANU leadership. In a speech on December 29, 1960, Nyerere argued that the TFL and its constituent unions were formed in cooperation with TANU during the drive to independence, and the idea that the unions could be independent from TANU was thus "an absurdity."[52] In private Nyerere expressed a less theoretical motivation. Describing a heady atmosphere with labor leaders promising an industrial utopia where citizens would be given motorcycles and European wages, Vedastus Kyaruzi recalled a conversation with Nyerere around the time "labor was getting wild." Kyaruzi asked how he was going to handle them. Nyerere's response echoed both European statism and chiefly labor management—with a healthy dose of the authoritarian preferences of the colonial state: "The duty of government is to govern. We are going to govern."[53]

Nyerere had begun quiet consultations with Ghanaian labor leaders over how to manage trade unions. John Tettegah, the general secretary of the Ghana Trades Union Congress, visited in October 1960 and extolled the virtues of close cooperation between the government and trade unions. He showed how employers could not fight a union supported by the government, and how the government could mandate a "check-off system" for collecting union dues. Some TFL members, led by Tumbo, resisted Tettegah's visit and his message, but moderates began to move toward greater cooperation with the government.[54] A later report by the Tanganyika Salaries Commission, chaired by another Ghanaian adviser, Dr. A. L. Adu, made similar recommendations, but the times were inauspicious for disciplined cooperation.

Victor Mkello had made some progress toward a cooperative Joint Council of union and employer representatives in the sisal industry, but the plan fell apart due to the rivalry of leaders within the union.[55] TFL plans to centralize union funding and decision making drove Tumbo to break with the TFL, taking several powerful unions with him.[56] Tumbo condemned proposals to strengthen TFL ties with the government, accused moderate leaders of misusing union funds, and threatened to sever ties between the TFL and its biggest constituent unions.[57] TFL moderates accused Tumbo of creating dissension with an aim toward taking over the union, and they tried to expel him and his colleagues from the TFL. But Tumbo's popularity in the larger unions prevented his ejection, and the TFL was split between TANU loyalists and Tumbo supporters.[58] Hehe chief and TANU supporter Adam Sapi was elected to chair a mediation commission. His report advocated that TFL and TANU remain separate organizations and called for a vote of confidence within the TFL. Kamaliza narrowly won the vote, but Tumbo and his race-baiting populism continued to make headway and gain influence.[59]

Settling Differences until Independence

Because of the racial politics of the labor movement, many of its activists found common cause with the ANC and its racial rhetoric.[60] When dockworkers threatened to take over the port to show their dissatisfaction with an arbitration agreement that failed to put enough Africans in management positions, TANU's minister for health and labor Derek Bryceson, a British farmer, reminded them of TANU's position that "did not recognize dual loyalties in nationalism." He explained that the new government policy was to "localize" the civil service, filling positions with people who considered themselves future citizens of Tanganyika regardless of race. He called Africanization "the battle cry of the followers of Mr. Mtemvu."[61] In the ensuing months, reports circulated that trade union members formerly loyal to TANU began joining the ANC "because of dissatisfaction over the Government's policy on Africanisation."[62]

In the effort to restrain racialist populism, Nyerere again raised the prospect of a single-party system. With TANU dominating the Legislative Assembly and guaranteed support for every bill, he argued that the opposition would be nothing more than "these five innocuous fellows there." In such a situation the opposition was only window dressing, he contended. "Therefore, in our circumstances an Opposition becomes ridiculous. It rules out debate."[63] Nyerere hoped that an authentic opposition would emerge with time and told the American consul that he expected a new opposition to emerge when the TANU faction that already sided with Mtemvu broke off to support or displace Mtemvu. He hoped only that the opposition would be "responsible, straightforward." He had been smoothing over disputes within TANU in order to present a united front for the achievement of responsible government, and for now it was "necessary to settle differences."[64]

At his first press conference after assuming office as prime minister in May 1961, Nyerere confirmed comments he had made while in West Africa that if any group based their opposition on race, religion, or tribe, he would "lock it up—and if I did not have a law to do so, I would make one." He argued that to be legitimate, opposition must aim at improving government functions but always remain "loyal" to the country, implying treason on the part of the ANC.[65] For Nyerere, Mtemvu's disloyalty was not that of secession but of racial exclusion.[66] With an uneducated electorate—at once frightened, frustrated, and euphoric about the prospect of independence—the constraints of rational choice were difficult for voters to gauge. As he had argued before the National Assembly, Nyerere saw in Mtemvu's ideology of racial citizenship a contagious threat to national unity and peace. "They are beginning to draw a distinction between Africans too," he said. "This is the beginning of breaking that major principle, and going downhill until you break up the country."[67]

The ANC's pressure for immediate Africanization of government and industry threatened the delicate political balance that had brought about the rapid and friendly end of colonial rule. Nyerere's pressure on Britain to move more quickly than expected toward independence was successful in large measure because of the goodwill he had cultivated with TANU's strong stand against race-baiting. "We have no intention of risking good government just for the sake of Africanisation."[68] But in the Legislative Assembly in October 1961, racialist sentiments sprung up even among his own party members when a proposal was brought forward to delay citizenship for non-Africans for five years after independence. Christopher Tumbo urged for a distinction between "natives" and "immigrant races."[69] A TANU member from Mbeya, J. B. Mwakangale, went so far as to call for the resignation of non-African ministers after independence. "We have no proof of their loyalty. They are bluffing and cheating us," Mwakangale alleged.[70]

In response, Nyerere threatened that he and his ministers would resign if the assembly did not support TANU's policy.[71] Nyerere denounced the hypocrisy of a policy favoring Africans in a country that was just about to emerge from a racially prejudiced colonial state. Visibly angry, he argued that once racial bias was introduced to Tanganyikan politics its logic would take on a life of its own, leading to widespread ethnic animosity.

> A day will come when we will say all people were created equal except the Masai, except the Wagogo, except the Waha, except the polygamists, except the Muslims, etc.... You know what happens when people begin to get drunk with power and glorify their race, the Hitlers, that is what they do. You know where they lead the human race, the Verwoerds of South Africa, that is what they do.... I am going to repeat, and repeat very firmly, that this Government has rejected, and rejected completely any ideas that citizenship

with the duties and rights of citizenship of this country, are going to be based on anything except loyalty to this country. We, sir, the Government are committed to this principle, and I repeat (since some people having got drunk, claim that they are speaking for the vast majority of the people in this country, and I never like being challenged on a matter of principle) that the vote here is going to be a completely free vote. No question of an artificial whip here, party machinery, it is a question of principle, a serious matter of principle here. The view of the Hon. Members and those of the Government could not be further apart. I am therefore asking for a free vote, and the moment the majority of the representatives of our people show that their views are different from ours, we resign.[72]

In response to Nyerere's denunciation of racially defined citizenship, Tumbo gave a speech to the Railway Workers' and Postal Workers' Unions criticizing the government for supporting only nonracial "localization" rather than a racially defined "Africanization" program. He threatened that if no change in policy were made, the government "should not blame us for anything that might happen between now and December 9."[73] Numerous unions began striking or threatening to do so in the weeks preceding independence, all with support from the TFL, reflecting Tumbo's influence within that organization.[74] Nyerere stayed the growing labor crisis, prevailing on the labor leaders to hold off at least through the independence celebrations. But the internal debate over Africanization only intensified and threatened to tear apart the TANU government on the eve of independence. A Muslim organization decried Nyerere's resignation threat as "blackmail."[75] Meanwhile, TANU's leadership drifted further from their grass roots as their governmental duties grew.

Having solidified TANU's position with his threat to resign to prevent the racially prejudiced citizenship bill from passing, Nyerere moved to weaken Mtemvu's democratic chances by excluding him from the public agenda. The TANU government began to actively hinder ANC activities, refusing to air their advertisements on Radio Tanganyika and banning the party from holding public meetings because of inflammatory speeches. It expelled Esau Omindo, a Kenyan working with the ANC in the weeks before independence, on the grounds that he was inflaming racial animosities. TANU ministers said that a young country like Tanganyika could not afford exposure to destructive attacks aimed at their own sense of "nationhood."[76] Nyerere's commitment to unity was a strategy to preclude ethnic and class conflict. He was convinced that an inclusive political party would provide a workable vehicle to manage political conflict peacefully. TANU was his instrument. Built up over the previous six years into the most powerful political organization in the country, it commanded popular support at all levels of society. Its bylaws provided not only a forum for civil debate but also a structure of authority that could restrain irresponsible politics. No other organization had that capacity, including the government itself, which he noted was "still tinged with colonialism."[77] Nyerere was willing to put his own political career on the line to ensure that TANU's fundamental ideological orientation remained intact.

Independence celebrations on the night of December 8, 1961, were a photogenic success, full of foreign dignitaries and solemn stagecraft.[78] With great ceremony, Richard Turnbull in colonial dress uniform handed over power to Nyerere, who wore colorful Ghanaian cloth in homage to Kwame Nkrumah, the hero of African nationalism. At midnight on December 9, the day of *Uhuru*, the Union Jack was lowered and the new Tanganyikan flag fluttered in the tropical breeze. Meanwhile, Lieutenant Alex Nyirenda planted the national flag at the summit of Mount Kilimanjaro. The new Swahili national anthem, commissioned by a government-sponsored competition, used as its basis the South African hymn of the anti-apartheid movement, "Nkosi Sekelele Afrika."[79] Mentioning Tanganyika only in its second verse, the song was a paean to Pan-African ideals and nondenominational divinity. A British newsreel announced, "'God Save the Queen' would be replaced by 'God Bless Africa.'"[80]

Nyerere's Resignation

In the lead-up to independence, as cabinet member Job Lusinde recalled, the intense focus of TANU's leadership on administering and reforming the government had left the grassroots party adrift. Its primary task had been the mobilization for independence; with that job accomplished, rank-and-file members no longer had a clear purpose. Nyerere did not want to lose this massive territory-wide organization, or ignore the invaluable contribution of those million members.[81] His Independence Day message in the party newspaper was that the government would provide direction and planning just as the TANU leadership had done. "But in the same way as the TANU National Executive would have been helpless without the activity in every village of the country, so the Government can achieve nothing by itself."[82] Lusinde explained Nyerere's concerns about the party in terms of the primary vehicle for local transport in rural Africa:

> It's like if you were in a bicycle race, and you win, and then you put the bicycle aside in order to celebrate the victory.... This was like the party, most of them were focused on the government positions and fighting over who would get ministerial positions and the like. Nyerere saw this happening and wanted to make sure they did not lose the party or let it turn into an "election party" only.[83]

Lusinde also noted that one "hot issue" in particular represented the bigger problem posed by the loss of the coherent and disciplined party of the independence struggle. For many African Tanganyikans, independence meant at minimum that members of minority races who had once been their social superiors should show respect. Even moderate members of the TANU government like Paul Bomani and Rashidi Kawawa issued warnings that "anybody who cannot adjust himself to this (racial equality) should pack up and go because this Government will not tolerate the behavior of those who live between two worlds."[84] In this context, minimal slights were taken as evidence that a white or an Asian individual had not comprehended the new reality. This sensitivity created political pressure for government action against insufficiently deferent minorities, and the pressure for such action easily slid into divisive race-baiting that threatened Nyerere's carefully cultivated racial harmony.

The deportation of Felix Arensen, a Swiss hotel manager, was the first in a series of punitive expulsions of Europeans that came as the TANU executive committee met in the first weeks of 1962. They evinced a bitter debate between racial moderates and extremists in the party. Nyerere spoke in support of the deportations, placating the extremists, saying that even if immediate economic change was not possible, Africans had a right to respect from other races and that the government's patience on this matter was exhausted.[85] Arensen had failed to recognize Amri Abedi as the new mayor of Dar es Salaam and ejected him from the hotel when he refused to order a drink.[86] The following day, three more foreign motel owners were served with deportation notices for refusing lodging to Jacob Namfua, a former TFL official recently become parliamentary secretary to the Ministry of Finance.[87] Given the bitter strikes in the sisal industry, the political change had only heightened the sense of antagonism between white business owners and African workers—and their youthful and newly empowered representatives. The next day, another Swiss sisal plantation engineer was expelled for pinning a TANU pin on his dog.[88]

TANU racialists began compiling a list of eighty-seven whites and Asians to be expelled.[89] While some of the slights were real, the spiraling race-baiting reflected a trend of entitlement and disrespect for the law on the part of the new government officials. George Kahama, minister of home affairs at the time, reported that some of the ire was directed at him for prosecuting new government officers for traffic violations and other minor offenses. Oscar Kambona, Bhoke Munanka, and Nsilo Swai led an attack to remove Kahama from his post. Only Nyerere's advocacy retained a place for him in the cabinet.[90] Over the course of 1962, Nyerere began to build the institutions and ideologies of bureaucratic authority to replace the intensely personal politics that favored the fiery rhetoric of radicals like Tumbo and populists like Kambona and Munanka.

Figure 3.2. The independence cabinet, 1961. *Rear, from left:* Minister of Local Government Job Lusinde; Minister without Portfolio Rashidi Kawawa; Minister of Commerce and Industry Nsilo Swai; Minister of Education Oscar Kambona; Minister of Lands, Forests, and Wildlife Tewa Saidi Tewa; Cabinet Secretary Charles Meek. *Front, from left:* Minister of Agriculture Paul Bomani; Minister of Legal Affairs Abdallah Fundikira; Prime Minister Julius Nyerere; Minister of Finance Ernest Vasey; Minister of Communications, Power, and Works Amir Jamal. *Not pictured:* Minister of Home Affairs George Kahama and Minister of Health and Labour Derek Bryceson. © Tanzania Information Services (MAELEZO).

The attack on Kahama, however, was a broader one. Although the matter was tied up with personal rivalries, here was a fundamentally ideological issue at stake. Despite their vanity, Kambona, Munanka, and Swai were all TANU members and loyal to Nyerere; but for them TANU's racial tolerance had been a tactical position that helped bring about early independence, not the stand of principle that Nyerere so firmly advocated.[91] Behind the closed doors of TANU's first general meeting of the independence era, the debate over race and citizenship that had taken place in the National Assembly just a few months before boiled over.[92] When members advocating racialist policy again proclaimed that they "spoke for the people," Nyerere replied that they would not speak for him.[93] He reminded them of his earlier threat to resign and made the same threat in this meeting. This time he had the very real intention of doing so because he also wished to get out of Dar es Salaam for a few months in order to rebuild the party.[94] Frustrated with the way top TANU officials and ministers were behaving, in the words of one observer, "as a law unto themselves, disregarding the people's wishes," Nyerere sought to reconnect with TANU's grass roots.[95] He used that decision to his best advantage in the fight against racialism. He told an American diplomat that he remained optimistic despite "a hard fight." Unhappy about the fervor for expulsions, Nyerere confided that "the controversy is my fault but I had too many problems at once."[96]

For the same reasons, he was equally uncomfortable about the possibility that Kambona would become head of the Ministry of Home Affairs and be placed in charge of the police and internal intelligence service.[97] In the end, Nyerere conceded to Kambona's placement in Home Affairs and accepted the ouster of Ernest Vasey from his position as minister of finance because Vasey was not a Tanganyikan citizen. The latter concession was easier to face because Vasey's successor, Paul Bomani, was one of TANU's most competent moderates and had worked well with Vasey, who agreed to stay on as an adviser.[98] In exchange for these placements, Nyerere was able to retain in the cabinet Amir Jamal and Derek Bryceson, Tanganyikan citizens of Indian and British descent, respectively. Both were TANU loyalists, as well as visible symbols of racial unity.[99]

While threatening resignation, and possibly in preparation for such a move, Nyerere asked Kambona to step down from his ministerial post in order to travel the country to rebuild TANU.[100] Kambona refused and Nyerere stepped down instead, arranging for Rashidi Kawawa to replace him as prime minister. Nyerere retained his parliamentary seat, as a "backbencher," and called for Tanganyika to become a republic "as soon as possible," with the expectation that he would become its first president.[101] He summoned the chiefs of the diplomatic missions to his office the following day to give advance notice of his resignation, emphasizing that it was purely voluntary, but necessary for the sake of the party. His reassurance only partly assuaged the doubts of the diplomats who worried about the direction the country was taking and the potential for public disturbance.[102] The ongoing presence of Richard Turnbull as an executive governor-general made the decision easier as well, since between Kawawa and Turnbull the government could be expected to keep order.[103] Nyerere began to prepare for a public announcement while the government mounted "massive police precautions" around Dar es Salaam.[104]

When Nyerere announced his resignation to gathered journalists at his Dar es Salaam home, people reacted with "shock and bewilderment" despite his efforts to emphasize that it was a voluntary decision and that TANU remained steadfastly united in all matters. If there had been disagreement, he assured his audience, "I would not be placing my confidence in them." He said he spent three days convincing TANU members of the need for him to rebuild the party personally. His goal was to develop an "able, elected Government that has the full support and cooperation of the people" by allowing his ministers to run the government on their own. He took the opportunity to praise Vasey's service to the country and to define his removal as a merely technical issue related to his citizenship status, not his race, emphasizing that Bryceson by contrast was a citizen and a full member of the cabinet. He stressed that he was resigning in order to build a "strong political organization active in every village, which acts as a two-way all-weather road along which the purposes, plans and problems of Government travel to the people at the same time as ideas, desires and misunderstandings of the people can travel direct to Government."[105]

The metaphor of the all-weather road echoed for years in the halls of TANU offices around the country, giving a concrete image to the party's bureaucratic authority and its necessary dependence on grassroots political participation. The image arose in part through Nyerere's conversations with his advisers. Just before independence, Vedastus Kyaruzi had offered some practical advice after a big upcountry rally: "The people surrounding you are often position-seekers; they are not going to tell you the truth. So if you want to know the people really, the grassroots, you must establish your own line of communication between the root and you." He suggested Nyerere cultivate a set of private, unsalaried advisers modeled on the Haya chiefly informants called *baramata*.[106]

In the ensuing months, Nyerere's absence from Dar es Salaam deflected public blame for the lack of dramatic transformation in the society and economy that some expected. His absence also allowed the passage of strong legislation against the labor movement and opposition, without the appearance of it being his initiative. Tending to the day-to-day administration of government, the extremists moderated their positions on Africanization as they realized the need for expatriate competence in their own ministries.[107] Nyerere credited this tactic to Kawawa, who took the approach of "give the fellows a job and they will learn."[108] He remained in close touch with the Dar es Salaam leadership, and they consulted him on major issues.[109] In the meantime, Nyerere was free to travel the country, bolstering his already overwhelming public support and steering public opinion toward his own positions of nonracial egalitarianism.[110] The effect of the move was powerful, keeping racialist opponents off balance and giving notice to outside observers that his loyalties lay in the rural countryside, not in the interests of superpower patrons.[111]

Bureaucratic Authority

Over the course of 1962, the Tanganyikan government passed laws and instituted practices that helped to construct a bureaucratic authority that was independent of Nyerere's prodigious personal authority. Nyerere's absence from Dar es Salaam allowed governmental functions to appear as institutional initiatives, and not his personal ones, even as they prepared a more powerful presidency for him. The government began working out the details of the new republican constitution. The minister for legal affairs, Chief Abdallah Fundikira, envisioned a weak executive separate from the president of TANU. In such a ceremonial role, Nyerere would become "father of the nation" and be above petty political strife and thus an "objective dispenser of justice and advice."[112] But Ernest Vasey reported that Nyerere envisioned "strong executive powers and necessary control of the legislature," with Kawawa serving as vice president and chair of the Parliament.[113] In the end, the bill followed Nyerere's vision.[114]

Kawawa proved an able administrator as he began organizing agricultural resettlement schemes and foreign relations using his authority of office rather than the charismatic authority that Nyerere held in abundance.[115] American embassy officials saw quicker action on aid programs and observed a "greater sense of urgency apparent among frequently dilatory expatriate officials probably partially due to feeling Nyerere's resignation removed their protection."[116] In response partly to Africanization pressures and partly to train more Africans for the civil service, Kawawa's government exchanged recently appointed Africans functioning as upcountry commissioners for European civil servants based in Dar es Salaam, making government halls in Dar es Salaam look more African while the regions were treated to "the unusual sight of seeing their very recently-appointed African administrative officers being replaced by Europeans."[117] Less than a month later, a different set of African Regional Commissioners were appointed for the whole country.[118]

Meanwhile, Kawawa arrested the attention of the trade unions. Both Tumbo and Kamaliza appeared to take the former TFL leader more seriously than they had Nyerere, whom they saw as an interloper, lacking roots in the movement.[119] Early in the year the government had been preparing more stringent labor legislation and had delayed its introduction due to the party turmoil in January. By late February Kawawa, Jamal, and others were voicing strong warnings against illegal strikes, urging labor to cooperate with the government for the sake of developing the economy.[120] Balancing these warnings was the formation of a commission on Africanization. Kawawa told the National Assembly that he hoped the measure would halt the "ill-directed public clamor" for immediate Africanization.[121] In March Kawawa beheaded the labor movement by offering the moderate Kamaliza the Ministry of Health and Labour and sending the radical Tumbo off as the high commissioner to London, reasoning, "If I cannot convince a man of the error of his ways, I promote him in the hope that responsibility will steady him."[122] He did the same with TANU firebrand Nsilo Swai, giving him a position in Tanganyika's UN office in New York.[123] Labor unrest

Figure 3.3. Second Vice President, Rashidi Kawawa, in his office, mid-1960s. Reproduced with permission from the Borthwick Institute, York, United Kingdom.

continued to frustrate not only TFL moderates but also TANU officials of all stripes who responded caustically to labor's criticisms of Nyerere.[124] TANU leaders sought to defuse labor unrest with rapid economic development, prevailing upon friendly diplomats to seek loans and foreign investors, assuring them security for their investments.[125]

In June TFL called for mandatory arbitration to promptly resolve a large-scale work stoppage in the sisal industry that had further angered Nyerere. Nyerere advocated for antistrike legislation despite opposition in both the cabinet and the TFL.[126] Responding to Nyerere's frustration, and with Tumbo exiled to London, Kawawa proved his loyalty by introducing and defending more stringent restrictions on labor than he personally thought necessary. The legislation was modeled on Ghana's labor laws and placed strict limits on legal strikes. The law subjected all industrial relations to compulsory arbitration under a government-controlled TFL and, in return, introduced a mandatory "check-off" system to deduct dues automatically from workers' paychecks.[127] To help prop up Kamaliza's waning popularity, the restrictive law was given more political counterweight in the form of workers' compensation legislation and a social security fund.[128] Following directly on the heels of the labor law, Kawawa presented the white paper on constitutional changes for a republic that followed Nyerere's preference for a strong president.[129]

Kambona, newly placed in the Ministry of Home Affairs, proceeded on an active but measured Africanization program in the police force, accelerating the appointment of an African to head the force and recruiting three Ghanaian police advisers to begin training what quickly became an effective all-African force.[130] He also put an African in charge of the Tanganyika Information Service, overseeing the Tanganyika Broadcasting Corporation. While these changes removed competent expatriates, they also opened the way for these bureaucracies to take a more complementary role in Tanganyika's nascent foreign policy, managing refugees, training militants, and broadcasting propaganda into neighboring countries under white-minority rule. Balancing the popular demand for Africanization with the realities of administration was difficult for even supporters of the policy like Kambona. Extreme demands, like the position of the Union of Public Employees that all expatriate employees abandon their jobs for replacement by Africans, were impossible to fulfill.[131]

An Africanization commission that was appointed in February 1962 announced in May that 30 percent of middle- and upper-grade civil service positions were filled by Africans, but nearly 20 percent of middle-grade posts were also vacant, lacking willing expatriates or qualified Africans.[132] Nyerere continued to work from behind the scenes to check the pace of Africanization because of its destructive effects on governmental efficiency and economic growth. He still held his own political prestige in reserve, saying he would remove himself from politics if TANU took positions that he could not accept. He took a long-term view of his principled effort to quell the racialist hue and cry, according to an American diplomat: "[Nyerere] said that if the country is in bad economic straights [*sic*] five or more years from now, he does not want to be held responsible for this condition. Moreover, it will mean little to his people at that time to tell them that he concurred in the disastrous Africanisation policy."[133]

After the experience of political exclusion during colonialism, many Africans understood African sovereignty to be the right to exclude non-Africans. It was difficult for TANU moderates, educated and relatively wealthy, to explain to populist masses that a simple African majority, as opposed to monopoly, in government constituted African sovereignty. Even more difficult was the reality that prestigious jobs paid well because of their requisite qualifications of education and technical skill, not because of the color of those who held the job; after all, the colonial government had structured education such that most white-collar positions were filled by Europeans and Asians, in practice reserving them on the basis of color. The positions remained, nevertheless, technical positions on which the government and economy depended, and placing uneducated people of any race in those positions would be calamitous. Labor leader and TANU loyalist Mustafa Songambele described the dilemma and the process that followed, patriotically attributing perhaps too much advocacy for Africanization to Nyerere:

> Question: why doesn't this government look like a government of Tanganyikans? . . . Even work that a Bantu can do, there is an Indian. Even work that an African can do, there is a European. We said no. Mwalimu opened up Africanization. . . . Africanization is to remove the colonialist who is there now, and put an African there who can do the work. This was done well. Because at that time all the government offices were either an Indian or a European. But this [imbalance] was necessary because there were not enough educated people. And the first task before us was to build primary and secondary schools. Everyone who was taught would know that he would take a leadership job of some kind. . . . We continued like this until Africanization was completed, until in most places patriots themselves held the power to govern their own country.[134]

Songambele's conclusion here is telling. Education was the key to Africanization, yet its result was the placement not of Africans, even if that is his general implication, but of "patriots" in government positions. His choice of a nonracial word here marks the TANU effort to displace racial affinities with loyalty to the party and country. Until enough Africans could be educated, the Europeans and Asians had to be retained; moreover, as "patriots," they could potentially continue as full members of the society indefinitely.[135] But what, in that case, did sovereignty mean? For many among those uneducated masses, without a sophisticated understanding of the international system and the rights of states, it was easy to imagine sovereignty as the division of colonial spoils offered by the proponents of immediate Africanization.

In another attempt to defuse the racial logic of Africanization with cultural intervention, Nyerere also translated Shakespeare's play *Julius Caesar* into Swahili. His goal was to prove the legitimacy of a widely spoken African language as an official language. The Asian Speaker of the Assembly, A. Y. A. Karimjee urged that Swahili introduction be delayed until after the next general elections so members, including himself, could withdraw if they did not feel fluent.[136] Kawawa announced in September that the first presidential speech on December 10 could be given in English or Swahili so that the nation's citizenry would feel the National Assembly was really their own.[137] Nyerere reinforced this point by refusing to allow interpreters to translate his Swahili speeches into local languages for upcountry crowds.[138] Making an appearance in Arusha on Nyerere's behalf, Oscar Kambona urged a rural crowd to put their trust in the new government and to put aside historical fears inscribed in ethnic tensions: "There is no need to fear the Masai any longer, your cattle will be protected by the police—and you must learn to speak, read, and write Kiswahili."[139]

It was likewise difficult for many Europeans and Asians, so inured to the colonial state, with its racial logic and dependent status, to imagine how radically the situation had changed with independence. African sovereignty meant the complete reorientation of internal and external policy toward the issues that resonated most among the populist masses. Africanization was but one issue among many, but was central to creating a legitimate image of bureaucratic authority. A sovereign foreign policy, oriented toward the interests of Africans rather than the superpowers, guided the new nation to consider the ideals of Pan-Africanism and African liberation above all else in its external affairs. The expression of African priorities in the form of government policy and ideology helped cultivate a more thorough transition than the simple acquisition of the state promoted by the racialists. Nyerere took pains to avoid the creation of a racially African state; it offended him just as much as the racially white state of South Africa for its violent and divisive implications. Even so, his passion for independence and African nationalism arose from his commitment to a state that democratically reflected the culture of the African majority occupying the territory. If successful, his vision could drown out the racialist urge. The question was how to harmonize that indigenous cultural vision with the requirements of sovereignty in the international community.

Suppressing the Opposition

Nyerere's actions during the year following his resignation suggest that he had no intention of bowing out of politics, and that such a decision would amount to the betrayal of everything he desired for the people of Tanganyika. What he believed to be best, however, required an ominous sacrifice of democratic principle. It was the first hint of the authoritarian streak that accompanied Nyerere's idealism throughout his career.[140] Throughout 1962, the TANU government intimidated and suppressed the racialist opposition.

The same day as Nyerere's resignation in January 1962, a new party announced its inauguration. The People's Democratic Party (PDP) was an initiative of Christopher Kasanga Tumbo, the erstwhile Railway Union leader, and Hassan Nkupe of the Miners' Union.[141] The PDP sought to support and supersede the racialist ideals of the ANC.[142] Echoing the rhetoric of racialist voices within TANU, the PDP's leaders in their manifesto declared themselves in favor of a nonracial society, but said they "strongly feel that this can not be brought about immediately because there is a very wide gap in both economic, education, political and social between the people of local origin and the immigrants." Its constitution called for "more opportunities to citizens of Local origin . . . African tradition and culture to be preserved, improved, and encourage[d] ... [the] immediate africanisation of both civil service and commerce ... [and] the development of democratic trade unions and co-operative movements without prejudice."[143]

TANU leadership viewed the emergence of the PDP with a mix of cynicism and alarm. This apprehension grew from Tumbo's menacing comments in the National Assembly only three months earlier as he resisted pressure to merge the trade union movement with TANU: "If trade unions are merged with major political parties and there should be political instability, the whole nation would collapse."[144] Tumbo's proven capacity to mobilize workers made the prospect of his political ambitions a source of deep unease for the TANU moderates, while TANU extremists, like Kambona, bristled at this potential challenger. Referring to Tumbo, Mustafa Songambele recalled that "one of our own tried to tempt us to form an opposition party out of the labor unions, and we refused, I refused. We said we will stick with Mwalimu only, and TANU."[145] TANU's success in bringing the TFL to heel under Michael Kamaliza had left Tumbo without a job, but still in possession of a large following within the labor movement, and he attracted the attention of those who grew frustrated with the lack of progress by Mtemvu's ANC.[146] Although he had not yet publicly announced his connection to the PDP, Tumbo stated in the National Assembly that his Railway Union was proceeding with a "master plan" to turn the comparatively educated and mobilized trade union movement into a political party.[147]

The Tanganyika government suspected that Tumbo was receiving pay and advice from the Soviet Union.[148] While they had little specific evidence, it was clear that both the United States and the Soviet Union were attempting to lure the labor movement into support for their policies.[149] A pamphlet by I. H. Potekin published by the Friedrich Ebert Foundation suggested that Soviet policy in sub-Saharan Africa would focus on trade unions in the absence of a clear line between a broad-based worker class and an indigenous landed gentry.[150] Through his friendship with labor leaders like Tom Mboya in Kenya and John Tettegah in Ghana, Nyerere was fully aware of American pressure on East African trade unions through the ICFTU and warned repeatedly against foreign intrusion in Tanganyika's internal politics.[151] Chinese agents were likewise active, and a few weeks after his resignation from the prime minister's office, Nyerere visited the Chinese Embassy in Dar es Salaam with a warning that they should stop giving cash to Tanganyikans who claimed to have political influence, a snide reference to Mtemvu, who had been sponsored for two visits to China.[152] Tumbo's appointment as high commissioner to London had effectively removed his voice from the political scene temporarily. This hardly quieted the Railway Union, however. Communist influence became evident when Tumbo's successor, S. J. Katungutu, returned from East Germany. He hailed a work stoppage in the sisal industry called by Victor Mkello, secretary general of the Plantation Worker's Union. Katungutu urged the government to nationalize all sisal plantations, opining further that Tanganyika should model its development after East Germany.[153]

In June Zuberi Mtemvu, before a rally of seven thousand followers in Dar es Salaam, outlined his own "master plan" for the ANC, "which aims to obtain a purely African government in Tanganyika within 12 months." The ANC announcement clearly supported Tumbo's February announcement, their parallel language intended to publicize their challenge to TANU's dominance and prepare for the PDP's unveiling. Mtemvu protested a temporary ban on ANC rallies and laid out a policy of civil disobedience. "If [the ban] continues we will be forced to take positive action. We will hold meetings and go to jail."[154] The ANC's ideology remained much the same and differed little from the PDP's manifesto, favoring racial policy in the interest of Africans. Both parties courted chiefs whose powers were being undermined by the TANU government. On a conciliatory note, Mtemvu acceded that the ANC would cooperate with TANU in the aid of African-majority rule in the Rhodesias.[155]

In response to Mtemvu's patriotic support for TANU foreign policy, Kambona announced in July that the ANC would be allowed to hold rallies and contest the election. Nyerere's instinct was to ban the ANC and PDP altogether and conduct an uncontested election dominated by TANU's nationalist vision.[156] Foreign observers and old TANU hands argued for ANC participation on democratic principle. Nyerere conceded this point for all of a month. In August, Kambona placed a renewed ban on ANC rallies until September 3 on the grounds that they were inciting violence.[157] In a show of determination, Mtemvu held a meeting the following day to announce his candidacy and the acceptance of his presidential nomination petition by the Electoral Commission.[158] All the while, racial advocates within TANU continued to push their cause, threatening to expel the government's preeminent non-Africans, Jamal and Bryceson, after the general election.[159]

In the lead-up to Mtemvu's candidacy, Tumbo resigned his position as high commissioner in London and returned to declare his split with TANU and his leadership of the PDP. With the passage of restrictive labor legislation, Tumbo had promptly understood that his appointment was a form of exile and said he resigned "for political reasons."[160] He held a public rally upon his return. Carrying a flywhisk and wearing African-styled dress, in line with the neotraditionalist clauses in the PDP manifesto, he prominently used an African name, Kasanga, rather than his English name, Christopher. He attacked TANU for leading Tanganyika into "corruption" and an "economic slump" by failing to bring about more rapid economic development. He protested the new labor law and pronounced that the PDP would represent "democratic socialism." He criticized TANU for allowing non-Africans to still sit in the National Assembly, saying that "multiracialism" of the tripartite election had not been abolished. He attacked "foreign traders" who sent their profits abroad and local investors who refused to support workers for fear of reducing their profits. Yet he also upbraided Mtemvu for participating in the upcoming elections, emphasizing that the PDP would boycott. Tumbo's brazen dismissal of the elections was perhaps stiffened by the reality that, at age twenty-eight, he was too young to run for president under the existing constitution.[161]

Even so, Tumbo worried the TANU leadership very deeply, more so than Mtemvu. Rashidi Kawawa, in conversation with the American ambassador, "spoke with some bitterness of Tumbo and his People's Democratic Party. . . . Kawawa obviously regards him as a greater threat than Mtemvu."[162] Othman Shariff, a Zanzibari moderate with the Afro-Shirazi Party, told US Embassy officers that "an opposition party headed by Tumbo might gain wide support in Tanganyika, since Tumbo would take an extreme racist line that would have popular appeal."[163] The PDP grew rapidly, selling thousands of membership cards in just a few weeks.[164] While TANU was a stronger organization, Nyerere doubted whether he could keep his own members from amplifying populist racialism. Furthermore, Nyerere's pressure for a powerful executive alienated others, like TANU supporter Chief Fundikira, who feared a creeping dictatorship.[165] Tensions were evident in TANU. More extreme TANU members, led by Bhoke Munanka, aimed to oust moderates like Vedastus Kyaruzi and Dunstan Omari despite their senior status in the party.[166] Nyerere's desire to constrain Tanganyikan politics and silence the voices of racial prejudice led him to continually advocate for the suppression of TANU's opposition.

Despite his election boycott, Tumbo began to work with Mtemvu to court influence among chiefs like Francis Masanja with neotraditionalist gestures that complemented his claims to African authenticity. Tumbo found further support from Chief David Kidaha Makwaia, who was one of the first Africans to sit in the colonial Legislative Council and among the most prominent African politicians in the country.[167] Building on the PDP's platform, Tumbo advocated a racial distinction for citizenship, arguing that non-Africans should be neither citizens nor members of the National Assembly, and be disallowed from holding land.[168] These populist positions had the potential to justify continued chiefly authority and were attractive to some who believed that TANU's hostility toward traditional governance threatened not only their own positions but also, as colonial governor Twining also had feared, the very stability of rural society.

From TANU's standpoint, politicized ethnic identities represented a challenge to state sovereignty and a threat to national unity. But popular resentment toward the demands of colonial chiefs provided an opportunity for the new leadership to eliminate chiefly roles in government. Initially the government simply planned to rationalize local governance with elected village and district councils and appointed executive officers under the new TANU-appointed area commissioners. But the policy was still under development. In November Job Lusinde, the minister of local government, issued a more far-reaching paper, titled "Position of Chiefs," announcing that, beginning January 1, 1963, chiefs and chiefdoms would no longer be elements of local governmental authority or organization. However, chiefs "would not be prevented from continuing their traditional functions"—which in practice tended to die out when they were no longer elements of practical authority.[169]

TANU's intention was to undermine traditional nobility and colonial chieftainship without demonizing chiefs as individuals. "We killed the administrative functions of chiefs," recalled Lusinde. "We took them out of administration for some time, but those who had some education, we inserted to take various positions in the society." Several traditional chiefs, notably Abdallah Fundikira and Adam Sapi Mkwawa, took positions in the new government, and many local positions were filled by members of the noble families that formerly had governed village society.[170] A significant exception was Chagga chief Thomas Marealle, who filed suit against the new government claiming a £2,000 annuity or a £20,000 lump-sum payment. Petro Njau, the kingmaker who helped create in 1951 the office of the paramount chief that Marealle occupied, wrote an acid response to Marealle's suit saying that his refusal to recognize democratic principles was the source of his own problem. In 1953 Njau had withdrawn from the ethnic orientation of Chagga politics and had begun to mobilize the panethnic Tanganyika Citizens' Union, a precursor to TANU.[171] Njau explained that the independent government had no responsibility for maintaining colonial policies toward chiefs and sardonically suggested Marealle should sue the Queen's government in London instead.[172] Subsequent legislation retroactively declared that chiefs would not be compensated for the loss of their former powers.[173] In the latter half of 1962, as the government moved to undermine chiefly authority, it was watchful for signs of resistance, most intensely so among those traditional authorities who had thrown their support to the racialist opposition.

Drawing on the newly Africanized police department, Kambona had initiated a secret investigation of Tumbo and his key supporter, the former Sukuma chief David Kidaha Makwaia, who criticized TANU's strong-arm tactics. Makwaia's enemies circulated rumors that he was organizing an armed rebellion with Arab supporters, but he mocked the image of a ragtag bunch of Arab traders camping out in the bush with rusty muzzle loaders. Nevertheless, Kambona promoted his assistant Leonard Bakuname to be a magistrate specifically to take evidence concerning Makwaia. The investigation brought Shinyanga chief of police Emil Mzena to Kambona's attention, and he promoted Mzena to head the investigative Special Branch the following year. The investigators found only that Tumbo had sought money from East German contacts he had made in London, but that these proved reluctant to fund him because of his opposition to Nyerere.[174] Given the fragile nature of the new state and Makwaia's political prominence, Nyerere took even farfetched rumors of "another Katanga" in Sukuma country as a threat to Tanganyika's stability.[175] Such rumors fed Nyerere's fears of political division that increasingly influenced his decision making.

As the investigation into Makwaia proceeded, Kambona introduced legislation for a Preventive Detention Act, quickly modeled on Ghana's, with strong support from Nyerere. Citing internal disorder in other newly independent countries as justification for the law, Prime Minister Kawawa guided the bill through the National Assembly as "an urgent matter," suggesting that it wasn't nearly as harsh as Northern Ireland's law in response to the Irish Republican Army.[176] Kambona acknowledged that the bill went against Tanganyika's declared interests in human rights and democracy, but that "where the State is not secure there can be no security for personal liberty." He proposed that preventive detention "must ultimately be subject to the control of Parliament." All detentions would be reviewed by an Advisory Committee that had the right to interview detainees, and that a quorum of the committee would have to include an appointee of both the governor-general and the chief justice.[177]

Kambona argued that where in the past there was little need for such an act (ignoring the powers of the colonial government to arrest and detain people at will), "the complexity of a modern state, the increase in knowledge and power, now makes even individuals and small groups capable of being a serious menace to society." With Tanganyika's active foreign policy and the racially divisive nature of internal political opposition, both internal and external threats to even the most fundamental vision of a racially harmonious democracy were many. An amendment was also added to the penal code making it an offense to interfere with a "self-help" scheme, some of which were to serve as cover for training camps for the Mozambique liberation movement.[178] Kambona accurately presented the bill as representative of powers held by most nations, even in the democratic West, and asserted that Tanganyika could therefore not be blamed for undermining democratic principle. "The right of power of a State in appropriate circumstances to detain people for the sake of the safety of the State itself is undeniable," Kambona proclaimed. "It is an attribute of Sovereignty."[179]

Some took issue with the bill immediately. "Now the Government tends to follow dictatorship instead of democratic principles," Chief Francis

Masanja thundered. But most voices in Parliament that day came in behind the bill. Barbro Johansson, a Swedish educator long resident in Tanganyika, struck a note of reasoned resignation, acknowledging that the fragile political reality of the new state demanded such a law. Preventive detention was intended to "prevent the activities of those in a country who do not believe in the Ballot Box," but she pleaded that preventive detention be used only "in such a way that it maintains people's trust and belief in the Ballot Box."

In response, Joseph Nyerere introduced the possibility that foreign subversion could undermine democratic processes, noting that during World War II Great Britain had used such powers of detention. "We do not yet have a nation," he submitted, citing the diversity of ethnicities and languages within the new nation's borders. Then, presenting nation-building as the moral equivalent of war, he addressed the internal and external attributes of sovereignty: "We are trying to build up this nation from 127 tribes. . . . Now this is a big war, Sir. And not only that, we are trying to see that we in Tanganyika build up a nation that people from outside will look upon as a nation."[180] At a press conference the next day, Julius Nyerere echoed his brother's point, arguing that the act was necessary to preempt threats to the fragile new nation, with its carefully cultivated ethnic and religious harmony. "If we succeed in creating a nation, we can stand criticism. But if we fail we will be ridiculed."[181]

After the bill's passage, Julius Nyerere took an unusual step as a "backbencher" to call a press conference to justify the new act as a measure against subversive activity. Citing evidence from Kambona's investigation of "people inside and outside the country who wish to use undemocratic means to overthrow the government," Nyerere argued that in a country without deep roots of nationalism, it was better to risk the detention of innocent people than allow irreparable harm to the young nation. Acknowledging that the act violated the principle of due process, he hoped the mere passage of the act would make its use unnecessary. Belying this sunny optimism, Nyerere intended to use the act to detain Tumbo on December 10, the day after the inauguration of the republic when the president would take over the duties of the governor-general, and thereby avoid having a detention mar the election.[182]

The Detention Act further inflamed political discourse. While Mtemvu supported preventive detention as a necessary measure needing only fair administration, Tumbo denounced the act as "a declaration of emergency on the peaceful people of Tanganyika." With sly sarcasm regarding Ghana's reputation as the leader of decolonization, Tumbo raised the same doubts Nyerere had about the viability of the Tanganyikan nation. "I have no reason to doubt that Tanganyika has become another Ghana, but the question remains, is Ghana successful—a country where states of emergency are declared?"[183] Meanwhile, Nyerere began to wield the mere threat of detention, telling crowds that it was aimed at traitors. Before a crowd of TANU elders and Youth League members in late September, Nyerere stirred up resentment toward Tumbo, while carefully avoiding the opposition leader's name. Tumbo had earlier assured crowds that he was independently wealthy but refused to invest in a company so as not to be a capitalist. Nyerere twisted this into a condemnation, asking how someone who had been given an ambassadorship could turn and betray the government, while the crowd replied with shouts of "Imprison him!" and "Hang him!" Nyerere wielded his rhetorical skills to great effect: "A man from Tanganyika, a poor country, to have money sufficient to keep him going without employment for the rest of his life? Where did he get his money from? How do we know this person has not betrayed us? How can we know whether he has not disclosed our State secrets?"[184]

The next day Nyerere initiated a dramatic step to intimidate Tumbo and the PDP on the pretext that that they were involved in Makwaia's supposed plot. In Tumbo's presence, police arrested Makwaia and his brother and secretly rusticated them to remote southern safehouses. Tumbo had been staying with Makwaia in Shinyanga during the campaign, and when they returned the next night, they found an armed plainclothes police officer standing outside Makwaia's house with a Land Rover running. The officer carried an order signed by Governor-General Turnbull deporting Makwaia to a mining settlement in Tunduru, and his brother to Chunya, under a colonial law for political rustication.[185] Another Sukumaland chief, Francis Masanja, was also rusticated and placed under house arrest in Geita. Masanja had been a TANU member allied with the racialist faction, and his opposition to the Preventive Detention Act had caused him to quit TANU and join the ANC.[186] It was not until a month later, as the election approached, that the government publicly announced the deportations alleging that Makwaia and his brother had attempted "not only to stir up opposition to [the] Government's policy with regard to chiefs but to inflame local feelings by conduct calculated to endanger peace and good order."[187]

Makwaia's arrest was motivated by unproven rumors of rebellion that were never announced publicly beyond the vague references to subversion in the debates about the Preventive Detention Act. If those rumors were true, then Nyerere carefully kept their details from the public in order to defuse any potential support for a broader rebellion. If, as is more likely, the rumors were invented, then the arrests were dramatically successful in scaring away opposition voters. Mtemvu's ANC received only 140 out of 21,500 votes in Shinyanga in November.[188] To avoid tainting the election, Nyerere had not used the new Preventive Detention Act, or arrested Tumbo himself, but clearly the arrests were meant to intimidate anyone actively campaigning for the opposition, let alone subversive action. With

Tumbo boycotting the elections, and TANU overwhelmingly popular even in Shinyanga, the arrests were probably unnecessary if their only aim was to ensure Nyerere's electoral victory in November. Of more concern, given Fundikira's criticisms of Nyerere's authoritarian presidency, is that such repression was probably counterproductive.

Repression and the Republic

With the suppression of the opposition, the November 1962 elections were a foregone success for Nyerere. He won 98 percent of the vote, with Mtemvu polling only twenty thousand votes nationwide.[189] While the results were coming in, Nyerere was jubilant, foreseeing a "brighter period opening for Tanganyika."[190] He told the American ambassador that "he had accomplished [the] mission he had set himself when he resigned as Prime Minister last January." He began to set his sights on how "to reorganize the government" and "catch up with the people" through rural development and economic planning; if he had a choice, he said, "the cities could go to hell" while he focused on the rural sector.[191] Nyerere still worried about racial prejudice, but he used the election results to argue that the Tanganyikan public had overwhelmingly rejected racism. People had ignored Tumbo's and Mtemvu's emotional appeals, which in turn made any TANU member who espoused racialism appear dangerously close to the discredited opposition. According to an American embassy staff member, Nyerere's opponents had mistakenly "imagined that TANU's weakest point was its total commitment to the principle of nonracialism, its refusal to stoop to any emotional revenge against those races which had formerly practiced racial discrimination against the Africans."[192]

The elections punctuated the drive to independence with a final formal separation from the Queen of England and removal of the British governor-general. Tanganyika became a republic under Nyerere's presidency. The celebrations were a success with many regional leaders in attendance. Tanganyikans proudly spoke of the birth of the republic as a moment of sovereignty: "at last truly independent." After the ceremonies were all over, Nyerere was perhaps a little too effusive with the American ambassador, who came to his house to deliver a message from the US president. Nyerere read the message aloud in Swahili to gathered family and friends. Contemplating the passage of an era, and anxious about the tasks at hand, he took the new ambassador by both hands and confessed, "I was all right until I said [my] last good-bye to Turnbull this morning. It was what I wanted, but I almost broke down. For [the] first time, I felt alone."[193]

The following week, Nyerere proposed to open TANU to all races and to invite opposition members back into the party, in preparation for the one-party state. "To all those who knock, we will say welcome!" The party debated and concluded, "Since unity was necessary during the campaign for independence, unity will continue to be necessary as we secure our independence, and it will be used as we build our country."[194] Nyerere's overwhelming electoral victory paved the way to his long-held vision of a racially diverse one-party state. By veiling the government's suppression of the opposition and Tumbo's subsequent electoral boycott, the TANU majority reinforced his consistent argument that the official opposition was too impotent to function as an opposition, though assertions hardly proved that ideological debate and watchdog functions could happen within a single nationalist party.

Nyerere was disappointed in the low voter turnout, attributing public apathy to voter fatigue as national elections had been held several times in recent years.[195] Low campaign contributions in TANU district branches seemed to reflect this sense of popular exhaustion, leaving the party nearly broke.[196] It was possible that Tumbo's appeal for an election boycott prevented some voters from registering, but observers saw little evidence of broad participation in the boycott.[197] The problem, as Kawawa put it in a meeting of TANU leadership, appeared to be "the rot" within TANU itself. "Contributions don't come in, the number of party members is decreasing, and the result of the party's condition is that TANU was not very successful in the District Council elections in Bukoba, Songea, and Moshi."[198] Despite Nyerere's travels the previous year, maintaining popular enthusiasm for the task of governance was proving much more difficult than the campaign for independence. A loyal TANU member complained of the acrimony in Tanganyikan politics becoming increasingly evident after the successful independence drive:

> One thing that grieves us now is to see that there are leaders of other political parties, really nothing more than little reeds that I venture to say, when the time of politics started in 1954, were still in schools learning algebra, and now these little children are walking the streets to entice some TANU members and pull them into their party. This is done openly, and it is because of the rottenness of TANU today that they are just watching while the country is taken over by fools.[199]

In an informal meeting of low-level ministers and district commissioners in mid-1963, Mustafa Songambele bluntly suggested a central problem: "People don't see their leaders." The party's leadership, now engulfed in duties of state, could not visit upcountry branches as frequently as they had done when their sole task was popular mobilization. But it was more than that. Chief Theresa Ntare said that district and regional commissioners were behaving like "bush governors," who did not listen to their constituents, squandered public funds, and acted as if they were not members of

TANU. She proposed better party supervision to eliminate the problem. "The people are watching our steps closely," she warned.

Michael Kamaliza pointedly asked the group to "look where we came from. Back then we were all of one accord . . . and a TANU shirt was something to be proud of. Now a TANU card is nothing to be proud of and our goals are no longer united." He suggested that the distribution of new government jobs created jealousies. "Our people have got the idea that since we got independence, well, we'll sit and wait for the Government to bring us something." He urged TANU to create jobs for its members by building industries under the newly formed Mwananchi Development Corporation. Abbas Sykes supported the push to provide something tangible for the citizenry and emphasized that the problem was not with the people, but rather with "leaders who have cared for them poorly. Let us cease our discord and try to please our citizens. We need only tell the people the truth." He suggested a full-time salaried secretary-general without the distraction of governmental duties to lead the party. Joseph Nyerere was convinced that even more radical restructuring was necessary, and he began laying out the case for what became the TANU "ten-cell" system: "a communist-style party, in groups of 10, 100, and 1,000 people, etc., and that each group should have its leader who knows his people by name, where they live, what work they do, and their monthly contributions." Sheikh Amri Abedi urged resolve: "We must stand firm, because complaints will continue, because the seeds we are planting will only bring fruit after some time." Until then he advised, in echo of Nyerere's colorful speech that compared independence to a successful hunt, "the name TANU should be seen and spread everywhere. . . . Let us love each other, let us not be like dogs who hunt with one will, but then when they capture their prey they begin to fight."[200]

Seeking to foster a unitary party at the January 1963 general meeting, Nyerere garnered unanimous votes in the face of contentious debate to invite opposition members back to the party and to open TANU to non-Africans.[201] Mtemvu, Makwaia, Tumbo, and others were welcomed back into TANU's now firmly nonracial fold. Makwaia and his brother were released in March and invited to dinner with Nyerere at the statehouse, while Tumbo quietly dissolved the PDP, took a trip to Europe, and then settled in Mombasa, Kenya.[202] With labor moderates empowered by the TANU victory, the government rusticated two popular trade union radicals who had instigated a massive unapproved strike in the sisal industry and opposed the new labor legislation. TFL likewise suspended two unions that had supported Tumbo.[203]

At the meeting, Nyerere also called on TANU delegates to approve his resolution for a one-party state that would rule out "factional parties" and allow civil servants to run for office within competitive local elections among members of the same party.[204] Two days later, he published his carefully constructed argument in a pamphlet titled "Democracy and the Party System," repeating his points that two-party systems had arisen in European societies riven by class conflict, and that competitive elections within one party would avoid factional conflict while preserving the democratic process.[205] With Tumbo abroad, Mtemvu held the ANC line that eliminating the opposition would lead to dictatorship, and menacingly cited the assassination of Olympio Sylvanus in Togo as a possible consequence to the drift toward authoritarianism.[206] The reference to Togo was a particularly sharp jab. Nyerere had opened the TANU conference the day before with comments on the Sylvanus assassination, and a moment of silence turned into a five-minute pause while "the Father of the Nation sat down very sadly and wept."[207]

The Muslim party AMNUT also equated a one-party state with "absolute dictatorship" and disputed Nyerere's claim to an overwhelming mandate, citing the low voter turnout in the November election.[208] Chief Fundikira had long protested Nyerere's authoritarian impulse, while other TANU moderates quietly voiced their doubts to Nyerere personally.[209] Fundikira's prominence created particular anxiety within TANU. Many linked AMNUT's opposition with Fundikira, seeing the threat of religion-based politics. In particular, Fundikira had been supporting a Muslim effort to block cooperation between Tanganyika and Israel and promote an "African Chamber of Commerce" that would aim to promote trade with the Muslim world to the exclusion of Israel.[210] TANU leaders took offense, as Israel was supporting training for TANU Youth League members and rural settlement schemes. While acknowledging the right of people to maintain religious organizations, TANU leaders asserted that "they can help build the country, but in the same way they can also bring the great danger of planting the seeds of hatred." TANU advised the government to issue "strong warnings" to those who would mix politics and religion.[211]

The "warning" took the form of the arrest of Fundikira on questionable charges of corruption in his role as chairman of the National Agricultural Products Board.[212] The drastic arrest might have backfired had Fundikira been a less principled man. In June the Nyamwezi chief had spoken eloquently in Parliament of his patriotism and abjured racial or religious prejudice. He then pointed out a very serious concern in the Muslim community—that the new government was dominated by Christians educated in mission schools. Although the party's National Executive Committee was majority Muslim, an influx of Christian civil servants threatened to marginalize Muslims. Fundikira proposed that the government take affirmative action to educate Muslims for the civil service.[213] This proposal, however, was not wholly new. Kawawa responded by pointing out that Nyerere had already made the same argument in his inaugural presidential speech six months before, and a law had already been passed requiring all schools to accept students of any religion and to offer religious lessons to children in their own religion.[214] The TANU leadership attacked the speech as religious demagoguery that only served to fuel Muslim complaints that the independence government favored Christians. The next day Fundikira was arrested.

At trial in August 1963, Fundikira appeared in Muslim attire, which was unusual for him, and held forth as a popular Muslim leader escorted by crowds of agitated supporters. Upon his acquittal, "he ascribed his vindication to the intercession of the one true God."[215] Despite the acquittal, Nyerere relieved Fundikira of his position as head of the state investment vehicle, the Tanganyika Development Corporation.[216] Late in the year, and certainly after some private discussions with Nyerere, Fundikira graciously rejoined TANU, lending his stately influence back to the party, only to be accused again a few months later of conspiring with the mutineers when his name showed up on a list of their preferred governmental appointments.[217]

For its part, the government continued to take stern action against any hint of religious politics, as they had with ethnic politics.[218] It is clear that Muslim political activism worried the government more than Christian meddling, but it acted to restrain both. It deported the prominent Muslim leader Sharif Hussein Ahmed Badawy back to his native Kenya, and put two leaders of a newly established Muslim advocacy organization, Dawa al-Islamiyya, under house arrest in upcountry villages.[219] Similarly, the government also replaced the heavily Catholic and uncooperative District Council in Bukoba with a more mixed membership. It then pressured the Tanganyikan Bishops' Council to issue a pastoral letter to its clergy warning them "not to use their sacred position of spiritual leadership in their communities to influence political elections by persuading their flocks to support a particular candidate or party."[220] By December a TANU area secretary in Mwanza told constituents that "political conditions are good now, even though there was gossip about religious politics . . . [and] opposition parties . . . but everything has been worked out and things are cool."[221]

Legislative innovation, political cunning, and crass intimidation all contributed to establishing sovereign government over a Tanganyikan nation whose very diversity also bore the seeds of division. The cost of capturing this authority was not only the immediate sacrifice of democratic debate but also the long-term undermining of democratic principles in the country's political structure. In retrospect, it appears as a particularly depressing spectacle of repression at the very moment of Tanganyika's birth as an independent republic. Moreover, the suppression of opposition was not merely opportunistic; it was strategic. Political repression allowed Nyerere to pursue his openly stated goal of a single-party state. For him, and the many TANU leaders who supported him, unity was more important than democracy during the transition to independence. Nyerere's authoritarian impulse cannot be separated from his idealism. Likewise, broader fears of a Congo-like collapse at the moment of liberation cannot be extricated from the personal animosities fueling the suppression of the independent labor movement and the political opposition as independence dawned. Fear of racialism's populist charms was also real as it threatened the new country's economic and social viability. A sense of fragility pervaded the postcolonial government and shaped the choices of its leadership.

Nyerere and his colleagues were also cognizant that mere repression could never be a nation-building strategy, and that unified nationhood would not last long without an ideological focal point. Across the country, over the course of 1962, Nyerere also began to articulate *Ujamaa* as a theory of citizenship that offered a nonracial and nonreligious alternative to Africanization as an image of African sovereignty.

4

The Invention of Ujamaa

Suggesting that Tanganyika should have a single-party system for at least fifteen years after independence, Nyerere argued that the key to a sustainable democratic system was not to be found in constitutional safeguards, no matter how ingeniously devised. He had come to the conclusion that any electoral system could be easily manipulated into dictatorship, and that for a democratic system to work at all there had to be a consensus, shared among people and leaders alike, about the constraints on political decisions within the nation-state.[1] Nyerere introduced the idea of a "national ethic" while endorsing the new republican constitution and the powerful executive it envisioned:[2]

> The safeguard of a people's right, the people's freedom and those things which they value ... is the ethic of the nation. ... If the people do not have that kind of ethic, it does not matter what kind of constitution you frame. They can always be victims of tyranny. ... What we must continue to do all the time, is to build an ethic of nation, all the time to build an ethic of this nation, which makes the Head of State whoever he is to say, "I have the power to do this under the Constitution, but I cannot do it, it is un-Tanganyikan."[3]

Given the shallow constitutional tradition in the newly independent country, Nyerere sought a popular philosophy of basic civil and economic rights balanced by an ideology of citizen obligation that would define what it meant to be Tanganyikan and thus designate the limits of legitimate politics.[4] Moreover, a philosophy of state articulated with an identifiably "African" sensibility would represent an integrative route to Africanness, as opposed to a divisive racial route.[5] During his travels in 1962, Nyerere composed a language and logic for a national ethic that would make sense as both grassroots and cosmopolitan discourse.

Without a popular democratic tradition in place, Nyerere believed it would take time for people to learn the rhythms, pitfalls, and limitations of democratic politics, and make the necessary commitment to maintain democratic principles despite their weaknesses. He was also concerned that racial extremists could win democratic elections, as had happened in Rwanda, and plant the seeds of division that would destroy any possibility of a stable democratic society.[6] A deeper legitimacy had to be established to guarantee the sovereignty of the racially harmonious and economically equitable society that Nyerere envisioned. For educated Africans who followed global events, socialism provided a vision of futuristic idealism: an egalitarian and productive alternative to colonial capitalism. Nyerere's commitment to socialism was both long-held ideal and tactical response to Cold War discourses of capitalism and communism.

Claiming socialist philosophical territory allowed him to constrain socialist rhetoric within Tanganyika and engage an international ideological realm rhetorically marked by the conflict between capitalism and communism. But that sort of external orientation was insufficient for the needs of Tanganyika, where most of the population consisted of illiterate farmers in small scattered homesteads across a vast dusty land. Nyerere's task was to find a language that spoke to rural and uneducated Tanganyikans about political choices amid the ideological battles of the age. During 1962 Nyerere introduced the term that would be identified with him his entire political career: *Ujamaa*, meaning both socialism and "familyhood." The word was not his invention; rather, he found it by wading into the life of the new nation looking for a set of reference points that would define what it meant to be Tanganyikan.

During his travels that year, it seems that Nyerere ran across Petro Itosi Marealle's book *The Life of the Chagga: Here on Earth and after Death*.[7] A meditation on the rapidly passing traditions of rural life, the book dealt fundamentally with families, from birth to death and beyond. Marealle's opening statement justified his purpose: "It is clear that all tribes or nations on earth have the responsibility to raise children and teach them how to live a good life of benefit to themselves and their neighbors." A local proverb expressed not only a psychological truism but also the anthropological concept of social reproduction: "As the child is raised, so he will be."[8] Explaining the impact of foreign immigrants on Chagga society, Marealle protested foreign stereotypes of African customs as "barbarous." He said the outsiders did not understand that the "Chagga are people of a tribe that could not live without familyhood amongst them; and this familyhood depends on clan and house."

Taking a Swahili word for extended family, *jamaa*, and turning it into the abstraction *ujamaa*, as Emma Hunter has noted, Marealle coined the term that came to define Tanzanian political culture.[9] Its utility arose from its claim as a distinction that defined African civilization. "The White civilization does not depend on *Ujamaa* of people with customs and traditions like these." The term defined African society by something other than negative attributes of race and linked stereotypes of barbarism. Furthermore, it provided an ideology of governance. "If you look at the history of Chagga ujamaa you will see that it begins in the house, then in the clan, and the peak of this ujamaa is the chieftaincy of the country." Like the peak of Mount Kilimanjaro, whose pyramidal shape loomed so prominently over Chagga country, the hierarchy of family created around its base a uniquely fertile land into which children were raised in a structure of authority and agricultural productivity. Each nested unit of this edifice constituted the elements of a bigger collectivity. As his train of thought gained momentum, Marealle seemed entranced by his own invention, and its impressive ideological reach. "Chagga did all their work by Ujamaa, and the harvest of this work was used in Ujamaa as well."[10] His new term provided a bridge from provincial isolation to cosmopolitan ambition. Ujamaa would bring people together and overcome racial prejudice caused by nothing more than a simple lack of familiarity between different groups.

In the course of conversations with such thoughtful elders, Nyerere began to elaborate Petro Marealle's metaphor of family as the bedrock of social virtue. The metaphor provided an immediate point of contact for the views about social ethics and governmental responsibility that he wanted to convey. Writing in an edited volume titled *Africa Speaks*, Nyerere argued for the intermediary virtues of a one-party state during the first years of independence in a postcolonial country. Like Marealle, he proposed that social structure in Africa was "a direct extension of the family."[11] These ideas are key to understanding the development of Nyerere's thought and its relation to the development of a Tanganyikan identity. Nyerere understood, or at least promoted the idea, that the familial vision of society in Africa conflicted with the oppositional politics of Europe, whether in the contentious politics of multiparty democracy in Western Europe or in the ideological premise of class conflict in Eastern Europe.[12] Nyerere's insistence on consensual politics for Tanganyika was based in part on an awareness of the bitter political divisions in neighboring countries and the suffering that turmoil was causing. His vision of a political family was accurate enough to resonate with many Tanganyikans who lived within extended families that functioned as organizations of great social and economic importance to them. Within the ideology of family also resided a memory of precolonial sovereignty—of the family's relationship to a chief or decentralized structure of governance negotiated among leading members of familial segments.[13]

The ideological utility of these familial references had been evident to Nyerere for some time. At home, after returning from Edinburgh in 1952, he had regular conversations with his mentor, Father Richard Walsh, whose thoughts in a 1953 publication evinced their probing conversations:

> In the history, languages and folklore of Africa is found reflected the genius and soul of the African people.... It is by seeking first what is good in these

> that we can hope to lay lasting foundations for the Africa of tomorrow. We might just mention in this connection the strength of family ties and tribal organization, the respect for laws, custom, authority and native wisdom.... And so it is nature herself which urges families to seek the mutual support of other families; thus we find people grouped into clans, tribes, and, ultimately, into that more highly organised society we call the State.... The State is in fact a commonwealth of families.[14]

This presentation of African community, romanticized as it was, fit anthropological theory of the time, and as one of several children of one of several wives of a minor chief, Nyerere had grown up amid the real thing. In Edinburgh, he had become familiar with the scientific language of anthropology to describe social structures in universal and comparable terms. Ujamaa, however, was a political invention, a very deliberate ideological resource to minimize conflict during the transition to independence. While the generalized terms of Ujamaa's anthropological inventions may have misrepresented the complexity and variation of actual life, his language certainly caught the imagination of people who recognized in it aspects of their own daily lives. An elderly Muslim woman in Buhaya a few years later was not alone in trumpeting Ujumaa discourse: "I identify with the nation because I know I belong to one big family of Tanzanians with one leader, Mr. Nyerere."[15] Even where villagers didn't agree with the interpretation and implications of Ujamaa, it provided a language of symbol and reference that aptly served to describe political ideas for rural, unlettered people.[16] Simultaneously, it was a language that resonated with foreign-educated audiences who could comprehend its anthropological logic. Ujamaa offered a language of mediation, providing two very different audiences with a system of reference in which their different understandings about the very nature of politics could be addressed within a single statement comprehensible to both.[17] With this language Nyerere could minimize the need to rationalize statements for one audience in terms acceptable to another and so avoid politically damaging contradictions.[18]

The romanticization of rural life, however, reinforced a popular image of cities as sites of decadence.[19] As symbols of the colonial order, cities were contradictory spaces for many Tanganyikans, filled with hope for a cosmopolitan future and anxiety about the loss of indigenous cultural coherence. Colonial legacies reinforced this ambivalence. Colonial rule had created a distinct divide between the administrative legal order of the cities and the notionally "customary" law in rural areas.[20] Urban economic opportunities had accelerated a well-established trend of rural young people moving into cities, and molding them as places of distinctly youthful ambition while prompting a reaction among colonial elites that regarded youth as vectors of disorder and crime.[21] This trend created a deep-seated challenge for the new government, which itself was prominently youthful and urban. Many in the TANU leadership, Nyerere among them, worried that a government built on an insular class of urban elites would quickly grow alienated from the country's vast rural majority, who in 1962 were mostly illiterate. Ujamaa's elevation of rural images in nationalist ideology aimed to reassure rural citizens that their presence, their desires, and their needs would be central considerations of an independent government dominated by an educated, Westernized, and increasingly urban professional class.

By filling the nominal political identity of "Tanganyikan" with a new political philosophy, expressed in local terms, Nyerere also gave life to a conception of national sovereignty that went beyond identification with him as a person or TANU as a source of patronage or protection. In Ujamaa lay a philosophical source for what it meant to be Tanganyikan beyond the simple accident of birth in a colonial territory. It defined an institution of Tanganyikan sovereignty. As with the chiefs and clan elders of old, a sovereign Tanganyikan government would be the representative of an ostensible family.[22] This was an eminently acceptable proposition for people who accorded the first president the honorific title "father of the nation." Even so, Ujamaa—denoting not a family as such but a theoretical state of familyhood—was clearly an abstraction, impersonal, not meant for the provincial reality of kinship but rather for the nationalist aspiration for institutions that could legitimately represent Tanganyika at home and abroad.

Land at the Heart of Familyhood

An element of Ujamaa's power as an ideological vessel of sovereignty was that land, with all its ideological freight, was generally vested in families at the most local level in many areas of the territory.[23] This ideology of land tenure often extended into traditional practices of local governance.[24] In Nyerere's Zanaki tradition, foundational prophets established possession over the land, an inheritance managed through "generation-sets"—elders who "walked around the boundaries of the land," defining the *ekyaro* of each new ruling generation and ensuring its peace and fertility.[25] British administrators remembered Nyerere's father as an amiable old chief primarily concerned with adjudicating land disputes.[26] This general orientation can also be found in southeastern districts populated by decentralized matrilineal Makonde people, where land devolved through family authorities. Such clan authority, according to women in the region today, was itself subject to a hierarchy of authority with its apex in the divine. Since "land can only be called the property of God," earthly delegation of divine authority was seen in clan-based allocation of land. Scholars interviewing these women summarized land tenure in the region in terms of access and control. "Access is guaranteed by being a member of a clan, while control is an attribute of the sovereign status of the clan."[27] Access to land was understood as an emblem of political rights in a community, and its allocation an attribute of authority.[28] Because of this, the question of land inhered in the philosophy of Ujamaa.

All of Nyerere's major statements about Ujamaa made reference to land. In fact, the question of land preceded Ujamaa. His first major pronouncement on postcolonial policy, before any talk of familyhood, was a statement on land tenure. In 1958 TANU published a pamphlet containing Nyerere's essay *Mali ya Taifa* (National Property). Reasoning that land was a gift from God that people occupied only temporarily while they lived and worked on it, Nyerere rejected freehold land tenure for postcolonial Tanganyika. He argued that freehold ownership would quickly devolve into foreign ownership of much of the land with the rest monopolized by a few wealthy property holders, a process British administrators had long seen happening along the coast.[29] "This dangerous situation occurred in Uganda and many other places in the world," he wrote.[30] The danger was the division of society into a propertied class and a landless class that would lead to conflict and possible bloodshed. The solution, argued Nyerere, was for land to be granted under leasehold, not freehold, conditions.

Nyerere did not, however, support customary leasehold, administered by ethnically identified authorities. "Africans have to forget about political considerations when thinking of the advantages and disadvantages of the present traditional system or the system of leasehold." Acknowledging that people's loyalty to customary tenure was in part due to their sense that signing over land to the government was equivalent to selling one's birthright, Nyerere suggested that this equation would fundamentally change with independence. Signing land over to a foreign colonial government had meant the total alienation of the land from the community, but after independence "our population will be united as one nation, and the land will belong to the nation." The hierarchical logic of land tenure, so fundamental to political organization and individual autonomy, was also inscribed in the sovereignty of the new nation.

The circularity of reasoning here recalls the self-referential quality of the ideology of national sovereignty. But it also addressed real conflicts such as those in Buhaya, west of Lake Tanganyika, in the 1950s, where peasants claimed the land was theirs long before its control was taken over by landlords in the quasifeudal *Nyarubanja* system that they called "secret slavery." Landless peasants in Buhaya, who believed that colonial customary law had transformed communal landholding into mere serfdom, had already suggested that they "fight each other with machetes" to "see who will win and take this land."[31] As a result of their protest, they successfully created an elected chieftainship in Buhaya like the one that took form in Kilimanjaro under Petro Njau's leadership.[32] Whether Nyerere made specific reference to the complaints reaching the district commissioner's office in Bukoba is unclear, but certainly he understood their sentiment, and the dangers such frustration boded for the new nation: He asserted: "The leasehold system is the best, and even if we must pay a small price for it, we have the obligation to do so in order to rid ourselves of the old customary system and to avoid the slavery associated with the freehold system."[33]

The "National Property" pamphlet served as a campaign platform, published as TANU gathered legislative power before independence. Announcing an intention to eliminate freehold tenure might well have backfired and undermined TANU's still contested leadership of the nationalist movement. Instead, the argument seemed to appeal to a vast rural constituency that associated authority with land allocation but resented the unequal access granted to colonial chiefs. It assured that independence would not simply be a transfer of power to a new set of exploitative authorities eager to alienate the wealth of the land to themselves. The essay established a culturally legitimate basis for TANU's nationalist authority, identifying it as sovereign—the rightful *Ng'wenye Shi*, the Shambaa term for chief that signified the "owner of the land."[34] Touring central Tanganyika, Nyerere echoed the identification of local leaders in Gogo communities, who were known as *wazengamatumbi*, or "settlement builders."[35] In April or May 1962, he gave a speech in Tabora, the next major city along the central railway. He took an old Nyamwezi song from the area and gave it new words: *Ohh TANU Yajenga Nchi* (TANU Builds the Country). A young publicity officer had recorded the crowd singing the song and sent the recording immediately to Radio Tanganyika.[36] The song raced through the country on the lips of the party's youthful supporters, becoming a powerful statement, not only of TANU's ideology, but of its hegemony.

Independence, as Nyerere described it in the TANU newspaper *Uhuru*, was "like obtaining the land on which to build a house."[37] The question was "what sort of house we want to build on this land." Given the centrality of land as a context for political authority in East Africa, and as a key symbolic attribute of social maturity within a family, it is unsurprising that Nyerere compared independence to the acquisition of real estate.[38] Given that land "was the property that we had," TANU activist Mbuta Milando asked, "Why did the British want to control our land?" His question arose from his overarching sentiment that "land has all the meaning; if you don't have land you don't have food."[39] Likewise, references to land and its role in the social order became central to the national identity Nyerere hoped to cultivate.[40] The colonial Land Ordinance was revised to vest all ownership of land in the president.[41] The allocation of land as an attribute of legitimate political authority was key to articulating a Tanganyikan national ethic that would resonate in the villages, transforming provincial bonds into national ones. A few years later, Nyerere told an audience in Cairo that "the only change which our law effected as far as the masses were concerned was that the land became national instead of tribal."[42]

The TANU government retained control over land from the beginning by simply changing the word "Governor" to "President" in updating the colonial Land Ordinance. But where the colonial state justified this in the name of paternal trusteeship, Nyerere's government couched this claim in rhetoric meant to appeal to rural citizens. Almost immediately after independence, the new government began to transform colonial policy that had separated land under customary law in rural areas from freehold estates held by foreigners. The general direction of land policy had already been defined, but the first steps were rather tentative. The move toward long-term leasehold was a concrete step away from the tribal basis of customary law, but at the same time it was a move toward a nationalized restatement of the indigenous idiom of land allocation. Although it was eager to distribute land to Africans, the new government cautioned that doing so would be useless if people were not prepared to develop it. So they would thoroughly investigate the productive potential of all applications for land registration. Nyerere initially promised to recognize existing freeholds but would avoid granting further large areas to individuals. Within weeks, however, the government reversed this stance, stating its intention "to convert freehold titles to some such form of leasehold."[43] The elimination of freehold put the government in the culturally resonant role of final allocator and arbitrator of land. The new policy, using the language of the colonial dichotomy, explained that "freehold is an alien conception to Africans, associated in their minds with exploitation and privilege."[44] Freehold, in this presentation, was contrary to the ethic of work that attached to the new land policy.

Family, land, and citizenship were social institutions that needed to be fused together in a new national ethic that could pierce the Cold War ideological structure—not only communism and capitalism, but also the modernist imagination that both strove to claim. To modernize, and yet retain an African cultural orientation sufficient to restrain a racial concept of Africanization, required the sort of ideological innovation that characterized the great nationalist leaders of Africa. Leopold Senghor, Kwame Nkrumah, Abdel Nasser, and Nyerere all articulated visions reflecting John Lonsdale's observation that the "dialectic between tradition and modernity at the core of political science's old evolutionary myth was a self-serving construction."[45] Senghor elaborated *Négritude*; Nasser mobilized *Al-Ishtirākiyya*; Nyerere appropriated *Ujamaa*.[46] Ujamaa would be his primary discursive tool to confront racialism, to restructure government, and to navigate the ideological battles of the Cold War.

Ujamaa and the Ideological Upper Hand

At the new TANU ideological college at Kivukoni in Dar es Salaam on April 16, 1962, using the term borrowed from Chagga commentator Petro Itosi Marealle, Nyerere proclaimed his new state ideology.[47] In a combative speech defending the leasehold system for land, he introduced Ujamaa as a translation for African socialism. He then continued: "In rejecting the capitalist attitude of mind which colonialism brought into Africa, we must reject also the capitalist methods which go with it. One of these is the individual ownership of land. . . . To us in Africa land was always recognised as belonging to the community."[48] With its intimacy of kinship and equitable allocation of land, Nyerere's metaphorical translation of socialism channeled a powerful ideological confluence.

The first protest against Ujamaa complained specifically about the implications of the policy for land tenure. Asserting that individual land ownership in the Bukoba and Moshi areas was ancient, a letter to the editor of the *Tanganyika Standard* stressed, "Mr. Nyerere's highly coloured presentation of 'African Socialism' cannot go unchallenged." The writer went on to hypothesize that the lack of individual tenure would cause land degradation.[49] For his part, Nyerere toured the country incessantly, preaching his new gospel of Ujamaa. In public and even in private, the language of Ujamaa became the language of government policy. It served as an explicit rejection of the conflict at the heart of European Marxist dogma, but more importantly, it was also a philosophical marker of the state's Africanness, directly opposing racialism as a basis for the postcolonial state.

Ujamaa was a manner of articulating a generic Africanization of culture instead of a racialized purge of non-Africans. Participation in Ujamaa rather than ethnicity might establish one's loyalties to a sovereign African government, and so defuse the explosive issue of race. In November 1962 Lucy Lameck, parliamentary secretary to the Ministry of Co-Operative and Community Development, urged a Dar es Salaam crowd to patronize the new Magomeni Cooperative Shop. Without making any racial references, her charge that people should not buy from those who "have exploited and overcharged the Tanganyikan people" clearly fingered the Asian shopkeepers who monopolized retail trade in Dar es Salaam. The problem with the consumer cooperatives was that they could not extend credit the way the Asian shopkeepers did and so were unable to attract African customers.[50] Because of this frustration and in response to a spike in maize flour prices blamed on Asian speculators, the government established the Co-operative Supply Association for Tanganyika in January 1963 to buy basic foodstuffs and retail them nationally.[51] By highlighting social practice rather than race and by establishing nonracial institutions in response to populist xenophobia, the Ujamaa policy discursively displaced a racial context, introducing a more manageable political one, rooted in a philosophy of government that Nyerere himself defined.

By mapping "socialism" onto Marealle's obscure term for "familyhood," Nyerere found the rhetorical freedom to draw from each of these connotations while being bound closely to neither. Familyhood represented a system that would meld an African moral world with a European material one, as he had described at Wellesley College the previous year, before he found Petro Marealle's powerful term: "Our problem is just this: How to get the benefits of European society—benefits which have been brought about by an organization of society based on an exaggerated idea of the rights of the individual—and yet retain the African's own structure of society in which the individual is a member of a kind of fellowship."[52]

Ujamaa as African socialism gave Nyerere and his government a political language that encompassed both the concerns for Africanization at the domestic level and the Cold War at the international level, and thus set the terms of their debate. A concern of Africanization, in addition to placing more Africans into positions held by British expatriates, was the aim to make government practices and institutions cohere more closely to political and economic habits perceived as "traditional" by African citizens. The wide ideological range across the dozens of cultural zones of Tanganyika could be endlessly manipulated to frame policy innovations by the new government. Policies could be defined in terms of transformations of existing modes of thought among rural citizens whose interaction with the colonial state had been limited to often unpleasant encounters with state bureaucracies and overly insistent agricultural extension officers.[53] With Ujamaa's ideological innovation, even Europeans working in the government ceased to be symbols of neocolonial imposition and became instead participants in a sovereign African society. By June 1963 Vice President Kawawa announced the imminent end of all race-based discrimination in government hiring.[54]

The personal language of "familyhood" powerfully expressed the ideals of socialism most attractive to Nyerere in an intimate manner that gave Tanganyikans an immediate mental picture of family and clan, so fundamental to most people's sense of identity and social place.[55] Additionally, and by no means unnoticed, Ujamaa distanced TANU's socialism from atheistic Soviet communism. Conversely, the web of traditions, patrons, and dependents that formed the *habitus* of clans in Tanganyika could be avoided and even directly critiqued with the "scientific" language of socialism.[56] Echoing the concerns of the 1955 Royal Commission report, Ujamaa promised to break Africans from traditions perceived as backward and provincial, and at the same time preserve those traditions during a process of modernization. Kambona painted the issue of village settlement as an effort analogous to the American space program—at once both development and defense. Where Americans were "sending their rockets to the moon to explore other colonies, the Tanganyika Government's rockets were to be sent to the villages with a view of developing the country as a whole."[57] Building directly on Marealle's initial brainstorm, the philosophy of Ujamaa brought positive resolution to the contradiction between the desire to invoke pride in African culture and the perception of Europe as the apotheosis of the modern scientific world.

A pamphlet inaugurating the new state philosophy for public consumption introduced Ujamaa as the self-sufficient "basis of African Socialism," denoting specifically Nyerere's philosophy. The pamphlet declared: "The basic difference between a socialist society and a capitalist society does not lie in their methods of producing wealth, but in the way that wealth is distributed."[58] Opposed to both "doctrinaire socialism" and exploitative capitalism, Ujamaa bestowed a usable ideological autonomy. "We, in Africa, have no more need of being 'converted' to socialism than we have of being 'taught' democracy. Both are rooted in our own our past."[59] Ujamaa was instant tradition, harnessed for the nationalist cause. In Ujamaa Nyerere created a philosophical sovereignty, engaged in the ideological conflicts of the world but at the same time independent of them, needing no one but himself and his party to define Tanganyikan orthodoxy. He was thus free not only to dismiss the capitalist orthodoxy of British colonialism but also to avoid the dogmatic need for class conflict that was the transformative force of socialist history. "Brought up in tribal socialism, I must say I find this contradiction quite intolerable," he wrote.[60]

Nyerere used the same language repeatedly to describe Ujamaa throughout the decade. Land, and the colonial distinction between European and African thought in regard to it, retained its power as a reference point for the logic of African socialism. "To us in Africa" Nyerere wrote, "land was always recognized as belonging to the community."[61] Inherent to this notion was the entire epistemology of the alien nature of freehold and the moral hazards of ownership. In its place, government-leased land symbolized a concept fundamental to local governance. "Each individual within our society had a right to the use of the land, because otherwise he could not earn his living and one cannot have the right to life without also having the right to some means of maintaining life."[62] Making good on his campaign promises of 1958, Nyerere articulated the logic of land allocation, arguing that, under Ujamaa, "unconditional or 'freehold,' ownership of land (which leads to speculation and parasitism) must be abolished. We must, as I have said, regain our former attitude of mind—our traditional African socialism—and apply it to the new societies we are building today."[63]

Nyerere contrasted the European class system with the habits of gerontocracy that prevailed in much of East Africa. "This respect for age and service will be preserved," he averred, emphasizing that traditional elders in the past held wealth in trust for their people, and that in the same way the rich in modern society should hold wealth "only in so far as it is a necessary aid to the carrying out of their duties." In this manner, the state, functioning as bureaucratic elder, would allocate land and wealth to foreigners at its own prerogative. The language of socialism and the vision of land policy superseded both the racialist and socialist positions taken by Christopher Tumbo's PDP, which predictably stated in the first clause in its manifesto, "We believe all land belongs to the clans."[64] Refining these ideologies to his liking, Nyerere maintained his prerogative to set the dominant tones of political rhetoric in Tanganyika.

After the inauguration of the Tanganyikan Republic on December 9, 1962, a year to the day after the independence celebrations, Nyerere gave a speech to Parliament as the nation's new president. He praised Kawawa and the cabinet ministers who had led the government during his absence for their "splendid example of unhesitating acceptance of responsibility, and the use of that responsibility in the service of our country." He defended TANU against accusations that it was a party of illiterates, saying that TANU could never be the party of an educated minority but rather represented the whole of a mostly illiterate population. He invited alienated members of TANU, those who left of their own accord and those who were expelled, to rejoin the party, as well as civil servants who hitherto had been legally barred from participation in politics. All of this was evident preparation to build the most inclusive one-party state possible. But he spoke primarily on this occasion in more abstract terms of his thought during the preceding year. He defined the task of the nationalist movement not as a technocratic agent of development but as an agent of national consciousness and the source of national identity. Nation building, he proclaimed, was fundamentally "an attitude of mind which will enable us to live together with our fellow citizens of Tanganyika, and of the whole world, in mutual friendliness and co-operation."[65]

Ujamaa displaced racialism as an avenue to a culturally African state. Internal sovereignty, in popular discourse and in Nyerere's philosophical intention, was fundamentally a cultural construction built on the fertile local implications of land and family-based authority bound to modernist conceptions of development and socialism. It was a national ethic designed to guide and govern the one-party state that he believed was necessary to establish a united national sentiment in the new citizenry. Ujamaa proposed to guide the development of a new national culture, which would be practiced in economic and foreign policy, government-sponsored youth activities, and countrywide villagization. All of these became visible signs of sovereignty, enacted by citizens on a daily basis throughout the land.

5

The Origins of Villagization

TANU Youth League settlement schemes were constantly praised by Nyerere and other government ministers, and their ideological force only continued to increase in official rhetoric. In his inaugural presidential speech on December 10, 1962, Nyerere made reference to "the work being done by the people themselves through self-help schemes" while, ironically, also emphasizing that rural development would be "directly under my control." Placing the work of these model citizens in a generational framework of family, he told the gathered parliamentarians, "It will be from their children and their grand-children that they will in the end receive the thanks they deserve." Village development was a major theme of the speech:

> The growth of village life will help us in improving our system of democratic government. . . . Although the methods may be democratic, the operation of democracy itself is not yet what it should be, nor can it be while the majority of our rural population remains so widely scattered. . . . I intend first to set up a new department: the Department of Development Planning. This Department will be directly under my control, and it will make every effort to prepare plans for village development for the whole country as quickly as possible.[1]

A divisional executive officer in northern Tanganyika used TANU rhetoric to encourage the populace to support "self-help" settlements, "for the sake of fighting our enemy 'poverty.'"[2] These schemes also served a national security purpose modeled on an optimistic understanding of the moshav settlements in Israel.[3] Nyerere's new Department of Development Planning was an institutional expression of Ujamaa's merging vectors of patriarchal land allocation in local discourse and foreign prescriptions for economic development. The new villages represented not only attempts to enact modernist ideas of development but also pragmatic strategies to secure borders for national defense. Government-directed village settlement was only partly an economic development policy; it was also a locally legible effort to establish sovereignty at the grass roots.

State-directed rural development in Africa has been characterized as an "anti-politics machine" by James Ferguson, who argued that the language of "developmentalism" suppresses political debate and so authorizes unidirectional state action toward rural farmers.[4] James Scott saw villagization as an aspect of a broader disciplinary trend that he called "high modernism," marked by a Utilitarian inheritance that Michel Foucault identified as panopticism.[5] Leander Schneider has argued that these dynamics lay at the heart of Tanzanian villagization, and attached themselves to the self-regard of civil servants who bound their personal authority to institutional roles provided by developmentalist practice. In Schneider's view, however, this confluence between political and institutional authority explains the policy's increasingly authoritarian implementation, which by the 1970s had become forced resettlement.[6] This critique, while accurate, is also too one-sided. As Mahmood Mamdani pointed out, an authoritarian orientation emerged not only from state-level prescriptions of foreign provenance but also from local discourse as well. He concluded, "To understand the centralized despotism that the Tanzanian experience turned into we need to bear in mind that it was the bitter fruit of a failed reform."[7]

In the 1960s Goran Hyden observed village-level state institutions absorbing and displacing local authority structures, and thereby replacing ethnic loyalties with nationalist attachments. In practice, this meant that the meaning of nation took root in local values, and was therefore infused by grassroots themes.[8] Clyde Ingle also noted villagization's core "political socialization" function in service to the nation.[9] The initial settlement schemes offered a modernist dramatization of Nyerere's mantra of the era, "Freedom and Work," which recalled the prerogatives of land allocation and familial obligation widely rooted in structures of local authority. Introducing the policy in his inaugural presidential speech, Nyerere pointed to the challenge of impressing the values of the independence movement into a new independent polity, making an implicit comparison to ethnic division and political violence in neighbouring Congo and Rwanda. "We are in no way different from others. We have the same difficulties and the same temptations here which lead people of any country to fall out with each other instead of working together, and to hate each other instead of being friends."[10] The government could no longer be considered the hostile presence of the colonial state. State authority had to emerge as a vernacular expression, each citizen taking the presidential oath with him that day. "Every one of us has an equal duty to do the work entrusted to him—whatever that work may be," Nyerere demanded in a voice of patriarchal authority, "as if he too had taken a solemn oath."

Villagization as a policy for agricultural development was not a Tanzanian invention; it emerged from international consensus on rural policy in developing countries. The policy grew directly from the World Bank's modernist recommendations on the eve of Tanganyika's independence to pursue a centrally planned "transformation" strategy that would create a more productive and profitable rural sector:

> The transformation program should rely to a considerable degree on securing quicker and higher returns on investment and effort by using selected, sparsely populated areas for planned settlement schemes and cattle ranches. In some places it is in any case already desirable to move people from overcrowded and deteriorating areas into others which are at present little used and such action will become increasingly necessary in the future. Many of the larger schemes would be best organized on a partnership basis in which individual Africans farm the land but a public authority provides capital works, productive services and an element of skilled management.[11]

In 1960 the TANU-led government embarked on its first experiments in transformative settlement, including a village in Sonjo country bordering on the Serengeti near the Kenyan border.[12] Young unemployed men from Dar es Salaam were offered farms in Sonjo, but they arrived to find nothing but wilderness. Even though the government hired out machinery to clear the land, the settlement was quickly abandoned.[13] The failed scheme ominously foreshadowed future travails of the villagization policy, but it also highlighted the mutually reinforcing discourses of authority that fueled Nyerere's faith in state-directed settlement. The Sonjo settlement clearly reflected the modernizing intent of World Bank "transformation" as well as the ongoing perception of Dar es Salaam's unemployed youth as criminals and hooligans.[14] A further motivation for the Sonjo settlement may have been the nascent national security logic of villagization. A government-sponsored settlement in Sonjo could provide an observation point for the troubling seed of a Maasai separatist movement encouraged by Father Eugene Hillman, who was based in neighboring Monduli and was traveling widely in the area.[15] Finally, the scheme also adhered closely to the widespread discourse of land allocation as an attribute of authority.[16]

In providing farmland to young people, the state emulated the patriarchal authority of many rural communities that offered land and the tools to bring out its fertility. Emerging from this discourse, an agricultural settlement in Sonjo presented the possibility of reversing the "multi-generational process by which Sonjo agriculturalists became pastoral Maasai."[17] In a precolonial period of Maasai ascendancy east of Lake Victoria, various ethnic groups adopted Maasai cultural markers for safety and status, even as they kept their agricultural ways. Sonjo refugees from these nineteenth-century conflicts fled across the Serengeti to settle in areas bordering on Nyerere's Zanaki country, which was also under Maasai pressure by the late nineteenth century. Farming communities in the western Serengeti began to define themselves "as 'Sonjo-peoples' within a Maasai world."[18]

The reinforcement of agricultural customs in these northern communities through government-sponsored "modernization" must have been appealing to Nyerere's Zanaki elders, who could remember the deleterious effect of Maasai dominance on the culture of farming communities.

In the early independence era, public clamor for tractors sprouted from both a grassroots longing for visible symbols of modernization and long-standing expectations of political leaders to produce fertility from the land, whether by organizing the manufacture of iron implements or by assuring rainfall. These democratic expectations demanded in turn a representative response. Although the government did not have tractors to simply hand out, it sought to fulfill this popular demand within its administrative and ideological limits. It called on people's participation in the national vision, not as colonial subjects, but as citizens, through the material enactment of this ideology in planned villages. Nyerere conflated these symbols of modernism and fertility in his inaugural presidential speech: "The first and absolutely essential thing to do, therefore, if we want to start using tractors for cultivation, is to begin living in proper villages. . . . If you were to ask me what Government proposes to do in the next few years, I would tell you that it intends to enable our country people to resettle in village communities so as to speed up rural development."[19]

In "proper villages," under the direct authority of the president, people would associate with the new nation, looking to the national government rather than parochial figures of authority for access to the fertility of the land. This, at least, was the ideal: enthusiastic citizens, voluntarily digging in to build a new nation in which all would live in egalitarian peace and prosperity, sprouting from a participatory structure of village democracy. But the Department of Development Planning had authoritarian roots in two intertwined cultural sources: in the compulsory drive of colonial production and in chiefly feudalism. Girded by colonial customary law, regimes like the *nyarubanja* system on the western shore of Lake Victoria and the *kihamba* system around Mount Kilimanjaro had gained bureaucratic authority during the early twentieth century over peasants who lost their means of redress against government-sponsored chiefly offices. Colonial indirect rule had conspired to bind its production demands to these most hierarchical examples of local practice in the territory. With independence, local politicians tried to impress the new president by singing the praises of communal self-help schemes, and pushing them to be more productive. They thereby filled the role of both state official and chiefly authority.

Local government administrators sought powers commensurate with those of the former colonial officers, and almost immediately began lobbying for authority to enforce participation in communal work. A district commissioner at a Regional Development Committee meeting asked for "guidance as to how far Government would be content to rely upon persuasion only to achieve production targets, and how far it would go in backing the use of stronger methods." A central government representative in attendance at the meeting assured him that "Government was quite prepared to use methods stronger than persuasion if persuasion failed."[20] Peasants bowed to pressure from local political elites to chip in on village development projects, much as they had been forced to do under colonial chiefs. "Self-help" lost some of its voluntary élan. Portuguese spies in southern Tanganyika reported in 1962 that people were already complaining about "being obligated to work on roads and bridges without remuneration."[21]

At a party at the British high commissioner's house in October 1962, Nyerere set aside the jocular small talk of the diplomatic social scene to address Andrew Cohen, an influential member of the British Colonial Office, asking, "May I raise a piece of shop?" Nyerere probed him on the possibility that a donor could "adopt" a settlement scheme by providing aid and expertise.[22] His idea was to develop land in each district for landless residents, who would then adopt modern farming methods and serve as models for rural development.[23] Cohen immediately suggested the Irish "Freedom from Hunger" organization, which eventually did provide start-up funds and expertise for pilot projects along the southern border. The British were skeptical, however, not so much of the idea itself but of the possibility of its implementation given the Sonjo experience and other depressing precedents. In particular, they questioned the logic of "'villagisation' as it is, regrettably, becoming known here."[24] It was a fallacy, argued British economists, that village development could stimulate economic growth in the surrounding countryside. If anything, the opposite was true.[25] But, they reported, "Nyerere made it plain in his December speech that his objectives are as much political and social as economic."

The British suspected that the main pressure came from local administrators who saw settlement schemes as a way to offer patronage to unemployed youth.[26] In any case, at least one precedent augured for success—at a price. During the Mau Mau rebellion in Kenya, "peasants were concentrated into villages so that they could be kept under observation on the one hand and protected on the other." Landholdings were consolidated and "farming machinery was made available but the strictest compulsion was employed to ensure that the owners of the land did what the Director of Agriculture thought best."[27] The lesson for Tanganyika, concluded one commentator, was that "an element of compulsion is needed if such schemes are going to make any real progress, but perhaps Dr. Nyerere is prepared to exert this."[28]

British calls for "compulsion" and comparisons to Kenya leave little doubt that the prescriptive power of such development policies went hand in hand with their potential to impose state authority in rural communities. Schneider is correct in identifying the developmentalist dynamic at work, but we must also acknowledge indigenous sources of inspiration that reinforced the political potential of villagization to enhance state authority. The ability to allocate land was a widely recognized attribute of political authority in East Africa, and the government's enactment of this power in rural settlement was a claim to sovereignty that displaced the powers of the former colonial native authorities in rural areas. The authority generated by developmentalist discourse was not just the subconscious side-effect of economic modernization policy. It was also the consciously desired result of a government seeking to project its presence more deeply into rural society.

Nyerere gradually accepted and endorsed the sort of compulsion that British diplomats suggested, but it took another decade. In the short term, new vice president Rashidi Kawawa took on day-to-day responsibility for villagization, with notable urgency. Not coincidentally, one of Kawawa's first government jobs in the early 1950s was as a clerk in the Social Development Department working in Kikuyu refugee camps in northern Tanganyika during the Mau Mau rebellion. There he saw the British policy of compulsory collectivization in action on a smaller scale.[29] In January 1963 Kawawa inaugurated a series of regional seminars on "villagisation" as "the second phase of our rational development plan" and the creation and functions of Village Development Committees (VDCs) as instruments of governance. His vision clearly reflected the British Kikuyu project, but he retained a labor leader's sense for moderation in regard to people's livelihoods—a respect for community initiative that seemed to fade in later years as the policy foundered on economic obstacles. Kawawa's speech was paraphrased by a British observer.

> Revolutionary changes of this nature are never easy especially for older people and I rely on your tact, good humour and understanding in winning the people's confidence at all stages of the various schemes. We cannot expect them to show interest in our big plans unless we have first supported their little ones. If people want water for their cattle it is no good first giving them a school. By patient understanding and sometimes giving way in small things we will sow the seeds of the right ideas throughout the villages.[30]

Kawawa and Nyerere sat down with Ambassador Leonhart in May 1963 to feel out US support. The conversation resulted in a multiyear collaboration with Syracuse University whereby young scholars would "act as brokers between the modernizing policy of Government and other large-scale institutions, and the masses of people towards whom commands and suggestions for technical and social and administrative changes are directed."[31] Clearly whatever authority resided in the customs of land allocation was equaled by the expert-driven vision of modernization. The new policy for rural development intended to formalize self-help work into a system that was not simply coercive, but incorporative—"improving our system of democratic government." Instituting this plan, a Rural Settlement Commission with the Village Settlement Agency as its executive organ was established in 1963 under Kawawa's authority. The commission's task was to define a general policy for villagization and to "co-ordinate the activities of all who are concerned with such settlement." The plan explained that "in order to provide a sound basis for all future rural settlement, the first task of the Rural Settlement Commission will be to select sites for, plan, and subject to the availability of the necessary finance, to establish a series of Pilot Village Settlements in rural Tanganyika."[32]

With a vision of farmers working cooperatively in equitably allocated villages, the plan aimed to "to ensure that each farmer is able to earn enough from the land allocated to him to improve his standard of living." To achieve such results, it would be "essential that rural settlements be planned on sound economic lines." The allocation of land was a language that communicated to an illiterate peasantry the principles of modern economy. The villages were envisioned as a line of defense against unproductive subsistence economies cut off from the cash circulation that enabled participation in national and global economies. By rationalizing the allocation of land, authorities envisioned a thoroughgoing reorganization of the rural economy. Lacking sufficient planning officers, written instructions offered guidance to local government and party staff in the "siting, layout and size of rural settlements." Land allocation offered the possibility of etching modernist government instructions into the soil of illiterate village culture, and in turn mapping village life into a national political structure: "To prevent the spread of subsistence agriculture, no settlement must be allowed to take place until it has been approved by the Regional Development Committee concerned and laid out by Regional departmental staff in accordance with instructions contained in this booklet."[33]

Preliminary notes for a booklet to be distributed to all regional commissioners laid out the model for a cautious plan of establishing one pilot scheme per region along the lines of the World Bank's recommendations. Each village would be laid out according to strict guidelines concerning its likelihood of success—its economic basis and a ready set of volunteers to work the new settlement. Volunteers were essential to any scheme, and they understood that they would live in a "comparatively concentrated settlement (where they will be subject to a stricter discipline than to which they have been accustomed)." The sites were not necessarily new settlements. Existing villages could be transformed into planned settlements "to provide experience in reorganizing and consolidating existing land holding." Promulgating the language of village settlement, the transformation of existing villages would "assist in spreading the idea of organized village settlement." The government intended to experiment with pilot projects before expanding nationwide in pursuit of the transformative goals defined by the World Bank—in hopes that "the final result . . . will amount to a rural, economic and social revolution of the whole country."[34]

The mode of land tenure outlined in the notes communicated governmental priorities and emphasized the government's allocative authority. Settlement volunteers would be given title to their land through a long process based on the World Bank recommendation that effectively filtered allocative authority down from the initial right of occupancy taken out by the government. Occupation rights would be transferred over time to the village cooperative society "when it assumes responsibility for the settlement." Finally "the cooperative would then issue titles to each farmer over the land allocated to him." The titles were tools of compulsion, and were "conditional upon the land being farmed according to regulations laid down by the society."[35] When the actual booklet was released, it was accompanied by a letter reminding the reader that "no settlement in your Region is allowed to take place until it has been approved by the Regional Development Committee."[36] This reminder underlined the message that all new villages needed to apply for permission from the Village Development Council, which would forward the request to the district and regional levels.[37] Through a regulated process of land allocation, the terms of national citizenship and state authority were written into local custom and widespread understandings of political power were expressed in local cultural memories of land and its governance.

Preparing a Modernist Ground

Like Ujamaa, villagization possessed an allure that arose from its promise to enhance both economic production and governmental authority on several cultural planes. The modernizing expectation of planned settlement was shared by Europeans and Africans alike; both groups saw in villagization a technology to improve agricultural production. As a result of the American ambassador's facilitation, Nyerere asked his expatriate commissioner of village development to visit Syracuse University in 1963 to put together a study team and arrange for a long-term project to support village development in Tanganyika.[38] The Syracuse faculty was quietly supportive of Tanganyika's broader goals, in part because Nyerere had recruited one of their own, in the person of Eduardo Mondlane, to lead the freedom struggle across the border in Mozambique. A preliminary study by Nikos Georgulas, a Tanganyikan whose Greek parents had been granted farms in the Tanganyika territory after World War II, articulated the rationalist terms that Nyerere usually used with foreigners: "In order to minimize the prohibitive costs involved in providing such services to the scattered rural population, the government's policy envisages a gradual redistribution of the dispersed population into rural village settlements."[39]

Villagization was also a mode of governance.[40] A press release relating to government assistance for settlement schemes in mid-1963 urged the virtues of democratic governance upon the councilors for the new villages, reflecting Nyerere's intention that the villages form the backbone of a democratic Tanganyika. Mahmood Mamdani has argued that the colonial state was "bifurcated" and treated rural and urban populations very differently. Most rural people lived under "customary law," which kept them a legal step removed from the state. Urban residents lived under the same law code as whites, such that, even if that code treated them unequally, they were in direct legal relationship with the state. Although Mamdani's simplification here has been criticized, resolving this dichotomy between rural and urban political cultures was fundamental to the creation of an integrated sovereign authority. Mamdani suggested that villagization was "first and foremost an attempt at a reform of the bifurcated state, at linking the rural and the urban, through the apparatus of the party."[41] Michael Kamaliza's description of rural policy at the time suggests that TANU was fully aware of this dichotomy and intended villagization to mitigate its divisive effects: "The aim of present socialist government [is] to give closer consideration to development between rural areas so as to remove [the] imbalance in development between urban and rural areas which was created by the colonial government."[42]

Villagization was not just economic. It was also a governmental attempt to demonstrate its authority in terms of both land allocation and economic production. Anthony Rwenyemamu, a Tanganyikan involved in the Syracuse University study, summarized the governmental aims for villagization thus: (a) the need for governmental approval for all new settlements, (b) provision of social services, (c) land clearing, and (d) agricultural training. Quoting from the government circular sent out during the launch of the pilot schemes, he emphasized the transformative nature of villagization as a nationalist project: "During the preliminary period, while the villages are being established and the farmers trained, settlers will be subject to strict discipline, and most work will be carried out communally."[43] Some of the researchers were assigned to look specifically at the political effort "to effectively regroup and organize its rural citizenry to enable them to profit from and contribute to nation-building activities." They also sought to understand how a power structure would develop in the villages.[44]

Villagization provided a means of disciplining peasants into virtuous participation in the nation of "freedom and work." Such villages were also meant to serve reciprocally as a means to police the government itself. Tewa

Saidi Tewa, head of Tanganyika's Ministry for Land, Forests, and Wildlife, told graduates of a leadership training course to remember their "responsibilities to the citizens." He implored them to respond quickly and efficiently to citizens' concerns, cautioning them against the vices of power: "For example, if a person needs a plot in a certain place, instead of dealing with him with respect and generosity you start to answer him imperiously." Warning the graduates profusely against corruption, he acknowledged that squatter settlements around many cities could be blamed partially on corrupt officers in his ministry whose prejudiced allocations had angered many people.[45] Organized villages were thus envisioned to help citizens monitor the integrity of government officials. Land policy anchored the rule of law in the new nation, not only by writing law and policy into the practice of village life but also by implementing a culturally rooted infrastructure of surveillance.

With the passage of the Freehold (Conversion) Act, which nationalized freehold land, the need for incorruptible officers to oversee land transactions and disputes became essential to good governance. Enforcing the new legislation helped to define government's role in resolving land disputes and thus formalized its assumption of allocative authority. The legislation granted the minister of lands, forests, and wildlife authority to resolve the inevitable disputes arising from the elimination of freehold tenure. Declaring eight white-owned farms in western Tanga District as disputed areas, the minister appointed a commission of inquiry to judge each case on the basis of whether the land was being used according to policy, "fully for the benefit of the people." Under this rationale, the reduction of European holdings could be effected with neither personal nor racial motives. Instead, land redistribution theoretically emanated from the just judgment of unprejudiced governmental policy, with no "intention of the government to rob anyone's land." The issue was presented in a nonconfrontational manner. "[The minister] told European farmers that if they held vast undeveloped land they could surrender it to the government and their action would very much help solve problems of land shortage in the Usambara mountains."[46] The new bureaucratic policy took on the populist pressure for land redistribution with its unresolved resentment on the part of many African peasants against white landholders. The policy temporarily defused the explosive and unwanted issue of race by subsuming it under the acceptable authority of the government in regard to land allocation. The nationalization of land dramatized, in recognizable local idiom, the government's role as impartial mediator.

Conforming the sovereign territory to the hegemonic form of the nation-state, Nyerere's government laid claim to allocative authority through new legislation and government-sponsored settlement schemes. The new policies were not, and could not be, simple projections of an idealized precolonial society. Rather they resonated with deeply held cultural norms, using those norms as a means to communicate a novel national ideology to a scattered rural population and draw villagers into a manageable national economy.[47] "The villages were the pillars of our development," recalled Kawawa.[48] The history of land allocation as a discourse of political authority helps explain Nyerere's early claim to presidential ownership of all land and his growing obsession with villagization. By laying claim to land and allocating it through villagization, the new government unified a state authority that had never been fully integrated in the colonial confluence of customary law and state authority under indirect rule. Through villagization, Goran Hyden observed, "TANU tends to get dragged into every matter, large or small, at the village level."[49]

Vihamba and Vijiji

The confluence of moral and political implications in the administration of land were nowhere more visible than along the fertile slopes of Kilimanjaro, where TANU youth and others eagerly petitioned the government to set aside land for settlement schemes.[50] The late colonial period had seen intense competition for land in the areas around Mount Kilimanjaro in Moshi and Mount Meru near Arusha.[51] This did not change with the coming of independence, but the nature of the authorities allocating these scarce homesteads, or *vihamba*, changed dramatically due to government policy to develop the administrative functions of villages, or *vijiji*. It was not necessarily the individuals who changed, but the source of their authority.

Before independence Paramount Chief Thomas Marealle had instituted a system of land boards to aid in local governance around Kilimanjaro. Those seeking land submitted forms to their local chiefly agent, or *mchili*, who forwarded it to the boards under local chiefs who reported to the Chagga Council, which had been under Marealle's authority until it changed to an elected president in 1960.[52] Under the old system, the duties of the *wachili* on the land boards was clearly understood in terms of their task of allocating vihamba, farms bearing ties of obligation and patronage to a patriarchal chief: "Every chief, with his chairman, should have his Land Board to allocate vihamba in his area; one person from every area . . . and agricultural instructors . . . will be members of this Chief's Land Board. . . . It is upon the Chief's Land Board, when allocating vihamba, to leave places for future use, like schools, hospitals, and a place to move a certain person [i.e., a troublemaker] for the good of everyone."[53]

Local councils were in place under the colonial administration when they answered to the Chagga Council in Moshi. After independence, the Chagga Council was disbanded and replaced by a district council advising an appointed district (or area) commissioner. The wachili oftentimes continued their tasks in local government positions after independence. While still occasionally (and incorrectly) called wachili, these former chiefly agents no longer reported to the chief, but rather executed their duties as local magistrates, land officers, and tax collectors on behalf of the nationalist government. A local council chairman noted the name of his mchili when he wrote the Kilimanjaro regional commissioner in 1963, requesting one thousand acres of land to distribute among several families near Moshi. The conceptual overlap between wachili and village officer was clear in local perspective. A resident at the time informed his regional commissioner that "village chairmen are like little wachili."[54] A former mchili recalled, "I was an mchili until the government came and I was chosen by the council to measure plots that would be within the town ... so that people could stay in the town."[55] During Nyerere's absence from the statehouse in 1962, Prime Minister Kawawa saw the government's main task to be the reformation of local government, which meant taking functions away from chiefly agents and investing them in elected local councils. Chiefs could remain in their customary roles, but outside of government administration. Some chiefs protested this loss of authority, but most were supportive, recognizing TANU's extraordinary mass appeal.[56] Minister of Home Affairs Oscar Kambona, before a crowd of six thousand in Kondoa, announced the government's intentions:

> In the past, during the colonial regime, chiefs were used as civil servants, they were used in collecting taxes, maintaining law and order and administering local government; now with the establishment of District Councils, it is found that chiefs have no part to play in the administration of local government, therefore when the present chiefs resign, retire or die, no other chiefs will be installed, they will be replaced by Executive Officers, who will be responsible for government in their areas.[57]

In mid-1963 this trend accelerated when the government renamed the local council system and gave it a uniform mandate and structure across the country in Village Development Committees. VDCs combined party and government functions at the local level. In Kilimanjaro, this meant that "the Divisional Land Boards ceased to operate as from September 1963."[58] Assuming the duties of chiefly governance also meant that all requests for traditional land grants, or vihamba, were to be directed to the village councils. The VDCs would now "investigate to see whether the petitioner deserves a *kihamba* or not, and all recommendations of the Committee should be written on the request forms and be signed by the Chairman and Secretary of the Village Development Committee."[59] The first VDC meetings in Mtaa Mriti in the South Rombo district of Kilimanjaro met where local elders used to meet, at the residence of the former mchili.

There they discussed the construction of a new clinic, burglaries in local stores, and potential police measures. They decided that anyone who did not come out when someone called for help to fight off a thief would be brought before the mchili's court.[60] The VDCs, inheriting the fundamental power to allocate land, also inherited preexisting governance responsibilities, and even the individual authorities that inhered in that power.

The Kilimanjaro executive officer explained to the divisional officers under him that the new VDCs should consist of the local TANU branch chairman and district council representative, a TYL member, local religious leaders and civil servants, and representatives from every constituent village. "And the *mchili* of that neighborhood will be the Secretary."[61] Each VDC was directed to prepare a work plan for developing their area. The Kibosho Plan of Work was typical, representing an area of 3,332 people of various religions, mostly farmers whom the plan's authors described as habitually "reluctant to listen or change their minds." The problems facing the community, from their perspective, stemmed from this habit. Development, at the grassroots level in Kilimanjaro, was seen as an essentially moral enterprise that called for local patriarchs to teach these stubborn farmers how to live like civilized people. Their plan evinced the worries of patriarchal elders overseeing villagers whom the elders viewed as miscreants:

Problems That Are Facing Them:

1. These people usually don't get along well enough, everyone concerns himself with those who are against him instead of anyone else.
2. They get angry for no reason without giving themselves the chance to think.
3. They are reluctant to change their ways, when a person from around here has made up his mind on something, he will follow up on it even if it means killing someone; in the past killings were very frequent around here.
4. They like to walk with weapons, especially knives.
5. They like to drink a lot, and they waste their time drinking.
6. They don't see the problems that are affecting them.
7. They don't know good ways to use money even though they have money.
8. Their houses are a problem; even if their neighbors have nice houses they are reluctant to imitate them.
9. They suffer from digestive diseases especially because they don't cook their meat enough.
10. Small children suffer from malnutrition, and many die.
11. They don't have good toilets.

They should be taught so that they realize:

1. They should understand their conditions and the problems they face.
2. They should think about their lives and future generations.

3. They should have a heart to work together with their wives and not leave all the work for their wives.
4. They should like to cooperate with other religions.
5. They should know the reasons for the deaths of their children and be ready to take care of them and feed them good food.
6. They should know how to use their time to benefit themselves and their country.
7. They should know how to use their money especially to build good houses.
8. They should learn how to read and write for their own benefit; so they can study magazines and books and learn about developments in other areas.[62]

Development, in the eyes of the Kibosho elders who attended the meeting, was primarily a question of improving social cooperation in accordance with local mores.[63] In each list, it is only the last few items that address TANU's priority areas of poverty, ignorance, and disease. Instead, these lists offered the grassroots concerns of a system of governance that was collegial in its organization but disciplinary in its execution. In protesting the choice of two non-TANU VDC members in Uru North, a villager wrote a letter invoking the "Nine Promises" of the TANU creed while defending his right to free speech—in order to insist that only TANU members be allowed on the VDC as government policy dictated. He signed his letter with his own variation of Nyerere's motto for TANU that is suggestive of exaggerated local conceptions of modern governance: "Freedom and Rigid Organization."[64]

Elsewhere, a VDC debated extensively the moral habits of youth, banning young women from drinking clubs and fining them 50 shillings for wearing short skirts.[65] The job of government, as seen by leaders in small patriarchal communities in northern Tanganyika, was to improve morals.[66] This reflected a combination of colonial influence and memories of precolonial authority. A similarly moral trajectory comes across in a Mwanza area secretary's year-end report in 1963, which echoed official propaganda: "[Village Development] Committees should be built well so that they can remove the problems of the village by sharing ideas, strength, and sweat."[67] Ujamaa's moral imperatives were every bit as important as its economic and developmental goals. This suggests that the disciplinary impetus of villagization was not simply a top-down order of a neocolonial state, but rather a "convivial" urge deeply shared with grassroots communities.[68]

Vice President Kawawa sent out a circular letter in November 1963 explaining the urgency and method of establishing VDCs in all localities.[69] The instructions explained how the VDCs fit into the hierarchy of government authority, and how they unified government and party authority by building them from existing TANU branches and limiting their membership to TANU members. But at the neighborhood level the main agents of the VDCs were wachili whose primary duties remained tax collection and land allocation, much as they had been before independence.[70] The only difference after independence was that the wachili served as agents for the national government and not ethnic chiefs. The announcement of the new system clearly echoed the governance structure marked by the hierarchy of Chagga land boards that had been under local chiefs. The new system changed them into nationally constituted VDCs, built on the same structure as colonial-era land boards that existed in areas like Kilimanjaro with highly bureaucratic chiefly systems. A government press release instructed that "persons wishing to move into an unoccupied area or to establish a new settlement must first seek the approval of the nearest Village Development Committee which would refer the matter to the Regional Development Committee through the District Council or the District Development Committee."[71]

Job Lusinde, the minister of local government who implemented these changes, explained that they were part of the broader effort of the independence movement to democratize politics from top to bottom. "In order to prepare people to receive new ideas, it was necessary to assure that our councils, both urban and rural, would have people who were elected by the citizens themselves." To do this they had to separate local authority from the undemocratic institution of chief, where the colonial government had vested many local government functions. The intention of this strategy was not simply the removal of competing institutions of authority that could potentially threaten the new government, but the preparation of rural citizens of the new country with the skills necessary to participate in a democratic government.

Undermining chiefly powers at independence was easy enough, since the chiefs were tainted by their association with the colonial government and were widely unpopular. The TANU government was aware of this and moved quickly to take advantage of this perception before ethnic authorities regained new legitimacy that could divide the national society. By custom, chiefs had inordinate authority over their subjects, powers that were enhanced by the colonial government's use of them. For people brought up in that culture, the difficulty of envisioning their own role in participatory democracy, without a chiefly referent, presented a particular challenge to the viability of the new government. Lusinde explained that rural habits of submission to chiefly authority obstructed participatory democracy: "These ideas would go on forever, so we had to remove this passivity, for the weak to be able to recognize their own humanity. How do you help this person so that his humanity is recognized, so that he doesn't continue with the mentality of slavery?"[72]

Although the tasks of the VDCs were often carried out by the same people who had executed these tasks under the chiefs and the new subdistrict units mostly had the same boundaries as the old chiefdoms, the VDCs were understood as the new sovereign entities. Commoners could be elected to the council and thus could execute its functions. The VDC system, Lusinde maintained, was intended to help people understand their new condition as citizens of a democratic country. In mid-1963 the party also recommended the creation of a new grassroots institution, the ten-cell system that assigned locally elected party representatives the task of monitoring all activities and providing a channel of communication between the party and the people for the theoretical "ten houses" under their jurisdiction.[73] It served an evident security function by channeling local observations into an intelligence hierarchy, but it was also an extension of the VDC. In 1964 preparations for the one-party state combined party and government functions. TANU village committees were folded into the VDC structure.[74] The village councils and the ten-cell system both contributed to Nyerere's goal to connect party leadership to the grass roots.

Ujamaa inserted a new nationalist ideology directly into the culturally rooted discourse of land allocation.[75] But there was another colonial concern that interacted with the nationalists' desire to reinvigorate a sense of local African culture. The colonial state had maintained a policy of sending unemployed young men back to villages from cities, motivated in part by the fear of "detribalization" that alienated young men from the authority of elders and family and made them unproductive delinquents in the cities.[76] To a large extent, this was a fiction of colonial governance, a vestige of colonialists' eagerness to maintain the cities as places with a distinctly European character. But "detribalization" fears also reflected coastal prejudices against upcountry immigrants, who were seen in local eyes as uncivilized and unsanitary and, in former times, best fit for slavery.[77] In the postcolonial era, this policy continued in service to a logic little altered from colonial rhetoric as it aimed to provide salutary rural work for the urban unemployed.[78]

The thrill of TANU's victory was the African possession of the state's command of technocratic mastery; and yet that very command placed the party in opposition to the realm of familial authority where it had been nurtured. TANU Youth League members brought forth a set of expectations more familial than political in conversation. Given TANU's successful occupation of the state, the technocratic hiring policies of the state seemed like a betrayal to the loyal party servants. Party youth members, in a telling statement about expectations for political patronage, complained that they were treated no different from opposition party members: "The thing that made people even more sad was to see that those who did not participate in TANU, and even those who opposed TANU, became the ones who were given posts and good jobs above the TANU members themselves. So the TANU member and the opposition member became the same."[79]

Such provision of work to youth served as a ritual substitute for a plot of land, which anchored adult independence like the vihamba farms in Kilimanjaro, allocated by chiefly councils and bearing moral obligations between the chief and the settler.[80] In a speech on Ujamaa in the villages a few years later, Nyerere made this connection explicit, referring to the many young people moving into towns looking for work and not finding any. "Frankly, the only way to help these young people and other families without enough land in their home areas, is to start new settlements in areas with plenty of land."[81] There being no way to expand Mount Kilimanjaro, he suggested young people move to other parts of the country.

The government sought aid from the World Food Programme of the United Nations and the Oxford Committee for Famine Relief to resettle two hundred young families from Kilimanjaro to Handeni District. Intended as a new model farm, the government had planned on sending experienced and well-equipped farmers to found the settlement. Instead, local councils sent poor farmers who went "in a very low state of morale and arrived with only the clothes on their backs." As in Sonjo, many of the settlers quickly abandoned the scheme and returned home, leaving seventy-six hardy souls to make the best of it.[82] In the end, the party recruited TANU Youth League members to start a cotton farm in Handeni, inauspiciously telling them to bring their farming implements with them.[83] While the government had placed a high priority on the project, it was unable to mobilize citizens and turned instead to the party's loyal cadres.

Another early TYL settlement scheme near the Kenyan border, just north of Nyerere's home, illustrates the manner of culturally rooted patronage that animated the villagization drive. The Mara TANU Youth Settlement Farm began as a direct outgrowth of a party decision in August 1963 "to look into ways and means of strengthening the Youth Movement." Bhoke Munanka, a TANU activist from Musoma, took on this task and proposed a diverse agricultural project oriented toward cash crops. The volunteers, chosen for "loyalty and enthusiasm," were unpaid apprentices, receiving training in modern farming skills for future employment on new settlement schemes nationwide.[84] The Mara Youth Farm betrayed an almost willful blindness to the failure of the preindependence Sonjo scheme. The patron's devotion to the hapless project became the mark of his loyalty to the youth and to the party.[85]

As a member of Parliament and statehouse aide, Munanka was well placed to herd people into service for the two committees he recommended to manage the scheme. The top-heavy management may have been an attempt to avoid the Sonjo outcome, but its necessity grew from Munanka's very lack of pragmatism. Before party leaders in early January 1964, Munanka explained that the funding goal of £50,000 (1 million shillings) was "too much . . . but this is not to say that we won't do anything and use anything that we have in order to raise this money." He announced that several highly placed political friends had donated a total of about 3,500 shillings. He then called on every citizen to donate 10 shillings each.[86] Moral commitment, not practicality, was the order of the day. By March the farm manager reported that few of the local donors had followed through on their pledges.[87] Munanka then arranged for Nyerere's wife, Maria, to act as "patron" of the project. Letters sent out under her signature prevailed upon prominent Dar es Salaam businessmen to donate toward a revised estimate for a £35,000 budget.[88] A photo of a new tractor donated to the Mara Youth Farm in September 1964 illustrated the summary of a speech by Rashidi Kawawa under a headline surprising only for its lack of irony: "Self-help a moral obligation."[89]

A few years later, the farm had yet to produce anything beyond a crop of "seed" beans and maize for the subsistence of the youth, who were still desperate to raise funds.[90] In early 1965 the farm had started a cattle herd with 1,000 calves donated by local farmers. Within a year they had to sell off 250 head to pay off debts. To make matters worse, they could not find buyers for the cattle because of transport difficulties in Musoma, and their primary customer for eggs had not received a shipment for five weeks.[91] The farm's volunteers were clearly exhausted, and they wrote ceaselessly to Munanka for aid. One young volunteer who spent three years on the farm sarcastically questioned flaccid government rhetoric that work was somehow its own reward: "Even if I live as poor a life as this, I volunteered to build our country, and our country then builds me. Now if the farm exploits me like this, does [the party] mean to say that it builds [my character]?"[92] Another writer dipped even more deeply into official culture, past the discourse of development and into the moral assumptions of land allocation and its particular meaning as a national policy: "Truly, father, I am the nation and you are indeed father and mother. My mother and father have died. Sir I pursued the building of our nation so that the nation would help me. I have no place to go. Thank you, I am an obedient child and builder of the nation."[93]

The nature of local authority that interacted with TANU directives varied across the territory, and the priorities and concerns of TYL youth and Kilimanjaro villagers cannot be taken to be universal. Even so, villagization was going on nationwide, and its interactions at the village level infused TANU with local culture while at the same time investing local authorities in a unitary national political hierarchy governed under Ujamaa. The material realities of village initiatives were minor and often misdirected, but their enforced popular participation made national priorities a reality of day-to-day life where ethnically identified authorities had once defined local politics.[94] Villagization brought together multiple political currents into a seductive theory of nation building.

The Model of the Israeli Moshav

Nation building, both physically in terms of infrastructure and ideologically in terms of citizen participation in the allocative authority of government, also found expression in the interests of national defense. Settlement, in this sense, was a locally bounded expression of the classic definition of the state as bearing a monopoly on the legitimate use of force. A Portuguese spy in Mtwara, along the border with Mozambique, reported that audience members at an official speech asked about the Portuguese military presence across the border.[95] The question hinted at the fragile security of the new state and the challenge of securing its southern border against a hostile neighbor. Developed under the guise of dealing with urban unemployment, Tanganyika made plans for village settlements in southern border regions in support of its interventionist policy toward Mozambique.[96] Nsilo Swai, the minister of health and labor, indicated that the government was prepared to force people to move into the settlements.[97] Settlement planning along the border accelerated in the months following the establishment of the OAU Liberation Committee in Dar es Salaam in 1963.

Tanganyika began to secure border regions and sites key to national security through pilot village settlements. One of the first focal points for villagization was along the southern border in the Ruvuma and Mtwara regions. The commissioner for village settlement notified the regional commissioner for Ruvuma in September 1963 that "immediate action" was necessary to prepare for the Mlale/Litenga Pilot Village Settlement. Forwarding plans of the settlement, similar to pilot projects in Kilimanjaro and Handeni, the commissioner for village settlement requested the selection of "250 farmers who are prepared to go to Mlala/Litenga [sic] on the terms and conditions laid down in the agreement." An initial group of 50 farmers were needed within a month, and another 200 by the beginning of November, in time to prepare for planting season. The order included a draft agreement for the farmers, as the final agreement was still being vetted by government lawyers. When the final agreement was prepared, it would be sent with Swahili translations "for each farmer to sign it in triplicate." The program received funding from the Irish "Freedom from Hunger" Campaign, which sent a "voluntary service manager."[98] The British government was reluctant to provide funds but estimated that "there was so much ministerial (and Presidential) prestige bound up in this scheme that it could not be allowed to fail. If the local and the national came into conflict, the local ones would lose."[99] The comment was ominously prescient as the government continued to pursue settlement schemes with overweening hopes for success.

The rushed urgency of the project might have been in response to the budgetary demands of the Irish donors, but the placement and the intensive legalism attached to the scheme evinced a parallel logic in its defense. The Irish government provided a fortunate infusion of funds for an incipient Tanganyikan strategy to populate the border area with government-allocated villages. In September 1963 Oscar Kambona restated Tanganyika's villagization intentions as a response to refugee inflows from Mozambique, asking the American ambassador for aid to build agricultural villages for Mozambican refugees in cooperation with the UN High Commission for Refugees.[100] Loyal Tanganyikans would provide support for military activities along the border, which were quietly being initiated by internal security contingents under Tanganyikan officers rather than by the regular military forces still under British command until February 1964.[101]

Intensive villagization in this region continued for several years, implemented through the Rural Settlement Commission, but directed by Kawawa's vice presidential office in consultation with the Ministry of Defence. Israel gave key support to Tanganyika in many fields, particularly defense and economic development. The villagization program had strong support from Israel; Tanganyikan leaders toured Israel, and party leaders were trained there.[102] A government memorandum on rural settlement directed that villages be organized to follow a "suitably adapted form of the Israeli 'Moshav' or gathered Cooperative Agricultural Settlement."[103]

The use of villagization for military purposes along the border was inspired by the Israeli moshav system, but it was equally built on notions of long-standing village policing and security. The head of the Ministry of Home Affairs, Job Lusinde, who oversaw these efforts, made several visits in the early 1960s to Israel to study the moshav system there and observed both its economic and military roles. "The idea that a village could begin to defend itself, if not with guns at least with intelligence," Lusinde recalled, came from these trips, though he added, "it was nothing new." Village society had always maintained habits of reporting visitors and strangers to local authorities, and organizing methods of dealing with local crimes through local chiefs and their councils, who could call on local residents, especially youth, to execute police functions. A household facing an attack could call out to neighbors, who were obligated to come to their aid. The ten-cell model found a natural fit in village culture. "So for us it was easy to combine what we were doing traditionally with these new ideas about defense," Lusinde explained.[104] He was on a cabinet-level committee in early 1964 that made recommendations on rebuilding the army after the January army mutiny. One of its recommendations was the creation of a military reserve "in every city and every new village."[105]

Despite their unlikely prospects with poor soils and extremely isolated locations, the agricultural schemes were considered of "highest importance" by the government because of their defensive function.[106] Communications in regard to the schemes were normally directed through the agricultural director's office in the Ministry of Land, Forests, and Wildlife, but copies were regularly forwarded to the permanent secretary for defense serving under Kawawa. In addition to the Irish funding, China and Yugoslavia were sending aid and advisers into the border settlement schemes.[107] Plans for proposed settlements received direct and detailed attention from Kawawa himself in consultation with Chinese advisers.[108] Where voluntary settlers could not be recruited, National Service youth were rapidly deployed from other parts of the country.[109] On the basis of Chinese advice, Kawawa ordered that settlements too close to the southern border be moved back "at least ten miles from the border and not more than 20 miles from the border."

Paying little attention to the actual terrain, Kawawa was concerned primarily with village placement relative to the border and the provision of "tractors, bulldozers, water pumps etc." needed to develop the settlements. Hard-pressed civil servants scrambled to implement the orders, which paid little heed to the advice of agricultural experts. The director of agriculture sheepishly informed numerous operations around the country that he would require all their surveying personnel. "I have not been left with any other alternative at this stage but to deploy all Land Planning Units . . . in order to plan the Village settlement schemes in Ruvuma and Mtwara Regions." All of the projects reflected the allocative authority of the government bureaucracy, a point made clear in the directive's conclusion: "The availability of finance to run these schemes is the concern of the Vice President's office and should not be given as an excuse for not being able to report conclusively."[110] The first major training camp for foreign "freedom fighters" from southern Africa was in Nachingwea, the district represented in Parliament by Kawawa himself, securely located just north of Mtwara.[111]

In September 1964, in response to rebel incursions supported by Nyerere's government, Portugal began a scorched-earth campaign to establish a cordon sanitaire in northern Mozambique, leading to another influx of thousands of refugees across the southern border.[112] Village development intensified in October to take pressure off the scattered local families caring for the impoverished refugees. Earlier requests for aid from UNHCR had been turned down because of the political and military nature of many of the refugees, but American foodstuffs were made available to the World Food Programme for their sustenance in December.[113] Settlements along the border offered a defensive observation point for Portuguese harassment, as reported to the American ambassador: "Rifle shots fired across river at houses in URTZ [United Republic of Tanganyika and Zanzibar] territory; increasingly large number of assaults on URTZ fishermen, raids from Portuguese side, attempts at intimidation, and regular violation URTZ airspace by daily air reconnaissance patrols."[114]

Rashidi Kawawa continued to coordinate village development policy, putting his experience working with Kikuyu refugees in the 1950s to immediate use. Over the course of the following two years, numerous settlement schemes along the southern border were ordered established with similar urgency "at the highest level." The new villages offered a first line of defense. With his customary reticence, Kawawa attributed the idea of defensive villages to Nyerere, noting only that he, "as the executive,"carried out the policy. The government had enough confidence in the political training offered to the villagers that it had no reservations about arming them. On October 1, 1964, the government created a village reserve force, "to protect and organize national projects, to set an example in discipline and determination to fulfill the objectives of nation building." Units of about 150 men were to be set up in villages along the borders with Mozambique, Congo, and Malawi.[115] Villagers were given military training and weapons that eventually included antiaircraft guns to defend against Portuguese threats. "We transformed all the villages," Kawawa explained, "from the Indian Ocean to Lake Nyasa, all along the border, all the citizens became guards of the country; every village was turned into a garrison."[116] A few years later, Kawawa proposed to expand the training program countrywide. TANU Central Committee planning notes describe the expansion of a program that was already in place in forty-four villages along the southern border:

> It was accepted that in regards to this military training that will be conducted in these villages, it would be wise if TANU ideology were taught as well.
>
> Weapons and Armories:
>
> a. Immediately after villagers are instructed on how to use weapons and receive appropriate military training they should be given weapons like rifles that they will keep in the village;
> b. A special armory should be built for these rifles in the village before the rifles are distributed;
> c. In order to make sure there are enough rifles for all the villages that will be given this training, the Chairman ordered the General Secretary to order 50,000 rifles from China for this program.[117]

Along the southern border, villagization had a particular use in developing facilities for guerrilla training camps and general security. But elsewhere in the country such villages, established under government authority and design, served the ideological purpose of acculturating people into a new national vision through an enactment of the moral authority to allocate land. Villages served as a culturally resonant administrative structure through which national policies for democracy, development, and defense could be implemented in Tanganyika's vast rural interior.

6

The 1964 Army Mutiny

The week began with a strike at the state; it ended with a forceful reinstatement of sovereign authority. The final blow came at the hands of a British commando. It was not an invasion, however, but a spectacle of power by a sovereign head of state, exercising authority both within the nation and as a member of the international community. A day-by-day account of the events of the mutiny of the Tanganyika Rifles from January 20 to 27, 1964, brings out the fluid nature of perception amid even more fundamental frameworks of understanding—the passage of time and the anxiety that inheres in the knowledge that the clock is ticking. Sovereignty inhered in the thinking and response of Nyerere and his main advisers during the crisis. This episode makes the slippery nature of state authority, and the discursive strategies of maintaining it, visible in the midst of turmoil. The issue at hand, racial policy, struck at the very identity of the state and at one of Nyerere's most closely held moral virtues. The mutiny was initially little more than a labor strike to protest the continued presence of British officers in the army. But the turning point that led to the invitation of British intervention was the Tanganyikan discovery of evidence of a plot to assassinate top politicians and overthrow Nyerere's government. As a military rebellion and an attack on Nyerere's national ethic, the mutiny directly threatened the race-blind state he had built.

In a study of the three cascading army mutinies in Tanganyika, Uganda, and Kenya that week, Timothy Parsons suggested that "Nyerere was eventually forced to accept the British offer after radical leaders of the Tanganyika Federation of Labour and renegade TANU politicians made contact with the striking askaris [soldiers]." Such a turn of events could have blown up the mutiny into a full-fledged coup d'état that could have fundamentally changed the course of national politics. Parsons acknowledged as much: "With the soldiers behind them, the rogue trade unionists would have the resources to topple Nyerere's government."[1] Yet, lacking further evidence, Parsons largely ignored the implications of a labor-led coup plot. In his account, the Tanganyika mutiny, like subsequent events in Uganda and Kenya, remained a strike action by disgruntled soldiers due to the "incomplete integration of colonial soldiers into the societies of independent East Africa." Parsons's interpretation reinforces official narratives that downplayed political motives in the mutinies and, in Tanganyika's case, fails to explain the crackdown on the labor movement that followed and the replacement of the Tanganyika Rifles with the highly politicized Tanzania People's Defence Forces (TPDF), established in the months after the mutiny.

Overseeing a detailed reassessment of the mutiny in the 1980s on behalf of the TPDF, Nestor Luanda concluded that evidence substantiating persistent rumors of a "conspiracy between trade unionists and mutineers is hard to come by," and that the crackdown on the labor movement that ensued reflected the government's overweening fear of the labor-led opposition. The mutiny, in his view, "was a god-sent opportunity" for the government "to make a final clampdown on the movement."[2] He noted that government leaders reacted to the mutiny in consideration of recent events in Togo, where Sylvanus Olympio was assassinated by his army in January 1963, and in the Republic of Congo (Brazzaville), where a trade union alliance with the military overthrew the one-party state of Fulbert Youlou in August that year.[3] Evidence of a labor connection to the 1964 mutiny was, for Luanda, the "proverbial needle in a haystack."

However, archival evidence suggests just such a needle—and the Tanganyikans found it. Carefully, if blindly, managing the crisis, the Tanganyikan leadership successfully navigated a complex war of perceptions. They maintained the government's initiative throughout the week, and with it the principle of nonracial citizenship. Both of these, together with the civilian government's ability to maintain its tenuous grip on the military, constituted discursive signs that reinforced the TANU government's ability to maintain "the code of sovereignty" under trying circumstances.[4] This interpretation undermines the widely held view that the week between the mutiny and the British intervention was the result of "irresolute leadership."[5]

Africanization in the Tanganyika Rifles

Since independence, tension had been rising over the continued presence of British commanding officers in the Tanganyikan army. Unequal pay scales and British privileges caused disenchantment among African officers.[6] One young, Sandhurst-trained African officer, Mirisho Sarakikya, who later became the commander of the TPDF, recalled having to share living quarters while British officers of similar rank did not.[7] African salaries for ranks below officer ranged from 106 shillings per month (about $15, the equivalent of about $100 today) for third-class privates to 460 shillings (about $64, or $430 today) for senior warrant officers, supplemented by rent-free housing in the barracks with education and medical services provided by the army.

While the official minimum wage in the civil sector had been 150 shillings per month, lower-level civil servants faced a pay decrease starting in 1962 to 100 shillings a month, and even that was not being paid regularly in rural areas.[8] Mine workers were making about 165 shillings per month. So army wages were at least a third lower than salaries for skilled labor in the private sector, but not out of line with civil service wages that had been brought down to army wage levels. However, Nyerere's 3,000-shilling presidential monthly salary signaled a wide income disparity in the young country.[9] Without a doubt, young recruits felt underpaid and fearful of future pay cuts and frustrated with an army that seemed to be stuck in colonial habits under British authority while the rest of the country moved into independence and Africanization. "We in the army were left at the bottom of the rung," recalled one soldier.[10] Moreover, intense labor activity and the politics of Mtemvu and Tumbo had an effect on enlisted men.[11] Free housing seemed like a joke compared to the facilities given to British officers, who treated the enlisted men with scorn. Frustration in the ranks was less about pay than respect.

Kambona's Africanization of the police command in 1962 heightened soldiers' expectations for similar progress for the military, and Kambona made the army a priority for 1964.[12] The British commander of the Tanganyika Rifles, Patrick Sholto Douglas, resisted rapid Africanization for fear of a breakdown in discipline. He had just recruited new soldiers to fill the two existing brigades and begin building a new brigade to guard the southern border with Mozambique.[13] In the middle of 1963, a new British officer, Lieutenant Colonel Rowley Mans, had arrived to command the First Brigade at Colito Barracks just north of Dar es Salaam.[14] In December 1963 Kambona requested Mans to prepare for Africanization in the force. Mans proposed that Alex Nyirenda, an African from Kambona's home area near Lake Nyasa, and S. M. A. Kashmiri, of Pakistani descent, be promoted to major. Kambona initially rejected both. The Asian Kashmiri was resented by African enlisted men and rankled Kambona, who did not accept him as a legitimate Africanization placement. Kambona refused Nyirenda ostensibly because he wanted older officers like Elangwa Shaidi, the recently promoted commissioner of police, to advance. Kambona relented on these two placements only after Nyerere terminated the Africanization policy with his pronouncement on January 7, 1964, "that discrimination in civil service employment, both as regards recruitment, training, and promotion, must be brought to an end immediately."[15] Nyerere's "localization" policy demanded only that leadership positions be filled by citizens, regardless of race.

Figure 6.1. *From left:* Minister of External Affairs Oscar Kambona, Second Vice President Rashidi Kawawa, and President Julius Nyerere consult with a military adviser, circa 1964. © Tanzania Information Services (MAELEZO).

Nyirenda and Kashmiri had been the first Tanganyikans to receive officer training at Sandhurst in Britain.[16] Lieutenant Colonel Mans regarded Nyirenda as one of the "young intelligent officers" of the new generation and took Kambona's rejection of the British-trained captain as the last straw in a series of frustrations during his short tenure. Mans prepared to submit a request for transfer "since this was personal animosity, humiliating to loyal and efficient Nyirenda."[17] Kambona first met Nyirenda in Britain while both were studying there—Nyirenda at Sandhurst and Kambona in London. Kambona's main activity in London was less studying than recruiting and fund-raising for TANU, and Nyirenda had refused to join, which made him suspect in Kambona's eyes. Upon his return to Tanganyika, Nyirenda exhibited an air of pride in emulation of senior British officers that verged on scorn for younger officers trained locally or in Israel.[18]

The Israeli-trained officers were recruited the year before out of the TANU Youth League. Nyirenda's dismissive attitude toward them reflected not only the British view that the education level of these young men was "far below what is necessary for commission in Tanganyika Rifles" but also disgruntlement among veterans that these young politicians lacked military experience.[19] The Youth League recruits had been hastily transferred into the army during their training in Israel without the basic training that had built esprit de corps among the Tanganyikan recruits. As long-standing members of TANU, the TYL recruits were so offended by Nyirenda's scorn that they complained to Kambona.[20] Peter Walwa, serving under Kambona in the Ministry of Defence, called in Nyirenda and upbraided him for "treasonable utterances" in his criticism of the younger officers' training and because Nyirenda had allegedly informed British officers of an Algerian arms shipment.[21] To mitigate the tensions, Kambona requested a plan to replace all British officers with Africans, thus diluting the influence of Nyirenda and Kashmiri. Brigadier Douglas complied and submitted a complete plan for the Africanization of the Tanganyika Rifles on January 14, 1964.[22] Whatever impact it might have had was completely overshadowed by the revolt in Zanzibar that same week.

From a Coup d'État to a Coup de Grâce

After the Zanzibar revolution, Kambona ordered Douglas to keep one army company on alert, ready to move to Zanzibar on a four-hour notice to restore law and order there. With the dramatic events on the islands being the talk of the town, and the army's ranks spread thin, a few young noncommissioned officers contemplated action to bring attention to their demands, imitating strikes in other industries over the last few years. On the evening of January 19, Nyerere hosted a statehouse reception for the new Zanzibari leaders and considered the implications of the brutal racial violence that had accompanied the revolution. While Nyerere lounged on the veranda with the American ambassador, the mutineers struck.

Lady Chesham summarized the enigmatic days that followed:

> From Monday to Friday no one liked the sight of soldiers on guard duty at the State House instead of Police. But the President and his wife drove around the city stopping to talk to people and the city carried on, a little nervously but quietly. Children went to school, shops were open, Government machinery moved as usual, and on Friday evening (January 24th) the president delivered the Hammarskjöld Lecture according to schedule.[23]

January 20

At 1:30 a.m. on Monday, January 20, 1964, someone pulled the fire alarm in the barracks of the Tanganyika Rifles stationed north of Dar es Salaam. Mutinous soldiers took control of the camp and locked the camp's commanding officers, both British and African, in a storeroom. The telephone lines had already been cut, and patrols guarded the roads leading to the barracks. Around 3:00 a.m., Vice President Rashidi Kawawa received word of the mutiny, alerted Nyerere, and then made his way to the base. The mutineers greeted him with hostility and derision, threatening to lock him in the storeroom as well.[24] A little while later, soldiers surrounded the statehouse seeking the president, who had already been evacuated to a Catholic mission across the bay in Dar es Salaam, according to a preexisting emergency plan.[25]

The impressively executed mutiny had been developed by a group of midlevel noncommissioned officers calling themselves the "Army Night Freedom Fighters." Having come up through the ranks, they lacked formal education and were bitter about being passed over for promotions by both the young British-trained officers like Nyirenda and Sarakikya, and the completely inexperienced TANU youth returning from Israel. The ringleader was a five-year veteran sergeant named Francis Hingo Ilogi, who had a smoldering resentment toward his British officers and a record of insubordination.[26] Sergeant Ilogi had originally trained as a wireless operator and recently returned for further training as an education instructor.[27] His experience, leadership training, and technical skills all contributed to the initial countrywide success of the mutiny. Ilogi held the racialized command in the army in contempt, but he was otherwise a professional soldier. He staged the mutiny as a nonviolent strike and, despite churlish indiscipline, rank-and-file soldiers obeyed Ilogi's command throughout the week.[28]

In the predawn hours, mutineers set up roadblocks blocking access to the airport and took control of the telegraph office. A concerned Nyirenda called Robert Hennemeyer, a well-connected American diplomat, told him about the mutiny, and advised him, "Keep your people off the streets." Hennemeyer passed on the message and went out seeking more information, only to be detained together with Job Lusinde and the British Acting High Commissioner Steven Miles by drunken mutineers.[29] Mutineers also deployed in the European neighborhood of Oyster Bay and began arresting senior British army officers in their homes. Brigadier Douglas briefly escaped on foot, before being arrested shortly thereafter.[30] As the morning light broke, mutineers in battle dress and enigmatic white baseball caps began to exercise control in town, taking command of the police station and detaining its British officers, while occupying the post office, the phone exchange, and the Tanganyika Broadcasting Corporation.[31] Police Commissioner Shaidi consulted with the mutineers outside the barracks, convincing them to release the African officers in the storeroom, while leaving the British officers locked up. The mutineers telegrammed the Second Battalion of the Tanganyika Rifles in Tabora inviting them to join in a strike against the European officers. "Our men here striking. Please join us. Police, airport, State House, Government store captured and Tanganyika Broadcasting Corp. Because men do not like Europeans in their

Army."[32] The young signals officer who received the message proceeded to communicate secretly with the mutineers in the capital while informing a small group of sympathetic soldiers in Tabora, who then began planning a takeover of the Second Battalion.[33]

From his undisclosed location at the Catholic mission across Dar es Salaam Harbor, Nyerere requested support from Kenya via the regional police commander in Tabora, who relayed the message to Lieutenant Colonel Miles Marston, the commanding officer of the Second Battalion in Tabora.[34] Reversing the request a short while later, Job Lusinde contacted the Kenyan foreign minister, Joseph Murumbi, and canceled the call for Kenya Rifles support as "he was certain they would be unreliable," since, like the Tanganyika Rifles, the Kenyan ranks also chafed under their British officers.[35] In response to these mixed signals, Kenyan prime minister Jomo Kenyatta requested precautionary authority for Royal Air Force transport for the battalion if the need should arise to move them.[36]

At the statehouse, Special Branch director Emil Mzena arranged for the mutineers to negotiate with Oscar Kambona, recently appointed as minister of external affairs and defense. Kambona was sympathetic to the mutineers' demand for the removal of British officers, and he began cautiously negotiating with them. The mutineers elected a young lieutenant, Elisha Kavana, as their commanding officer, overstepping Douglas's favorites, Nyirenda and Kashmiri.[37] Ilogi would be second in command.[38] Saying he had to consult with Nyerere to approve the appointment, Kambona returned to the statehouse. The gesture signaled Kambona's continued loyalty to Nyerere, but with Nyerere absent, Kambona approved the appointments in consultation with Mzena only. To strengthen his hand, Kambona again contacted Kenya for support—not for the suspect Kenya Rifles, but for a civil police intervention force.[39] At 10:00 a.m. a sleep-deprived Kambona, under heavy armed guard, summoned the British high commissioner and explained that he intended to fly all the British military officers out of the country immediately.[40] This was necessary, he said, "to restore situation," which meant not only bringing the troops back to civilian control but also minimizing external influences. Wynn Jones Mbwambo, the American-trained chief of protocol and security, contacted foreign embassies, summarizing the work-related demands of the troops and the government's inclination to negotiate with them. He requested: "Do not send troops. Have them stand by. Better developments in progress."[41]

The mutineers struggled to maintain control of the capital as the uncertain situation began to sow panic in the populace. Undisciplined mutineers had briefly arrested several TANU leaders, only to be told by their leaders, "We do not want ministers. We do not want to overthrow the government. We wanted to get rid of the British officers."[42] By midday there seemed to be "no effective government forces to maintain law and order," as Kambona arranged with the British high commissioner for the evacuation of British subjects. African crowds cheered as British expatriates were driven through the town in the back of a lorry. About thirty British officers were flown to Nairobi, arriving haggard and exhausted around lunchtime; their families followed in the evening.[43] For Asian and Arab residents unable to evacuate, nerves were on edge, especially after the racially directed violence in Zanzibar the week before. In Bagamoyo and Dar es Salaam, crowds began targeting Arab merchants. Mutineers put a stop to looting in Asian trading areas of the city with brutal force. When one frightened Arab shopkeeper shot and killed a soldier entering his shop, the soldiers burned it down killing his entire family except for the youngest girl, who was taken into police custody.[44]

Meanwhile, the government took its own measures to restore order to the city. Field Force police that were still loyal to the government warned people to stay inside and rounded up anyone on the streets.[45] The British high commissioner began to sound notes of panic, appealing to the Commonwealth Relations Office in London that massacres of Europeans might begin unless European soldiers intervened "before night fall, without fail."[46] At one o'clock in the afternoon, Kambona finally made a radio broadcast, announcing "some misunderstandings between African and British soldiers of the 1st Battalion of the Tanganyika Rifles. After my intervention the [mutinous] soldiers have now returned to Colito Barracks." He assured listeners that the army and police were still loyal to the Tanganyika government and appealed for calm and the normal execution of public services.[47] Nyerere remained eerily absent, and Kambona appeared as the nation's loyal savior.[48]

At the Catholic mission in Kurasini, a bewildered Nyerere recorded a statement for broadcast the next day, urging calm, reflecting on the disgrace the incident had brought the nation.[49] The recording session offered a moment of ministerial consultation and coincided with a number of decisions to deescalate the situation. The state of emergency was put into abeyance, avoiding a precedent for the suspension of the constitutional order.[50] Lusinde continued to argue against the introduction of outside forces, including Kenyan detachments. Kambona communicated with Kenyatta, repeating that Kenyan troops were not necessary. In Tabora, Marston and Sarakikya, unaware of communications between the mutineers and their own soldiers, gave orders to secure government buildings in preparation for an emergency transfer of government operations if Dar es Salaam became unmanageable.[51] Mutineers enforced a curfew in Dar es Salaam with a brazen show of authority, smoking marijuana openly and harassing citizens and expatriates alike.[52]

A struggle for control of the army and country was taking place, and it remained far from clear how the situation would be resolved. There was no clear authority in the territory of Tanganyika that day. The government maintained its sovereign initiative through cautious negotiation and refusal of outside help, retaining ideological clout even as it lost control of state-defining instruments of coercive force. The challenge of the days ahead was to reestablish the TANU state as the territorial sovereign and preclude a preemptive foreign intervention that would violate the state's external sovereignty and so undermine the legitimacy of its internal authority.

January 21

The night passed quietly, with mutineers patroling main areas but with no overwhelming military presence visible in residential areas and minor activity only in response to the sighting of a British warship anchored just over the horizon.[53] British warships had been brought to the region in the wake of the Zanzibar Revolution, and upon hearing news of the mutiny, the British military ordered an aircraft carrier to pick up a marine commando unit from their base in Aden and proceed with a destroyer escort to the East African coast.[54] Tuesday morning in Dar es Salaam brought a modicum of order as government ministers toured the city exuding a sense of normality.[55] Police patrolled the city "rounding up hooligans" and dispersing crowds.[56] In Tabora, Lieutenant Colonel Marston reported midmorning that the situation was under control but "dicey," with menacing rumors that the battalion in Nachingwea had mutinied.[57] Nachingwea troops had in fact mutinied at dawn. The British commanding officer got on what he thought was a secure army radio channel to Dar es Salaam to find out if the Tabora battalion was still loyal, but "someone intercepted my code," he recalled, "and told me to fuck off."[58] Kambona's permanent secretary, Peter Walwa, ordered British officers to stay at their posts. Despite his doubts, the British high commissioner confirmed that "the Government still exercised control through Mr. Kambona."[59]

By midmorning a group of low-ranking soldiers in Tabora had mutinied as well. Some rampaged through the town attacking Arab-owned businesses, while others at the airport were in such disarray that they appeared to be intoxicated.[60] Soldiers brandishing rifles kicked open a door at the Tabora district hospital, and seeing an American Peace Corps volunteer, they yelled, "Mama Mzungu, njoo!" (White woman, come here). Surrounded by the entire African staff, the volunteer's nursing aide stepped forward and refused to let her move toward the soldier. The soldier ordered the Americans to go home, and fired over their heads as they turned to leave the compound. The soldiers called out the whole staff for a salute of "Uhuru na Umoja"—Nyerere's motto had been twisted into a racial proclamation for a black African nation. "Then they drove wildly out of the compound and were gone in a cloud of dust." But they soon returned asking for the Americans, whom the staff had now hidden in a back office. Seeking another target, the soldiers took hold of a British doctor and trundled him out to the compound before a firing squad. The chief African orderly ran out as they were about to shoot, pleading that if they killed the doctor there would be no one to treat the soldiers' own injuries. Amid more shots in the air and another shout of "*Uhuru na Umoja,*" the soldiers again departed.[61]

Receiving word of mutinies in Tabora and Nachingwea, Kambona arranged for air transport to pick up British officers there. He considered traveling to the scene himself to assess the situation but instead sent a group of TANU men to calm upcountry stations. They stopped first in Mwanza, and then went to Tabora.[62] Hingo Ilogi claimed that Kambona consulted with him to approve and send orders for an African officer to take control in Tabora.[63] This may have been a necessary precaution on Kambona's part to ensure that the Tabora mutineers would accept the new appointment. Kambona sent a cable instructing Captain Sarakikya, the British-trained junior officer stationed in Tabora, to take command, which he did with impressive authority.[64]

Angered by the racially motivated violence in town, Sarakikya immediately placed his officers under arrest and ordered the troops to line up for roll call, where he asked one of the soldiers to read Kambona's message aloud. Upon instructions from Dar es Salaam, the captain released the African officers and placed a guard on the Europeans still locked in the storeroom with orders that "anyone wanting to molest them will be shot, and shot dead."[65] The British officers were transferred in the afternoon to the airport to await transport to Nairobi.[66] Sarakikya had arranged for trusted troops to be present at every stage, and he left a veteran NCO, David Msuguri, in charge at the airport.[67] By 12:30 p.m. the chief nurse at the Tabora hospital informed the Peace Corps volunteers that Sarakikya had stopped by to tell them there would be no more trouble. "We knew Mrisho well," one volunteer reported, "and trusted him without reservations."[68]

In Dar es Salaam, the government slowly began regaining the appearance of control; people returned to work, shops and ministries opened their doors. An Indian resident went to the central police station to plead for the release of some Sikh youths picked up the day before. At the station he ran into the head of the Arab Association, who had come to claim the girl rescued from the shop the mutineers had burned down. "There I saw the most unbelievable scene. The pretty Arab girl about 4 years old clung to the African police woman in uniform as if they were mother and daughter and happy in each other's company."[69] The Tanganyika Broadcasting Corporation was on the air again, playing three speeches by Kambona in rotation every half hour. The speeches scolded the looters and assured the public that the situation was in hand, that it was not a coup attempt but a demand for better pay. Ostensibly to reassure and inform the public, the broadcast gave some the impression that Kambona was about to take over the government.[70] While this possibility frightened minority residents, it may have had a calming effect on mutinous soldiers who saw in Kambona an ally to their Africanization cause.

Nevertheless, as the day passed, tensions gave way to renewed violence. By Tuesday afternoon, riots left as many as 30 people dead and 250 injured around the market area.[71] This led to another attempt by the mutineers to close off the city.[72] Kambona had been in touch with Nyerere and the cabinet but was still unsure about the whole affair—with good reason. Emotional tensions created an uncertain situation with soldiers, police, and mobs acting impulsively. In the confusion, police had detained and beaten Nyerere's brother, Joseph, together with Bibi Titi Mohamed and the minister of health.[73] The mutineers harassed journalists as mobs became increasingly combustible.

Holding on by its fingertips, the Tanganyikan government maintained its sovereign authority in the midst of the disorder, its leaders weighing what little strength they had against the compromises necessary to placate the mutinous army to preclude the very real possibility of a government overthrow. Kambona, with the help of statehouse aide Bhoke Munanka and Minister of Home Affairs Lusinde, had brought a modicum of control to the situation, getting troops back to their barracks and making a broadcast urging people to return to work as normal. British diplomats reported that the "Field Force is clearing mob from streets."[74] Kambona's recently Africanized police force proved its mettle, and its loyalty, enforcing law and order in the wake of the riots. The police commissioner accurately gauged both the political and the tactical balance of power, and he was reluctant to allow his elite Field Force troops to confront the mutineers because of the possibility that a direct engagement would spark a civil war if these two institutions became combatants.[75]

The rumor that Nyerere would make a speech had a calming effect: "Everything quiet in town. Police in control, soldiers back in barracks. Everyone is waiting on President's speech which he is expected to give this evening."[76] Nyerere's prerecorded Swahili broadcast at 8:15 p.m. expressed sentiments clearly typical of the president, but the voice was uncharacteristically subdued, leading some to suspect that he was drugged or under duress, or perhaps not Nyerere at all, but an imposter.[77] These rumors had subtle but significant effects. A countervailing suspicion of something more sinister could have spurred a British intervention ordered by a jumpy high commissioner, or further activity by the mutineers if the government appeared to be out of Nyerere's control. It is unclear why the government leadership waited until evening to broadcast the speech recorded the day before as they continued to control the radio broadcasts; it would seem they waited until they had a better sense of the situation so that the broadcast would not be embarrassingly premature if governmental authority deteriorated further. The president's whereabouts were still unknown to the public, as the disembodied voice crackled over transistor radios across the country: "Yesterday there were minor troubles in Dar es Salaam and that trouble ended yesterday. . . . I want to reassure you so that you may be calmed. . . . Countrymen, do not panic; panic is a sign of immaturity. . . . Yesterday, my countrymen, was a day of great disgrace for this young nation."[78]

Nyerere tread very softly, seeking to reassure the rank and file, whose general loyalty he accurately surmised, of his sympathies for their confusion and the deaths among them. Even in the feeble tone of the broadcast, Nyerere managed to take on the voice of a scolding father filled with an underlying tenderness toward his deviant children. This approach aimed to reestablish a sense of natural authority to himself personally and to the office of the president. The speech was "expected to have a steadying effect," but those looking for a demonstration of authority and strength were disappointed. "The impression we got was that he could have been forced to make it by the mutineers."[79] It was a weak discursive intervention, but his broadcast presence had an anesthetic effect, and the capital city was expected to be up and running in the morning. Reassuring news came in from upcountry: in Nachingwea, the two British officers there "were courteously treated, were allowed to take all luggage and were seen off by shamefaced group of own men";[80] while in Tabora, "new Commander Sarakikya [was] both popular and in firm control."[81] Five Europeans held in Dar es Salaam were released on instructions from Lieutenant Kavana, the new commander appointed by the mutineers the night before.[82]

Nyerere, in the meantime, had quietly returned to Dar es Salaam, perhaps to witness the effect of the broadcast and prepare for an appearance if necessary to prove his authority.[83] Late Tuesday night he met with the French ambassador, stressing that there had been no political motivations or significance to the events of the last two days, and that the mutiny stemmed from grievances about Africanization.[84] Nyerere consistently maintained this apolitical narrative of the mutiny, in order to minimize its implications for the sovereignty of the TANU-led government and its ideology, even after evidence emerged that events had taken a political turn.

January 22

With the mutineers only temporarily placated, Wednesday morning brought calm to Dar es Salaam but whispers of trouble in Uganda and

Kenya. For the Tanganyikan public, the day was remarkably normal. Dar es Salaam businessmen opened their shops, assurances went out that the disorders had been exaggerated, and the "situation [was] much better controlled than alarmist reports have suggested."[85] By midmorning it was publicly known that Nyerere was back in the statehouse. The cabinet met under Vice President Kawawa, and conditions seemed secure enough for Nyerere to publicly tour the city.

In the evening Nyerere invited British High Commissioner Miles and American Ambassador Leonhart to the statehouse.[86] "Nyerere was remarkably relaxed and gave appearance of complete frankness."[87] He lamented that in the seventeen years of struggle for independence, not a drop of blood had been shed, but there had been two dozen deaths in two days of armed recklessness.[88] Struggling to put an end to the rumors of intrigue, he emphasized that it was "a strike over workers' grievances, difference was that these were workers with guns."[89] He assured the diplomats that Kavana, the mutineers' selection for commanding officer, was a "good soldier," and prudently judged that "it would be unrealistic for me not to accept this situation in present circumstances." After things were settled, he could "weed out incompetent officers and educate the troops on the seriousness of their offence."[90] For the time being, he felt that it was worth accepting the officers elected by the mutineers in order to bring about a quick end to the violence, but he held the possibility of British assistance in reserve. He expressed some regret that the incident would frighten many of the British expatriate civil servants still on hand into leaving. Nyerere also vouched for the loyalty of Kambona and insisted that the incident was not a foreign initiative. "Poor Oscar," Nyerere told the diplomats, "had always been unlucky in that people were always saying he was trying to oust [the] President. Today, when this story had reached Kambona, he had been so distressed that he had broken down and wept and was now, after [the] exhaustion of last two days, resting at home."[91]

Both Miles and Leonhart briefed Nyerere on the presence of their respective naval vessels anchored just out of sight offshore, and their readiness to intervene if called on. Quietly expressing thanks for this reassurance, Nyerere responded, "If things do not seem to be working out the way I expect I promise to tell you." After the meeting Miles specifically requested that the commando unit remain stationed offshore, even as the captain of the HMS *Centaur* was anxious to return to Aden.[92] Nyerere was keen to resolve the situation without resorting to outside help, but even keener to reestablish governmental authority. His dilemma was that while outside help could be effective in arresting the mutineers, it could also undermine governmental legitimacy, thereby turning a limited mutiny into a deeper crisis of sovereignty.[93]

January 23

On Thursday morning, the Tanganyikan government began engaging in damage control, reestablishing a visage of sovereign authority. Nyerere made further public appearances around Dar es Salaam and held meetings with the diplomatic community, setting a tone of cautious assurance. In a midmorning press conference, he addressed the Tanganyikan people in person, appearing "to be much more candid," again taking on the character of a scolding father or patient schoolmaster.[94] He restated his urgent priority: "We have to restore confidence in our country and win back the reputation we had as a peaceful and mature country"; but he carefully avoided the issue of how the mutineers would be punished.[95] He and his ministers continually emphasized that the incident was basically a labor dispute and not a threat to civilian authority.[96]

As the dust began to settle in Tanganyika, African troops in the First Battalion of the Uganda Rifles mutinied, arresting their British officers. Prime Minister Obote, fully aware of the unresolved events in Dar es Salaam, promptly called in British assistance. Troops under British officers stationed in Kenya arrived by evening to arrest the insubordinate soldiers. Promptly in succession, a battalion of the Kenyan Rifles mutinied in Lanét, and Kenyatta similarly allowed British-led troops to quickly capture the mutineers.[97] High Commissioner Miles met with Nyerere on Thursday evening to discuss the Uganda situation and to convey Douglas's view "that unless British intervene to restore TR [Tanganyika Rifles] discipline, situation cannot be reestablished and Tanganyikan Government will remain prisoner of army."[98] The British, in response to High Commissioner Miles's requests, had quietly gathered a small strike force just offshore. Douglas estimated that the present force was "sufficient for a quick settlement." Nyerere responded by saying he would talk it over with "the boys," presumably Kambona and Lusinde as well as Nyirenda and Sarakikya, whose authority he was also anxious to maintain.[99]

The decisions facing Nyerere undermined the core of his political beliefs and accomplishments. The events constituted a fall from grace for his idealistic vision of the young nation. Most worrisome, events illustrated how even trivial grievances could threaten the young country's sovereign government.[100] Governmental authority still hung tenuously in the balance, its command little more than a thin facade of rhetorical flourish. Still the government stood as the recognized authority in the land, and the situation was settled enough that Nyerere could begin to reflect on both its tragedy and its implications. Given the power of rumor and perception in the maintenance of sovereignty during the Cold War, reinforcing this facade of sovereign authority, no matter how thin, was a crucial accomplishment that week. Externally the Tanganyikan government portrayed a visage of mature calm in the face of the storm, while internally the performance of sovereign authority maintained the consensus around Nyerere's government, its ideology, and its autonomy in the face of foreign pressure. This appearance, however fragile, minimized the political risks of the fateful decisions to come.

January 24

A tense normality came to reign in Dar es Salaam by Friday morning, as the mutineers and the government gambled on bluffs and hedges, each standing precariously on the other's shoulders—none sure who was loyal and who was not, who was strong and who was weak, who was friend and who was false. The three East African presidents were evidently in communication, with Obote communicating through Kenyatta. Throughout the week, the presidents maintained a private channel of communication, studiously kept secret from European and American ears.[101] Obote's decision to call in British troops became an analytical touchstone for Nyerere. On the one hand, Nyerere felt that Obote's lack of "political control" of his country forced his hand, requiring him to call in outside assistance. On the other hand, he feared that Obote's use of British troops would make the Tanganyikan government look indecisive by comparison. He told the British high commissioner that "he had not closed [his] mind to requesting British intervention."[102]

The ambiguous situation was contributing to a breakdown of discipline as ambitious noncommissioned officers sought popularity and power through increasingly radical demands. It was becoming increasingly evident that many nonranking soldiers were as surprised as anyone with the turn of events and were only reluctantly following orders given the reprimands of the popular and admired president. "Indeed, there is evidence," a British officer reported, "that the army as a whole was both astonished and ashamed at the consequences of its action."[103] Rumors spread that dockworkers intended to strike and that the police might ally themselves with the mutineers.[104] The lack of central authority created an impulse toward agitation as leaders sought advantageous positions in expectation of a realignment of power in the country.

Indeed, such a realignment may have been under way. The mutiny had begun as a localized labor action within the army, but that description was not nearly so benign as Nyerere and his ministers made it appear. As one former labor stalwart recalled, "Some of our leaders had a desire to rule."[105] Using the mutiny as a springboard, labor leaders gave speeches at the barracks, trying to redirect the mutineers' grievances into a full-scale rebellion.[106] Presidential security chief Wynn Jones Mbwambo understood the radical labor plan for a coup d'état to have entailed four steps: The first was to instigate a similar mutiny in the police force that had hitherto been an effective counterweight to the mutineers. With the police on their side, the mutineers could then retake control over Dar es Salaam. They hoped for sympathetic strikes by the dock and railway workers, and civil servants if possible, leading to a general government shutdown. Then the mutinous police and army personnel could arrest and assassinate Nyerere and his cabinet ministers.[107] In the aggressive investigations that followed the mutiny, Emil Mzena's Special Branch reported the discovery of two lists in the house of a labor leader. One list was of a "government to be established following a coup planned for January 25 or 26," with the names of potential new cabinet members—including PDP chairman Christopher Tumbo, TFL president Victor Mkello, and Chief Abdallah Fundikira, who had just announced his resignation from his post as minister of justice in a forceful speech in Tabora, in which he expressed disapproval for Nyerere's autocratic policies.[108] The other list was of "leaders scheduled for assassination."[109]

Despite the gravity of the reports, Nyerere was anxious that this evidence not be used to cast suspicion on Chief Fundikira or intimate any alliance between racial extremists and the widely respected elder statesman. Fundikira had been a fervent and loyal nationalist throughout the independence period, despite his personal ambitions and religious sympathies. His recent break with TANU resulted from his growing distaste for Nyerere's harassment of political opponents and proposals for a one-party state. But Fundikira himself had always been a moderate who had never allied with the younger TANU radicals or the racialists of Mtemvu's ANC and Tumbo's PDP. With the mutiny, Fundikira cast his considerable authority back with Nyerere and TANU until the crisis settled down.[110]

In order to retain control of the discursive implications of the disturbances, Nyerere and his associates carefully presented the whole sequence of events as a simple labor action within the army for Africanization and better pay, and not a strike at the state.[111] None of the evidence of the coup plot was made public.[112] During the week of the mutiny, Mzena had told Ambassador Leonhart only of "disloyal civil servants" in the government. The following week, Security Chief Mbwambo acknowledged privately to Leonhart that by January 24, "it [was] clear [that] a full-fledged revolutionary plot against the government [was] in progress."[113] Beneath a nonchalant public face, Nyerere's government downplayed political motivations, despite the harboring of intense doubts about the deeper crisis at stake. Publicly Nyerere pursued a nonconfrontational policy, aiming "to educate [the] average soldier about [his] loyalties and responsibilities to [the] state."[114] But privately, recognizing the looming threat of a labor-initiated coup d'état, he cast another stone. He requested a British force to disarm the mutineers.[115]

The formal request for British assistance came from Vice President Kawawa, as chairman of the Military Council, and was delivered by Minister of External Affairs Oscar Kambona in the company of Paul Bomani, minister of the treasury.[116] Kambona requested that only British forces be used, and that the operation be mounted immediately. He was agreeable to the British request that Nyerere make a public statement the morning immediately after the action to ward off accusations of neocolonialism.[117] Mirisho Sarakikya flew in briefly from Tabora for consultations, accompanied by Nyerere's childhood friend David Msuguri, a veteran sergeant who had also been promoted by the mutineers to lieutenant. They were scheduled to return early the next morning to maintain security at the upcountry barracks.[118] Sergeant Ilogi was instructed to drive them to the airport at 4:30 a.m., keeping them out of harm's way and Ilogi out of touch with his troops. Job Lusinde and Paul Bomani were charged with working out new wage levels in accord with civilian pay scales that were to be announced at a celebration scheduled for that evening, where free liquor would leave the troops inebriated and hungover the following morning.[119] Kambona then met with High Commissioner Miles, Brigadier Douglas, and Major Brian Marciandi; he reconfirmed Douglas as commander of Tanganyika Forces, creating an immediate chain of command upon successful completion of the action. They decided to move immediately, before dawn on Saturday, January 25. Upon approval from London, Douglas and Marciandi boarded a launch sent from the HMS *Centaur*, which picked them up at the president's pier. Mobilizing the strike force aboard the *Centaur* that night, they prepared a plan to take control of Colito Barracks and the city.[120]

Having approved the intervention, in a remarkable feat of mental discipline and political dissimulation, Nyerere kept his appointment to deliver a scheduled address at the Dag Hammarskjöld Foundation dinner. Delivering a scholarly speech with his characteristic ease, he outlined a Lockean theory of sovereignty for Africa, focusing on contract rather than conflict, under the title "The Courage of Reconciliation."[121] "He was given a standing ovation by an audience of all races," noted one observer. Another reported, "This caused the President to smile for the first time."[122]

January 25

At dawn, the British ship lobbed artillery fire at Colito Barracks, while a commando unit landed and promptly took control of the base. The Tanganyika Rifles troops were hungover, their weapons locked down according to normal procedure, and their leader occupied as a chauffeur for Sarakikya. The disoriented Tanganyikan soldiers offered little resistance and within an hour were sitting on the soccer field with their hands above their heads.[123] Upon returning from the airport and witnessing the scene at the barracks, Sergeant Ilogi made his way to the telegraph office and sent a message to the United Nations requesting help because "the Army of Tanganyika has been attacked by an unknown force."[124]

Meanwhile, Leonhart reported, downtown Dar es Salaam was "oblivious to British action. Schools, shops, traffic, normal."[125] Nyerere acted as if nothing unusual was underway, keeping his appointments and ignoring the echo of explosions that city residents had heard around dawn.[126] By midmorning Lawi Sijaona and Bhoke Munanka visited the high commissioner requesting no further action.[127] Nyerere waited until midafternoon to broadcast a speech, rather than immediately at dawn as he had promised.[128] This delay, as well as the deliberately informal nature of his written request for British assistance, handwritten and signed by Rashidi Kawawa on unmarked stationary, both suggest that Nyerere was prepared to deny that British intervention was invited if it went badly. The intervention, no matter how friendly, coming from a former colonial power, was a blow to Tanganyikan pride, if not its sovereignty.[129]

The British attack, coming at Nyerere's request, gave the impression that he had acted with restraint and control during the week, reining in British forces while his government responded first to the demands of its own African citizens.[130] The image he cultivated of fatherly forbearance for misbehaving children neither denied the fundamental validity of the mutineers' grievances of low pay and discrimination nor legitimated the tactic of rebellion. The African public and the government were largely sympathetic to the former, while Nyerere repeatedly scolded the latter. The attack's dramatic demonstration of British proficiency did not come with a rush on Monday immediately following the mutiny, but rather upon the authoritative request of the president, who claimed his rightful place to call for such action.

In mildly profane humor, Nyerere later tried to brush off the grave political risks that British intervention entailed. He compared the use of foreign troops to wearing someone else's clothes, with the risk that those clothes might turn out to be head-to-toe covering worn by some Muslim women, known in Swahili as a *buibui*. With a victor's panache, Nyerere joked:

> Our soldiers stripped us of our clothes and left us naked. This guy [the British] says he can lend us some clothes.... One of our mates warned us that we might ask to borrow clothes and be given a *buibui*, then what will you do! So we wrestled [with this question] from that first day on Monday, Tuesday, saying if I borrow from them, I don't know if I'll be given pants or what. But by Friday, there was no alternative, if it turns out to be a *buibui*, we'll just have to wear it and lose it somewhere down the road. Someone will think that it is Fatuma and you take it off and he'll know that it's Juma![131]

Fatuma is a woman's name, Juma a man's. The speech echoed the gendered logic of his youthful essay on women with its hint that a threat to sovereignty was a threat to manhood. But like the female clothing that disguised a male symbol of sovereignty, the British action had demonstrated the Tanganyikan government's possession of the powers formerly held by the colonial state, including command of its metropolitan emergency capabilities. The lingering fear and respect for the former colonial ruler contributed to the psychological force of the action, and implied Nyerere's unique intimacy with foreign powers. The attack demonstrated that even if the mutineers had captured the state, with its accompanying administrative apparatus, Nyerere personally commanded its metropolitan faculties. Summarizing a government statement issued a few days later, the American ambassador noted this emphasis, reporting in the staccato sytax of Amercan diplomatic cables: "It is apparently also necessary to repeat that British troops entered Tanganyika at request of Tanganyika Government with purpose of disarming with minimum bloodshed troops who were terrorising towns of Dar es Salaam, Tabora, and Nachingwea. Far from violating sovereignty of Tanganyika, British troops have upheld sovereignty of people, at request of people. They will leave as soon as satisfactory alternative arrangements can be made."[132]

This overwhelming strength, demonstrably at his command, reinforced his patriarchal power and made a mockery of the mutiny. To those in the know—the cabinet and the foreign diplomats—the initial mutiny had been impressive. "Plot was laid, and plan to envelop city and take all key positions designed and carried out with maximum surprise and in apparent complete security."[133] The mutineers' competence was obscured after a week of derision and scolding, punctuated by their impotent defeat at the hands of a small British force. "At this point there is wholly new situation in Tanganyika. British action has returned levers of command to Nyerere."[134] As salutary as this situation was, part of Nyerere's hesitance to call in British aid during the week had been to avoid the invocation of colonial force and the further personalization of political power this entailed.

Where Western powers were interested in the instrumental strength of a singularly powerful leader as an ally in Cold War competition, Nyerere's distress arose not from personal failure but from the institutional failure of the military command.[135] If anything, it was the political and ideological structure of his government, and in particular his own prestige, that held strong. During the week he had met with his cabinet and delegated power to his ministers, and he was pleased with Kambona's ability to wield his ministerial power loyally and effectively. The week of relative inaction demonstrated the continued political competence of his government to resolve the situation on its own moral authority even when it lost its military capacity. There was no starker reminder of the dangers posed by postponing the transformation of colonial institutions. Lusinde recalled that they consciously chose not to bring back the Field Force from Zanzibar because to do so would have created a confrontation between the police and the army that could have escalated the mutiny into a civil war.[136] With the government's continuity of moral authority achieved during a week of forbearance, the call on the former colonial power became a disciplinary action against an army that was an unreconstructed leftover from the colonial period, with its British officers still in place. The action, in the end, allowed Nyerere and his cabinet to use the occasion to reclaim, without irony, Tanganyika's sovereignty: "Any Independent country is able to ask for the help of another Independent country." He turned his shame back on the mutineers. "Those who brought this shame upon us are those who tried to intimidate our Nation at the point of a gun."[137]

Dismantling the Labor Movement

On Sunday afternoon, two hundred British soldiers took control of the Tabora barracks and armory and arrested twenty-four mutineers.[138] Leonhart opined that the "main and most encouraging development of the day was rapidity with which Nyerere moving to reassert control."[139] On Monday morning, another British commando unit, with support by air from HMS *Centaur* fighters, disarmed the remaining mutineers in Nachingwea. On Thursday Captain Sarakikya was promoted to brigadier and made commander of the Tanganyikan army. The mutineers' choice, Major Kavana, was named second in command, and Brigadier Douglas was asked to stay on as a military adviser.[140] Two weeks later Nyerere asked Nigeria, Algeria, and Ethiopia to send troops to train a new officer corps for the Tanganyikan army, and a few days later he made a similar request of Britain.[141] Douglas commanded the Tanganyikan force for exactly six days after the mutiny, and the ongoing British presence was carefully structured to be nothing more than the sort of training mission requested by other African countries, and later by China.

The government remained very cautious about disclosing the evidence of the coup plot. The day after the British intervention that ended the mutiny, Nyerere privately confirmed reports that "some trade union officials and other persons have been detained by police . . . to enable them to be questioned on certain activities and events which are causing concern to the Government."[142] Under the authority of the Preventive Detention Act, the Special Branch arrested more than five hundred trade union members, police, and civil servants of all ranks in an effort to uncover the reality and extent of the plot to overthrow the government.[143] "This step was taken," Kawawa explained, "after discovering a number of people who were starting to use the language of terrorism with seditious intent, so we decided to detain them."[144] Announcing Sarakikya's promotion, Nyerere made the only public admission that the mutiny was something more than a labor strike, hinting at "some mischievous people here and there." He added: "There are some of these amongst the number of people who have been arrested and placed in detention, because after last Monday they have been conspiring with ringleaders of the armed revolt in the hope that a further revolt would bring the downfall of our country. These people include some Trade Union leaders and one Area Commissioner."[145]

Aside from the mutiny leaders under arrest, the rest of the First Battalion of the Tanganyika Rifles was discharged, and Nyerere announced that the army would be rebuilt with loyal citizens of "the new Tanganyika" who would be "carefully selected and trained for the services of our people."[146] Meanwhile, the investigation took place "in almost complete secrecy."[147] Neither the British nor the Americans knew anything more than what the Tanganyikan officials told them.[148] British troops were tasked with tracking down several dozen mutineers who had fled Dar es Salaam.[149] Christopher Kasanga Tumbo, expelled from Kenya as "an undesirable immigrant," was arrested by Tanganyikan police at the border.[150] Labor detainees were investigated individually, and then released if their innocence was ascertained—most within weeks, while others languished for much longer.[151] Four months later, 190 people remained in prison, including Tumbo.[152] At the time, Kawawa privately betrayed a sense of how close the government had come to collapse and hinted at a steely new attitude toward potential subversion. "It could have been much worse," he said in his typically understated manner. "We have learned a lesson. We intend to see that this sort of thing doesn't happen again."[153]

The focus of government concern was the labor movement and remnants of the opposition parties. The mutineers by contrast were largely ignored. Most soldiers were sent back to their home areas and told to report to the government once a week, and a few of the leaders were put on trial before a special judicial panel created by a law hastily pushed through the Parliament in February. In response to those who called for him to issue harsher penalties, Nyerere responded, "I don't punish the person, it is the law that punishes the person."[154] Seeking to avoid publicizing the labor plan to overthrow the government, the panel called on neither Kambona nor Mzena to testify. Since the mutiny's leaders had not actually killed anyone, they were let off with light sentences of ten to fifteen years, and most were released early. Hingo Ilogi was one of the few who actually served his full sentence.[155] Christopher Tumbo languished in prison without trial for two years. He was released in April 1966 along with eight remaining detainees from the mutiny when Nyerere declared an amnesty for some ten thousand prisoners.[156] Tumbo was then sent into internal exile and kept under police surveillance until the time of Nyerere's retirement in 1985. Upon release he continued to advocate for multiparty democracy.[157]

A former labor activist who was briefly detained in the roundup recalled, "There were none that protested, because the leaders were inside. By the time they were let out, a single workers' party had been created, NUTA."[158] Within weeks of the mutiny, Nyerere disbanded the TFL and placed all labor unions under a new government-controlled union, the National Union of Tanganyika. NUTA's constitution, prepared in just seven days, was based on detailed proposals under development since mid-1963 for "making the TFL a Division of the Ministry of Labour and staffing it, in part, with paid officials who would hold office at the pleasure of the President."[159] On January 28, Nyerere also announced the composition of the presidential commission on the proposal for a democratic one-party state he had announced the year before. The commission, chaired by Rashidi Kawawa, included party loyalists like Kambona and Lucy Lameck together with a diverse group of lawyers and elders like Petro Itosi Marealle. Their terms of reference highlighted Nyerere's concept of a "national ethic" of civil rights and equality.[160]

Two months later, in a mass rally defending the creation of NUTA, Rashidi Kawawa studiously avoided any mention of labor involvement in the mutiny. He merely invoked the paternal metaphor of political leadership so common in Africa: "No reasonable father can let his children do as they like and similarly no responsible government can let its citizens do as they like regardless of the results." He said the government could not sit idle while the trade unions were mismanaged and cited new minimum wages, unemployment insurance, annual leave, public holidays, and protection from sudden layoffs. Addressing the trade unions, he claimed, "The trouble was that your workers allowed your leaders to struggle for power and personal ambitions at your expense. Yet in spite of that, the Government did more than your leaders did for you." Labor leaders Alfred Tandau and Mustafa Songambele claimed that workers had long desired a national union. Songambele brusquely cautioned former labor leaders against undermining the new union: "If they are found out, their punishment will be known. And if there are any wolves in sheep's skins among the new leaders, they should resign now."[161]

The final chapters of the mutiny brought a forceful demonstration of presidential power, both the ability to call on foreign expertise and the internal capacities of the Tanganyikan state. The use of foreign troops came only after establishing a public impression that the situation was in hand, under the firm control of the elected civilian government. Foreign intervention came only after intelligence—never publicly disclosed—pointed to a more elaborate plan under way to violently oust the legally established government. While immediate intervention might have seemed so natural a course of action as to obscure the violation of sovereignty, the delayed intervention did just the opposite: it chiseled into sharp relief the boundaries of Tanganyikan authority.[162] In order to reinforce this message, Nyerere invited all African heads of state to meet in Dar es Salaam, allowing him to reestablish his reputation and demonstrate his control of the country while entreating African countries to avoid divisive Cold War entanglements.[163]

From a British and American perspective, the assertion of sovereignty was hardly so categorical, depending as it did on the conflation of personality and polity so common to the Western relationship to the newly independent countries of Africa. The American ambassador drew an important tactical conclusion from the incident, in support of small deployments to effect instrumental change in small countries: "Case for conventional capabilities and role of the [aircraft] carrier as flexible instrument for application of limited force could scarcely have been better demonstrated."[164] Leonhart immediately began suggesting a parallel action in Zanzibar leveraged on a request for British military support from Zanzibari president Karume.[165] Noting his "immediate impressions" after the British intervention, Leonhart also commented on the appearance of instability: "Nyerere's request for British military assistance was product not only of army mutiny and deadlocked negotiations with military ringleaders but of situation moving totally out of control." It had been apparent to foreign diplomats that dockworkers and police were about to strike, "disloyal civil servants" wanted to emulate the Soviet Union, Asian residents were on the verge of panic, and the cabinet and president were absent at the moment of crisis. By contrast, they saw a flattering image of cool-headed Europeans hunkering down for a moment of neocolonial trouble that their supreme competence could readily resolve.[166]

This self-serving assessment reinforced local gossip of moral turpitude in the Tanganyikan government. Such rumors presented a threat that was much more difficult to control than the mutiny itself. The coup plans undeniably hinted at constitutional weakness in the state, but observers made much of the apparent ineptitude of the African mutineers and the exceptional ease of British intervention. In truth, the Africanized police and Special Branch had acted effectively during the crisis and the TANU youth were not implicated in the rebellion. Criticisms of Nyerere's hesitance failed to acknowledge that the British action went so smoothly in part because the government had spent the week reestablishing its preeminence and legitimacy—and because of the canny "celebration" the night before the intervention that left the mutineering soldiers hungover when British troops landed.

Most of the criticism in the diplomatic community saw in Nyerere's delayed call for British troops a debilitating indecisiveness, a moral weakness symbolizing the state's weakness. Leonhart observed somewhat ruefully that "Nyerere had waited for negotiated settlement as long as he could, longer than he should, and his own hesitations and failure to take public lead must I think be regarded as contributing to crisis and collapse."[167] This statement seeded a reputation for weakness that stuck with Nyerere for the better part of a decade. Leonhart's opinion of "the mutiny, and [Nyerere's] own timorous role in it" repeated itself ever more emphatically as it ascended the American diplomatic hierarchy.[168]

For Nyerere, the key lesson of the incident was the need to prevent internal threats because they undermined his government's credibility. He sought to reverse the force of American scorn and preempt any cause for further intervention. Over and over he emphasized the need to "work doubly hard so as to reduce as much as possible the damage which has been done to our country." Consistently minimizing the subversive threat of the labor plot, he kept the evidence discovered by the Special Branch secret. Maintaining the position that the mutiny was fundamentally a labor strike preserved the image of a united and sovereign government with no precedent of internal threat. He likewise made no mention of investigations into Chinese and Cuban activities in the weeks before the mutiny, including suspicions surrounding a Chinese news correspondent named Kao Liang.[169] Meanwhile, the government announced evasively "that there is no evidence whatsoever to suggest that 'communists' were responsible for the events of last week."[170] Nyerere's official line also included "categorical statements [of] his own confidence in Kambona," who many suspected of instigating the mutiny in order to promote his own ambitions for power.[171] Meanwhile, competing and equally unsupported rumors circulated that "it may have been an Nkrumah–Oginga Odinga operation to remove Nyerere, who was considered too moderate."[172]

The rumor-mongering of the week of the mutiny had given way to competing presentations of officially sanctioned truth—each, like a rumor, seeking to prove its context. The underlying concern of these debates, ultimately, was the limit of sovereignty in postcolonial Africa during the Cold War. The reality was that the mutiny had indeed spawned a "revolutionary situation" in the capital, but it was initially not a strike at the head so much as a strike against his nonracial policies, which were the focus of intense political debate. The mutiny was intended to precipitate a limited change in those policies in the army, and in that it succeeded. But in the midst of the disorder, a coup attempt had begun to take shape as various groups united by a racialist ideology assembled around the mutiny to instigate an alternative vision for the country that could easily have replaced the multiracial state that TANU had established. At every step, Nyerere and his colleagues maintained the state's delicately balanced sovereignty, delaying the intervention long enough to credibly claim it was their autonomous initiative and not a foreign imposition.

7

The National Youth Service

Immediately following the resolution of the January 1964 mutiny, Nyerere made a speech calling on TANU Youth League (TYL) members to enlist in a new army that would replace the suddenly defunct Tanganyika Rifles. A few weeks later, during the first parliamentary session after the mutiny, Nyerere brought parallel bills for the establishment of a national labor union, NUTA, and the rapid expansion of the nascent National Service, Jeshi la Kujenga Taifa (JKT), or literally, "The Army to Build the Nation."[1] The legislation allowed the president to mobilize the JKT for military service, but most JKT activities involved articulating Ujamaa into action domestically, communicating TANU's ideology through the modernist rituals of military drills directed toward rural development rather than combat.

On January 30, 1964, a special committee met to brainstorm the creation of a new army. The committee recommended that all new recruits for the police or army should spend three months in the JKT, and that TYL youth should register in the JKT. Furthermore, they proposed that military training be introduced in all teachers' colleges and some secondary schools, that national security awareness should be taught widely, and that some honorary military ranks be introduced "for those who have served the country." They would develop an elite "commando" corps, promote the president to commander-in-chief with his own military uniform, incorporate the heads of security organs into the National Executive Committee of the party, and create a special commission for military grievances. They also suggested a dedicated military airport, emergency radio station, and the need to identify and secure national security assets, including water sources. They also floated the idea that the Tanganyika Electric Supply Company (TANESCO) and potentially other major industries be nationalized. Finally they proposed what came to be known as *mgambo*, a village-level military reserve.[2]

The new army was trained as an explicitly politicized force, in contrast to the British tradition of a politically neutral force. British military historian

Hew Strachan has argued that the dubious ideal of an apolitical military only applied once a modern British sovereign had been established above local politics sometime after the Glorious Revolution, and even then its vaunted neutrality was itself a political claim.[3] With the nature of national sovereignty still undefined, the army needed political training to defend a sovereign ideal rather than subnational interests like class, ethnicity, or institutional loyalty.[4] In June 1964 Rashidi Kawawa reversed colonial policy by announcing that soldiers and police officers could participate in politics and join TANU—which they did en masse, under orders from their officers.[5] Later that year, membership in TANU became a prerequisite for joining the army.[6] Political doctrine was a primary component of training for the new army. The new commander, Brigadier Mirisho Sarakikya, explained that political training was intended to build an army that would understand their duty to protect the people of the country, not any one individual. "If there are problems affecting the *wananchi* [citizens] then they are problems that affect the military too."[7] The TANU leadership seems to have been concerned about the situation Timothy Parsons later observed: that the old East African armies had been left aside in the nationalist mobilization. Paul Bomani articulated the task before them: "The mutiny occurred because . . . there were among [the soldiers] people who had not identified themselves with the new Tanganyika. Our problem now is to create a new army which shares the nationalism of the rest of the country, and which is fully and consciously involved in the development of the nation."[8]

A party structure was inserted into the military, with military officers wearing "two hats," one according to military rank and one according to TANU hierarchy. Sarakikya insisted that if the party was to be supreme in the military, its authority structure must follow the military chain of command. "The military is a complete chain," he explained; "if there is any break then there is no army." In November 1964 Selemani Kitundu, then coastal regional commissioner, was granted an honorary rank of colonel in order to act as the political commissar of the newly inaugurated Tanzania People's Defence Forces.[9] For new recruits, the vehicle for politicization was the JKT. The army, previously a colonial construction of deliberately balanced ethnic identities, was made subject to a contentious nationalist vision. TANU defined a particular nonracial orthodoxy, and the mutiny offered proof that racialist populism had the potential to destroy the fragile new state. As a part of its response, the TANU government institutionalized culturally rooted roles for youth into state functions tied fitfully to its developing ideology.

Like the Ghananain Builders Brigades, upon which it was based, the JKT guided Tanganyikan youth toward state priorities, and thereby helped displace the raucous youth movement with a more authoritative state institution. The JKT rooted itself in local culture while providing a means for redefining the social roles of young men and women. However, further research, like that of Jeffrey Ahlman on Ghana's Builders Brigades or Jay Straker on Guinea's youth policies, would be needed to examine the manner in which JKT participants contested its administration and ideology.[10] Certainly there are more subtle contestations than the famous protest when university students marched to the statehouse in 1966 to oppose the new mandate that all higher education students would have to serve in the JKT for two years. Andrew Ivaska has shown how an emerging class consciousness among university students intersected with local discursive habits that accorded paternalistic authority to age.[11] In 1966 protesting students arrived to find an angry Nyerere, who scolded them and suspended them indefinitely, telling them to go back to their home villages where their self-consciously modern sensibilities might confront the old-fashioned mores of rural families.

Closely allied with the military, the JKT further subordinated the army to the political ideology of TANU while incorporating yet another aspect of local culture into state practice. The JKT helped displace the colonial military model of a "neutral" autonomous and technocratic army with one more specifically allied to TANU's nationalist vision. Using language deeply rooted in East African discourse about youth, Nyerere proposed an institution of deep philosophical relevance, built on a widely held idea that young men were by definition available for quasimilitary functions, providing such service in preparation for their leadership role as elders. Lawrence Gama, one of the JKT's founding administrators, said that its effectiveness was in "modernizing cultural activities . . . not to destroy but to improve."[12] As Lawi Sijaona proposed in presenting the JKT bill to Parliament, their training in this regard was less vocational than moral: "The pride and strength of our Nation are in the hands of the youth of this country, because the youth of today are indeed the leaders of tomorrow. So it is clear that we must prepare these youth so that they can be ready to take on the tasks that face our nation."[13]

The politicization of the army was a major step in expanding TANU's role beyond the political and policy realms that characterized its activities in the brief period of multiparty politics following independence. Calling on the TYL to rebuild the new army was the first act in direct preparation for a one-party state, followed closely by the creation of the National Union of Tanganyika. In order to fold the restive labor movement into the government, Nyerere had previously cajoled the leadership of the Tanganyika Federation of Labour into close alliance with TANU, and passed legislation to make it effectively a government institution. After the mutiny, Nyerere dissolved the TFL and created NUTA as a branch of government. A system of political commissars was later developed for unions, parastatal factories, and the army.[14] Similarly, the JKT pulled the TYL constituency out of the party and into the state structure to help enforce the parameters of legitimate politics, which the TYL was wont to overreach.

James Brennan has argued that during the late colonial period, the TYL drew on culturally authorized roles to practice "managed vigilantism" and thereby challenge the colonial state's Weberian monopoly on legitimate force in support of TANU political dominance. After independence, Brennan suggests, TANU tried to constrain the TYL with nationalist rituals and institutions like the JKT, but the TYL remained difficult to control in large part because ambitious politicians could use TYL cadres as "a potentially autonomous patrimony" to increase their political influence both locally and nationally.[15] One contemporary observer speculated that, in an effort to avert such a development, Joseph Nyerere, the brother of the party leader, was placed deliberately at the head of the TYL to keep it from becoming an independent militia.[16] Joseph Nyerere's appointment as TANU administrative secretary for youth affairs suggested a symbolic hierarchy that reinforced TANU's gerontocratic authority over the TYL.[17] Such an orientation hints at an awareness of the TYL's utility for that very purpose. TANU maintained the TYL as a secondary guarantor of its authority over the state as a ruling party. With the crisis of the mutiny, TANU moved into an ever more explicit supervision of the state at all levels. It then used the state to constrain civil society, including TANU-affiliated organizations like the TYL and the TFL. This process consolidated state sovereignty at the cost of institutional autonomy.

Youth and the Socialization of Governance

In East Africa, there was a widespread cultural expectation that a primary task for youth was armed service to the community. Expanding this effort into recruitment for a new army and the construction of the National Youth Service, government youth policy began to absorb local ideologies of gerontocracy and initiation rites, and their role in social order.[18] While the Youth League structure bore inspiration from European party youth leagues, the members who made up the rank and file of the TYL were local semiliterate youth with little exposure beyond the confines of a peasant upbringing. Their participation gave shape and identity to the Youth League, and their expectations found sympathetic ears among the politicians overseeing the organizations who were consciously seeking to build culturally African institutions that would be effective for governance in a predominantly rural and unlettered population. TANU institutions took on ritual relationships to each other, inventing an instant age structure, not rooted in hoary cycles of epic time but emanating from the perceived institutional needs of people for whom the structural implication of age was taken as an inherent aspect of human society.[19] The TANU government cultivated a new nationalist culture at the local level, but that very process meant that local cultures also shaped the nation.

A clan historian from Nyerere's home area explained how "eight Generation Sets, rotating in eight-year cycles, led the country effectively. They watched over the security of the country, if there was danger or an enemy, hunger or any kind of crisis."[20] In the regions east of Lake Victoria, on the western edge of the Serengeti where Nyerere came from, two distinct age-denominated political structures overlapped, one of a thousand years standing and the other of more recent vintage. Generation-sets and age-sets are different conceptions, but both tie a cyclical understanding of human lifetimes to a structure of governance.

The long-standing generation-sets of Zanaki tradition, alternating between two symbolic generations every twenty-five years or so, retained precedence over sequential age-sets, which were a recent import coinciding with the rise of Maasai power in the area. Under Maasai military dominance in the western Serengeti, local agricultural groups formed themselves into a Maasai system of governance that incorporated age-sets of youth who were initiated together through circumcision every five to ten years.[21] The Maasai initiation memorialized a point in history, prepared a group of future leaders, and marked time for the current generation of leaders. But the new Maasai system did not replace older systems of governance in the subjected communities. Rather the Maasai system functioned parallel to the old system, with the newer overlay considered somewhat superficial, not unlike the way people submitted to a later conquest by European colonialists. The Maasai system, in its time, was at the locus of power; people participated in it to gain influence, to seek peace, and to negotiate their social position. It came into wide use among the generation-sets of Zanakiland as a way for young men from various ethnic groups in the region to get ahead in life during a time of Maasai dominance.[22]

Maasai terms merged with Bantu terminology among the peoples of Musoma District. Whether the Maasai term for an elders' council, *ol kiama*, was absorbed by local Bantu languages as *chama*, or vice versa, the gerontocracy of age-sets came to define politics in the region.[23] In turn-of-the-century Swahili, the word *chama* lost its reference to councils of elders and took on a more general connotation as a social association.[24] By the mid-twentieth century chama came to mean "political party," which is its predominant connotation today.[25]

The Maasai presence in the western Serengeti was politically instrumental, but never hegemonic. Local agricultural groups, like Nyerere's Zanaki, viewed their generation-set system as being authoritative. Despite the visibility of the Maasai-styled age-sets, elders taught that the older generation-sets were preeminent, because through them they controlled access to land.[26] The two systems both mobilized young men into military service and other collective tasks and united people across clan and ethnic boundaries. Maasai age-sets were assimilated in Zanakiland to socialize youth and train them for military service during a period of Maasai hegemony. But the rituals of healing the land and guarding its fertility were vested in local generation-sets, whose authority superseded even that of the chiefs. The elder governing generation formed a political class for the small, localized "nations," whose boundaries were inscribed as each new governing generation took power. As one governing generation reached retirement age, an appropriate moment was chosen for the ceremony of *kung'atuka*, the passing of administrative power from one generation to another, while the remaining elders took on advisory roles as moral authorities.

Both age-sets and generation-sets, although different in function and practice, inscribed in ritual and in physical settlement an age-delimited structure representing a normative view of human society in many areas of Tanganyika. Gerontocracy was enforced in age-observant greetings of respect, rituals, seating arrangements at feasts, and judicial matters.[27] Age structures were common, if not universal, throughout East Africa.[28] Nyakyusa children in the south near Lake Nyasa were taught to build their own villages at a very young age, which they occupied on an increasingly permanent basis as they matured. In the villages they cultivated a habit of sharing their lives and resources, building strong fraternal loyalties. When the older generation was ready to retire, the entire geographical organization of the society would shift, reinscribing the society onto a map defined by the younger generation, who resided in the villages they had begun building as children.[29] Across the border in Malawi, Yao children undergoing the period of isolation that accompanied (male) circumcision—known generally in Swahili as *jando*—were taught social mores of hospitality and obedience, hygienic practices, history, and the obligations of tribal membership in a camp in the wilderness beyond the village.[30] Girls received a similar initiation, but among the Yao were not circumcised as in other groups across East Africa. After their isolation, both boys and girls returned to the village and marched to the house of the local chief and sang, "The door is shut, o Father, come and let me enter." The chief would appear, and as the youth demonstrated their new skills before him, he would ransom them from the elders who had been their instructors in their bush camp.[31] Thus rescuing them from the ageless disorder of the camp, the chief returned the young people, transformed from children into youthful adults, to the established civilization of the village. Similar rituals existed in Chagga communities, near Mount Kilimanjaro. Upon being initiated into an age-set, children listened to a song by the elder who had guided them through the initiation. The song framed their experience in terms of the cycle of the generations that gave form to society.[32]

Ee, you who come out from the teachings,
I have taught you weighty matters carefully,
Thus teach ye your successors in the future,
That they in turn may teach their children.
Ee ye my children, Be my children!
I tell you, teach the age sets
From generation to generation, let them have understanding.[33]

Children of Chagga elites were offered an additional asset in their coming of age. They inscribed marks into a sacred stone, where youth who would become confidants of chiefs were sworn to keep ritual and state secrets. The period of youth included a time of revolt against parental authority that included the organization of a semi-independent "child republic" governed by a generation of youth in preparation for their role as governors of the society. The ritual of initiation, with its coded lessons for elite children, served to reinstate the authority of elders.[34] In Haya society, boys went through an education program that prepared them for leadership and military activities and served to winnow out those deemed unsuited to leadership.[35] The cohort of youth was nearly universally understood as a military corps, under the authority of the governing generation. Arusha elders, near Mount Meru, told young men before being circumcised, "You are the police of the country. You are depended upon in every kind of danger, an enemy attack or when dangerous animals molest the people in your *boma*."[36]

The revolt of youth against elders was an expected turning point in the rhythm of generational power; its ritual aspect helped to highlight and define social and governmental order.[37] Even in decentralized or egalitarian societies like the Maasai or the Gisu of eastern Uganda, initiation was a time of emphasizing self-control, a fundamental virtue where the police powers of a centralized sovereign did not exist. Instead, the use and control of force was shared by all, a lesson dramatized in the fearful experience of adolescent circumcision.[38] In Kenya, the memory of colonial conquest in Kikuyu country, with its disruption of initiation rituals involving circumcision, found expression in popular songs about the erosion of generational order and its role in governing human and agricultural fertility. "The disciplines of reproduction and production were indivisible," according to John Lonsdale. "Without initiation, fertility went out of control and civilization collapsed."[39] An equally apocalyptic vision of the changes that independence would bring was recorded in southwestern Tanganyika in the early 1960s, in a cultural context similar to that of the Nyakyusa youth who built their own villages. A Fipa prophet told his listeners: "O you people, you're going to be robbed of your country." He showed them his clenched fists asking what they thought he held in them. "Now I'll open up: let's see what rubbish we have here! ... They're grasshoppers, and see! They fly away! ... The grasshoppers are your children, and they are flying away, all of them! YOU remain behind, old and dying!"[40]

Nyerere grew up in a rural village amid both generation- and age-sets that were still functioning during colonial rule. David Msuguri, Nyerere's age-mate and childhood friend, entered the army in 1942 and spent his life rising through the ranks, becoming TPDF commander in the 1980s. He recalled how young people were socialized to think in terms of age grades in the political structure. He called the filed teeth that both he and Nyerere sharpened when they came of age mere "fashions" of youth. Speaking of the governing institutions of old Zanaki society, he referred to the "neikulu," which he noted was a variation of the word *Ikulu*, meaning "statehouse."[41] As Msuguri explained:

> It was not a council. *Neikulu* was young men. You go until you reach a certain stage, then you progress (*kung'atuka*). Now these become elders. And here elders of another kind, senior elders. You will find there are *wenyekura, wenyebireti*, these are regions, or they are fashions of change, as I told you earlier, we go with the times. Those *wenyekura* didn't just disappear, they didn't just end; youth move on. When they reach their age they step back. Now those who were herded behind them come forward. Those others [behind them] continue in same way.[42]

Referring to generational groups as both "regions," using the same word used for administrative regions today, and "fashions of change" evokes the structural conception of time in age-sets and generation-sets. The passage of cohorts was not just a manner of election or succession to a distinct institution of authority; generational dynamics were the nature of government itself as conceived by the Zanaki.

Future Kenyan president Jomo Kenyatta drew from the same discursive well in his functionalist description of age-sets in Kikuyu society during his childhood.[43] Kenyatta maintained that the *irua* initiation ceremony in Kikuyuland marked "the commencement of participation in various governing groups in the tribal administration." The naming of age-sets, Kenyatta asserted, was the main record of local history. Kenyatta represented the generational system as a form of democracy in contrast to a legendary royal despotism that it replaced, deposed by the *iregi* generation-set, so named for the revolt. Kenyatta enumerated a set of principles of government that he claimed were formalized in the mythical first meeting of the Kikuyu Council following the overthrow of the foundational "King Gikuyu." Nearly all the principles make reference to age-sets as the central point of social organization, and the fourth principle states explicitly: "The government should be in the hands of councils of elders (*kiama*) chosen from all members of the community, who had reached the age of eldership, having retired from warriorhood. And the position of elders should be determined by a system of age-grading."[44]

Nyerere certainly contemplated this deeply politicized ethnography by his fellow head of state, with whom he shared a British higher education.[45] Generational change, in Nyerere's home village and in much of the country, inhered in the memory of precolonial government and was deployed to justify the postcolonial government.[46] Taken in this sense, sovereignty rested neither in an office nor in an individual, but in the passage of political time. Like European theories of divinely ordained kingship or natural law, the attachment of sovereign authority to generational change or the regular rhythm of age-sets made such authority an organic part of the world of nature. Age-graded structures were holy in this sense, progenitors of an essential world. Such a construction does not simply legitimate authority but fixes a structure of authority into a conceptual environment. The colonial state naturalized its authority in ideas of civilization and race that justified the role of the colonial ruling class. The 1964 mutiny was an attack on colonial legacies, and their racialized nature. By creating a new army out of the new nation's "youth," Nyerere replaced the latent racial authority of the colonial army with a generational logic, now inserted into the institution most fundamentally representative of sovereignty—the military.

An Army in Embryo: The TANU Youth League

TANU was viewed as a young people's movement, and youth was a category initially dominated by grassroots enthusiasts rather than young people still in school. It was not so much age but their lack of schooling and status that marked them as youth. The moderates close to Nyerere tried to pull these young supporters toward an inclusive vision of nation by constructing an exclusive political establishment defined by TANU control. Other political leaders encouraged a more racialist national identity, and the rifts in TANU found parallels in the Youth League.

During the TYL's first year, radical young supporters calling themselves "Bantu groups" pushed for a return to what they imagined as a pre-Islamic, pre-Christian African culture, and styled themselves as the party's nascent praetorian guard.[47] Such atavistic enthusiasms notwithstanding, the manner in which youth involved themselves politically in TANU did bear a clear connection in ideology and practice to the precolonial age structures. In Sukuma country, the youthful executors of chiefly decisions, the *basumba batale*, joined the TANU Youth League in large numbers.[48] In the western part of the country, Kimbu people described the Uwuxala *ing'oma* (royal dance society) as *siasa*, or "politics."[49] Aylward Shorter quotes one modern

Kimbu man as saying, "We used to belong to the *ing'oma* of the Uwuxala. Now we belong to the *ing'oma* of TANU.'[50] Like the overlapping meanings of the Maasai *ol kiama* and the Swahili *chama*, previously existing institutions took on new meanings as the politics of independence approached. Party leaders sought to both absorb the energies of young supporters and redirect them toward their preferred ideological positions. In this sense, a young man from Korogwe seeking a job noted that since 1959 he had been a "servant in our army of unity, the TANU Youth League."[51]

The TYL knit together a number of informal youth auxiliaries that supported TANU during the drive to independence, mobilizing youth for rallies and propaganda, and also providing security for TANU gatherings, enforcing party discipline, and harassing political opponents with brazen independence from party leadership.[52] Hadija Binti Kamba, who joined the Youth League in the 1950s, explained that the youth were "the soldiers for every occasion," providing both security and intelligence while distinguishing strong party supporters from uncommitted hangers-on.[53] According to its constitution, TYL members understood their task to "encourage the Youth to sacrifice and work for TANU." The Youth League was subsidiary to the party, with all its property held in trust by TANU.[54] TYL members sought a place for themselves as local police, but also as TANU's enforcers, harassing political opposition. With the onset of TANU leadership in responsible government in 1960, TYL youth played an increasingly aggressive role as the "police of the country," opportunistically wielding the sovereign sword of the TANU government. Their racially motivated searches of Asian shop owners undermined TANU's struggle to cleanse its ranks of racialism. Reflecting their local cultural roots as armed appendages to local authority, TYL members seemed to care less for democracy than for their role in constituting and executing TANU's political power. Their wanton interference in local communities and businesses had begun to breed resentment toward TANU by 1964.[55] In typically condensed telegraphic writing, an American consul reported on the overenthusiastic Youth League efforts to enforce justice and keep the peace: "Number of incidents reported from all over Territory of groups Africans taking 'police' action, including making 'arrests,' searching houses and ejecting occupants, stopping and searching cars, holding 'courts' and carrying out punishment. Most of persons 'arrested' have been Africans. Also number of official reports of groups drilling with imitation rifles, patrolling streets at night. Incidents, which began shortly after formation of responsible government, attributed in nearly every case to TYL."[56]

TANU worked constantly to rein in the TYL, emphasizing its role as an auxiliary, not an initiator of policy. Speaking to the Makerere Students' Guild shortly after independence, Nyerere pointed out that the tinge of colonial resentment still clung to the new government, so "TANU is the great source of power."[57] The government's legitimacy and authority still rested in the party, an authority that tempted ambitious TYL leaders to overreach. The ambiguity of sovereignty in the new nation bore the threat of institutional disorder, whether caused by the Youth League, labor unions, the army, or opposition parties. The new district commissioner responded diplomatically: "The support of the TYL in the preservation of the law and order is most valuable but they should clearly be shown what they should and should not do."[58]

The creation of an "elders" section helped anchor TANU's legitimacy in the eyes of the older generation and avoided the impression that the party was just a group of rowdy young men. Sheikh Sulemani Takadir was the first leader of the elders, but his authority was limited. He was expelled from the party when he questioned the lack of Muslims among TANU election candidates. Nyerere felt that such questions invoked religious partisanship.[59] Although meant to tamp down religious politics, Nyerere's sensitivity to religious discussion often had an opposite effect of ratcheting up religious confrontation. A TANU official in Dar es Salaam called on the TYL to "carry out investigations" of the All-Muslim National Union of Tanganyika (AMNUT) in the days following its creation. The ambitious young men of the Youth League could be useful in TANU's confrontation with alternative institutions, but the TYL also threatened the somewhat insecure cadre of still-youthful party leaders like Kambona and Kawawa and local community elders who felt bewildered in the rush to independence.[60]

Within the TYL, the category of "youth" was not necessarily designated by age but by seniority and status. Reflecting the variety of hierarchical age structures embedded in latent precolonial systems of governance, some TYL "youth" were middle aged, no younger than many of the top governmental officials.[61] Even as they restrained TYL autonomy, TANU leaders reinforced the fundamental expectations of youth as a coercive instrument of governmental authority, seeking not to erase youthful ambitions but to direct them. Edward Barongo praised the Youth League for being more effective than the police. He exhorted them to be "the eyes, ears, and nose of TANU. . . . Every word said about TANU, whether bad or good, they should quickly bring a report."[62] Rashidi Kawawa called on the TYL in one of the first public statements of Tanganyika's southern Africa liberation policy, just after the beginning of internal self-government in May 1961: "Although colonialism is leaving Tanganyika it is still around the corner. . . . Therefore if nations like the Portuguese go on with their discriminatory policies the TANU Youth League will one day be required to go and forceably [*sic*] evict them out of Mozambique and thus complete the efforts of freeing the whole African continent from the slavery of being ruled."[63]

After independence, the TYL began to settle in to roles and relationships fully cogent with preexisting ideologies of the political role of youth as well as TANU ideological priorities. TANU Youth League branches in Tanga and elsewhere expressed great enthusiasm for setting up communal farms under the patronage of local government in 1962.[64] The Tanga District TYL branch forwarded memos to the TANU area headquarters from its Council for Youth Development and Security Council. They proposed the communal tasks of building party offices and village latrines and improving the local dance societies "that will bring benefits and also be ready to tour outside the country." The local TYL Security Council proposed to harmonize the Youth League's activities and official policing through seminar presentations by police officers, and through the creation of a police "reserve" made up of TYL members.[65] In Handeni, as elsewhere, TYL members assigned themselves to collect taxes and enforce controls on the export of food from the district. The local regional commissioner advised TYL leadership that their enforcement activities would kill the party by alienating the local citizens who resented the continued need for state taxes. "There are officers in the District Council with this job," he told them.[66] In Mwanza, TYL enthusiasm led to a deliberate misinterpretation of judicial orders: the youth insisted that messengers of the district court were not to arrest anyone without a TYL official present. The misunderstanding hinted at their desire to contribute to the ambiguous authority of the postcolonial state.

In response to this need to establish clear lines of authority, one of the party's regional secretaries circulated an extended meditation on the nature of government and democracy in the new condition of independence. He began by noting that although the police were now under a TANU government, "it is difficult for regular citizens to understand the meaning of this division that should not be separable." The secretary went on to define government as "a group of people who volunteer to do the work of the people on behalf of the people themselves and are paid by the people themselves." But in order to create a government there first had to be a party that defined policy, which in Tanganyika's case was TANU. However, he noted, "when we delegate a certain party to be in Government it is clear that this does not mean every party member should be called [a representative of] the government." In order to do the work of government, civil servants, including police and jail guards, needed to operate without interference. The TYL contribution in this regard, he argued, was that of ordinary citizen, not civil servant. Youth League members could make citizen's arrests for basic crimes when police were not nearby, but they were not to use force unless the accused resisted with violence, nor were they to use party buildings as "lockups." The memo tactfully constrained the legal and political scope of TYL policing without questioning members' general duty to do "this meaningful work of guarding security in the country."[67]

Although possession of the colonial state was what TANU sought, the relationship youth initiated toward the state through the TYL was envisioned in the moral terms of patriarchy. TYL members expected patronage as they would expect of patriarchal village authorities. They lobbied for building projects and businesses to employ TYL members.[68] In a letter to the regional commissioner of Tanga in 1963 requesting that he visit their settlement scheme in Muheza, a TYL area secretary addressed the commissioner in terms almost subversive to the technocratic order of the state, but in full accord with patriarchal local culture. "Here in our region of Tanga, we all recognize that we have no other Father but you, so fill our hunger, in all types of problems we cannot cry to anyone but you."[69] The youth addressed the top regional government executive as father, incorporating him into a moral world that legitimated his authority and placed expectations on it.

As TANU took over the reins of government, the mass structure of its organization with the cultural load that it carried with it, strained against the technocratic inheritance of the colonial state. This tension found expression in the contradictory speeches of Oscar Kambona, serving as both minister of Home Affairs and general secretary of the party at the time of independence. A popular figure among the youth and the TANU grass roots, Kambona called on all citizens to help the police, and for TYL to be the "torch light of TANU" enforcing the new order, while pointedly limiting TYL ambitions to merely reporting criminals to the police. He announced the publication of a booklet to guide citizen policing "which I hope will solve the present problem." In the end, to avoid offending the politically active youth, the version of the speech distributed in a press release removed almost all reference to the TYL.[70] The rhetorical expectations for youth nevertheless remained strong in Kambona's speeches, and he continued to call on the TYL to actively help the police in catching lawbreakers.[71] In Tanga, the regional police commander approached the TYL to help reduce marijuana usage.[72] In Mwanza, the regional commissioner appreciated the TYL for providing an alternative instrument for law and order while acknowledging that "strong measures had to be taken" to improve discipline in the police.[73] Despite TYL's members' occasionally disruptive nature, their role was firmly established as "guardians of the party."

The ideological pressure of elder authority and obligation and the policing role of youth began to infuse the technocratic structures inherited from the colonial state. TANU branches were expected to maintain distinct roles for the entire gerontocratic structure of village society and were faulted for not supporting elders' committees.[74] Statehouse aide Bhoke Munanka met with TYL members during a fact-finding session on the "deterioration of the Youth Movement" in Musoma, on the western edge of the Serengeti in early January 1964. The attendees complained that "the top leaders of TANU don't care much about the youth of the TYL, whereby in the past they were shoulder to shoulder.... These days they think of [the youth] as just a bunch of singers and that their tasks have ended." Party youth continued to pine for a role in internal security, a desire that had brought about continued clashes with the organs of the state. "Until now the youth aren't helping the Government in the capture of criminals," one TYL representative told Munanka. "When they capture a criminal it is always turned around and it is they who are arrested and jailed. The relationship [between the TYL and local government] has not been straightened out, especially when [the youth] are brought before a colonialist judge they are punished severely. This situation is discouraging those who want to help."[75]

The authority of elders existed in tension with the legal institutional structures of the party and the state, not unlike the overlapping age structures of the western Serengeti. As TANU took uncertain possession of the inherited state, its composition as a mass party formed an uneasy marriage with its structure as a ruling party. In the past, village community had also offered a layer of protection, sheltering villagers from the invasive demands of an overarching state, but with TANU the state became uncomfortably intimate. The village hierarchies that made up so much of TANU's grassroots structure no longer communicated with the state through the discredited detours of indirect rule. Nor did village communities become immediately amenable to direct incorporation into the new government; rather, they gave way to a frustrated incoherence in the ideology and expectations of freedom (*uhuru*) that would continue for the rest of the decade. In early 1964 Musoma youth explained their expectations to Munanka as national party representative with rural roots: "In the past, all the speeches suggested that immediately after *Uhuru*, all youth of the TYL would be soldiers, moreover the leaders of the villages and the Districts looked forward to holding the status of the *wangwana*, the chiefs, and the District Commissioner and others. But this did not happen. This was against the expectations of many people in the country."[76]

The colonial state had a series of overlapping authorities spread across a motley patchwork of communities great and small—some widely dispersed, some concentrated in a region. The *wangwana*, or "civilized" elite, was one mode of social order along the Swahili-speaking coast and up and down the trade routes piercing the country to the Great Lakes. The chiefs were an assortment of prominent men granted administrative status by the colonial state, some of them having a much broader authority rooted in a historical office. Under indirect rule, as the youth noted, these authorities were tied to the colonial state—the tin-pot omnipotence of the district commissioner—and stitched into a territorial fabric. Independence and its direct discursive link to sovereignty was bound to Tanganyika as a whole, but it was a shallow status. For an ethnic community or a local web of alliances among prominent patriarchies, uhuru would constitute something very different from independence. These unofficial entities functioned on very different principles and depended on very different relationships to neighboring communities.

TANU's ambition was over the mandate territory itself. Power lay with the colonial state, and leaders did not seek to reestablish precolonial forms, but rather to insert themselves and their culture into the inherited state. To achieve its ambition, the party needed also to incorporate the myriad entities of local order, whose functioning was rooted in the everyday habits and beliefs of people. Youth establishing a TYL village suggested the manner by which the territorial state could be transformed into a culturally resonant nation. They expected and intended to bring to life the old campaign song "TANU builds the country." Like the Yao, Chagga, and Nyakyusa children of days past, TYL youth created a politicized village that symbolized their new republic. One TYL leader explained, "For me and my fellow youth of the TANU Youth League, our main goal is to build our young Nation in order to try to remove that thing called Poverty and we faithfully decided to leave town to live here in the wilderness together with one common goal in the name of that song *Ooo TANU Yajenga Nchi*."[77]

With TYL members clashing with police and lobbying for land that they were ill prepared to use, TANU leaders searched for a solution that would integrate youthful yearning for a role in national security with the state's need to command legitimate violence. In February 1962 Oscar Kambona made a suggestion that went beyond the regulated compromise guiding citizen cooperation with the police. He announced an intention to formalize a specific role for youth in the national government through the creation of a "constructive army of the TANU Youth League whose objectives would be based on building the nation."[78] Such an army promised to institutionalize two roles for youth, which had begun developing immediately with the advent of self-rule but still existed in an inchoate and contested state: establishing politicized villages in "settlement schemes" and contributing to military and police functions. Through the TYL, TANU's nationalist goals found expression in locally resonant ideas about the political role of youth. In turn, TANU's character absorbed an amalgam of local cultures that further distinguished it from a generic political party in the European sense and deepened its character as a distinctly African political institution.

Jeshi la Kujenga Taifa: The National Youth Service

Oscar Kambona had first mentioned the idea of a National Service for public works in a press conference after a TANU executive committee meeting in July 1960.[79] It is unclear whose idea it was, but it was formulated within TANU before independence. Rashidi Kawawa recalled that he and Nyerere were impressed with Golda Meir's account of Israeli youth policy after a conversation with the Israeli prime minister at a 1958 celebration of Ghana's first anniversary of independence.[80] After attending an International Labor Organization conference in Lagos in December 1960, Derek Bryceson visited Accra for three days to study Ghana's "builder's brigades" that extended precolonial ideas about youth into postcolonial political structures.[81] He returned "even more enthusiastic . . . after having seen for himself what they were doing in Ghana," reassuring an American consular officer that "the project was not merely an idea of his. It had considerable support among the leaders of TANU."[82] In June 1962, in the midst of debates about preventive detention and the single-party state, Kawawa forwarded a bill for the National Youth Service to the National Assembly as a means to channel the energies of Tanganyika's youth.[83] The task of developing the idea was passed, appropriately, to the Ministry of National Culture and Youth under Lawi Sijaona, himself a former TYL leader. In introducing legislation in Parliament, Sijaona declared, "In the past youth of the country had helped in the struggle for independence but now it was time to give them some useful constructive part in the building of the nation. . . . For a long time we have heard of people asking, what has the government done for me? I think now is the time to teach youth to be able to ask, what can I do for my country?"[84]

There were a number of models for the JKT, and as Tanganyika was already a major recipient of Peace Corps volunteers, it is unsurprising that Kennedy's stirring phrase entered into Sijaona's vision for the new National Youth Service. Sijaona sought the prestige of precedent by referencing such youth corps institutions abroad: "In our holy continent of Africa, countries like Ghana and Mali and others have armies of this sort." Citing such programs further afield, Sijaona described the healing power of the Yugoslavian youth service that rebuilt their country after World War II, and the quasibiblical power of Israeli youth to cultivate fertility, turning deserts into a country of trees, flowers, and farms. "Here, Mr. Speaker," Sijaona extemporized," let me say that the National Youth Service is not something foreign in this world, nor here in our Africa." The vision for the Jeshi la Kujenga Taifa also grew out of colonial versions of European scouting movements, which had small numbers of Tanganyikan youth involved. The headmaster of the Tanga Boys' Secondary School sought to build up the Magamba Youth Brigade as "a very militant section of the TYL for it will carry out national building projects in the villages around the school. . . . In other words it acts as Scouts did in the past."[85]

The JKT was designed to socialize youth into the nationalist vision of the TANU government. Lawrence Gama, an early director of the JKT, recalled, "In this way we could mold a Tanzanian way, to have one direction in life."[86] The JKT was seen as a fertile source of soldiers, police, civil servants, and university students, making youth service a modern rite of passage for the new state. "In this army," Sijaona proclaimed in Parliament, "one thing which we want to emphasize is teaching our youth to have a heart of good citizenship and service to the Nation."[87] Peter Siyovelwa, a member from Iringa, insisted that this orientation should be encouraged from childhood. Since "the upbringing of a person to love his country starts when he is a child not when he is already an adult," he proposed a nationalist education program for each school, requiring teachers to go through the JKT and teach children "the importance of serving their country." It would be necessary, as in the army, "for each recruit to take an oath of loyalty to the President of the Republic and that he would serve his Nation."[88] In the debate, Bibi Titi Mohamed acknowledged the fear that arming youth in the JKT would create a potential threat to national security, but she contended that this danger was easily managed. In the voice of a stern Swahili mother, she simply expected patriotic loyalty from the youth, echoing the context of mature self-control inculcated in initiation rites. "It will be a great danger," she said. "But we don't fear that danger, except that we should lay down 'discipline' that will have the strength to strike fear into those who might think that they will find pleasure and recreation. They will have to leave those ideas behind, and understand that there are things to learn to support our country and build our country."[89]

While basic military instruction in light weaponry had always been envisioned for the JKT, the mutiny reemphasized the need for its military purpose. Israel sent advisers to help establish the JKT as a nationalist institution. Job Lusinde helped to integrate the policy with existing security institutions as "a sort of reserve army . . . that was very good for citizenship and nationalism."[90] One parliamentarian suggested that all adults under age forty-five should receive some military training and that each regional headquarters should house a JKT regiment. The National Youth Service began to root itself in conceptions of precolonial structures for defense and security of a militarized society under a controlling culture of patriarchal nationalism. "Things that the chiefs, or let's say, the Ngoni were doing, or the Maasai were doing," noted former JKT director Gama, citing the martial attributes of prominent precolonial ethnic groups, "we turned that into defense. . . . We trained them now properly. . . . This is how we used the ideas of culture and worked them into the modern world."[91] Kawawa explained that youth "would understand our culture, how defense was in the past, and why it needs to continue today."[92] Some years later, TANU guidelines made this assumption explicit: "The idea of basing defence on the people themselves was easily understood by Tanzanians, because it was not new to them. The traditional societies were simple structures where every able-bodied man was also a fighter when the need arose."[93]

The nascent JKT, rooted in the grassroots TYL, brought with it the possibility for a reenvisioning of the resolutely male institutions of defense and security. Both men and women signed up for the new Special Constabulary Service of the TYL across the country.[94] The age-structure vision for the TYL did not exclude women. Even if dominated by men, its composition and targets for recruitment were always defined by the nongendered word *youth*. Two female European members of the National Assembly commented favorably on the JKT bill, their views illustrating the feminist flavor of undifferentiated inclusion of women in the JKT. Lady Chesham, Nyerere's friend and supporter, promoted a vision deriving from a memory rooted in the gendered division of labor of the war years in Europe. She suggested that girls be given different training than boys, allowing them to take over the work of men in a national emergency should the men be drafted into war. The Swedish leader of the Girl Guides scouting organization, Barbro Johansson, disagreed. The seasoned educator took a more fundamentally feminist perspective on the bill, thrilled to note that girls were going to be considered the same as boys. "Women should also learn obedience, discipline, since in the army this sort of learning is needed even more than for men."[95]

The JKT brought together youth from around the country and from various economic and educational backgrounds, subjecting them all to deliberately harsh training in the territory's rural wilds. "It was not to humiliate," Lusinde insisted, "but to teach them to be humble, and to have *discipline*."[96] The word "discipline," when used untranslated as an English word interposed in a Swahili sentence (rather than *adabu, utii*, or the more formal *nidhamu*), as Lusinde did here and Bibi Titi did before the National Assembly, signifies good manners, maturity, and dignified conduct. These traits have an ethical implication in gerontocratic culture where the difference between *maadili mema* (good ethics) and *tabia njema* (good habits) is very slight. This initiatory task of the JKT combined national identity with the inculcation of proper respect for civil government. Kawawa, who went through JKT training himself as a model citizen and civil servant, said that cadets were taught "patriotism, to love their country, to be trustworthy and hard-working, and to guard their nation."[97] In practice, JKT instructors were often harsh and arbitrary, and it could be argued that the skills learned by the young cadets were to submit to tyrannical state authority. But this was not the intention. Rather, the severe experience of cadets represented a combination of the break-and-rebuild dynamic of military basic training, and the often frightening aspects of traditional rites of initiation. The JKT mobilized both of these historical contexts in support of a nationalist vision of participatory citizenship.

Figure 7.1. President Julius Nyerere greets National Service (JKT) members. JKT Director Lawrence Gama stands to Nyerere's left. © Tanzania Information Services (MAELEZO).

The nation itself was not a natural entity, but a political one. The vision of nation, conceptualized and communicated through TANU, developed as a conversation between the state and its citizens. The terms of patriarchal fealty became a normative conception of nation, which in turn bore an ideological force that transformed state institutions inherited from colonial rule. When parents in Mtae village objected to their children receiving military training for fear that they would be sent into war, the area commissioner assured them that the government fully shared their sense of proper upbringing, and reminded them of the martial duties of youth.

> In the same way I want to inform all the people and elders of the way the TANU Youth of Mtae brought praise to the whole district of Lushoto for their courage, their wisdom, and their obedience in serving the Nation. All these praises go to the parents of Mtae and the way they have brought up their children with good manners. We would be very grateful if this spirit would continue without being undermined by belligerents who don't have the behavior of our Nation.[98]

The commissioner's exchange with the parents of Mtae was typical of the tensions built in to the hybrid institution of the JKT, its purpose deliberately ambiguous, depending as much on local cultural expectations as on national administrative needs as it defined its shifting civil, military, and educational objectives. Building the JKT became a means of working out the challenges of administration in the postcolonial situation and resolving the organic cultural ideals of political and administrative power. Building equally on European models of youth service programs and African traditions of age-sets, the politicians and civil servants administering the JKT struggled through the adjustments necessary to create a wholly new institution. The JKT, like the new independent state, was to be an amalgam of ideas from many different models, foreign and domestic, civil and military, old and new.

The Moral Core of Government

Max Weber influentially proposed that all state power derives from military discipline and that the defining attribute of the state is its monopoly on the legitimate use of force.[99] But Weber's observations of the European state system should be taken as constitutive not descriptive. As Nyerere endeavored to bring his country into full sovereign membership in the international system, he had to conform the new country to these constitutional attributes of nation-states. By rebuilding a nationalist military structure upon a culturally defined category of youth, he established new organs of state security that were also legitimate in local conception.

Under the same British officership as it had before independence, the Tanganyika Rifles had virtually been a foreign institution only bound to the new government by tenuous constitutional fetters. In the mutiny, the non-commissioned African soldiers rebelled against their foreign leadership and made a direct appeal to Nyerere for an improvement in working conditions. The initial rebellion implicated Nyerere's patriarchal obligations to his African children rather than an ideological struggle of the Cold War. Rallying the proponents of Africanization, the labor movement sought to turn this appeal into a deeper protest against the legitimacy of the TANU government and its rejection of racial favoritism. Nyerere's government responded by instituting a new army built on long-standing notions that were already present in TANU of the authoritative role of elders and the paramilitary tasks of youth in East African society.[100]

With the elements of Tanganyika's national identity and ethic still under debate, the nature of patriotism remained undefined: to some it meant loyalty to Nyerere, to others it meant democratic process, and for still others it meant a defense of race or ethnic homeland. Patriotism, under these circumstances, was political. The mutiny had demonstrated both the danger of an apolitical military and the need for a citizenry politicized into a unified national identity. In response, Nyerere sought to build a new military in an organic cultural relationship to the nation defined by his national ethic, embodied in TANU. Even before the mutiny, the Tanganyikan government had turned to TANU to recruit a military core loyal to TANU's vision, sending TYL members to Israel for training. On the same day the British disarmed the mutineers, Nyerere announced a plan already in formation: "Clearly, it is essential that we should build up the Republic's Army again. I call on members of the TANU Youth League, wherever they are, to go to the local TANU office and enroll themselves. From this group we shall try to build a nucleus of a new Army for the Republic of Tanganyika."[101]

Brigadier Douglas, in his final tenure at the head of the army, frowned on the drastic change in orientation that TYL recruitment would mean for the constitution of the military in Tanganyika. He told the American ambassador that the TYL core would "necessarily center on unemployed Dar-es-Salaam youth which he considers [a] most unreliable lot." More to the point, "recruitment on this basis would upset careful tribal balance British had tried to maintain in TR [the Tanganyika Rifles]."[102] The new policy for military recruitment took an opposite tack on each of these issues. Party loyalty replaced tribe as an administrative category, and through the auspices of the TYL and the military, the constructive engagement of unemployed youth provided them a social role that was both culturally rooted and nationalist. In the National Assembly, the member from the West Lake Region praised the TYL for their close cooperation with the police in the weeks after the mutiny "to guard peace in our country."[103] In response to the government's call for TYL members to join the new army after the mutiny, a regional party secretary proudly reported his efforts to mobilize young people over the course of 1964.

> The work that has been done by the TANU Youth League has been helpful and commendable to the party. It will be remembered that around the 20th of January 1964 the army of the Tanganyika Rifles mutinied and that around the 25th of January 1964, just after this mutiny this Army was disarmed and those found guilty were dismissed, and others were judged. The Father of the Nation Julius K. Nyerere, President of the Republic of Tanzania and our holy party of TANU, called for our youth of the TYL to register their names to establish a new Army to replace the old one that was broken up. I am glad and proud to report to this holy council that a total of 77 men and 6 women from our region have entered the army. Sir Chairman and this holy council, you will see that the number of youth that joined the army is very small. This stems from the total spaces we were allocated by our holy government. It should not be forgotten that others of our youth we have sent to the Army to Build the Nation.[104]

After the mutiny, the JKT absorbed some of the martial ambitions of the TYL and developed in conjunction with the new army, offering both a fount of new recruits and a model for a new nationalist army.[105] With the urgent priority to rebuild the army, it took almost a year to put the JKT plan into motion on a countrywide scale. In 1964 the JKT developed in discrete limited operations, establishing strategically placed villages and camps in preparation for a wider expansion. An inaugural group of 511 young people marched from Dar es Salaam to Ruvu, in a manner reminiscent of the *ekyaro*, or ritual walk of Nyerere's home culture, to begin their training in April 1964. A second group of 500 drilled at Mugulani Camp in Dar es Salaam, both groups being in preparation for a competitive selection for military careers.[106] The expansion of the initial pilot projects began with two 300-member "coys" named Operation 700 and *Maendeleo* (Development) that were mobilized rapidly in part so they could be displayed on Republic Day celebrations in early December.[107] Regional commissioners visiting the capital toured the JKT training farm at Ruvu.[108]

As a last stage in the training of the new "people's" army, 400 of the new soldiers were sent to the Ruvu Training Center for a three-week course named "Operation Kujenga" (Operation to build). The stated intention of the course was "to train and inspire the Soldiers with the spirit of brotherhood building and working for the nation and loyalty." The syllabus for the soldiers featured two main activities: "a) participating in developing Ruvu; b) Political indoctrination." The content of the Ruvu training course had been developed in a brainstorming session on July 30, 1964, in the midst of the planning and envisioning of the new military to replace the Nigerian troops on loan in the wake of the mutiny.[109] The Ruvu center was preparatory for the later training of four thousand elite reservists to be "highly trained activists to meet special emergencies." The goal of the program, expressed in an editorial in the *Nationalist* newspaper, echoed longstanding TYL desires: "to enable TANU Youth League members to accept their full responsibility for implementing program of the organization and equip themselves in fullest sense to face whatever challenges they may have to meet wherever they happen to be stationed."[110]

With its homegrown authenticity, the JKT provided a fundamental ethic for the new army under Brigadier Sarakikya. The structure of the JKT was modeled in part after European military traditions, but its roots in the TYL and traditions of youthful military service in age-sets became the core ethic for a loyal new military. This was a significant rupture from the ambiguous neutrality that was the goal of the former Tanganyika Rifles. The gerontocratic ethic, although some distance removed from the pragmatic organization of the military, replaced the royalist ethic that had guided the vaunted "neutrality" of what had once been tellingly named the King's African Rifles. The Tanganyikan approach combined the communist ideal of a people's defense force with the ethic and authority structure of rural African age structures, which had been sovereign in precolonial times and whose habits were still inscribed in everyday life. The JKT's goal of "discipline" was an essential component of its broader ethical ambitions. Bringing its broad developmentalist urge to improve the lives of citizens through civil works, the JKT became the moral foundation for the narrower tasks of military deployment.[111]

Under the direction of the office of Second Vice President Kawawa, these first companies were stationed in Nachingwea, Kawawa's own ministerial district in the south. It was twelve miles west of an army base, but more important, not far north of the Mozambique border. The JKT was one of a series of policies intended to settle and militarize the border regions: the Congolese border in the west, and especially the southern border where Tanganyika's open support of the Mozambican liberation movement, FRELIMO, had made it a low-intensity war zone with regular Portuguese incursions into Tanganyikan territory.[112] At the Nachingwea site the vice president ordered the JKT to clear land and start farming. "By this the first National Service Regional Unit will be established," he said.[113]

The controlling bureaucratic influence of Rashidi Kawawa in every state policy is hard to overstate, especially given the understated manner with which he administered vast transformations in the structure and methods of government in the early years of independence. This humble éminence grise was the key executive for almost all the administrative innovations of the decade. Indeed, the goal of all the discipline exerted upon the young recruits aimed largely to induce in them the simple administrative competence exhibited by this most loyal aide to President Nyerere. He was the model citizen par excellence. As the nationalist ideology urged the government toward ever greater influence over all social institutions, the ritual of the youth camp was drawn into the second vice president's purview (the first vice president, after the union with Zanzibar, was the Zanzibari president ex officio). Like village subchiefs of former times, he represented on a national level the ideals of bureaucratic office; the president, like a chief, was an office, not a personality. It was easy, on the one hand, to personalize the presidency in the outsized public persona of Nyerere representing the nation to a bigger world. Kawawa, on the other hand, perfected the persona of a domestic bureaucrat, enfolding the intense trust that Nyerere had in him into the simple authority of office.

The second vice president's office exemplified the presidential delegation of power, modeling both efficacy and the limits of ministerial authority. Through the JKT, with Kawawa as its paramount authority, the ethic of delegated ministerial authority could be carried down to young people at the beginning of their lives as citizens. JKT leaders were sought from existing TYL structures; the police conducted four-month leadership courses for proven and healthy TYL leaders.[114] The JKT thus provided a proving ground for future TANU leaders.[115] JKT leaders using the channels of the Mtwara Police called for recruits from the neighboring coastal region, copying the message to the Ministries of Defence and Youth: "25 boys and 10 girls are needed from each of your districts to join the Jeshi la Ujenzi wa Taifa (National Service). They should be citizens of Tanzania and unmarried. They should be upstanding members of TANU and TYL of appropriate age."[116]

A JKT camp was divided into four sections: the Nyerere Brigade, the Karume Brigade, the Kawawa Brigade, and the Kambona Brigade.[117] The recruits' daily tasks implicated them in the personalized body of a civil nation. Not only did the multiplicity of these political figures offer a chart of ministerial bureaucracy, but the youth became the agents of these nationalist icons and their ministerial goals for the country. They emulated Kawawa, who himself sweated through JKT training as if he were none other than an enthusiastic villager. The JKT companies were at once the completion of the ministerial order down to the most isolated parts of the country and the earliest stages of citizenship for young people reaching the age of majority. They also represented the bureaucratization of a culturally rooted moral order with ministers playing the role formerly held by village elders. In a speech at his former teaching post at St. Francis Secondary School in Pugu, Nyerere told the assembled students, "A boy who has good manners and respect brings praise to his parents, and that applies too to the nation." The newspaper reported the speech under the headline "Nation Your Parent."[118] In these familial terms, ideas about "discipline" merged with the ethics of life in the nation.

With the maturation of the JKT, the postcolonial state provided itself with a means to socialize youth into a nationalism that found legitimacy both in the appropriation of an internationally recognizable form of National Youth Service and in a locally familiar form as the Jeshi la Kujenga Taifa, imbuing the new government with a sense of the age structures perceived by many as inherent to the natural order of things. The new institution provided a civil counterpart to the party's Youth League, directing the TYL's desired participation in security activities toward a culturally relevant and politically manageable bureaucratic entity. "The National Service trained our youth in the direction this country was going," explained the former JKT director Lawrence Gama.[119] The JKT also fundamentally reshaped the government's relation to the military, replacing the technocratic alienation of the army from local social structures with a process that went beyond politicization and entered the realm of enculturation.

Nyerere routinely referenced his rural upbringing in his speeches and discourse throughout his career, and famously used the Kizanaki verb *kung'atuka* to refer to his retirement in 1985 from the office of the presidency. The term referred to the act of an elder generation ceding authority to a younger age-set. He also met regularly with friends and elders from the village before and after independence and his tenure as president. He had cultivated the rural political imaginary of his upbringing in his theory and practice of statesmanship, opening national policy to practices rooted in local memory and perception. The TYL's further role in reforming the military and founding the National Youth Service (JKT) extended age structures into a cultural, rather than racial, mode of African governance. As a training ground for future soldiers, civil servants, and politicians, the JKT served as the moral core of government.

Part 3
External Sovereignty

8

A Realist Foreign Policy

Among TANU's leaders, a regional vision to safeguard nationalist politics took form even before independence. Nyerere and his colleagues were aware of the internal and external weaknesses of the new state they governed, and they charted a realist course within these limits. Tanganyika's limited military and economic resources, its nonexistent diplomatic corps, and its newly minted statehood made any independent policy goal somewhat improbable, and its leaders were certainly overly optimistic in many regards. Nevertheless, their ideals were meant to stabilize the TANU government and to broadcast its influence abroad, both of which were fundamentally realist policy goals. Their strategy accords with current conceptions of realism that take into account the "multitiered nature of threat assessment."[1] Rashidi Kawawa recalled an international strategy that was a necessary complement to TANU's domestic goals.

> Our commitment was to the liberation of Africa. . . . This was the commitment of all our citizens. TANU educated all our citizens to make a small contribution to help [neighboring minority-ruled countries]. . . . If we had left them it would have taken a long time for them to liberate themselves, and our independence would not have been complete. . . . The shame of being ruled was shared by all of us . . . so it was necessary to help them to get complete independence.[2]

Tanganyika's early approach sought to use ideological power in concert with its limited diplomatic force in the interest of sovereign autonomy. After the founding of the TPDF in 1964 and the arrival of military aid from China, the newly renamed Tanzania began to exercise significant military force through the liberation movements it supported. However, until the first incursions into Mozambique in September 1964, its influence existed almost entirely in its fluent engagement of diplomatic discourse. The position taken by TANU was that the nation would not be truly free unless neighboring countries were also free, and that a bigger political unit would wield more clout in the international realm. While ideological in its analysis of global political dynamics, it was no less realist in its orientation than the ideologically driven policies of the superpowers. A labor leader and party activist recalled the down-home imagery that communicated this policy at TANU's ideological training center, Kivukoni College: "If you have a farm, and your are guarding against birds; if you don't watch the field of your neighbor . . . then they will come to your farm as well. So we thought that if the belt [of independence] gets closer to the enemies, and many nations get independence, then even Tanzania's independence would be peaceful. So we were helping them *kwa hali na mali.*"[3]

With few exceptions, the details of this early period of Tanganyika's foreign policy have not been documented by scholars.[4] Yet the broad outline of what became Tanzanian foreign policy was already formulated by TANU a year before independence. As elaborated by Oscar Kambona, it consisted of "(1) Socialism and progressive reforms at home; (2) Pan-Africanism and Federation within Africa; and (3) Neutralism, with reliance on the United Nations in the world at large."[5] With the addition of support for southern African liberation movements, the period set a trajectory that changed little for nearly three decades.[6] As one of the country's first diplomats explained, "We were preparing for a fight that might last a hundred years."[7] Nyerere advocated on behalf of African nationalist movements within the international legal framework organized around the United Nations, which he felt was key to peace in global politics. Addressing the United Nations just days after Tanganyika's independence in 1961, Nyerere expressed his pleasure in accepting "the right to join in the search for greater understanding and greater harmony between the peoples of the world," and pledged to "do what little we can to enhance the status of this Organization."[8]

Nyerere's personal idealism, and the idealism latent in the rhetoric of Pan-Africanism and liberation, easily masks the fundamental realism of his thinking and Tanganyikan policy.[9] Nyerere believed both regional unification and southern African liberation were necessary to ensure peace and security within Tanganyika and enhance its influence in the international system, buttressing the internal and external pillars of sovereignty. With international clout, Tanganyika could more effectively seek the foreign aid necessary for its internal development and the diplomatic support for the regional strategy that Tanganyikan leaders saw as crucial to the country's security. Nyerere pursued these policies with a tactical and effective prudence that underscored his realist assessment of both the geostrategic environment and Tanganyika's place within it.

Liberation in Southern Africa

While still at Edinburgh University in Scotland in the early 1950s, Nyerere wrote a pamphlet titled "The Race Problem in East Africa." The essay argued that continued racial discrimination would bring traumatic violence in Africa on the order of the French Revolution. He framed an argument about racial relations in Tanganyika within a broader canvas of "East and South Africa."[10] This regional context took on a more distinctly political form in the Pan-African Freedom Movement of East and Central Africa, or PAFMECA, formed on September 17, 1958, as one of Nyerere's initiatives and funded mostly by TANU.[11] Its first meeting took place in Mwanza on the heels of massive protests against the colonial state and subsequent government suppression, when independence was still seen as being five to ten years off.[12] Its aim was to initiate "positive action" toward the liberation of white-dominated territories of southern Africa. In addition to diplomatic efforts, it would also "organize the masses into militant mass movements under dynamic leadership."[13] Although it did not become an organizational center for militant movements, PAFMECA began to articulate the strategy that was later taken up by the Organization of African Unity's Liberation Committee, established in 1963 in Dar es Salaam in recognition of Tanganyika's leadership.[14] Among the first policies PAFMECA advocated was the boycott of South African goods, spearheading what became a thirty-year campaign for international economic pressure on the apartheid system.[15]

South Africa

Nyerere, emerging as a leader of an international effort, was the keynote speaker at a London meeting of South African exiles and other supporters initiating an economic boycott in protest of apartheid in South Africa in June 1959.[16] As prime minister of a self-governing Tanganyika in 1960, Nyerere had access to the threat of legislation to galvanize a consumer boycott, with the hope that importers would join in as well. Answering a question about the effect of the boycott on the economy, Nyerere took a tone of moral outrage that he hoped consumers, importers, and unions alike would internalize and believe. "If you think it is a serious moral matter, you have to be willing to pay the price."[17] The boycott was exemplary of Nyerere's sense of mass mobilization. It was not a question of economic force. Even a full boycott of South African goods would cause little pain in Tanganyika and bring little pressure on the apartheid state. South African imports represented only 2 percent of Tanganyika's total imports, and only 4 percent of Tanganyika's exports.[18] Rather, the boycott was meant to mobilize moral indignation through participation and so encourage bigger economies to join in. His position on the issue cost him nothing politically but planted a seed for legitimizing future sacrifices. Indeed, by 1963, British High Commissioner Miles commented that the self-sacrifice of Tanganyika's boycott put pressure on Britain to put actions behind their words: "Britain's distinction between the arms she supplies to South Africa for defensive purposes and those which could be used to enforce apartheid, cuts no ice with them at all." Tanganyika was now "in a position to point to Britain's vast and lucrative trade with, and investment in, South Africa, and to contrast this with our public utterances on apartheid."[19]

In the meantime, Tanganyika continued to cultivate an institutional base to direct a concerted strategy for southern Africa while refugees from political repression flowed into the country. Nelson Mandela was one; he came in 1962 seeking support for his African National Congress (ANC) and recalled meeting Nyerere, who recommended that armed struggle be postponed until the South African militant movements could be united.[20] In January 1961 the South African United Front settled into an office in Dar es Salaam to be shared with the one-person staff of PAFMECA. Heading the office was James Hadebe, a former school principal and official in the South African ANC. Part of his task, at TANU's behest, was to limit the continued influx of refugees into Tanganyika that party leaders were finding burdensome to manage.[21] The partnership moved toward a policy of targeted immigration, recruiting skilled South Africans to work in Tanganyika. TANU also helped funnel South African dissidents to London and elsewhere.[22] Top students received university education abroad, often in communist countries, while others went for shorter leadership courses and military training.[23]

As independence approached, Nyerere established opposition to apartheid rule as a nation-defining value. "To be successful . . . in our country, we must therefore make our detestation of the South African system apparent in every action," Nyerere exhorted at a meeting of Commonwealth prime ministers in March 1961.[24] Nyerere insisted that Tanganyika would withdraw from the Commonwealth if South Africa were admitted. "To vote South Africa in is to vote us out." He said that South Africa's admission would push Africans toward communist supporters of the liberation movement.[25] The conference duly rejected South Africa's application. The successful outcome made it appear that Nyerere's stand was decisive, and it demonstrated his allegiance to principle. His international stature enhanced, he began to lobby in foreign capitals for support of liberation policies, paying a visit to Accra and Lagos in April 1961 to discuss these issues with Kwame Nkrumah and others.[26] He convinced Nkrumah to allow the Pan-African Cooperative Alliance, which had hitherto only met in West Africa, to meet in Dar es Salaam in 1962.[27] The South African ANC used the occasion to meet in Dar es Salaam in August 1962, establishing Tanganyika as a base of operations and quickly founding training facilities for young militants.[28] Members of numerous liberation movements from across southern Africa were invited to open offices in Dar es Salaam and begin training in secret camps. Nyerere's policies had created a recognizable sovereign identity for Tanganyika on the global stage, symbolizing the hopes for independence and democracy in southern Africa.[29]

Mozambique

PAFMECA began to implement the military strategy envisioned in its initial meetings by supplying Mozambican liberation movements with weapons. Soon after the onset of responsible self-government on May 1, 1961, the Tanganyikan government began threatening military action against Portuguese colonialism.[30] This orientation also drew Dar es Salaam authorities deeper into Mozambican politics, where they quickly marginalized the Russian-trained Adelino Gwambe.[31] The twenty-one-year-old Gwambe represented the União Democrática Nacional de Moçambique (UDENAMO), but he did not have strong support in Mozambique, instead relying on outside help funneled through Tanganyika from the Soviet Union and on favor from Nkrumah for recruiting bilingual Africans on behalf of the Ghanaian government.[32]

TANU sought to cultivate a Mozambique African National Union (MANU) under Tanganyikan leadership reporting to Oscar Kambona.[33] By January 1962 MANU leaders credibly reported "7–8 offices in Tanganyika, with approximately 2,000 members in Tanganyika and 700 in Mozambique."[34] MANU's strongest support came from Makonde people in northern Mozambique, who had strong cultural ties to southern Tanganyika. Seeking support from Kazumu Banda in Nyasaland (Malawi), one MANU member probably exaggerated significantly when he estimated 2,560 members within Mozambique, adding "I have the support of all the African people from north of Mozambique from Zumbo to Queinga."[35] MANU's leadership averred that support was weak among Makonde elders along the border where the Portuguese maintained spies in Tanganyika and kidnapped suspected militants to repatriate them.[36] Reluctant to antagonize the Portuguese government, Makonde elders eventually expelled MANU leaders, refusing likewise to cooperate with the conspiratorial Gwambe and UDENAMO.[37]

To counter the phlegmatic progress of the Mozambique movement, Nyerere began working with Eduardo Mondlane, a like-minded Mozambican scholar based at Syracuse University, to establish a new party, the Frente de Liberação de Moçambique, or FRELIMO, to unite these fractious organizations and lead the liberation struggle there.[38] Mondlane, a former UN diplomat who had strong contacts in the US State Department, had toured Mozambique in 1961, and UDENAMO had unsuccessfully tried to recruit him.[39] Mondlane preferred to work with Nyerere if he could be provided with a house and living stipend.[40] Christopher Ngaiza, stationed at the United Nations, recalled Nyerere's entreaty to Mondlane in December 1961.

> Our independence won't be complete if Mozambique is not free. . . . I can't match the salary you are now getting as a professor. But I can give you these things: I will give you a house, for free (and indeed they went to prepare it), I can give you an allowance (I don't recall how much, but it was basic), and the leadership in educating your people, so that Tanganyika can be like a springboard to penetrate [Mozambique], and we'll help you. But beyond that we won't go any further.[41]

Under tight secrecy, with Mondlane one of only three people within his organization knowledgeable about the initial preparations, FRELIMO set up camps in southern Tanganyika along the Mozambique border to train refugees in sabotage and guerrilla warfare under the tutelage of Tunisian instructors.[42] With US funding, Mondlane's American wife set up a school for refugees that provided nonpolitical education to Mozambican refugees, providing the literacy skills necessary for indoctrination and military training and acting as a conduit to fund military activities.[43] Using Tanganyikan contacts, FRELIMO began organizing tactical instruction abroad in January 1963, flying militants to Algeria for training.[44] In subsequent years, Algeria became a strong supporter of the liberation struggle, offering weapons and training conducted through Tanzania.[45]

Northern and Southern Rhodesia (Zambia and Zimbabwe)

Conflict with Mozambique was only the most immediate facet of a wider confrontation with South Africa's strategy of buttressing white-minority regimes to its north as a response to the threat of African independence. The Portuguese colonies, together with Southwest Africa (Namibia) and Roy Welensky's nascent Central African Federation of Northern and Southern Rhodesia, comprised a "cordon sanitaire" blocking action against South Africa from majority-ruled states.[46] As with the South African strategy, the Tanganyikan government moved deliberately from symbolic measures toward more concrete actions, coordinating and provisioning the militant movements regionally while advocating for them abroad.[47]

In February 1962 an expanded version of PAFMECA had been founded in Addis Ababa, the Pan-African Freedom Movement of East, Central, and Southern Africa (PAFMECSA). The new organization represented an effort to convert the movement-based PAFMECA, founded under colonial rule, into an organization of sovereign governments in support of liberation movements in white-ruled areas of southern Africa.[48] With independence, countries like Tanganyika, Algeria, and Guinea could acquire weapons and financial support for the liberation movements, and thereby put some teeth into threats of armed resistance, increasing the attractiveness of moderate approaches in negotiation. In September PAFMECSA made its first weapons shipments into central Africa. The leader of the Zimbabwean African People's Union (ZAPU), Joshua Nkomo, boarded an Air France flight in Cairo for Dar es Salaam with two dozen assault rifles in his checked luggage and "ammunition and grenades—unprimed, I checked that—as hand baggage."[49] Tanganyika's minister for local government, Job Lusinde, made arrangements to transport the materiel through Northern Rhodesia with Kaunda's assistance, and on into Southern Rhodesia.

Militancy was integral to Nyerere's broader strategy and not just a rhetorical co-optation of antiwhite sentiment. Tanganyika's geopolitical tactic sought to outflank a white-dominated Central African Federation that would block Tanganyikan influence in southern Africa. Nyerere judged "that Northern Rhodesia was the key to the situation," and prepared a push in support of Kaunda for early independence there. Nyerere's private goal was simply to assure that in subsequent elections an African majority would emerge even if some gerrymandering were necessary. "The objective was so desirable," the British high commissioner reported, "that [Nyerere] would prefer all means to be examined rather than see the situation in Northern Rhodesia boil up to an explosion."[50] Tanganyika made the most of its membership on a UN subcommittee, pressing for a series of resolutions urging Britain to call a constitutional conference in Southern Rhodesia.[51] Welensky wanted to isolate East Africa by connecting Congo's Katanganese separatists more closely to the Central African Federation.[52] Nyerere sensed that Northern Rhodesia was a realistic short-term goal that would prevent an outbreak of violence, push white domination farther south, and facilitate further inroads into Mozambique, Angola, and Southern Rhodesia. Each territory represented a small step toward the isolation of South Africa.

Tanganyikan intelligence suggested that Welensky was supporting the Northern Rhodesian ANC party and its erratic candidate Harry Nkumbula in the upcoming elections, funding them with help from Katanganese separatist leader Moïse Tshombe, who was also arranging for military training and for Nkumbula's party members.[53] Welensky hoped that an alliance with a friendly Nkumbula would divide African votes and allow continued European domination even if whites lost legislative control in the territory.[54] With Tshombe's bond to foreign mining firms and his interest in capturing the entire copper belt, such an alliance would seal off southern Africa and set back the liberation movement indefinitely.[55] As anxious as the Tanganyikans were to prevent this, they also understood that any actual violence in Northern Rhodesia would favor Welensky and weaken Britain's moderating influence. Kaunda's participation in racially imbalanced elections mirrored

TANU's late colonial strategy that had brought about its peaceful ascent to legislative power.[56] Tanganyika's threats were calibrated to sway the elections and subsequent constitutional negotiations, but not instigate immediate violence as in Mozambique. But if Welensky's strategy proved victorious, then the depressing prospect of widespread violent conflict would become a necessity, and the threats would not be empty ones.[57] In the end, Tanganyika's support contributed to the territorial dominance of Kaunda's United National Independence Party (UNIP) in Northern Rhodesia. UNIP's popularity eventually pulled even Nkumbula's ANC into a coalition. Nkumbula's "breach of faith" greatly disappointed Welensky, who fruitlessly set about to destroy him by supporting an oppositional faction within the ANC.[58]

With peaceful progress in Northern Rhodesia, Tanganyika's representative at the United Nations, Dr. Vedastus Kyaruzi, quietly lobbied Britain for positive action in Southern Rhodesia. Arguing that current policies of the Southern Rhodesian government would leave long-lasting emotional scars, he suggested that the Southern Rhodesian prime minister, Sir Edgar Whitehead, should renew contact with ZAPU leader Joshua Nkomo, "if only over a cup of tea."[59] Nkomo articulated the general Tanganyikan strategy of balancing imminent violence against British arbitration, but he refused to participate in an election with a second-class African franchise.[60] Tanganyika's Rhodesia strategy aimed to pave the way for British action that would ensure progress toward majority rule in both territories, putting pressure on Southern Rhodesia by means of a successful strategy for Northern Rhodesia.[61] Continual lobbying of the British government eventually brought about a declaration that Northern Rhodesia had the right to opt out of Welensky's federation. Britain's position solidified the autonomy of Kaunda's government, which finally ruled independent Zambia upon the dissolution of the Central African Federation on New Year's Day 1964.

As Welensky began to accept the inevitability of African government in Northern Rhodesia, Southern Rhodesia became the white redoubt with an increasingly reactionary settler community preparing to capture power in the December 1962 elections. Despite Edgar Whitehead's attempts to placate white extremists by suppressing black political activism, the extremist Rhodesian Front won the election with Winston Field's promise to declare independence if Britain continued to urge compromise with African nationalists. ZAPU was banned and Joshua Nkomo was placed under house arrest. Meeting with political activists, Nkomo concluded "that the time for peaceful protest was over, and we must get ready to fight."[62]

While the humble saber rattling of a nearly unarmed former colony was merely tactical at this point, with no military action envisioned, the Tanganyikan government continued its propaganda campaign by means of radio broadcasts. TBC began broadcasting tapes of Kaunda's speeches at

10:00 p.m., preempting domestic programming. In November, following the banning of ZAPU, TBC began political broadcasts aimed at Southern Rhodesia, granting Nkomo's then colleague Ndabaningi Sithole a prime slot, where he warned about the possibility of violence, in line with Tanganyika's strategy of balancing threats with a willingness to compromise. "In Algeria guns and police were used but they failed," Sithole averred; "and in Zimbabwe and Zambia guns and police are used, but they will fail and fail lamentably."[63] Instead, ZAPU's TBC broadcasts urged people to boycott the upcoming elections in Southern Rhodesia, condemning Welensky and outlining his ties to South Africa, Mozambique, and Katanga.

For its part, the Tanganyikan government urged moderation to those who pushed for immediate military action. Ignoring Nkomo's insistence that Southern Rhodesia's settler establishment was implacable, Nyerere insisted that British pressure could bring about a breakthrough in negotiations with Southern Rhodesia. In a letter to the British prime minister, Nyerere suggested that Britain had the right to quash a Rhodesian settler revolt, just as it had suppressed the Mau Mau revolt in Kenya.[64] Rashidi Kawawa spoke in Parliament to moderate Tanganyika's position in the face of more militant views in TANU, saying that a threat to withdraw from the Commonwealth and commit to a military offensive was premature without an international African consensus and "while all doors are not yet closed." He expressed confidence in a UN delegation to London that included a Tanganyikan representative and reiterated his position that "our objective at the moment should be to help our brothers achieve their independence without bloodshed."[65]

TANU's commitment to negotiation reflected a widening divide between Nyerere's incrementalism and Nkomo's militancy. In July 1963 Nkomo broke with the ZAPU leadership after Nyerere opposed his idea of a "government in exile," and ZAPU leaders allied with Sithole lost faith in Nkomo's "poor management of the party."[66] Nyerere told Nkomo to return home to Salisbury, despite the threat of arrest, to organize his grass roots as his "efforts to organize the armed struggle from Dar es Salaam were not practical."[67] Kambona felt much the same, considering Ndabaningi Sithole to have shown the requisite political courage by going back to Rhodesia knowing that he and his allies would be immediately arrested. Moving to Highland, Rhodesia, upon their release, they quietly founded the Zimbabwe African National Union on August 8, excluding Nkomo and signaling their alliance with TANU. Nkomo meanwhile called a ZAPU meeting to rally his supporters in Salisbury on August 10.[68] The split aggravated divisions in Dar es Salaam, and on August 12 Kambona sent police to close down the ZAPU offices in the city, saying they would stay locked until "things had cooled down." ZAPU representatives came to shore up relations in Dar es Salaam later that month, and offices for both organizations soon reopened.[69]

The OAU Liberation Committee

Nyerere's efforts on behalf of Mozambique and the Rhodesias stemmed from a very real belief not only in the ideals of Pan-Africanism but also in its tactical utility. Nyerere believed that Tanganyika would never be fully sovereign or safe unless the whole of Africa were under majority rule. This required fundamental changes to the geostrategic map of southern Africa. When Kaunda came to visit in September 1963, they had begun to envision a railroad linking Zambia to Dar es Salaam, thereby reducing central Africa's dependence on the transport systems of South Africa and the Portuguese colonies.[70]

Because of its diplomatic experience and militant commitment, Dar es Salaam was chosen as the headquarters for the Liberation Committee, or "Committee of Nine," created at the second meeting of the OAU in 1963 to organize a Pan-African effort on behalf of territories still under minority or colonial rule.[71] The committee moved into repurposed offices of the now defunct PAFMECSA.[72] Kambona was unanimously elected to chair the committee, and a number of countries pledged financial support, from Nigeria's leading pledge of £100,000 to Uganda's more humble offering of £10,000.[73] Kambona's financial management left much to be desired, and the Liberation Committee was not particularly effective until after his departure, but TPDF efforts to secure the southern border and supply weapons to the liberation armies sharpened strategies that continued to grow in their impact.[74]

The establishment of the Liberation Committee brought the leaders of most of the militant movements to Dar es Salaam, much to the chagrin of Kwame Nkrumah, who had held their loyalties in Accra. A British diplomat in Dar es Salaam, who had formerly been posted in Accra, reported that Nkrumah actively sought to subvert East African federation and the Liberation Committee.[75] By the end of the year, Nyerere turned a biting speech toward Nkrumah's opposition to regional federation and "the curious argument that the continued balkanization of East Africa will somehow help African Unity."[76] Nyerere's annoyance with Nkrumah stemmed from a growing frustration shared by many African leaders with the latter's obstructionism. Nkrumah had long advocated for the creation of a continental African government, and continued pushing this idea long after most of his fellow heads of state had abandoned the idea as impractical.[77] Nyerere repeatedly emphasized that he agreed with Nkrumah's ostensible goal of a unitary African government, but he argued that such unity had to be built in practice. One could not simply will an African government into existence with the godlike pronouncement "Let there be unity."[78]

Figure 8.1. President Julius Nyerere of Tanzania with President Kwame Nkrumah of Ghana during the Organization of African Union (OAU) Heads of Government Meeting held in Accra in 1965. © Tanzania Information Services (MAELEZO).

Nyerere supported the limited goals of the OAU, as envisioned in Addis Ababa in May 1963. He continually encouraged multilateral attempts at broader cooperation, including regional federations. Nyerere did not regard regional groupings as ideal arrangements, but rather as appropriate stepping-stones on the way to continental unity. Nkrumah feared that regional federations would derail momentum for continental union. But his opposition to East African federation struck Nyerere as an attempt "to rationalize absurdity."[79] In the end, the feud that developed between Nyerere and Nkrumah was not particularly ideological, but personal.[80] Although Nkrumah proclaimed continental unity, in Nyerere's view he had become a source of "divisive propaganda"—and possibly worse as it was widely suspected that he had a hand in the assassination of Sylvanus Olympio of Togo in January 1963.[81] Out of respect for Nkrumah's accomplishments and vision, Nyerere avoided naming him publicly, but it is clear that by May he voiced the feelings of many when he told his fellow heads of state in Addis Ababa, "None of us is prepared in the name of unity to invite a Napoleon to come and bring about unity by conquest."[82]

East African Federation

The impressive scope of the Liberation Committee's mandate grew out of Tanganyika's ambitious leadership toward the creation of a large, militant, and independent African state in East Africa. The committee had begun working toward this vision even before independence. A PAFMECA map from 1960 showed the southern border of an East African Federation along the Lúrio River in Mozambique, south of Lake Nyasa.[83] PAFMECA's preindependence vision was of a united East Africa stretching from Somalia, Ethiopia, and the Sudan borders in the north to the southern end of Lake Nyasa in the south, from Zanzibar in the east to Northern Rhodesia in the west. It is doubtful whether Nyerere's ambitions were as extensive.[84]

As Nyerere worked toward independence for Tanganyika, he began consulting with leaders in other territories about the possibility of bringing a unified East Africa to independence as a single nation. Colonial administrators had promoted territorial integration for almost forty years as a commonsense administrative structure for East Africa.[85] In the 1950s David Stirling planted the seed of what became Welensky's Central African Federation, with the hope that it would also incorporate British East Africa in a sprawling federation.[86] In the late 1950s Nyerere blamed British colonial "*divide et impera*" for East African divisions, but his rhetoric was somewhat duplicitous. After all, the opponents of federation had from the beginning been East African residents: Buganda monarchists, Kenyan leftists, and Dar es Salaam manufacturers fearing competition.[87]

The Kenyan politician Achieng Oneko, who was imprisoned with nationalist icon Jomo Kenyatta in the 1950s, recalled Nyerere visiting them during Rawson Macharia's trial in Kitale in 1959 and mentioning his willingness to delay Tanganyika's independence in order for East Africa to become independent as a single unit.[88] In a paper for the Conference of Independent African States in June 1960, which he later presented for approval at the third annual meeting of PAFMECA, Nyerere argued forcefully for preindependence federation. He understood, and was very explicit in emphasizing, that "Federation after complete independence means the surrender of sovereignty."[89] Pointing out that such surrender would be very difficult for new national leaders, he cited Buganda secessionism in Uganda as an example of the divisive effect of a colonial territory advocating for independence with the idea of trying "to put it together later." He suggested instead that as soon as each country had achieved responsible self-government, it could then vote itself into a federation prior to being accorded independence. He cited precedent in the Horn of Africa where the British hastened independence for Somaliland so that it could become independent as a single entity with the UN trusteeship territory of Somalia.

On a more garrulous note, Nyerere pointed out that his East African federation policy was meant to undermine Welensky's Central African Federation and its implications for southern Africa: "There is not the slightest doubt in my mind that a popular Federation cannot but hasten the collapse of an unpopular Federation next door."[90] Marion Chesham, a member of the Tanganyika National Assembly and strong TANU supporter, doubted Kenyan and Ugandan commitment to federation and urged federation with Northern Rhodesia and Nyasaland. She felt that many Asians and Europeans were ready to support a move to create "a bulwark of strength and peace in the trouble that may lie ahead" if Welensky should succeed in allying with Katanga.[91]

However, Nyerere's proposals for preindependence federation were opposed by many rank-and-file members of TANU who flooded his office with telegrams urging independence sooner rather than later. The combative Christopher Tumbo announced that "TANU is misleading us."[92] Specifically, Tumbo and many in the labor movement believed that Nyerere's federation plan would simply perpetuate the British East African High Commission in Nairobi, which they saw as favoring Kenya over other constituent states.[93] With both Uganda and Kenya struggling with internal politics just to establish stable governments, Nyerere found little practical success toward federation, even as both countries voiced their support.[94] Rumors in Dar es Salaam suggested that Luo leftist Oginga Odinga accused Nyerere and Mboya of being American stooges engaged in "a plot to frustrate African nationalism in Kenya by submerging it in a federation."[95] In December 1960 an American diplomat relayed Nyerere's comments on the confused state of affairs: "Oginga Odinga is flat out against it; Gichiru is shy; Nyerere says 'Tom (Mboya) is for it, unless he is double-crossing me.' The Zanzibaris claim they will talk about it after their own independence."[96]

As a practical matter, Nyerere asserted that the "key to Federation is Kenya; once Kenya agrees, Uganda, possibly others will follow." Privately Nyerere intimated that he would promote Jomo Kenyatta to lead an East African federation if he would commit to it.[97] Ideally he hoped Kenyatta could commit to the plan after the February 1961 elections, and thus negotiate the union before Tanganyika's independence. But in the absence of Kenyatta's cooperation, Nyerere was working on a "much less satisfactory" alternative plan.[98]

The alternative plan was a more scattershot approach of pulling smaller neighboring states into a federation with Tanganyika, building up a set of legal and political precedents that would attract the bigger countries to join in the future.[99] In January 1961, in the absence of a firm commitment from Kenyatta or Obote, Nyerere began floating the idea of what he called a "pilot project" for federating Tanganyika with the Belgian-governed trust territory of Ruanda-Urundi.[100] The traditional kings of both territories expressed support for Nyerere's plan.[101] Beyond the geostrategic concerns of federation and Pan-Africanism, two other pressures spurred Nyerere's push for federation: refugee flows and ethnic separatist movements. These two related trends signaled the need for a stronger African hand to manage regional politics and reflected Nyerere's prescient fears that divided polities were vulnerable to outside manipulation.

Ethnic violence tended to create refugees and destabilize the peripheral areas that were already the most difficult to govern effectively. While the numbers of Ruanda-Urundi refugees in Tanganyika remained small compared to those fleeing to other neighboring countries, they still bore the threat of spreading violence.[102] Violence in Ruanda-Urundi had pushed out a hundred thousand Tutsis, including some who entered Tanganyika.[103] Cross-border ethnic loyalties threatened the notional integrity of colonial boundaries. Uganda faced secessionist Buganda, which balked at broader federation for fear of losing clout if the kingdom were subsumed within ever-larger political units.[104] In Tanganyika, Maasai representatives, under the young and inexperienced Chief Edward, were urged on by an ambitious American priest, Father Eugene Hillman, to organize an appeal to the UN Trusteeship Council for the creation of a Maasai state encompassing parts of both Tanganyika and Kenya. Nyerere was aware of the strong influence of Catholic priests in planting the seeds of recent ethnic division in Ruanda-Urundi and contended that likewise Father Hillman was the Maasai "Richelieu."[105]

Ethnicity-based movements ignored the broader Pan-African goals that sought to enhance African power on the world stage. They served as further proof of Nyerere's analysis that any orientation other than the voluntary creation of bigger units would lead to "balkanization," and a destructive cycle of defensive appeal to ethnic politics.[106] This dynamic, as events in the Congo had shown, was vulnerable to outside manipulation. Nyerere sent repeated cables to the UN Trusteeship Council arguing that the conflict in Ruanda-Urundi was a political one being misrepresented as primordial strife by Belgian administrators who sought to "repeat the old colonial routine of claiming their presence to be essential for the prevention of bloodshed between the tribes. . . . There is no rigid line of demarcation between Batutsi 'overlords' on the one hand and Bahutu 'serfs' on the other."[107] Nyerere's analysis was matched by US intelligence that noted "local Belgian involvement in stimulation and manipulation of certain latent inter-tribal animosities and ambitions for purpose of obscuring, confusing, and defeating strong and rapidly growing multi-tribal nationalism."[108]

Nyerere hoped that political support for the nationalist Union Nationale Rwandaise (UNAR) party, despite its alliance with the Tutsi royals, could guide Ruanda-Urundi politics away from ethnic animosity and toward nationalist liberation. He had previously criticized the Belgian government of "turning the Mwamis into puppets," but as independence approached, he hoped that the influence of a progressive and nationalist nobility would offer a path to stability. In the end, UNAR never exhibited a unifying potential; violence escalated and the trend in Ruanda-Urundi continued to veer toward social schism. Hutu spokesman Gregoire Kayibanda spouted ethnically divisive rhetoric aimed at mobilizing Hutu resentments and alienating Tutsis inclined to support a nonethnic nationalist government.[109] Kayibanda benefited from a continued Belgian presence that effectively weakened Tutsi elites and opened a path to Hutu postcolonial dominance.[110] The divisive policy succeeded in 1961, and UNAR boycotted the elections leading to an overwhelming victory by the Belgian-supported Parti du Mouvement de l'Emancipation Hutu under Kayibanda, whom the Belgians cast as "another Nyerere."[111]

After Tanganyikan independence, Nyerere's frustration was palpable in a speech for TANU's annual meeting in 1962. Referring to another flood of refugees, he told the delegates that African countries were doing their best to help them but that people were "obeying orders [from] foreigners who benefit when Africans take up the Panga (big knife) against fellow Africans." Lamenting the assassination of Prince Rwagasore in Urundi as a strike against nationalist progress, he drew a comparison with the Congo, telling a TANU meeting, "We should not be surprised if we have another Tshombe in Ruanda-Urundi."[112] In the meantime, Tutsi supporters of the former Rwandan king gathered in southern Uganda and began launching cross-border raids.[113] The Kayibanda government considered Tutsi support of federation as a plan to reestablish "the old Tanganyika-Rwanda-Burundi empire" and accused Tanganyika of harboring members of the "terrorist Inyenzi organization."[114]

In Uganda and Kenya, powerful political minorities concerned about losing their political influence continued to pull away from federation.[115] In anticipation of future cooperation, Nyerere also began unilaterally to initiate policy precedents that would favor future amalgamation. In late 1962 Tanganyika proposed a cooperative approach to external relations and defense with Uganda, sending two ministers to discuss the issue with Ugandan officials. The idea met with an initially favorable reaction in Uganda, and a public announcement of the plan was scheduled for February 1963 with a proposed joint ministry to be located in Arusha in northern Tanganyika. The heir to the old British High Commission in Nairobi, the East African Common Services Organisation (EASCO), was reborn as the weak and largely symbolic East African Community, which collapsed in the following decade, never having absorbed any of the sovereign powers of the individual states as Nyerere had envisioned.[116]

Despite a categorical joint statement in support of political federation by the three East African leaders in June 1963, Nyerere ultimately found little success in amalgamating the various East African territories even after independence.[117] TANU had supported independence activism in Zanzibar, especially that by the Afro-Shirazi Party, which became a close ally. The union with Zanzibar in 1964 represented a truncated federation that Nyerere promoted as a token step toward the bigger goal.[118] Never losing hope in the possibility of federation, Nyerere continued to prepare the ground for increased cooperation. But as these hopes waned, he also took pragmatic steps to gain national control over the economy, inaugurating a national currency in 1965 in a step that hindered, rather than aided, progress toward regional unity.[119]

Foreign Aid and Diplomacy

TANU's rise to power brought with it a delicate dance of administrative authority and diplomacy as the new Tanganyikan government sought to fulfill the goals it set for itself, fully aware that it had neither the administrative capacity nor the financial ability to do so.[120] Instead, Nyerere and his colleagues arranged foreign aid and technical expertise while constantly asserting their own freedom of decision. Initially dependent almost exclusively on Britain, TANU gradually broadened the scope of its diplomatic efforts so that its varied sources of aid reduced dependence and subservience to any one donor. Casting a wide net allowed it to find funding for its various activities, many of which were opposed by one or another of its benefactors. Balancing multilateral dependence with its independent efforts on behalf of liberation and federation, Nyerere and Tanganyika grew rapidly in prestige and influence on the international scene and with the United Nations, replacing what it lacked in hard power with the soft attributes of respect and intellectual influence.

Tanganyika's first soundings of development aid under a TANU government signaled Nyerere's commitment to Cold War neutrality. In May 1960, just after the start of responsible self-government, TANU women leaders, Bibi Titi Mohamed and Lucy Lameck, made an unpublicized visit to the Soviet Union and China, the first such visit by TANU representatives. Bibi Titi reinforced TANU's nonaligned position, telling the Swahili newspaper *Mwafrika* after the trip that "Tanganyikans are not Communists, but if Russia offers us education, we shall not hesitate to send our children. Tanganyika is greatly in need of technicians, agricultural experts, scientists and chemists."[121] Both women tried to hide the trip from Western diplomats, but Tanganyikan opposition politicians exposed them, publicizing a photo of the two women in a group with Mao Zedong.[122] The visit initiated a robust long-term relationship with China. Late in life, Bibi Titi, in her song of praise for her colleagues in the women's movement, celebrated her travels with Lameck, declaring, "We are the discoverers of China!"[123] The following year the Chinese press noted Tanganyika's achievement of responsible government as "an initial victory of the anti-colonialist struggle."[124] In 1962 China sent a cultural delegation, and then several Tanganyikan ministers traveled China in late 1963, making plans for a Dar es Salaam visit by Zhou Enlai in January 1964 and a reciprocal visit by Nyerere to Beijing in February.[125]

Cultivating communist support was intended to balance the reality of structural dependence on Western aid. Nyerere's British expatriate minister of finance, Sir Ernest Vasey, inquired in Washington in January 1961 about the possibility of the United States contributing fully funded agricultural extension offices that would function in a countrywide network. Vasey also expressed interest in ways to build up secondary schooling with the expectation that many British teachers would return home, and suggested that a highly regarded American university sponsor some secondary schools in Tanganyika to produce top-quality graduates.[126] Nyerere visited Germany the following month with Nsilo Swai, the minister of commerce and industry, both making a strong impression. "It came as a surprise, and a pleasant one," a British diplomat in Bonn reported, "that a near neighbor of the Congo Republic should appear to be in a very different state of peace and orderly development."[127] Nyerere pressed for West German aid for his new Three-Year Plan, made a strong case for German private investment in Tanganyika, and sought aid for agricultural processing industries. Such rural-oriented industries were part of a broader effort to restrain popular demands for expensive externally built projects and urban industry in favor of strategies to make rural life more economically productive.[128] In August Nyerere made similar entreaties in Washington, explaining that even with British assistance and the hope of German aid, he still faced a deficit of £14 million in his £24 million budget for economic development.[129]

As independence approached, one of the most troubling questions Tanganyika faced as a soon-to-be sovereign nation was its financial and technical dependence on its colonial ruler and its weakness in the nation-state system. Tanganyika's entire government bureaucracy relied on a coterie of British expatriate civil servants, and its budget was planned and subsidized through the Colonial Office in London. With a lack of personnel or funds for foreign embassies, Tanganyika depended on the British High Commissions for representation in most places.[130] The military, like many governmental departments, remained under British officers even though both countries shied away from the discomfiture of a formal military agreement between an administering power and a trust territory.[131] Nyerere understood the need for continuity and the invaluable role of the expatriates as well as the political necessity of Africanization, without which the government could not sustain legitimate sovereignty internally or externally. To create a legitimately sovereign government, he actively promoted African civil servants where possible, but also lobbied Western governments to provide him with a "brain trust" of expatriate technical advisers.[132] The concern to fill midlevel civil service positions also informed his push for an East African federation. An open question at the time of independence was how to renegotiate the services of the unpopular East African High Commission, which maintained a variety of governmental tasks, including communications, railways, customs, and research. Sharing these tasks both reduced the burden of the civil service and bound the East African territories together, potentially forming the "nucleus for East African federal institutions" that could overcome the divisions of national sovereignty through the practicalities of cooperation.[133] Eventually the question of the East African High Commission services was resolved with the creation of EASCO.[134]

Five days after independence, Tanganyika sought admission to the United Nations, a necessary step in the legal ascription of sovereignty in the post–World War II world.[135] Tanganyika's first UN representative was Dr. Vedastus Kyaruzi, a TANU stalwart who had led the former Tanganyika African Association into a more militant phase while Nyerere was still studying in Edinburgh. Kyaruzi later attended Edinburgh as well to continue his medical training. Kyaruzi's experience and education singled him out for travel to New Zealand for training as a diplomatic officer, where he observed the New Zealand delegation at the United Nations.[136] He was assisted in New York by Christopher Ngaiza, a young man from Kyaruzi's home area who had been previously employed grading coffee for an agricultural marketing cooperative.[137] Tanganyika's early diplomats were from the small cohort of educated Africans in the territory, many of whom were already acquaintances of the TANU leadership. They were deployed conservatively as Tanganyika initially opened only three foreign missions in 1961 with a total of thirty-five staff abroad and an equal number in the newly established Foreign Office in Dar es Salaam. Embassies in New York, London, and New Delhi were followed by an office in Bonn in 1962, and in Leopoldville (Kinshasa) in 1963.[138] The Tanganyikan government opened only a few embassies to minimize diplomatic expenses. These first posts were necessary, Nyerere explained, because of historical ties and the numbers of Tanganyikan citizens in these countries. "Failure to open offices there would mean, in a sense, a breaking of an existing relationship rather than simply a failure to expand."[139] Staff members rotated between stations quite frequently, as a means of both training new officers and maintaining experienced figures in strategic posts.

Tanganyika's admission to the United Nations also brought its first taste of the quiet power game that was the Cold War in the halls of the United

Nations; its admission was nearly derailed by the question of Chinese representation at the United Nations. Nationalist China (Taiwan) threatened to veto Tanganyika's application in the Security Council because of Nyerere's position that Communist China should be admitted to the United Nations.[140] Despite British discouragement of his taking a stand on principle, Nyerere stood firm and risked Tanganyika's exclusion from the United Nations by a Taiwanese veto. In exchange for Taiwanese support, Nyerere instructed Kyaruzi to promise a vote against an upcoming Soviet resolution supporting Communist China's admission while voting for a nonbinding resolution calling for the "recognition" of mainland China.[141] Acceding to Kyaruzi's reasoning that blocking Tanganyika's admission would create even more problems for Nationalist China, Taiwan abstained, despite Tanganyika's continued support for Communist China's claim.[142] "That they were able to do so is largely due to the restraint and discretion shown by the Tanganyika Government and its representatives here, in preventing the [Taiwanese] threat from becoming generally known."[143] Nyerere's negotiation of this hurdle impressed the British and others yet again with his stand on principle, a personal trait that was also a key aspect of his public persona. At the same time, he pragmatically avoided the dispiriting scandal of a rejected application to the United Nations, and the negative precedent it would represent for African independence.

Within the country, Tanganyikan leaders tried to minimize foreign influence by restricting embassies to just ten foreign employees in order to avoid the massive foreign missions that seemed to be directing a proxy war in the Congo.[144] Upon his return to Dar es Salaam to take up an advisory post, Kyaruzi assigned a note taker to sit in on any meeting between a Tanganyikan minister and a foreign diplomat.[145] Since well before independence Nyerere had proclaimed his commitment to nonalignment in the Cold War, refusing to bow to the "scarecrow" of communism. "The fact that one may disagree with the policies of the Communist Party," Nyerere emphasized, "is not a valid reason for refusing to examine a particular argument on its own merits simply because the communists do not happen to have rejected it."[146] Tanganyikan Federation of Labour trips to the Eastern Bloc were balanced by trips to Israel and scholarships in the United States.[147] But nonalignment did not mean "not caring," Nyerere emphasized. "Although our policy will not be passive neutrality, it will be independent."[148] Just before independence, Nyerere's first visit to a communist nation was to Marshal Tito's nonaligned Yugoslavia, where editorials praised Tanganyika for its nonaligned stance.[149] This public visit was carefully chosen for its symbolic value. The quiet journey to China by Bibi Titi and Lameck may have yielded a more concrete relationship, but Nyerere's trip to Yugoslavia identified Tanganyika's neutralist geostrategic location in the Cold War.[150]

Sovereign Influence

Nyerere's carefully cultivated reputation as a leader of uncommon eloquence and principle, together with his assertive foreign policy, gave him an outsized presence on the world stage, while Tanganyika took on the image of a particularly hopeful case of African independence. Nyerere's ambitions for African unity and liberation enhanced his international influence, especially since his desire for East African unity and liberation in southern Africa still seemed achievable in the near term. With his stands of principle at the United Nations and within the Commonwealth, his peaceful multiracial society, and his down-to-earth amiability, his stature rose in Africa, where he avoided public insult to his nationalist colleagues even in the midst of their disagreements. He sought to capitalize on his reputation to move the world's great powers to act in support of his goals. He quietly built channels of communication with China, cultivating prospects for future cooperation in aid of a military strategy for southern Africa. With the United States and Britain he sought political support for economic sanctions against South Africa and federation for East Africa.

Nyerere had met John Kennedy on previous visits to the United States, when the young senator was known as a friend of African nationalists. In May and June 1963, Nyerere wrote two letters to President Kennedy seeking US support for his primary foreign policy goals. The first concerned southern Africa. While acknowledging that Africa was a minor issue for American foreign policy, Nyerere framed the issue as a threat to peace in the whole region, echoing his thoughts from the pamphlet on race relations he wrote ten years before in Edinburgh. He also appealed to Kennedy's sympathy for civil rights and pointed out that civil rights in all of southern Africa, including in his own country, were under threat because of South African policy. In reaction to South African extremism, he argued that African racial extremists found a more receptive ear among the masses, undermining the possibility of peaceful multiracial societies in Africa. Finally he pressed the case for a strengthened boycott to bring about a peaceful solution for southern Africa and smother an incipient regional war. Nyerere asked Kennedy to take a stronger diplomatic stand at the United Nations and elsewhere against South Africa, and urged the United States to join the boycott of South African goods that PAFMECA had begun a few years before.[151]

Expressing his appreciation for Nyerere's thoughts on South Africa, Kennedy invited Nyerere for an "informal visit."[152] Before Kennedy's reply arrived, Nyerere composed a second letter about East African federation. In the letter, he briefed Kennedy on the progress of the Organization of African Unity, explaining its aim "to increase the immediate capacity of Africa to improve the conditions of life for the people without falling prey to the intrigues of the neocolonialists and without becoming unduly dependent on any outside states." He also expressed hope that the OAU would help Africa remain aloof of "world conflicts which do not concern us," saying that individual African countries were too weak "to avoid being used by those whose help we need" but that as a unit they could accept aid and investment and still retain "national integrity and independence."[153] In Washington the following month, the United States gave Nyerere a full state visit. His speech at the National Press Club in Washington on Tanganyika's policy of supporting the liberation movements caught the attention of the British high commissioner in Dar es Salaam, who recommended it to his superiors as showing Nyerere "in his characteristic vein, namely as champion of African rights and African unity. On a theme of this kind his eloquence and facility of expression are remarkable."[154]

Nyerere's diplomacy strengthened Kennedy's resolve to take some minimal symbolic steps. The following month, the United States banned all small arms sales to South Africa in support of the UN call for a voluntary embargo sponsored by the OAU.[155] Cultivating a friendly relationship with Kennedy, Nyerere increased his own influence in Africa as someone who could command the attention of the superpowers, but he also pursued the tactical goal of cultivating Western support for a nonaligned East African federation. The fulcrum of this vision was the question of sovereignty. A surrender of sovereignty was necessary to create the larger units that Pan-Africanists envisioned, but Nyerere understood the goal of Pan-Africanism was to solidify broader continental sovereignty in the international realm. Nyerere's letters to Kennedy were realist and tactical. As a key ideological goal, regional federation constituted a point of national interest. "Tanganyika's power to influence the course of events in East Africa," wrote an American embassy officer in echo of Nyerere's views, "will largely depend upon . . . close economic relations among the East African territories and upon the possibility of eventual political federation."[156]

Nyerere was perhaps more aware than his peers at home and abroad of the avenues by which African countries could best leverage influence despite their political weakness on the international stage. Leaders like Jomo Kenyatta in Kenya and Joseph Mobutu in Congo leveraged not so much influence as material support through firm loyalty to the United States as a benefactor within the Cold War landscape. Later regimes in Congo-Brazzaville, Somalia, and Ethiopia pursued a similar policy in relation to the Soviet Union. Nyerere's acid description of UN politics captured his disdain for neocolonial condescension toward the nonaligned world: "It's almost as if these giants expect to produce little men out of their pockets, who then run through voting lobbies before being safely gathered up again."[157] Realism for Nyerere did not mean simple capitulation to either side in the Cold War. At the Addis Ababa OAU conference,

Nyerere emphasized that realism and idealism could go hand in hand, but he argued against Nkrumah's "revolutionary" vision of an immediate Pan-African state. Instead Nyerere advocated gradualism, saying that "no good mason would complain that his first brick did not go far enough," but insisting, rather, that each brick was essential to the final edifice. "A true revolutionary is not an unrealistic dreamer."[158]

Nor did he take kindly to the arrogance of office that frequently accompanied the new nationalist leaders who celebrated their new powers with the trappings of former authorities, kings, and district commissioners. The quasireligious celebration of nationalist icons was as often a grassroots swell as a despotic imposition; people looked for saviors and could turn fiercely against them when their transformative personalities proved all too human.[159] Aware of his uniquely symbolic role as leader of the independence movement and head of state, Nyerere tolerated a cult of personality built around him in the comparatively humble role of mwalimu. But he complained of "the growing tendency within the Government to confuse dignity with what I consider to be sheer pomposity." What had begun as a bearable level of "overenthusiasm" in singing the national anthem every time Nyerere entered a room had become a disruptive ritual of state for every occasion. "Indeed, if it is true that over-familiarity breeds contempt then we are ourselves guilty of exposing the anthem to ridicule." In a major speech on Saba Saba Day, a holiday celebrating the formation of TANU, Nyerere bemoaned this trend and warned of the unintended consequences of excessive anthems, motorcades, and the like: "The office of the President, in this or any other sovereign republic, carries with it the duties and responsibilities of the Head of State. It does not, or most certainly should not, oblige its holder to become also the greatest public nuisance in the capital city!"[160]

But the problem spoke to the essential fragility of nationalism. The nation was a symbolic construct, dependent less on policies than on the constant communication and popular acceptance of its rituals and their meaning in the lives of its citizens. Politicians and many of their supporters insisted on the reassuring performance of state power amid the most mundane activities of national life. Nationalism had to be made ubiquitous before it could become banal.[161] Yet Nyerere seemed conveniently blind to the despotic potential lurking in his new commands as mwalimu-in-chief. "Even if it were proved that the people really did enjoy [disruptive displays of nationalism]—which I very much doubt . . . it would still be our duty to put a stop to it, and to tell the people that what they had learned to enjoy was wrong."[162]

Nyerere's visit to Washington did little to ease his weariness with state ceremony. But the more familiar cultural territory in London offered a welcome respite, where he chose to forgo the "swarms of motor cyclists buzzing around distinguished visitors as they do in the United States." After meeting members of the British government and greeting representatives of the royal family, Nyerere took the opportunity to enjoy a rare night of anonymity. "They decided to go on a 'pub crawl' in the East End," where they met a gregarious pub owner who took them for a walk, regaling them with tall tales of the neighborhood's history. "They managed to put back a good deal of beer and had got on famously. The interesting thing was that the pub manager had no idea who the President actually was; his reception had been entirely spontaneous."[163] It was also the highlight of the London visit, which produced little of substance; Nyerere believed his conversations on Southern Rhodesia were more productive in the United States. He continued to place great hope on an East African federation but lingering artifacts of decolonization such as a border dispute between Kenya and Somalia bespoke continued frustration.[164]

Nyerere's foreign policy aims from 1960 to 1963 were to expand sovereign power in Africa by building bigger, stronger political units through regional cooperation and by unifying African efforts to liberate the minority-ruled areas of southern Africa. Tanganyika was the leader of this effort, and the success of the liberation effort required that Tanganyika be stable and secure, internally and externally. In Nyerere's understanding, this very stability required both regional federation and southern African liberation. Abroad, his advocacy for pragmatism in regard to Pan-Africanism and his eloquent diplomacy brought him accolades. His international reputation conferred upon Tanganyika a freedom of action in the international sphere that other recently independent countries did not enjoy. Ideology was Nyerere's articulation of national interest, and his foreign policy was fundamentally realist in its orientation as he pursued Tanganyika's sovereign interests with a tactical prudence throughout his tenure.

9

The Cold War and the Union Treaty

Within a week of the Zanzibari Revolution in January 1964, Oscar Kambona reported that the new Zanzibari leader Abeid Karume, together with Kassim Hanga and the influential Abdulrahman Babu, expressed interest in the idea of a "union or federal relationship with Tanganyika in the near future."[1] After the mutiny on the mainland, which had ironically left Nyerere in a strong position both internally and externally, Tanganyika entered into a tense period of diplomatic jockeying over the fate of revolutionary Zanzibar. In the Union of Tanganyika and Zanzibar, the East African leadership found a solution that satisfied all sides enough to restrain an outside intervention, and so retain East African control over the islands. As Kambona explained, the key issue was to maintain local autonomy from foreign interference: "Our first concern was the growing Communist presence, and second, the danger of the Cold War coming in. The Cold War was in the Congo already—it would have been a straight line across Africa. . . . The problem was how to isolate Zanzibar from the Eastern countries, yet not be used by the West for its own purposes."[2]

The details of this account largely agree with those of Issa Shivji, Thomas Burgess, Ian Speller, Frederick Jjuuko, and Godfrey Muriuki, but my analysis suggests that both Nyerere and Karume were concerned about increasing superpower interference in Zanzibar and sought to minimize it, fearing that it would fuel further violence.[3] Western diplomats worked to retain a friendly government in Zanzibar as a strategic asset in the Indian Ocean, and Eastern countries made great efforts to cultivate the strong communist element in the Zanzibari leadership to create an ideological ally in East Africa. The Tanganyikan leadership sought only to keep Zanzibar from becoming dependent on either side. To accomplish this, Nyerere and Karume agreed to end revolutionary Zanzibar's tenuous sovereignty and place it within the ad hoc framework of a new sovereign state that came to be known as Tanzania.

Zanzibar, as petite as Congo was grand, was another key Cold War prize. East African leaders fought to maintain regional control over the course of events there. The weapons at their disposal were almost exclusively rhetorical. After the Zanzibar Revolution on January 12, 1964, the British colonial secretary paid a visit to Dar es Salaam to meet with Nyerere. In the meeting, the secretary indicated a suspicion that Tanganyika had aided the revolution and cautioned that the islands could become an "African Cuba," repeating a potent American metaphor that had also been cast about in the Congo in the months preceding Lumumba's assassination.[4] Kambona had been using the phrase for American audiences the year before, aware of its discursive power.[5] But communist takeover was only one of several concerns that burdened him in the months before the British turned over the islands to a government loyal to the sultan. "Tanganyika had several worries ... about an independent Zanzibar," Kambona explained during his visit to Washington in October 1963. "He thought that Zanzibar was thinking more of forming an Islamic Federation with Somalia and Sudan rather than joining the East African Federation."[6] But with the populist revolution of January 1964, aided by a few Cuban-trained militants and prominent Zanzibari communists, Cold War concerns emerged preeminent. The East African leaders kept superpower intrigue at bay through the careful manipulation of the discourse that governed the tense competition between East and West in the nonaligned world.

Revolutionary fervor on the islands boiled over when Britain granted independence to a government nominally under Prime Minister Mohammed Shamte, whose parliamentary coalition of landed interests was seen by many as nothing more than a return to the quasi slave regime of the former Arab sultans.[7] The former sultan had commanded more respect than his playboy successor, Jamshid bin Adbullah, who saw independence as a return to Arab hegemony.[8] During the last decade of colonial rule, bitter electoral politics had raged around racial resentments between those who felt at least partially bound to their indigenous African roots and those who identified most strongly with their Arab heritage.[9] These groups were not easily separated, however. Despite his association with an ostensibly Arab government, Shamte looked incontestably African. For those who claimed African roots, some saw themselves as mainlanders whose forefathers had been brought over as slaves, and others saw themselves as Shirazi, whose ancestors had occupied the islands since medieval times when they intermarried with legendary Persian traders. The popular leader of the Afro-Shirazi Party (ASP), Abeid Karume, was a former sailor and bandleader with a knack for populist performance. He had the broadest base of support.

Abdulrahman Babu and Ali Sultan Issa had recently formed the Umma Party as a radical break with the Arab interests who controlled the Zanzibar National Party (ZNP). They were Stone Town boys, friends since childhood, who had become global citizens in the adventurous travels of their youth. They saw the promise that international communism offered to the proletarian masses whom they had encountered in seaports and servant quarters around the world, and they were inspired by the reform of formerly feudal societies in Russia and China and their rapid rise to power. For Babu and Issa, these societies differed from Zanzibar only in scale. They hoped such a revolution could transform Zanzibar. They arranged for a group of Zanzibaris to go to Cuba for training and smuggled in a shipment of Czech weapons from Egypt.[10] The comparison to Cuba, we should recall, did not come after the Zanzibar Revolution, but before.

In the predawn hours of January 12, neither Babu nor Issa was present when a small army of about one thousand day laborers and ASP Youth League members under the dubious leadership of John Okello captured weapons from the Ziwani and Mtoni police stations, occupied banks and post offices, and embarked on an ill-disciplined reign of terror.[11] In a handwritten autobiography received by the US Embassy in October that year, and later published as a book, Okello told his story: a Ugandan itinerant worker, semiliterate in several languages, who had landed in Zanzibar in 1959 and took up work in a quarry.[12] In December 1963 he proclaimed himself the "field marshal" of a plan to "revolute this Govnment." He put unemployed laborers to the task of recruiting a ragtag army. "When you go in the farms and get somebodey with no food and with no job you just tell him that you will get everything you just come with us and become a soldia or Askari." By the end of the year, he claimed nearly two thousand recruits for his proletarian army.

Okello offered his services to Seif Bakari and the ASP Youth League leadership, who were quietly planning a revolution with guidance from a group of their own members who had just returned from training in Cuba.[13] Bakari was the coordinator of the subversive "Group of Fourteen" that had been working on general plans to weaken or overthrow Shamte's government with quiet support from at least a few members of Nyerere's mainland government.[14] It seems that the Youth League intended to allow the naive day laborers to take the blame should the attack fail and permitted Okello to lead the initial midnight raid. The senior ASP leadership was only vaguely aware of the Youth League's plans, but they hurriedly organized a party on the evening of January 11. It is not clear if the party was to provide cover for the Youth League's activities, or to distract them from carrying them out.[15] Okello instructed his men to "fight with all Arabs starting on the idge of 15 years," but not women or children or religious leaders; to loot all Arab businesses, but not to "sleep with any woman nor girl of there's though you have arrested her for that will look a sin on us all." He promised them "when the war is over its when I will start giving you all the farm." After years of frustrated ambitions among the African working classes, the ramshackle revolution captured control of the government, sent the sultan's court fleeing, and resulted in the deaths of several hundred, and possibly a few thousand, Arab Zanzibaris and sympathizers.[16] At Britain's request, Nyerere sheltered the sultan on the mainland and arranged his escape into exile.[17]

While there may have been a few other radical immigrants to the islands like Okello, there is no evidence of imported troops from the mainland. This was a local rebellion premised on local resentments. On the morning of the revolution, Okello claimed that his men took Abeid Karume and Aboud Jumbe at gunpoint to the radio station to announce that Shamte's government had been overthrown. Okello consistently promoted Karume as the new leader, even though some reports indicate that Karume had tried to warn the ZNP government of the Youth League plot.[18] Taken by surprise with the rapid turn of events, Karume made his way to Dar es Salaam for safekeeping and consultations with Nyerere. Two days later, he returned to take control with a core group of senior ASP loyalists and Umma Party supporters. Karume put a stop to the massacres, buried the bodies, and shepherded the squabbling coalition of communists, nationalists, and populists into a loosely organized revolutionary government.[19]

Atrocities by Okello's men were one worry; foreign intervention in support of the old government was another. On January 16, Karume and Babu confronted Frederick Picard and Don Petterson, the American consul and vice consul, respectively, placing them and several journalists under house arrest.[20] Karume had word of alarmist reports sent out that morning by the journalists that suggested his leadership was merely a facade for Babu's communist ambitions, and that Okello controlled the military.[21] Karume was astute enough to realize that both communism and atrocities would offer convenient justification for the United States and Britain to support a countercoup. The diplomats were released the following day, with a formal request that Picard be replaced because of his "direct intervention in internal affairs."[22] Picard flew to Dar es Salaam that same afternoon, and Petterson took over the post for the time being.[23]

On January 17, Karume put Okello on a flight to Dar es Salaam as well, but the mutiny there brought the unstable quarry worker back to the island.[24] Karume tolerated him for several weeks under close observation, reading his mail, keeping him off the radio, and generally making it clear, in Okello's recollection, that Karume "was not huppey with me."[25] Failing to disarm Okello's scattered men, the revolutionary government sought to incorporate them into a new revolutionary army, cut off from Okello's command.[26] Karume sent Okello to Kenya in February where he was warned against returning. But the indomitable "field marshal" made his way back and was met at the Zanzibar airport by Karume and Babu and a group of armed men. Karume escorted him directly back into the plane and headed to Dar es Salaam.[27] On the mainland, Karume brought him to the statehouse, and Okello reported that "Nyerere said to us that there is no use of us to have such Creules in the Ilands [Cruelties on the Islands]." Okello was sent penniless back to Kenya, where finally an Ethiopian man took pity on him and lent him a car to get him back to Uganda.[28] Okello never returned to Zanzibar.

Between pragmatic nationalists like Karume and idealists like Issa and Babu, Nyerere hoped a progressive nationalist government could be established. He spent the first week after the revolution trying, in Leonhart's words, "to use his leverage to reestablish order in Zanzibar and prevent a racial bloodbath." By the end of the week, before the mutiny threatened his own government, Nyerere had begun to consider longer-term options. "Left to himself [Karume] would merely replace Arabs with Africans in same feudal structure," he told Leonhart. "This is not enough. If real social reform did not [happen], Communists would take over. Babu had ideas necessary for thoroughgoing social reform."[29] But the Tanganyikan leadership was also keen that Umma Party leftists did not lead Zanzibar into communist neocolonialism under the Soviet Union or China. Whether coincidentally or not, the revolution seems to have been timed when Issa and Babu were both off the island.

Meanwhile, the superpowers scrambled to garner influence.[30] American secretary of state Dean Rusk floated the idea, in typical bureaucratic staccato, that communist Chinese were "seeking exploit fragile political situation for their own ends and in particular to establish base in Zanzibar for further subversive activities, particularly in East Africa."[31] As the British made preliminary plans for an intervention, Rusk signaled that the United States was prepared to support such a move.[32] "A communist Zanzibar would serve them as a base for subversion and insurgency operations against mainland from Kenya and to the Cape."[33] The British, secretly "considering whether we ought not to seek a respectable excuse for intervening and eliminating ... extremist elements" from Zanzibar, ordered a small aircraft carrier armed with a marine commando unit to sail south from its position in Aden and await further orders in East Africa. The marine commando unit was used a week later to put down the Tanganyika Rifles Mutiny.[34]

The British plan for Zanzibar hinged on the cover of an invitation, however ill-informed, from the new Zanzibari president Abeid Karume. To force his hand, British authorities deviously suggested that Nyerere withdraw the stabilizing Tanganyikan police presence in Zanzibar as a caution against disorder in Dar es Salaam, when their real purpose was to plant an armed British force in Zanzibar. London instructed the high commissioner in Dar es Salaam to approach Nyerere: "You could add that if Karume felt in need of a replacement we would be prepared to send a detachment of British soldiers to take over from Tanganyika police. No indication would of course be given of political objective."[35] We can assume that the "political objective" entailed greater British control over the new Zanzibari government. For the time being, Nyerere put their advice aside.

For over a month after the revolution, it remained the view of the British prime minister that there was "not really a responsible government there at all." Britain hesitated to extend diplomatic recognition to the revolutionary government that had displaced the constitutional measures left in place when power was handed over in December 1963. The US followed the British lead, but the Americans became increasingly impatient as Nyerere warned that without US support Zanzibar could become "another Congo," and that Karume was looking to communist powers for support.[36] In mid-February the Zanzibari government declared British and American diplomats persona non grata because of the lack of diplomatic recognition. Concerned that the lack of Western representation would make a communist takeover more likely, President Lyndon Johnson personally called Prime Minister Alec Douglas-Home to urge recognition.[37]

In the meantime, with Nyerere's help, the United States negotiated a delay in the expulsion of its diplomats, and a trusted young Foreign Service officer named Frank Carlucci was dispatched carrying a personal letter from Johnson to Karume. Ambassador Leonhart accompanied Carlucci to meet with the Zanzibari cabinet. The new president, flattered to receive the apologetic greeting from Johnson, promised not to expel the ambassador so long as there was an immediate announcement of recognition. But he doubted the US leaders understood how the delayed decision had affected the delicate situation following the revolution. "Some people have guns," Karume intoned. "Some have spears. They have conflicting views. Which group should I turn to?"[38] The delay caused Karume to turn openly to communist countries for aid.

The Soviet Bloc was certainly interested in Zanzibar. None other than Markus Wolf, the renowned head of East German foreign intelligence, packed his bags for an extended undercover stay on the islands. He accompanied General Rolf Markert, who had been appointed as an adviser to the new Zanzibari security service. Wolf was initially overwhelmed by culture shock in Zanzibar's bitter political environment, with its myriad racial, religious, and ideological tensions. "Coming from a country where everyone in the ruling party was united in support of established goals, we were unfamiliar with a government of individuals who were divided by contradictory goals and interests."[39] From the Soviet Bloc's perspective, a primary concern was to deny China a foothold on the African continent, and for that reason the East Germans carried a deep suspicion of Abdulrahman Babu, who had strong connections to Communist China. Wolf and his colleagues "conducted a senseless exercise" of counting portraits of Mao hanging in Zanzibari governmental offices.[40]

To oversee US interests, the somewhat more adaptable Frank Carlucci was transferred to Zanzibar as chargé d'affaires, eager to assess the situation and plan a course of action. Carlucci had begun his diplomatic career during the Suez Crisis in 1956, and then rose to the rank of vice consul in South Africa between 1957 and 1960. In 1960 he landed in the Congo and was present during the destruction of Lumumba's government. He stayed in Congo until early 1964, just before deployment to Zanzibar.[41] Carlucci's background made him highly suspect in the eyes of the Zanzibari leadership, an intuition that was only reinforced by his subsequent career path.[42] Upon being expelled from Zanzibar in early 1965, Carlucci spent the next four years as a counselor for political affairs in Rio de Janeiro while the Brazilian military dictatorship hardened its repression of leftist elements. He served in various policy positions in the United States under Richard Nixon and was posted as ambassador to Portugal after the overthrow of the dictator António de Oliveira Salazar. In the 1980s he became a prominent Washington insider as deputy director of the CIA and served briefly as secretary of defense after the Iran-contra scandal. But in an interview in 2005, he still recalled Africa as the "crucible" of the Cold War.[43] Upon transfer to the Congo in 1960, the extroverted Carlucci became known for his familiarity with the local people, his facility in foreign languages, and his assertive negotiations with the main players of the Congo drama.[44] Carlucci, who knew many of Congo's political leaders personally, was widely suspected of being a CIA agent.[45]

Ideological pressure suffused the daily work of both American and Soviet diplomats in Africa, and their obsessions were easily legible to foreign leaders.[46] In Zanzibar, this Cold War competition seemed juvenile to Karume, who asked Carlucci, not long before his departure, why the "Americans and Russians always wanted to outdo each other. . . . Why do [you] have this tug of war? Why do [you] have to compete in every field?"[47] As he had done in Congo, Carlucci quickly developed close relationships with the key players Zanzibar, impressing Karume with his fluent Swahili; touring by day, drinking by night with the radical playboy Ali Sultan Issa; and meeting "clandestinely" with the apprehensive attorney general, Wolfgang Dourado, "in hushed tones on a darkened roof."[48]

In concert with US pressure, Britain made several offers to Nyerere of military support for an intervention in Zanzibar, but the Western diplomats worried that their repeated suggestions had led him to suspect "an intention by the West to intervene in Zanzibar even if unasked."[49] Pressing him to agree to Western support for action in Zanzibar, Leonhart warned Nyerere of concerns that Zanzibar would reach a "point of no return" in a month and that s "Communist takeover would follow." Nyerere replied by scolding Leonhart about the early delays in Western aid and recognition for Zanzibar: "Bloc doubtless offering aid for its own purposes, but what was West offering?"⁵⁰ Meanwhile, from the islands, Carlucci reported that Karume was informed but uninterested in the British offer of military aid to take action against communist influence on the islands.⁵¹

In light of Karume's refusal, Carlucci suggested a plan familiar to CIA operatives of the era. "Believe we should develop alternate plans if intervention contemplated," Carlucci wrote in clipped prose that garnered praise from his State Department superiors.⁵² "One possibility might be create local incident. Problem would be generate one of sufficient proportions to make case credible."⁵³ Nyerere and his colleagues were well aware that the CIA had used local agents to create disorder and overthrow left-leaning governments several times in the early years of the Cold War. There was every reason to believe such a plan coordinated with the sultan's loyalists could work on an island nation of three hundred thousand people where, as Lyndon Johnson put it, "appropriate support can surely be found within Zanzibar itself, both before and after any necessary action."⁵⁴ Carlucci's inquiries must have circulated widely. From exile, the decommissioned field marshal John Okello got word of rumors that Americans "might support a counter-revolution" in Zanzibar.⁵⁵ But the feared intervention never happened, overtaken by Tanganyika's sudden embrace of Zanzibar in a lopsided treaty just a few weeks later.

Yet the union plan did not come about as suddenly as it appeared.

The Threat of Intervention

Immediately after the Zanzibar Revolution, conversations between Kambona, Karume, Babu, and Hanga broached the possibility of a bilateral union, which remained a debated strategy as Cold War pressures on the islands mounted.⁵⁶ Their goal at that point may have been less international than local. The bloody revolution had created a combustible situation under Okello's erratic leadership. "That situation was fraught with danger," recalled a member of the legal team that drew up the Union Treaty, noting the parallel possibility that the sultan's supporters would stage a counterrevolution. "It needed to be handled because otherwise Zanzibar could end up being torn to pieces."⁵⁷ A union would provide security, an institutional infrastructure for the government, and a more robust means of sidelining Okello.

TANU had been a strong supporter of Karume's Afro-Shirazi Party, and for some time Nyerere and Karume had been discussing the possibility of Zanzibar joining a broader East African federation.⁵⁸ The union idea appealed to many in the island nation where much of the population was made up of people with mainland roots whose ancestors had been brought in as slaves for clove plantations.⁵⁹ But to sympathizers of the former government, federation with the mainland seemed like an attempt simply to annex Zanzibar by force. Because of this, Kambona resisted pressure from the Zanzibari leaders for a quick federation. He said that "Zanzibar should exist independently for some months at least before federation discussions resumed."[60] The US eventually came to see the union as an attractive "long-range solution . . . as a possible way to strengthen Karume and reduce Babu's influence."[61] Nyerere expressed hesitance about a bilateral union absent regional federation, and insisted that the "Zanzibar boys would not be stooges of anyone. They want to be independent and neutralist. The things they talk about most are a new Hilton hotel and an international airport."[62] The Americans initially absorbed this view, and came to see Karume as a sort of coastal Kenyatta, a "moderate" strongman that the United States could live with, "President of GOZ in fact as well as in name."[63]

In Karume, Nyerere found a bluntly effective politician who could keep racial violence from turning into genocide internally while maintaining a policy of nonalignment externally through cautious engagement of both sides in the Cold War. Markus Wolf, the East German spymaster, later remarked, "Karume was much more adept than we had suspected at playing off external powers against each other."[64] Minister for Foreign Affairs Oscar Kambona pursued this delicate diplomatic balance in a conversation with the British representative in Dar es Salaam, emphasizing that "Western recognition would help to keep Zanzibar unaligned."[65] Tanganyika held its hard-earned autonomy at the pleasure of the superpowers, and sought to set them against each other, carving out sovereignty in between them. "It is more important to me than to you that Zanzibar be non-aligned. Chinese on Zanzibar threaten me more directly," Nyerere reassured Leonhart after the revolution. "You Americans must help me keep some sort of balance there."[66] He did not use "balance" as a euphemism for neocolonial dependence; in fact, just the opposite. Nyerere continually maintained that the old racially stratified regime of the sultan's loyalists "was far more likely to produce an 'east African Cuba'" than Karume's new government. He insisted from the beginning that "new Zanzibar would be 'socialist and independent' but not Communist."[67] While the United States and Britain contemplated armed intervention in Zanzibar, Nyerere opted for an awkward union between the islands and the Tanganyikan mainland to preempt superpower control.

By the time of the Zanzibar Revolution, Nyerere had a set of governing institutions prepared to respond professionally and diplomatically to the twin crises he faced that month. He sought and implemented a response to the Zanzibar crisis that would establish consistent patterns of diplomacy for postcolonial Africa. He had already begun using TANU institutions in parallel to government institutions, binding a party constructed internally in a grassroots movement to the externally constructed government inherited from colonialism. Their interpenetrations animated the sterile colonial state into fecund nationhood. Using the power of nation-state diplomacy, Nyerere delayed Tanganyikan recognition of Zanzibar briefly in order to accord with the thin precedent of the Republic of Congo (Brazzaville), and thus encourage the new regime to restore law and order with due seriousness. "They could not apply one set of rules to African situations far from Tanganyika and another to those near," Nyerere told Ambassador Leonhart.[68] With a mischievous grin, Nyerere used the TANU National Executive Committee to address a question more fitting to a government institution: "They will love to argue for Zanzibar recognition and persuade me to change my mind."[69]

Despite Nyerere's assurances, Carlucci's alarms from Zanzibar pushed Ambassador Leonhart to doubt Karume's ability to fend off the communists in his government and Nyerere's ability to protect him. Privately Leonhart opined that "neither we nor British believe Tanganyika-Zanzibar Federation practical possibility ... and agree elimination of Babu prime objective."[70] If American diplomats seriously considered the union plan, it was only as a ruse paving the way for further Western action. Commenting on an upcoming meeting of East African heads of state with Karume in Dar es Salaam, Leonhart speculated about the possibility of a "take-over by Babu in Karume's absence but Karume would still be President and then could invite our intervention in Zanzibar."[71] They hoped Jomo Kenyatta would facilitate their plans, but he insisted on East African consensus before any action.[72] The Kenyan president bought time, calming American urgency by sending a high-level delegation with a letter telling Karume that the situation on the islands was "unstable" and warning that Babu was "like a cobra on your neck," conspiring against him.[73]

Babu and Hanga were painted among those that Leonhart and Carlucci referred to as the "wild men on the Revolutionary Council," an echo of American prejudices about Patrice Lumumba as "insane."[74] Like Lumumba, the issue was not so much whether they were "wild" or "insane" but that they were too independent-minded for American liking. An Indian representative estimated that Babu "is real boss of island."[75] Babu's imposing intelligence and ties to Communist China made him both a target and a justification for outside intervention.[76] But in the face of facts that overwhelmed the simplicities of Cold War strategy in African countries, American policymakers hid behind colorful clichés of disdain, in the same way the Congo had become a "comic opera" in the eyes of the Eisenhower White House. This phrase reappeared in March 1964 when the American ambassador in London, summarizing a conversation about British colonial secretary Duncan Sandys's trip to Zanzibar, described much of it as being "of a comic opera character." With this characterization, he could comfortably dismiss the Zanzibari government's reason to exist. "Sandys believes the government as presently constituted is almost completely incompetent to administer its affairs."[77] Under such circumstances, Westerners could view intervention as a favor.

Certainly both sides in the Cold War jockeyed for influence in the islands, each thinking the other had the advantage. East Germany sent two undercover military consultants in early March in response to a Zanzibari request for Soviet and East German support in building its armed forces. Later that month the Soviet Union sent a shipload of arms, vehicles, and instructors.[78] East Germany provided strategic support and intelligence training, but they were concerned "that the People's Republic of China is exercising a considerable ideological influence . . . and has announced the provision of material aid."[79] In March the East Germans still saw the situation as favorable, judging that "an open intervention by imperialist powers seems unlikely." Zanzibari politicians told them promisingly that Tanganyika would "embark on a similar course in its domestic and foreign policy." But the East Germans did pick up on American machinations of the sort of scenario that Carlucci had proposed. They expressed concern that "the imperialist powers use frustrated elements from within the revolutionary movement to form armed gangs who could make attempts at intervention."[80] More dispiritingly, the East German deputy foreign minister visited and concluded that "some politicians from Zanzibar seem to overestimate their influence on the mainland" and were unlikely to persuade Nyerere's government into alliance with Eastern Bloc countries despite the efforts of the socialist true believers like Babu and Ali Sultan Issa.[81]

Carlucci had indeed been searching for divisions within the Zanzibari ruling group, but he had begun to doubt his ability to exploit ideological differences among the Zanzibari leadership. "It no longer useful to think in terms of precipitating immediate showdown between moderate and extreme elements," read his assessment. "We must now think in terms of a longer term operation in Zanzibar."[82] In a deluge of daily reports, he made much of communist influence, British inaction, and East African hesitance, eventually provoking a response from Washington. After spending two days with Issa in late March, Carlucci reported, "[I] believe we have reached point where it no longer practical think of people's republic of Zanzibar as a non-aligned member of African family." He warned that "US ability influence situation has been limited," and judged that the "East African Governments now becoming alarmed but have no program for concerted action."[83] Two days later, the White House developed two plans for covert action in Zanzibar, one assuming British support and another "for action through Tanganyika if the British hold back."[84] In secret, the United States turned to Carlucci to prepare an intervention even as Nyerere was directing Kambona quietly to prepare the Union Treaty. He had Karume's assent, but otherwise little input from Zanzibar.[85]

Carlucci's continual reports of communist activity echoed in a State Department memorandum to Secretary Dean Rusk about the "rapidly deteriorating situation in Zanzibar." The memo recommended that the "best bet appears to be a covert action program which is in process." The aim of the action was to bend Karume toward the United States, but "if Karume proves to be a man with whom we are unable to work, explore alternatives and find someone else."[86] Britain was prepared to cooperate in support of action against Zanzibari communists, but not the overthrow of Karume. So long as Nyerere or Karume approved, Britain offered assistance to stabilize the situation after a military intervention.[87] The British apprised Kambona of their readiness to supply military support for a takeover of Zanzibar.[88] Disregarding British caution, President Johnson grew impatient and proposed unilateral action: "We should have as much help from our friends in East Africa as possible, but I wish to make it clear that if they are not responsive, I believe that action should be taken just the same."[89]

In the last week of March, Nyerere convened a heated emergency meeting of the TANU executive committee, just before the party's annual meeting. Acknowledging the urgent discussions, he told the American ambassador only that there would be major cabinet changes in the coming month.[90] One topic at hand apparently concerned foreign intervention in Zanzibar and the inclusion of the islands in a federation as a solution. Press releases after the party meeting emphasized African unity and an East African federation, preparing the ground for such an announcement.[91] Zanzibari leaders had already broached the subject in late March with the East German deputy foreign minister and head of foreign intelligence. Wolf, who opposed the idea, reported in April, "If a union did come to pass, we suspected that the British government would put pressure on Zanzibar to end its association with us."[92] From that point on, the East Germans were told nothing about the union negotiations and were assured "that no such move was planned." Wolf only found out about the union on the eve of its announcement while he was off in a Pemba village, "sitting among new recruits at dusk answering questions about the relationship between Marxism and religion."[93]

Neither was the union mentioned to Americans, who were only notified of communist influence in Zanzibar, with an implication that at least some in Nyerere's cabinet would invite intervention if necessary.[94] Such leaks were intended to forestall American action with the assurance that East African leaders would address Western concerns. The British remained committed to acting only with approval from Karume and other East African leaders. From London, the American ambassador noted with resignation "that effective British military intervention in Zanzibar is not now feasible," admitting that he could "not see what overt political action is practical at this time."[95]

Nevertheless, Carlucci found support for more aggressive action among those concerned with the fates of minorities in Zanzibar. On April 12, he met with Wolfgang Dourado and R. K. Tandon, the Indian high commissioner to Zanzibar, both of whom reinforced Carlucci's opinion that the island was irreparably dominated by communists. "Tandon strongly urged US direct intervention as only feasible means of redressing situation," while Dourado had already been preparing subversive "action groups." With Indian support for intervention, Carlucci recommended "direct action," arguing that "sufficient rationale could be found in GOZ persecution of local Indians and Goans."[96] On April 15, Thomas Hughes, in the State Department's Bureau of Intelligence and Research, issued a set of policy alternatives for Zanzibar highlighting Carlucci's pessimism. The report presented an unappealing choice between maintaining a mere "listening post" on the islands if they went communist or a potentially counterproductive "unilateral application of Western military force to topple the present Karume-Babu regime."[97] These two unattractive alternatives cast a flattering light on covert action through a third force of Zanzibari exiles.

Aware of these pressures, if not their details, Nyerere was clearly agitated by reports of 2,500 Zanzibari Arabs training in the Middle East to invade Zanzibar and reinstall the sultan.[98] He probed the American ambassador for information. Leonhart denied any knowledge, but Nyerere believed the reports to be "well based," and reinforced Tanganyikan police units seconded to the islands. Likewise fearing communist interference, he also warned the East German deputy foreign minister "not to send additional arms to Zanzibar and not to try to re-export revolution to Tanganyika."[99] Nyerere then spent most of early April traveling widely upcountry to consult with regional authorities and party members on the challenges of regional cooperation. In Nairobi, he arranged a meeting of the three East African heads of state, in hopes that the pressure of foreign intervention might bring them on board for an East African federation treaty that could include Zanzibar.[100] Kenyatta and Nyerere voiced readiness to postpone negotiations about economic imbalances between their countries for the sake of immediate federation. However, caught between Buganda's intransigence and Ghanaian pressure opposing regional blocs, Milton Obote remained reticent to commit Uganda to the plan.[101] An East African federation remained out of Nyerere's grasp, and Kenyatta refused to support a proposed Kenyan union with Zanzibar.[102] So negotiations continued between Tanganyika and Zanzibar under Kambona's guidance, and in mid-April Kambona informed the

American ambassador "of closely held talks . . . to revive [the] possibility [of a] Tanganyika-Zanzibar Federation."[103]

This timely leak cut off an imminent American-supported intervention plan based on Carlucci's recommendations, and likewise cultivated American favor to oppose Soviet pressure. Nyerere and his colleagues had some awareness of the level of superpower intrigue surrounding Zanzibar, if not the specifics of timing and tactics. American and British officials had suggested various intervention schemes to Karume, Kenyatta, and Nyerere, and all three were in continual confidential communication. Ambassador Leonhart in Dar es Salaam repeatedly pressed Nyerere to take action in Zanzibar, and the British High Commission informed him of their readiness to act militarily upon his request.[104] Nyerere communicated American sentiments to Kambona, who sought to pacify the American itch to intervene. Kambona reassuringly informed the Ambassador Leonhart that "he was more worried about Zanzibar than [the Americans] were." Turning the tables on Western impatience, Kambona noted that a request for arms from Britain still had received no reply. "If I had asked the Russians, they would have had them here in a week."[105]

In reality, the Tanganyikan leadership distrusted Russian intentions in light of the experience of fellow African foreign ministers who had dealt with imperious Soviet demands. Communist Bloc support came almost exclusively in the form of weaponry and military training, while a grandiose East German housing project lingered untended.[106] Kambona feared that the Soviets were seeding distrust, and that Karume had come to think the "Tanganyika Government [was] working too closely with Americans and British." Guinean diplomat Achkar Marof visited Zanzibar, at the behest of the Americans, for consultations in mid-April and gave a compelling presentation relating Guinea's frustrating experiences with Soviet interference.[107] Nyerere's own intelligence contacts suggested that the Soviets intended to establish an airbase in Zanzibar, a move as worrisome as the satellite-tracking facility the United States had begun to establish on the island before the revolution.[108] In early April, Karume made a show of ordering the American tracking station on the island to be dismantled and removed, setting precedence for making similar demands on Eastern powers.[109] Kenyan finance minister Gichiru had also informed Karume of intelligence about a far-fetched communist plan to replace all the current East African presidents as if they were so many chess pieces, "with Babu for Zanzibar, Odinga for Kenya, Kambona for Tanganyika, and Nekyon for Uganda."[110] With a hint of flattery for the American ambassador, Kambona took umbrage at Soviet scorn for African sovereign interests. "They're making the same mistake in Zanzibar they made in Guinea and Congo. They think Africans can't think for themselves."[111]

The Union Treaty

In January and February US plans had initially proposed to manipulate Karume's behavior with offers of aid and quiet threats of force, but by the end of March, Leonhart's doubts, Johnson's fears, and Carlucci's warnings pressed toward more direct action to overthrow the revolutionary government. Indian High Commissioner Tandon traveled to Kenya, where he spoke with Foreign Minister Joseph Murumbi, and then James Ruchti in the US Embassy in Nairobi. There he summarized his conversation with Carlucci and Dourado. Tandon urged the United States to work with Kenya to launch an intervention. Kenyan participation was unlikely in Ruchti's view, but he nevertheless prevailed upon Ambassador William Attwood to press Kenyatta to cooperate in such an action.[112]

The US began to prepare the ground among its NATO allies to welcome an intervention in Zanzibar, suggesting that East African leaders "have been reluctant to take effective action to prevent the continuing deterioration."[113] Aware that overt intervention would create resentment among communists and nationalists alike, the United States advocated covert action through local intermediaries, if they could be found.[114] Undersecretary of State George Ball sent word to London on April 16 recommending "that Kenyatta/Karume action be tried," requesting the cooperation of the British intelligence agency, MI-6, and the approval of colonial secretary Sandys. "If Sandys still demurs, you should ask him what other plans he has to avoid communist takeover Zanzibar. Time is running out. . . . You should bear in mind President Johnson's continued concern with sharply deteriorating Zanzibar situation."[115] The British authorized a plan the following day to act without the knowledge of Nyerere or Karume, so long as Kenyatta's cooperation could be assured to keep the operation secret.[116] They agreed with the Americans that "nothing could be expected from Karume now. Nyerere was also weak."[117] Kenyatta may have informed Nyerere of the British inquiry about intervention, which may be the reason Kambona leaked word of the union negotiations to Ambassador Leonhart that same evening.

Kambona proved an able foil to foreign intrigue, and he continued in furious negotiations, as Leonhart understood it, to "use Hanga to seal off Babu by some form of Tanganyikan Government-GOZ union."[118] Despite the intense Western interest in the union negotiations, the Zanzibari leadership kept the details of the plan away from prying eyes, in order to maintain local initiative. Karume excluded a suspected informant, Attorney General Dourado, from the legal negotiations and drafting of the Union Treaty; and the American-friendly Othman Shariff was deployed to the new Zanzibari High Commission in London in March.[119] On April 18, taking a cue from earlier British devices to force Karume's hand, Kambona threatened to withdraw all Tanganyikan police forces on the islands, arranging a dozen charter flights to haul them out that very day.[120] Much to Nyerere's relief, Kambona's gambit was successful. "At same time flight was sent from Dar-es-Salaam to pick up Hanga," Carlucci reported. "Hanga arrived at airport, then disappeared and returned with Karume. Karume proceeded to Dar-es-Salaam. Order for 12 charter flights was cancelled today."[121] In Dar es Salaam, the Tanganyikans briefed the Zanzibaris on Western plans to intervene, and Karume committed himself to the treaty.[122]

Nyerere and Kambona had repeatedly reassured Leonhart that Babu would be constrained in the envisaged union, keeping the ambassador apprised of their progress and nurturing his support. Leonhart did his best to urge cooperation from Washington, since "Kambona may request some assistance, direct or covert, from us in behalf of Hanga early next week. We may need to move swiftly."[123] This information was conveyed to Carlucci, who was instructed to communicate secretly with Kambona on April 20, pending the US State Department's decision.[124] Leonhart rustled up support in Washington for the union initiative, even though it "would not be most aromatic situation conceivable."[125] On April 20, the State Department sent word for Leonhart to communicate to Nyerere and Kambona "its blessing and support to the Tanganyika initiative: Tanganyika-Zanzibar Federation or incorporation," and promised aid upon Kambona's request.[126] In Kampala, American envoy Olcott Deming discussed the developments with his British and Indian associates. Their observations signal the fundamental discursive shift achieved by the Union Treaty: from a point where outside military action had been legitimately imaginable to diplomatic observers, it was now reported that "they regard intervention by outsiders entirely out of the question."[127]

Before the union plans were made public, Western powers had discursively defined Karume's government as incompetent in order to justify their interference. With intervention imminent, the East African leaders were able to subsume Zanzibari sovereignty under the more stable and reputable sovereignty of Tanganyika and thereby retain local control and short-circuit the machinations of foreign agents. This shift accords with Cynthia Weber's theory that, when confronted with a credible articulation of sovereignty, "intervention is prohibited and, when carried out, condemned by the supposed community of sovereign states."[128] The recollection of ASP secretary-general Thabit Kombo suggests that the East Africans understood this dynamic at the time. "In America they weren't happy, but the law does not give them permission to intervene with force, despite our smallness."[129]

The union proposal had deflected an American plan to force Karume to act as an American puppet or lose his government, and at the same time it incorporated Babu within the nationalist fold, despite his strong communist backing. In London, the Kenyan high commissioner, Josephat Karanja, disabused the American ambassador of the "African Cuba" portrayal of Zanzibar. "As regards the possibility of communists converting Zanzibar into another Cuba, he was frankly disdainful." The intellectually impressive Karanja, with his recent PhD from Princeton University, reinforced the idea that "some sort of economic or political union" was the best solution for Zanzibar. He assured the American that all the East African leaders "were thoroughly informed of what was going on in a fashion that no outsiders could be," and that they would not allow Zanzibar to house foreign missile bases.[130] His comments buttressed Kambona's leaked notice about the union negotiations to Leonhart and signaled a coordinated effort by the East African leadership to cultivate international support for the union as a means of keeping the Cold War at bay.

Throughout the uncertain negotiations by his energetic colleagues, Nyerere retained African initiative in the entire matter. When Leonhart asked whether he had discussed the union with the British, Nyerere said "he had not discussed it with any non-African," and then inquired of the ambassador whether it would be wise to inform the British. In the American ambassador's response, his elliptical reference to "force contingencies implicit in situation" gave Nyerere pause. Whether or not he knew the nature of those "force contingencies," Nyerere decided to inform the British promptly the following day. He visited Zanzibar on April 22 to finalize "talks on Tanganyika-Zanzibar 'union' which [are] now far along."[131] The cagey Kenyatta quietly buttressed the union plan, inviting Babu for a well-timed state visit that kept the radical leader out of Zanzibar while negotiations were finalized.[132] He also delivered a strongly worded letter to the British that Kenya "would view with great concern any movement of British troops from this country for offensive or war-like operation in another country without prior consultation."[133] Coincidentally, Karume gave Ali Sultan Issa, Babu's friend and radical associate, an opportune assignment to the new Zanzibari High Commission in London, where he joined his more conservative counterpart Othman Shariff. Both were kept in the dark about the union negotiations.[134]

Taking advantage of Babu's and Issa's absence, Nyerere corralled support for a speedy agreement. His presence was key to consolidating support between mainland moderates and the more radical coalition that supported the union: Karume, Hanga, Mwinyigogo, and Twala in Zanzibar; Kambona, Lusinde, Munanka, Tambwe, and Simba in Tanganyika. The negotiations were conducted in secret without public input, their haste driven by a fear that the sultan's supporters would find the resources to reinstall themselves in power.[135] Although later critical of the way the union was structured, Aboud Jumbe saw no alternative at the time to its hurried negotiation: "In 1964 the people were not consulted because the two leaders were in a race against time and could not afford the *luxury* of delay."[136]

Confident in a successful conclusion to the negotiations, Nyerere called an emergency sitting of the National Assembly two days hence to approve the treaty in principle. Both Soviet and Chinese reactions to the agreement caused some anxiety. Zanzibari students in Russia sent scripted telegrams to Karume and Hanga expressing displeasure in the union.[137] But Nyerere remained "hopeful [that the] Russians will accept [a] Tanganyika-Zanzibar union without too much fuss as [a] means [of] forestalling Chinese takeover."[138] As for the Chinese, Nyerere had his own prejudices about their intentions, since in his view they "have already selected Zanzibar's next government. Babu is a Chinaman."[139] Upon hearing that Agence France-Presse got word of the union, Kambona called in the American ambassador late at night on April 22 to tell him that the union would be announced the following day. Kambona expressed the hope that press reports could be delayed long enough to avert an "armed show-down on Zanzibar" with Babu's Umma Party followers. Having sent several Special Branch police to Zanzibar that day, with more to come, and doubled the number of bodyguards on Karume and Hanga, he requested US intelligence about possible violence. He was confident that if they could maintain the situation for the rest of the week, the union would be strong enough to stand.[140] Impressed by the efficient negotiation of the treaty and its hopeful prospects, Leonhart responded positively to talks with Minister of Home Affairs Lusinde about the provision of automatic weapons for the Tanganyikan police forces stationed in Zanzibar.[141]

In the absence of Attorney General Wolfgang Dourado, Dan Nabudere, a left-leaning, London-trained Ugandan lawyer, arrived in Zanzibar on April 24 to help Karume work out the legal structure of the union. He consulted with Karume, Nyerere, and Roland Brown working on behalf of the Tanganyikan government.[142] Mark Bomani, the Tanganyikan solicitor general, followed to finalize legalities the next day.[143] Since a simple federation of equals between tiny Zanzibar and the much larger Tanganyika would be unacceptable to mainlanders, and the wholesale incorporation of Zanzibar into Tanganyika would be equally offensive to Zanzibaris, the lawyers used the Northern Ireland–United Kingdom precedent for lack of a better model.[144]

Ali Sultan Issa in London only got word about the treaty from a journalist there.[145] Likewise taken by surprise in Nairobi, Babu voiced his support for the union before news reporters, but as the American ambassador quipped, the Zanzibari leader was "obviously whistling in the dark."[146] Carlucci's reaction was not much different, responding to British approval of the union with a sudden reversal of his own dramatic proclivities. Noting

Nyerere's request to Leonhart that "any US public statements on Tan Govt-Zanzibar union be avoided," Carlucci took credit for deflecting Duncan Sandys's desire to deliver a congratulatory message to Karume.[147] Carlucci reported, "UK HICOM agrees with me that we should not interfere at this stage and should keep our contacts to absolute minimum to avoid giving impression we involved."[148] With the Union Treaty articles unanimously ratified by the Tanganyikan National Assembly and pushed through the Zanzibari Revolutionary Council by Karume and Hanga on April 25 and 26, respectively, Nyerere had successfully preempted both American intervention and communist domination in Zanzibar.[149]

A Small Discursive Triumph

The next evening, in conversation with a British diplomat, Nyerere acknowledged "with a chuckle that as we knew from the mutiny, it was not in his character to reach this sort of decision without some qualms." But he had done so with the requisite foresight. "He said that over past few weeks he had been building up strength of Tanganyika police in Zanzibar. He was worried about the lightness of their armoury as compared with those of the Zanzibar Liberation Army." The US responded positively to a request for vehicles and light arms.[150] The British also urged Nyerere to strengthen the Tanganyikan police presence on the islands, which he did, though he declined to pursue the suggestion that he deploy Nigerian troops there.[151] A week later, the British gave the United States notice that they no longer supported outside intervention: "Please tell the State Department at an appropriately high level that in our view the likelihood of being asked to mount a full scale intervention operation in Zanzibar against organised armed opposition has receded with the ratification of the Act of Union by both Tanganyika and Zanzibar."[152]

Plans for intervention remained in place, but the British urged caution, suggesting that the Cuban-trained cadres now in place in Zanzibar would be a more formidable counterforce than had been in place in January when planning began. Reflecting on the new situation a month later, T. L. Crosthwait in the British Embassy averred, "I think we can take it that it is extremely unlikely that Karume will now ask us to intervene." These considerations all pointed "to the advisability of avoiding except in the last resort an operation in the nature of a *coup de main* from outside."[153]

Karume smiled broadly when he met with Carlucci after ratification of the Union Treaty, telling him the lack of US support at the time of the revolution had required him to invite communist support to defend the revolution. "What could I do when my friends let me down?" Karume asked Carlucci. "He hoped I now understood Zanzibar would not be communist." Karume emphasized that the "union with Tanganyika was in fact the beginning of EA Federation," but that for the time being he had "full authority" in Zanzibar.[154] In the ensuing months, Nyerere brought the Zanzibari communists into his cabinet and arranged influxes of both Western and Eastern aid.[155] Nyerere considered Karume as the legitimate political leader of the new regime, but saw him as "lacking in ideas and inclined toward conservatism." By contrast, "Babu would be a force for social and economic change," he said.[156]

Nyerere had professed his admiration for the Zanzibari radical since the revolution and expected that Babu would be of great benefit to the union government. As interpreted for Western ears, Abdulrahman Babu's appointment to "an unimportant ministry" in Dar es Salaam was "preferable to leaving Babu adrift and to his own devices."[157] Certainly Babu's appointment as minister of commerce and cooperatives seemed innocuous to the Americans, but this understanding underestimated the sincerity of the effort to integrate left-wing Zanzibari leaders in the more powerful union government. By September an American intelligence report lamented, "Instead of restraining the expansion of Communist influence, URTZ is probably facilitating the spread of this influence into Tanganyika," and mused somewhat ominously about the fragility of power in the new country: "Nyerere and Karume, perhaps Babu and Kambona, could be toppled overnight, and replaced by persons who may be unknown to us at present. Communists could be thrown out and Westerners invited in. Quick change and sheer chaos are always just over the horizon."[158]

A particularly infantilizing view of Africans helped justify foreign intervention and paternalist control over client strongmen. Intervention was an easy option given the judgment that "the institutions of government in black Africa are so precarious, and the dispositions of leaders so capricious, that estimates of the future are highly tenuous."[159] This dismissal of the possibility of a coherent African politics provided a rationalization for reliance on strongmen. The envisioning of African institutions and leaders as disposable created a logic of causation that both explained the overwhelming strength of superpowers relative to postcolonial states and made intervention seem free of consequences since any ensuing chaos was immediately attributable to local disorder, as in Zanzibar in the weeks following the revolution: "The inability of the new government to free itself of armed thugs and the resulting insecurity this brings provides a fertile field for Communist efforts to establish the kind of amenable government which promises future difficulties."[160] The Tanganyika-Zanzibar Union had forestalled the Western rationale for intervention by containing the influx of communist influence, but it did not do so by becoming subservient to American demands. Tanzania moved steadily to the left after the Union.

Figure 9.1. The Tanzania Union president, Julius Nyerere, swears in Sheikh Abeid Karume as first vice president of the United Republic of Tanzania, 1964. © Tanzania Information Services (MAELEZO).

Translating the hasty arrangement into a real country would take time, but it strengthened African control of Zanzibar's political trajectory. "Can't you see," explained another Tanganyikan minister, "that what we have done is first to build a roof. . . . After that, the window, walls and doors will come."[161] EASCO immediately began to work out the integration of the new Union into its structure. Nyerere estimated that "the initial organizing period" would last six months, but that it would take five years to fully harmonize the institutions of the two governments.[162] Major issues like defense, finance, foreign affairs, and ministerial appointments would be in the hands of the Union government based in Dar es Salaam under Nyerere's presidency, but Zanzibar would retain autonomy in its internal affairs under Karume as the first vice president. Tanganyika's laws were to be supreme, however, allowing its Preventive Detention Act to be used to detain any obstructionists in Zanzibar or the mainland.

After successfully concluding the treaty, Nyerere was elated, aware that he had forestalled outside intervention in Zanzibar, in what he called "the biggest gamble of my life."[163] More important, he had taken a step toward his closely held vision of progressively building an East African federation.

He expressed his joy to the Ambassador Leonhart in terms carefully phrased to resonate with an American perspective. Even in private talks with the ambassador he drew on his knowledge of audience and discursive skill to coin a phrase that worked its way up the information chain all the way to President Lyndon Johnson. Nyerere said the Union was a "miracle so good I can't believe it," but warned that his success in preventing a communist takeover was still a fragile reality. "I've worked one miracle but I can't go on working miracles alone. I didn't create mess in Zanzibar; I inherited it. I've arrested the rot and we have another chance."[164] He successfully shed a flattering light on himself and his country in stunning contrast to the perception that held forth in the days after the mutiny of an institutionally fragile country under a frail leader.

A few days later, the American undersecretary of state for political affairs, Averell Harriman, noted in a request to President Johnson seeking financial aid for Zanzibar that "the merger between Tanganyika and Zanzibar was a miracle.... We really need a second miracle—to have Tanganyika absorb Zanzibar in fact."[165] Just as the gossip on the ground in Leopoldville about Patrice Lumumba's "insanity" became a cipher at the White House level for the whole of the Congo in 1960, Nyerere's insertion of the image of a "miracle," as a reference point for the union with Zanzibar, trumped the troubling echo of the Congolese "comic opera" that had been circulating in early 1964. This small discursive intervention was as much the act of sovereign initiative as a military standoff; it served the same purpose, identifying the Union of Tanganyika and Zanzibar as a responsible and independent actor in the international community. The "miracle" set a precedent for the Union's continued autonomy that served Nyerere well as he struggled to keep the lid on subsequent diplomatic crises that year.

10

Contending with International Intrigue

The second half of 1964 brought continual contention with signs of intervention, spycraft, and planted rumors. Cold War powers enhanced their own freedom of action by sowing confusion that constrained the ability of other countries to ascertain the necessary intelligence to react. Eastern and Western powers used secrecy and misdirection to distract their rivals for both defensive protection and offensive tactics. Such deliberate distraction served to make the "Third World" countries they fought over look naive and irresponsible. For countries like Tanzania, this meant operating amid uncertainty, compelled to act even when confronted with evidence that beggared belief.

A key insight of discursive analysis is the idea that communication is a two-way street, where the speaker never quite knows how the hearer will interpret the message. In diplomacy and spycraft, this ambiguity is an asset deliberately deployed. Lies and secrets are not only a way of hiding information but also, as Luise White proposed, ways "to make certain information so charged that its value and importance is unlike that of other information."[1] In such a kaleidoscopic crucible, Tanzanian leaders struggled constantly throughout 1964 to divine superpower intentions and preempt foreign intervention, which from their perspective seemed imminent. In the Union Treaty, the Tanzanian leadership showed that they could respond to Cold War intrigue in kind. But the Union radicalized Tanzanian foreign policy, and brought with it a new awareness of the risks its ideology entailed. Tanzania successfully defended its autonomy during a year in which its newly constituted United Republic faced numerous inscrutable challenges to its sovereignty.

During this period, Tanzania's internal search for competent leadership could easily have been derailed by external actors, as had happened in the Congo.[2] Abdulrahman Babu's intelligence, idealism, and organizing ability impressed Nyerere and many others, but as elsewhere in the Cold War world, these very abilities became a hindrance to his advancement. Frank Carlucci reported, with typical theatricality, "Babu most dangerous of group because . . . he most able man in government."[3] Karume, whom American diplomats underestimated as "ignorant and inept," was a safer and preferable choice.[4] The promotion of mediocre leadership by Cold War powers provided an attractive means to restrain postcolonial autonomy and tended to produce dictators of limited political creativity.[5] Nyerere mused at a press conference whether "it is subservience and not friendship that western countries want."[6] After the intrigue that led to the union with Zanzibar, Nyerere learned to distinguish friendship from subservience in the face of bewildering levels of dissemblance on the part of his Cold War "friends" and ever more strongly pursued an independent course for his newly defined country.

Closely intertwined with the Cold War struggle in Zanzibar, Tanzania's active support for the liberation movements in southern Africa solidified the domestic legitimacy of its sovereignty and communicated its presence to the global community. After the Union, the year continued to bring turmoil, skirmishes, and heated rhetoric along the southern border with Mozambique. During an African visit by Portuguese president Américo Tomaz in August, Radio Tanganyika announced an armed offensive into Mozambique within five years.[7] In fact, FRELIMO's first attack within Mozambique came within the month, beginning with an attack on a Portuguese base in northern Mozambique on September 25.[8] Portuguese foreign minister Alberto Noguera responded by citing recent US bombardment in North Vietnam as justification for military action on Tanzanian soil.[9] Meanwhile, continued conflict in the Congo was fueled by military aid from both East and West, with Tanzania funneling Chinese aid to Congolese rebels. Increasingly frustrated with Western hesitance in regard to Tanzania's battles against white dominance in the South, Nyerere built a close relationship with China, in which he found an ideological ally. As Nyerere began to seek a donor that would build a railroad from Dar es Salaam to Lusaka, he found the Chinese more responsive than Western countries.[10] The mutiny temporarily disrupted this relationship by postponing an arranged visit by Chinese premier Zhou Enlai as well as Nyerere's reciprocal visit.[11] Both were rescheduled for the following year.

The January army mutiny was not so much a turning point as a reason to intensify policies and processes already in motion.[12] Nyerere's turn to a one-party state was already under way internally, and policies of liberation and regional federation were already high priorities externally. But the mutiny encouraged a much stronger executive orientation in the government to avoid future threats to the state. Tanzania's active role in the liberation movements further helped to channel military energy and burnish Nyerere's credentials against accusations from Kwame Nkrumah that he had become "an imperialist agent" after the British intervention.[13] Countering continued hostility from Ghana, including the circulation of a "malicious" pamphlet at the Cairo OAU meeting, Nyerere called Nkrumah's promotion of a Pan-African union a "cloak for unbrotherly activities." The *Nationalist* vented Nyerere's muscular counter to Nkrumah, highlighting Tanzania's militant credentials: "Let us not deceive ourselves. The struggle in colonial Africa today is a race for arms. If we cannot have an African liberation brigade, we can at least get the guns for the fighters."[14] Nyerere made good on his promises to arm liberation movements.[15] The activist foreign policy helped outflank African nationalist extremism at home, and cooperation with the Chinese defused leftist political pressure, which was particularly keen among the revolutionaries in Zanzibar.

The mainland leadership continued to be cautious toward all the Cold War powers. After a Tanzanian delegation led by Kawawa returned from Beijing in July 1964 with an agreement for military training, Nyerere "understood western friends would be concerned and acknowledged he also had worries," but he insisted such concerns would not dissuade Tanzania's burgeoning relationship with China.[16] Certainly the Tanzanians were impressed with Mao and his enthusiasm for the military struggle for southern Africa: the Chinese leader was "a very well-informed man," recalled the newly commissioned Brigadier Sarakikya.[17] But the Tanzanian leadership remained skeptical. On a subsequent delegation, Nyerere's brother Joseph was disturbed by the totalitarian state, with its enforced uniformity and constant surveillance. "I know we are supposed to be developing a system of African socialism," said another delegate upon his return, "but I do not think we could ever work under that kind of socialism."[18] President Nyerere told Leonhart that he "hoped US could view situation 'objectively' in Tanganyika's interests and for its own responsibilities in Africa."[19]

Seeking autonomy of action for Tanzania, its leaders hoped to carve out political space for the endogenous development of habits and institutions of governance, and they sacrificed administrative efficiency for political balance. Ambassador Leonhart reported Nyerere's repeated declarations of neutrality to Washington: "He believed in non-alignment and he must try to live by his faith. He could not defend his beliefs if he relied exclusively on western countries in the security field."[20] The difficulty of integrating divergent advice, mismatched machinery, incompatible weaponry, and conflicting ideologies from many donors was a small price for the political independence gained by casting this wide net. "There were some who said mixed training missions made no military sense, [and] they might be right," Nyerere told Leonhart, insisting he was merely a political leader. Leonhart paraphrased Nyerere's sarcastic response to such criticism: "If they want military doctrine they should replace him with military governor."[21]

Military governors were, of course, a fact of Cold War neocolonialism. Third World strongmen, working with pay and protection from superpower patrons to command territories, were counted as pawns in the Cold War chess match. Upon concluding that Congolese prime minister Patrice Lumumba would become an autocrat in the pay of the Soviets, the United States successfully sought his removal, a process that ended in his murder.[22] After several American-approved replacements in the prime minister's office, including the Katanganese separatist leader Moise Tshombe in mid-1964, Joseph Mobutu eventually emerged as a US-paid autocrat. Mobutu increased his control over the military and the people, eventually doing away with all pretense of civilian rule. Civilian governments seemed to slip away from the unwavering allegiance desired by superpower patrons. Civilian regimes, under these circumstances, were the exception rather than the rule, and enduring nonaligned regimes like the one Nyerere envisaged were practically nonexistent.

A New Militancy

As the year 1964 unfolded, Tanzania sought to maintain friendly relations with both sides in the Cold War, pursuing an independent foreign policy while rebuilding its army to become one of the most effective militaries in independent Africa. Kawawa emphasized the need for a strong military "to safeguard sovereignty and support anti-colonial struggle in accordance [with the] OAU."[23] Israeli advisers helped train police forces, while Nigerian soldiers under Lieutenant Colonel James Pam replaced the British commandos providing temporary national security.[24]

These measures provided stability while Mirisho Sarakikya oversaw the retraining of a "people's army." With Chinese, Yugoslav, West German, and Canadian help, he built the new United Republic Military Force, later titled the Tanzania People's Defence Forces (TPDF). During Kawawa's visit to China in June, Tanzania received offers of financial assistance, as well as Chairman Mao's personal promise to train "up to 2,000 officers" in support of the liberation movements.[25] An initial class of 1,300 soldiers graduated in September 1964 under the command of sixty officers, half of whom were trained in Britain and Israel.[26] "By any standards the troops put up a first class show," observed a British military adviser.[27] The new recruits spent 20 percent of their time in political training under Tanzanian instructors, who explained that their first obligation was to defend neither the government nor its representatives but the people of the country and the national ethic Nyerere sought continually to define.[28] At the TPDF's first graduation ceremony, Nyerere's speech illustrated that an army's loyalties could not be taken for granted, and that soldiers' sense of where their loyalties lay was a deeply political matter:

While I say that I inducted you, the actual truth is that WE INDUCTED YOU. Because when I inducted you I did so on behalf of every citizen of Tanzania. Every one of us, whether President of the Republic, politician or civil servant, farmer, teacher, or day laborer has the duty to serve our country to the best of their ability.... My last word comes as a teacher. Learn. Learn hard. Learn for the sake of your country and for the whole of Africa.[29]

Fifty mainland soldiers were sent to Zanzibar to help incorporate the People's Liberation Army into the new TPDF with the training of a three-hundred-man platoon by Chinese and Soviet military instructors. The Soviet Union offered $42 million worth of industrial aid, as well as significant military training, while China provided the equivalent of a $4.8 million grant and $39 million in interest-free credit. Over the course of 1964, China and the Soviet Union provided Tanzania with 2,500 tons of armaments.[30] Even with all the armaments and advisers from the communist world flowing into Tanzania, Nyerere assured British representatives that "he was determined to go to any length to stop the Communists from taking over in Zanzibar."[31] West Germany sent weaponry and a promise to develop a small air wing for the new army as well as four coast guard vessels.[32] The US and Britain sent machine guns for the Tanganyikan Field Force contingent still stationed in Zanzibar.[33] Balancing the Cold War powers was Tanzania's strategy to prevent any outside power from taking over in Zanzibar.

West Germany's aid, for example, hinged on the outcome of a slow diplomatic row about its insistence on the "Hallstein Doctrine," which prevented it from maintaining relations with any country that recognized East Germany. Since Zanzibar had an East German Embassy, and Dar es Salaam a West German one, Tanzania needed to find a new arrangement that would allow it to express its nonaligned policy.[34] When the Union Treaty was signed, Babu adamantly stated, "We will not sever relations with East Germany." If there was a problem with hosting representation for both East and West, it could be "sorted out."[35] In Bonn, Kambona tried to frame the issue to appeal to West German sentiments, emphasizing his government's commitment to the new Tanzanian Union. He told the West Germans that he "believed that it was more necessary to have the union of Tanganyika and Zanzibar, to control the extension of communism in the latter, than to force the issue of East German representation, and perhaps risk [a] rupture of the union."[36] Kambona made much the same case to the Soviets later that month, this time playing off the Sino-Soviet tensions, pointing out that Russian obstruction could destroy the Union and allow China even more access to Zanzibar.[37] Some years later, Kambona recalled:

> As Minister of Foreign Affairs of Tanganyika, I went to Cairo to consult with Khrushchev, who had gone there for the inauguration of the Aswan dam.

Previously I had met with Gromyko and other high Soviet officials. After two hours of fruitless argument the Russian Prime Minister observed: How do you think it is possible to achieve a union between a Conservative-Progressive regime and the militant regime of Zanzibar? I replied without hesitation: The Prime Minister of the USSR should know the response since Mao Tse-Tung accuses him of being Conservative-Progressive. Khrushchev broke into laughter at my response and said: You can go back to your country. The Soviet Union will not block your path.[38]

Upon his return, Kambona spoke to the Egyptian representative in Dar es Salaam in order to understand the diplomatic arrangements that had allowed a West German embassy to coexist in Cairo with an East German consulate lacking diplomatic recognition.[39] Following this model, the East Germans eventually allowed their Zanzibar embassy to be moved to Dar es Salaam and downgraded to a consulate general. In the end, it was the West Germans who refused to compromise, attributing their inflexibility to internal electoral politics.[40] Western diplomats saw all this maneuvering as a sign of Nyerere's weakness toward communists in Zanzibar, and urged him to threaten Karume with arrest in order to force a withdrawal of East Germans from Zanzibar.[41] Knowingly violating the Hallstein Doctrine, "to show [the] unity of Tanganyika and Zanzibar and non-alignment, Nyerere said he had to recognize both [East and West Germany]."[42] Tanzania held fast to this position despite West Germany's threats to withdraw military aid, which eventually it did the following year, whereupon Nyerere told the German ambassador, "Take the rest of your aid as well." Tanzania, he insisted, would not accept aid with strings attached.[43]

These spats contributed to American anxiety about Tanzania's relationships with communist countries. The US State Department fretted, "Nyerere [is] making a great mistake in inviting Chicom military presence," and began contingency planning for a new intervention, comprising "additional actions other than those now being worked on which US and Free World could usefully undertake if initial Chicom penetration cannot be avoided."[44] In response to American anxieties about his cooperation with China, Nyerere vented his views at a press conference with blunt impatience: "Frankly, I do not know why it is a problem." He emphasized that Tanzania was receiving aid from multiple countries from both East and West, and that the "mess" in the Congo was due in large part to Western meddling in response to "the communist bogey." Furious about the cynical choice that had placed Katanga's separatist leader in the prime ministerial office once held by Lumumba, he asked, "Why must Tshombe be rammed down our throats?" He proclaimed there was "a problem of conscience here," and that Western ambassadors needed to respect African decisions. He mocked the fear that Chinese instructors would destabilize the new Tanzanian army: "The maximum risk is army will revolt. My army revolted in January. It was not trained by Chinese.... The Chinese want to colonize Tanganyika, my foot! It is humiliating that I have to explain to Ambassadors any decision about accepting seven Chinese instructors. I do not expect other people to take decisions for this government. I am completely capable of looking after this country."[45]

With emboldened connections to the Soviet Union and China, and the urgency of the newly formed Liberation Committee, Tanzania worked assiduously to build up its support for the liberation movements, especially in Mozambique.[46] In October Kambona, speaking as chair of the Liberation Committee, acknowledged the September inauguration of FRELIMO's military campaign in Mozambique. "The resistance in Mozambique has started, and no amount of intimidation from Lisbon and NATO powers will stop it." FRELIMO officials then publicly acknowledged that a major offensive had begun three weeks earlier, neglecting to mention the heavy casualties taken among their troops.[47] Karume, accompanied by members of the Revolutionary Council, held a meeting at Chukwani Barracks in Zanzibar to discuss support for FRELIMO, after which he planned to accompany Nyerere to an OAU meeting in Cairo.[48] These activities caught the attention of Malcolm X, who paid a visit later that month during his Africa journey.[49]

Throughout September and October, arms and personnel were funneled toward the garrison villages along the southern border and a FRELIMO training camp in Nachingwea. Portuguese intelligence services reported extensively on Tanzania's activities in support of the Mozambican liberation movement.[50] Fighters in camps along the border were carefully investigated to root out spies, but a few individuals, hoping for payments, reported regularly to the Portuguese consul in Salisbury.[51] Amid the growing tension, suspicions abounded and rumors concerning national security threats were particularly potent. Several white missionaries were arrested in southern villages on charges of espionage arising from an anonymous, possibly forged, letter attributed to a student dissatisfied with his marks on an exam at a mission school. Nyerere arranged for the missionaries' release at the behest of the American ambassador.[52] Meanwhile, a Soviet-trained and Soviet-armed military contingent from Zanzibar relocated to Mtwara along the Mozambique border, but the ill-disciplined troops so harassed local shopkeepers and expatriates that they were immediately recalled.[53]

In November two dozen Chinese instructors traveled to a newly built training camp in Kongwa village near Dodoma, and another in Bagamoyo, just north of Dar es Salaam.[54] The camps aimed to train three thousand soldiers from Mozambique, Southern Rhodesia, and South Africa who were rotated through in cohorts of two hundred. FRELIMO sought to train sleeper agents who would lead the Mozambican population in a rebellion at a future date.[55] The Kongwa camp was built in a thinly populated area in the central part of the country that had been partially cleared in the late colonial era for peanut farming. Tanzania provided the trainees with room and board and weekly stipends of twenty shillings, partially paid through the inconsistent funds of the Liberation Committee. In response to shortages, camp residents sold their goods and clothes for cigarette money. Tensions between the freedom fighters in training and local villagers who found work constructing the camp resulted in occasional disturbances requiring police action.[56] About two thousand recruits were selected for infantry training with a hodgepodge of World War II–era firearms. Top recruits continued with sabotage training in Mpuku village, five miles south of Dar es Salaam, with Chinese, Soviet, and East German trainers. Some students went for further courses in Algeria, China, Cuba, and the Soviet Union.[57] In the camps, Algerian and Chinese instructors, assisted by local translators, taught from an illustrated manual titled "Curso de Guerrilhas," apparently translated from an Algerian original.[58] Amid all these preparations, Tanzania's new army inculcated Nyerere's nationalist ideals, including his commitment to nonalignment and liberation in southern Africa, both of which served to bind the army to the state as a legitimate expression of African-based sovereignty.

Rumors as Weapons

In November Nyerere's government was confronted with rumors deployed as psychological warfare, intended to cause uncertainty and paralysis in Tanzania's foreign policy. On November 9, three letters, ostensibly stolen from the office of the Congolese prime minister Moise Tshombe, were handed to Tanzania's newly placed ambassador in Kinshasa, Andrew Tibandebage.[59] Dated between October 2 and 21, they seemed to be planning documents for an American-initiated plan to "bombard all the strategic points being used by Communist China in Tanganyika," and "as a second measure and after the advice of Interpol to make special arrangements to overthrow the government of Mr. Julius Nyerere in the manner being studied by the Department of State." One letter, a sloppy imitation of an American diplomatic note from its embassy in Leopoldville, said the United States "counts on the support of the Congolese government for this affair, including the upcoming evacuation of American citizens from Albertville." Another letter in amateurish French, from an undisclosed regional embassy, gave information on communist weapons shipped into Dar es Salaam. The third letter, apparently a response to a request recently delivered by an American pilot, seemed to be from a mercenary named "Mülher" based in Coquilhatville who promised to "prepare all the mechanisms for the putsch." In error-ridden French, the mercenary explained that he would ask to be relieved of his military duties for the Congolese government and would travel to South Africa to recruit "seven specialists for an armed putsch who have already proven themselves in Africa." He requested an advance of "25.000₷."[60]

The forged letters, though sloppy, were clearly well informed. The mercenary's details accord with the movements of an ex-Nazi South African–based mercenary named Siegfried Mueller who was recruited by the notorious soldier-for-hire "Mad Mike" Hoare, also based in South Africa. Hoare later led the mercenary column from Kongolo in Katanga to Stanleyville in coordination with the American-Belgian paratroop operation on November 24. Hoare recalled meeting with Tshombe in mid-September "with a plan to give him Stanleyville by the end of October," and he described a scene in a Leopoldville nightclub later that evening when an "American journalist" handed 25,000 francs to "Miss Leo 1964," a suspiciously hefty amount for a Congolese courtesan.[61] Despite the hurried production of the letters themselves, the forger obviously had detailed access to locally produced intelligence, and their sloppiness may have been a deliberate tactic to mask their origins.

Tibandebage rushed back to show the documents to Nyerere, who shared them with Kambona. Despite the letters' outlandish language, their threat seemed real enough from Tanzania's perspective, given its support for FRELIMO. Just a week prior, Nyerere had "outlined his concern over the deterioration of the situation along the Mozambican border, and his fear of possible Portuguese military retaliation against Tanganyika."[62] Thousands of refugees were streaming into Tanzania fleeing a Portuguese scorched-earth campaign intended to disrupt Tanzanian activities along the border, while Portuguese airplanes conducted surveillance in Tanzanian airspace, tracking arms shipments from Chinese, Soviet, and Algerian ships.[63] The Portuguese Foreign Ministry had been drumming up support for intervention in a propaganda campaign that claimed, "Tanganyika is becoming a giant base for subversion."[64]

After looking over the dubious letters, Nyerere asked Kambona, "Oscar, do you remember what you did as a schoolboy when a bully threatened you?" Kambona responded, "I shouted as loud as I could."[65] Kambona flew to Dar es Salaam and called a press conference in the airport to condemn the documents and raise alarm about the alleged "plot." Years later, in an interview with a Portuguese journalist, Kambona claimed that he suspected the letters were forged and only publicized them at Nyerere's urging.[66] But at the time he took full responsibility for sounding the alarm. "Kambona said it was the African way to speak out immediately and publicly about anything that worried them," the British high commissioner reported. "It was for the Americans to say that there was no truth in the story."[67]

Within a week, Nyerere began to suspect that the forgeries were part of a psychological attack and not a military one. Tanzania's new representative at the United Nations, John Malecela, voiced the allegation that "the United States is plotting against Tanzania in a clever way which might not involve force."[68] After the incident had died down in early January, Waldo E. Waldron-Ramsey, another young officer working in the Tanzanian mission at the United Nations, expanded on this theory, telling G. Mennen Williams that Tanzania was "convinced now that evidence of [the so-called] American plot [was] planted by Portugal in [an] effort to create trouble."[69] Tanzania certainly suspected a "Western Plot"—not a military intervention, but a psychological ruse initiated by Portugal. Because the evidence surrounding this incident is still so vague, we cannot know the truth. The Tanzanians had reason to suspect Western powers as much as Eastern ones, but the real issue was the pervasive uncertainty besetting the leadership of a newly independent country with limited intelligence resources operating in the Cold War context.

The French embassy in Leopoldville suspected that the forged documents originated in the Czech embassy there.[70] This is certainly possible, as a defector from the Czechoslovakian intelligence service later claimed that one of his colleagues had forged these letters in a scheme to paint the United States as a "major conspirator and enemy of leftist African regimes." According to Ladislav Bittman, the scheme was concocted by a brilliant drunkard in the Czech intelligence service named Vaclav Louda, who disappeared for two days of "celebration" after the letters were made public. An Eastern Bloc origin would suggest an attempt to seed distrust about American intentions in Africa by highlighting its anticommunist alliances with Portugal and the southern African minority regimes. Bittman considered the forgeries a grand success because the Tanzanians publicized the letters in newspapers and marched in protest, while diplomats across Africa denounced American machinations.[71]

Other evidence, however, raises doubts about the Czech origin of the letters, suggesting that Bittman's account could have been a smokescreen obscuring what had been a Western-initiated deception designed to confuse and distract the Tanzanian leadership from American-sponsored military activities in eastern Congo. Bittman's book was published shortly after his defection by the Syracuse University Research Corporation (SURC), an institution set up to "work on research and development projects of significance to America's interests" and function as a "trusted advisor" to the US government.[72] CIA insiders Victor Marchetti and John D. Marks claimed that the agency funded the publication of many books as propaganda, and regularly subsidized publishers, "from Eastern European émigré organs to such reputable firms as Frederick A. Praeger, which admitted in 1967 that it has published 'fifteen or sixteen books' at the CIA's request."[73] Bittman's study of Eastern Bloc deceptions seems to fit a pattern of books that veiled American intelligence activities by providing well-informed accounts that highlighted publicly known information in a narrative that obscured still-secret operational details.[74]

The use of forgeries as disinformation was a common Cold War technique used by both sides, and this was not the first time Tanzania had been targeted.[75] E. Howard Hunt, later famous for his involvement in the Watergate scandal, upon being questioned about his work on a 1963 forgery of a State Department cable purporting to link John F. Kennedy to the assassination of South Vietnamese president Ngo Dinh Diem, told federal prosecutors that he "had been given some training in my past CIA career to do just this sort of thing . . . floating forged newspaper accounts, telegrams, that sort of thing." Marchetti and Marks suggested that similar documents presented as examples of Eastern Bloc forgeries may have served as disinformation for American purposes. In a 1961 Senate briefing on communist forgeries, Deputy Director of Clandestine Services Richard Helms noted thirty-two fraudulent documents "packaged to look like communications to or from American officials." As with the Tanzanian forgeries, certain documents on Indonesia that Helms presented appeared to be "rather crude forgeries," wrote Marchetti and Marks, "but their message was accurate. Not only did the CIA in 1958 support efforts to overthrow the Sukarno government, but Helms himself, as second-ranking official in Clandestine Services knew it well."[76] Disinformation was an essential tactic of preserving "plausible deniability" for covert operations, including American operations in eastern Congo in November 1964.[77]

The "Western Plot" forgeries coincided with efforts to create a distraction from the ongoing American-sponsored operations against rebel forces representing Lumumba's legacy in eastern Congo. These operations culminated in the joint Belgian-American raid on Stanleyville on November 24 timed to coincide with the arrival of Congolese military and mercenary columns in the city. Ostensibly intended to rescue hostages, the operation was actually a full-scale military attack to recapture Stanleyville from the rebels and secure the American-supported Congolese government in Leopoldville in preparation for territory-wide elections in February of the following year that would solidify the Leopoldville government.[78] An American-Belgian paratroop operation for a limited rescue of the hostages was agreed upon in principle in a meeting on November 8 with Belgian African policy experts, approved by the Belgian foreign minister on November 9.[79] The "Western Plot" forgeries were handed to Tibandebage that afternoon. On November 11, a US State Department memo to officers overseeing the Congo operation praised the "initiative in exploring with Belgians psychological warfare. . . . Immediate objective in psych war aimed at liberation of Stan is reduction of threat to security of US nationals in rebel hands." The memo recommended radio broadcasts "to blanket Stanleyville with messages designed for optimum psychological effect . . . including fabricated rumors . . . as offensive mounts."[80] The forged letters may have been intended to seed confusion about the target of Mike Hoare's mercenary column traveling north from Katanga toward Stanleyville.[81]

When facsimiles of the forgeries appeared in the Tanzanian press, the Dar es Salaam diplomatic community quickly realized they were fraudulent and began trying to ascertain their mysterious authorship. In an emergency meeting on November 11, the TANU Central Committee met to discuss the "secret plans of some Western countries desiring to attack Tanzania." Kawawa, chairing the meeting, explained the letters and the group decided to arrange protest marches and a public rally where Nyerere would speak on the issue.[82] Tanzania continued to support the rebellion in eastern Congo, and there is no evidence that it changed its military activities in response to the dubious threat intimated in the forgeries.

Since the union with Zanzibar, Tanzania had been supporting the Congolese rebellion by conducting weaponry and other aid to what they considered to be the "legitimate" government in rebel-held Stanleyville. In late August Kambona and Lusinde visited Congolese refugee camps in Kigoma, near the border on Lake Tanganyika, in order to arrange transport for Chinese weapons that were to be delivered in Dar es Salaam for transshipment to the Congo.[83] A planeload of weapons for the rebels flew from Dar es Salaam to Arua, Uganda, on November 14.[84] Tanzania continued to play a leading role in supplying and coordinating the Congolese rebellion.[85] This was a great frustration to the US and Belgian planners coordinating a major operation against the Stanleyville rebels.

One piece of evidence suggests that the Tanzanian forgeries were a deliberate ruse carried out by Portugal in coordination with the American "fabricated rumors" campaign. A classified Portuguese file originally labeled "Intervenção no Tanganica" dealt exclusively with intelligence about Oscar Kambona. The last document in the file was a secret memorandum, dated November 9, that was circulated to its intelligence services and its Western European embassies.[86] In the memorandum, circulated the day the letters were handed to Tibandebage, the Portuguese secretary of state recommended that "missions take advantage of the opportunities provided to them to discreetly feed the suspicions that already today reside upon the personality and work of this African politician," referring to Kambona who in Portuguese eyes was "the real mentor of the subversive Mozambique movements and one of our most dangerous enemies in Africa."[87] The memorandum seems to be a notice to Portuguese stations in Africa tacitly apprising them of the forged letter operation so that they would not be taken by surprise when its results became public. The details

Figure 10.1. National Service (JKT) members demonstrate in protest of the "Western Plot" intimated in the forged letters of November 1964. *First sign reads:* "We warn those who are plotting for Tanzania they never get a chance." *Second sign reads:* "Africa Is One Unity Strength. Imperialist Away from Africa." *Third sign reads, in part:* "May God curse you American, South African Boer, Portuguese, and Rhodesian Boer . . ." © Tanzania Information Services (MAELEZO).

of the actual plan were not mentioned, and it is not clear what types of actions were intended in this approved plan to smear Oscar Kambona.

The rest of the file dealt exclusively with intelligence about Kambona. The Portuguese were aware that both the British and the Americans regarded Kambona with deep suspicion, and sought to exploit those doubts by making him appear foolish and reckless.[88] The British harbored their own suspicion that Kambona had instigated the January mutiny himself. US intelligence services noted that a Pakistani doctor who had treated Kambona's wife reported that Hanga and Babu had visited Kambona, to propose he was the real "father of the nation," because Nyerere had become a Western puppet.[89] Kambona notably declined the Zanzibari entreaties on that occasion, but this did not wipe away the doubts that he harbored. Portugal evidently hoped its action against Kambona would drive a wedge between him and Nyerere, whose deteriorating relationship the Portuguese tracked closely before and after the smear campaign.[90] Ambassador Leonhart went so far as to surreptitiously record conversations with Nyerere and then play them back to Kambona to gauge his reaction. Kambona later said that he did not betray his shock at the recording, but clearly still felt burned by the incident and the American ambassador's attempt to drive a wedge between him and Nyerere.[91]

Other diplomatic gossip hints of a wider attempt to smear Kambona. On December 11, in a conversation with British prime minister Harold Wilson, Hastings Banda of Malawi fingered the Chinese ambassador in Dar es Salaam as the point man for Chinese operations in Africa, and opined without much basis that "in Kenya the Vice President Odinga as their man; in Tanzania it was Kambona." He went on to tell Wilson that Nyerere "was not tough enough" and that "this meant that it was not Nyerere who was the real ruler but Kambona."[92] Summarizing a similar conversation with Kenneth Kaunda, Dennis Grennan, who was known as an expert on the African copper belt, reinforced these same worries in a meeting with Prime Minister Wilson. Grennan said that Kaunda was "very anxious about the position of President Nyerere . . . and that a rescue operation was needed if Tanzania was not to be lost entirely to the Chinese." He repeated the Kambona-Babu-Chinese connection and conveyed Kaunda's intention "to talk to Wayne Fredericks of the United States State Department in order to try and persuade the United States not to throw Tanzania irrevocably to the wolves."[93] The British in particular were concerned that Kambona threatened to displace Nyerere, and Banda's characterization only reinforced these rumors. In fact, Kambona consistently surprised the British by not being the communist schemer that they thought him to be.[94] It is impossible to say for certain whether any of these rumors, or the forgeries themselves, were seeded in a Portuguese attempt to undermine Kambona, but clearly such a plan had been approved. Whatever its extent, the Portuguese smear campaign intervened in an ambiguous context of rumor and secondhand knowledge.

The mysterious operation contributed to a growing distrust between Nyerere and Kambona and marked the beginning of Kambona's political decline that ended in exile two years later.[95] Within a year Nyerere had taken over the foreign affairs portfolio personally, and Kambona was living semipermanently in The Hague, ostensibly for medical treatment.[96] Both Tibandebage and Nsilo Swai suspected that Kambona himself had fabricated the letters for his own "political reasons."[97] Regardless of their origin, they humiliated Nyerere's administration, which looked dangerously gullible with a measure of "comic opera" naiveté. Tanzania's impulsive public reaction to the forgeries seemed to reinforce this image of immaturity, even if their publication helped blunt their intended effect in the region.

If the forgeries were of Eastern Bloc origin, their purpose may have been to sow fear about Western-led preparations for military action in eastern Congo, but then presumably they would have highlighted action in Congo, not Tanzania. If of Western origin, the forgeries were intended to distract from operations in eastern Congo. Following the killing of an American missionary in mid-October and further threats to American and Belgian hostages held in Stanleyville, the US State Department was anxious to move on Stanleyville in early November.[98] "The best protection we can afford the Europeans," advised the US ambassador in Leopoldville, "is to move ahead with military campaign (coupled with psychological warfare) as quickly and efficiently as possible."[99] American planners were undecided whether to deploy a limited rescue mission before the arrival of Mike Hoare's mercenary column or to proceed with a joint operation like the one finally deployed on November 24. A delayed joint operation would coincide with the arrival of Congolese troops, but Europeans in the area pressed for an immediate paratrooper rescue.[100] While both the mercenary column and a unilateral American paratrooper operation were prepared to strike within days, the United States wanted to avoid the use of its own troops in the Congo. American military planners stressed their need to "maintain control over timing et cetera [of] their final assault on Stanleyville," but left their diplomats in Leopoldville "in [the] dark" about plans in Washington.[101]

The joint American-Belgian action plan "Dragon Rouge" was ready on November 15.[102] Two days later, Dean Rusk's office sent out an urgent but enigmatic memo to Leonhart in Dar es Salaam: "For tactical reasons connected with developments elsewhere in Africa it is of utmost importance to disprove Kambona allegations soonest, preferably in three or four days."[103] By November 17, Belgian paratroopers were assembled on Ascension Island off the West African coast for immediate deployment via American cargo planes, but were held "for period of 4–5 days prior to further execution order," apparently in order to allow a Congolese army contingent under Frederic Vandewalle to get into position.[104] Joseph Mobutu, commanding the Congolese army, was finally briefed and approved the plan on November 21, and Johnson ordered military planners to initiate when they saw fit.[105] These delays were clearly an effort to time the paratrooper landing and the arrival of the mercenaries and Congolese troops, but perhaps also to fan the flames of the forged letter conflagration in Tanzania. Hoare's column had been held up for nearly two weeks securing a bridge near Kindu, 250 miles south of Stanleyville. The mercenaries left Kindu on November 18, then stopped at Lubutu on November 22, a day's drive on a good road from Stanleyville. That same day the paratroopers were transferred to the Kamina airfield in Katanga, and Vandewalle's force joined Hoare's troops in Lubutu. They set out the following evening, intending to arrive with the paratroopers at dawn on November 24. Rain and rebel fire delayed the ground troops, and they arrived midmorning.[106]

While the drop on Stanleyville was being prepared, American forgery experts were trundled off to Tanzania with all the equipment they needed to construct a detailed analysis to prove the infamous forgeries to be forgeries indeed.[107] The experts' report seems incontestable, but just as easily contributes to a narrative of "plausible deniability" that was a planned part of all covert operations by Cold War powers. Algeria and the East Germans were fingered as favored suspects, as well as Kambona himself, still suspect since the mutiny. But his consultation with Nyerere, and the effect of their joint decision to publicize the documents, had instead made the president momentarily sympathetic to the challenges his young foreign minister faced in a world of cynical intrigue. In Dar es Salaam, Kambona broached the possibility with the American ambassador of a face-saving "exchange of notes" to quietly resolve the issue.[108]

At the behest of the Americans, the Tanzanians did not publicize another set of letters relating to the mercenary "Mülher" that were received from the Algerian ambassador on November 20.[109] Without knowing what the Tanzanians told the Congolese rebels in regard to the forged letters, it is difficult to evaluate their effect on rebel defensive preparations in Stanleyville. If there were significant exchanges of intelligence between Tanzania and the Congo rebels, the forgeries may have sown some short-lived confusion. But with the publication of the letters and the diplomatic furor that followed, they did not succeed in convincing anyone that the march of the mercenary column in eastern Congo intended to invade Tanzania. Few doubted that the real target was Stanleyville. If this account of the forgeries as a psychological operation is accurate, they mainly represented a discursive component of a broader military attack, meant to confuse the context of American and Belgian activity in the Congo.

At a planned demonstration against the supposed "Western Plot" on November 15, Nyerere gave a freewheeling two-hour speech before a large crowd at the national stadium. He appeared on stage with Kambona and Karume and other ministers, explaining the union and all rumors and controversies of the past year with earthy humor. If there were any truth to the unlikely rumor that the very men sitting behind him were the authors of the forgeries, the performance reinforced his persona as the face and voice of Tanzanian nationalism. In the speech, Nyerere took the opportunity to dissect the rumors and exaggerations of the publicity battle. "Only seven Chinese have been made the cause of spoiling all our friendship with the Western countries. . . . We have thousands of Britons working here . . . and the numbers of Peace Corps members will be 550 this year." Laying authoritative claim to his role as land allocator in chief, Nyerere also dwelt for some time on the issue of confiscating lands of colonial settlers, explaining that he did so not because of their race but because they were not using it productively. "A person is given land by his fellow countrymen to make

Figure 10.2. President Julius Nyerere speaks at a public rally in Dar es Salaam, November 1964. *From left:* Bibi Titi Mohamed, First Vice President Sheikh Abeid Karume, Nyerere, and Second Vice President Rashid Kawawa, with Minister of State Amir Jamal and Minister of State Nsilo Swai in the foreground. © Tanzania Information Services (MAELEZO).

use of it and not to sit on it like a mat." He also planted a seed of doubt in the public mind about the letters, opening the door to a future retraction without undermining the government's credibility, suggesting that the government reacted strongly to possible forgeries because so many other threats were real. "The Swahili say: A man who has been bitten by a snake startles if he sees a palm leaf."[110] Turning to Abeid Karume sitting behind him, Nyerere asked, "What do they do in Zanzibar when they see a palm leaf?" Karume gamely played along, "They get startled!"

A few days after the speech, Kambona enthusiastically lauded Nyerere: "Tanganyika needed Nyerere, Africa needed him."[111] Having learned a lesson, two weeks later Kambona experimented with a rumor attack of his own against American activities in Congo. According to a British diplomat, "Shortly after the Stanleyville operation [Kambona] personally concocted a story for the *Nationalist* by 'inventing' a Congolese rebel soldier who was said to have escaped from Stanleyville who with tears in his eyes described how the mercenaries killed every African in sight."[112]

After the shock of the Stanleyville operation had died down, and while Kambona visited the United States and the United Kingdom in early December, Nyerere publicly accepted the American finding that the "plot" documents were forgeries. The incident, however, very nearly led to a break in the friendly relations the two countries had enjoyed officially until then.[113] Portugal may have considered this break between Tanzania and the United States as a felicitous side-effect of the operation. Lisbon had grown especially frustrated with Kennedy's support for African nationalism, and saw no improvement under Johnson.[114] Indeed, discreet US support for a FRELIMO school for Mozambican refugees was being channeled through the African American Institute, a State Department creation, and the government urged the Ford Foundation to continue support for educating refugees despite Portuguese pressure on the foundation to cut off funding.[115] Foreign Minister Noguera had been quoted by a German magazine saying, "The primary enemy of Portugal in Africa is America."[116] Such conflicting goals aside, however, Portugal continued to cultivate its alliance with the United States, and to insist on its status as a full member of NATO. There was nothing surprising in a Portuguese minister complaining about US policy in an unguarded moment of an interview, even as his country still maintained close and cooperative relations with the United States.

After the fallout from the forged letter incident cleared, Nyerere and Leonhart agreed that they "had no other wish than have our relations return friendship mutual cooperation."[117] Nyerere himself was deeply frustrated with life in "rumourville."[118] When the Australian ambassador expressed bewilderment that all the evidence they had for the "Western Plot" was the three documents, Nyerere responded despondently: "What am I to believe—I don't know, I just don't know.... When I made the speech at the mass rally, everybody expected me to say either these are 100% true or 100% untrue—what was I to say—I don't know.... We are simple people. We have had no experience of forgeries."[119]

Fending off self-doubt, Nyerere could barely maintain his composure as he struggled to divine the truth behind the contradictory protestations of his foreign friends. Nyerere fretted that out-of-control white mercenaries originally hired by Tshombe in the Congo could become a danger to Tanzania. "No one knows what they may do next," he said. He turned instead to old friends. In late December, just before Christmas, Nyerere had traveled to Zanzibar and received enthusiastic receptions throughout his journey as he congratulated Zanzibaris for progress on self-help schemes, supported revolutionary efforts to redistribute land, and expressed sympathy for the populist resentment against former slaveholding classes. The journey marked the success of the initial bond that constituted the new nation of Tanzania.[120] Compared to the menacing uncertainty of foreign intrigue, the shaky coastal union seemed reassuringly stable, as the

Zanzibari government made formidable security arrangements in preparation for his visit.[121]

The Expulsion of Gordon and Carlucci

Another case of ambiguous evidence sparked the final crisis of Tanzania's external sovereignty during the tumultuous year following the Zanzibar Revolution. A couple weeks after Nyerere's December visit, Zanzibari intelligence services obtained recordings of what seemed to be a telephone call on January 11, 1965, between American consular officers Robert Gordon and Frank Carlucci planning a military intervention in Zanzibar under the code name "second twelfth." Although the Tanzanian leadership could not be certain whether their interpretation of the recordings was accurate, they perceived an external threat to the Zanzibari government and chose to act defensively. The Zanzibari Revolutionary Council recommended that the diplomats be expelled, and in the end Nyerere agreed. The expulsion was a risk Nyerere took for the sake of the Union.

The two diplomats had been under surveillance for some time, and Tanzanian intelligence suggested that their plan fell through only because Gordon had failed to arrange a shipment of weapons promised to Zanzibari rebels.[122] Gordon and Carlucci maintained that the phrase "second twelfth" referred to their attempt to convince the White House to release a congratulatory letter to Karume on the second anniversary of the revolution. They said they had failed to obtain a letter on January 12, and were trying to make a case for a letter for February 12, once it was clear which other governments would send congratulatory messages. The "second twelfth" was thought to be appropriate because the Zanzibari government had postponed the anniversary celebration until February 12 because January 12 fell during Ramadan.[123] Gordon told Carlucci that to make a strong case to the White House for a letter, he would rhetorically "need more ammunition."[124] This commonplace turn-of-phrase in American English was easy to misunderstand, especially if there was a good reason to do so for political ends.

The recordings were played in meetings of the Zanzibari Revolutionary Council and in Nyerere's cabinet. Job Lusinde heard the tape and recognized the phrase as a figure of speech, but was convinced that it was code and that Carlucci's diplomatic credentials were a front for his CIA employment.[125] Based on cabinet and council recommendations, Nyerere expelled both US diplomats immediately for "acts that would endanger the Government of Unguja, and beyond that, the Government of the Union."[126] In Zanzibar, Karume sent members of his party's Youth League to break open containers imported for the US Consulate in Zanzibar to check for weapons.[127] Carlucci protested that the recordings were doctored by Soviet or East German advisers, and Gordon denied any contact with Zanzibari dissidents or knowledge of shipping movements.[128] With direction from Washington, Leonhart told Nyerere that the charges were preposterous, and if Nyerere insisted on expelling the diplomats, it would lead to a downgrading of US relations with Tanzania.

The ambassador's report of the conversation to his superiors at the State Department took note of Nyerere's emotional state with a diagnostic economy, not unlike spurious evaluations of Lumumba's mental state during the Congo Crisis in 1960.[129] "Nyerere replied emotionally," Leonhart wrote, "that I must understand that in aftermath of plot, forged documents, last few difficult months in our relations, and his appreciation US restraint and patience, neither he nor his government would have taken this decision without positive and overwhelming proof. He and his closest advisers had met throughout the day on case and had no alternative but request immediate removal Gordon and Carlucci." Weeping and hardly able to speak, Nyerere stood by his decision, telling the ambassador, "This is one more damn period we just have to get through." With a scornful eye, Leonhart warned Nyerere "that [even] with all [the] good will [in the world,] none of us could continue to help him unless he helped himself."[130]

The incident presented an inauspicious beginning to a new year that both Nyerere and Leonhart had hoped would leave such awkward impasses behind them. After a year of troubled suspicions between two men who sought friendship, both personal and diplomatic, the ambassador cautioned, "This method of handling [the] affair could have [the] gravest effect on our relationship." The verdict was evidently a difficult one for Nyerere. But his strain stemmed not simply from indecision but also from the suspicion that the American ambassador, whom he considered a friend, was either lying to him or had no idea what his own government was doing. The expulsion threatened to upset the precarious balance Tanzania had struck between East and West in the Cold War, a fragile sovereignty punctuated by the possibility of foreign intervention.[131] "We are a small country, but we are as much a sovereign state as the U.S.," Nyerere insisted. "We do not bully, and we do not like being bullied."[132]

Nyerere made a difficult but prudent decision to support the Zanzibari Revolutionary Council's decision and expelled Carlucci and Gordon amid a wave of rumors and plots against his government's authority.[133] As with the forged letters incident, the reality behind the diplomatic row remains a mystery, but within a few months even the British found themselves "coming round to the view that there is almost certainly more to the matter than a single telephone call."[134] Nyerere's colleagues were sure that the Gordon-Carlucci plot was real, but suspected the two diplomats were working alone in direct communication with G. Mennen Williams without informing Ambassador Leonhart in Dar es Salaam.[135]

Aware of Carlucci's service in the Congo at the time of Lumumba's assassination, the Tanzanian leaders were convinced that he was a CIA agent and had had a hand in it.[136] His sudden appearance in Zanzibar after the revolution suggested that he was on a similar mission there, as he tracked everything from arms shipments to dissident politics.[137] Carlucci had proposed direct action against the revolutionary Zanzibar regime before the Union Treaty. He was disturbed by subsequent events on the islands and was aware of the efforts of Zanzibari royalist rebels to obtain materiel and American assent for an armed coup d'état. Robert Gordon was also posted to Dar es Salaam in the wake of the revolution in Zanzibar. A veteran Foreign Service officer, previously posted in Iraq and Sudan, Gordon arrived in Dar es Salaam in June. In preparation for his new assignment he had attended a short course during the first part of 1964 at the US War College, which ran regular training programs for CIA agents.[138] Even if the tapes were doctored, the incident provided an opportune reason to expel two diplomats made suspect by the context of Cold War intrigue, and despite his doubts Nyerere did so.

The East Germans had been tracking Carlucci's activities closely and marked him as a subversive agent. It is possible that East German agents in Zanzibar voiced their suspicions after their director of foreign intelligence recognized Carlucci when both showed up to harvest cassava at a mass event put on by the revolutionary government.[139] When Carlucci returned from a vacation after the Union Treaty, he tried to "establish a social relationship with my next door neighbor, Aboud Jumbe, now Minister of State in the URTZ Government." When Jumbe finally invited him over, having had a bit too much to drink, he apologized to Carlucci for not inviting him sooner, but he confessed, "If I had visited your house, I would have been shot."[140] As the East Germans were training Zanzibar's security forces, it is likely that they passed on to the Zanzibaris some of the information about Carlucci that they were reporting to their superiors: "The American consul Carlucci has become very active in Zanzibar. He contacted the secretary of the Revolutionary Council and tried to obtain internal information from Zanzibar's leading circles. The reason he gave for his activities was that he wanted to exploit rifts within the government for outside intervention."[141]

Many officials in Tanzania's security forces, including Kambona, had read David Wise and Thomas Ross's 1964 book *The Invisible Government*.[142] The exposé was a well-informed, if conspiratorial, portrait of Cold War espionage highlighting American interventions in the Third World. Wise and Ross argued that many operations were directed by a secret group, primarily in the CIA, that acted independently of the elected American government. One chapter detailed the story of "the innocent ambassador" to Burma who had been deliberately misled about covert US support for Nationalist troops there.[143] Given their experiences that year, the

Tanzanian leaders were inclined to believe that CIA agents might be operating independently of Ambassador Leonhart. The ambassador may have wondered about this himself. To clear the air, all three American ambassadors in East Africa were brought back to Washington in February for briefings and a private meeting with President Johnson.[144] British diplomats based in Dar es Salaam likewise complained about just this sort of planning without their knowledge. "We in DAR must be equally kept informed of any contingency plans, if only to vet their validity."[145]

In fact, regardless of whether Gordon and Carlucci's specific telephone conversation was related to a subversive plot, the British-American plan to invade Zanzibar had never been entirely set aside.[146] Western intelligence services were not convinced that the Union Treaty precluded communist influence in Zanzibar.[147] Beginning with the aborted intervention plans of April, British and US intelligence services continued to share detailed estimates of Zanzibari military capabilities.[148] In June a prepared plan for military intervention awaited only Nyerere's assent, but he was, according to a British embassy officer, "still determined to see things through" and avoid intervention. The officer, however, doubted the communists could be routed from Zanzibar "without ultimate show-down, including possible use of force."[149] This renewed possibility of Anglo-American intervention was publicized by the London *Financial Times*, which advocated an invasion of the islands in a well-informed editorial.[150] In July the British navy tested secure radio transmissions in Zanzibar in preparation for the order "to retain a warship within seven days' steaming of Zanzibar against the need to meet an emergency evacuation."[151] A diplomat stationed in Dar es Salaam discussed the complexities of a coup with his superiors in London in early August: "I assume that if by any chance Britain were involved in an intervention operation and asked to assist in the subsequent task of administering the island, we would have the support of the Tanganyika authorities to underpin the Zanzibar administration with a few experienced expatriate officers."[152]

In September the British had begun to revisit their pre-Union fears about Zanzibar after concluding that Nyerere had minimal influence on Zanzibari politics and that if he were unable to control events, "the Union will break up and Zanzibar will become a communist state and a dangerous shop window on the East African coast."[153] But three months later, after the forged letters fiasco, the attitudes of the British reversed course, their having concluded that Nyerere was now suspicious of Western intentions and would never ask for or support foreign action in Zanzibar. British officers in Dar es Salaam advised that "the undertaking which Mr. Sandys gave to President Nyerere through Kambona last March of military support over Zanzibar . . . is now so remote that there is no case for holding in readiness any plan which involved tying down British forces."[154]

When the expulsion of Gordon and Carlucci occurred, Tanzania had detained and was interrogating a Cuban exile named Luis Toribio Cosme, who was cited in *Invisible Government* as the lead Cuban pilot in the Bay of Pigs operation.[155] Tanzanian authorities had arrested Cosme on Christmas Eve in Tabora, when he entered the country flying a UN plane ostensibly full of Burundian refugees. The Tanzanians were aware of Cosme's mercenary activities in the Congo, in part from the testimony of his own wife, who said he was a spy.[156] Secretary of State Rusk inquired anxiously about Cosme's fate, in a manner supportive of *Invisible Government*'s contention that US intelligence activities operated without the knowledge of local ambassadors. Rusk deceptively indicated to Ambassador Leonhart that any bad publicity arising from Cosme's capture was propaganda, hinting at the unlikely possibility that Tanzanians were forcing information out of this staunch anticommunist officer from the pre-Castro Cuban Air Force of Fulgencio Batista.[157] Rusk, in the department's typical telegraphic style, urgently requested "any information about what Cosme may be saying while he is in custody. . . . It possible we may face surfacing operation accompanied by propaganda barrage linking Congo, Tanzanian Plot, Cosme and Gordon/Carlucci affair in effort discredit us."[158] His concern betrayed a fear that such allegations could not be easily dismissed. However tenuous the actual connections, to the Tanzanians these events appeared to be linked, and in the African Cold War context they spelled danger.

In addition to Cosme's presence, there had been plenty of evidence that year of plots to upset the fragile Union, which Westerners feared was trending toward communist domination. In April, while trying to mobilize Western aid to strengthen the Union, Nyerere had raised the unlikely possibility "that there might be a coup in Zanzibar led by pro-Chinese Communist supporters of Babu to undo the union with Tanganyika."[159] Similar rumors circulated again in August that Babu was training a personal army under Soviet supervision "to carry out a coup against the present Government and Karume in particular."[160] Meanwhile, East German intelligence observed "a noticeable increase of imperialist activity in Zanzibar."[161] In September a "little mutiny" was disrupted in the coastal district of Tanga where labor leaders arrested during the January mutiny were being held. Among the thirty people arrested were Major Kavana and Captain Chacha, two officers of the old Tanganyika Rifles who had been favorites of the mutineers in January. Also implicated was the local area commissioner, who was promptly replaced by a TANU loyalist.[162] In October word spread that an American ship had offloaded weapons to a dhow, which delivered them to Zanzibar where they were seized.[163] Another set of mainland police reinforcements were deployed to the islands, and the Zanzibari Revolutionary Council approved the mass arrest of more than a hundred local residents accused of subversion.[164] Carlucci heard that some of the detainees had been tortured and had confessed to a counter-revolutionary plot, and noted: "From time to time we and British have both had approaches (which we promptly rebuffed) from Arab groups planning subversion, it [is] possible that these stories are correct."[165] The ambassador to Kenya likewise recalled repeated visits by "a bearded Arab patriarch from Mombasa who asked, always in vain, for help in restoring the sultan to Zanzibar."[166]

Indeed, Prince Mohamed Abdullah, the brother of the deposed sultan Jamshid bin Abdullah, was a regular visitor to the US Embassy in London in search of support. He encouraged a US intervention and US advocacy for a referendum in Zanzibar on the union with Tanganyika. Barring other action, he proposed that £100,000 would be sufficient to recruit a mercenary army to overthrow Karume's government.[167] On a visit on November 9, Prince Abdullah informed Philip Kaiser in London that he had "sufficient finances now available from another source" to hire foreign mercenaries to overthrow Karume's government. The promised funds for the November invasion were contingent on obtaining an agreement that the "US would give new government such support as necessary (including military) to assure that Tanganyika or any other country did not move against it." Kaiser forwarded the request to Washington: "In view serious nature of request . . . appreciate prompt reply."[168] Washington's reply is unavailable, but rebellion in Zanzibar was fermenting.

That same day, a week after the seizure of the dhow carrying weapons to the islands, Zanzibari authorities detained an Irish Catholic priest together with 150 "Arabs arrested following fears counterrevolutionary plot and suspicions ZNP (repeat ZLP) [sic] smuggling arms and money into Zanzibar from Mombasa."[169] The next day, as the forged letters made their way to Nyerere's hand, Carlucci wired warning to London that "if word gets to Karume that Prince Mohammed frequenting U.S. Embassy, this would greatly complicate our situation here."[170] The following week, during the uproar on the mainland over the forged letters plot, the Zanzibari government imprisoned another fourteen members of a subversive organization called the "Peace Fighters' Union," sentencing five of them to death.[171] The arrests largely targeted members of the former ZNP government, and the executions were carried out a few days later. At least one detainee was released upon being found innocent and went to see Carlucci. The freed detainee said he had received a personal apology from Karume, who had asked if he knew Carlucci and cautioned, "Avoid him, he is a very dangerous man."[172]

The Tanzanian leadership already held Carlucci in great suspicion, potentially linked to various subversive activities up and down the coast, and the recorded telephone conversations were a pretext for a longer-standing desire to remove him from the scene. In early January, about a week before the Gordon/Carlucci affair surfaced, a part-time Swahili announcer for Voice of America stationed in Cairo, Ahmed Hamoud, representing a group of Zanzibari exiles calling themselves the Zanzibar Liberation Front, made a renewed approach to the American ambassador in Egypt. "Their object," he observed, "since they see no other recourse, is revolution. For this they need money and arms, and a guarantee that outsiders will be kept away from the islands while they launch their armed insurrection."[173]

Hoping for US support, Hamoud brought copies of publications documenting complaints about the revolutionary Zanzibari regime. The first was an undated pamphlet published shortly after the January revolution titled "Zanzibar: A Lesson to Freedom Loving Peoples," which had been released by the Zanzibar Liberation Front. In erudite English, the pamphlet interpreted Zanzibar's recent history and offered both a critique of communism and a declaration that Zanzibari revolutionaries were in fact fascists. It offered information on Algerian arms shipments to Zanzibar that had been reported in secret American and Portuguese intelligence documents, but only announced publicly in a Portuguese press conference in late 1964, well after the pamphlet was published.[174] The pamphlet also cited the former Zanzibari prime minister Mohammed Shamte, who was perturbed when Nyerere asked him, "Why not annex Zanzibar to Tanganyika? After all, it is no bigger than Moshi."[175]

Hamoud also had in hand a subsequent broadside that referred to the pamphlet, and accused Karume of turning the islands into "a labour camp" with mass arrests, rapes, and floggings. It pointed out that the Union Treaty was signed while Abdulrahman Babu was abroad, and argued that hidden weapons, used as the pretext for Karume's arrests of Arab counterrevolutionaries, were in fact stashed by Babu, Ali Mafoudh, and their compatriots in preparation for a communist overthrow of Karume.[176] This second counterrevolutionary broadside was originally released on November 9, 1964, coinciding with Prince Abdullah's entreaty to the American representative in London, the psychological operations in preparation for the American attack on Stanleyville, and the Portuguese initiation of the plan to smear Kambona, and the forged letters. Christopher Ngaiza, stationed in London as the Tanzanian high commissioner, was also aware of these publications and had concluded that they were published in the United Kingdom, with the support of the deposed sultan, who was living there in exile.[177] Even if these events were not connected, to Tanzanian observers at the time they appeared to be linked.

In January, the day after Carlucci's departure, the chief American consular officer in Zanzibar reiterated Carlucci's innocence to Karume, who responded by recalling Tanzanian suspicions that Carlucci and Gordon aimed to arm an invasion by the former sultan's Arab partisans. "Does the

US want to reimpose Arab slavery on Africans? ... Of course not, there could be no possible reason for this, no benefit for USG."[178] Karume's final answer to his own rhetorical question was either a sign of ongoing worries about reinvasion by the sultan's loyalists or a sly hint that he caught on to the American diplomatic sleight of hand in its protestations of innocence. Then, to assuage worries of reprisals against Americans in Zanzibar, Karume reassured the officer that his intelligence services informed him of everything that happened in Zanzibar. "Nobody will do anything against any American," Karume intoned with a note of triumph. "No one can deceive me."

Tanganyikan and Zanzibari politicians responded effectively to the ambiguous currents of Cold War intrigue. As with much else that busy year, it is still unclear whether there was an authorized plan for American-supported intervention in Zanzibar in 1964, but the evidence is sufficient to suggest that the Tanzanians reacted prudently to well-grounded suspicions that their country's sovereignty was threatened. The tone of diplomatic communication, the psychological operations, and the cooperation with disgruntled loyalists of the old regime in Zanzibar are strikingly similar to American intrigue in Iran, Guatemala, and Indonesia that brought about the overthrows of Mohammad Mosaddeq, Jacobo Arbenz, and Sukarno, all leftist nationalists like Nyerere and Karume.[179] While the overthrow of the revolutionary Zanzibari government in an American-supported coup by loyalists to the former sultan's regime may seem far-fetched today, at the time the Tanzanian leadership considered it a distinct possibility.[180] Cold War historian Odd Arne Westad's observations reinforce the plausibility of Tanzanian concerns about foreign interference: "By the late 1950s the United States had established an interventionist policy with global reach. Only regimes that accepted the American hegemony in foreign policy and in development strategy were seen as viable, and some of the 'unviable' states were condemned for voluntarily or involuntarily opening up for communism, and thereby provoking a US intervention."[181]

The Cold War powers cultivated uncertainty as a tactic of their interventionist strategies. Nonaligned countries had to act despite this uncertainty. In the Union of Tanzania, East African leaders created a state that could be read as "viable" to the Cold War powers, and thus resistant to overt intervention. By late 1964, however, many in the US government were clearly arguing that the Tanzanian union no longer served American purposes, even if it remains unclear what steps they took in attempts to redirect Tanzanian policy.

Often acting on nothing more than hunches, Tanzanians took proactive steps to reshape the strategic situation and communicate the sovereignty of their territory in an ambiguous diplomatic struggle. East African leaders shared intelligence among themselves as effectively as the superpowers did, and they displayed a strategic sophistication that kept Zanzibar firmly within an East African sphere of influence while escalating the battle for the liberation of southern Africa. They supported armed rebellion in Mozambique, having rhetorically prepared the ground for a broader regional confrontation with white minority governments that neither side in the Cold War could oppose publicly. Beginning in 1965, Tanzania embarked on a more explicitly socialist path and deeper bilateral relationship with China without sacrificing productive relationships on either side of the ideological divide. To the extent that they could prevail in these battles of rumor and intrigue, they cultivated favorable conditions for sovereign autonomy in domestic and foreign policy.

Conclusion

> In 1961, what was our major ambition? Our major ambition was obviously to survive as a nation. We have survived as a nation, we have consolidated ourselves as a nation, and we have consolidated our independence.... Only as an independent country could we do such things as raising standards of living, increasing education, and so forth. Well I can't say we have achieved all we would have liked to achieve.
>
> —Julius Nyerere, 1971

Amidst innumerable ongoing challenges, the union with Zanzibar is still the most contentious issue that the Tanzanian state faces. A 2013 constitutional commission proposed an end to the "two-government" system put in place by the Union Treaty of 1964, to be replaced by a "three-government" system that would offer both Zanzibar and the mainland more autonomy under an overarching federal government.[1] This is a response to continued complaints about the asymmetric union agreement and its enforcement by the ruling party. In 2000 and 2005 an opposition party, the Civic United Front (CUF), accused the ruling party of election fraud, while TANU's heir, Chama Cha Mapinduzi (CCM), accused CUF of campaigning to break up the Union. Violence and intimidation on the islands marred both elections. Throughout this period the two parties have endeavored to come to an agreement ("*Muafaka*") to improve electoral machinery and institute a power-sharing government on the islands, a process that brought about a more tranquil, if no less contested, election in 2010.[2] CUF never openly advocated secession, but the party has been outspoken in favor of autonomy in the recent constitutional debates. The cry for Zanzibari independence in recent years has been led by the Association for Islamic Mobilisation and Propagation (popularly known as Jumiki or Uamsho), which proclaims: "We want our country of Zanzibar and we want the full sovereignty of Zanzibar."[3] In the midst of this there is a religious tension between a mainland government that many Muslims see as dominated by Christians, and a Zanzibari opposition that many Christians consider too tolerant of Islamic fundamentalism.

This tension finds expression in opposing accounts of history, particularly that of the Union.[4] Typical of old-guard members of Nyerere's government, Thabit Kombo defended the Union as a natural reunification and the continued defense of a people artificially separated by colonial borders and the slave regime of the former sultan. "Without the Union, the enemies of Zanzibar would have increased their machinations, and there would be neither security nor peace, neither in Zanzibar nor on the mainland."[5] In Harith Ghassany's collection of oral histories of the Zanzibar Revolution, memories fade into alternating praises and denunciations of the founding fathers. Karume is acclaimed as a "leading participant" in planning the revolution and also painted as a simpleton who knew nothing of the revolution and was hoodwinked into signing the Union Treaty. Nyerere is credited with initiating the revolution and discussing a pragmatic union with a cooperative Karume, while being blamed for sinister machinations to dilute Muslim influence by subsuming Zanzibar under a Union government with its supposed preponderance of mainland Christians. In these memories, Oscar Kambona, who later broke with Nyerere and moved into exile as a vocal opponent, emerges as a curious hero. He seems to symbolize an alternative national mythology that removes Nyerere from his saintly throne and thereby liberates political rhetoric from his stubborn insistence on Ujamaa and the Union. It is a discursive strategy that veers into extremist scapegoating not unlike the violent rhetoric that Jonathon Glassman documented in prerevolutionary Zanzibar. One of Ghassany's informants portrays Kambona, after his return from exile to run for office in 1995, as fixing the blame on Nyerere for training Hutu extremists in mainland refugee camps "so that they would go attack Tutsis" in the Rwandan genocide. "I think there is no problem in Africa in which Nyerere did not have his hand," Ghassany's interviewee concludes histrionically.[6]

In these minimally edited and highly politicized testimonies, such wild accusations coexist with credible insights into the bewildering events of 1964.[7] What is striking in all of these perspectives is the memory of two former sovereignties, and the ongoing central concern of CCM to reinforce the Union as the new sovereign. The odd arrangement of the Union Treaty, with a semisovereign government for Zanzibar under an overarching Union government with no separate governing structure for mainland Tanganyika, evinces the compromise that made the treaty possible. Nyerere was keen to retain a unitary sovereign authority, and he did so by sacrificing a separate political identity for Tanganyika and allowing for the obvious incongruity of the agreement.

Some of the Zanzibari revolutionary leaders, having briefly controlled a sovereign power, regretted the relinquishment of that sense of control and possibility, despite their initial support for federation in principle. Aboud Jumbe argued that neither Tanganyika nor Zanzibar "committed suicide after the marriage which gave birth to the United Republic," and therefore the "two-government" system that gave Zanzibar limited autonomy under the Union government of Tanzania lacked a legal constitution.[8] Despite Abdulrahman Babu's initial support for the idea, the treaty was consummated very deliberately while he was out of the country for fear that he would torpedo the arrangement if his socialist ambitions were constrained. Summarizing this history from exile years later, Babu elided his early support for the Union.[9] Where Babu thrived in the ideological negotiations of Cold War diplomacy, Abeid Karume, under continuous contradictory pressure from American, Chinese, and Soviet diplomats, was more prepared to hand over these headaches to a Union government. Nyerere credited "Karume's generosity of spirit" for making the treaty possible by relinquishing the main markers of Zanzibari sovereignty: "presidential office, powers over foreign affairs, finance, army and police, citizenship, even his harbors."[10] In his New Year's speech in January 1965, Nyerere presented the union as he always wanted it to be, the first baby step toward regional federation: "The Union between Tanganyika and Zanzibar is the event which history will record for 1964. For us, the people of Tanzania, it has enormous importance; the stupidity of two separate sovereign states when the people have a common history, culture, and language, has been ended by our own action."[11]

The Tanganyika-Zanzibar Union overcame the fundamental challenge of Pan-African unity that Nyerere frequently pointed out: the sacrifice of existing sovereignty for the sake of federation. And in this regard Zanzibar is the exception. East African federation foundered against various subnational interest groups that believed their authority would be diluted, from the king of Buganda to the residents of coastal Kenya, and then the rival nationalist leaders themselves.[12] Tanganyika was by far the most unified of the former British colonies in East Africa, a unity Nyerere meticulously cultivated in nearly every speech. Even so, independence across East Africa meant a confrontation with powerful colonial-era chiefs who retained a sense of authority thought to have been only temporarily subject to British authority. For them, independence became a moment to reclaim lost thrones and lost lands, even if the idea of what was lost was largely imaginary. The end of colonialism meant an end to myriad memories of sovereignty that had been kept alive during the brief period of British indirect rule. For Nyerere, this fundamentally destructive erasure of former authorities was a feasible and necessary first step toward Pan-African unity. The core problem was how to reconcile nationalist authorities to the reality that Pan-African government would require a Pan-African sovereign. "One of the hard facts we have to face on our way to African Unity," Nyerere wrote, "is that this Unity means—on the part of countries—the surrender of sovereignty, and—on the part of individual leaders—the surrender of high positions. We must face quite squarely the fact that so far there has been no such surrender in the name of African Unity."[13]

Such international unity begged the question of effective internal sovereignty. In Tanganyika—through the power of the nationalist movement with its deft management of ideology and institutional development, and its Machiavellian marginalization of all rivals—Nyerere had established overarching authority. With his resignation of the prime minister's office in 1962 and his conscientious cooperation with his party and governing structure, he laid the groundwork for the depersonalization and institutionalization of Tanganyikan sovereignty. The nation became, in Bibi Titi's words, "not the country of Nyerere," but rather "the country of the Nation of Tanganyika." The price of Nyerere's strategy was the elimination of multiparty democracy. The Tanganyikan sovereign would be nationalist sentiment itself, a moral vision borne primarily in the institutions of the ruling party, and only secondarily in the government.

Having established nationalist sentiment, the subsequent Union with Zanzibar required the imagination of an entirely new nation: that of Tanzania. Just as two individuals choosing to cooperate for mutual benefit each sacrifice a measure of their individual autonomy for the sake of a new agreement to govern their relationship, Nyerere argued, so also the incorporative agreement between two nations created something wholly new in their union. Nyerere perceived that if a separate Union government were created to govern the two contributing states, it would not inherit their sovereignty but only manage it as the agent of two paymasters. Instead the two governments had to somehow be combined into a single sovereign, even if it had two vice presidents. One served as an assistant to the president of the republic, the other as the president of what would otherwise be either a constituent political region or an independent country. The key was that the Zanzibari president did not wield sovereign power but was rather limited to legal and regulatory powers proportionate to those of a federal governor. The awkward compromise that emerged, for all its failings, structured the Union as a unified state under one president.

In an epic historical poem about the Tanzanian army from the Stone Age to modern times, Minael Mdundo acclaimed the Union Treaty's clever institutional innovation that communicated the overarching sovereignty of Tanzania to the residents of its unbalanced constituencies: "Tanganyika and Unguja [Zanzibar] then became one country, a Republic with rights, and much strength in the country."[14] In an introduction to the poem, Tanzanian historian Isaria Kimambo divided it into three thematic sections that seem to consolidate the official CCM party line into historical vocabulary: (a) the time in *Tanzania Bara* (continental Tanzania, what had been the Mandate Territory of Tanganyika) before the Union of Tanganyika and Zanzibar, (b) *Tanzania Visiwani* (Island Tanzania, i.e., Zanzibar) before the Union, and (c) *Tanzania Nzima* (Complete Tanzania) after the Union.[15] The creation of the Union is portrayed as the moment of sovereignty.

For Abdulrahman Babu the Union Treaty became just the opposite: "a murky story of political cunning and skullduggery," Cold War intrigue in which "the active instigator was the United States government." Despite his frustration with its implementation, even Babu addressed the Union in terms of the same ideal of African unity that Nyerere espoused, with the implication that if had it been "created in a genuine spirit of Pan-Africanism," it would then represent a viable sovereignty. Babu expressed these views from exile in Britain in the mid-1980s, writing the preface to an account of the Zanzibar Revolution and the Union written by an amateur historian, Amrit Wilson. Quoting extensively from the American diplomatic correspondence on file in the Lyndon Baines Johnson Library in Austin, Texas, Wilson endeavored to "tell the real story through these perceptions and through US reports of its own actions, letting the voices of officials speak for themselves as they conspire, gloat, boast, confide and panic to each other in these curiously phrased telegrams and messages."[16] In fact, Wilson offered a very powerful historical critique, arguing that Nyerere launched Tanzania onto a neocolonial path politically and economically, to the detriment of Zanzibari interests. Written during the deregulated denouement of the one-party state, Wilson's account ended with a Zanzibari commentator explaining that Zanzibar was ripe for another revolution. "The present rulers can't rule the country any more. . . . A major explosion is on its way. . . . Nobody wants the union."[17] Implying a neocolonial origin of the Tanzanian Union, Wilson's condemnation hinged on the idea that the bond between sovereignty and political legitimacy had been broken.[18]

In a recent reevaluation, Tanzanian legal scholar Issa Shivji found that the basic shortcoming of the Union agreement was the lack of democratic participation in its implementation, which has left the legitimacy, not to mention the constitutionality, of the Union perennially crippled.[19] Karume made the decision to join Tanganyika on behalf of the Zanzibari people without public input, and then indefinitely postponed constitutional revisions to establish the Union in law.[20] In the meantime, the Union government incrementally took control over an increasing number of governmental powers. Tanzania's 1977 constitution formalized ongoing contradictions between the powers of the Union and the laws of Zanzibar. The merger of the ASP and TANU to form CCM in 1977 made it easy to pass the new constitution with minimal democratic participation, leaving it as doubtful as ever in the eyes of many. However, Shivji still presents the broader issue of the Union in the same light as Nyerere did, in the tension between narrow nationalism and Pan-African integration. The bridge between the two, Shivji urges, should be the legitimating force of democratic choice.

As this account has shown, assertions that the idea for the Union came from Americans seeking to thwart communist intentions are incorrect. The Union was initially proposed by the Zanzibari leadership, including both Abeid Karume and Abdulrahman Babu, who had already been in conversation with Nyerere and other mainland leaders. Babu's (and Jumbe's) later criticism of the Union arose from subsequent disagreements, not from its original vision. The hasty imposition of the Union Treaty was a result of the emergency created by foreign intrigue in the region in 1964 and the counterrevolutionary activities of Zanzibari exiles who had been the victims of the revolution. The Union was ultimately the rushed result of the decision and subsequent pronouncement to merge the two countries. It was a discursive intervention that fundamentally preserved local authority in the two countries, which chose voluntarily to unify under the banner of Pan-Africanism. Whatever its shortcomings, the Union strategically stabilized East Africa in 1964 and deflected superpower influence in Zanzibar.

"The Price of Social Living"

The first years of Tanzania's independent history show that the production of supreme institutional authority in a territory and its coincident broadcast abroad are both products of discursive agency, which lies at the heart of all political leadership. It is a question of how well the ideals and practice of political leadership accord with the expectations of the people subject to the authority of that leadership.[21] This subjection is nominally voluntary, in the limited sense of people's conformity to an existing power structure. It stems from people's best judgment of the facts at hand—facts that continually shift in meaning and interpretation as they disseminate through society. In the modern world of Shivji's retrospective and legalistic interpretation of the Union Treaty, it is democratic procedure that legitimately expresses the concept of Rousseau's *volonté générale* that Nyerere wrestled with at Edinburgh. But we must also account for how public representatives in general make decisions in times of crisis, and in particular how public consensus is formed in an East African cultural environment, where precolonial modes of social organization retain a cogent presence in the political system. Minael Mdundo's poem, rooting modern Tanzanian history in a politicized memory of a precolonial past, asserts that people saw the benefits of central authority and so produced central authorities for themselves: "In the many tribes," she wrote, "they saw that it was beneficial for there to be a Chief in place to lead in peace."[22] Hers is a highly politicized and constructed memory, but it signals a popular discourse about political leadership that scholars cannot ignore.

The chiefly offices created in the colonial period, like the one Nyerere felt called to create in the Zanaki country in his youth, were as much the result of construction as of conquest. New regimes can be instigated by force, just as Maasai military power transformed the structure of sovereignty in Zanaki country in the nineteenth century. But conquering powers initially capture only a very superficial sovereignty, which allows prior systems of authority to retain their supremacy in local affairs. Until a deeper legitimacy can be established, conquered people continue to imagine their reemergence once the conquering power can be expelled, rendering the conqueror's sovereignty incomplete. Such belief in a reemergent sovereignty was evident in the dual discourse of gerontocracy that Jan Shetler found in Zanaki country. There Maasai age-set systems operated superficially over the deeper and more authoritative generation-sets of the Zanaki people.[23] But even there the slow discursive change from conquest to legitimacy was already in motion. With each generation the incorporation of Maasai age-sets into local practice blurred the lines between Maasai and Zanaki practice, creating a new hegemony. Likewise in today's world, democratic practice must attain hegemony before it can function.

The discursive concept of hegemony is a key point of debate between conquest and legitimacy in the postcolonial state.[24] The only difference between a delimited territorial hegemony and sovereignty is the additional legal ascription of autonomy granted to sovereigns in the international community. This then reminds us that the mere ascription of "flag" sovereignty is not sufficient, and that a proper definition of sovereignty must entail the powers understood in the concept of hegemony. This is true both within nations and in the international system. Sovereignty only functions because it is a hegemonic construct in the world today.[25]

At the heart of the Union debate is the question of whether the United Republic of Tanzania has gained hegemony or not: Is Tanzania a permanent polity or just a superficial result of a coercively enforced "Nyerere-Karume coup d'état" (as Babu called it)?[26] The question itself cannot be answered; it is, rather, constitutive of the society created by the Union. The question anchors the continual negotiation of the awkward terms of the Union Treaty that constitutes the Tanzanian nation-state. Shivji suggests that democratic choice might have provided the answer then, and must now anchor efforts to define new polities, whether national or Pan-African. But in regard to the current Union, it would be a traumatic separation even if democratically chosen. As the treaty reaches its fiftieth anniversary, a new proposal to revise the Tanzanian constitution offers the chance for a democratic ratification of an ongoing Union in some form, but an actual separation is not officially contemplated.[27]

Nyerere sought to define the Union within an ideal of incremental Pan-Africanism framed by his articulation of African socialism rather than Cold War alliances. This idea held a certain coercive hegemony while Nyerere remained in power in a single-party state. In a thoughtful essay on the Union and its legacy, Haroub Othman pointed out that the Union is part-and-parcel of the stabilizing hegemonic construct that Tanzanian nationhood represents.

The national language, the ethics of equality and human dignity, and the Union of Tanganyika and Zanzibar are what overcame the ethnic hatred, religious bigotry, regional parochialism and national differences and forged national cohesion and unity. It is these that have made Tanzania an example in a continent beset with secessionism, ethnic violence and religious pogroms. One hopes that there is capacity, honesty and patriotism within Tanzania that will look beyond the sectarian interests. The alternative is too horrendous to contemplate.[28]

Contemplating hegemony, Steven Feierman took issue with Antonio Gramsci's original Marxist formulation that peasants are incapable of articulating a discursive critique of their situation and so rely on leaders rising above peasant consciousness to do so for them.[29] Instead, Feierman argued, in a prefiguration of Mbembe's work, that peasants themselves create and authorize the discourse and practice to which political elites must conform. In the integrated intellectual networks of rural Tanzania that were Feierman's site of investigation, the idea that hegemony emanates from an ideologically and socially alienated ruling class becomes impossible to sustain. In fact, Gramsci's definition of an intellectual is fairly expansive and encompasses the possibility of "peasant intellectuals." Feierman's critique is directed more at the "impoverished mechanistic concept which interprets each particular ideological element as caused or imposed by a particular set of class relations."[30] Feierman's study undermines the Marxist teleology of class conflict, and instead aligns with Nyerere's own critique of that aspect of socialist theory.[31] Nyerere and most of his colleagues, although not far removed from peasant society, were from families that somehow had access to education for their children. In many ways they were representative of both the transformative intellectuals of Gramsci's formulation and the elite of a peasant intellectual ferment, which Feierman suggests. Arguably, through their colonial education, they were also agents of a bourgeois notion of modernization. They were products of multiple discourses seeking, as Nyerere put it, "a new synthesis."

It becomes clear that, in many cases, conflict is not an objective state but a constitutive ideology that does not erase socioeconomic boundaries but rather constructs them in a hegemonic social intercourse. By presenting this process as veiled tyranny, Michel Foucault's disciplinary model of power intimated the presence of a Marxian false consciousness in the minds of people caught up in a "coercive apparatus." Late in his career, Foucault allowed that "when I was studying asylums, prisons, and so on, I insisted, I think, too much on the techniques domination. . . . We must not understand the exercise of power as pure violence or strict coercion."[32] In this perspective, power was always relational, "rooted deep in the social nexus, not reconstituted 'above' society as a supplementary structure."[33] Holly Hanson likewise took issue with the implications of these approaches in a critique of Pierre Bourdieu. "To assert that 'gentle, hidden exploitation is the form taken by man's exploitation of man whenever overt, brutal exploitation is impossible' naturalizes domination and makes it inevitable." Hanson insisted that assent was key to politics in precolonial East Africa.[34]

For Nyerere, sovereignty seemed to appear at a point of balance between Foucauldian discipline and consensual legitimacy. If Foucauldian discipline is taken to be the internalized norms that govern individual behavior in relation to the coercive power of the state, then legitimacy is the point at which the power of coercive force is evident and acknowledged but where it is held in abeyance through a conscious consensus about the nature of just relations between individuals and the state. One place such consensus becomes visible is in the circulation of resonant rumors and the conversations that shape mass opinion below the level of public opinion makers, which is why rumor was of such concern to Nyerere during the mutiny.[35]

In his speech on January 24, 1964, in memoriam of Dag Hammarskjöld during the week of his army's mutiny, Nyerere spoke at length about the nature of sovereignty and political order. Presaging postmodern approaches, he proposed that the voluntary cooperation of individuals for mutual benefit inevitably created a potential for conflict over the terms of their agreement that did not exist before their cooperation. Nyerere's conceptual intervention that evening turned on a more immediate concern: his authorization earlier that day of British military assistance and the coincident risk of his claim to sovereignty. In terms deriving from his midcentury Edinburgh education rather than postmodern deconstruction, Nyerere nevertheless articulated the quandary of Jacques Derrida's judge, caught between the uniformity of the law and the contingency of the case.[36] Governmental coercion, held in discursive balance among free individuals, was "the price of social living." Individual agency, in Nyerere's Utilitarian-derived view, was the elemental form of sovereignty, but an attribute existing only in theory since by force of biology and history people live in communities that limit individual freedom.

> It is law and authority which transform this situation—of co-operation constantly endangered by conflict—into a situation of expanding human development. Only a system of rules governing inter-personal behavior, and the enforcement of these rules makes co-operation between men possible and fruitful.... But the peace resulting from imposed law is short-lived.... The only system of law which brings stable peace is a system which is based on the fundamental human equality of all the people under its suzerainty, and which aims at reconciling to the greatest possible degree man's conflicting desire for individual freedom and the benefits of communal life.... Thus there is, and must always be, in every society a balance between that voluntary agreement which is necessary to give stability, and that element of force which ensures that people abide by their own decision to pay the price of social living.[37]

In any case, we can observe that as overarching authorities are constructed, individual political agency is accordingly diffused and emerges as the discursive potential to shape the constructed sovereign. However, we should note that the idea of individual agency, be it fiction or no, is the conceptual foundation upon which rests the elemental liberty of the sovereign citizen in a democracy. Electoral democracy is built on the belief in individual agency of the voter. If, however, diffuse agency is the reality, then we must argue that it is only simulated through the binary data of votes. A new democracy requires an infrastructure of basic political process to produce this compiled consensus communicating the diffuse collective agency of the society. Representative democracy likewise requires belief in the individual agency of elected leaders to act effectively on behalf of those who choose them. Elected officials in this sense signify the diffuse agency of a constituency, which justifies and enables their institutional power under the guise of individual agency.

Cynthia Weber's simulacrum of external sovereignty then corresponds to this discursive construct of internal authority, which by definition is an imposition on individuals whose sovereign initiative is the defining counterpoint to institutional power. On a similar point, Foucault maintained that "the relationship between power and freedom's refusal to submit cannot, therefore, be separated. . . . A society without power relations can only be an abstraction."[38] A perceived reality of agency—in both the free will of the voter and the elected representative's ability to institute power relations with and over others—is the consensual premise of democracy. Since this premise allows for an emergence of tyranny, constitutional limits emerge as corollary. However, such limits are anchored by fickle consensus rather than law. At the point of constitutional impasse, law becomes a simple threat of force and so performs the very tyranny it seeks to prevent.[39] Discursive intervention, despite the contextual constraints on its agents, is the only effective force to shape this consensus short of destroying and remaking it. This was Nyerere's task, and the historical question is whether his resort to state coercion reinforced his discursive impact at key moments, or destructively undermined it.

This question cannot be answered here, but it can guide further evaluation of Nyerere's postcolonial tenure. Intellectuality at all levels of society, as so many historians of Africa have argued, is a decisive factor of historical change. To that extent, ideas and their expression have been a key focus of this study. But their context is the defense of initiative and competition for influence that constitute political activity. Nyerere's manipulation of cultural understandings of race, ethnicity, economy, land, youth, and ethics shaped a legitimate civic nationalism marked by a nonethnic definition of citizenship that avoided the divisive and violent conflicts of Tanzania's neighbors. His country's circumstances may have been easier than its neighbors', but in taking on the liberation struggle and the ambitions of Pan-Africanism, Tanzania also invited conflict. The key to its internal peace is that the conflicts that ensued did not break the institutional structure put together in the first years of independence.[40]

The deep penetration of Swahili language and culture in the late precolonial era and the relatively benign neglect of the colonial era both contributed to the ease with which a multiethnic nationalist coalition was formed in Tanzania. But we cannot assume that a peaceful political environment in the postcolonial period was therefore inevitable. We acknowledge, on the one hand, the possibility that Nyerere's suppression of the labor movement and opposition politics were necessary impositions of sovereign authority that allowed the formation of a stable political culture from which democracy could emerge in the 1990s. On the other hand, as James Brennan has pointed out, the inverse is certainly true as well: the constraints on opposition politics put in place in the early 1960s continue to debilitate the emergence of truly competitive democracy.[41] It is a burden that Tanzania will bear for a long time to come, and the patient fight for a competitive democracy will remain preeminently the task of a principled opposition.

The ruling party may have a role to play here as well. Pointing to the fate of other ruling parties that wore out their welcome, the chairman of the CCM Elders' Committee recently suggested that if the time had come for CCM to lose a presidential election, then it should confront that possibility honestly, and become an effective opposition party.[42] Debates within CCM can be as powerful as interparty debate. Visiting CCM Headquarters in 2013, I was given a small book printed in 2007 by Makwaia wa Kuhenga, apparently representing the views of party elders.[43] It is a deeply critical commentary on the ruling party, disparaging the attitude that simply winning elections by hook or by crook is the goal of a political party, and probing the role of ideology and ethics. The book reprints an extended letter from Nyerere's former private secretary Joseph Butiku to outgoing president Benjamin Mkapa arguing that internal debates about proposed presidential candidates masked underlying corruption within the party. Kuhenga proposed that CCM lead an effort to write a new constitution with more robust checks and balances. For all the attention given to the nature of the Union in the 2013 constitutional draft, it may be that changes in bureaucratic structures and electoral procedures will turn out to be more important.

The Limits of Sovereignty and Discourse

We must confront the limitations both of sovereignty and of discursive agency, as analytical concepts and as political strategies. Certainly wide-ranging debates about sovereignty point to its shortcomings as a means of analyzing power, let alone as a means of understanding the transnational complexities of the global political economy. Sovereignty fails us when we confront some of the rebel movements of the early twenty-first century whose leaders do not seem to be motivated by a claim to sovereignty at all but rather a variety of narrower goals, from religious dogma to mere gangsterism. Groups like Uganda's Lord's Resistance Army or Somalia's Al Shabaab are at different points in a field of localized goals. Discourse also falls short, even though there are those who will argue that human experience is exclusively perceived through discourse. Such an abstraction seems ill suited as historians confront the cynical machinations of the South African–supported rebel group Resistência Nacional Moçambicana (RENAMO) in Mozambique, the crass scramble for marketable resources in the Congo, the endemic malnutrition across the continent, or famines in the Horn. Despite the insufficiency of the concepts, however, all of these point to crises of sovereignty and struggles for discursive agency in their concern for the establishment of authority and the mobilization of human resources. Sovereignty cannot explain all politics or all conflicts, but within the nation-state system it is a necessary component of all analysis because the concept is fundamental to the system's very functioning. The discursive power of violence, its ability to instill fear or awe or honor, is oftentimes far greater than its immediate impact on a finite number of human lives. And as many have argued in regard to the Rwandan genocide, the mobilization of mass violence builds upon a discursive foundation.[44]

So neither sovereignty nor discursive agency offers a prescription for political stability. Like all political strategies, they too easily overreach themselves. We can leave aside the excesses of a totalitarian state like Mobutu's Congo or the desperate attempts of apartheid South Africa to defend the sovereignty of its minority government. More humble excesses plagued Tanzania's quest for sovereignty. Beginning with Nyerere's repression of the opposition during the transition to independence, Tanzania grew only more authoritarian under his presidency. The 1965 elections were the first held under the newly instituted single-party system. Nyerere was the only presidential candidate, and TANU's Central Committee attempted to vet every candidate for local office. Over the following decades, increasing numbers of both critics and corrupt loyalists in Nyerere's government were detained without trial or charged with the broadly defined crime of "economic sabotage." The monopolization of political power allowed for the unproductive and unpopular policy of forced villagization. Its hasty implementation was at once a product of the state's robust sovereignty and an emblem of its limits.

Villagization, as Leander Schneider pointed out, was the product of a discursive strategy run amok. Ujamaa had been invented for particular political reasons in 1962, and deployed loudly again in 1967 to gird the Arusha Declaration. Its translation as socialism pulled it ever more firmly into fruitless debates about dogma as it justified ever more unrealistic demands on the Tanzanian populace. Ujamaa, after all, had never really been a language of policy; it was a language of power. As Joel Samoff observed in the early 1970s, Ujamaa easily ignored the very ethics it sought to instill and served instead as a rhetorical field where notables competed for control of the local party. James Brennan more recently demonstrated that Ujamaa offered rhetorical cover for a racially targeted policy of nationalizing buildings that were 98 percent Asian-owned. Similarly, Andrew Ivaska revealed how Ujamaa's claims to Africanness justified the harassment of women in Dar es Salaam who had the temerity to sport miniskirts during their fashion heyday of the late 1960s.[45] We might find that all discursive agency is prone to these sorts of excesses because it is not the controlled agency of an individual will. Discourse is by definition multifarious, and in the attempt to deploy its power its users are drawn toward ever more extreme iterations. The very success of a discursive strategy drives it toward excess, which in policies like villagization can turn reasonable social experiments into upheavals.

Herein lies the challenge that discursive insights offer us. The very ideals that we hold with the highest esteem are those most prone to blind us and draw us into abuse. Discourse, in the Saussurean sense, is not merely a way of *speaking about* experience; it is the means by which we *perceive* experience. It is monumentally difficult to imagine a world outside the discursive framework that we construct, or to experience the world without its structure of meaning. Because of this, the ideals we define within that framework tempt us ever toward overstatement. Whether in wars of religion, implacable policy imperatives, or genocidal dreams of purity, we find ourselves constantly called on to constrain our discursive strategies and seek balance. The acknowledgment of discursive agency, as Elizabeth Ermarth suggests, undermines the philosophical foundations of our modern political arrangements.[46] This realization calls us to confront even our most treasured ideals. While democracy, with its checks and balances and free press, offers a stubborn defense of discursive excess, it cannot be excluded here. Our absolute faith in its virtues cautions us to be wary of exaggerated expectations for its efficacy.

For Issa Shivji, good political leadership must risk the dangers of discourse in order to present an inspiring vision around which a social consensus can precipitate. In this sense, Shivji argues, Nyerere provided leadership: "The ideology of Ujamaa, notwithstanding its many pitfalls, was one of the few postindependence constructs in Africa which provided such a vision or consensus."[47] Contemplating such "transformative agency" in East African political leadership, Eric Aseka proposed that the articulation of a consensus inevitably precedes democracy. "It is in such distinct communities that democracy has always emerged since democracy consists of rules whose validity depends on the willingness of a certain community to observe them."[48] The question is how to construct a consensus around a fair and inclusive set of rules.

Staffan Linberg's recent work suggests that democracy is a learned culture that is established over time as a pattern of popular participation in political campaigns and elections takes root.[49] Even when campaigns and elections are not truly democratic, they effectively prepare a population and political system for more democratic elections over time. The question that Lindberg cannot answer is whether long periods of constrained democracy create such a powerful prejudice against political opposition that the eventual emergence of robust democratic competition is prevented. It may be, but Lindberg's work nevertheless suggests that we pay attention to the efforts of states to create circumstances of political stability within which democracy can be cultivated. Democracy is not sufficient to its own dual ambition of legitimation and administration. A deeper national consensus must precede it in order to constitute a state executor of democratic choice and define the inclusive ground rules necessary for democratic competition. What Lindberg's research shows is that practice of regular elections can inculcate the idea of democratic procedure as the necessary basis for legitimate politics.

Tanzania's regular electoral cycle, despite the constraints of a one-party system between 1965 and 1995, established democratic procedure as a normative political ritual, and multiparty elections since 1995 have become increasingly competitive. We can argue that the routinization of elections under a stable and sovereign government paved the way for the progressively robust democratic practices emerging today. Such an interpretation of Tanzanian history would risk legitimizing the authoritarian constraints on democracy that most African countries imposed after independence, and offer justification for more current examples like post-Soviet Russia under Vladimir Putin—or, for that matter, nineteenth-century America with its white male electorate. So we must be very cautious here. The legitimation of authoritarian constraints in the name of political stability poses myriad dangers to democracy, and leads almost inevitably to excess. But confronting (and critiquing) the utility of such constraints points us toward the very real issues at stake in processes of democratization and thereby guides us toward better thinking and better policies in support of functional democracy instead of blind insistence on democratic ideals.

Nyerere paired a critical perspective on democracy's application in a newly decolonized country with an awareness of the artificiality of the nation-state system and its ideological claim to territorial sovereignty. He proposed viable steps toward Pan-African unity and global cooperation that would change the nature of this system by sacrificing aspects of the sovereign power held by territorial authorities. He was realistic enough to understand that Tanzania's ability to conform to the expectations of territorial sovereignty was not only a fundamental task of decolonization, but also the only practical starting point to garner the influence necessary to construct the supranational sovereign proposed in Pan-Africanism.

Nations, he told his audience at the Dag Hammarskjöld lecture, were an "intermediate stage" toward a harmonious international system governed by the United Nations. He pictured the international system as an extension of the nested hierarchy of family-based institutions that Petro Itosi Marealle had imagined as the source of Ujamaa. As utopian as Nyerere's speech was, it was fundamentally practical and political. His promotion of the United Nations was in part targeted to the narrow purpose of bringing international pressure to bear on the apartheid South African regime. But he also maintained his theoretical position, which by the end of the speech became likewise an overtly political position, put into practice that very night in his invitation to Britain to intervene against the mutiny. "The challenge of the twentieth century is the conversion of nationalism into internationalism," he concluded.

Between nationalism and internationalism lies the concept of sovereignty, regulating the relationship between the two. The establishment of sovereignty in a postcolony does not represent an accomplishment predicated on modernization theory, but rather the pragmatic attempt by a political leadership to conform to the international system as constituted in the "UN World," of Kelly and Kaplan's conception.[50] If sovereignty is simply a "dense political practice," as Rob Walker described it, then it is not only a debated theoretical construct but also a useful analytical concept for interpreting historical events.[51] Sovereignty has a well-developed theoretical literature; but the term also has a commonsense meaning that makes it accessible to nonspecialist readers. In the interaction of its internal and external aspects, sovereignty offers a broad and inclusive framework for historical analysis of the postcolonial state. Sovereignty can provide the basis for studying everything from international relations to civil wars to grassroots movements. Paired with an analytical concept of discursive agency, sovereignty becomes a robust and nuanced concept for studying not only the constitution of postcolonial states but also the inevitable internal and external contestations to nationalist claims.

Discursive agency also provides a flexible and broad approach to politics, with a similarly rich theoretical literature. In this frame, politics becomes much more than the parties, politicians, and production goals of modernization theory, and also something more than the well-worn trope of popular resistance. Discursive analysis reminds us of the reciprocal quality of political power that, in the end, is nothing more than a surface sheen on a deep pool of cultural knowledge. At the international level, the concept of discursive agency allows us to see the manipulations of the "code of sovereignty," and so escape the narrow materialism of political power conceived as a crass manifestation of military and economic clout or a simplistic dichotomy of rulers and ruled. National sovereignty conceived as an expression of discursive agency provides a powerful analytical approach to the postcolonial African state from both the top down and the bottom up, as well as the constant "convivial" interactions everywhere in between. This study of the early years of independence in Tanzania illustrates how this approach helps us to move beyond the analytical categories that have long guided political scientists in Africa, and turn toward a more comprehensive historical approach.

Sovereignty, with its assumption of institutionally congruent units in the nation-state system, implies the possibility of comparison between states. This account of Tanzania may offer a point of comparison for the ways in which other countries negotiated and established sovereign authority. The utility of sovereignty as a category of analysis is precisely in its breadth. We can seek gradations of sovereignty, both internal and external, as a means of comparing postcolonial states. In the Congo, sovereignty was clearly a facade brought to the breaking point; in Uganda, sovereignty was fundamentally disputed between a radical central government and an atavistic Buganda kingdom; in Kenya, sovereignty was highly personalized in a bureaucracy of patronage. In Tanzania, popular authority was deliberately cultivated into a relatively robust sovereign government. Amid these gradations, discursive agency may provide a means of comparing the construction of political "ecologies" in different countries, but discourse also implies irreducible complexity specific to particular constellations of actors.[52] While this account may provide a basis for comparison between postcolonial countries, I also hope it would be disruptive of simplistic equivalencies.

The policies forged by Nyerere and his colleagues between 1960 and 1964 established a sovereign nation that effectively governed inside its borders and took its place in the global nation-state system. This achievement entailed discursive fluency in multiple contexts, both indigenous and international. The efficacy of this "way of the lips" resulted from its legitimacy in both arenas, which emanated in part from the disciplinary powers expected in both. Nyerere's success in establishing Tanzanian sovereignty, in the classic sense of internal authority and external identity, made possible the construction of Tanzania as one of the most stable and influential countries in Africa. This accomplishment created the peaceful conditions necessary to anchor a developing democratic practice. Because of this, the evaluation of the history and policies of the Tanzanian state must start with the foundational establishment of sovereignty.

Notes

Acknowledgments

1. Given the conflicts in the Congo in the last decade, this is certainly a regular occurrence. A similar incident was reported more recently in "DRC Soldiers Held for Illegal Entry," *Guardian*, November 7, 2011, viewed at http://www.ippmedia.com/frontend/?l=35140. A local commander told journalists that "we have seized their arms and arrested them because they have violated the laws of our land. . . . The armed DRC soldiers entered the country illegally."

Introduction

Epigraph. Marion, Lady Chesham, general letter, January 27, 1964, Papers of Marion, Lady Chesham, File 25 (hereafter cited as CHE-25), BI.
 1. Issa interview; see also Shivji, *Pan-Africanism or Pragmatism?*, 45.
 2. William Leonhart, Dar es Salaam (DAR), to Department of State (DOS), January 20, 1964, National Security Files, Country Files, Box 100, File 1, No. 64 (hereafter cited as NSF/CF 100-1.64), LBJ.
 3. DAR to DOS, January 23, 1964, NSF/CF 100-1.4, LBJ; Nyerere (Maria) interview; Nyerere (Makongoro) interview.
 4. DAR to Commonwealth Relations Office (CRO), London, January 24, 1964, Dominions Office (DO) 226/10, PRO; Elena to Lady Chesham, January 24, 1964, CHE-25, BI.
 5. Elena to Lady Chesham, January 24, 1964, CHE-25, BI.
 6. DAR to CRO, January 24, 1964, DO 226/10, PRO.
 7. Ibid.
 8. DAR to CRO, "Tanganyika Fortnightly Summary," April 24, 1964, Foreign and Commonwealth Office (FCO) 141/14044.134, PRO.
 9. Rosnow, "Rumor as Communication"; Rosnow, "Inside Rumor"; Kapferer similarly proposes that rumors have a "hidden symbolic message" in contextual implications that are at the heart of their emotional impact. Kapferer, *Rumors, Uses, Interpretations, and Images*, 93.
 10. White, *Speaking with Vampires*, 56–88; White, *Assassination of Herbert Chitepo*. See also Knapp, "Psychology of Rumor"; Allport and Postman, *Psychology of Rumor*, 159–99; Gluckman, "Gossip and Scandal"; Shepperson, *Myth and Reality in Malawi*; Fine, "Goliath Effect"; Musambachime, "Impact of Rumor"; and Boyer, "Conspiracy, History, and Therapy."
 11. Kampala to CRO, January 24, 1964, DO 226/10, PRO.

12. See Iliffe, *Modern History of Tanganyika*, 318–34, 487–507.
13. G. O'Connor to Executive Officer, Kilimanjaro District Council, "Compensation Mangi Mkuu," December 27, 1963, Accession 555, File 2/1/3, No. 33 (hereafter cited as 555: 2/1/3.33), TNA.
14. Hansard, *18th February 1964 to 21st February 1964*, February 18, 1964, Member Abdallah Fundikira, Member Peter Siyovelwa, 126; Robert Hennemeyer, DAR to DOS, "Fundikira Rejoins Tanganyika African National Union," March 19, 1964, Record Group (RG) 59, Box 2687, POL-POLITICAL AFFAIRS & REL-TANGAN, 1/1/64, NARA.
15. In Tanzania, the terms "National Assembly" and "Parliament" are used interchangeably for the institution known in Swahili as the *Bunge*.
16. Hansard, *18th February 1964 to 21st February 1964*, Bibi Titi Mohamed, 122.
17. Young, "Colonial State."
18. Quoted in Baregu, "Perception," 47.
19. Cooper, *Decolonization and African Society*, 20; Hargreaves, *Decolonization in Africa*.
20. Noer, *Cold War and Black Liberation*; Young and Turner, *Rise and Decline*.
21. Macqueen, *Decolonization of Portuguese Africa*; Newitt, *History of Mozambique*; Mondlane, *Struggle for Mozambique*.
22. Anglin, *Zambian Crisis Behaviour*; Horne, *Barrel of a Gun*.
23. Price, "Pretoria's Southern African Strategy," 14.
24. Barber, *South Africa*; Bauer and Taylor, *Politics in Southern Africa*.
25. Mutibwa, *Uganda since Independence*; Jorgensen, *Uganda*; Ibingira, *African Upheavals since Independence*; Uzoigwe, *Uganda*.
26. Londsdale, "Moral Economy."
27. Anderson, *Histories of the Hanged*, 279–88; Elkins, "Struggle for Mau Mau Rehabilitation," 25-57.
28. Branch, *Defeating Mau Mau*; Odhiambo and Lonsdale, *Mau Mau and Nationhood*; Maloba, *Mau Mau and Kenya*.
29. Spear and Waller, *Being Maasai*.
30. Lonsdale, "KAU's Cultures."
31. Prunier, *Rwanda Crisis*; Lemarchand, *Burundi*.
32. Westad, *Global Cold War*.
33. See Renda, *Taking Haiti*, 14. Chinua Achebe noted similarly that "[Joseph Conrad's novel] *Heart of Darkness* projects the image of Africa as 'the other world,' the antithesis of Europe and therefore of civilization, a place where man's vaunted intelligence and refinement are finally mocked by triumphant bestiality." Achebe, "Image of Africa."
34. Emotionalism in a foreign leader had also helped justify American intervention in Iran in 1953. See Roosevelt, *Countercoup*, 77.
35. Meeting of the National Security Council, September 15, 1960, in *Foreign Relations of the United States*, 14:489; "Foreign News: Third Man Up," *Time*, September 26, 1960.
36. Dag Hammarsköld and Pierre Wigny, quoted in "An Analytical Chronology of the Congo Crisis," pp. 18, 38–39, NSF/CF 86-1.1a, LBJ.
37. Witte, *Assassination of Lumumba*; Monje, *Central Intelligence Agency*, 52-55.

38. The phrase "comic opera" turns up later in reference to Zanzibar, and also in relation to Indonesia, where the US contemplated intervention in 1958, and did intervene in 1965. See Foote (Batavia) to DOS, January 13, 1947, reprinted in *Foreign Relations of the United States*, 6:893; the phrase was repeated in a magazine story: "Indonesia: Waiting Game," *Time*, May 31, 1958.

39. See Pandey, *Remembering Partition*, 55.

40. Elena to Lady Chesham, January 24, 1964, CHE-25, BI.

41. Robin Miller to David Owen, Microfilm, CSAS.MF.107–8, Ivan-Smith Papers, BI.

42. "Congo Army Offensive on Katanga: 30 Mile Thrust in Bid to End Secession," *Tanganyika Standard*, November 3, 1961, 1; "Congolese Troops Run Riot: UN Threatens to Quell Them by Force," *Tanganyika Standard*, November 16, 1961, 1; "Congolese Murder Italians: Dismembered Bodies Thrown into River," *Tanganyika Standard*, November 17, 1961, 1.

43. "Congo Horror 'Example' to Zanzibaris," *Tanganyika Standard*, October 4, 1961, 1.

44. Kyaruzi interview. This is Kyaruzi's own translation of his recollection of the Swahili original "usilie mwana usilie, uliyataka mwenyewe." See also Mwakikagile, *Nyerere and Africa*, 391.

45. In my 2006 interview, Ali Sultan Issa reported that while he was stationed in Cairo around this time, an American diplomatic officer threatened him that if Zanzibari leaders were anything like Lumumba they would be killed in the same way.

46. See Kirk-Greene, "His Eternity."

47. Marion, Lady Chesham to Julius Nyerere, undated, CHE-7, BI. For Chesham's biography, see Ross, *Guide to the Tanganyikan Papers*.

48. Jackson and Rosberg, *Personal Rule in Black Africa*; Wrong, *Footsteps of Mr. Kurtz*; Holland, *Dinner with Mugabe*.

49. Anderson, "State of Terror."

50. Abu Bakarr Bah provides a nice formulation in "State Decay."

51. Herbst, *States and Power in Africa*, 254.

52. Kelly and Kaplan, "Nation and Decolonization," 427.

53. See Anderson, *Imagined Communities*. Kelly and Kaplan suggest that Anderson's groundbreaking critique of nationalism falsely projected the image of the nation-state into an imperial past. This may be unfair to Anderson, whose focus was the "origins and spread of nationalism" rather than its institutional consolidation as a global order.

54. Smith, *Nationalism*, 13.

55. Brennan, *Taifa*; Aminzade, *Race, Nation, and Citizenship*.

56. Mbembe, *On the Postcolony*, 89.

57. Mwijage interview.

58. Mbembe, in "On the Postcolony," acknowledges his debt here to Edward Said's thesis from his *Orientalism* (6).

59. Geiger, *TANU Women*, 8.

60. For gendered critiques of sovereignty see Pateman, *Sexual Contract*; Boucher, "Male Power and Contract Theory," Fraser, "Beyond the Master/Subject Model"; and Hoffman, *Gender and Sovereignty*.

61. Mbembe's project bears the imprint of Anne McClintock's insights into the construction of imperial power in *Imperial Leather*.

62. Mbembe, "On the Postcolony," 6, 19–20, 26–27.

63. See Lindberg, "Forms of States." Lindberg writes, "Sovereignty also lies at the heart of democratization. Rule by the people demands a spatial unit to be identified containing the people and juridical autonomy in political space. Democracy, as we know it, makes little sense if there is no clearly defined state and few issues for the people's political representatives to decide on" (177). Lindberg's pragmatic empiricism serves as evidence supporting Rob Walker's suspicions that our faith in democracy is ontologically suspect. See Walker, *Inside/Outside*.

64. My approach responds to Herbst's concern that "scholars have generally been unsuccessful in developing a view of African politics that takes the precolonial period seriously while still acknowleging the traumas created by white rule," as well as Mbembe's critique that analysts tend to ignore "what African agents accept as their reasons for acting." See Herbst, *States and Power in Africa*, 29; Mbembe, *On the Postcolony*, 7. See also Bayart, *State in Africa*, 108–10, 193, 207–8, 248–51, 270–71.

65. See Kelly and Kaplan, *Represented Communities*, 1–29.

66. Morefield, "States Are Not People," 659.

67. Grovogui, "Secret Lives of the 'Sovereign,'" 272–74.

68. Walker, *After the Globe*.

69. This phrase is heard commonly today and appears in Tanzania's 1977 constitution, but it was in use soon after independence. For example, in a debate about East African federation, Amri Abedi referred to the OAU policy of respecting the "mamlaka ya nchi za Afrika, yaani wa kuheshimu, Territorial integrity and sovereignty." Hansard, *16th June 1964 to 3rd July 1964*, Minister of Community Development and National Culture, 317. *Mamlaka* commonly means authority, but can also refer to dominion or jurisdiction. The 2013 draft for a new constitution provides a more defined approach, referring to specific *mamlaka za nchi* in various regards. *Enzi* is another word for sovereignty, but in everday usage this bears a more archaic connotation usually reserved for divine sovereignty. Related to the concept of sovereignty is that of the state, or *dola* in Swahili.

70. Jackson, *Sovereignty*, 1–23.

71. Weber, *Simulating Sovereignty*, 127.

72. Ermarth, "Agency in the Discursive Condition."

73. See chapter 1 for details on Nyerere's teacher.

74. Mbembe, *On the Postcolony*, 128–33.

75. Pratt, *Critical Phase in Tanzania*, 202.

76. Chachage, "Mwalimu in Our Popular Imagination." Similarly, Eric Aseka has noted that Nyerere composed a transformational conception of what it meant to be Tanzanian, a unique accomplishment of postcolonial sovereignty. Aseka, *Transformational Leadership in East Africa*, 21, 249.

77. My fundamental point of reference here is Saussure's distinction between *langue* and *parole*, but we might also take note of Wittgenstein: "If we had to name anything which is the life of the sign, we should have to say that it was its *use*." Saussure, *Writings in General Linguistics*; Wittgenstein, *Wittgenstein Reader*, 60 (emphasis in original).

78. See Shapiro, Bonham, and Heradstveit, "Discursive Practices Approach."

79. Ermarth, *History in the Discursive Condition*, 48–55.

80. Reflecting on Michael Sonnenscher's study of public discourse during the French Revolution, Gareth Jones noted, "The loss of linguistic and political authority generally amount to the same thing." Jones, "Determinist Fix," 71.

81. See Geiger, *TANU Women*; Feierman, *Peasant Intellectuals*; Spear, *Mountain Farmers*; Askew, *Performing the Nation*; and Ivaska, *Cultured States*.

82. This follows on the approach in Chabal and Daloz, *Culture Troubles*, while bearing in mind the Orientalist dangers addressed in Rotter, "Saidism without Said."

83. See Mbembe, *On the Postcolony*, 14–17. The "cultural turn" looked to people's interaction in a system of meanings (culture) to identify agency after the intensely structural implications of the earlier "linguistic turn." See Steinmetz, *State/Culture*.

84. Ekeh, "Colonialism and the Two Publics"; Geertz, "Integrative Revolution"; Vaughan, *Nigerian Chiefs*; Falola, *Power of African Cultures*, 100–105.

85. Reckwitz, "Theory of Social Practices," 257; Bourdieu, *Distinction*, 170–72.

86. See Walker, *After the Globe*, 13–18.

87. Guha, *Elementary Aspects of Peasant Insurgency*, 15–17; Dean, *Imperial Brotherhood*, 13.

88. See Branch, *Kenya*, 19–22. For explorations of the interactive nature of colonial sources, see Hamilton, *Terrific Majesty*; Spear, "Neo-Traditionalism"; and Lekgoathi, "'Colonial' Experts, Local Interlocutors." More broadly, see Stoler, *Along the Archival Grain*; and Chatterjee, *Nation and Its Fragments*.

89. For a critical questioning of archives as institutions, see Hamilton, *Refiguring the Archive*.

90. See also Allman, "Phantoms of the Archive."

91. Duggan and Civille, *Tanzania and Nyerere*, 42; Kissinger, *Years of Renewal*, 931–36; James, *Nkrumah and the Ghana Revolution*, 223; Wenner, *Shamba Letu*; Sahnoun, "Nyerere," 143.

92. Bienen, *Tanzania*, 203–57; Pratt, *Critical Phase in Tanzania*, 5–8; Mathews and Mushi, *Foreign Policy of Tanzania*, 35.

93. Jumbe, *Partner-Ship*, 114.

94. Lofchie, *Zanzibar*, 207–8; This line of thought has become increasingly prominent in Tanzanian political debates, with Nyerere's heroic reputation being countered with portraits of him as a villain in various guises, including that of a "Catholic zealot." See Mohamed Said, "Tanzania: A Nation without Heroes," presented at the Seminar on the Fiftieth Anniversary of the African Independences Marginalized, Forgotten, and Revived Political Actors, British Institute in East Africa, September 24, 2013, available for download at http://www.jamiiforums.com/jukwaa-la-siasa/528609-tanzania-a-nation-without-heroes-by-mohamed-said.html (accessed July 21, 2014).

95. Deogratias Mushi, "Is Nyerere's Process to Sainthood Timely?" *Guardian* (Dar es Salaam), January 24, 2006, http://web.archive.org/web/20060509023340/http://www.ippmedia.com/ipp/guardian/2006/01/24/58455.html.

96. Parsons, Review of *Youth, Nationalism*, 644.

97. Lee, *Making a World after Empire*, 19.

98. Bjerk, "Sovereignty and Socialism in Tanzania." I deliberately avoided reading Smith's work until the late stages of this manuscript so as not to bias my reading

of the sources. Points of agreement with his account are therefore corroborative rather than derivative. Smith, *We Must Run.*

99. See Jones, "Word and Deed."

Chapter 1

An earlier version of this chapter appeared in Bjerk, "Julius Nyerere and the Establishment of Sovereignty."

1. Tibandebage interview; Lusinde interview, November 7, 2006; Kawawa interview, August 9, 2006.
2. Irenge interview, August 20, 2003.
3. Cooper, *Decolonization and African Society*, 1.
4. "Nyerere of Butiama," Musoma District Book, p. 71, Reading Room, TNA.
5. Listowel, *Making of Tanganyika*, 172–77; Smith, *We Must Run*, 37–52; "British High Commission Biographic Data," DAR to DOS, July 13, 1965, RG 59, Box 2692, POL 15-1 TAN, NARA.
6. Irenge interview, August 20, 2003.
7. Ibid.
8. He took his Christian name after his baptism in 1943 just before he left for Makerere University in Kampala, Uganda.
9. "Dreams That Never Died," *Monitor* (Kampala), October 20, 1999.
10. "'African Socialism' by JUKANYE, Kampala," *Tanganyika Standard*, July 23, 1943, cited in Brennan, "Youth," 26. Other thoughts in the letter reflect Nyerere's sentiments expressed elsewhere that he owed a great debt to the African people who paid the colonial taxes that paid for his education there.
11. Nyerere, *Uhuru wa Wanawake*, ii.
12. For a sense of the moral discourse of patriarchal elders in northwestern Tanganyika, see Peterson, *Ethnic Patriotism.*
13. "Dreams That Never Died," *Monitor* (Kampala), October 20, 1999.
14. Nyerere, *Uhuru wa Wanawake*, 27.
15. Ibid., 63.
16. One line of critique here would be to suggest that Nyerere's use of women's oppression as a proxy for the colonial oppression of Africans created a gendered conception of political power, which saw sovereignty as a male prerogative. Such a critique, however, would mean that Nyerere's argument for women's rights was merely meant as an insult to politically emasculated African men, and that under an independent state the liberation of women would not only be curtailed but opposed for the sake of constructing a philosophically masculine sovereign state.
17. "Father Richard Walsh: 1910–1979"; Sivalon, "Roman Catholicism."
18. Shetler, "Interpreting Rupture in Oral Memory," 396.
19. James Irenge, "Historia: Uhusiano kati ya walimu," 5–6, James Irenge Papers, MNF.
20. Shetler, *Imagining Serengeti.*
21. Iliffe, *Modern History of Tanganyika*, 492; Hyden, *Tanu Yajenga Nchi*, 118. A similar debate emerged in eastern Tanganyika with the rise of the Usambara

Citizens' Union, which worked closely with the leaders of the Chagga political organization, Petro Njau, and Paramount Chief Thomas Marealle. See Tanganyika Citizens' Union to Marealle II, August 26, 1956, 555: 10/1.1, TNA. See also Steven Feierman, *Peasant Intellectuals*, 205–22.

22. Irenge, "Historia," 5–6, James Irenge Papers, MNF.

23. Smith, *We Must Run*, 43.

24. Marginal note on file by G. G. Campbell to Mrs. Barberton, Colonial Office (CO) 981/34, PRO.

25. Julius Nyerere to Mrs. P. M. Mitford-Barberton, April 22, 1949, CO 981/34, PRO.

26. Marginal note on file by Miss Campbell to Mr. Carmichael, June 21, 1949, CO 981/34, PRO.

27. Sivalon, "Roman Catholicism."

28. The Musoma District Book, now in the Tanzania National Archives, summarized official knowledge about Zanaki culture for incoming colonial officers, noting that "politically they are truculent and difficult to handle" (7). Caroll Houle, a Maryknoll priest long stationed in Nyerere's hometown of Butiama, also recalled that the culture there supported an exasperating love for argumentation. Houle interview.

29. Radcliffe-Brown, preface to *African Political Systems*, xxi.

30. Namier, "Richard Pares."

31. Nyerere's Student Notebook on British History, October 11, 1950–May 30, 1951, CHE, BI.

32. Edinburgh University Calendar, 1949–50 (Edinburgh: James Thin, 1949), EUA; *Tacitus on Britain and Germany*; Bagehot, *English Constitution*.

33. Mill, *Basic Writings*, 130. Thomas Molony is probably correct to suggest that Nyerere's reading of Hsiao-Tung Fei's *Peasant Life in China* was as influential as his reading on British history. Molony, *Nyerere*, 168–70.

34. Julius Nyerere to George Shepperson, May 5, 1960, File 1, Shepperson Files, EUA.

35. Axel Stern to George Shepperson, File 4, Shepperson Files, EUA. Presumably Stern was the lecturer that Nyerere elsewhere remembered as "a continental gentleman who had lost an arm."

36. See Bradley, *Ethical Studies*.

37. Green, *Lectures*, 13, 65–66, 168–69, 192.

38. A. M. K. Kalinjuma to George Shepperson, February 16, 1988, File 4, Shepperson Files, EUA; Julius Nyerere to George Shepperson, May 5, 1960, File 1, Shepperson Files, EUA; Collins, *Coloured Minorities*; Macmurray, *Conditions of Freedom*; Costello, *John Macmurray*; Grey, *Socialist Tradition*; Stern, *Science of Freedom*.

39. Article on Nyerere, 22–25, File 4, Shepperson Files, EUA.

40. George Shepperson, draft of article for *Africa Events*, October 1985, File 4, Shepperson Files, EUA.

41. George Shepperson to A. M. K. Kalinjuma, March 1, 1988, File 4, Shepperson Files, EUA.

42. Rev. Kenneth MacKenzie to Alison Truefitt, March 11, 1964, File 4, Shepperson Files, EUA.

43. "Edinburgh University's First African Prime Minister" by George Shepperson, *University of Edinburgh Gazette*, No. 28, October 1960, 22, File 3, Shepperson Files, EUA.
44. Jean W. Wilson to George Shepperson, File 1, Shepperson Files, EUA. Molony, *Nyerere*, 122.
45. Carter, *T. H. Green*, 165–68.
46. Article on Nyerere, 22–25, File 4, Shepperson Files, EUA; Nyerere, *Freedom and Unity*, 23–29.
47. Nyerere article on the Race Problem, File 1, Shepperson Files, EUA.
48. Article on Nyerere, 22–25, File 4, Shepperson Files, EUA.
49. Mill, *Basic Writings*, 12; see also Stokes, *English Utilitarians and India*.
50. Nyerere, *Freedom and Unity*, 27.
51. Joan Wicken, "African Contrasts: Report of the Alice Horsman Travelling Fellow, 1956–1957," Somerville College, Oxford, January 1958, 29–36, Papers of Lloyd Swantz, Madison, WI.
52. T. H. Betts to Julius Nyerere, July 29, 1958, Foreign Colonial Bureau (FCB), File 121/3, No. 32 (hereafter cited as FCB 121/3.32), RH; Butiku interview.

Chapter 2

1. Kisumo interview, June 12, 2006.
2. Iliffe, *Modern History of Tanganyika*, 486.
3. See Pratt, *Critical Phase in Tanzania*, 63–89.
4. Brennan, "Short History of Political Opposition."
5. Bender, "Being 'Chagga.'"
6. "The Unity of Lake Tanganyika Nations Association Ujiji," Tabora District Book, TNA.
7. Japhet and Seaton, *Meru Land Case*; Spear, *Mountain Farmers*; Taylor, *Political Development of Tanganyika*, 97–106; Richards, *East African Chiefs*.
8. Japhet and Seaton, *Meru Land Case*.
9. Iliffe, *Modern History of Tanganyika*, 491–94, 568–69.
10. Tanganyika Citizens' Union, Mwakungwi Office, Lushoto to Marealle II Mangi Mkuu wa Wachagga, Kilimanjaro, August 26, 1956, 555: 10/1.1, TNA.
11. See Mwakikagile, *Life under Nyerere*, 20–21.
12. Spear and Waller, *Being Maasai*, 16. Also, Barth, *Ethnic Groups and Boundaries*.
13. See Peterson, *Ethnic Patriotism*.
14. Bienen, *Tanzania*, 66–67.
15. Barongo interview.
16. Barongo, *Mkiki Mkiki wa Siasa*, 211–15.
17. Iliffe, *Modern History of Tanganyika*, 482–83.
18. Ibid., 569; Maguire, *Toward "Uhuru" in Tanzania*, 279–82.
19. Iliffe, *Modern History of Tanganyika*, 395–576; Geiger, *TANU Women*; Pratt, *Critical Phase in Tanzania*; Barongo, *Mkiki Mkiki wa Siasa*; Iliffe, "Breaking the Chain"; Maguire, *Toward "Uhuru" in Tanzania*; Coulson, *Tanzania*; Said, *Life and Times*; Listowel, *Making of Tanganyika*.

20. In my interview with Vedastus Kyaruzi, he said both he and Dr. Saleh were transferred by British administrators, because "they feared trouble in Dar es Salaam."

21. See also Iliffe, *Modern History of Tanganyika*, 505–15.

22. Karago interview.

23. Bernard Mapalala, "Chief Patrick Kunambi: The Julius Nyerere that I Knew," *Guardian* (Dar es Salaam), October 15, 2009.

24. "TANU Denies Allegations," *Tanganyika Standard*, October 13, 1954, 1.

25. Kunambi interview.

26. Brennan, *Taifa*, 146.

27. Mathews and Mushi, *Foreign Policy of Tanzania*, 516.

28. Budodi interview; interviews with Lubala, Kibuana, Salim (Hamid), Shija, and Sigamba (interviewed together as Tanzanian Foreign Legion representatives). Iliffe suggests that elders across the south were initially reluctant to support the nationalist movement because they feared another traumatic defeat as had happened in the Maji Maji rebellion at the beginning of the century. Iliffe, *Modern History of Tanganyika*, 519–20.

29. Sykes (Abbas) interview.

30. Geiger, *TANU Women*; Suwedi interview.

31. Mwarabu interview.

32. Kyaruzi interview; Kamba interview; Suwedi interview; Said, *Life and Times*; Iliffe, *Modern History of Tanganyika*; Geiger, *TANU Women*.

33. Stirling, "Capricorn Contract"; Ross, "Capricorn Africa Society"; Phiri, "Capricorn Africa Society Revisited"; Hughes, *Capricorn*.

34. "The Philosophy of the Tanganyika National Society," *Tanganyika Standard*, January 21, 1956, 2–3.

35. Kisumo interview.

36. Kawawa interview, June 12, 2006.

37. See "Kenya: Infiltration of Mau Mau into Tanganyika," FCO 141/5881 and FCO 141/5882—both in PRO.

38. Sunseri, "Statist Narratives."

39. Sigamba and Shija interview. See also Iliffe, *Modern History of Tanganyika*, 520.

40. Kapilima interview.

41. Kawawa interview, August 9, 2006.

42. Interviews with Kawawa, August 9, 2006; Kisumo, June 12, 2006; Mogella; and Songambele.

43. Budodi interview. Much of the early political organization began in the large ethnic organizations that had also petitioned earlier UN delegations. The Sukuma Union, the Chagga Council, and the Bahaya Union were prominent organizations of literate elites identified with their ethnic origins. Maguire, *Toward "Uhuru" in Tanzania*, 72–83; Iliffe, *Modern History of Tanganyika*, 487–99, 568–69.

44. Kisumo interview, June 12, 2006.

45. Barongo interview.

46. "T.A.N.U.," *Tanganyika Standard*, January 21, 1956, 2.

47. "T.A.N.U.," *Tanganyika Standard*, February 1, 1956, 2.

48. "TANU and UTP," *Tanganyika Standard*, February 12, 1956, 2.

49. Zuberi Mtemvu, External Affairs Secretary of TANU, to FCB, March 12, 1957, FCB 123/3.48, RH.
50. Makwaia interview; see also Smith, *We Must Run*, 86–89.
51. Barongo interview.
52. Kawawa interview, August 9, 2006.
53. "Mtoto Akililia Kisu Wacha Kimkate," *Sauti ya TANU* 40, September 25, 1958, FCB 121/3.39, RH; see also Iliffe, "Breaking the Chain."
54. Julius Nyerere of TANU to Jimmy (T. F. Betts), September 26, 1958, FCB 121/3.36, RH.
55. Letter from Mshana Chairman of UTP Tanga to District Commissioner Tanga District, October 24, 1958, 493: A.6/38 1.21, TNA.
56. Brennan, "Short History of Political Opposition"; Chande, *Islam, Ulamaa and Community Development*; Nimtz, *Islam and Politics*.
57. Leys, "Tanganyika," 251–68.
58. TANU Election Manifesto, 1960, cited in Maazimio ya Mikutano ya Mwaka 1959–64, February 25, 1964, 589: BMC 11/03/A.12, TNA.
59. Brennan, "Realizing Civilization through Patrilineal Descent."
60. See Miller, "Political Survival of Traditional Leadership."
61. Nyerere, *Freedom and Unity*, 121.
62. World Bank, *Economic Development of Tanganyika*.
63. *East Africa Royal Commission Report*, 290, 369.
64. Lusinde interview, November 7, 2006.
65. Iliffe's account of "The Creation of Tribes" under indirect rule and his overview of tribal associations in the late colonial era are important background information for this analysis. Iliffe, *Modern History of Tanganyika*, 318–34, 487–507.
66. "Stop Defying the Law—Nyerere," *Tanganyika Standard*, November 25, 1958, 1.
67. Nyerere, *Freedom and Unity*, 39.
68. Maguire, *Toward "Uhuru" in Tanzania*, xxvi–xxvii.
69. Cranford Pratt, by contrast, tends to isolate his discussions of Ujamaa and Nyerere's governing philosophy so that they appear as ideals that he presents as being put into practice in political events. Pratt, *Critical Phase in Tanzania*, 63–89.
70. Eckert, "Regulating the Social." The government's circumscription of political activity was a little duplicitous given its evident support for the United Tanganyika Party, which represented white privilege in the guise of racial parity.
71. Tsuruta, "Urban-Rural Relationships"; Tsuruta, "African Imaginations of Moral Economy."
72. Mutual obligations formed a "moral economy" that John Lonsdale has argued was the basis for ethnic identity in Kikuyu country in Kenya, where "arguments about virtue and power, property and labour reinforced each other" in historical imagination, understandings of colonial rule, and religion. Over the course of colonial rule, the violence of Mau Mau emerged from unresolved tensions in Kikuyu society as the bonds of obligation broke down in the face of governmental demands and social change. "What inspired Kikuyu nationalists to seize the exterior architecture of tribe was the coarsening of its colonial interior." Lonsdale, "Moral Economy of Mau Mau," 348–53.
73. Giblin, *Politics of Environmental Control*, 114–16, 136–41.

74. Ingle, *Village to State*, 73.

75. Letter from President of MUNA Office Chanika to Provincial Commissioner Tanga and Handeni, October 23, 1958; Letter from District Office Handeni to Provincial Commissioner Tanga, November 18, 1958; Letter from c/o A. O. Mwelinguza Secretary of Chama cha Ukoo wa Wazigua, Tanga to Seuta to the Tribal Council, Zigua and Nguu Council, March 8, 1961—all in 493: A.6/62, TNA.

76. On "homespun history" see Peterson and Macola, *Recasting the Past*, 15.

77. A Detailed History of "The Origin of the Bukwimba Country" as written by Kadasson Mange in 1931 and partly translated by Edward Shillinde Kadasso, edited and cyclostyled at the Nyegezi Social Research Institute by the Mwanza Research Team, January 1967, History of Origin of Bukwimba Country, 6, TNA.

78. Compare this situation to the popular politics of midcentury Pare country, where citizens met in illegal *barazas* to discuss ways of influencing or deposing colonial chiefs, while community leaders contemplated a tribal association. See Kimambo, *Penetration and Protest in Tanzania*, 96–97, 116.

79. Giblin, *Politics of Environmental Control*, 70–86; Bender, "Being 'Chagga.'"

80. Willis, *State in the Making*, 165–79. In Sukumaland, Andrew Maguire observed that "the necessity for a fundamentally approving consensus on the part of the people, and certain privileges and sanctions enjoyed by groups within the traditional political order, limited the autocratic tendencies of chiefs." Maguire, *Toward "Uhuru" in Tanzania*, 2. Likewise, Holly Hanson has argued that in precolonial Buganda, chiefly authority was constructed in a "heterarchal" system based on assent rather than mere tyranny. Hanson, *Landed Obligation*, 17.

81. Milando interview, June 14, 2006.

82. Kyaruzi interview.

83. N. Pritchard noted both Nyerere and Kawawa citing village discussion as a justification for consensus-oriented debate in a one-party state in "Note by the High Commissioner: The One Party State System in Tanganyika," January 19, 1963, FCO 141/6931.62, PRO.

84. Feierman, *Peasant Intellectuals*, 181–203.

85. Cooper, *Decolonization and African Society*, 11.

86. Nyerere, *Freedom and Unity*, 105.

87. R. Pembo to Secretary-General TANU, "Baraza kuu la Wazee limevunjwa, jipya limeundwa," August 14, 1961, 589: BMC 11/01 A.6, TNA.

88. Mill, *Basic Writings*, 12.

89. Nyerere, *Freedom and Unity*, 106.

90. "Opposition in a Democracy," *Tanganyika Standard*, November 25, 1959, 4.

91. "Opposition Party," *Tanganyika Standard*, December 7, 1959, 2.

92. "The Task of the Opposition," *Tanganyika Standard*, December 14, 1959. For reference to Ghana see Rathbone, *Nkrumah and the Chiefs*.

93. A. Mbatina, "Opposition Party," *Tanganyika Standard*, February 3, 1960, 2.

94. Kasella Bantu, "Opposition Party," *Tanganyika Standard*, February 10, 1960, 2.

95. Barongo, *Mkiki Mkiki wa Siasa*, 230.

96. Weber, *Social and Economic Organization*; see also Foucault, "Governmentality."

97. Nyerere, *Freedom and Unity*, 105–6.

98. Ibid., 85.

99. For more on consensual decision-making, see Snyder, "Being of 'One Heart.'"

100. Clutton-Brock, *Dawn in Nyasaland*.

101. See Green, *Lectures*, 65–66; Rousseau wrote in *The Social Contract*, "When, among the happiest people in the world, bands of peasants are seen regulating affairs of State under an oak, and always acting wisely, can we help scorning the ingenious methods of other nations, which make themselves illustrious and wretched with so much art and mystery?" (bk. 4, p. 1).

102. Nyerere, *Freedom and Unity*, 106; see also "Africa's Place in the World," a speech at Wellesley College in February 1960, in Nyerere, *Africa Today and Tomorrow*, 10; and "The African and Democracy," originally published in Duffy and Manners, *Africa Speaks*. Nyerere originally framed this argument publicly as part of a series of pedagogical articles in the party newsletter, *Sauti ya TANU* (no. 76). See Barongo, *Mkiki Mkiki wa Siasa*, 228–31.

103. Nyerere, *Freedom and Unity*, 196–202.

104. Ibid., 150.

105. Carter, *T. H. Green*, 165–68.

106. Joan Wicken, Tanganyika Education Trust Fund to Lady Hilda Selwyn-Clarke, Fabian Commonwealth Bureau, November 12, 1960, FCB 121/5.7, RH.

107. Wicken, "College at the Crossing Place." Wicken notes that they raised £105,000 within Tanganyika, presumably including the Karimjee donation.

108. George Bennett, "An Outline History of TANU," *Makerere Journal* 7 (1963), Paul Lubeck Papers, Box 3, File 14, HI.

109. Likewise, the current holder of the Zanaki chieftainship, a rainmaker on a once-sacred hill near Nyerere's hometown, reports that the chief depended on an elders' council that had the power to remove him from office. Ihunyo interview.

110. Brennan, *Taifa*.

Chapter 3

1. "Sitaki Kutishwa Kwa Migomo," *Ngurumo*, November 20, 1961, 1.

2. Bayart, *State in Africa*; see also Schatzberg, *Political Legitimacy in Middle Africa*.

3. "Sitaki Kutishwa Kwa Migomo," *Ngurumo*, November 20, 1961, 1.

4. "Self-Rule Day Dead: Cameroons Violence," *Tanganyika Standard*, January 3, 1960, 1.

5. "Guerrilla War in Congo: Tribes Clash, Many Dead," *Tanganyika Standard*, October 17, 1959, 1.

6. Sadleir, *Tanzania, Journey to Republic*, 235.

7. William C. Canup, "An Analysis of the Ruanda-Urundi Political Situation"; Brussels to DOS—both in RG 59, Box 2027, 778.00/6-360, NARA.

8. Tanganyika Information Services press release, November 17, 1961, 593: CB/5/1.17, TNA.

9. "Uhuru Means Exploitation Says Mtemvu," *Tanganyika Standard*, October 5, 1961.

10. Nyerere, *Africa Today and Tomorrow*, 5.
11. See Iliffe, *Modern History of Tanganyika*; Giblin, *Politics of Environmental Control*; and Feierman, *Peasant Intellectuals*.
12. Gulliver, *Neighbours and Networks*, 192–94; see also Liebenow, *Colonial Rule and Political Development*, 165.
13. Juma, "Sukuma Societies"; see also Knudsen, "Dance Societies."
14. Makwaia interview.
15. Mponzi, "Continuity and Change," 4.
16. Feierman, *Peasant Intellectuals*, 124.
17. Giblin, *Politics of Environmental Control*; Giblin, *History of the Excluded*, 107–37; see also Ingle, *Village to State*, 73–75.
18. Bjerk, "Building a New Eden."
19. Iliffe, *Modern History of Tanganyika*, 539.
20. Sunseri, *Vilimani*, 173–78; Deutsh, *Emancipation without Abolition*.
21. Abrahams, *Political Organization of Unyamwezi*, 34, 169–70.
22. Sadleir, *Tanzania, Journey to Republic*, 228.
23. Iliffe, *Modern History of Tanganyika*, 573; Sadleir, *Tanzania, Journey to Republic*.
24. Maazimio ya Mkutano Mkuu wa Mwaka, April 27 to May 2, 1962, attachment to T. A. Kibhogoya Msonge to Wajumbe Wote, January 12, 1963, 589: BMC 11/03 PRT A.1, TNA.
25. Songambele interview; Mang'ombe interview.
26. "Teamwork Essential Says Nyerere," *Tanganyika Standard*, January 18, 1960, 1.
27. 2 Thess. 3:10: "For even when we were with you, this we commanded you, that if any would not work, neither should he eat."
28. Tumbo, "Towards NUTA," 8–13.
29. Iliffe, *Modern History of Tanganyika*, 541.
30. See also Coulson, *Tanzania*, 137–40; Friedland, *Vuta Kamba*.
31. Willliam R. Duggan, DAR to DOS, October 4, 1960, RG 59, Box 2027, 778.00/6-360, NARA.
32. William R. Duggan, DAR to DOS, "Postal Strike Developments," January 2, 1960, RG 59, Box 2772, 878.062/1-260, NARA; "Mobile Post Offices Go into Action," *Tanganyika Standard*, January 14, 1960, 1.
33. William R. Duggan, "Probability of a Major Strike in Tanganyika," DAR to DOS, January 18, 1960, RG 59, Box 2772, 878.062/1-260, NARA.
34. "Dockers: We Will Strike," *Tanganyika Standard*, January 20, 1960, 1; "Dar Dockers Union Withdraws Strike Notice," *Tanganyika Standard*, January 26, 1960, 1.
35. "Dockworker's View," *Tanganyika Standard*, February 6, 1960, 2.
36. "Strike Almost Inevitable on Railway," *Tanganyika Standard*, January 4, 1960, 1.
37. "Tanganyika 'Being Held Ransom,'" *Tanganyika Standard*, January 27, 1960, 1.
38. "Apologise for This Insult, Says Tumbo," *Tanganyika Standard*, February 5, 1960, 1; "We Go Ahead—Tumbo," *Tanganyika Standard*, February 9, 1960, 1.
39. "African Rail Workers Start Strike," *Tanganyika Standard*, February 10, 1960, 1; "Railmen Start Work," *Tanganyika Standard*, May 2, 1960, 1; Robert Huddleston, DAR to DOS, February 10, 1960, RG 59, Box 2772, 878.062/1-260, NARA; Robert Huddleston, "Labor Summary of the Month of January, 1960," DAR to DOS, February 17, 1960, RG 59, Box 2772, 878.062/1-260, NARA.

40. "Union Talks Today with Manager," *Tanganyika Standard*, February 13, 1960, 1, 3.

41. "Iringa Ends Boycott," *Tanganyika Standard*, February 19, 1960, 3.

42. "Stop This Strike, Says TANU," *Tanganyika Standard*, February 26, 1960, 1.

43. "Dock Workers Return to Work Today," *Tanganyika Standard*, March 11, 1960, 1; "7,000 Out on Sisal Strike," *Tanganyika Standard*, April 4, 1960, 1.

44. "We'll Help You, UK Railmen Tell Tumbo," *Tanganyika Standard*, April 5, 1960, 1.

45. Robert Huddleston, DAR to DOS, April 2, 1960, RG 59, Box 2772, 878.062/1-260, NARA.

46. "Tumbo Hands Over," *Tanganyika Standard*, April 15, 1960, 1; "Railmen Start Work," *Tanganyika Standard*, May 2, 1960, 1.

47. "Minutes of TRAU meeting, July 1960," William H. Friedland Collection, Box 8, "TRAU" Folder, HI.

48. William R. Duggan, DAR to DOS, October 30, 1960, RG 59, Box 2027, 778.00/6-360, NARA.

49. Barongo, *Mkiki Mkiki wa Siasa*, 255. In his book, Barongo transcribed and included the entire speech in Swahili. The speech appears in edited form in Nyerere, *Freedom and Unity*, 99–102.

50. "Extract from Tanganyika Intelligence Report, Sept. '60," CO 822/2673.4, PRO; "Extract from Tanganyika Intelligence Report, Dec. '60," CO 822/2673.7, PRO. See also Iliffe, *Modern History of Tanganyika*, 542.

51. William R. Duggan, "View of Michael Kamaliza, the Former President, on Reorganization of the Tanganyika Federation of Labour," DAR to DOS, RG 59, Box 2772, 878.062/1-260, NARA.

52. "Unions Are Part of the Party Says Nyerere," *Tanganyika Standard*, December 30, 1960; see also Rashidi Kawawa, "The TFL, TANU, and Unity," *Spearhead* (Dar es Salaam), December 1961, 14–16.

53. Kyaruzi interview; also, in his interview Songambele said that Nyerere could be "mkali kama serikali," or severe in his governmental role. Kyaruzi's recollections here are also recounted in Mwakikagile, *Nyerere and Africa*, 391.

54. "Extract from Tanganyika Intelligence Report, Jan. '61," CO 822/2673.8, PRO; "Extract from Tanganyika Intelligence Report, Nov. '60," CO 822/2673.6, PRO; "Chronological Outline of TFL Meetings, 1960–64," Friedland Collection, Box 6, HI.

55. Iliffe, *Modern History of Tanganyika*, 541.

56. "Extract from Tanganyika Intelligence Report, May '61," CO 822/2673.11, PRO.

57. "Extract from Tanganyika Intelligence Report, March 1961," CO 822/2673.13, PRO; "Extract from Tanganyika Intelligence Report, February '61," CO 822/2673.12A, PRO; 'No Confidence in Government Says Tumbo," *Tanganyika Sunday News*, April 16, 1961.

58. "Extract from Tanganyika Intelligence Report, March 1961," CO 822/2673.13, PRO; "Extract from Tanganyika Intelligence Report, April 1961," CO 822/2673.14, PRO; "Extract from Tanganyika Intelligence Report, May '61," CO 822/2673.11, PRO; Kisumo interview, September 7, 2006.

59. "Extract from Tanganyika Intelligence Report, July 1961," CO 822/2673.15, PRO; "Extract from Tanganyika Intelligence Summary, September 1961," CO

822/2673.17, PRO; Robert Hennemeyer, Dar es Salaam, "Political Implications of Recent Developments in the Tanganyika Trade Union Movement," July 24, 1961, RG 59, E3266, Box 12, 560 LABOR—Outgoing, NARA.

60. Pratt, *Critical Phase in Tanzania*, 111.

61. Willliam Duggan, DAR to DOS, October 4, 1960, RG 59, Box 2027, 778.00/6-360, NARA.

62. "Tanga Reports of Trade Union Men Quitting TANU," *Tanganyika Standard*, December 22, 1960; extracted in CO 822/2673.7B, PRO.

63. Nyerere, *Africa Today and Tomorrow*, 5–7, 13; Nyerere, *Freedom and Unity*, 103–6.

64. Barrington King to DOS, January 4, 1961, RG 59, Box 2029, 778.13/1-461, NARA; see also Songambele interview.

65. William Duggan, DAR to DOS, May 3, 1961, RG 59, Box 2027, 778.00/5-161, NARA.

66. Brennan, "Short History of Political Opposition"; Barongo interview; Barongo, *Mkiki Mkiki wa Siasa*.

67. Nyerere, *Freedom and Unity*, 128.

68. "'We Don't Intend to Risk Good Rule'—Kawawa," *Tanganyika Standard*, July 10, 1961, 3.

69. Hansard, *10th October–20th October 1961*, October 17, 1961, 313–14.

70. "Nyerere Threatens to Resign: Angry Intervention in Citizenship Debate," *Tanganyika Standard*, October 19, 1961, 1.

71. "Nyerere Asema Nitajiuzulu," *Ngurumo*, October 19, 1961, 1; "Sheria ya Uraia Ingoje Miaka 5," *Ngurumo*, October 19, 1961, 1.

72. Nyerere, *Freedom and Unity*, 128. David Kidaha Makwaia claimed to have given Nyerere a copy of Hitler's *Mein Kampf* around this time, which may account for the caustic reference here in relation to the racialist faction.

73. Robert Hennemeyer, DAR to DOS, November 8, 1961, RG 59, Box 2772, 878.062/1-260, NARA.

74. William Duggan, DAR to DOS, November 24, 1961, RG 59, Box 2772, 878.062/1-260, NARA; "Chronological Outline of TFL Meetings, 1960–64," Friedland Collection, Box 6, HI.

75. "Blackmail—AMNUT," *Tanganyika Standard*, October 21, 1961.

76. "Government Expels ANC Man," *Tanganyika Standard*, November 15, 1961, 1.

77. DAR to DOS, "Julius Nyerere Speaks at Makerere College during Visit to Be Installed as Honorary Fellow," April 10, 1962, RG 59, Box 2028, 778.00/1-262, NARA.

78. Sadleir, *Tanzania, Journey to Republic*, 245–48.

79. Press release, "Cash Award for Prize-Winning Lyrics in National Anthem," July 31, 1961, 593: CB/10/1.5, TNA.

80. British newsreel quoted in the documentary "The Legacy of Julius Nyerere," dir. Abdulrahman Kinana, 2011, posted on YouTube by the Institute of African Studies Carleton College, March 11, 2011, https://www.youtube.com/watch?v=c8QkgDzfvlo&list=PL78CA46645B57160D.

81. Iliffe, *Modern History of Tanganyika*, 573.

82. Nyerere, *Freedom and Unity*, 140.

83. Lusinde interview, June 30, 2013.
84. Robert Hennemeyer, DAR to DOS, January 12, 1962, RG 59, Box 2773, 878.254/6-2960, NARA.
85. Robert Hennemeyer, DAR to DOS, January 17, 1962, RG 59, Box 2773, 878.254/6-2960, NARA.
86. Andrew Nyerere, who was a student at a nearby school at the time, heard that the new mayor was refused entry at the door, where a sign was posted "No Africans and dogs allowed inside." See Mwakikagile, *Life under Nyerere*, 46.
87. Robert Hennemeyer, DAR to DOS, January 18, 1962, RG 59, Box 2028, 778.00/1-262, NARA.
88. Robert Hennemeyer, DAR to DOS, January 19, 1962, RG 59, Box 2773, 878.254/6-2960, NARA. These incidents are briefly discussed in Barongo, *Mkiki Mkiki wa Siasa*, 291.
89. Robert Hennemeyer, DAR to DOS, January 19, 1962, RG 59, Box 2773, 878.254/6-2960, NARA; Robert Hennemeyer, DAR to DOS, January 20, 1962, RG 59, Box 2028, 778.00/1-262, NARA.
90. Robert Hennemeyer, DAR to DOS, February 6, 1962, RG 59, Box 2029, 778.13/1-461, NARA.
91. DAR to DOS, January 25, 1962; David Bruce, London to DOS, January 25, 1962—both in RG 59, Box 2028, 778.00/1-262, NARA.
92. See also Manners, "Africanization, Neo-Racialism and East Africa," 4–6, 15.
93. F. H. Page-Jones, "Comment on Tanganyika Government Changes," attachment to Paul O'Neill to DOS, January 26, 1962, RG 59, Box 2029, 778.13/1-461, NARA.
94. William Duggan, DAR to DOS, November 24, 1961, RG 59, Box 2772, 878.062/1-260, NARA.
95. F. H. Page-Jones, "Comment on Tanganyika Government Changes," attachment to Paul O'Neill to DOS, January 26, 1962, RG 59, Box 2029, 778.13/1-461, NARA.
96. Robert Hennemeyer, DAR to DOS, January 22, 1962, RG 59, Box 2773, 878.254/6-2960, NARA.
97. Robert Hennemeyer, DAR to DOS, January 20, 1962, RG 59, Box 2028, 778.00/1-262, NARA.
98. Robert Hennemeyer, DAR to DOS, January 19, 1962, RG 59, Box 2773, 878.254/6-2960, NARA.
99. DAR to DOS, January 23, 1962, RG 59, Box 2028, 778.00/1-262, NARA.
100. Memorandum of Conversation, DOS, June 25, 1962, RG 59, Box 2028, 778.00/1-262, NARA.
101. Robert Hennemeyer, DAR to DOS, January 22, 1962, RG 59, Box 2773, 778.00/1-262, NARA.
102. Frederick Picard, DAR to DOS, January 23, 1962, RG 59, Box 2029, 778.13/1-461, NARA; DAR to DOS, January 24, 1962, RG 59, Box 2028, 778.00/1-262, NARA.
103. Pratt's view in *Critical Phase in Tanzania* (91), that the resignation represented a break from a pattern of dependency on the British, seems premature. He is more accurate in describing the resignation as dealing mostly with internal issues, in particular racialism (117–18). The effect of the resignation tended to

support British interests, even if it was also a means of preparing for a republican declaration that would remove Turnbull as governor-general.

104. DAR to DOS, January 22, 1962; DAR to DOS, January 23, 1962—both in RG 59, Box 2028, 778.00/1-262, NARA.

105. Robert Hennemeyer, DAR to DOS, January 24, 1962, RG 59, Box 2773, 778.00/1-262, NARA.

106. Kyaruzi interview; see also Kashangaki interview; Selemani interview; Nyamwaga interview.

107. DAR to DOS, March 5, 1962, RG 59, Box 2029, 778.13/5-2962, NARA.

108. Pratt, *Critical Phase in Tanzania*, 121.

109. Lusinde interview, June 30, 2013.

110. Robert Hennemeyer, DAR to DOS, January 25, 1962, RG 59, Box 2029, 778.13/1-461, NARA; F. H. Page-Jones, "Comment on Tanganyika Government Changes," attachment to Paul O'Neill to DOS, January 26, 1962, RG 59, Box 2029, 778.13/1-461, NARA; Pratt, *Critical Phase in Tanzania*, 118.

111. Duggan and Civille, *Tanzania and Nyerere*, 73.

112. Robert Hennemeyer, DAR to DOS, February 17, 1962, RG 59, Box 2029, 778.03/10-1460, NARA.

113. Thomas Byrne, DAR to DOS, April 24, 1962, RG 59, Box 2028, 778.00/1-262, NARA.

114. Thomas Byrne, DAR to DOS, May 31, 1962, RG 59, Box 2028, 778.00/1-262, NARA.

115. Robert T. Hennemeyer, interview for Foreign Affairs Oral History Project (FAOHP), Association for Diplomatic Studies and Training, 1989, accessed July 24, 2014, http://www.adst.org/OH%20TOCs/Hennemeyer,%20Robert%20T.toc.pdf.

116. Robert Hennemeyer, DAR to DOS, February 1, 1962, RG 59, Box 2029, 778.13/1-461, NARA.

117. Robert Hennemeyer, DAR to DOS, February 8, 1962, RG 59, Box 2028, 778.00/1-262, NARA.

118. Robert Hennemeyer, DAR to DOS, February 27, 1962, RG 59, Box 2028, 778.00/1-262, NARA.

119. DAR to DOS, March 5, 1962, RG 59, Box 2029, 778.13/5-2962, NARA.

120. Robert Hennemeyer, DAR to DOS, February 26, 1962; Robert Hennemeyer, DAR to DOS, February 12, 1962—both in RG 59, Box 2772, 878.062/1-260, NARA.

121. Robert Hennemeyer, DAR to DOS, February 24, 1962, RG 59, Box 2029, 778.13/5-2962, NARA.

122. DAR to CRO, March 12, 1962, DO 181/31, PRO; DAR to CRO, March 12, 1962, DO 181/31, PRO; Listowel, *Making of Tanganyika*, 410.

123. Mark D. Tennant to W. S. Bates, September 8, 1962, DO 183/145.42A, PRO; Robert Hennemeyer, DAR to DOS, March 12, 1962, RG 59, Box 2029, 778.13/1-461, NARA; "Cabinet Changes," DAR to CRO, March 12, 1962, DO 181/31, PRO; Olcott H. Dening, "New Cabinet Changes in Tanganyika," letter to Governor "Soapy" Williams, March 13, 1962, RG 59, Box 2029, 778.13/1-461, NARA; "Biographical Note on Hon. A. Z. N. Swai," DO 181/31.14, PRO; "Dr. Vedasto Kyaruzi's Appointment in Prime Minister's Office," press release by

Tanganyika Information Services, March 24, 1962, DO 181/31.13, PRO; Thomas Byrne in DAR to DOS, April 21, 1962, RG 59, Box 2029, 778.13/1-461, NARA.

124. Thomas Byrne, "Trade Union–Government Controversy Flames Anew: Tumbo Resigns as London High Commissioner," to DOS, August 28, 1962, RG 59, Box 2772, 878.02/10-461, NARA.

125. Memorandum of Conversation, "Israeli Business Ventures in Tanganyika," April 6, 1962; Robert Hennemeyer, "Commerce Minister Reassures Private Investors," DAR to DOS, March 14, 1962; Robert Hennemeyer, "Ford Considering Assembly Plant in East Africa," DAR to DOS, July 24, 1961; William R. Duggan, "Tanganyika Minister Seeks American Financial Assistance for Proposed Co-Operative Bank," DAR to DOS, January 6, 1960—all in RG 59, Box 2772, 878.02/10-461, NARA.

126. Thomas Byrne, DAR to DOS, June 7, 1962, RG 59, Box 2773, 878.062/3-1564, NARA; Thomas Byrne, DAR to DOS, June 18, 1962, RG 59, Box 2773, 878.062/3-1562, NARA.

127. Thomas Byrne, DAR to DOS, June 9, 1962, RG 59, Box 2773, 878.062/3-1562, NARA; Pratt, *Critical Phase in Tanzania*, 123–24.

128. Thomas Byrne, DAR to DOS, September 10, 1962, RG 59, Box 2028, 778.00/8-262, NARA.

129. DAR to DOS, June 6, 1962, RG 59, Box 2028, 778.00/1-262, NARA.

130. Thomas Byrne, DAR to DOS, May 2, 1962; and Thomas Byrne, DAR to DOS, July 10, 1962—both in RG 59, Box 2028, 778.00/1-262, NARA; Thomas Byrne, DAR to DOS, May 12, 1962, RG 59, Box 2029, 778.13/5-2962, NARA; Thomas Byrne, DAR to DOS, "Police Assistance Program, Tanganyika," September 14, 1962, RG 59, Box 2029, 778.2/10-160, NARA.

131. Robert Hennemeyer, DAR to DOS, February 14, 1962, RG 59, Box 2029, 778.13/5-2962, NARA.

132. Report of the Africanisation Commission, 1962, 590: EB 18/056.1, TNA; Thomas Byrne, DAR to DOS, May 12, 1962, RG 59, Box 2029, 778.13/5-2962, NARA.

133. Thomas Byrne, DAR to DOS, May 12, 1962, RG 59, Box 2029, 778.13/5-2962, NARA.

134. Songambele interview.

135. A more detailed account of the racial implications of educational policy appears in Bertz, "Educating the Nation."

136. Thomas Byrne, DAR to DOS, July 17, 1962, RG 59, Box 2029, 778.2/10-160, NARA.

137. Robert Hennemeyer, DAR to DOS, September 9, 1962, RG 59, Box 2029, 778.2/10-160, NARA.

138. Maryogo interview, June 6, 2006.

139. Oscar Kambona, press release, July 19, 1962, 593: CB/8/1.12, TNA.

140. Pratt, in *Critical Phase in Tanzania*, noted that "there is little in Nyerere's political ideas to check the vehemence with which TANU has tended to reject any who wish to be active in public affairs but who wish to remain outside of TANU" (80).

141. Kisumo interview, September 7, 2006.

142. DAR to Secretary of State, January 25, 1962, RG 59, Box 2028–778.00/1-262, NARA.

143. Attachments to Hennemeyer, DAR to DOS, "New Political Party Announced," January 31, 1962, NARA, RG 59, Box 2028–778.00/1-262.

144. "Unions Will Not 'Sell Dignity for Political Ideologies,'" *Tanganyika Standard*, October 21, 1961, 1.

145. Songambele interview.

146. Thomas Byrne, DAR to DOS, September 18, 1962, RG 59, Box 2773, 878.062/3-1562, NARA.

147. Robert Hennemeyer, DAR to DOS, February 15, 1962, RG 59, Box 2773, 878.062/1-260, NARA; Kisumo interview, September 7, 2006; *Tanganyika Standard*, February 14, 1962, cited in "Chronological Outline of TFL Meetings 1960–64," Friedland Collection, Box 8, HI.

148. Thomas Byrne, DAR to DOS, September 28, 1962, RG 59, Box 2029, 778.2/10-160, NARA; Walter Townsend to Ronald Donovan, January 28, 1962, Friedland Collection, Box 8, "TRAU," HI.

149. Robert Hennemeyer, DAR to DOS, February 8, 1962, RG 59, Box 2772, 878.062/1-260, NARA; Robert Hennemeyer, DAR to DOS, November 20, 1962, RG 59, Box 2028, 778.00/8-262, NARA.

150. Thomas Byrne, DAR to DOS, May 29, 1962, RG 59, Box 2773, 878.062/3-1562, NARA.

151. J. K. Tettegah to Tom Mboya, June 10, 1960, Scheinmann Papers, File: Mboya, Tom, HI.

152. "Chinese Reportedly Warned to Cease Distributing Funds," DAR to DOS, February 27, 1962, RG 59, Box 2028, 778.00/1-262, NARA; Brennan, "Short History of Political Opposition," 257.

153. Thomas Byrne, DAR to DOS, June 7, 1962, RG 59, Box 2773, 878.062/3-1562, NARA.

154. Thomas Byrne, DAR to DOS, June 4, 1962, RG 84, E3266, Box 10, 350.1 African National Congress, NARA.

155. Thomas Byrne, DAR to DOS, June 4, 1962, RG 59, Box 2028, 778.00/1-262, NARA.

156. Thomas Byrne, DAR to DOS, July 18, 1962, RG 59, Box 2028, 778.00/1-262, NARA.

157. Thomas Byrne, DAR to DOS, August 2, 1962, RG 59, Box 2028, 778.00/8-262, NARA.

158. Robert Hennemeyer, DAR to DOS, September 6, 1962, RG 59, Box 2028, 778.00/8-262, NARA.

159. Thomas Byrne, DAR to DOS, July 24, 1962, RG 59, Box 2029, 778.13/5-2962, NARA.

160. Thomas Byrne, "Trade Union–Government Controversy Flames Anew: Tumbo Resigns as London High Commissioner," to DOS, August 28, 1962, RG 59, Box 2772, 878.02/10-461, NARA.

161. William Leonhart, DAR to DOS, October 13, 1962, RG 59, Box 2028, 778.00/8-262, NARA.

162. William Leonhart, DAR to DOS, October 13, 1962, RG 84, E3266, Box 7, 350 Tanganyika, NARA. Tumbo had previously referred to expatriate civil servants as "mercenaries." Manners, "Africanization, Neo-Racialism and East Africa," 4.

163. Memorandum of Conversation, September 20, 1962, RG 59, Box 2028, 778.00/8-262, NARA.

164. William Leonhart, DAR to DOS, October 6, 1962, RG 59, Box 2773, 878.062/3-1562, NARA; Kamba interview.

165. Memorandum of Conversation, DOS, September 25, 1962, RG 59, Box 2028, 778.00/8-262, NARA.

166. Thomas Byrne, DAR to DOS, September 14, 1962, RG 59, Box 2028, 778.00/8-262, NARA.

167. William Leonhart, DAR to DOS, October 3, 1962, RG 59, Box 2028, 778.00/8-262, NARA; William Leonhart, DAR to DOS, October 6, 1962, RG 59, Box 2773, 878.062/3-1562, NARA; "Chief David Kidaha Makwaia: Respected Tanzanian Leader Whose Influence Extended from Colonial Rule to Independence," *Times* (London), May 11, 2007.

168. Thomas Byrne, DAR to DOS, September 11, 1962, RG 59, Box 2773, 878.062/3-1562, NARA.

169. Makwaia interview; Maguire, *Toward "Uhuru" in Tanzania*, 321–37.

170. Lusinde interview, November 7, 2006.

171. Iliffe, *Modern History of Tanganyika*, 491–94.

172. Petro Njau, Kilimanjaro District Council to Thomas Marealle, OBE, November 26, 1962, 555: 2/1/3.16, TNA.

173. G. O'Connor to Executive Officer, Kilimanjaro District Council, December 27, 1963, 555: 2/1/3.33, TNA.

174. Thomas Byrne, DAR to DOS, September 28, 1962, RG 59, Box 2029, 778.2/10-160, NARA; William Leonhart, DAR to DOS, October 13, 1962, RG 59, Box 2028, 778.00/8-262, NARA; William Leonhart, DAR to DOS, October 22, 1962, RG 59, Box 2029, 778.13/5-2962, NARA; Robert Hennemeyer, DAR to DOS, "No Evidence of Bloc Financial Assistance to Tumbo; Special Branch Seeking Evidence That Mtemvu Receiving Chicom Support," November 20, 1962, RG 59, Box 2028, 778.00/8-262, NARA.

175. Makwaia interview; Robert Hennemeyer, DAR to DOS, "Two Chiefs Deported," November 10, 1962, RG 59, Box 2028, 778.00/8-262, NARA.

176. Thomas Byrne, DAR to DOS, September 27, 1962, RG 59, Box 2028, 778.00/8-262, NARA; Thomas Byrne, DAR to DOS, September 26, 1962, RG 59, Box 2029, 778.2/10-160, NARA.

177. See also "An Act to Amend the Local Governance Ordinance," Enacted by the Parliament of Tanganyika, September 25, 1962, RG 59, Box 2028, 778.00/8-262, NARA.

178. Thomas Byrne, DAR to DOS, September 27, 1962, RG 59, Box 2028, 778.00/8-262, NARA.

179. The Hansard records Kambona's final word in this sentence as "undesirable," which does not make sense. The same speech is also quoted verbatim in American diplomatic correspondence, and the word recorded there is "undeniable." See "Mr. Kambona Moves Second Reading of Preventive Detention Bill," September 27, 1962, RG 59, Box 2028, 778.00/8-262, NARA.

180. Hansard, 25th September 1962–27th September 1962, 112. Compare to the comment of Massimo d'Azeglio, the Italian politician and novelist, after the

Risorgimento, "We have created Italy; now we must create Italians." Quoted in Haste, "Constructing the Citizen," 417.

181. Thomas Byrne, DAR to DOS, September 28, 1962, RG 59, Box 2029, 778.2/10-160, NARA; William Leonhart, DAR to DOS, October 13, 1962, RG 59, Box 2028, 778.00/8-262, NARA.

182. Thomas Byrne, DAR to DOS, September 28, 1962, RG 59, Box 2029, 778.2/10-160, NARA; William Leonhart, DAR to DOS, October 13, 1962, RG 59, Box 2028, 778.00/8-262, NARA.

183. William Leonhart, DAR to DOS, October 3, 1962, RG 59, Box 2028, 778.00/8-262, NARA.

184. Thomas Byrne, DAR to DOS, September 28, 1962, RG 59, Box 2773, 878.062/3-1562, NARA.

185. Makwaia interview.

186. Maguire, *Toward "Uhuru" in Tanzania*, 351–52.

187. Makwaia interview; "Chief David Kidaha Makwaia," *Times*, May 11, 2007. The government announcement of the rustication came a month later. A week after the announcement, reports emerged that the arrests were made on September 29. Robert Hennemeyer, DAR to DOS, "Two Chiefs Deported," November 10, 1962, RG 59, Box 2028, 778.00/8-262, NARA.

188. Robert Hennemeyer, DAR to DOS, "Two Chiefs Deported," November 10, 1962, RG 59, Box 2028, 778.00/8-262, NARA.

189. Barrington King, "Results of Tanganyika's Presidential Election," November 14, 1962, RG 59, Box 2028, 778.00/8-262, NARA.

190. William Leonhart, DAR to DOS, November 7, 1962, RG 59, Box 2028, 778.00/8-262, NARA.

191. William Leonhart, DAR to DOS, November 3, 1962, RG 59, Box 2028, 778.00/8-262, NARA.

192. Barrington King, "Results of Tanganyika's Presidential Election," November 14, 1962, RG 59, Box 2028, 778.00/8-262, NARA.

193. William Leonhart, DAR to DOS, December 12, 1962, RG 59, Box 2028, 778.00/8-262, NARA.

194. Taarifa ya Mkutano wa Halmashauri Kuu ya Taifa, November 26, 1962, 589: BMC 11/02 PRT A.1, TNA.

195. Robert Hennemyer, DAR to DOS, October 29, 1962, RG 59, Box 2028, 778.00/8-262, NARA.

196. Taarifa ya Halmashauri Kuu ya Taifa, January 10–14, 1963, 589: BMC 11/02 PRT A.2, TNA.

197. William Leonhart, DAR to DOS, October 29, 1962, RG 59, Box 2028, 778.00/8-262, NARA.

198. E. A. Kisenge to Bhoke Munanka, July 20, 1963, 589: BMC 11/02 PRT A.3, TNA.

199. Letter from T. A. Tuwa ("on behalf of 100 party members whose signatures, if needed, will follow") to TANU Regional Secretary, Tanga, September 29, 1962, 493: A.6/34.230, TNA.

200. E. A. Kisenge to Bhoke Munanka, July 20, 1963, 589: BMC 11/02 PRT A.3, TNA.

201. Minutes za Mkutano Kuu wa Mwaka wa TANU, 16–19 January 1963, 589: BMC 11/02 PRT A.33, TNA; Hart, DAR to DOS, November 28, 1962, RG 59, Box 2028, 778.00/8-262, NARA.

202. Makwaia interview; William Leonhart, DAR to DOS, January 17, 1963, RG 59, Box 2028, 778.00/1-163, NARA; Maguire, *Toward "Uhuru" in Tanzania*, 338–60; William Leonhart, DAR to DOS, February 10, 1964, RG 59, Box 2688, POL 36 TANGAN 1/1/64, NARA.

203. The suspended unions were the Railway Union and the Mine Workers Union. See Robert Hennemeyer, DAR to DOS, November 12, 1962; William Leonhart, DAR to DOS, January 7, 1963; Thomas Byrne, DAR to DOS, "Government Relations with TFL Enter New Phase"—all in RG 59, Box 2773, 878.962/3-1562, NARA.

204. William Leonhart, DAR to DOS, January 15, 1963, RG 59, Box 2028, 778.001/-163, NARA.

205. Robert Hennemeyer, DAR to DOS, "Transmittal of Text of President Nyerere's Address, 'Democracy and the Party System,'" January 17, 1963, RG 59, Box 2028, 778.00/1-163, NARA; see also Nyerere, *Freedom and Unity*.

206. William Leonhart, DAR to DOS, January 17, 1963, RG 59, Box 2028, 778.00/1-163, NARA.

207. Minutes za Mkutano Kuu wa Mwaka wa TANU, 16–19 January 1963, 589: BMC 11/02 PRT A.33, TNA.

208. William Leonhart, DAR to DOS, January 17, 1963, RG 59, Box 2028, 778.00/1-163, NARA.

209. William Leonhart, DAR to DOS, January 28, 1963, RG 59, Box 2028, 778.00/1-163, NARA.

210. Fr. Schildknecht, "Final Report," Papers of Lloyd Swantz, Madison, WI.

211. Mkutano wa Halmashauri ya Ofisi Kuu Mbele ya Halmashauri Kuu ya TAifa, January–July 1963, 589: BMC 11/02 PRT A.11, TNA.

212. Smith, *We Must Run*, 111.

213. Bates, "Tanganyika," 458; Hansard, *11th June 1963–26th June 1963*, 760–62.

214. Nyerere, *Freedom and Unity*, 181.

215. Robert Hennemeyer, DAR to DOS, "Religion and Politics Disturb Tanganyika's Leaders," undated [ca. September 1963], RG 84, E3266, Box 10, Afro-Asian People's Solidarity Conference, 350.1, NARA.

216. Robert Hennemeyer, DAR to DOS, "Fundikira Deposed as Chairman, Tanganyika Development Corporation (TDC)," October 6, 1963, RG 84, E3266, Box 11, 361.2 Kambona 1963, NARA.

217. Maazimio ya Halmashauri Kuu ya Taifa, undated [mid-1964], 589: BMC 11/02 PRT A.30, TNA.

218. For background on ethnic politics, see Iliffe, *Modern History of Tanganyika*, 523–51.

219. High Commission, DAR to CRO, "Tanganyika Fortnightly Summary," September 13, and October 25, 1963, FCO 141/6931.100, 126, PRO; Chande, "Muslim-State Relations," 107.

220. Robert Hennemeyer, DAR to DOS, "Religion and Politics Disturb Tanganyika's Leaders," undated [ca. September 1963], RG 84, E3266, Box 10, Afro-Asian People's Solidarity Conference, 350.1, NARA.

221. I translated the slangy "mambo yamekuwa shwari" as "things are cool." Taarifa ya Area Secretary, Mwanza, December 31, 1963, 246: 6/14.246, TNA.

Chapter 4

1. See Pratt, "Julius Nyerere," 141.
2. Thomas Byrne, DAR to DOS, June 29, 1962, RG 59, Box 2028, 778.00/1-262, NARA.
3. Nyerere, *Freedom and Unity*, 174.
4. This argument contrasts with other studies of Nyerere's thought, like that of Cranford Pratt, that focus on his relevance to theoretical debates about socialism.
5. See also Brennan, "Blood Enemies."
6. See Robert MacKinnon, Brussels to DOS, July 27, 1960, RG 59, Box 2027, 778.00/6-360, NARA.
7. Early the next year, Nyerere appointed P. I. Marealle to a commission to reform local government and later to the commission tasked with making recommendations for a single-party state. Magotti, *Rashidi Mfaume Kawawa*, 71.
8. Marealle, *Maisha ya Mchagga*, 1–2. For further discussion see Hunter, "Pursuit of the 'Higher Medievalism.'"
9. Hunter, "Pursuit of the 'Higher Medievalism,'" 157.
10. Marealle, *Maisha ya Mchagga*, 99–100. Clyde Ingle, in *Village to State* (75), found a similar discourse of communal cooperation, or "chiwili," present in Zigua areas near Handeni in the early 1960s.
11. Duffy and Manners, *Africa Speaks*, reprinted in Nyerere, *Freedom and Unity*, 103–6.
12. Nyerere, *Africa Today and Tomorrow*, 13.
13. Giblin, *History of the Excluded*, 55–71.
14. Walsh, *Africans and the Christian Way of Life*, 18–19. The Vatican Archives entry for this document reads, "letter drafted by Fr. Walsh, and approved and issued by the bishops." Walsh was appointed "Secretary for the Tanganyika Bishops to represent the Catholic Missions at the Department of Education" in 1946. In other publications, Walsh presented an essentially socialist economic ethic for government, urging lawmakers "to guarantee ... a reasonable standard of comfort" for all people as a "sacred right," and in one case, restated nearly word for word, Nyerere's thinking on the need for a one-party state. See "Father Richard Walsh, 1910–1979"; Sivalon, "Roman Catholicism," 92, 99, 113.
15. Hyden, *Tanu Yajenga Nchi*, 149–50.
16. See Giblin, *History of the Excluded*, 363.
17. Ujamaa corresponds in many ways to T. H. Green's philosophy of government as relationship of mutual obligation.
18. Compare to Berman and Lonsdale's insights in "Custom, Modernity," 173–98.
19. Ivaska, *Cultured States*, 17.
20. Mamdani, *Citizen and Subject*.
21. Burton, *African Underclass*.

22. See Lal, "Self-Reliance and the State."
23. See, for example, Giblin, *History of the Exluded*, 227–33; Spear, *Mountain Farmers*, 192–202; and Gulliver, *Neighbours and Networks*, 63–73.
24. Bjerk, "Allocation of Land."
25. Shetler, *Imagining Serengeti*, 118–19.
26. "Nyerere Burito," Musoma District Book, Page 71, Reading Room, TNA.
27. Dondeyne et al., "Changing Land Tenure Regimes," 16–17.
28. Budodi interview. This theme is strong in Kenya and Uganda as well. See Kibwana, "Land Tenure," 233; and Hanson, *Landed Obligation*.
29. Extract from Annual Report, 1934, Tanga District Book I, Appendix No. 4, TNA.
30. Nyerere, *Freedom and Unity*, 53–54.
31. Letter from Residents of Kymutwara Chiefdom to District Commissioner, Bukoba, October 4, 1955, 619: Land *Nyarubanja*, vol. 3.322, TNA.
32. Hyden, *Tanu Yajenga Nchi*, 113–20.
33. Nyerere, *Freedom and Unity*, 58.
34. See Feierman, *Peasant Intellectuals*.
35. Mnyampala, *Gogo*, 17.
36. Mbita interview, December 9, 2006.
37. Nyerere, *Freedom and Unity*, 138.
38. For other comments on the social qualities of land, see Spear, *Mountain Farmers*; and Weiss, *Making and Unmaking*, 192.
39. Milando interview, June 14, 2006.
40. Fimbo, "Land, Socialism and the Law."
41. Mugerwa, "Land Tenure in East Africa," 5, 110–11; cf. Freehold Titles (Conversion) and Government Leases, Chap. 523, Tanzania, Revised Laws, Annual Supplement, 1963–65 (Dar es Salaam: Government Printer, 1964–69).
42. Nyerere, *Ujamaa—Essays on Socialism*, 85.
43. "Statement of Policy on Freehold Land," 593: CB/9/1 No. 4, TNA.
44. Ibid.
45. Lonsdale, "Moral Economy of Mau Mau," 316. Ujamaa responded to the "general dialectics of national culture in the postcolony," described by Andrew Apter, in "The Subvention of Tradition: A Genealogy of the Nigerian Durbar," in Steinmetz, *State/Culture*, 248.
46. See Rejwan, *Nasserist Ideology*; and Markovitz, *Léopold Sédar Senghor*.
47. Nyerere, *Freedom and Unity*, 170.
48. "Ujamaa is Tanganyika's Aim," *Tanganyika Standard*, April 16, 1962, 1.
49. E. Tibesigwa, "Mr. Nyerere's Socialism," *Tanganyika Standard*, May 1, 1962, 2.
50. Robert Hennemeyer, DAR to DOS, "Disappointing Response to Consumer Co-Operative," November 19, 1962, RG 59, Box 2772, 878.02/10-461, NARA.
51. DAR to Secretary of State, January 21, 1963, RG 59, Box 2772, 878.02/10-461, NARA.
52. Nyerere, *Africa Today and Tomorrow*, 13.
53. Feierman, *Peasant Intellectuals*, 149, 182–92.
54. Kawawa announced: "The giving of preference to Tanganyika citizens of African origin as a temporary expedient will continue, but the Government has publicly stated its aim that eventually there shall be no distinction as between

Tanganyikans in the public service whatever their origin." Statement on Africanisation, June 10, 1963, 590: EB/18/056 PART A.7, TNA.
55. Swantz, *Blood, Milk, and Death*.
56. Weiss, *Making and Unmaking*.
57. Press release, July 17, 1962, 593: CB/8/1.15, TNA.
58. Nyerere, *Freedom and Unity*, 162.
59. Ibid., 170.
60. Ibid., 169.
61. Ibid., 166.
62. Ibid., 166.
63. Ibid., 167.
64. "Manifesto," attachment to Robert Hennemeyer, DAR to DOS, "New Political Party Announced," January 31, 1962, RG 59, Box 2028, 778.00/1-262, NARA.
65. Nyerere, *Freedom and Unity*, 178.

Chapter 5

1. Nyerere, *Freedom and Unity*, 184.
2. Divisional Executive Officer, East Hai to Area Commissioner, Kilimanjaro, October 2, 1963, 555: 9/23.142, TNA.
3. Ze'ev Derori describes the Israeli *moshavim* as being relatively insecure in the 1950s in *Israel's Reprisal Policy*, 75–82.
4. Ferguson, *Anti-politics Machine*.
5. Scott, *Seeing Like a State*. See Foucault, *Discipline and Punish*.
6. Schneider, *Government of Development*; Ferguson, *Anti-politics Machine*. Schneider's insights echo Clyde Ingle's observations of enforced communal labor in the 1960s in *Village to State*.
7. Mamdani, *Citizen and Subject*, 172.
8. Hyden, *Tanu Yajenga Nchi*. Hyden's later work retreated somewhat from his 1960s portrait of a state successfully laying claim to rural political loyalties. In the 1970s Hyden portrayed a state unable to convert political loyalties into lifestyle commitments to a new economic order. See Hyden, *Beyond Ujamaa in Tanzania*.
9. Ingle, *Village to State*, 195–99.
10. Nyerere, *Freedom and Unity*, 178.
11. World Bank, *Economic Development of Tanganyika*, 7.
12. See Listowel, *Making of Tanganyika*, 381. Sonjo is also an ethnonym, and there are several villages known as Sonjo, of which one was designated for "transformation."
13. F. A. Reynolds to J. A. Molyneaux, September 1, 1963, DO 166/61, PRO.
14. Burton, *African Underclass*.
15. "Murmurings in Masailand," DAR to DOS, August 2, 1960, RG 59, Box 2027, 778.00/6-360, NARA; Hillman, "Inculturated Life." Tension between Maasai people and Sonjo people has continued in more recent times as well. See Shivji, *Not Yet Democracy*, 21.
16. See Bjerk, "Allocation of Land."

17. Berntsen, "Maasai and Their Neighbors," 6–7; J. E. G. Sutton, "Becoming Maasailand," in Spear and Waller, *Being Maasai*, 52–54.
18. Shetler, "Interpreting Rupture in Oral Memory," 408.
19. Nyerere, *Freedom and Unity*, 183.
20. Minutes of the Regional Development Committee, Tanga, April 6, 1962, quoted in Ingle, *Village to State*, 96.
21. Senhor Dr. João Monteverde Pereira Bastos, Consul de Portugal em Salisbury, January 9, 1963, 607 PAA, Ministério dos Negócios Estrangeiros, Proc 945, 135 Moçambique, UL 11, AHD.
22. Cohen was at that time representing the British Department of Technical Co-Operation. Sir Andrew Cohen, "Development Areas in Districts; Dr. Nyerere's Views," attachment to Sir Andrew Cohen to Sir Algernon Rumbold, January 3, 1963, DO 166/61.3, PRO; see also Iliffe, *Modern Tanganyika of Tanganyika*, 438.
23. Despite Tanzania's disastrous fifteen-year experiment in rural "transformation," the basic idea that Nyerere articulates here remains very much alive. Compare Jeffrey Sachs's Millennium Villages project, accessed July 21, 2014, http://www.unmillenniumproject.org/mv/index.htm.
24. Sir Neil Pritchard, DAR to L. B. Walsh-Atkins, CRO, January 18, 1963, DO 166/61.5, PRO.
25. Alan Dudley, Department of Technical Co-Operation, to Sir Neil Pritchard, Dar es Salaam, February 1963, attachment to W. A. C. Mathieson to F. A. Reynolds, February 8, 1963, DO 166/61.10, PRO.
26. J. L. F. Buist to L. B. Walsh-Atkins, CRO, January 18, 1963, DO 166/61.5, PRO.
27. F. A. Reynolds to J. A. Molyneaux, January 9, 1963, DO 166/61, PRO. The colonial Kenyan villagization project was also commended in the *East Africa Royal Commission Report*.
28. J. A. Molyneaux to L. B. Walsh-Atkins, January 9, 1963, DO 166/61, PRO.
29. Kawawa interview, August 9, 2006; Curtis Strong to US Secretary of State, "British High Commission Biographic Data," July 13, 1965, RG 59, Box 2692, POL 15-1 TAN, 7/1/65, NARA.
30. "Vice President's Speech, Seminar," January 12, 1963, DO 166/61.8, PRO.
31. Syracuse University, "Proposed Multi-Disciplinary Team Research on Rural Village Settlement in Tanganyika," 26, Paul Lubeck Papers, Box 3-13, HI.
32. "Rural Settlement Commission Established," press release from Tanganyika Information Services, May 9, 1963, 548: R.20/1.1, TNA.
33. Ibid.
34. "Rural Settlement in Tanganyika," attachment to Commissioner for Village Settlement to Ruvuma Regional Commissioner, September 11, 1963, "Village Pilot Settlement Scheme—Ruvuma Region" Memorandum, 640: P/sch/v/ruv ada II Part I.2, TNA.
35. Rural Settlement Commission Circular to All Regional Commissioners, Appendix B, "Notes on the Establishment of Pilot Village Settlements," April 5, 1963, 548: R.20/1, TNA.
36. Commissioner for Village Settlement to All Regional Commissioners, January 8, 1964, 548: R.20/1.34, TNA.

37. Halmashauri Kuu ya Makazi ya Vijijini, Booklet "Makazi ya Vijijini," received by the Regional Commissioner, Moshi, January 10, 1964, 548: R.20/1, TNA.

38. Fred Burke, Syracuse University, to William Leonhart, January 13, 1964, Leonhart Papers, Box 38, File: Tanganyika 1964–65 (1 of 2), JFK. Ingle, *Village to State*, 51.

39. Nikos Georgulas, graduate student, Fall 1963 (Syracuse University), "An Approach to the Economic Development of Rural Areas in Tanganyika with Special Reference to the Village Settlement Program," Leonhart Papers, Box 38, File: Tanganyika 1964–65 (1 of 2), JFK.

40. Shivji, "Reforming Local Government"; Ingle, *Village to State*, 169.

41. Mamdani, *Citizen and Subject*, 177. See Leander Schneider's critique in "Colonial Legacies and Postcolonial Authoritarianism."

42. Press release, July 24, 1963, 593: CB/7/2, Safaris, Public Engagements Personal Affairs: Mr. M. Kamaliza, TNA.

43. Program of East African Studies at Syracuse University, Project Proposal: "Proposed Multi Disciplinary Team Research on Village Development in Tanganyika," Leonhart Papers, Box 38, File: Tanganyika 1964–65 (1 of 2), JFK.

44. "Village Pilot Settlement Scheme—Ruvuma Region" Memorandum: "Rural Settlement in Tanganyika," 640: P/sch/v/ruv ada II Part I, TNA.

45. "Maonyo Yaliyotolewa na Waziri wa Ardhi Misitu na Wanyama Alhaj Tewa Saidi Tewa kwa Maafisa Tisa Waliomaliza Mafunzo Mjini Dar es Salaam," September 27, 1963, 593: CB/9/1.29, TNA.

46. Tanganyika Information Services, press release, "Minister to Appoint Inquiry into Disputed Lands," October 17, 1963, 593: CB/9/1.30, TNA; Tanganyika Information Services, press release, "Minister to Appoint Inquiry into Disputed Lands," October 18, 1963, 593: CB/9/1.31, TNA.

47. Wily, "Political Economy," 9.

48. Kawawa interview, November 10, 2006.

49. Hyden, *Beyond Ujamaa in Tanzania*, 88.

50. TANU Secretary Kahe to Executive Officer, Kilimanjaro District, September 4, 1964, 555: 9/23 No. 163, TNA; Vijana Wakristu Wafanya Kazi wa Kibosho Singa to Executive Officer of Kilimanjaro District Council, October 7, 1964, 555: 9/23 No. 166, TNA; Umoja wa Wakulima wa Mwaawe to Chief Executive Officer, Kilimanjaro, October 17, 1964, 555: 9/23 No. 171, TNA.

51. Spear, *Mountain Farmers*.

52. Provincial Commissioner, Northern Province, to Secretary of Chagga Council, April 1, 1960, 555: 2/1/3.1, TNA.

53. "Kumbukumbu za Mkutano wa Kwanza wa Rombo Land Board," June 1, 1954, 555: 9/15.1, TNA.

54. Michaeli Maeda to Regional Commissioner, Kilimanjaro, September 28, 1963, 555: 9/23.143, TNA.

55. Mandare interview.

56. Kawawa interview, September 5, 2006.

57. Oscar Kambona, press release, July 17, 1962, 593: CB/8/1.15, TNA.

58. Executive Officer, Kilimanjaro, to Chair, KFCU, April 24, 1964, 555: 9/5.242, TNA.

59. Executive Officer, Kilimanjaro District, to All Divisional Executive Officers, April 22, 1964, 555: C.5/1A.281, TNA.
60. Divisional Executive Officer, South Rombo Division, to Executive Officer, Kilimanjaro District, January 16, 1964, 555: C.5/1A.219, TNA.
61. Executive Officer, Kilimanjaro, to Divisional Executive Officers, October 30, 1963, 555: C.5/1A.190, TNA.
62. Plan of Work, Kibosho (Narumo and Lyamungo), 555: C.5/1A.251, TNA.
63. See Peterson, *Ethnic Patriotism*; and Ivaska, *Cultured States*.
64. Peter S. Herman to Area Commissioner, Kilimanjaro, April 13, 1964, 555: C.5/1A.284, TNA.
65. VDC Minutes from East Vunjo, July 27, 1964, 555: 1/37/II.58, TNA.
66. See Ivaska, "In the 'Age of Minis.'"
67. "Taarifa ya Area Secretary, Mwanza," December 31, 1963, 246: A 6/14.246, TNA.
68. Villagization represented a "capillary" communication that helps us see beyond the unidirectional implication of the panoptic rationale suggested by James Scott, in *Seeing Like a State*.
69. H. A. Mwakangale, Area Commissioner, Kilimanjaro District, to Divisional Executive Officers of Kilimanjaro District Council, February 12, 1964, 555: 1/37/II.1, TNA.
70. Divisional Executive Officer, East Hai, to TANU/Village Development Committees of East Hai, May 7, 1964, 555: 1/37/II.32, TNA; Divisional Executive Officer, South Rombo, to Executive Officer, Kilimanjaro District Council, June 10, 1964, 555: 1/37/II.38, TNA; "Mkutano wa 2 wa VDC Samanga Chini," February 22, 1964, 555: C.5/1A.266, TNA.
71. Tanganyika Information Services, press release, May 9, 1963, 548: R.20/1, TNA.
72. Lusinde interview, November 7, 2006; see also Bienen, *Tanzania*, 204.
73. Maazimio ya kupelekwa Katika Mkutano wa Halmashauri kuu ya taifa, 589: BMC/11/02 PRT A.13, TNA.
74. Wilbert Klerruu, quoted in *Nationalist*, November 6, 1964, cited in Bienen, *Tanzania*, 356.
75. See Bjerk, "Allocation of Land."
76. Mumford, "Education."
77. Glassman, *Feasts and Riot*.
78. Burton, *African Underclass*.
79. "Haya yafuatayo ni majina ya waliohudhuria mkutano wa TANU youth league huko musoma tarehe January 10, 1964," 589: BMC/11/04/A.38, TNA.
80. Spear, *Mountain Farmers*; Samoff, *Tanzania*, 79.
81. Nyerere, *Ujamaa Vijijini*, 30.
82. Commissioner for Village Settlement to Regional Commissioner, Arusha and Kilimanjaro, August 13, 1963, 555: 9/23.144A, TNA; Field Assistant to Executive Officer, Kilimanjaro, October 17, 1963, 555: 9/23.144, TNA.
83. Settlement Manager, Handeni, to Area Commissioners in Kilimanjaro, March 6, 1965, 555: 9/23 No. 201, TNA; Divisional Executive Officer, West Vunjo, to Area Commissioner, Kilimanjaro, March 29, 1965, 555: 9/23.203, TNA.
84. "The Mara TANU Youth Settlement Farm," 589: BMC 12/01/B.99, TNA.

85. Bhoke Munanka, "Settlement Scheme for the TANU Youth League," November 21, 1963, 589: BMC 12/01 B.61, TNA.

86. "Hotuba ya Mheshimiwa I.M. Bhoke Munanka Kuhusu Ufunguzi wa Mara TANU Youth Settlement Farm," January 9, 1964, 589: BMC 12/01/C.37, TNA.

87. Executive Secretary, Mara TANU Youth Farm, to Bhoke Munanka, March 21, 1964, 589: BMC 12/01/B.1, TNA.

88. Maria Nyerere to D. W. B. Stroud, Ottoman Bank, August 14, 1964, 589: BMC 12/01/B.78, TNA.

89. "Self-Help a Moral Obligation," *Tanganyika News Review*, September 1964, 589: BMC 12/01/B.151, TNA.

90. C. M. Nyirabu, Assistant to Bhoke Munanka, to Tara S. Dogra, June 9, 1966, 589: BMC 12/01/C.200, TNA.

91. E. W. Root to Executive Officer, North Mara District Council, May 5, 1966, 589: BMC 12/01/C.181, TNA; Secretary, Mara TANU Youth Farm, to A. Baumann, Uganda Meat Packers, April 5, 1966, 589: BMC 12/01/C.159, TNA; Wildialim to Administrative Secretary, Mara Region, May 31, 1966, 589: BMC 12/01/C.194, TNA; Bhoke Munanka to Area Commissioner, Tarime, June 8, 1966, 589: BMC 12/01/C.195, TNA.

92. Wambura Paulo Mkono to Chairman, M.T.Y.S.F. Board, October 4, 1967, 589: BMC 12/01 E.146, TNA.

93. Pathis Mangara, M.R.T.S.F., to President's Office, March 31, 1967, 589: BMC 12/01 E.91, TNA.

94. Mbita interview, December 9, 2006.

95. Ministério dos Negócios Estrangeiros to Senhor Dr. João Monteverde Pereira Bastos, Consul de Portugal em Salisbury, January 9, 1963, Information Received by Ministry of Ultramar, November 2, 1962, 607 PAA, Relações com o Tanganika, Processo 945, 124 1962/63, AHD.

96. Mbita interview, December 9, 2006; Robert Hennemeyer, DAR to DOS, January 26, 1962, RG 59, Box 2773, 878.10/8-1662, NARA; Thomas Byrne, "Prime Minister's Policy Speech to National Assembly," DAR to DOS, June 26, 1962, RG 59, Box 2029, 778.13/5-2962, NARA; Barrington King, "Tanganyika Minister Threatens Action Against Portuguese Territories," DAR to DOS, May 22, 1961, RG 59, Box 2027, 778.00/5-161, NARA.

97. Robert Hennemeyer, "Possible Use of Compulsion in Agricultural Resettlement Program," DAR to DOS, March 3, 1962, RG 59, Box 2773, 878.10/8-1662, NARA.

98. Cover Letter to Memorandum from Commissioner for Village Settlement to Regional Commissioner for Ruvuma Region, September 11, 1963, 640: P/sch/v/ruv ada II Part I "Village Pilot Settlement Scheme—Ruvuma Region," No. 2, TNA.

99. F. A. Reynolds, DAR to CRO, September 23, 1963, DO 166/61.31, PRO.

100. William Leonhart, DAR to DOS, September 21, 1963, RG 59, Entry 3266, Box 11, 361.2 Kambona 1963, NARA.

101. Sarakikya interview, June 26, 2006.

102. Kreinin, *Israel and Africa*.

103. "Village Pilot Settlement Scheme—Ruvuma Region" Memorandum: "Rural Settlement in Tanganyika," 640: P/sch/v/ruv ada II Part I, TNA. A number of Tanzanian leaders and TYL youth had visited moshav settlements in Israel,

and Israel conducted much of its military training for African militaries in such settlements. See Levey, "Israel's Involvement in the Congo," 20. See also Weingrod, *Reluctant Pioneers*; Klayman, *Moshav in Israel*; and Willner, *Nation-Building and Community*.

104. Lusinde interview, November 7, 2006.

105. "Mapendekezo ya Halmashauri Maalum ya Kuunda Jeshi Jipya ya Jamhuri ya Tanganika," January 30, 1964, 589: BMC11/02 A.29, TNA.

106. D. A. Mwakosya to Regional Agricultural Officer, Ruvuma, October 22, 1964, 640: P/sch/v/ruv.12, TNA; Director of Agriculture to Senior Research Officer, Ilonga, October 22, 1964, 640: P/sch/v/ruv.13, TNA.

107. Director of Agriculture to Regional Agricultural Officers of Mtwara and Songea, November 16, 1964, 640: P/sch/v/ruv.18, TNA; J. L. F. Buist to J. W. Howard, Department of Technical Co-operation, "Village Settlement," December 17, 1963, DO 166/61.42, PRO.

108. S. J. Galinoma for Principal Secretary in the Office of the Second Vice President to Principal Secretary in the Ministry of Agriculture, March 24, 1965, 640: P/sch/v/ruv.29, TNA.

109. NSHQ Operation order 9/65, Nachingwea Project, October 12, 1964, 482: VP/N.40/5.13, TNA.

110. Director of Agriculture to Regional Agricultural Officers in Mtwara and Songea, September 13, 1965, 640: P/sch/v/ruv.35, TNA.

111. Sarakikya interview, June 26, 2006.

112. Jesse MacKnight, "Movement of 4,000 Refugees into Southern Tanganyika," October 8, 1964, RG 59, Box 32, REF REFUGEES AND MIGRATION TANG, NARA.

113. Mr. Dawson, "World Food Program Assistance to Mozambique Refugees in Tanzania," December 4, 1964, RG 59, Box 32, REF REFUGEES AND MIGRATION TANG, NARA.

114. William Leonhart, DAR to DOS, October 2, 1964, RG 59, Box 2694, POL 32 TANZAN, 1/1/64, NARA.

115. DAR High Commission to Ministry of Defence (Army), October 23, 1964, DO 185/51.148, PRO.

"Report No. 2 by Defence Adviser, Dar es Salaam, Period I: October to December 31, 1964," attachment to B. G. Pugh to High Commissioner, DAR, March 8, 1965, DO 213/160.2, PRO.

116. Kawawa interview, November 10, 2006.

117. "Kumbukumbu ya mkutano kuhusu mafunzo ya kijeshi katika vijiji uliofanyika katika ofisi ya makamu wa pili wa rais," October 14, 1968, 589: BMC/11/04/F.19, TNA.

Chapter 6

1. Parsons, *1964 Army Mutinies*, 125.
2. Luanda, "Playout of the Mutiny," 107–8, 160.
3. Research on the overthrows of Sylvanus Olympio in Togo and Fulbert Youlou in Congo-Brazzaville is remarkably thin, as with the overthrow of Hubert Maga

in the Republic of Dahomey (now Benin) in October 1963. For a summary see Nugent, *Africa since Independence*, 206–7, 201–11, 244–45; Decalo, *Coups and Army Rule*, 52–53, 95–99, 136–48; and Houngnikpo, *Determinants of Democratization*.

4. Weber, *Simulating Sovereignty*, 127.
5. See Pratt, *Critical Phase in Tanzania*, 178–79.
6. Parsons, *1964 Army Mutinies*, 67–75.
7. Sarakikya interview, June 26, 2006.
8. The rates of military pay are recorded in 482: PM.18/62/0168, TNA. This figure is repeated in British correspondence around the time of the mutiny, comparing the 106-shilling rate to 150 shillings as a minimum government wage for civilians. The exchange rate is calculated in accord with the official exchange rate of 20 East African shillings to 1 British pound sterling in 1964, which was equivalent to US$2.77 in 1955 (per PACIFIC Exchange Rate Service, accessed July 21, 2014, http://fx.sauder.ubc.ca/etc/USDpages.pdf). This seems to be accurate, as an American diplomatic memorandum in 1960 quoted an equivalency of $21 and 150 EA shillings, which yields the same rate. See DAR to DOS, February 16, 1960, RG 59, Box 2772, 878.062/1-260, NARA; DAR High Commission to CRO, January 23, 1964, DO 226/10, PRO. See also Slater, *African Odyssey*, 254.
9. See Press release, Lake Region, March 21, 1962, 593: CB/8/1 No. 5, TNA.
10. Luanda, "Playout of the Mutiny," 27.
11. Cooper, *On the African Waterfront*.
12. DAR to CRO, January 23, 1964, DO 226/10, PRO.
13. Robert Hennemeyer, DAR to DOS, October 27, 1963, RG 84, E3266, Box 11, 570.1 Military 1963, NARA.
14. "Report of Mutiny by 1st Battalion Tang Rifles 20th January 1964 by Lt. Col. RSN Mans, MBE" from Nairobi, January 22, 1964, Microfilm, CSAS.MF.107–8, Ivan-Smith Papers, BI; now also available in FCO 141/140143, PRO.
15. Ibid.; Nyerere, *Freedom and Unity*, 259. Nyerere was acting to stem the extreme shortage of qualified personnel in the ministries. See Elizabeth Tolman, "Civil Service Manpower Shortages," DAR to DOS, January 1, 1964, RG 59, Box 2687, POL 15-4 TANGAN, NARA.
16. "Sandhurst Man's New 'First,'" *Tanganyika Standard*, November 16, 1961, 1.
17. "Report of Mutiny by 1st Battalion Tang Rifles, 20th January 1964," FCO 141/140143, PRO.
18. Ibid.; "Intelligence Briefing Memorandum Check Bulletin," DEFE 64/5, PRO.
19. For background on Israel's increasing involvement in East Africa, see Levey, "Israel's Strategy in Africa."
20. Luanda, "Playout of the Mutiny," 92, 94.
21. Parsons, *1964 Army Mutinies*, 104.
22. "Report of Mutiny by 1st Battalion Tang Rifles, 20th January 1964," FCO 141/140143, PRO; "Israeli Assistance for Tanganyikan Police," Memorandum of Conversation, January 14, 1963, RG 59, Box 2028, 778.00/1-163, NARA.
23. Marion, Lady Chesham, general letter, January 27, 1964, CHE-25, 12, BI.
24. "Report of Mutiny by 1st Battalion Tang Rifles, 20th January 1964," FCO 141/140143, PRO.
25. Nyerere (Makongoro) interview; Luanda, "Playout of the Mutiny," 90.

26. BLFK Nairobi to War Office, January 20, 1964, DO 226/10, PRO; William Leonhart, DAR to DOS, January 3, 1964, NSF/CF 100-1.27, LBJ; DAR to CRO, January 22, 1964, DO 226/10, PRO.

27. Luanda, "Playout of the Mutiny," 80; see also Parsons, *1964 Army Mutinies*, 90–112.

28. See Parsons, *1964 Army Mutinies*, 108–9.

29. Hennemeyer, FAOHP interview.

30. BLFK to War Office, January 20, 1964, DO 226/10, PRO.

31. DAR to CRO, January 20, 1964, DO 226/10, PRO.

32. BLFK to C in C in Mideast and War Office, January 20, 1964, DO 226/10, PRO.

33. "Report by Lt. Col. H. N. M. Marston MC on the Events in 2nd Battalion the Tanganyika Rifles, Tabora, 20/21 January 1964," FCO 141/14043, PRO.

34. DAR to CRO, January 21, 1964, DO 226/10, PRO; BLFK to C in C in Mideast and War Office, January 20, 1964, DO 226/10, PRO.

35. William Leonhart, DAR to DOS, January 24, 1964; William Leonhart to DOS, February 9, 1964—both in RG 59, Box 2687, POL 23-9 TANGAN, NARA.

36. DAR to CRO, January 20, 1964, DO 226/10, PRO.

37. DAR to Nairobi, January 20, 1964, DO 226/10, PRO.

38. "Akena Aona Maiti Sita Magomeni," *Ngurumo*, May 1, 1964, 2–3.

39. DAR to CRO, January 20, 1964, DO 226/10, PRO.

40. Ibid.

41. William Leonhart, DAR to DOS, January 20, 1964, NSF/CF 100-1.56, LBJ.

42. Luanda, "Playout of the Mutiny," 96.

43. H. S. H. Stanley to D. N. Ndegwa, Nairobi, January 21, 1964, DO 226/10, PRO.

44. A Canadian diplomat morbidly reported that "when the Arab's little six-year old daughter stumbled out thirty full grown men shot her down with automatic rifles. This incident was witnessed by the Head of CID, Akena." High Commissioner, DAR, to Undersecretary of State for External Affairs, May 15, 1964, RG 25 8928-20-TAN-1-3-ZAN pt. 1, LAC.

45. Robin Miller to David Owen, January 21, 1964, Ivan-Smith Papers, BI; Jhaveri, *Marching with Nyerere*, 209.

46. DAR High Commission to CRO, January 20, 1964, DO 226/10, PRO.

47. Ibid.

48. William Leonhart, DAR to DOS, January 20, 1964, NSF/CF 100-1.52, LBJ.

49. Luanda, "Playout of the Mutiny," 118; DAR to CRO, January 23, 1964, DO 226/10, PRO.

50. DAR to CRO, January 23, 1964, DO 226/10, PRO.

51. Sarakikya interview, June 26, 2006.

52. Robin Miller to David Owen, January 21, 1964, Ivan-Smith Papers, BI; William Leonhart, DAR to DOS, January 24, 1964, RG 59, Box 2687, POL 23-9, Rebellion Coups, TANGAN, 1/1/64, NARA.

53. Telegram received by Col. Legge at Dar es Salaam High Commisssion, January 21, 1964, DO 226/10, PRO.

54. Luanda, "Playout of the Mutiny," 127–31.

55. Robin Miller to David Owen, January 21, 1964, Ivan-Smith Papers, BI.

56. Telegram received by Col. Legge at Dar es Salaam High Commisssion, January 21, 1964, DO 226/10, PRO; DAR to CRO, January 21, 1964, DO 226/10, PRO.
57. DAR to CRO, January 21, 1964, DO 226/10, PRO; SCCI Boletim de Difusão de Informações, October 7, 1964, SR 082 Tanzania 1964/NOV/20–1965/JAN/13 H.2.26 MU/GM/GNP/082/Pt.1, AHU.
58. Luanda, "Playout of the Mutiny," 104.
59. "Report by Lt. Col. H. N. M. Marston," PRO.
60. Luanda, "Playout of the Mutiny," 101–2.
61. Jean Read, "The Mutiny in Tabora," Paul Lubeck Papers, Box 3-8, HI; William Leonhart, DAR to DOS, January 22, 1964, RG 59, Box 2688, POL 36 TANZAN, 1/1/64, NARA.
62. T. W. Aston to DAR High Commission, January 21, 1964, DO 226/10, PRO.
63. Luanda, "Playout of the Mutiny," 102n52.
64. "Report by Lt. Col. H. N. M. Marston," PRO. The cable read: "Prevent all British officers to leave Captain Sarakikya to become CO."
65. Sarakikya interview, June 26, 2006; DAR to CRO, January 21, 1964, DO 226/10, PRO.
66. DAR to CRO, January 21, 1964, DO 226/10, PRO.
67. "Report by Lt. Col. H. N. M. Marston," PRO.
68. Jean Read, "Mutiny in Tabora," HI.
69. Jhaveri, *Marching with Nyerere*, 210.
70. DAR to CRO, January 21, 1964, DO 226/10, PRO; DO 183/155, PRO.
71. Robin Miller to David Owen, January 21, 1964, Ivan-Smith Papers, BI; Situation Report, January 21, 1964, NSF/CF 100-2.93, LBJ.
72. Robin Miller to David Owen, January 21, 1964, Ivan-Smith Papers, BI.
73. William Leonhart, DAR to DOS, January 24, 1964, RG 59, Box 2687, POL 23-9, Rebellion Coups, TANGAN, 1/1/64, NARA.
74. DAR to CRO, January 21, 1964, DO 226/10, PRO.
75. DAR to CRO, January 23, 1964, DO 226/10, PRO.
76. DAR to CRO, January 21, 1964, DO 226/10, PRO.
77. BLFK to War Office, HQ Mideast; Nairobi to CRO; and DAR to CRO—all January 22, 1964, DO 226/10, PRO.
78. DAR to DOS, January 21, 1964, NSF/CF 100-1.49, LBJ.
79. Elena to Lady Chesham, January 24, 1964, CHE-25, BI; see also DAR to CRO, January 23, 1964, DO 226/10, PRO.
80. BLFK to CINC Mideast and War Office, January 22, 1964, DO 226/10, PRO.
81. DAR to CRO, January 21, 1964, DO 226/10, PRO.
82. HQ BLFK to CRAF (EA) Nairobi, January 21, 1964, DO 226/10, PRO.
83. DAR to CRO, January 23, 1964, DO 226/10, PRO.
84. DAR to DOS, January 23, 1964, NSF/CF 100-1.42, LBJ.
85. Robin Miller to David Owen, January 22, 1964, Ivan-Smith Papers, BI.
86. Situation Report, January 21, 1964, NSF/CF 100-2.93, LBJ.
87. DAR to CRO, January 23, 1964, DO 226/10, PRO.
88. DAR to DOS, January 22, 1964, NSF/CF 100-1.47, LBJ.
89. Ibid.
90. Ibid.
91. DAR to CRO, January 23, 1964, DO 226/10, PRO.

92. Nairobi to CRO, January 22, 1964, DO 226/10, PRO.
93. Robin Miller to David Owen, January 21, 1964, Ivan-Smith Papers, BI.
94. Situation Report, January 23, 1964, DO 226/10, PRO.
95. Nyerere Press Conference, January 23, 1964, DO 226/10, PRO.
96. Oscar Kambona to Duncan Sandys, CRO, January 23, 1964, DO 213/236, PRO.
97. Parsons, *1964 Army Mutinies*.
98. See also Luanda, "Playout of the Mutiny," 116, 125.
99. Miles later spoke with Kambona and Lusinde on the use of British force. While Kambona expressed some openness to intervention, Lusinde remained fixed against outside involvement, as he had since the crisis began. William Leonhart, DAR to DOS, January 24, 1964, NSF/CF 100-1.40, LBJ.
100. Robin Miller to David Owen, January 21, 1964, Ivan-Smith Papers, BI.
101. Oscar Kambona to CRO, January 24, 1964, DO 226/10, PRO.
102. Leonhart in DAR to Secretary of State, January 24, 1964, NSF/CF 100-1.40, LBJ.
103. Robin Miller to David Owen, January 21, 1964, Ivan-Smith Papers, BI.
104. William Leonhart, DAR to DOS, January 24, 1964, NSF/CF 100-1.40, LBJ.
105. William Leonhart, DAR to DOS, January 26, 1964, NSF/CF 100-1.31, LBJ. Lusinde used the same phrase to describe the situation in a discussion after the mutiny; William Leonhart to DOS, February 9, 1964, RG 59, Box 2687, POL 23-9 TANGAN, NARA; see also Mogella interview.
106. William Leonhart, DAR to DOS, January 27, 1964, RG 59, Box 2688, POL 36 TANGAN, 1/1/64, NARA. See also Ginwala, "The Tanganyika Mutiny," 93–97; Sadleir, *Tanzania, Journey to Republic*, 271; Parsons, *1964 Army Mutinies*, 125, 133.
107. William Leonhart, DAR to DOS, January 28, 1964, RG 59, Box 2687, POL 23-9 TANGAN, 1/1/64, NARA.
108. Robert Hennemeyer, "Recent Activities of Chief Fundikira," DAR to DOS, January 11, 1964, RG 59, Box 2687, POL – TANGAN, 1/1/64, NARA.
109. William Leonhart, DAR to DOS, February 22, 1964, NSF/CF 103-4.107, LBJ; copied in RG 59, Box 2687, POL 15 TANGAN, 1/1/64, NARA. It seems the lists were real, and they were certainly taken to be so by Nyerere and his government. They were discovered by the Tanganyikan Secret Service and never made public. News of them only came belatedly to the attention of the American ambassador in a comment by Protocol and External Security Chief Mbwambo and a more specific report in February from E. E. Bellege, a former general secretary of the National Union of Post Office and Telecommunications Employees. Bellege had been a moderate in the TFL, advocating that it remain independent of any political party and opposing attempts to ally the TFL with Tumbo's PDP. In 1962 Bellege threw his loyalties in with TANU. He spent time that year in both the Unite States and the Soviet Union on grants offered by both countries to influential young leaders in the government and labor unions. As a well-informed source in the labor movement, he had several contacts with the American ambassador in 1962. By mid-1963, he was a sitting member of the Central Committee that controlled TANU. We must also consider, of course, the possibility that the lists were forgeries. Even if they were forgeries, it is still unlikely that they were planted by forces loyal to Nyerere, as they would have undermined the very appearance of stability and legitimacy

that Nyerere so carefully cultivated. Additionally, Nyerere's government kept the lists secret; if they were forgeries they certainly would have publicized them for an intended political effect. It is equally unlikely that the lists were forgeries produced by communist agents, as they only served to undermine the labor forces that were friendly to communist interests. It is possible that lists were forgeries planted by British or American intelligence officers to create pressure for outside intervention and instigate a crackdown on the labor movement in the wake of the Zanzibar Revolution. Even if this were true, Nyerere and his government took the lists to be real, and their response was measured against the perceived reality of a coup plot by labor leaders. See William Leonhart, DAR to DOS, February 1, 1964, RG 59, Box 2687, POL 23-9 TANGAN, 1/1/64, NARA; "Tanganyika Labor Opposition to Government Control," Memorandum of Conversation, June 25, 1962, RG 59, Box 2028, 778.00/1-262, NARA; Thomas Byrne, DAR to DOS, September 26, 1962; Robert Hennemeyer, DAR to DOS, November 19, 1962; DOS, "Countering Soviet Bloc Entry into Tanganyika Labor Field," June 20, 1962—all in RG 59, Box 2773, 878.062/3-1562, NARA; Wajumbe wa Central Committee, June 10, 1963, 589: BMC/11/04/A.17, TNA; Cabrita, *Mozambique*, 18–19.

110. Hansard, *18th February 1964 to 21st February 1964*, Member Abdallah Fundikira, Member Peter Siyovelwa, 126. Some rumors suggested that Chief Fundikira, having received word of this evidence, briefly fled the country as the arrests of labor and opposition leaders began. William Leonhart, DAR to DOS, January 29, 1964, RG 59, Box 2688, POL 36 TANZAN, 1/1/64, NARA.

111. Peter Kisumo's recollection in 2006 of these events is illustrative of the TANU leadership's evasive approach; at different points in our conversation he suggested that (a) Tumbo was a principled man who believed in the need for a political opposition, (b) Tumbo was already in detention when the mutiny happened, and (c) the country's first coup attempt followed on the heels of the mutiny. Kisumo quickly retreated from this final suggestion of a sequential relationship between the mutiny and a coup plan and talked instead about Oscar Kambona's effectiveness and loyalty in dealing with the mutineers. In an unrecorded conversation on July 13, 2013, however, Kisumo acknowledged an assassination list that included Nyerere and Kawawa, and a house arrest list including Lusinde and Bomani.

112. In a recorded interview with the author, Pius Msekwa acknowledged that Tumbo was arrested after the mutiny for treason. A few years after the incident, Nyerere told William Edgett Smith that members of the opposition "were talking with the army" during the mutiny. Smith, *We Must Run*, 165. But there is no evidence supporting the rumor that Tumbo had been directing the mutiny secretly from Morogoro, as reported in Listowel, *Making of Tanganyika*.

113. William Leonhart, DAR to DOS, January 26, 1964, NSF/CF 100-1.31, LBJ.

114. Robin Miller to David Owen, January 21, 1964, Ivan-Smith Papers, BI.

115. Duncan Sandys, CRO Circular to High Commissions, January 25, 1964, DO 226/10, PRO.

116. Luanda, "Playout of the Mutiny," 126. Luanda's account is based largely on interviews conducted in the mid-1980s, and his chronology seems to be a little bit off in several places. My account is based on a close reading of dated diplomatic correspondence from the time.

117. DAR to CRO, January 24, 1964, DO 226/10.153, PRO.

118. William Leonhart, DAR to DOS, January 25, 1964, NSF/CF 100-1.36, LBJ.
119. Luanda, "Playout of the Mutiny," 121–26.
120. DAR to CRO, January 25, 1964, DO 226/10, PRO. For a detailed account of the British operation, see Lawrence *Dar Mutiny of 1964*.
121. Nyerere, *Freedom and Unity*, 267–69.
122. Marion, Lady Chesham, general letter, January 27, 1964, CHE-25, BI; "The Week of January 20–25 in Dar es Salaam," Paul Lubeck Papers, Box 3-8, HI.
123. Luanda, "Playout of the Mutiny," 135.
124. "Hingo Alipiga Simu UNO Ilete Jeshi," *Ngurumo*, May 5, 1964, 1.
125. William Leonhart, DAR to DOS, January 25, 1964, NSF/CF 100-1.36, LBJ.
126. "The Week of January 20–25 in Dar es Salaam," Paul Lubeck Papers, Box 3-8, HI.
127. William Leonhart, DAR to DOS, January 25, 1964, NSF/CF 100-1.37, LBJ.
128. Mikidadi Mdoe, then a program director at the Tanganyika Broadcasting Corporation, was ordered by the director of the TBC to broadcast a statement that the British action had been requested by the Tanganyika government. Uncertain if the instructions were genuine, Mdoe delayed the broadcast. Luanda suggests that this statement was handed to Mdoe the morning of January 24, but that seems highly unlikely given the secrecy of the operation, let alone the fact that Nyerere did not make the decision to request British help until later in the day. More than likely, he was given the statement on January 25. See Luanda, "Playout of the Mutiny," 123.
129. Report of D/Inspector Thorne, January 28, 1964, DO 183/155.
130. In a 1989 interview Nyerere said that he had feared losing his "semblance of control" had the British intervened unilaterally if he delayed his request too long. "As it is, I did not have much [control]: but at least I would 'play' I had invited them!" See Baregu, "Perception," 68n81.
131. Quoted in Luanda, "Playout of the Mutiny," 126. There may have been an inspiration for Nyerere's remark here. Mwamvita Salim recalled a preindendependence event where a TANU women's group dressed Nyerere in a *buibui* in order to bring him in unnoticed to speak with them. Geiger, *TANU Women*, 117.
132. William Leonhart in DAR to Secretary of State, January 31, 1964, RG 59, Box 2687, POL 23-9 TANGAN, 1/1/64, NARA.
133. William Leonhart, DAR to Secretary of State, January 26, 1964, NSF/CF 100-1.31, LBJ.
134. Ibid.
135. Ibid.
136. Lusinde interview, July 6, 2010.
137. Julius Nyerere, speech, January 26, 1964, DO 226/10, PRO.
138. DAR to CRO, January 25, 1964, DO 226/10, PRO; DAR to CRO, January 27, 1964, DO 226/10, PRO.
139. William Leonhart, DAR to DOS, January 27, 1964, RG 59, Box 2687, POL 23-9 TANGAN, 1/1/64, NARA.
140. DAR to CRO, January 30, 1964, DO 226/10, PRO.
141. William Leonhart to DOS, February 12, 1964, NSF/CF 100-1.21, LBJ; William Leonhart to DOS, February 14, 1964, RG 59, Box 2687, POL 15 Government TANGAN, NARA.

142. DAR to CRO, January 26, 1964, DO 226/10, PRO; William Leonhart, DAR to DOS, January 27, 1964, RG 59, Box 2688, POL 26 TANGAN, 1/1/64, NARA.

143. William Leonhart, DAR to DOS, February 12, 1964, NSF/CF 100-1.23, LBJ; Hansard, *18th February 1964 to 21st February 1964*, 75.

144. Kawawa interview, September 5, 2006.

145. "Speech by Nyerere," PAA 32-A PAA, AHD.

146. Ibid.

147. William Leonhart, DAR to DOS, January 31, 1964, RG 59, Box 2688 POL 36 TANGAN, 1/1/64, NARA.

148. William Leonhart, DAR to DOS, February 1, 1964, RG 59, Box 2687, POL 23-9 TANGAN, 1/1/64, NARA.

149. William Leonhart, DAR to DOS, January 28, 1964, RG 59, Box 2687, POL 23-9 TANGAN, 1/1/64, NARA.

150. William Leonhart, DAR to DOS, February 10, 1964, RG 59, Box 2688, POL 36 TANGAN, 1/1/64, NARA.

151. Mogella interview; William Leonhart, DAR to DOS, February 14, 1964, RG 59, Box 2688, POL 36 TANGAN, 1/1/64, NARA.

152. William Leonhart, DAR to DOS, May 13, 1964, RG 59, Box 2694, POL 29, Arrests, Detention, TANZAN, NARA.

153. "The Week of January 20–25 in Dar es Salaam," Paul Lubeck Papers, Box 3-8, HI.

154. Luanda, "Playout of the Mutiny," 158.

155. Ibid.; Parsons, *1964 Army Mutinies*, 155–57.

156. T. L. Richardson, Canadian High Commission to R. H. Hobden, CRO, "Tanzania Union Day," April 27, 1966, DO 213/103.84, PRO.

157. Tumbo, "Civic Awareness," 50.

158. Mogella interview.

159. "Organisation of the Tanganyika Federation of Labour (TFL) as a National Workers' Movement Integrated with the Ministry of Labour," RG 59, Entry 5235, LAB Labor & Manpower TANG LAB1—General Policy Plans, NARA; "Kumbu kumbu ya NUTA kwa tume ya rais juu ya NUTA," 548: A.60/65/II.59, TNA; DAR to DOS, February 22, 1964, RG 59, Box 2687, POL 17, TANGAN, NARA.

160. "Report of the Presidential Commission on the Establishment of a Democratic One-Party State," 1965, RG 59, Box 2689, POL 12 TANZAN, 1/1/64, NARA.

161. "Mr. Kawawa Replies to Critics of Tanganyika's New Union," press release by Tanganyika Information Service, March 7, 1964, Paul Lubeck Papers, Box 3-4, HI.

162. Weber, *Simulating Sovereignty*.

163. "Speech by Nyerere," PAA 32-A PAA, AHD; Lagos to DOS, January 31, 1964, RG 59, Box 2687, POL 23-9 TANGAN, 1/1/64, NARA.

164. DAR to DOS, January 26, 1964, NSF/CF 100-1.31, LBJ.

165. DAR to DOS, January 28, 1964 (Section 2), NSF/CF 103-1.3, LBJ.

166. DAR to DOS, January 26, 1964, NSF/CF 100-1.31, LBJ; DAR to CRO, January 25, 1964, DO 226/10, PRO.

167. DAR to DOS, January 26, 1964, NSF/CF 100-1.31, LBJ.

168. "Prospects for the Tan-Zam Railway," November 8, 1965, NSF/CF 100-7.102a, LBJ. Even five years later, insinuations of Nyerere's weakness lingered in the

British Foreign and Commonwealth Office even as his power at home and abroad was at its zenith in 1969. See Phillips to Tebbit, August 19, 1969, FCO 31/438, PRO.

169. William Leonhart, DAR to DOS, January 28, 1964; William Leonhart, DAR to DOS, February 1, 1964—both in RG 59, Box 2687, POL 23-9 TANGAN 1/1/64, NARA.

170. William Leonhart, DAR to DOS, January 27, 1964, RG 59, Box 2687, POL 23-9 TANGAN, 1/1/64, NARA.

171. DAR to DOS, February 5, 1964, NSF/CF 103-4.145, LBJ; John Osman, "Moscow Boss in East Africa—Kambona Runs Forces in Tanganyika," *Daily Telegraph*, January 23, 1964, DO 226/10, PRO; T. D. O'Leary to Mr. Costley-White, January 30, 1964, DO 213/236, PRO.

172. Intelligence Brief, Salisbury, undated, 32-A PAA, AHD.

Chapter 7

1. William Leonhart, DAR to DOS, February 22, 1964, RG 59, Box 2687, POL 15-4 TANGAN, 1/1/64, NARA.
2. "Mapendekezo ya Halmashauri Maalum ya Kuunda Jeshi Jipya la Jamhuri ya Tanganika," 589: BMC11/02 A.29, TNA.
3. Strachan, *Politics of the British Army*.
4. See Luanda, "Playout of the Mutiny," vii–ix, 156.
5. Bienen, *Tanzania*, 376–67.
6. "Taarifa ya Secretary-General Mbele ya Halmashauri Kuu 15 Dec 1964," 589: BMC/11/02/B.3, TNA.
7. Sarakikya interview, June 26, 2006.
8. Quoted in Parsons, *1964 Army Mutinies*, 168.
9. Bienen, *Tanzania*, 377; Luanda, "Playout of the Mutiny," 157.
10. Ahlman, "New Type of Citizen"; Straker, *Youth, Nationalism*.
11. Ivaska, *Cultured States*, 124–47.
12. Gama interview.
13. Hansard, *18th February 1964 to 21st February 1964*, 135.
14. Mogella interview.
15. Brennan, "Youth." This was clearly a relationship cultivated by both sides. In 2006 I witnessed a local TYL chapter in Musoma Rural District honor the member of Parliament for the district with the title "Commander of the Youth," giving him a spear, a fly-whisk, and a shiny green robe.
16. Bates, "Tanganyika," 454.
17. Leadership of the TYL seems to have been a bit ambiguous, but from 1960 to 1967 we can assume that Joseph Nyerere was effectively in charge. James Brennan suggests that Lawi Sijaona served in TANU as Youth League secretary from 1956 to 1960, but then has other sources that suggest that Joseph Nyerere was in charge of the TYL as early as July 1958. Abeid Sakara places Rashidi Kawawa as the first leader of the TYL when it was formally instituted in 1958. Brennan, "Youth," 221, 239; Sakara, *Rashidi Mfaume Kawawa*, 189.

18. See also Carthew, "Life Imitates Art"; Burgess, "Young Pioneers"; and Ivaska, "Of Students."
19. See also Bjerk, "Building a New Eden."
20. Mturi, "Historia ya Ikizu," in Shetler, *Telling Our Own Stories*, 52.
21. Spencer, *Time, Space, and the Unknown*, 15–42; Thomson, *Through Masailand*.
22. Shetler, "Interpreting Rupture in Oral Memory," 399.

23. A colonial official took the term *mchama*, meaning the elder responsible for calling a council, to be "possibly concocted" from the Maasai term for a council of elders, *ol kiama*—and he may have been correct. The *k-i-a* combination at the beginning of a word is often pronounced as "cha" around Lake Victoria. In the Bantu language of Kenya's Meru people, the *kiama* (pl. *biama*) was a basic political unit that, like the Zanaki generation-sets, ran parallel to a system of age-sets. While a Bantu noun class is evident in the *ki-/bi-* prefix in Meru usage, this does not necessarily mean that the word is of Bantu origin, as borrowing into this noun class is common in Swahili. The Arabic word for book/books, *kitab/kutub* (كتاب/كتب) comes into Swahili as *kitabu/vitabu*; the English word for drinking club/clubs is used in colloquial Swahili as *kilabu/vilabu*. In a personal communication, Christopher Ehret suggested that Swahili borrowed the term *kiama/chama* from the Bantu language Thagiicu in the middle of the second millennium. He noted that while it is possible that Maasai communitites borrowed *kiama* and its social implications from Thagiicu, that is unlikely as all the known borrowing between the two languages has been from Maasai to Thagiicu, not vice versa, and that if it had been borrowed from the Bantu *ama root, it would appear in Maasai usage as *keama* not *kiama*. In his textbook, Ehret notes that age-sets had ancient roots in both Bantu and Nilo-Saharan languages. See R. S. W. Malcolm, "System of Government," Musoma District Book, Reading Room, TNA; and Fadiman, *When We Began*. I appreciate the help of Kathryn Deluna and Rhiannon Stephens on this question as well.

24. *Chama*, meaning guild or association, appears as an entry in Madan, *English-Swahili Dictionary*, but does not appear appear in Krapf, *Dictionary of the Suahili Language*. *Kiama*, presumably pronounced with a hard *k*, is defined in Krapf's dictionary as an apocalyptic deluge, from an Arabic root (قام), while *kiama* does not appear in Madan's dictionary. It is possible that a coastal semantic shift from elders' council to political association was aided by the presence of the Arabic *jama't* (جمع) which can mean association, creating a phonic gateway for *kiama* to become *chama*.

25. *Kiama* had been employed in early colonial Kenya as a government-sponsored elders' council for resolving local disputes, but the Mau Mau movement adopted the term to designate its executive committee in Nairobi as the *Kiama kia Wiathi*, or Freedom Council. In Tanganyika, the 1950s remained a transitional period for the word *chama*, as elders' councils began to take on increasingly administrative roles in formalized tribal hierarchies like the Chagga Council, and political innovators began to create European-style political parties. The Chagga Council created land boards that absorbed some of the roles of community elders. Members of the Rombo Land Board suggested in 1955 that its name should be changed to "Halmshauri ama Chama cha Arthi." The Tanganyika Citizens' Union (TCU) created an elected party structure, perceived as a *chama* (like the Tanganyika African Association), to displace ethnic politics in Chagga country. In 1956 Shambaa

representatives looked to the TCU for guidance on how to create a "chama halali" (party proper) under leaders elected by its members. See Kershaw, *Mau Mau from Below*, 105; Lonsdale, "Moral Economy of Mau Mau," 396, 436; "Kumbukumbu ya Mambo ya Mkutano wa Rombo Land Board Uliiokutanika Hapa Rombo, March 1, 1955, 555: 9/15, No. 7A, TNA; and "Mkutano wa President Tanganyika Citizens' Union Ulifanyika Makungwi—Lushoto District 26'8'56," attachment to Tanganyika Citizens' Union, Mwakungwi Office, Lushoto to Marealle II Mangi Mkuu wa Wachagga Kilimanjaro, August 26, 1956, 555: 10/1, No. 1, TNA.

26. Shetler, "Interpreting Rupture in Oral Memory," 398.

27. See Aguilar, *Politics of Age and Gerontocracy*; Baxter and Almagor, *Age, Generation, and Time*; Muller-Dempf, "Generation-Sets"; Worthman, "Interactions of Physical Maturation"; Spencer, "Opposing Streams"; and Juma, "Sukuma Societies."

28. One researcher observed that the Ankole people in Uganda are an outlier in this regard, having no gerontocratic system. Elam, "Family and Polity in Ankole."

29. Wilson, "Nyakyusa Age Villages."

30. Recently, riding in a car with some old men in Dodoma, we passed some children out in the dry wilderness along a dusty district road. They were there for *jando* apparently. I asked whether the JKT experience was like *jando*, and the old men heartily agreed. "JKT ni jando kabisa," one said.

31. Heckel, "Yao Tribe."

32. Wimmelbücker, *Kilimanjaro—a Regional History*, 82–87.

33. Fosbrooke and Marealle, "Engraved Rocks of Kilimanjaro," 179–81.

34. Raum, *Chaga Childhood*. See also Moore and Puritt, *Chagga and Meru of Tanzania*.

35. Hyden, *Tanu Yajenga Nchi*, 81.

36. Thomas, "Formal Education of Arusha 'Murran,'" 87.

37. Almagor, "Charisma Fatigue," 635–49.

38. Suzette Heald's *Manhood and Morality* adds an indispensable analytical layer to colonial policies that criminalized urban youth described by Burton in *African Underclass*.

39. Lonsdale, "Moral Economy of Mau Mau," 393; see also Thomas, "Imperial Concerns and 'Women's Affairs.'"

40. Willis, "Kaswa," 253.

41. Okuth, in *Africa*, suggests that the word "ikulu" was adopted from the Sukuma language (70). "Ikulu" does not appear in colonial-era Swahili-English dictionaries, but only in Charles Rechenbach's 1967 dictionary, defined as "the State House in Dar es Salaam."

42. Msuguri interview; see also Musoma District Book, TNA, which summarizes Baxter's work on Zanaki age-sets.

43. See a parallel study in Gulliver, *Social Control*.

44. Kenyatta, *Facing Mount Kenya*, 134, 187–89; see also Fadiman, *When We Began*.

45. The Fabian Society in London had supported both Nyerere and Kenyatta as a part of their opposition to colonialism and had hosted Kenyatta in a conference in London a few years before Nyerere's arrival in Edinburgh. See Berman and Lonsdale, "Custom, Modernity," 192.

46. See Brennan, "Youth," 237.

47. Mbita interview, November 2, 2006; Brennan, *Taifa*, 147.
48. Maguire, *Toward "Uhuru" in Tanzania*, 317–18.
49. See also Knudsen, "Dance Societies."
50. Shorter, *Chiefship in Western Tanzania*, 140–47.
51. Abdallah Shabani, Korogwe to Secretary-General of TANU, August 21, 1963, 481: A6/74.34, TNA.
52. Brennan, "Youth," 228–29; Magotti, *Rashidi Mfaume Kawawa*, 43; Iliffe, *Modern History of Tanganyika*, 532; Sakara, *Kawawa Mfaume Kawawa*, 188.
53. Kamba interview. See also Geiger, *TANU Women*, 118.
54. Barrington King, "Background Information on the TANU Youth League," DAR to DOS, January 21, 1961, RG 59, Box 2027, 778.001/-461, NARA.
55. Brennan, "Youth," 229, 236.
56. Barrington King, DAR to DOS, November 22, 1960, RG 59, Box 2027, 778.00/6-360, NARA.
57. DAR to DOS, "Julius Nyerere Speaks at Makerere College during Visit to Be Installed as Honorary Fellow," April 10, 1962, RG 59, Box 2028, 778.00/1-262, NARA.
58. C. W. B. Costeleo, District Commissioner, Mwanza, to District Secretary, TANU, July 18, 1962, 246: A 6/14.147, TNA.
59. George Bennett, "An Outline History of TANU," *Makerere Journal* 7 (1963), Paul Lubeck Papers, Box 3-14, HI.
60. Brennan, "Youth," 228, 231.
61. Barrington King, "Background Information on the TANU Youth League," DAR to DOS, January 21, 1961, RG 59, Box 2027, 778.00/1-461, NARA.
62. "TYL Macho, Masikio, Pua ya TANU," *Ngurumo*, September 12, 1961, 9.
63. Barrington King, DAR to DOS, May 22, 1961, RG 59, Box 2027, 778.00/5-161, NARA.
64. H. S. Ngalweson, Area Secretary TYL, Same, to Area Commissioner, September 19, 1962, 481: A6/74.28, TNA.
65. "Halimashauri ya Maendeleo ya Vijana wa TYL Imeshauri Haya Yafuatayo Hapa Chini Ambayo Yakifuatwa Yatasaidia Maedeleo ya Vijana Wilaya Hii ya Tanga," "Halimashauri ya Usalama Inashauri Haya Yafuatayo Hapa Chini Ambayo Yakifuatwa Yatasaidia Kuhifadhi Usalama na Amani Wilayani," 481: A6/74.32, TNA.
66. Regional Commissioner Tanga to Area Secretary for TANU, September 4, 1962, 481: A6/74.27, TNA.
67. R. S. Wambura, Regional Secretary, Lake Region, to All District Secretaries, August 1, 1962, 246: A6/14.148, TNA.
68. K. Ibrahim Abdallah, Area Secretary TYL to Chief Executive Officer, Mwanza District Council, August 23, 1963, 246: A 6/14.204, TNA.
69. Area Secretary for TYL in Settlement Scheme, Muheza, to Regional Commissioner, August 23, 1963, 493: A.6/34.279, TNA.
70. Draft press release, February 4, 1962, from Morogoro, "'A good citizen must help police'—Kambona," 593: CB/8/1.2, TNA.
71. Press release from Information Officer, Lake Region, March 21, 1962, 593: CB/8/1.5, TNA.
72. Regional Police Commander, Tanga, to District Secretary TYL, June 29, 1962, 481: A6/74.14, TNA.

73. Mwanza Annual Report 1963, 15, Reading Room, TNA.
74. Taarifa ya Area Secretary, Mwanza, December 21, 1963, 246: A 6/14.246, TNA.
75. "Haya yafuatayo ni majina ya waliohudhuria mkutano wa TANU youth league huko musoma tarehe January 10, 1964," 589: BMC/11/04/A.38, TNA; "Shida Zilizotolewa na TYL Musoma District Kuhusu Kulegea kwa Umoja wa Vijana, mbele ya Mheshimiwa Bhoke Munanka, Financial Secretary wa TANU," January 10, 1964, 589: BMC/12/01/C, TNA.
76. "Haya yafuatayo ni majina ya waliohudhuria mkutano wa TANU youth league huko musoma tarehe January 10, 1964," 589: BMC/11/04/A.38, TNA.
77. Area Secretary for TYL in Settlement Scheme, Muheza, to Regional Commissioner, August 23, 1963, 493: A.6/34.279, TNA.
78. Draft press release, February 4, 1962, from Morogoro, "'A good citizen must help police'—Kambona," 593: CB/8/1.2, TNA.
79. "Mr. Oscar Kambona Developing as TANU Spokesman," DAR to DOS, July 19, 1960, RG 59, Box 2027, 778.00/6-360, NARA. See also William Duggan, "Some Recent Labor Developments in Tanganyika," DAR to DOS, December 9, 1960, RG 59, Box 2772, 878.02/10-461, NARA.
80. Magotti, *Rashidi Mfaume Kawawa*, 43.
81. See Allman, "Youngmen and the Porcupine"; and Li, "Asafo and Destoolment."
82. Barrington King, "Tanganyika Minister of Labour Plans the Use of 'Builders Brigades,'" DAR to DOS, January 6, 1961, RG 59, Box 2772, 878.02/10-461, NARA.
83. Thomas Byrne, "Prime Minister's Policy Speech to National Assembly," DAR to DOS, June 26, 1962, RG 59, Box 2029, 778.13/5-2962, NARA.
84. Thomas Byrne, "Tanganyika's Youth 'Army' Plan," DAR to DOS, December 31, 1962, RG 59, Box 2029, 778.210/-160, NARA; Hansard, *18th February 1964 to 21st February 1964*, 135.
85. Headmaster, Tanga Boys' Secondary School, to Regional Commissioner, November 12, 1965, 481: A6/74 3.87, TNA.
86. Gama interview.
87. Hansard, *18th February 1964 to 21st February 1964*, 135.
88. Ibid., 143.
89. Ibid., 141.
90. Lusinde interview, November 7, 2006.
91. Gama interview.
92. Kawawa interview, November 10, 2006.
93. In 1971 *Mwongozo* continued: "Some societies were better organised than others. The Wasukuma of central-northern Tanzania developed a thorough system of defence and security in this manner, with the village community constituting a single unit. In the event of any crime, perpetrators were summoned before the village council and interrogated. If found guilty, they were ostracised along with every member of their household. They were not to speak to any member of the community. They were forbidden to join any activity or make contact with any other village member. They remained outcasts until they were pardoned. In case of external threats, the able-bodied were the fighters. These societies were well-knit and could

satisfy their needs for defence and security internally." See Lupogo, "Tanzania: Civil-Military Relations."

94. Tabora Region Annual Report, 1964, 1, Reading Room, TNA; Chris Pappas, "TANU Youth Leaguers to be Appointed Special Constables," DAR to DOS, April 19, 1964, RG 59, Box 2687, POL 14 TANGAN, 1/1/64, NARA.

95. Hansard, *18th February 1964 to 21st February 1964*, 137, 139.

96. Lusinde interview, November 7, 2006.

97. Kawawa interview, November 10, 2006.

98. H. A. Mwakangale, Area Commissioner Lushoto, to Branch Chairman, TANU Mtae Branch, Lushoto District, March 22, 1965, 481: A6/74.58, TNA.

99. Weber, *Social and Economic Organization*, 156.

100. Bienen, *Tanzania*, 188.

101. Speech by Julius Nyerere, DAR to CRO, January 26, 1964, DO 226/1019, PRO; Bienen, *Tanzania*, 374–80.

102. William Leonhart, DAR to DOS, February 6, 1964, NSF/CF 100-1.26, LBJ.

103. Hansard, *18th February 1964 to 21st February 1964*, 216.

104. Hon. L. P. Dante-Ngua MP, Regional Secretary, Singida, "Taarifaa ya Khatibu wa Mkoa: Kazi za TANU Kipidi cha 10th January 1964–9th January 1965," 589: BMC/11/01/B.34, TNA.

105. DAR to DOS, February 10, 1964, RG 59, Box 2687, POL 14 TANGAN, NARA.

106. Chris Pappas, "National Youth Service in 'Nation-Building Exercise," DAR to DOS, April 16, 1964, RG 59, Box 2687, POL 14 TANGAN, 1/1/64, NARA; Ministry of Defence and National Service to NSHQ Nkulila, June 8, 1964, 482: VP/N.40/5.4, TNA.

107. NSHQ Operational Order 8/65, Movements and Reorganization, November 12, 1964, 482: VP/N.40/5.15, TNA; Peter Fishbein, "Tanganyika National Service—Visit of Joseph Nyerere," March 28, 1964, RG 59, Box 32, POL 13-2 TANG "National Service" Youth Organization, NARA.

108. "Operation Order 6/65, October 26, 1964, Staff "A" monthly meeting," 482: VP/N.40/5.11, TNA.

109. NSHQ Operation Order 1/65, Operation Kujenga, August 3, 1964, 482: VP/N.40/5.8, TNA.

110. William Leonhart, DAR to DOS, October 2, 1964, RG 59, Box 2694, POL 32 TANZAN, 1/1/64, NARA.

111. Gama interview.

112. William Leonhart, DAR to DOS, October 2, 1964, RG 59, Box 2694, POL 32 TANZAN, 1/1/64, NARA.

113. NSHQ Operation Order 9/65, Nachingwea Project, October 12, 1964, 482: VP/N.40/5.13, TNA. See also NSHQ Operation Orders 14–23, detail deployments in batches of 90 servicemen to Ruvuma, Nachingwea (Mtwara), Dodoma, Nyumba ya Mungu, Mbarali (Mbeya), Nyatwari (Mwanza), and Kigoma, 482: VP/N.40/5, TNA; and "Annual Programme January–June 1965 (Amendment to Annual Programme 64/65) from Ministry of Defence and National Service to Tanzania National Service Headquarters, written by D. S. Nkulila, Director of National Services, January 4, 1965, 482: VP/N.40/5.24, TNA.

114. Telegram to all police from all administrators, October 22, 1965, 481: A6/74.80, TNA.

115. Gama interview.
116. Tanganyika police message from Mtwara to Utawala, October 16, 1965, 481: A6/74.78, TNA.
117. Jerome Mwakifuna, Commander Lushoto Youth Work Camp, to Regional Commissioner, Tanga, May 2, 1966, 481: A6/74.112, TNA.
118. "Nation Your Parent," *Tanganyika Standard*, September 23, 1964, 1.
119. Gama interview.

Chapter 8

1. Williams, *Realist Tradition*, 8; Lobell, Ripsman, and Taliaferro, *Neoclassical Realism*, 46.
2. Kawawa interview, September 5, 2006.
3. Mogella interview. *Hali na mali* is a Swahili phrase meaning, here, literally moral and material support, but generally referring to a commitment of heart and soul.
4. Okwudiba Nnoli, in *Self Reliance and Foreign Policy*, discusses diplomatic milestones and foreign aid arrangements during this period. Joseph S. Nye, in *Pan-Africanism and East African Integration*, gave a compelling account of the efforts to bring about an East African federation. An edited volume by University of Dar es Salaam scholars does not cover this period beyond a few mentions; see Mathews and Mushi, *Foreign Policy of Tanzania*.
5. "Mr. Oscar Kambona Developing as TANU Spokesman," DAR to DOS, July 19, 1960, RG 59, Box 2027, 778.00/6-360, NARA.
6. For veterans of this policy, the 1994 democratic elections in South Africa represent the successful conclusion of Tanzania's contributions to the liberation struggle, while recent progress toward East African cooperation demonstrates the ongoing influence of this early goal. Mbita interview, November 2, 2006; Zacarias, *Security and the State*; "An East African Federation: Big ambitions, Big Question-Marks," *The Economist*, September 3, 2009.
7. Ngaiza interview.
8. Nyerere, *Freedom and Unity*, 145.
9. Several observers have noted Nyerere's overwhelming influence on foreign policy. See Bienen, *Tanzania*, 159; Pratt, *Critical Phase in Tanzania*, 6; Mushi, "Tanzania," 35; and Ngaiza interview.
10. Nyerere, *Freedom and Unity*, 27.
11. Letter from I. M. Bhoke Munanka, September 23, 1958, FCB 121/3.40, RH; Bates, "Tanganyika," 457.
12. Julius Nyerere to Jimmy (T. H. Butts), July 23, 1958, FCB 121/3.28, RH; Julius Nyerere to Jimmy (T. H. Butts), August 16, 1958, FCB 121/3.32, RH.
13. "Freedom Charter of the Peoples of East and Central Africa," FCB 121/3.41, RH; "Resolutions Passed by the Tanganyika, Nyasaland, Kenya and Zanzibar, and Uganda Delegates Who Attended the Pan-African Conference Held at Mwaza, Tanganyika from the 16th to 18th September 1958," FCB 121/3.43, RH.
14. Nye, *Pan-Africanism and East African Integration*, 119–27; Sahnoun, "Nyerere."

Notes to pp. 185–187 315

15. Taapopi and Keenleyside, "West and Southern Africa"; Pfister, "Gateway to International Victory."

16. Julius Nyerere, letter to the editor, *Africa South*, October–December 1959, online at the website of the African National Congress, accessed July 21, 2014, http://www.anc.org.za/show.php?id=6901&t=Boycotts.

17. "Nyerere's Comments on South African Boycott," DAR to DOS, September 4, 1960, RG 59, Box 2029, 778.03/10-1460, NARA.

18. Ibid.

19. F. S. Miles, DAR to Duncan Sandys, CRO, November 5, 1963, DO 213/123, PRO.

20. Mandela, *Long Walk to Freedom*, 279–81, 284–85, 294–95; see also Ndlovu, "ANC in Exile," 411–78, and "ANC and the World," 541–72.

21. Memorandum, "Student Refugees," attachment to Jesse MacKnight to Mr. Mulcahy, November 23, 1964, RG 59, E5253, Box 31, Refugees and Migration, REF 10-1 Refugee Training, NARA; "South African United Front Opens Dar es Salaam Office," DAR to DOS, January 24, 1961, RG 59, Box 2027, 778.00/1-461, NARA. The American document misspelled his name as "Hadeby." James Hadebe's biography can be found on *South African History Online*, accessed July 21, 2014, http://www.sahistory.org.za/people/james-jobe-hadebe.

22. "Skilled Africans Being Smuggled to Tanganyika," DAR to DOS, February 5, 1962, RG 59, Box 2772, 878.062/1-260, NARA.

23. See also Bopela and Lulthuli, *Umkhonto we Sizwe*.

24. Nyerere, *Freedom and Unity*, 109–12.

25. "People's Daily Commentator Greets Tanganyika's Achieving Self-Government," Hong Kong to DOS, May 3, 1961, RG 59, Box 2027, 778.00/5-161, NARA; "Communist Activities with Kenya Students," DAR to DOS, June 18, 1962, RG 59, Box 2029, 778.00/7-1761, NARA.

26. William Duggan, DAR to DOS, April 17, 1961, RG 59, Box 2029, 778.13/1-461, NARA.

27. Thomas Byrne, "Pan-African Cooperative Alliance to Meet in Dar es Salaam in October or November," DAR to DOS, July 24, 1962, RG 59, Box 2028, 778.00/1-262, NARA.

28. Thomas Byrne, "South African Congress Men to Hold Dar Talks," DAR to DOS, August 16, 1962, RG 59, Box 2028, 778.00/8-262, NARA; Bopela and Lulthuli, *Umkhonto we Sizwe*, 28–38.

29. Tambo, *Preparing for Power*, 95.

30. Barrington King, "Tanganyika Minister Threatens Action against Portuguese Colonies," DAR to DOS, May 22, 1961, RG 59, Box 2027, 778.00/5-161, NARA.

31. Thomas Byrne, "An Impression of Oscar Kambona, Minister of Home Affairs," DAR to DOS, July 10, 1962, RG 59, Box 2028, NARA; Gabinete dos Negocios Politicos, Ministerio do Ultramar to Director Geral dos Negocios Politicos e da Administração Interna in Ministerio dos Negocios Estrangeiros, October 9, 1961, 607 PAA, AHD; "Recrutamento de nativos portugueses para fins subversivos," August 1963, 1033 PAA, AHD.

32. Thomas Byrne, "Report from Mozambique Refugees on National Democratic Union of Mozambique," DAR to DOS, April 16, 1962, RG 59, Box 2028,

778.00/1-262, NARA. For a more detailed account of these organizations, see Cabrita, *Mozambique*, 5–20.

33. "'Let African States Handle Mozambique,'" *Tanganyika Standard*, May 15, 1962, 1; "A 'M.A.N.U.' (Moçambique African National Union)," undated, 32-A PAA, AHD; Chilcote and Mondlane, "Eduardo Mondlane," 5.

34. "Anti-Portuguese African Movements in Tanganyika," Memorandum of Conversation, DOS, February 13, 1962, RG 59, Box 2028, 778.001/-262, NARA.

35. Jose Baltazar da Costa (Chagonga) to Hastings Kamuzu Banda, May 6, 1962, 1033 PAA, AHD.

36. "Portuguese Have Spies, Says Refugee," *Tanganyika Standard*, April 12, 1962, 1; 608 PAA, Proc 945, 17, AHD; Consulado de Portugal, DAR to Senhor Ministro do Negocios Estrangeiros, July 20, 1961, 607 PAA, AHD.

37. Malyn Newitt reports that Gwambe was later proven to be a Portuguese agent. See Newitt, *History of Mozambique*, 524. See also Consulado de Portugal, DAR to Senhor Ministro do Negocios Estrangeiros, July 20, 1961, 607 PAA, Relações com o Tanganika, Processo 945, 124 1962/63, Proc P/3 No. 116, AHD; Thomas Byrne, "Gwambe Banned Again by Tanganyika Government," DAR to DOS, August 2, 1962, RG 59, Box 2028, 778.00/8-262, NARA.

38. "Registration of Societies Lushoto District," Registrar of Societies to Regional Commissioner, Tanga, April 18, 1963, Accession unknown, H.6/70.69, TNA.

39. See also Mwakikagile, *Nyerere and Africa*, 206–22.

40. Cabrita, *Mozambique*, 16.

41. Ngaiza interview; see also Cabrita, *Mozambique*, 9.

42. Thomas Byrne, DAR to DOS, July 31, 1962, RG 59, Box 2773, 878.254/6-2960, NARA.

43. George S. High to Lloyd H. Ellis, Lourenço Marques, August 18, 1964; Mozambique Institute, "Progress and Plans, 1963–1964"—both in RG 59, E5253, Box 31, Refugees and Migration, REF 10-1 Refugee Training, NARA; F. S. Miles, DAR, to Duncan Sandys, CRO, November 5, 1963, DO 213/123, PRO; Cabrita, *Mozambique*, 18; Hennemeyer, FAOHP interview.

44. Robert Hennemeyer, "Further Information Concerning Mozambicans Receiving Military Training in Algeria," DAR to DOS, January 29, 1963, RG 59, Box 2029, 778.2/10-160, NARA.

45. Mondlane, *Struggle for Mozambique*; SCCI Boletim de Difusão de Informações, October 7, 1964, SR 082 Tanzania 1964/NOV/20–1965/JAN/13 H.2.26 MU/GM/GNP/082/Pt.1, AHU; "O Tanganica É Uma Base de Subversão e Porque somos um dos Vizinhos Ameaçados," December 30, 1964, 278 PAA, AHD.

46. Mlambo, "Second World War to UDI," 86–93, 104–12.

47. See Nkomo and Harman, *Nkomo*, 109; and Sibanda, *Zimbabwe African People's Union*, 97–103.

48. Wallerstein, *Africa*, 58–59, 68; and "Pan-African Freedom Movement of East and Central Africa (PAFMECA)."

49. Nkomo and Harman, *Nkomo*, 102.

50. DAR High Commissioner, "Talk with Mr. Nyerere on the 4th May," DO 183/145, PRO.

51. Kay, "Politics of Decolonization," 796–98.

52. Wood, *Welensky Papers*, 994, 1052; Hughes, "Fighting for White Rule."

53. H. S. H. Stanley, DAR, to K. A. East, CRO, May 18, 1962, DO 183/145.24, PRO; "News Talk Following the News Broadcast from Radio Tanganyika on Saturday December 1, 1962," DO 183/145, PRO.
54. Mulford, *Zambia*, 245, 268–72.
55. Marion, Lady Chesham, to Julius Nyerere, September 24, 1961, CHE-7, BI.
56. Iliffe, "Breaking the Chain," 168–97.
57. See Sibanda, *Zimbabwe African People's Union*, 95–100.
58. Mulford, *Zambia*, 229–312.
59. Report of conversation by Mark Tennant with Vedastus Kyaruzi, attachment to W. S. Bates to K. A. East, CRO, September 12, 1962, DO 183/145, 42A, PRO.
60. Wood, *Welensky Papers*, 1076; Good, *U.D.I.*, 40–41. Sibanda, *Zimbabwe African People's Union*, 90, 115n53.
61. S. C. Mwakang'ata, President, Kivukoni College Students' Council to the Prime Minister, London, "Memorandum on Southern Rhodesia," October 9, 1962, DO 183/145.50, PRO.
62. Nkomo and Harman, *Nkomo*, 105.
63. "Z.A.P.U. Political Speech Broadcast from Radio Tanganyika, Saturday, 12th November 1962," DO 183/145, PRO.
64. Julius Nyerere to Harold Macmillan, April 4, 1963, DO 183/145.90, PRO.
65. "Speech in National Assembly, Vice President," April 25, 1963, DO 183/145, PRO.
66. William Leonhart, DAR to DOS, June 20, 1963, 84, E3266 Box 10, 350 Southern Rhodesia 1963, NARA; Scarnecchia, *Urban Roots of Democracy*, 130–32.
67. Nkomo and Harman, *Nkomo*, 115.
68. Sibanda, *Zimbabwe African People's Union*, 91–94.
69. DAR High Commission to CRO, "Tanganyika Fortnightly Summary," August 16, 1963, August 30, 1963, October 11, 1963, FCO 141/6931.95, 99, 116, PRO.
70. DAR High Commission to CRO, "Tanganyika Fortnightly Summary," September 27, 1963, FCO 141/6931.104, PRO.
71. Wolfers, *Politics*, 163–80.
72. F. S. Miles, DAR, to Duncan Sandys, London, "Tanganyika and the Liberation of Africa," November 5, 1963, DO 213/123, PRO; Wallerstein, *Africa*, 162–63.
73. SCCI, "Relatório da Reunão do Comité de Coordenação Para a Libertação de África, em Dar-es-Salaam, em Junho de 1963," SR 176, AHU; F. S. Miles, DAR, to Duncan Sandys, CRO, November 5, 1963, DO 213/123, PRO.
74. Kyaruzi interview; Kawawa interview, September 5, 2006; Mbita interview, December 9, 2006.
75. F. S. Miles, DAR, to Duncan Sandys, CRO, November 5, 1963, DO 213/123, PRO.
76. Nyerere, *Freedom and Unity*, 253.
77. Thompson, *Ghana's Foreign Policy*, 305–56; "I Did Not Sabotage East African Federation: Interview with Milton Obote," *Monitor* (Kampala), April 10, 2005, reprinted in Mwakikagile, *Life under Nyerere*, 18.
78. Nyerere, *Freedom and Unity*, 216.
79. Ibid., 253.
80. F. S. Miles, "The Influence of Ghana in East Africa," October 4, 1963, FCO 141/6931.107, PRO.

81. Walraven, *Dreams of Power*, 124.
82. Nyerere, *Freedom and Unity*, 214.
83. Consulado de Portugal, DAR, to Senhor Ministro do Negocios Estrangeiros, July 20, 1961, 607 PAA, Relações com o Tanganika, Processo 945, 124 1962/63, Proc P/3 No. 116, AHD; "Prospects for East African Federation," Brief for Talks with Julius Nyerere, July 1963, DO 168/81, PRO.
84. This may be the map mentioned by Nyerere that Hastings Banda showed him, depicting Mozambique territory distributed to neighboring countries. Nyerere said he ridiculed it. Mwakikagile, *Tanzania*, 192; Shivji, "Pan-Africanism in Mwalimu Nyerere's Thought."
85. Nye, *Pan-Africanism and East African Integration*, 86–94.
86. Phiri, "The Capricorn Africa Society Revisited"; Hughes, *Capricorn*.
87. "Prospects for East African Federation," July 1963, DO 168/81, PRO; Jelmert Jorgensen, *Uganda*, 140–45; Mutesa, *Desecration of My Kingdom*.
88. Oneko interview; see also Odaka interview; and Kiano, "Pan-African Freedom Movement."
89. Nyerere, *Freedom and Unity*, 85.
90. Ibid., 91.
91. Marion, Lady Chesham, to Julius Nyerere, September 24, 1961, CHE-7, BI.
92. Nye, *Pan-Africanism and East African Integration*, 175–83; William Duggan, DAR to DOS, November 1, 1960, RG 59, Box 2029, 778.001/7-1761, NARA; Kisumo interview, September 7, 2006.
93. Minutes of TRAU Meeting, July 30, 1960, Friedland Collection, Box 8, "TRAU," HI; Mtei interview, September 9, 2006.
94. Howell, "Analysis of Kenyan Foreign Policy."
95. R. E. Collins, Ottawa, to N. Berlis, Dar es Salaam, September 23, 1963, RG 25, 10068-20-TAN-2-2, LAC.
96. "Thoughts on Conclusion of Tour: An Epilogue," DAR to DOS, December 6, 1960, RG 59, Box 2027, 778.00/6-360, NARA.
97. Kyaruzi interview; Nyerere (Maria) interview; Karume interview.
98. Barrington King, DAR to DOS, January 4, 1961, RG 59, Box 2029, 778.13/1-461, NARA.
99. Barrington King, DAR to DOS, February 3, 1961, RG 59, Box 2027, 778.00/1-461, NARA.
100. William Duggan, DAR to DOS, February 15, 1961; London to DOS, February 10, 1961; Barbour, DAR to DOS, January 31, 1961—all in RG 59, Box 2027, 778.00/1-461, NARA.
101. Barrington King, DAR to DOS, April 8, 1961, RG 84, E3266 Box 9, 350 Ruanda-Urundi 1963, NARA.
102. "Views of Julius Nyerere on African Questions," Memorandum of Conversation, February 1, 1960, RG 59, Box 2029, 778.03/10-1460, NARA; William Duggan, DAR to DOS, September 18, 1961, RG 59, Box 2029, 778.5 MSP/2-2761, NARA; Macarthur, Brussels to DOS, November 28, 1961, RG 59, Box 2773, 878.254/6-2960, NARA.
103. "Analysis of Ruanda-Urundi Political Situation," Elizabethville to DOS, October 12, 1960, RG 59, Box 2027, 778.00/6-360, NARA.

104. "Prospects for East African Federation," Brief by CRO for Talks with Nyerere, July 1963, DO 168/81, PRO.
105. Canup, Elizabethville to DOS, June 14, 1960; "Murmurings in Masailand," DAR to DOS, August 2, 1960—both in RG 59, Box 2027, 778.00/6-360, NARA.
106. London to DOS, February 10, 1961, RG 59, Box 2027, 778.00/1-461, NARA.
107. "Nyerere Blames Belgium," *Tanganyika Standard*, December 6, 1959, 1.
108. Kampala to DOS, June 14, 1960; "Analysis of Ruanda-Urundi Political Situation," Elizabethville to DOS, October 12, 1960; Herter, DOS to Elizabethville, June 6, 1960—all in RG 59, Box 2027, 778.00/6-360, NARA.
109. Timberlake, Usumbura to DOS, February 13, 1961, RG 59, Box 2027, 778.00/1-461, NARA; Prunier, *Rwanda Crisis*, 41–54.
110. Newbury, *Cohesion of Oppression*, 195–96.
111. Barrington King, DAR to DOS, November 7, 1960, RG 84, E3266 Box 9, 350 Ruanda-Urundi 1963, NARA; "Communal Elections in Ruanda," Brussels to DOS, July 27, 1960; "Communal Elections in Ruanda—II," Brussels to DOS, July 27, 1960; "Analysis of Ruanda-Urundi Political Situation," Elizabethville to DOS, October 12, 1960—all three in RG 59, Box 2027, 778.00/6-360, NARA.
112. Kumbukumbu ya Mkutano Mkuu, April 27–May 2, 1962, attachment to T. A. Kibhogya Msonge to Wajumbe Wote, January 12, 1963, 589: 11/03 PRT A.1, TNA; Thomas Byrne, DAR to DOS, April 28, 1962, RG 59, Box 2028, 778.00/1-262, NARA; "The Assassination of Prince Louis Rwagasore, Prime Minister of Burundi," Brussels to DOS, October 18, 1961, RG 59, Box 2029, 778.13/1-461, NARA.
113. Kigali to DOS, July 7, 1962, RG 84, E3266 Box 9, 350 Rwanda (Kigali), NARA.
114. Memorandum of Conversation, August 22, 1962; Thomas Byrne, DAR to DOS, "Tanganyika Denies Inyenzi Launching Raids from Its Borders," August 28, 1962—both in RG 84, E3266 Box 9, 350 Rwanda (Kigali), NARA.
115. "Prospects for East African Federation," Brief for Talks with Julius Nyerere, July 1963, DO 168/81, PRO.
116. Mtei interview, September 9, 2006.
117. D. Wadada Nabudere, "The Role of Tanzania in Regional Integration in East Africa—Old and New Patterns," in Mathews and Mushi, *Foreign Policy of Tanzania*, 123–51.
118. See Ghassany, *Kwaheri Ukoloni*; Glassman, *War of Words*, 159; and Shivji, *Pan-Africanism or Pragmatism?*, 70.
119. Mtei interview, September 9, 2006.
120. William Duggan, DAR to DOS, June 18, 1960; "Aid for Tanganyika and East African Federation," Memorandum of Conversation, January 9, 1961—both in RG 59, Box 2029, 778.2/10-160, NARA.
121. Barrington King, "Visit to Moscow and Peking by Women Leaders of TANU (May 1960)," DAR to DOS, January 14, 1961, RG 59, Box 2773, 878.413/7-560, NARA.
122. Barrington King, "Further Developments Regarding Visits to Communist China by Tanganyikans," DAR to DOS, January 19, 1961; Barrington King, "Photograph of TANU Women Leaders with Mao Tse-tung," DAR to DOS, April 8, 1961—both in RG 59, Box 2773, 878.413/7-560, NARA.

123. Geiger, *TANU Women*, 186.

124. "People's Daily Commentator Greets Tanganyika's Achieving Self-Government," Hong Kong to DOS, May 3, 1961, RG 59, Box 2027, 778.00/5-161, NARA.

125. These high-profile journeys were postponed because of the mutiny of the Tanganyika Rifles in January 1964. Niblock, "Tanzanian Foreign Policy," 25.

126. "Aid for Tanganyika and East African Federation," Memorandum of Conversation, January 9, 1961, RG 59, Box 2029, 778.2/10-160, NARA.

127. British High Commission, Bonn, to Foreign Office (FO), February 2, 1961, FO 371/161126, PRO.

128. DAR to DOS, August 23, 1960, RG 59, Box 2029, 778.00/17-1761, NARA. Two years later, Nyerere told American ambassador Leonhart that he needed "to reorganize government [to] catch up with [the] people" through rural development and economic planning; if he had a choice, he said, "the cities could go to hell" while he focused on the rural sector. See William Leonhart, DAR to DOS, November 3, 1962, RG 59, Box 2028, 778.00/8-262, NARA.

129. "Tanganyikan Request for Economic Assistance," Memorandum of Conversation, July 14, 1961, RG 59, Box 2029, 778.5 MSP/2-2761, NARA; see also Listowel, *Making of Tanganyika*, 391–98.

130. B. E. Rolfe to P. A. Carter, CRO, March 6, 1961, FO 371/154703, PRO.

131. Saukey-Wraght, "Mr. Nyerere's Attitude towards the Date of Independence of Tanganyika; Establishment of Military Facilities in Tanganyika," FO 371/154703, PRO.

132. William Leonhart, "Tanganyika Braintrust," to DOS, November 22, 1962, RG 59, Box 2772, 878.00/2-1660, NARA.

133. London to DOS, June 16, 1961, RG 59, Box 2029, 778.03-10/-1460, NARA; W. S. Ryrie, Colonial Office to Barbara Miller, FO, March 15, 1961, FO 371/154703, PRO; Nye, *Pan-Africanism and East African Integration*, 119, 177.

134. Nye, *Pan-Africanism and East African Integration*, 133; Mtei interview, September 9, 2006.

135. P. Dean, New York to London, January 16, 1962, DO 181/31.2, PRO; Kelly and Kaplan, "Nation and Decolonization."

136. "New Zealand Assistance to Tanganyika: Training of Tanganyikan Diplomatic Officer," Wellington to DOS, September 21, 1961, RG 59, Box 2029, 778.5 MSP/2-2761, NARA.

137. Ngaiza interview.

138. Nnoli, *Self Reliance and Foreign Policy*, 35; see also "The Hon. Joseph K. Nyerere's Speech Delivered during Debate on Prime Minister's Policy Statement," Tanganyika, May 1961, Tom Mboya Papers, Box 38–38.4, Representatives in Africa Tanganyika, vol. 1, HI.

139. "Representation Overseas," Paul Lubeck Papers, Box 3-7, HI.

140. Kyaruzi interview.

141. Robert Hennemeyer, DAR to DOS, December 22, 1961, RG 59, Box 2029, 778.13/1-461, NARA.

142. Kyaruzi interview.

143. P. Dean, New York to London, January 16, 1962, DO 181/31.2, PRO.

144. "The Hon. Joseph K. Nyerere's Speech Delivered during Debate on Prime Minister's Policy Statement," Tanganyika, May 1961, Tom Mboya Papers, Box 38–38.4, Representatives in Africa Tanganyika, vol. 1, HI.

145. Kyaruzi interview.
146. "Public Statements of Nyerere on Major Issues," DAR to DOS, September 11, 1961, RG 59, Box 2029, 778.131/-461, NARA.
147. "Trade Union Delegation Visit Israel, Soviet Union, East Germany and the U.K.," DAR to DOS, July 18, 1962; "Bloc Trade Union Program," DAR to DOS, May 29, 1962—both in RG 59, Box 2773, 878.062/3-1562, NARA; Thomas Byrne, DAR to DOS, May 29, 1962, RG 59, Box 2028, 778.00/1-262.
148. "Representation Overseas," Paul Lubeck Papers, Box 3-7, HI.
149. George Kennan, "Yugoslavia Recognizes Tanganyika," Belgrade to DOS, December 13, 1961, RG 59, Box 2029, 778.001/7-1761, NARA.
150. See also Willets, *Non-aligned Movement*.
151. Julius Nyerere to John Kennedy, May 16, 1963, NSF Box 124A, Tanganyika 1962–64, JFK.
152. John Kennedy to Julius Nyerere, June 14, 1963, NSF Box 124A, Tanganyika 1962–64, JFK.
153. Julius Nyerere to John Kennedy, June 18, 1963, and June 18, 1963, NSF Box 124A, Tanganyika 1962–64, JFK.
154. P. A. Carter, DAR to N. Aspin, CRO, July 17, 1963, DO 168/81, PRO.
155. Clarizio, Clements, and Geetter, "United States Policy," 251; Schlesinger, *Thousand Days*, 559, 580–83.
156. Robert Hennemeyer, "Politico-Economic Assessment," DAR to DOS, April 4, 1962, RG 59, Box 2028, 778.00/1-262, NARA.
157. "Representation Overseas," Paul Lubeck Papers, Box 3-7, HI.
158. Nyerere, *Freedom and Unity*, 216–17.
159. Mazrui, "Poet-Presidents and Philosopher-Kings"; Furlong, "Azikiwe and the National Church."
160. Nyerere, *Freedom and Unity*, 223–26.
161. Billig, *Banal Nationalism*.
162. Nyerere, Freedom and Unity, 226.
163. P. A. Carter, "Note of Talk with Mr. G. Rockey on President Nyerere's Visit to London," August 12, 1963, DO 168/81, PRO. The "convivial manager" was at the George Inn in Southwark. They also visited the Old King's Head and the Anchor.
164. "Visit to London of the President of Tanganyika: 21st to 25th July, 1963," October 31, 1963, DO 168/81, PRO.

Chapter 9

1. William Leonhart, DAR to DOS, January 17, 1964, NSF/CF 103-1.20, LBJ. This early formulation of the idea, and Babu's involvement, belies many accounts of the Union that present it as a sudden imposition from Tanganyika intended to sideline Babu. See, for example, Pratt, *Critical Phase in Tanzania*, 138–39.
2. Smith, *We Must Run*, 176–77. Timothy Parsons cites a similar conversation the following year between Kambona and the recently retired governor-general of Kenya, Malcolm J. McDonald, who reported that "according to Oscar Kambona,

Nyerere used the federation of the two countries to keep the region out of the Cold War by limiting the extent of communist influence in Zanzibar." See Parsons, *1964 Army Mutinies*, 164. See also R. W. D. Fowler to Malcolm Macleod, Nairobi, March 17, 1965, DO 213/245, PRO; Lourenço Marques to DOS, "Oscar Kambona Interview," March 2, 1973, RG 59, Box 2618, POL 29 TANZAN, 1/1/70, NARA.

3. Both Mark Bomani and Mirisho Sarakikya in conversation with the author in June 2013 explained the situation in these terms. See also Shivji, *Pan-Africanism or Pragmatism?*; Burgess, "Socialist Diaspora"; Speller, "African Cuba?"; and Jjuuko and Muriuki, *Federation within Federation*.

4. CRO to DAR High Commission, January 25, 1964, DO 185/51, PRO; Weissman, "CIA Covert Action," 266.

5. During his October 1963 visit to the US to lobby for support for an East African federation, Oscar Kambona, half in jest, referred to Zanzibar as "Tanganyika's Cuba." However, William R. Duggan, then an embassy officer in Dar es Salaam, claims to have coined the phrase in July 1963, in conversation with Nyerere during his visit to the US. Duggan and Civille, *Tanzania and Nyerere*, 76. See also Kyaruzi interview.

6. Memorandum of Conversation, October 16, 1963, RG 84, Entry 3266, Box 11-361, NARA.

7. Kombo, *Masimulizi*, 131–32.

8. Clayton, *Zanzibar Revolution*, 46–47; Petterson, *Revolution in Zanzibar*, 43.

9. Glassman, *War of Words*, 275–81.

10. Issa interview; Burgess, *Race, Revolution and the Struggle*, 70–77; Clayton, *Zanzibar Revolution*, 45–46.

11. The number of soldiers given is based on estimates by both Okello himself and by an anonymous member of the ASP and the Young African Social Union (YASU). William Leonhart, DAR to DOS, January 15, 1964, NSF/CF 103-1.34, LBJ.

12. Chris Pappas, DAR to DOS, "The Field Marshal John Okello Story," October 3, 1964, RG 59, Box 2691, POL 15-1 Head of State, Executive Branch, TANZAN, 8/1/64, NARA; Okello, *Revolution in Zanzibar*.

13. Olcott Deming, Kampala to DOS, January 30, 1964, NSF/CF 103-1.2, LBJ.

14. See Ghassany, *Kwaheri Ukoloni*, 163–64. The oral history testimonies that Ghassany collected are highly politicized and often based on hearsay, but the recollections of Ahmed Othman Aboud (or Aboud "Mmasai") seem fairly credible on this point. See also Lusinde interview, July 6, 2010; and William Leonhart, DAR to DOS, February 5, 1964, NSF/CF 103-1.19, LBJ. Thabit Kombo lists the names of the "Committee of Fourteen" as follows: Seif Bakari, Abdallah Said Natepe, Ramadhani Haji, Mohamed Abdallah (Ameir Kaujore), Mohamed Mfaranyaki, Khamis Daruwesh, Said Ali Bavuai, Hamid Ameir, Hafidh Suleiman, Pili Khamis, Said Washoto, Khamis Hemed (Nyuni), Yusuf Himid, and then John Okello. Ludovick Mwijage adds several more contributors: Hassan Nassor Moyo, Edington Kisasi, Ibrahim Makungu, and Khamis Hemed. See Kombo, *Masimulizi*, 133; and Mwijage, *Julius Nyerere*, 131.

15. Kombo, *Masimulizi*, 131–38; William Leonhart, DAR to DOS, January 15, 1964, NSF/CF 103-1.34, LBJ.

16. The number of deaths has never been accurately estimated. In February Karume claimed that 230 Africans and 305 Arabs were either killed or wounded,

and another 1,200 Arabs were detained in former schools in Zanzibar town and in prison buildings on Tortoise Island. This coincides with a "conservative" estimate" of 500 dead by a "reliable" source in the Zanzibari government on January 16. On January 15, however, the American consul reported an anonymous Zanzibari Arab source estimating 2,100 dead, and a British estimate of 5,000. Donald Petterson later estimated 5,000 as well. Abdulrahman Babu claimed that the numbers of deaths in the revolution were greatly exaggerated, due to Okello's "wild claims on the local radio of thousands of casualties" that were intended to incite fear. However, Ludovick Mwijage points to a mass burial of victims in a dry well in Bambi, on Unguja island. Mwijage's claim finds support in film footage appearing in the scabrous Italian film *Africa Addio*. Allegedly filmed from January 18 to 20, 1964, the footage shows multiple sites of massacres and mass graves, each containing scores of bodies. See A. L. Adu to David Owen, "Report on Visit to Zanzibar, February 10, 1964," Smith File, BI; DAR to DOS, January 15, 1964, 1964, NSF/CF 103-1.32, LBJ; and William Leonhart, DAR to DOS, January 16, 1964, NSF/CF 103-1.26, LBJ. See also Glassman, *War of Words*, 282–84; Babu, "1964 Revolution," 241; Petterson, *Revolution in Zanzibar*, 107; and Mwijage, *Julius Nyerere*, 131.

17. Kombo, *Masimulizi*, 135.
18. Burgess, *Race, Revolution*, 22.
19. William Leonhart, DAR to DOS, January 15, 1964, NSF/CF 103-1.35, LBJ; William Leonhart, DAR to DOS, January 16, 1964, NSF/CF 103-1.27, LBJ; Meffert interview.
20. William Leonhart, DAR to DOS, January 16, 1964, NSF/CF 103-1.26, LBJ.
21. William Leonhart, DAR to DOS, January 18, 1964, NSF/CF 103-1.12, LBJ.
22. Zanzibar to DOS, January 17, 1964, NSF/CF 103-1.17, LBJ.
23. William Leonhart, DAR to DOS, January 17, 1964, NSF/CF 103-1.18, LBJ.
24. "Report of Mutiny by 1st Battalion Tang Rifles, 20th January 1964," FCO 141/140143, PRO.
25. Chris Pappas, DAR to DOS, "The Field Marshal John Okello Story," October 3, 1964, RG 59, Box 2691, POL 15-1 Head of State, Executive Branch, TANZAN, 8/1/64, NARA.
26. William Leonhart, DAR to DOS, January 30, 1964, NSF/CF 100-1.27, LBJ.
27. Ali interview.
28. Chris Pappas, DAR to DOS, "The Field Marshal John Okello Story," October 3, 1964, RG 59, Box 2691, POL 15-1 Head of State, Executive Branch, TANZAN, 8/1/64, NARA.
29. William Leonhart, DAR, to Department of State, January 20, 1964, NSF/CF 103-1.6, LBJ.
30. Clayton, *Zanzibar Revolution*.
31. Dean Rusk, DOS to All African Diplomatic Posts, January 30, 1964, NSF/CF 103-3.22, LBJ.
32. See Speller, "African Cuba?," 290–91.
33. Dean Rusk to London, January 30, 1964, NSF/CF 103-"Zanzibar Vol. 2" No. 191a, LBJ; see also Gleijeses, *Conflicting Missions*, 57–58; and Shivji, *Pan-Africanism or Pragmatism?*, 73–75.
34. Lawrence, *Dar Mutiny of 1964*; Baregu, "Perception."
35. CRO to DAR High Commission, January 25, 1964, DO 185/51, PRO.

36. William Leonhart, DAR to DOS, February 15, 1964, NSF/CF 103-4.133, LBJ.

37. Telephone conversation between Lyndon Johnson and Alec Douglas-Home, February 19, 1964, White House Tapes, 2115 ALEC DOUGLAS HOME 2/19/64 12:00P WH6402, LBJ.18 PNO 4, see also Lyndon Johnson telephone recording no. 2115 online at the Miller Center's Presidential Recording Program, University of Virginia, accessed July 21, 2014, http://millercenter.org/scripps/archive/presidentialrecordings/johnson/1964/02_1964.

38. William Leonhart, DAR to DOS, February 20, 1964, NSF/CF 103-4.121, LBJ.

39. Wolf, *Man without a Face*, 285. Wolf recalls traveling in February and staying for several months, not leaving until after the Union Treaty. But he mentions that he traveled with East German deputy foreign minister Wolfgang Kiesewtter, whose visit was from March 19 to April 1, 1964. "Report on Trip by Kiesewetter to Zanzibar and Tanganyika," April 8, 1964, DY 30/IV A 2/20-1176, SAPMO.

40. A concern with portraits of Mao in Babu's offices arose in a Stasi report: "Informal Mission Report," April 21, 1964, MfS/HA I/17493, BStU.

41. Smith, *Encyclopedia*, 44–45.

42. Issa interview.

43. Carlucci interview.

44. "Dynamic Diplomat; Frank Charles Carlucci 3d," *New York Times*, February 24, 1964, attachment to Leopoldville to Ministro do Negicios Extrangeiros, July 21, 1964, 32 PAA, AHD; Bourderie, "Tough Little Monkey."

45. Frank Carlucci, interview for Foreign Affairs Oral History Project (FAOHP), Association for Diplomatic Studies and Training, 1997, accessed July 24, 2014, http://www.adst.org/OH%20TOCs/Carlucci,%20Frank%20Charles%20III%20_April%201,%201997_.pdf.

46. See Gromyko, *African Countries' Foreign Policy*.

47. Frank Carlucci, "Conversation with URT First Vice President Karume," Zanzibar to DOS, December 8, 1964, RG 59, Box 2691, POL 15-1 TANZAN, NARA.

48. Frank Carlucci, Zanzibar to DOS, March 6, 1964, NSF/CF 103-3.69, LBJ; Frank Carlucci, Zanzibar to DOS, March 26, 1964, NSF/CF 103-4.137b, LBJ; Issa interview; "Intelligence Update," October 20, 1964, MfS/HVA/203, BStU.

49. R. W. D. Fowler to L. B. Walsh Atkins, January 14, 1965, 185/51, PRO; L. B. Walsh Atkins to R. W. D. Fowler, December 31, 1964, DO 185/51, PRO; J. Bourn, B.L.F.K. Liaison Conference, Zanzibar and Pemba, September 23, 1964, DO 185/51, PRO.

50. William Leonhart to DOS, March 28, 1964, NSF/CF 100-2.93, LBJ.

51. See also Speller, "African Cuba?," 292.

52. A National Security Council member recommended Carlucci's reporting to presidential aide McGeorge Bundy as "staccato, to the point, and highly useful." Peter Jessup to McGeorge Bundy, March 27, 1964, LBJ NSF/CF 103-6.237.

53. Frank Carlucci, Zanzibar to DOS, March 31, 1964, NSF/CF 103-3.57, LBJ.

54. Lyndon Baines Johnson, draft letter to British Prime Minister, March 26, 1964, NSF/CF 100-2.72, LBJ. US interventions in Iran (1953), Guatemala (1954), and the Congo (1960), and the failed Bay of Pigs intervention in Cuba (1961), had used similar tactics.

55. Okello, *Revolution in Zanzibar*, 165.
56. William Leonhart, DAR to DOS, January 17, 1964, NSF/CF 103-1.20, LBJ; Jumbe, *Partner-Ship*, 15.
57. Bomani interview.
58. Kombo, *Masimulizi*, 80–92, 138–40; Clayton, *Zanzibar Revolution*, 44; Ghassany, *Kwaheri Ukoloni*, 176. See also Karume interview; William Leonhart, DAR to DOS, April 25, 1963, RG 84, E 3266, Box 10, 350 Zanzibar, 1963, NARA.
59. Karume interview; Kawawa interview, September 5, 2006.
60. William Leonhart, DAR to DOS, January 30, 1964, NSF/CF 100-1.27, LBJ.
61. Dean Rusk, DOS to DAR, March 6, 1964, NSF/CF 103-4.100, LBJ. In 1997, Frank Carlucci claimed that the Union idea was initiated by William Leonhart. Carlucci, FAOHP interview. This does not seem to be correct. Clearly the idea had already been developed by Nyerere and Karume before the Zanzibar Revolution, and Leonhart first heard about the idea in January when Kambona told him about his meeting with Karume, Babu, and Hanga. It would seem that subsequently Leonhart advocated for the Union as an alternative to Carlucci's recommendations for an armed intervention of the type initially envisioned by the British just after the revolution.
62. Jesse McKnight to Governor Williams, January 25, 1964, RG 59, Box 2687, POL 15-4 TANGAN, 1/1/64, NARA.
63. William Leonhart, DAR to DOS, March 8, 1964, NSF/CF 103-4.115, LBJ; J. Bourn, B.L.F.K. Liaison Conference, Zanzibar and Pemba, September 23, 1964, DO 185/51, PRO.
64. Wolf, *Man without a Face*, 285.
65. Oscar Kambona, from Stephen Miles to CRO, February 6, 1964, quoted in R. W. D. Fowler to Malcolm Macleod, Nairobi, March 17, 1965, DO 213/245, PRO.
66. William Leonhart, DAR to DOS, February 22, 1964, NSF/CF 103-4.106, LBJ.
67. William Leonhart, DAR to DOS, January 13, 1964, NSF/CF 103-1.40, LBJ.
68. William Leonhart, DAR to DOS, January 14, 1964, NSF/CF 103-1.40, LBJ.
69. William Leonhart, DAR to DOS, January 20, 1964, NSF/CF 103-1.6, LBJ.
70. William Leonhart, DAR to DOS, March 8, 1964, NSF/CF 103-4.98, LBJ.
71. Ibid., quoted in Shivji, *Pan-Africanism or Pragmatism?*, 75, 78.
72. Nairobi to DOS, March 9, 1964, NSF/CF 103-5.112, LBJ.
73. Quoted in Shivji, *Pan-Africanism or Pragmatism?*, 75, 78; see also "Report from GDR Ambassador in Zanzibar to Foreign Ministry in Berlin," March 1964, DY IV A 2/20-1171, SAPMO; Vass, Nairobi to DOS, April 2, 1964, NSF/CF 103-5.209, LBJ.
74. See, for example, Frank Carlucci, Zanzibar to DOS, November 10, 1964, RG 59, Box 2693, POL 23-8, Demonstrations, Riots, TANZAN, NARA.
75. Vass, Nairobi to DOS, March 24, 1964, NSF/CF 103-5.211, LBJ.
76. William Leonhart, "Two Notes," Box 38, File: Tang. Think Pieces, JFK.
77. David Bruce, London to DOS, March 10, 1964, NSF/CF 103.5, LBJ.
78. "Soviet Aid to the Government of Zanzibar," CIA Intelligence Information Cable, date sanitized (approx. March 26, 1964), NSF/CF 100-1.14, LBJ; Zanzibar to DOS, April 11, 1964, NSF/CF 103-3.39, LBJ.
79. Informal Mission Report, April 21, 1964, MfS/HA I/17493, BStU.
80. "Report from GDR Ambassador in Zanzibar to Foreign Ministry in Berlin," March 1964, DY IV A 2/20-1171, SAPMO.

81. "Report on Trip by Kiesewetter to Zanzibar and Tanganyika," April 8, 1964, DY 30/IV A 2/20-1176, SAPMO.

82. Frank Carlucci, Zanzibar to DOS, March 17, 1964, NSF/CF 103-3.62, LBJ.

83. Frank Carlucci, Zanzibar to DOS, March 26, 1964, NSF/CF 103-6.237a, LBJ.

84. McGeorge Bundy to Colonel Connell, March 28, 1964, NSF/CF 103.234, LBJ. It is possible that the "action through Tanganyika" referred to the Union plan, but I do not believe this to be the case. While Leonhart may have encouraged the Union plan, it was not his initiative. The idea had been in place since before the Zanzibar Revolution, and the actual Union negotiations developed in secret without Leonhart's being informed until April. The East African leadership excluded from the negotiations the very people the US depended on as informants, in particular Wolfgang Dourado and Othman Shariff. Additionally Carlucci's communications suggest that he was likewise unaware of any "concerted action" in East Africa. Leonhart tended to look favorably on Nyerere's views, and he may have advocated for the Union plan after April 15 as a moderate solution to allay American fears while Carlucci pushed for a more aggressive armed intervention in cooperation with local agents. See Frank Carlucci, Zanzibar to DOS, March 26, 1964, NSF/CF 103-6.237a, LBJ. See also Hennemeyer, FAOHP interview.

85. U. Alexis Johnson, "Summary of Action Taken on Zanzibar Question during Week of March 29," April 6, 1964, NSF/CF 103-6.227, LBJ; Shivji, *Pan-Africanism or Pragmatism?*, 78–81.

86. J. Wayne Fredericks, "Rapidly Deteriorating Situation in Zanzibar," March 25, 1964, RG 59, Box 2693, POL 23-8 TANZAN, 1/1/64, NARA.

87. "In this respect," opined T. L. Crosthwait from Dar es Salaam, "it seems to me that intervention in Zanzibar is a more difficult operation than was the suppression of the Tanganyika mutiny which I think left most of the Government machine unimpaired." T. L. Crosthwait to L. B. Walsh Atkins, CRO, June 9, 1964, DO 185/51, PRO.

88. R. W. D. Fowler, DAR to L. B. Walsh Atkins, CRO, January 14, 1965, DO 185/51.152, PRO.

89. Lyndon Baines Johnson, draft letter to British Prime Minister, March 26, 1964, NSF/CF 100-2.72, LBJ; McGeorge Bundy, "Memorandum for the President," March 29, 1964, NSF/CF 103-6.233b, LBJ.

90. DAR to DOS, March 31, 1964, RG 59, Box 2687, POL 14 TANGAN, 1/1/64, NARA; William Leonhart, DAR to DOS, April 4, 1964, RG 59, Box 2687, POL 15-4 TANGAN, 1/1/64, NARA.

91. Chris Pappas, DAR to DOS, "TANU Annual Conference," April 20, 1964, RG 59, Box 2687, POL-POLITICAL AFFAIRS & REL-TANGAN, 1/1/64, NARA.

92. "Report on Trip by Kiesewetter to Zanzibar and Tanganyika," April 8, 1964, DY 30/IV A 2/20-1176, SAPMO.

93. Wolf, *Man without a Face*, 284.

94. William Leonhart, DAR to DOS, March 29, 1964, RG 59, Box 2687, POL 15 Government TANGAN, 1/1/64, NARA.

95. David Bruce, London to DOS, March 31, 1964, NSF/CF 103-5.164, LBJ.

96. Frank Carlucci, Zanzibar to DOS, RG 59, Box 2687, POL 23-9 TANGAN, 1/1/64, NARA.

97. Thomas Hughes, Research Memorandum, "Growing Communist Influence in Zanzibar: US Policy Alternatives," April 15, 1964, NSF/CF 103-6.225, LBJ.
98. G. E. Millard, April 9, 1964, FO 371/176569, PRO.
99. William Leonhart, DAR to DOS, April 6, 1964, NSF/CF 103-3.9a, LBJ.
100. William Leonhart, DAR to DOS, April 16, 1964, RG 59, Box 2687, POL 15-4 TANGAN, 1/1/64, NARA; William Leonhart, DAR to DOS, April 22, 1964, NSF/CF 103-3.78, LBJ.
101. James Ruchti, Nairobi, to DOS, April 10, 1964, NSF/CF 103-5.206, LBJ.
102. William Leonhart, DAR to DOS, April 23, 1964, NSF/CF 100-4.109, LBJ.
103. William Leonhart, DAR to DOS, April 17, 1964, RG 59, Box 2694, POL TANZAN U-Z, 1/1/64, NARA.
104. See also Speller, "African Cuba?," 292.
105. William Leonhart, DAR to DOS, April 17, 1964, NSF/CF 103-3.84, LBJ.
106. Frank Carlucci, Zanzibar to DOS, July 7, 1964, NSF/CF 100-4.124, LBJ.
107. Ali Sultan Issa also indicated to me that the Soviets were viewed with much more suspicion than the Chinese. William Leonhart, DAR to DOS, April 17, 1964, NSF/CF 103-3.84, LBJ.
108. DOS to Zanzibar, April 7, 1964, NSF/CF 103-3.51, LBJ; Frank Carlucci, Zanzibar to DOS, April 11, 1964, NSF/CF 103-3.37, LBJ; Frank Carlucci, Zanzibar to DOS, April 19, 1964, NSF/CF, 103.17a, LBJ; Zanzibar Information No. 31, August 19, 1964, DO 185/51, PRO.
109. Bill Brubeck to McGeorge Bundy, "Zanzibar," April 7, 1964, NSF/CF 103-6.226, LBJ.
110. Gichiru suspected that Kambona would not cooperate with such a plan, a confidence that later proved correct when some members of the Zanzibar Revolutionary Council approached Kambona about becoming a new "father of the nation" in November, in a conversation overheard by a Dr. Nasir-Ud-Din Quairashi, who was treating Kambona in Nairobi. William Attwood, Nairobi to DOS, April 18, 1964, NSF/CF 103.18, LBJ; William Attwood, "Tanzania," Nairobi to DOS, November 20, 1964, RG 59, Box 2693, POL 23 TANZAN, 1/1/64, NARA; Washington High Commission to Foreign Office, November 23, 1964, DO 213/30, PRO; DAR High Commission to CRO, November 26, 1964, DO 213/30, PRO; High Commission, Nairobi, to CRO, November 28, 1964, DO 213/30, PRO.
111. William Leonhart, DAR to DOS, April 17, 1964, NSF/CF 103-3.84, LBJ.
112. James Ruchti, Nairobi to DOS, April 15, 1964, RG 59, Box 2687, POL 23-9 TANGAN, 1/1/64, NARA.
113. "NATO Secret—United States Delegation to the North Atlantic Council: Situation in Zanzibar," April 15, 1964, 32 PAA Proc 950, 123, AHD. The Portuguese referred to the NATO memorandum as a proposal for "intervention." "Projecto—Aerograma: Secreto Urgente," 32 PAA Proc 950, 123, AHD.
114. A key document in this drama in American archives is still entirely "sanitized": Zanzibar to DOS, April 14, 1964, RG 59, Box 2687, POL 17, TANGAN, 1/1/64, NARA.
115. George Ball, DOS to London, April 16, 1964, NSF/CF 103-3.6a, LBJ.
116. What Johnson called the "Kenyatta/Karume action" was apparently the British plan for a Kenya-based paratrooper invasion of Zanzibar, code-named Operation Boris. The British also had a contingency plan code-named Finery, which was never

Notes to pp. 220–224

authorized, for a sea-based invasion of Zanzibar that would not require Kenyatta's approval and the subsequent risk of exposure. Speller, "African Cuba?," 293.

117. Memorandum of Conversation, April 17, 1964, NSF/CF 103-6.245a, LBJ.
118. William Leonhart, DAR to DOS, April 18, 1964, NSF/CF 103-3.82, LBJ.
119. Shivji, *Pan-Africanism or Pragmatism?*, 79; Issa interview; Meffert interview.
120. William Leonhart, DAR to DOS, April 22, 1964, NSF/CF 100-4.113, LBJ.
121. Frank Carlucci, Zanzibar to DOS, April 19, 1964, NSF/CF 103-3.28, LBJ.
122. See also Jumbe, *Partner-Ship*, 15.
123. William Leonhart, DAR to DOS, April 18, 1964, NSF/CF 103-3.82, LBJ.
124. William Leonhart, DAR to DOS, April 19, 1964, NSF/CF 103-3.81, LBJ.
125. William Leonhart, DAR to DOS, April 17, 1964, NSF/CF 100-1.4, LBJ; Frank Carlucci, Zanzibar to DOS, April 19, 1964, NSF/CF 103-3.17a, LBJ; William Leonhart, DAR to DOS, April 19, 1964, NSF/CF 103-3.81, LBJ.
126. Quoted in Wilson, *US Foreign Policy and Revolution*, 73.
127. Olcott Deming, Kampala to DOS, April 21, 1964, NSF/CF 103-3.3a, LBJ.
128. Weber, *Simulating Sovereignty*, 4.
129. Kombo, *Masimulizi*, 139.
130. David Bruce, London to DOS, April 22, 1964, NSF/CF 103-5.156, LBJ.
131. William Leonhart, DAR to DOS, April 22, 1964, NSF/CF 103-3, No. 78, LBJ.
132. William Attwood, Nairobi to DOS, April 25, 1964, NSF/CF 100-4.166, LBJ; Frank Carlucci, Zanzibar to DOS, April 25, 1964, NSF/CF 100-1.148, LBJ.
133. High Commission, Nairobi, to CRO, "Zanzibar," April 25, 1964, DO 185/51, PRO.
134. Issa interview.
135. Bomani interview.
136. Jumbe, *Partner-Ship*, 13; emphasis in original.
137. Frank Carlucci, Zanzibar to DOS, April 26, 1964, NSF/CF 100-4.140, LBJ.
138. William Leonhart, DAR to DOS, April 22, 1964, NSF/CF 103-3.78, LBJ; William Leonhart, DAR to DOS, April 22, 1964, NSF/CF 100-4.113, LBJ.
139. William Leonhart, DAR to DOS, April 22, 1964, NSF/CF 100-1.3, LBJ.
140. William Leonhart, DAR to DOS, April 22, 1964, NSF/CF 100-4.113, LBJ.
141. William Leonhart, DAR to DOS, April 24, 1964, NSF/CF 100-4.104, LBJ; CRO to DAR High Commission, July 4, 1964, DO 185/51.96, PRO; CRO to DAR High Commission, July 3, 1964, DO 185/51.94A, PRO.
142. Frank Carlucci, Zanzibar to DOS, April 25, 1964, NSF/CF 100-4.146, LBJ; Jjuuko and Muriuki, *Federation within Federation*, 20. See also Jumbe, *Partner-Ship*, 105; Shivji, *Pan-Africanism or Pragmatism?*, 80–81; and Bomani interview.
143. Othman, "Tanzania: Beyond Sectarian Interests"; William Leonhart, DAR to DOS, April 25, 1964, NSF/CF 100-4.97, LBJ.
144. William Leonhart, DAR to DOS, April 22, 1964, NSF/CF 103-3.78, LBJ.
145. Issa interview.
146. William Attwood, Nairobi to DOS, April 25, 1964, NSF/CF 100-4.166, LBJ; see also Jjuuko and Muriuki, *Federation within Federation*, 20–21.
147. William Leonhart, DAR to DOS, April 23, 1964, NSF/CF 100-4.110, LBJ; William Leonhart, DAR to DOS, April 24, 1964, NSF/CF 100-4.105, LBJ; William Leonhart, DAR to DOS, April 23, 1964, NSF/CF 100-4.109, LBJ.

148. Frank Carlucci, Zanzibar to DOS, April 25, 1964, NSF/CF 100-4.147, LBJ.

149. See Shivji, *Pan-Africanism*, 76–94. The "Acts of Union of Tanganyika and Zanzibar" were published April 27, 1964, citing their approval by the Revolutionary Council. The votes approving the Union Treaty are noted in Nyerere, *Freedom and Unity*; DAR to DOS, April 26, 1964, NSF/CF 100-4.97, LBJ; and Zanzibar to Central Intelligence Agency, "Babu's Agreement to Union with Tanganyika," April 26, 1964, NSF/CF 100-4.164, LBJ.

150. DAR High Commission to CRO, "Tanganyika/Zanzibar Union," April 24, 1964, DO 185/51.1, PRO.

151. DAR High Commission to CRO, "Nigerian Troops and Zanzibar," May 13, 1964, DO 185/51.24, PRO.

152. CRO to DAR High Commission, May 3, 1964, DO 185/51.9, PRO.

153. T. L. Crosthwait, DAR, to Maj. Gen. C. R. Price, CRO, May 15, 1964, DO 185/51, PRO.

154. Frank Carlucci, Zanzibar to DOS, April 28, 1964, NSF/CF 100-4.139, LBJ.

155. W. Averell Harriman, Undersecretary of State for Political Affairs, "Memorandum for the President," May 4, 1964, NSF/CF 100-5.178, LBJ; Frank Carlucci, Zanzibar to DOS, May 2, 1964, NSF/CF 100-4.136, LBJ; William Leonhart, DAR to DOS, June 10, 1964, NSF/CF 100-3.45, LBJ.

156. William Leonhart, DAR to DOS, January 14, 1964, NSF/CF 103-1.40, LBJ.

157. William Attwood, Nairobi to DOS, April 25, 1964, NSF/CF 100-4.167, LBJ.

158. Sherman Kent, "Implications of Growing Communist Influence in URTZ," September 29, 1964, Board of National Estimates, CIA, NSF/CF 100-5.172, LBJ.

159. Ibid.

160. Dean Rusk, DOS to DAR, February 2, 1964, NSF/CF 103-4.149a, LBJ.

161. John Spencer to Richard Nolte, August 18, 1964, RG 59, Box 2690, POL 15 Government TANZAN, NARA.

162. William Leonhart, DAR to DOS, June 10, 1964, NSF/CF 100-3.115, LBJ.

163. John Spencer to Richard Nolte, August 18, 1964, RG 59, Box 2690, POL 15 Government TANZAN, NARA.

164. DAR to DOS, April 29, 1964, NSF/CF 100-4.88, LBJ.

165. W. Averell Harriman to President, May 4, 1964, NSF/CF 100-5.178, LBJ.

Chapter 10

1. White, "Telling More."

2. In the effort to avoid a flash point that might destabilize Zanzibar politics and undermine the Union, Nyerere quietly ordered the transfer of imprisoned members of the sultan's former government to mainland prisons in June 1964, "to insure their greater safety." William Leonhart, DAR to DOS, July 15, 1964, RG 59, Box 2694, POL 29 Arrests, Detention, TANZAN, NARA.

3. Frank Carlucci, Zanzibar to DOS, March 13, 1964, NSF/CF 103-3.65, LBJ. Duncan Sandys was the British colonial secretary.

4. William Leonhart, DAR to DOS, January 16, 1964, NSF/CF 103-1.28, LBJ.

5. Nzongola-Ntalaja, *Congo from Leopold to Kabila*, 152.

6. William Leonhart, DAR to DOS, July 29, 1964, RG 59, Box 2691, POL 15-1 TANZAN, 1/1/64, NARA.
7. "Conferência de Imprensa do Ministro dos Negócios Estrangeiros Pronunciada a 7 de Agosto de 1964," Ministério dos Negócios Estrangeiros, Serviços de Informação, 278 PAA, AHD.
8. Newitt, *History of Mozambique*, 523.
9. Editorial, *Nationalist*, November 13, 1964, quoted in DAR to CRO, November 13, 1964, DO 213/30, PRO.
10. Robert Foulon, "George Ivan-Smith's Views on Mr. Babu and the Zambia-Tanganyika Railway," Lusaka to DOS, July 9, 1964, RG 59, Box 2689, POL 7 TANZAN, NARA; see also Monson, *Africa's Freedom Railway*.
11. William Leonhart, DAR to DOS, January 28, 1964; Stevenson, Tokyo to DOS, January 6, 1964—both in RG 59, Box 2687, POL TANGAN, 1/1/64, NARA; "Kawawa's Visit to Communist China," Hong Kong to DOS, November 29, 1965, RG 59, Box 2689, POL 7 TANZAN, NARA; Sarakikya interview, June 26, 2006.
12. Lusinde interview, November 7, 2006.
13. Boswell, DAR to DOS, July 24, 1964, RG 59, Box 2691, POL 15-1 TANZAN, 1/1/64, NARA.
14. William Leonhart, DAR to DOS, July 22, 1964; William Leonhart, DAR to DOS, July 23, 1964—both in RG 59, Box 2691, POL 15-1 TANZAN, 1/1/64, NARA.
15. "Preparativos de Subversão do Tanganica"; Circular, January 14, 1965—both in 32 PAA, Politica Interna Externa Republica Unificada do Tanganica Zanzibar, AHD.
16. William Leonhart, DAR to DOS, July 30, 1964, NSF/CF 100-3.59, LBJ. The following month, Kawawa traveled to Prague and Moscow to court foreign aid but was unimpressed with Soviet offers. Pratt, *Critical Phase in Tanzania*, 159.
17. Sarakikya interview, June 26, 2006.
18. Robert Gordon, DAR to DOS, October 10, 1964, RG 59, Box 2689, POL 7 TANZAN, 8/1/64, NARA.
19. William Leonhart, DAR to DOS, July 30, 1964, NSF/CF 100-3.59, LBJ.
20. Ibid.
21. Ibid.
22. Witte, *Assassination of Lumumba*; "The Congo," Policy Briefing Book for Secretary of State, December 1960, NSF/CF 86 File 1.3, LBJ.
23. P. A. Carter, DAR to R. de Burlet, CRO, August 1, 1964, DO 185/51.109, PRO.
24. W. Averell Harriman to Mr. Bell, "US-Israeli Coordination in URTZ Police Training," October 23, 1964, RG 59, Box 32, POL 2 TANGANYIKA ISRAEL, NARA; F. S. Miles, DAR, to Duncan Sandys, CRO, "Tanganyika: The Military Situation," April 15, 1964, FCO 141/14044.120, PRO.
25. William Leonhart, DAR to DOS, July 28, 1964, RG 59, Box 2690, POL 15 Government TANZAN, 7/1/64, NARA; Memorandum for Governor Williams meeting with Governor Harriman, October 6, 1964, RG 59, Box 32, POL 2 CHICOM-TANGANYIKA, NARA; Notice to Dr. António de Madeiros Patricio, Nações Unidas, September 24, 1964, 32 PAA, AHD; "Fornecimento de Armas À República

Unida do Tanganica e Zanzibar," September 23, 1964; CIA, "Tanzania Taking the Left Turn," May 21, 1965, NSF/CF 100.111, LBJ.

26. London to Ministro dos Negocios Estrangeiros, Lisbon, August 26, 1964, 1033 PAA, AHD.

27. "Report by Defence Adviser, United Republic of Tanganyika and Zanzibar," DO 213/160.1, PRO.

28. Sarakikya interview, June 26, 2006.

29. "Askari Waombwa Kuwa Watii, Waminifu, na Mashujaa," *Nchi Yetu*, August 1964, 11.

30. CIA, "Tanzania Taking the Left Turn," May 21, 1965, NSF/CF 100.111, LBJ.

31. DAR High Commission to CRO, "Tanganyika/Zanzibar Union," July 15, 1964, DO 185/51.99, PRO.

32. Thomas Hughes, Annex to "Significance of Chinese Communist Arms Aid to Tanganyika," August 4, 1964, RG 59, Box 32, AID 6 TANG—Communist Bloc Aid, NARA.

33. CRO to DAR High Commission, July 4, 1964, DO 185/51.96, PRO; CRO to DAR High Commission, July 3, 1964, DO 185/51.94A, PRO; William Leonhart, DAR to DOS, April 24, 1964, NSF/CF 100-4.104, LBJ.

34. William Leonhart, DAR to DOS, April 29, 1964, NSF/CF 100-4.88, LBJ.

35. William Attwood, Nairobi to DOS, April 25, 1964, NSF/CF 100-4.166, LBJ.

36. Bonn to Foreign Office, May 6, 1964, FO 371/176521, PRO. Kambona reinforced this view in a conversation with the British foreign secretary. "Record of Conversation between the Foreign Secretary and Mr. Oscar Kambona, Foreign Minister of Tanganyika," February 9, 1965, DO 213/114.7, PRO.

37. Lord Harlech to Foreign Office, May 28, 1964, FO 371/176521, PRO.

38. Lourenço Marques to DOS, "Oscar Kambona Interview," March 2, 1973, RG 59, Box 2618, POL 29 TANZAN, 1/1/70, NARA.

39. Millard to Foreign Office, May 29, 1964, FO 371/176521, PRO.

40. Memorandum of Conversation, "United Republic of Tanganyika and Zanzibar (URTZ)," July 15, 1964, RG 59, Box 2690, POL 15 Government TANZAN, NARA; P. A. Carter, DAR to Norman Aspin, CRO, July 11, 1964, FO 371/176521, PRO; Bonn to Mansfield, Foreign Office, October 29, 1964, FO 371/176521, PRO.

41. Millard to Foreign Office, May 29, 1964, FO 371/176521, PRO.

42. William Leonhart, DAR to DOS, January 26, 1965, NSF/CF 100-3.7, LBJ.

43. Taarifa ya Mkutano wa Halmashauri Kuu ya Taifa, March 3, 1965, 589: BMC/11/02/B, TNA.

44. DOS to DAR, August 4, 1964, NSF/CF 100-3.54, LBJ.

45. William Leonhart to DOS, September 1, 1964, RG 59, Box 2691, POL 15-1 TANZAN, 8/1/64, NARA.

46. DAR High Commission to CRO, "Military Equipment in Zanzibar," October 13, 1964, DO 185/51.143, PRO; J. Bourn to Mr. Dawson, October 13, 1964, DO 185/51.145, PRO.

47. James L. O'Sullivan to Wayne Fredericks, October 19, 1964, RG 59, Entry 5253 Box 31, POL 26 MOZ, 1964, NARA.

48. J. Bourn to Mr. Dawson, October 14, 1964, DO 185/51.147, PRO.

49. William Leonhart to DOS, October 12, 1964, NSF/CF 100-3.37, LBJ.

50. By 1962 Malawi's president, Hastings Kamuzu Banda, had befriended Portugal, recruiting spies embedded in the liberation movements on Portugal's behalf. Some Portuguese intelligence appears to be pretty unsound. One notice suggested that weapons shipped by dhow from Zanzibar were intended for a "putsch" against Nyerere organized by southern Makonde people in June or July 1964. This report could either represent deliberate misinformation or was a part of the ongoing political turmoil in Zanzibar. See Hastings Kamuzu Banda to Jose B. da Costa (Chagonga), April 25 and May 9, 1962; Jose Baltazar da Costa (Chagonga) to Hastings Kamuzu Banda, May 6, 1962; Norman Amed, Boletin de Informações July 2, 1964; Carta de "Gino"—all in 1033 PAA, AHD.

51. "Exército de Libertação: Recrutamento e Treino," August 5, 1964; Bastos to Consulado Geral de Portugal em Salisburia, August 11, 1964; Lt. Col. Fernando Sequeira, Salisbury, "Liberation Army: Recruiting and Training; A. Ivens-Ferraz de Freitas, Salisburia to Serviços de Centralização e Coordenação de Informações (SCCI) April 9, 1964; A. Ivens-Ferraz de Freitas, Salisburia to Serviços de Centralização e Coordenação de Informações (SCCI) April 9, 1964; S. M. A. Lindi, June 9, 1964; "Jornada de Angola," February 4, 1964, *Boletim de Informação* 6 (March 1964), p. 11—all in 1033 PAA, AHD.

52. Meagher, "Items for Inclusion in Briefing Memorandum for Mr. Ball," December 2, 1964, RG 59, Box 32, INF—INFORMATION ACTIVITIES (GEN), NARA. A Mozambique national spying for the Portuguese reported that the missionaries had little contact with the foreign soldiers in the training camps. See Johnny Tumbo, July 30, 1964, 1033 PAA, AHD. The letter may well have been a forgery intended to seed distrust and confusion along the Tanzanian border.

53. DAR High Commission to Ministry of Defence (Army), October 23, 1964, DO 185/51.148, PRO.

54. "Report No. 2 by Defence Adviser, Dar es Salaam, 1 October to December 31, 1964," attachment to B. G. Pugh to High Commissioner, DAR, March 8, 1965, DO 213/160.2, PRO.

55. "Report in Brief" Radio-Escuta, "Support" da União Sociética [*sic* Soviética], 1033 PAA, AHD; "Report No. 2 by Defence Adviser, Dar es Salaam, 1 October to 31 December 1964," DO 213/160, PRO.

56. Johnny Tumbo worked as a low-paid spy for Portugal; his letters of June 1, July 2, July 12, and July 24, 1964, can be found in 1033 PAA, AHD.

57. J. Bourn to Colonel Pugh, November 1, 1964, DO 185/51.149, PRO.

58. "Curso de Guerrilhas Livro II," 1033 PAA, AHD.

59. Lourenço Marques to DOS, "Oscar Kambona Interview," March 2, 1973, RG 59, Box 2618, POL 29 TANZAN, 1/1/70, NARA.

60. This enigmatic currency symbol is what appears in the facsimile of the mercenary's letter in an American report. "The Tanzanian Forgeries, November 1964," April 1965, NSF/CF 100, 7, LBJ. See also "Annex 'B'. The three forged letters as printed and translated in the 'Nationalist,'" DO 213/30, PRO.

61. See Hoare, *Congo Mercenary*, 75–81; see also Bunnenberg, *Der "Kongo-Müller."*

62. "Developments in AFC Countries during Your Absence," November 4, 1964, RG 59, Box 23, POL 2, 1964, NARA.

63. "Portuguese Military Build-Up," *Tanganyika Standard*, October 10, 1964, 1; "O Tanganica É Uma Base de Subversão E Porque somos um dos Vizinhos

Ameaçados," *Diario de Noticias*, December 30, 1964, 278 PAA, AHD; Ministério dos Negócios Estrangeiros, Transmissão Imediata de Noticias, November 12, 1964, SR 082, AHU.

64. "Lisbon Cry for 'Intervention' in East Africa," *Tanganyika Standard*, October 25, 1964, 1; "Mozambique Freedom Fighters 'Caught,'" *Tanganyika Standard*, October 12, 1964.

65. Pratt, *Critical Phase in Tanzania*, 145.

66. Lourenço Marques to DOS, "Oscar Kambona Interview," March 2, 1973, RG 59, Box 2618, POL 29 TANZAN, 1/1/70, NARA.

67. High Commissioner, DAR to CRO, December 3, 1964, DO 213/30, PRO; London to DOS, December 8, 1964, RG 59, Box 2689, POL 7 TANZAN, NARA.

68. Washington, DC, to Foreign Office, November 20, 1964, DO 213/30, PRO. Andrew Tibandebage said that Nyerere immediately suspected the letters were forged, but thought that perhaps "the Americans had something to do with some trick on Tanzania"; Tibandebage himself suspected the letters were "one of Kambona's tricks . . . to damage Nyerere in some way or other." Tibandebage interview.

69. UN to DOS, January 13, 1965, RG 59, Box 2688, POL 1 TANZAN, 1/1/64, NARA. Waldron-Ramsey was a young British Labour Party activist, raised in England by a West Indian father and Tanganyikan mother, who had taken Tanzanian citizenship and become an influential adviser and provocative speechwriter in the Tanzanian UN mission. Plimpton, UN to DOS, "Waldo E. Waldron-Ramsey, Secretary Legal Affairs and Research, Tanzanian UN Mission," February 4, 1965, RG 59, Box 2695, POL 17 TANZAN-US, 1/1/64, NARA.

70. William Leonhart to DOS, November 30, 1964, RG 59, Box 2695, POL 9 Intervention TANZAN-US, 11/16/64, NARA.

71. Thanks to James Brennan for this reference. Bittman, *Deception Game*, 80–85.

72. "Syracuse Research Corporation Celebrates 50 Years," Syracuse Research Corporation, February 15, 2007, archived online January 8, 2013, http://archive-com.com/page/1094800/2013-01-08/http://srcinc.com/news/article.aspx?id=265.

73. Marchetti and Marks, *CIA*, 164.

74. See, for example, Reed, *111 Days in Stanleyville*. David E. Reed was a "roving editor" for *Reader's Digest* who reported from various Third World locations; in May 1964 he had also interviewed Abdulrahman Babu, after which he met with Ambassador Leonhart in Dar es Salaam. William Leonhart, DAR to DOS, May 22, 1964, RG 59, Box 2688, POL 6 TANZAN, 1/1/64, NARA; "David Reed, 63, Editor for *Reader's Digest*," *Washington Times*, November 27, 1990. See also Roosevelt, *Countercoup*, and a series of Praeger publications: Vittachi, *Fall of Sukarno*; Hunter, *Sukarno and the Indonesian Coup*; Hunter, *Zanzibar*; and Schneider, *Communism in Guatemala*. See also Cribb, Review of *Sukarno and the Indonesian Coup*.

75. CRO Circular, "Alleged Western Plot against Tanzania," November 19, 1964, PREM 13/614.166, PRO. See also Andrew and Mitrokhin, *World Was Going Our Way*, 465–66. This account of the KGB archive given to the British by Mitrokhin, a Soviet defector, is compelling but somewhat dubious. Andrew was apparently hand-selected by the British government to study and summarize the Mitrokhin archive in two publications. He was given exclusive access to the still-classified archive, so other scholars have not been able independently to evaluate his presentation,

which he notes was thoroughly reviewed and edited by the British government before publication.

76. Marchetti and Marks, *CIA*, 163–65. In the 1950s, the US was willing to instigate the breakup of Indonesia in order to prevent a socialist government there. Westad, *Global Cold War*, 129–30.

77. On plausible deniability, see Karabell, *Architects of Intervention*, 40; and Bissell, *Reflections of a Cold Warrior*, 205–13; see also Fryxell, "Psywar by Forgery."

78. A close study of unclassified American documentation of this operation explained that the plan was "more than just an evacuation operation. [Gen. Paul DeWitt] Adams hoped to end the rebellion with it." Odom, "Dragon Operations," 14; see also Westad, *Global Cold War*, 142; Wagoner, *Dragon Rouge*, 67; Weissman, *American Foreign Policy*, 237–52; James L. O'Sullivan to Governor (G. Mennen) Williams, November 9, 1964, RG 59, Box 23, CWG- American Personnel and Stanleyville, NARA; and Wayne Fredericks and Joseph Palmer, Memorandum for Governor Harriman, "The Congo Problem—ACTION MEMORANDUM," RG 59, Box 23, Intelligence General Policy Congo, NARA.

79. James L. O'Sullivan to Governor Williams, "American Personnel in Stanleyville," November 9, 1964; Matthew Looram to Governor Williams, "American Personnel in Stanleyville," November 10, 1964—both in RG 59, Entry 5235, Box 31, POL 23-9, NARA.

80. Dean Rusk, DOS to Leopoldville, November 11, 1964, NSF/CF 83-1, Congo Cables (1 of 2).93, LBJ.

81. This interpretation would counter most interpretations of this incident, which suggests that gullible Tanzanians were taken in by clumsy forgeries that could not have been the work of a professional CIA agent. See Pratt, *Critical Phase in Tanzania*, 145. In my interpretation, the letters' apparent clumsiness may have been deliberate, thereby contributing to plausible deniability.

82. Minutes of Central Committee Meeting, November 11, 1964, 589: BMC/11/04/A.72 (also No. 73 Central Committee Meeting of November 13, 1964), TNA.

83. USARMA Leopoldville GDRC to RUEAHQ/DIA, November 15, 1964, NSF/CF 83-3.245, LBJ.

84. Leopoldville to RUEHCR/SECSTATE, November 14, 1964, NSF/CF 83-1.7, LBJ.

85. CIA, "Tanzanian Support for the Congo Rebels," April 7, 1965, NSF/CF 87-4.6, LBJ.

86. When this file was released at my request on January 18, 2004, it was numbered 32-A PAA and labeled (according to my notes) "Intervenção no Tanganica." James Brennan reports that these docments now appear in a file numbered 33 PAA, titled "Politica Externa e Interna do Tanganyika—Oscar Kambona, Ministro dos Negocios Estrangeiros do Tanganyika," and that 32-A PAA is labeled "Interferencia de Tanzania," declassified on January 22, 2004. In NARA, a file titled "Intervention" contains internal correspondence dealing with the forgeries, including several markers where documents have been removed for national security purposes. See RG 59, Box 2695, POL 9 Intervention TANZAN-US, 1/1/65, NARA; and Bjerk, "African Files in Portuguese Archives."

87. The Potuguese "as Missões" (Missions) seems to be code for the Portuguese secret service, PIDE. Ministério dos Negócios Estrangeiros, Circular, November 9, 1964, 32-A PAA [now in 33 PAA, see previous note], AHD.

88. An American embassy officer in Lisbon talked with a Portuguese foreign ministry officer, Soares de Oliveira, about the documents. Oliveira "smilingly asked if Embassy officer implying GOP [Government of Portugal] responsibility," and then blamed the Chinese. Anderson, Lisbon to DOS, November 21, 1964, DOS RG 59, Box 2695, POL 9 Intervention TANZAN-US, 1/1/65, NARA.

89. William Attwood, "Tanzania," Nairobi to DOS, November 20, 1964, RG 59, Box 2693, POL 23 TANZAN, 1/1/64, NARA; Washington High Commission to Foreign Office, November 23, 1964, DO 213/30, PRO; DAR High Commission to CRO, November 26, 1964, DO 213/30, PRO.

90. The United States took much effort to gauge the impact of the incident, instructing all its embassies in Africa to ask about local views on the incident. William Witman II, Lome to DOS, "Tanzanian 'Plot' Allegations against US," January 13, 1965; Robert A. Remole, Bamako to DOS, "Tanzanian 'Plot' Allegations against US," January 13, 1965; Claude G. Ross, Bangui to DOS, "Tanzanian 'Plot' Allegations against US," January 12, 1965—all in RG 59, Box 2695, POL 9 Intervention TANZAN-US, 1/1/65, NARA. Curtis Strong, "Further Evidence of Trouble within GURT," DAR to DOS, April 6, 1965; William Leonhart, DAR to DOS, December 16, 1964—both in RG 59, Box 2691, POL 15-1 TANZAN, 1/1/65, NARA. See also Governo Geral de Angola, SCCI to Gabinete dos Negócios Políticos no Ministerio do Ultramar, December 29, 1964, SR 082, AHU.

91. Lourenço Marques to DOS, "Oscar Kambona Interview," March 2, 1973, RG 59, Box 2618, POL 29 TANZAN, 1/1/70, NARA.

92. "Record of a Conversation between the Prime Minister and the Prime Minister of Malawi, Dr. Hastings Banda," December 11, 1964, PREM 13/614.122, PRO.

93. Grennan also carried an enigmatic handwritten letter from Kaunda to the prime minister saying he was not ready to "formalize" his thoughts. He wrote simply, "Dennis [Grennan] will explain to you that I am getting more and more encouragement from our mutual friend. What he promised he would do is precisely what he has done and we could not expect anything more at the moment from a man in his position." Memorandum of Conversation, February 25, 1965, PREM 13/614.115, PRO; Kenneth Kaunda to Harold Wilson, February 20, 1965, PREM 13/614.120, PRO.

94. See, for example, R. W. D. Fowler, CRO, to Malcolm MacDonald, Nairobi, March 17, 1965, PREM 13/614.111, PRO.

95. Chris Pappas, "Kambona in Difficulty," DAR to DOS, February 2, 1965, RG 59, Box 2691, POL 15-1 TANZAN, 1/1/65, NARA.

96. *Africa 1966* No. 10, attachment to J. A. Shepherd, CRO, to T. L. Richardson, Canadian High Commission, June 10, 1966, DO 213/103.90, PRO.

97. Tibandebage interview; William Leonhart to DOS, June 30, 1965, RG 59, Box 2695, POL TANZAN-US, 3/27/65, NARA.

98. Lyndon Johnson did not want to move before the American election on November 3 for fear that an embarrassment in Africa could undermine his chances. Wagoner, *Dragon Rouge*, 69; George Godley, Leopoldville to DOS, November 7,

1964, NSF/CF 83-1.28, LBJ; George Godley, Leopoldville to DOS, November 6, 1964, NSF/CF 83-1.26, LBJ.

99. George Godley, Leopoldville to DOS, October 27, 1964, NSF/CF 83-1.51, LBJ.

100. USSTRICOM to RUCOCR/CINCARSTRIKE, November 1, 1964, NSF/CF 83-3.235, LBJ; USSTRICOM to RUEHCR/SECSTATE, November 1, 1964, NSF/CF 83-3.247, LBJ; Bill Brubeck to McGeorge Bundy, "Stanleyville Hostage Problem," November 9, 1964, NSF/CF 83-3.260, LBJ; Samuel E. Belk to McGeorge Bundy, "The Congo," October 27, 1964, NSF/CF 83-3.266, LBJ; George Godley, Leopoldville to DOS, November 14, 1964, NSF/CF 83-1.6, LBJ; George Godley, Leopoldville to DOS, November 7, 1964, NSF/CF 83-1.24, LBJ.

101. George Godley, Leopoldville to DOS, November 11, 1964, NSF/CF 83-1.20, LBJ.

102. Wagoner, *Dragon Rouge*, 133.

103. Dean Rusk, Secretary of State to DAR, November 15, 1964, NSF/CF 100-3.25, LBJ; Lt. Col. W. H. Glasgow, "Operations Dragon Rouge and Dragon Noire," US Army, Europe, Operations Division, Historical Section, 1965, 15, accessed July 14, 2014, http://www.history.army.mil/documents/glasgow/glas-fm.htm.

104. USCINCEUR to RUFPAG/CINCUSAREUR, November 15, 1964, NSF/CF 83-3, No.232, LBJ.

105. Namikas, *Battleground Africa*, 205–6.

106. Reed, *111 Days in Stanleyville*, 182–83, 209–10; Hoare, *Congo Mercenary*, 103–35; Villafana, *Cold War in the Congo*, 71–97.

107. Dean Rusk, Secretary of State to DAR, November 17, 1964, NSF/CF 100, 3, 24, LBJ; "The Tanzanian Forgeries, November 1964," April 1965, NSF/CF 100, 7, LBJ.

108. Washington, DC, to Foreign Office, November 20, 1964, DO 213/30, PRO.

109. R. W. D. Fowler, DAR to CRO, November 23, 1964, DO 213/30, PRO; William Leonhart, DAR to DOS, November 26, 1964, NSF/CF 84-5.92, LBJ. See also Bittman, *Deception Game*, 84–86.

110. "Speech by Nyerere at 15 November Rally, Kijangwani Playing Fields," November 15, 1964, DO 213/30, PRO.

111. Washington, DC, to Foreign Office, November 20, 1964, DO 213/30, PRO.

112. R. W. D. Fowler to Malcolm Macleod, Nairobi, March 17, 1965, DO 213/245, PRO.

113. London to DOS, December 8, 1964; Jesse MacKnight to G. Mennen Williams, "Your Appointment with Oscar Kambona, Foreign Minister of Tanzania," December 17, 1964—both in RG 59, Box 2689, POL 7 TANZAN, NARA; Edward Mulcahy to G. Mennen Williams, November 12, 1964, RG 59, Box 32, POLITICAL AFFAIRS & REL TANG POL 2 Tanganyika US, NARA; R. H. Hobden, CRO, to K. E. Broadley, Washington, DC, December 11, 1964, DO 213/30, PRO; President Nyerere's Speech at Mass Rally, December 9, 1964, DO 213/30, PRO; "Mwalimu Buries That Plot," *Nationalist* (Dar es Salaam), December 10, 1964, 1.

114. George Loft to Wayne Fredericks, December 4, 1964, RG 59, Entry 5235, Box 31, REF 10-1, NARA; Memorandum of Conversation, "Portuguese Request to

HMG for Information on Mozambican Nationalist Preparations in Tanganyika," February 26, 1964, RG 59, Entry 5235, Box 31, POL-CF-Tanganyika, NARA.

115. G. Mennen Williams to W. Averell Harriman, "Cancellation of Ford Foundation Support to the Mozambique Institute: Action Memorandum," November 20, 1964; Matthew Looram to Wayne Fredericks, "Ford Foundation's Contributions to Mrs. Mondlane's Mozambique Institute," June 4, 1964; E. J. Beigel to William Blue, November 25, 1964—all in RG 59, Entry 5235, Box 31, REF 10-1, NARA.

116. "Conferência de Imprensa do Ministro dos Negócios Estrangeiros Pronunciada a 7 de Agosto de 1964," Ministério dos Negócios Estrangeiros, Serviços de Informação, 278 PAA, AHD; Memorandum of Conversation, NSF/CF 154, Portugal General, 10/19–11/31/62, JFK; Lisbon to DOS, May 20, 1961, NSF/CF 154, Portugal General 5/20–7/31/61, JFK.

117. William Leonhart, DAR to DOS, December 3, 1964, NSF/CF 100-3.22, LBJ.

118. "It's Up to West—Nyerere," *Tanganyika Standard*, November 16, 1964, 1.

119. Extract of conversation between Australian High Commissioner and Nyerere, November 26, 1964, DO 213/30, PRO.

120. Frank Carlucci, Zanzibar to DOS, December 21, 1964; Frank Carlucci, Zanzibar to DOS, December 29, 1964—both in RG 59, Box 2689, POL 7 TANZAN, 8/1/64, NARA.

121. Frank Carlucci, Zanzibar to DOS, December 22, 1964, RG 59, Box 1685, DEF 19 TANZAN, NARA.

122. "Statement Regarding Alleged USG Involvement In Plotting against the GURT," February 2, 1965, RG 59, Box 34, POL 2 Gordon-Carlucci Case, NARA.

123. Smith, *We Must Run*, 200.

124. "Statement by Robert C. F. Gordon," RG 59, Box 34, POL 2 Gordon-Carlucci Case, NARA.

125. Lusinde interview, June 30, 2013. US State Department diplomat Francis McNamara recalled an unnamed Tanzanian "well disposed toward the U.S." who said that the tape sounded "convincing," and that one of a pair of Israeli security agents who heard the tape also felt it to be genuine. It was McNamara's impression that Nyerere "was convinced that we were up to something, but did not wish to break with us." Francis Terry McNamara, interview for Foreign Affairs Oral History Project (FAOHP), Association for Diplomatic Studies and Training, 1989, accessed July 24, 2014, http://www.adst.org/OH%20TOCs/McNamara,%20Francis%20Terry.toc.pdf.

126. "Taarifa ya Mkutano wa Halmashauri Kuu ya Taifa," March 3, 1965, 589: BMC/11/02/B, TNA; William Leonhart, DAR to DOS, January 16, 1965, NSF/CF 100-3.14, LBJ; "Report to GDR Ministry of Foreign Affairs on TANU Annual Party Conference," March 10, 1965, DY IV A 2/20-954, SAPMO. Surprisingly, this seems to be the only mention of the Gordon-Carlucci expulsion in the East German records, and their names are not even mentioned by name in this report.

127. Donald Petterson, "A Brief Look at First Vice President Karume," Zanzibar to DOS, February 23, 1965, RG 59, Box 2691, POL 151-1 TANZAN, 1/1/65, NARA.

128. Carlucci interview. Carlucci acknowledged more recently that "beyond a doubt we were both wrong to double talk." Frank Carlucci, personal communication, April 17, 2009. In an FAOHP interview, Robert Gordon cited a letter from

Frank Carlucci in the 1980s in which Carlucci mentioned a conversation with a Soviet official who told him that they had doctored the recordings. Carlucci's account here is consistent with a contemporary Portuguese note on the incident. Robert C. F. Gordon, interview for Foreign Affairs Oral History Project (FAOHP), Association for Diplomatic Studies and Training, 1989, July 24, 2014, http://www.adst.org/OH%20TOCs/Gordon,%20Robert%20C.F.toc.pdf. See Washington to Ministerio dos Negócios Estrageiros, February 19, 1965, 31 PAA, AHD.

129. William Leonhart, DAR to DOS, January 16, 1965, NSF/CF 100-3.13, LBJ; Westad, *Global Cold War*, 143.

130. William Leonhart, DAR to DOS, January 15, 1965, NSF/CF 100-3.18, LBJ.

131. Julius Nyerere to Lyndon Johnson, January 28, 1965, NSF/SHSC 52-2.68, LBJ.

132. Smith, *We Must Run*, 199.

133. My presentation here argues against Okwudiba Nnoli's view that the expulsion of Carlucci and Gordon was imprudent. See Nnoli, *Self-Reliance and Foreign Policy*, 162–63.

134. F. S. Miles, DAR, to Norman Aspin, CRO, February 19, 1965, DO 213/114.15, PRO.

135. Lusinde interview, July 6, 2010; William Leonhart, DAR to DOS, January 15, 1965, NSF/CF 100-3.18, LBJ; Memorandum of Conversation, "Makame's View of Zanzibar Revolution and U.S.-Tanzania Relations," March 23, 1965, RG 59, Box 2694, POL 23-9 TANZAN, 1/1/64, NARA.

136. Chris Pappas, "Swai Discusses the Tanzania Political and Economic Scene," DAR to DOS, July 6, 1965, RG 59, Box 2688, POL 1 TANZAN, 1/1/64, NARA; Issa interview; Lusinde interview, July 6, 2010. In March 1965 TANU publicized its suspicions that Gordon and Carlucci were CIA agents in local newspapers. Curtis Strong, DAR to DOS, March 15, 1965, RG 59, Box 2689, POL 9 Intervention TANZAN 1/1/64, NARA.

137. Frank Carlucci to DOS, August 27, 1964, RG 59, Box 2691, POL 15-1 TANZAN, 8/1/64, NARA.

138. Gordon, FAOHP interview. See also Jones, "Working with the CIA."

139. Wolf, *Man without a Face*, 285–86; Petterson, *Revolution in Zanzibar*, 196–98.

140. Frank Carlucci, Zanzibar to DOS, June 3, 1964, RG 59, Box 2691, POL 15-1 TANZAN, NARA. Jumbe went on to become head of intelligence in Zanzibar, and took over the presidency of the island government after Karume was assassinated in 1972.

141. "Intelligence Update," October 20, 1964, MfS/HVA/203, p. 7, BStU.

142. Dean Rusk, DOS to William Leonhart, DAR, January 17, 1965, NSF/CF 100-3.11, LBJ; Smith, *We Must Run*, 200.

143. Wise and Ross, *Invisible Government*, 129–35; see also Schlesinger, *Thousand Days*, 427–28; Kaufman, "Trouble in the Golden Triangle"; and William Joseph Sebald Diary Extracts, HI.

144. Memorandum for Mr. McGeorge Bundy, "Presidential Meeting with US Ambassadors to East Africa," February 13, 1965, NSF/CF 91-1.133, LBJ.

145. B.G.D., DAR, to Col. Pugh, June 24, 1964, DO 185/51.88, PRO; see also T. L. Crosthwait, DAR, to L. B. Walsh Atkins, CRO, June 18, 1964, DO 185/51.87, PRO.

146. See Speller, "African Cuba?," 293–97.

147. P. A. Carter to R. de Burlet, CRO, August 1, 1964, DO 185/51.109, PRO; CRO to Zanzibar, June 17, 1964, DO 185/51.86, PRO; T. L. Crosthwait, DAR, to L. B. Walsh Atkins, CRO, June 9, 1964, DO 185/51, PRO.

148. E. L. Dickinson, CRO, to D. F. le Breton, High Commission, Zanzibar, April 21, 1964, DO 185/64.15A, PRO; T. L. Crosthwait, DAR, to T. D. O'Leary, CRO, June 29, 1964, DO 185/51, PRO; Joint Staff Intelligence, HQ Middle East Command, British Forces Office 69, "Zanzibar," July 9, 1964, DO 185/51.98A, PRO.

149. DAR High Commission to CRO, June 14, 1964, DO 185/51.72, PRO.

150. "Financial Times Suggests Invasion," June 6, 1964, DO 185/51.89, PRO.

151. F.O.M.E. to DAR High Commission, June 28, 1964, DO 185/51.90, PRO; CRO to DAR High Commission, July 4, 1964, DO 185/51.94, PRO.

152. P. A. Carter to R. de Burlet, CRO, August 1, 1964, DO 185/51.109, PRO.

153. J. Bourn, B.L.F.K. Liaison Conference, Zanzibar and Pemba, September 23, 1964, DO 185/51.139, PRO.

154. R. W. D. Fowler, DAR, to L. B. Walsh Atkins, CRO, January 14, 1965, DO 185/51.152, PRO. See also Speller, "African Cuba?," 297.

155. Wise and Ross, *Invisible Government*, 10. See also Trest and Dodd, *Wings of Denial*, 65; and Ruiz, *Diario de una Traición*.

156. The reference to mercenary activities and the testimony of Cosme's wife come from Dean Rusk, DOS, to William Leonhart, DAR, January 17, 1965, NSF/CF 100-3.11, LBJ. Details of Cosme's arrest in Tanzania are given in Beruvides, *Cuba, Anuario Histórico, 1965*, 1. The Americans were funding numerous Cuban pilots working with mercenary operations in the Congo. See also William Brubeck, Memorandum for the President, "American Pilots in Congo," June 20, 1964, NSF/CF 81-1, Congo vol. 1, 11/63-6/64.202, LBJ.

157. Joseph Brown, "Havana Daydreamin,'" *South Beach Magazine*, May 17, 1996, http://www.southbeach-usa.com/havana.htm.

158. Dean Rusk, DOS, to William Leonhart, DAR, January 17, 1965, NSF/CF 100-3.11, LBJ.

159. "Memorandum for the Minister: Zanzibar," May 4, 1964, RG 25 8928-20-TAN-1-3-ZAN pt. 1, LAC.

160. "Zanzibar Information—No. 35," August 22, 1964, DO 185/51.120, PRO.

161. "Intelligence Update," June 26, 1964, MfS/HVA/206, BStU.

162. William Leonhart, DAR to DOS, September 17, 1964; William Leonhart, DAR to DOS, September 12, 1964; William Leonhart, DAR to DOS, May 17, 1964—all in RG 59, Box 2694, POL 29, Arrests, Detention, TANZAN, NARA.

163. This coincides with the indefinite suspension of a British plan, code named "Giralda," for a unilateral invasion using only British troops. Speller, "African Cuba?," 295–97.

164. Frank Carlucci, Zanzibar to DOS, October 29, 1964; Frank Carlucci, Zanzibar to DOS, October 30, 1964—both in RG 59, Box 2694, POL 29 Arrests, Detention, TANZAN, NARA.

165. Carlucci betrayed some concern for what these interrogations might reveal, noting, "While we can be virtually certain Commies trying to implicate both Americans and British in 'counter revolutionary' plot we have no evidence Karume accepts these stories." Frank Carlucci, Zanzibar to DOS, November 6, 1964; and Frank Carlucci, Zanzibar to DOS, November 2, 1964—both in RG 59, Box 2694,

POL 29 Arrests, Detention, TANZAN, 1/1/64, NARA; and Frank Carlucci, Zanzibar to DOS, October 28, 1964; and Frank Carlucci, "Released Political Prisoner Tells of Detention," Zanzibar to DOS, December 22, 1964—both in RG 59, Box 2694, POL 29 TANZAN 1/1/64, NARA.

166. Attwood, *The Reds and the Blacks*, 189.

167. Wendell Coote, London to DOS, October 9, 1964, RG 59, Box 2694, POL 30-2 TANZAN, 1/1/64, NARA.

168. Philip Kaiser, "Zanzibar: Sultan's Brother Seeks U.S. Support," London to DOS, November 9, 1964, RG 59, Box 2694, POL 30-2 TANZAN, 1/1/64, NARA.

169. William Leonhart, DAR, to Secretary of State, November 9, 1964; and Frank Carlucci, Zanzibar to DOS, November 10, 1964—both in RG 59, Box 2694, POL 29 Arrests, Detention, TANZAN, 1/1/64, NARA.

170. Frank Carlucci, Zanzibar to DOS, November 10, 1964, RG 59, Box 2689, POL 9 Intervention TANZAN, 1/1/64, NARA.

171. "News received from radio Zanzibar on Sunday 15.11.64 at 1400 hrs.," DO 185/64, PRO. The leaders of the organization were listed as Mohamed Salum Barwani, Amour Zahor, Mohamed Hamoud Barwani, Saidi Dahoma Kombanyongo, Hamza Mohamed, Ali Awadh, Idi Juma Fumu, Abdulrehman Haid Malish, Nassor Mansour Mohamed, Awadh Salim, Abdulla Omar, Said Ali Humud, Mussa Lashoka, and Ali Ahmed Riyami. A.C.D.S. MacRae to Mr. Greatorex, "Executions in Zanzibar," November 19, 1964, DO 185/64, PRO. Thabit Kombo recalls the name of the organization as "People's Fighters Union," and he claimed they were organized by Amour Zahor of Kajificheni in Unguja. Kombo, *Masiumulizi*, 154.

172. Frank Carlucci, Zanzibar to DOS, November 15, 1964, RG 59, Box 2694, POL 29 Arrests, Detention, TANZAN, 1/1/64, NARA; Frank Carlucci, "GOZ Statement Regarding Sentencing of Accused Revolutionaries," Zanzibar to DOS, November 21, 1964, RG 59, Box 2694, POL 23-9 TANZAN, 1/1/64, NARA.

173. Donald Bergus, "Zanzibari 'Arab' Requests US Assistance for Planned Revolt," Cairo to DOS, January 9, 1965, RG 59, Box 2693, POL 23 TANZAN, 12/10/64, NARA.

174. "O Tanganica É Uma Base de Subversão E Porque somos um dos Vizinhos Ameaçados," Diario de Noticias, December 30, 1964, 278 PAA, AHD; SCCI Boletim de Difusão de Informações, October 10, 1964, SR 082 Tanzania 1964/NOV/20–1965/JAN/13 H.2.26 MU/GM/GNP/082/Pt.1, AHU.

175. Zanzibar Liberation Front, "Zanzibar: A Lesson to Freedom Loving Peoples," RG 59, Box 2693, POL 23 TANZAN, 12/1964, NARA.

176. Zanzibar Liberation Movement, "Zanzibar and Our Conscience," November 9, 1964, RG 59, Box 2693, POL 23 TANZAN, 12/1964, NARA.

177. "Subversion Leaflet in London," *Sunday News* (Dar es Salaam), November 15, 1964, cited in R. W. D. Fowler, DAR to CRO, November 15, 1964, DO 213/30.45, PRO.

178. Donald Petterson, Zanzibar to DOS, January 17, 1965, NSF/CF 100-4.117, LBJ.

179. Gasiorowski and Byrne, *Mohammad Mosaddeq*; Schlesinger and Kinzer, *Bitter Fruit*; Roosa, *Pretext for Mass Murder*.

180. Bomani interview.

181. Westad, *Global Cold War*, 130.

Conclusion

Epigraph. "The Nyerere Style," *Tanzanian Affairs*, January 1, 2012.

1. The new constitutional proposal is an ongoing topic in the news; see, for example, Sylivester Domasa, "3-Tier Govt Will Not Undo the Union, Says Warioba," *Guardian* (Dar es Salaam), February 13, 2014.

2. Burgess, *Race, Revolution and the Struggle*, 290–311; Jjuuko and Muriuki, *Federation within Federation*, 10–14, 48–66; Rawlence, "Briefing"; Cameron, "Zanzibar's Turbulent Transition"; Matheson, "Maridhiano"; "Zanzibar Elections," *Tanzanian Affairs* 98, January 1, 2011, http://www.tzaffairs.org/2011/01/zanzibar-elections/.

3. Uamshozanzibar, "Msimamo wa Jumuiya na Taasisi za Kiislamu Zanzibar Juu ya Mchakato wa Katiba," *Uamsho Zanzibar*, June 24, 2012, http://uamshozanzibar.wordpress.com/2012/06/24/msimamo-wa-jumuiya-na-taasisi-za-kiislamu-zanzibar-juu-ya-mchakato-wa-katiba/#more-219. See also "TANGANYIKA WATUWACHIEE TUPUMUWEEEEEEE," YouTube video, posted by Bin Seif, May 16, 2012, http://www.youtube.com/watch?v=q1Ndo_d-CqU; "UBAYA WA DUBWANA MUUNGANO—UAMSHO 'ALABAMA,'" YouTube video, posted by Bin Seif, April 27, 2012, http://www.youtube.com/watch?v=lA_PofmofqY; "MUHADHARA LUMUMBA 26 April 2012—UAMSHO '1,'" YouTube video, posted by Bin Seif, May 15, 2012, http://www.youtube.com/watch?v=6uHITwcG55E; and Fouéré, "Zanzibar Independent in 2015?," 1–4.

4. An insightful undergraduate honors thesis on this topic now circulates on websites debating Zanzibari politics. Daly, "Our Mother Is Afro-Shirazi." See also Myers, "Narrative Representations of Revolutionary Zanzibar."

5. Kombo, *Masimulizi*, 139.

6. Ghassany, *Kwaheri Ukoloni*, 214. Interestingly, I have heard similarly accusatory rumors that suggest Nyerere was in fact Tutsi, with the related implication that he sought to oppress common people in Tanzania like the Tutsi nobility traditionally had done in Rwanda.

7. There are a number of recent works by people questioning the hagiographic clichés surrounding Nyerere. Most of them portray Nyerere as a repressive leader who had a secret personal agenda. The most credible of these works, despite its distortions, speculations, and erasures, is Mwijage, *Julius Nyerere*.

8. Jumbe, *Partner-Ship*, 23–32.

9. Babu, "1964 Revolution."

10. DAR to DOS, April 29, 1964, NSF/CF 100-4.88, LBJ.

11. "President Nyerere's New Year Message," *Nationalist*, January 2, 1965, 1.

12. "Prospects for East African Federation," July 1963, DO 168/81, PRO; Mutesa, *Desecration of My Kingdom*; Brennan, "Lowering the Sultan's Flag."

13. Nyerere, *Freedom and Unity*, 85, 253.

14. Mdundo, *Utenzi*, 120.

15. Isaria Kimambo, "Utangulizi," 1.

16. Wilson, *US Foreign Policy and Revolution*, 2, 8–9.

17. Quoted in Wilson, *US Foreign Policy and Revolution*, 140.

18. Wilson has reaffirmed this thesis in an updated account of Zanzibari politics, in *Threat of Liberation*.

19. Shivji, *Pan-Africanism or Pragmatism?*; Shivji, *Where Is Uhuru?*, 79–92.

20. This argument was initiated by Attorney General Wolfgang Dourado, and elaborated by Jumbe in *The Partner-ship*. See Amizade, *Race, Nation*, 204.

21. Schatzberg, *Political Legitimacy in Middle Africa*.

22. Mdundo, *Utenzi*, 13.

23. Shetler, *Imagining Serengeti*.

24. See Bayart, *State in Africa*, 108–10.

25. Agnew and Corbridge, *Mastering Space*, 13–19, 80–95.

26. Wilson, *US Foreign Policy and Revolution*, 2.

27. This is an ongoing topic in the news, for example: Sylivester Domasa, "3-Tier Govt Will not Undo the Union, Says Warioba," *Guardian* (Dar es Salaam), February 13, 2014.

28. Othman, "Tanzania: Beyond Sectarian Interests." Othman's essay was apparently originally published in 1993 by the Danish Centre for Development Research.

29. Gramsci, *Gramsci Reader*, 164–85, 196–99, 422–24.

30. Feierman, *Peasant Intellectuals*, 26; see also Mouffe, *Gramsci and Marxist Theory*; Laclau and Mouffe, *Hegemony and Socialist Strategy*, and Mudimbe, "Review."

31. Nyerere, introduction to *Freedom and Socialism*.

32. Foucault, "About the Beginning," 204.

33. Foucault, "Subject and Power," 794.

34. Hanson, *Landed Obligation*, 17. T. C. McCaskie came to a similar conclusion in regard to the Asante kingdom of Ghana: "The state's ability to coerce society ultimately depended upon society being structurally complicit in, or consenting to, its subjection to the state's interventions." McCaskie, *State and Society*, 86.

35. Shibutani, *Improvised News*, 129–62.

36. Derrida's perspective builds on Carl Schmitt's idea of political leadership as the power to judge the exception. Schmitt, *Political Theology*. See also Derrida, "Force of Law"; Bates, "Crisis between the Wars"; and Sokoloff, "Between Justice and Legality."

37. Nyerere, *Freedom and Unity*, 267–69.

38. Foucault, "Subject and Power," 790–91.

39. See Schmitt, *Political Theology*.

40. Zambia, closely aligned politically and ideologically with Tanzania, provides a comparable case of a country with minimal potential for internal conflict that maintained a peaceful and stable postcolonial history.

41. Brennan, "Short History of Political Opposition," 269.

42. Unrecorded conversation with Peter Kisumo, July 13, 2013.

43. Kuhenga, *CCM*.

44. Taylor, *Sacrifice as Terror*.

45. Samoff, *Tanzania*; Brennan, *Taifa*; Ivaska, *Cultured States*.

46. Ermarth, "Agency in the Discursive Condition," 51–58.

47. Shivji, *Where Is Uhuru?*, 17.

48. Aseka, *Transformational Leadership in East Africa*, 1, 18, 229.

49. Lindberg, *Democracy and Elections in Africa*. Lindberg's view echoes those of Ottaway, in "Democratization in Collapsed States," and Chua, in "Markets, Democracy, and Ethnicity."

50. Kelly and Kaplan, "Legal Fictions after Empire," 169–95.

51. Walker, *Inside/Outside*, 154–55.

52. See Schneider, *Government of Development*.

Bibliography

Interviews

My interviews are being deposited on DVD at the Mwalimu Nyerere Foundation in Dar es Salaam, with the exception of those with Frank Carlucci, Robert Houle, Peter Kisumo (July 13, 2013), Patrick Kunambi, Benjamin Mandare, Saada Meffert, David Msuguri, and Abbas Sykes.

Ali, Ali Yusuf. July 10, 2013, Zanzibar, Tanzania.
Barongo, Edward. June 22, 2006, Dar es Salaam, Tanzania.
Bomani, Mark. June 19, 2013, Dar es Salaam, Tanzania.
Budodi, Tito. April 14, 2006, Mwanza, Tanzania.
Butiku, Joseph. November 4, 2006, Dar es Salaam, Tanzania.
Carlucci, Frank. November 20, 2005, Washington, DC, USA.
Forodhani, Mwanabibi. August 7, 2006, Songea, Tanzania.
Gama, Lawrence. August 11, 2006, Songea, Tanzania.
Houle, Robert. June 18, 2004, Ossining, New York, USA.
Ihunyo, Marwa. April 17, 2006, Busegwe (Musoma), Tanzania.
Irenge, James. August 20, 2003, April 17, 2006, Musoma, Tanzania.
Issa, Ali Sultan. August 23, 2006, Zanzibar, Tanzania.
Jembe, Al Hajj Abdallah Masudi. September 30, 2006, Bagamoyo, Tanzania.
Kafiti, William. April 14, 2006, Mwanza, Tanzania.
Kahatano, Rhoda. August 16, 2006, Bunju (Dar es Salaam), Tanzania.
Kamba, Hadija. August 1, 2006, Dar es Salaam, Tanzania.
Kapilima, Cassian. August 29, 2006, Dar es Salaam, Tanzania.
Karago, Al Hajj Tawaqal. September 19, 2006, Mayange-Matendo (Kigoma), Tanzania.
Karume, Fatma. August 24, 2006, Zanzibar, Tanzania.
Kashangaki, Desire. May 19, 2006, Karagwe, Tanzania.
Kawawa, Rashid. August 9, 2006, September 5, 2006, November 10, 2006, Songea and Tegeta, Tanzania.
Kazi, Fabian Shawa. August 9, 2006, Litowa Village (Songea), Tanzania.
Keen, John. May 3, 2006, Nairobi, Kenya.
Kibuana, Jacob John George (Tanzanian Foreign Legion). July 28, 2006. Dar es Salaam.
Kisumo, Peter. June 12, 2006, September 7, 2006, July 13 and 14, 2013, Moshi and Dar es Salaam, Tanzania.
Kunambi, George Patrick. August 21, 2004, Dar es Salaam.
Kyaruzi, Vedastus. May 21, 2006, Bukoba, Tanzania.

Lubala, Sylvester (Tanzanian Foreign Legion). July 28, 2006, Dar es Salaam, Tanzania.
Lusinde, Job. November 7, 2006, July 6, 2010, June 30, 2013, Dodoma, Tanzania.
Makbel, Al Hajj Mohamed Omar. November 8, 2006, Dodoma, Tanzania.
Makwaia, David Kidaha. April 29, 2006, Moshi, Tanzania.
Malecela, John. July 3, 2013, Dodoma, Tanzania.
Mandare, Benjamin Solomon. August 1, 2004, Dar es Salaam, Tanzania.
Mang'ombe, Ali Jaibu. August 8, 2006, Songea, Tanzania.
Marealle, Thomas. June 8, 2006, Moshi, Tanzania.
Maryogo, Esrom. June 1 and 6, 2006, Bweri Village (Musoma), Tanzania.
Matito, Simba Saidi. August 15, 2006, Morogoro, Tanzania.
Mbarika, Juma. August 21, 2006, Dar es Salaam, Tanzania.
Mbita, Hashim. November 2, 2006, December 9, 2006, Dar es Salaam, Tanzania.
Meffert, Saada. July 9, 2013, Zanzibar, Tanzania.
Mhagama, Geoffrey. August 10, 2006, Songea, Tanzania.
Mhunda, Joseph. May 30, 2006, Butiama (Musoma), Tanzania.
Milando, Mbuta. June 14 and 15, 2006. Dar es Salaam, Tanzania.
Millinga, John. August 11, 2006, Peramiho (Songea), Tanzania.
Mogella, Odilo Blasi. August 13, 2006, Morogoro, Tanzania.
Mohamed, Suleiman Ali. July 9, 2013, Zanzibar, Tanzania.
Mpili, Masudi. September 30, 2006, Bagamoyo, Tanzania.
Msekwa, Pius. June 19, 2013, Dar es Salaam, Tanzania.
Msuguri, David. August 19, 2003, Butiama, Tanzania.
Mtei, Edwin Isaac Mbiliyewi. September 9, 2006, June 26, 2013, Tengeru (Arusha), Tanzania.
Mwakawago, Daudi. September 26, 2006, Dar es Salaam, Tanzania.
Mwarabu, Asha Nyoni. August 8, 2006, Songea, Tanzania.
Mwijage, Ludovick Simon. July 21, 2013, Holstebro, Denmark.
Ngaiza, Christopher. May 22, 2006, Kamachumu (Bukoba), Tanzania.
Ngombale-Mwiru, Kingunge. July 12, 2013, Dar es Salaam, Tanzania.
Nhigula, George. August 31, 2006, Dar es Salaam, Tanzania.
Njau, Paul. April 29, 2006, Moshi, Tanzania.
Nyamwaga, Jack. September 27, 2006, Dar es Salaam, Tanzania.
Nyerere, Emil Magige. June 3, 2006, Butiama (Musoma), Tanzania.
Nyerere, Jacton. May 31, 2006, Butiama (Musoma), Tanzania.
Nyerere, Madaraka. June 3, 2006, Musoma, Tanzania.
Nyerere, Makongoro. April 3, 2006, Msasani (Dar es Salaam), Tanzania.
Nyerere, Maria. April 11, 2006, Butiama (Musoma), Tanzania.
Obote, Miria. May 24, 2006, Kampala, Uganda.
Odaka, Sam. May 27, 2006, Kampala, Uganda.
Oneko, Richard Ramogi Achieng. May 11, 2006, Kunya Village (Kisumu-Oyoma), Kenya.
Pandu, Abdulla Hussein. August 23, 2006, Dunga Village (Zanzibar), Tanzania.
Rupia, Paul. August 2, 2006, Dar es Salaam, Tanzania.
Salim, Hamid (Tanzanian Foreign Legion). July 28, 2006, Dar es Salaam, Tanzania.
Salim, Salim Said. July 9, 2013, Zanzibar, Tanzania.
Sarakikya, Mirisho. June 26, 2006, June 10, 2013, Arusha, Tanzania.

Selemani, Omari. November 7, 2006, Dodoma, Tanzania.
Shija, Gregory (Tanzanian Foreign Legion). July 28, 2006. Dar es Salaam, Tanzania.
Sigamba, Pascal (Tanzanian Foreign Legion). July 28, 2006, Dar es Salaam, Tanzania.
Siyovelwa, Peter. October 18, 2006, Iringa, Tanzania.
Soko, Joaquim Menas. August 9, 2006, Litowa Village (Songea), Tanzania.
Songambele, Mustafa. August 8, 2006, Songea, Tanzania.
Suwedi, Hadija. August 15, 2006, Morogoro, Tanzania.
Sykes, Abbas. July 29, 2006, December 13, 2006, Dar es Salaam, Tanzania.
Taratibu, Haruna. November 8, 2006, Dodoma, Tanzania.
Tibandebage, Andrew. May 19, 2006, Karagwe, Tanzania.

Archival Sources

Canada

Library and Archives Canada, Ottawa (LAC)

Germany (with assistance of Toni Weis)

Stasi Records Office, Berlin (BStU)
Stiftung Archiv der Parteien und Massenorganisationen der Deutschen Demokratischen Republik, Bundesarchiv, Berlin (SAPMO)

Portugal

Arquivo Histórico Diplomático, Lisbon (AHD)
Arquivo Histórico Ultramarino, Lisbon (AHU)

Tanzania

Chama cha Mapinduzi Library, Dodoma
East Africana Collection, University of Dar es Salaam
Mwalimu Nyerere Foundation, Dar es Salaam (MNF)
National Archives, Dar es Salaam (TNA)

United Kingdom

Borthwick Institute of Historical Research, York (BI)
Edinburgh University Archives, Edinburgh (EUA)

Public Record Office, National Archives, London (PRO)
Rhodes House, Oxford (RH)

United States

John F. Kennedy Library, Boston, MA (JFK)
Lyndon B. Johnson Library, Austin, TX (LBJ)
Hoover Institution and Russian Government Archive (with assistance of Ron Basich), Stanford University, Stanford, CA (HI)
National Archives and Records Administration, College Park, MD (NARA)

Published Sources

Abrahams, Ray G. *The Political Organization of Unyamwezi*. Cambridge: Cambridge University Press, 1967.
Achebe, Chinua. "An Image of Africa: Racism in Conrad's 'Heart of Darkness.'" *Massachussetts Review* 18 (1977): 782–94. Reprinted in *Heart of Darkness, an Authoritative Text, Background and Sources Criticism*, edited by Robert Kimbrough, 251–61. London: W. W. Norton, 1988.
Agnew, John, and Stuart Corbridge. *Mastering Space: Hegemony, Territory, and International Political Economy*. London: Routledge, 1995.
Aguilar, Mario, ed. *The Politics of Age and Gerontocracy in Africa*. Trenton, NJ: Africa World Press, 1998.
Ahlman, Jeffrey S. "A New Type of Citizen: Youth, Gender, and Generation in the Ghanaian Builders Brigade." *Journal of African History* 53, no. 2 (2012): 87–105.
Allman, Jean. "Phantoms of the Archive: Kwame Nkrumah, a Nazi Pilot Named Hanna, and the Contingencies of Postcolonial History-Writing." *American Historical Review* 118, no. 1 (2013): 104–29.
———. "The Youngmen and the Porcupine: Class, Nationalism and Asante's Struggle for Self- Determination, 1954–57." *Journal of African History* 31, no. 2 (1990): 263–79.
Allport, Gordon, and Leo Postman. *The Psychology of Rumor*. New York: Holt, 1947.
Almagor, Uri. "Charisma Fatigue in an East African Generation-Set System." *American Ethnologist* 10, no. 4 (1983): 635–49.
Aminzade, Ronald. *Race, Nation, and Citizenship in Postcolonial Africa: The Case of Tanzania*. New York: Cambridge University Press, 2013.
Anderson, Benedict. *Imagined Communities: Reflections on the Origin and Spread of Nationalism*. London: Verso, 1983.
Anderson, David. *Histories of the Hanged: Britain's Dirty War in Kenya and the End of Empire*. New York: W. W. Norton, 2005.
Anderson, Jon Lee. "State of Terror." *New Yorker*, July 1, 2013.
Andrew, Christopher, and Vasili Mitrokhin. *The World Was Going Our Way: The KGB and the Battle for the Third World*. New York: Basic Books, 2005.

Anglin, Douglas G. *Zambian Crisis Behaviour: Confronting Rhodesia's Unilateral Declaration of Independence, 1965–1966.* Montreal: McGill-Queen's University Press, 1994.
Aseka, Eric Masinde. *Transformational Leadership in East Africa: Politics, Ideology and Community.* Kampala: Fountain Publishers, 2005.
Askew, Kelly M. *Performing the Nation: Swahili Music and Cultural Politics in Tanzania.* Chicago: University of Chicago Press, 2002.
Attwood, William. *The Reds and the Blacks: A Personal Adventure.* New York: Harper and Row, 1967.
Babu, Abdulrahman. "The 1964 Revolution: Lumpen or Vanguard." In *Zanzibar under Colonial Rule,* edited by Abdul Sheriff and Ed Ferguson, 220–47. Athens: Ohio University Press, 1991.
Bagehot, Walter. *The English Constitution.* London: Oxford University Press, 1928.
Bah, Abu Bakarr. "State Decay: A Conceptual Frame of Failing and Failed States in West Africa." *International Journal of Politics, Culture, and Society* 25, nos. 1–3 (2012): 71–89.
Barber, James. *South Africa in the Twentieth Century.* Malden, MA: Blackwell, 1999.
Baregu, M. L. "Perception of Threat and Conception of Defence before the Mutiny." In *Tanganyika Rifles Mutiny January 1964,* edited by Tanzania People's Defence Forces, 35–69. Dar es Salaam: Tanzania People's Defence Forces, 1993.
Barongo, Edward. *Mkiki Mkiki wa Siasa.* Nairobi: East African Literature Bureau, 1966.
Barth, Fredrik, ed. *Ethnic Groups and Boundaries: The Social Organization of Culture Difference.* 1969. Reprint, Long Grove, IL: Waveland Press, 1998.
Bates, David. "Crisis between the Wars: Derrida and the Origins of Undecidability." *Representations* 90 (2005): 1–27.
Bates, Margaret L. "Tanganyika." In *African One Party States,* edited by Gwendolen M. Carter, 395–483. Ithaca, NY: Cornell University Press, 1962.
Bauer, Gretchen, and Scott D. Taylor. *Politics in Southern Africa: State and Society in Transition.* Boulder, CO: Lynne Rienner, 2005.
Baxter, P. T., and U. Almagor, eds. *Age, Generation, and Time: Some Features of East African Age Organizations.* London: Hurst, 1978.
Bayart, Jean-François. *The State in Africa: The Politics of the Belly.* Cambridge: Polity Press, 2009.
Bender, Matthew V. "Being 'Chagga': Natural Resources, Political Activism, and Identity on Kilimanjaro." *Journal of African History* 54 (2013): 199–220.
Berman, Bruce, and John Lonsdale. "Custom, Modernity, and the Search for *Kihooto*: Kenyatta, Malinowski and the Making of *Facing Mount Kenya.*" In *Ordering Africa: Anthropology, European Imperialism, and the Politics of Knowledge,* edited by Hellen Tiley, 173–98. Manchester: Manchester University Press, 2007.
Berman, Bruce, and John Lonsdale. *Unhappy Valley: Conflict in Kenya and Africa.* Bk. 2, *Violence and Ethnicity.* Athens: Ohio University Press, 1992.
Berntsen, John L. "The Maasai and Their Neighbors: Variables of Interaction." *African Economic History* 2 (1976): 1–11.
Bertz, Ned. "Educating the Nation: Race and Nationalism in Tanzanian Schools." In *Making Nations, Creating Strangers: States and Citizenship in Africa,* edited

by Sara Dorman, Daniel Hammett, and Paul Nugent, 161–80. Leiden: Brill, 2007.

Beruvides, Esteban M. *Cuba, Anuario Histórico, 1965.* Miami: Colonial Press International, 2002.

Bienen, Henry. *Tanzania: Party Transformation and Economic Development.* Princeton, NJ: Princeton University Press 1970.

Billig, Michael. *Banal Nationalism.* Thousand Oaks, CA: Sage, 1995.

Bissell, Richard M., Jr. *Reflections of a Cold Warrior: From Yalta to the Bay of Pigs.* New Haven, CT: Yale University Press, 1996.

Bittman, Ladislav. *The Deception Game: Czechoslovak Intelligence in Soviet Political Warfare.* Syracuse, NY: Syracuse University Research Corporation, 1972.

Bjerk, Paul. "African Files in Portuguese Archives." *History in Africa* 31 (2004): 463–68.

———. "The Allocation of Land as a Historical Discourse of Political Authority in Tanzania." *International Journal of African Historical Studies* 46, no. 2 (2013): 255–82.

———. "'Building a New Eden': Lutheran Church Youth Choir Performances in Tanzania." *Journal of Religion in Africa* 35, no. 3 (2005): 324–61.

———. "Julius Nyerere and the Establishment of Sovereignty in Tanganyika." PhD diss., University of Wisconsin, 2008.

———. "Postcolonial Realism: Tanganyika's Foreign Policy under Nyerere, 1960–1963." *International Journal of African Historical Studies* 44, no. 2 (2011): 215–46.

———. "Sovereignty and Socialism in Tanzania: The Historiography of an African State." *History in Africa* 27 (2010): 275–319.

Bopela, Thula, and Daluxolo Lulthuli. *Umkhonto we Sizwe: Fighting for a Divided People.* Alberton, South Africa: Galago Publishing 2005.

Boucher, Joanne. "Male Power and Contract Theory: Hobbes and Locke in Carole Pateman's 'The Sexual Contract.'" *Canadian Journal of Political Science* 36, no. 1 (2003): 23–38.

Bourderie, Jack. "A Tough Little Monkey." In *Dirty Work 2: The CIA in Africa*, edited by Ellen Ray, William Schaap, Karl Van Meter, Seán MacBride, and Louis Wolf, 208–14. Seacaucus, NJ: Lyle Stuart, 1979.

Bourdieu, Pierre. *Distinction: A Social Critique of the Judgment of Taste.* Translated by Richard Nice. Cambridge, MA: Harvard University Press, 1984.

Boyer, Dominic. "Conspiracy, History, and Therapy at a Berlin *Stammtisch.*" *American Ethnologist* 33, no. 3 (2006): 327–39.

Bradley, F. H. *Ethical Studies.* Oxford: Clarendon Press, 1927.

Branch, Daniel. *Defeating Mau Mau, Creating Kenya: Counterinsurgency, Civil War, and Decolonization.* Cambridge: Cambridge University Press, 2009.

———. *Kenya: Between Hope and Despair, 1963–2011.* New Haven, CT: Yale University Press, 2011.

Brennan, James R. "Blood Enemies: Exploitation and Urban Citizenship in the Nationalist Political Thought of Tanzania, 1958–1975." *Journal of African History* 47, no. 3 (2006): 387–411.

———. "Lowering the Sultan's Flag: Sovereignty and Decolonization in Coastal Kenya." *Comparative Studies in Society and History* 50, no. 4 (2008): 831–61.

———. "Realizing Civilization through Patrilineal Descent: African Intellectuals and the Making of an African Racial Nationalism in Tanzania, 1920–1950." *Social Identities* 12, no. 4 (2006): 405–23.

———. "The Short History of Political Opposition and Multi-Party Democracy in Tanganyika, 1958–64." In Maddox and Giblin, *In Search of a Nation*, 250–76.

———. *Taifa: Making Nation and Race in Urban Tanzania*. Athens: Ohio University Press, 2012.

———. "Youth, the TANU Youth League and Managed Vigilantism in Dar es Salaam, Tanzania, 1925–73." *Africa* 76, no. 2 (2006): 221–46.

Bunnenberg, Christian. *Der "Kongo-Müller": Eine Deutsche Söldnerkarriere*. Berlin: Europa-Übersee, 2007.

Burgess, G. Thomas. *Race, Revolution and the Struggle for Human Rights in Zanzibar: The Memoirs of Ali Sultan Issa and Seif Sharif Hamad*. Athens: Ohio University Press, 2009.

———. "A Socialist Diaspora: Ali Sultan Issa, the Soviet Union, and the Zanzibari Revolution." In *Africa in Russia, Russia in Africa: Three Centuries of Encounters*, edited by Maxim Matusevich, 263–92. Trenton, NJ: Africa World Press, 2007.

———. "The Young Pioneers and the Rituals of Citizenship in Revolutionary Zanzibar." *Africa Today* 51, no. 3 (2005): 3–29.

Burton, Andrew. *African Underclass: Urbanisation, Crime and Colonial Order in Dar es Salaam*. Oxford: James Currey, 2005.

Cabrita, João M. *Mozambique: The Torturous Road to Democracy*. London: Palgrave, 2000.

Cameron, Greg. "Zanzibar's Turbulent Transition." *Review of African Political Economy* 29, no. 92 (2002): 313–30.

Carter, Matt. *T. H. Green and the Development of Ethical Socialism*. Exeter, UK: Imprint Academic, 2003.

Carthew, John. "Life Imitates Art: The Student Expulsion in Dar es Salaam, October 1966, as Dramatic Ritual." *Journal of Modern African Studies* 18, no. 3 (1980): 541–49.

Chabal, Patrick, and Jean-Pascal Daloz. *Culture Troubles: Politics and the Interpretation of Meaning*. Chicago: University of Chicago Press, 2006.

Chachage, Chambi. "Mwalimu in Our Popular Imagination: The Relevance of Nyerere Today." *Pambazuka*, no. 452, October 13, 2009. http://pambazuka.org/en/category/features/59510.

Chande, Abdin N. *Islam, Ulamaa and Community Development in Tanzania: A Case Study of Religious Current in East Africa*. San Francisco: Austin and Windfield, 1998.

———. "Muslim-State Relations in East Africa under Conditions of Military and Civilian or One-Party Dictatorships." *Historia Actual Online* 17 (2008): 97–111.

Chatterjee, Partha. *The Nation and Its Fragments: Colonial and Postcolonial Histories*. Princeton, NJ: Princeton University Press, 1993.

Chilcote, Ronald H., and Eduardo Mondlane. "Eduardo Mondlane and the Mozambique Struggle." *Africa Today* 12, no. 9 (1965): 4–8.

Chua, Amy. "Markets, Democracy, and Ethnicity: Toward a New Paradigm for Law and Development." *Yale Law Journal* 108, no. 1 (1998): 1–107.

Clarizio, Lynda M., Bradley Clements, and Erika Geetter. "United States Policy toward South Africa." *Human Rights Quarterly* 11, no. 2 (1989): 249–94.

Clayton, Anthony. *The Zanzibar Revolution and Its Aftermath*. London: C. Hurst, 1981.
Clutton-Brock, Guy. *Dawn in Nyasaland*. London: Hodder & Stoughton, 1959.
Collins, Sidney. *Coloured Minorities in Great Britain: Studies in British Race Relations Based on African, West Indian, and Asiatic Immigrants*. London: Lutterworth Press, 1957.
Cooper, Frederick. *Decolonization and African Society: The Labor Question in French and British Africa*. Cambridge: Cambridge University Press, 1996.
———. *On the African Waterfront: Urban Disorder and the Transformation of Work in Colonial Mombasa*. New Haven, CT: Yale University Press, 1987.
———. "Possibility and Constraint: African Independence in Historical Perspective." *Journal of African History* 49, no. 3 (2008): 167–96.
Costello, John E. *John Macmurray: A Biography*. Edinburgh: Floris Books, 2002.
Coulson, Andrew. *Tanzania: A Political Economy*. New York: Clarendon Press, 1982.
Cribb, Robert. Review of *Sukarno and the Indonesian Coup: The Untold Story*, by Helen-Louise Hunter. *Contemporary Southeast Asia* 30, no. 2 (2008): 332–34.
Daly, Samuel. "Our Mother Is Afro-Shirazi, Our Father Is the Revolution: The 1964 Zanzibari Revolution in Tanzanian History." Senior thesis, Columbia University, 2009.
Dean, Robert D. *Imperial Brotherhood: Gender and the Making of Cold War Foreign Policy*. Boston: University of Massachusetts Press, 2001.
Decalo, Samuel. *Coups and Army Rule in Africa: Motivations and Constraints*. New Haven, CT: Yale University Press, 1990.
Derori, Ze'ev. *Israel's Reprisal Policy, 1953–1956: The Dynamics of Military Retaliation*. New York: Routledge, 2005.
Derrida, Jacques. "Force of Law." Translated by Mary Quaintance. In *Deconstruction and the Possibility of Justice*, edited by Drucilla Cornell, Michael Rosenfeld, and David Gray Carlson, 3–67. New York: Routledge, 1992.
Deutsh, Jan-Georg. *Emancipation without Abolition in German East Africa c. 1884–1914*. Athens: Ohio University Press, 2006.
Dondeyne, Stephanie, Els Vanthournout, John A. R. Wembah-Rashid, and Jozef A. Deckers. "Changing Land Tenure Regimes in a Matrilineal Village of South Eastern Tanzania." *Journal of Social Development in Africa* 18, no. 1 (2003): 7–31.
Dorman, Sara, Daniel Hammett, and Paul Nugent. *Making Nations, Creating Strangers: States and Citizenship in Africa*. Leiden: Brill, 2007.
Duffy, James, and Robert A. Manners, eds. *Africa Speaks*. Princeton, NJ: D. Van Nostrand, 1961.
Duggan, William Redman, and John R. Civille. *Tanzania and Nyerere: A Study of Ujamaa and Nationhood*. Maryknoll, NY: Orbis Books, 1976.
East Africa Royal Commission Report, 1953–1955. London: Her Majesty's Stationery Office, 1955.
Eckert, Andreas. "Regulating the Social: Social Security, Social Welfare and the State in Late Colonial Tanzania." *Journal of African History* 45, no. 3 (2004): 467–89.
Ekeh, Peter P. "Colonialism and the Two Publics in Africa: A Theoretical Statement." *Comparative Studies in Society and History* 17 (1975): 91–112.
Elam, Yitzchak. "Family and Polity in Ankole: The Hima Household and the Absence of Age-Sets." *Ethnology* 14, no. 2 (1975): 163–71.

Elkins, Caroline. "The Struggle for Mau Mau Rehabilitation in Late Colonial Kenya." *International Journal of African Historical Studies* 33, no. 1 (2000): 25–57.
Ermarth, Elizabeth Deeds. "Agency in the Discursive Condition." *History and Theory* 40, no. 4 (2001): 34–58.
———. *History in the Discursive Condition: Reconsidering the Tools of Thought.* New York: Routledge, 2011.
Fadiman, Jeffrey. *When We Began, There Were Witchmen: An Oral History from Mount Kenya.* Berkeley: University of California Press, 1993.
Falola, Toyin. *The Power of African Cultures.* Rochester, NY: University of Rochester Press, 2003.
"Father Richard Walsh: 1910–1979," *Petit Echo* 1 (1980): 44–51.
Feierman, Steven. *Peasant Intellectuals: Anthropology and History in Tanzania.* Madison: University of Wisconsin Press, 1990.
Ferguson, James. *The Anti-politics Machine: Development, Depoliticization, and Bureaucratic Power in Lesotho.* Minneapolis: University of Minnesota Press, 1994.
Fimbo, G. M. "Land, Socialism and the Law in Tanzania." In *Towards Ujamaa: Twenty Years of TANU Leadership,* edited by G. Ruhumbika, 261–64. Dar es Salaam: East African Literature Bureau, 1974.
Fine, Gary Alan. "The Goliath Effect." *Journal of American Folklore* 98 (1985): 63–84.
Foreign Relations of the United States (FRUS), 1958–1960. Vol. 6, *Asia;* vol. 14, *Africa.* Edited by Harriet Dashiell Schwar and Stanley Shaloff. Washington, DC: United States Government Printing Office, 1992.
Fosbrooke, H. A., and Chief Petro I. Marealle. "The Engraved Rocks of Kilimanjaro: Part II." *Man* 52 (1952): 179–81.
Foucault, Michel. "About the Beginning of the Hermeneutics of the Self: Two Lectures at Dartmouth." *Political Theory* 21, no. 2 (1993): 198–227.
———. *Discipline and Punish: The Birth of the Prison.* Translated by Alan Sheridan. New York: Pantheon Books, 1977.
———. "Governmentality." In *The Foucault Effect: Studies in Governmentality,* edited by Graham Burchell, Colin Gordon, and Peter Miller, 87–104. Chicago: University of Chicago Press, 1991.
———. "The Subject and Power." *Critical Inquiry* 8, no. 4 (1982): 777–95.
Fouéré, Marie-Aude. "Zanzibar Independent in 2015? Constitutional Revision, Politicized Islam and Separatist Claims." *Mambo! Recent Research Findings in Eastern Africa* 10, no. 2 (2012): 1–4.
Fraser, Nancy. "Beyond the Master/Subject Model: Reflections on Carole Pateman's *Sexual Contract.*" *Social Text* 37 (1993): 173–81.
Friedland, William H. *Vuta Kamba: The Development of Trade Unions in Tanganyika.* Stanford, CA: Hoover Institution Press, 1969.
Fryxell, Alma. "Psywar by Forgery." *Kent Center Occasional Papers* 5, no. 1 (1961). Last updated August 4, 2011. https://www.cia.gov/library/center-for-the-study-of-intelligence/kent-csi/vol5no1/html/v05i1a03p_0001.htm.
Furlong, Patrick J. "Azikiwe and the National Church of Nigeria and the Cameroons: A Case Study of the Political Use of Religion in African Nationalism." *African Affairs* 91, no. 364 (1992): 433–52.
Gasiorowski, Mark J., and Malcolm Byrne, eds. *Mohammad Mosaddeq and the 1953 Coup in Iran.* Syracuse, NY: Syracuse University Press, 2004.

Geertz, Clifford. "The Integrative Revolution: Primordial Sentiments and Civil Politics in New States." In *The Interpretation of Cultures: Selected Essays*, 255–310. New York: Basic Books, 1973.
Geiger, Susan. *TANU Women: Gender and Culture in the Making of Tanganyikan Nationalism, 1955–1965*. Portsmouth, NH: Heinemann, 1997.
Ghassany, Harith. *Kwaheri Ukoloni, Kwaheri Uhuru! Zanzibar na Mapinduzi ya Afrabia*. Self-published, 2010. Accessed July 14, 2014. http://www.scribd.com/doc/31875247/Kwaheri-Ukoloni-Kwaheri-Uhuru.
Giblin, James L. *A History of the Excluded: Making Family a Refuge from the State in Twentieth-Century Tanzania*. Athens: Ohio University Press, 2005.
———. *The Politics of Environmental Control in Northeastern Tanzania, 1840–1940*. Philadelphia: University of Pennsylvania Press, 1992.
Gifford, Prosser, and Wm. Roger Louis, eds. *Decolonization and African Independence: The Transfers of Power, 1960–1980*. New Haven, CT: Yale University Press, 1988.
Ginwala, Frene. "The Tanganyika Mutiny." *World Today* 20, no. 3 (March 1964): 93–97.
Glassman, Jonathon. *Feasts and Riot: Revelry, Rebellion, and Popular Consciousness on the Swahili Coast, 1856–1888*. Portsmouth, NH: Heinemann, 1995.
———. *War of Words, War of Stones: Racial Thought and Violence in Colonial Zanzibar*. Bloomington: Indiana University Press, 2011.
Gleijeses, Piero. *Conflicting Missions: Havana, Washington, and Africa, 1959–1976*. Chapel Hill: University of North Carolina Press, 2002.
Gluckman, Max. "Gossip and Scandal." *Current Anthropology* 4, no. 3 (1963): 307–16.
Good, Robert C. *U.D.I.: The International Politics of the Rhodesian Rebellion*. Princeton, NJ: Princeton University Press, 1973.
Gramcsi, Antonio. *A Gramsci Reader: Selected Writings, 1916–1935*. Edited by David Forgacs. London: Lawrence and Wishart, 1988.
Gray, Geoffrey. "'Piddington's Indiscretion': Ralph Piddington, the Australian National Research Council and Academic Freedom." *Oceania* 64 (1994): 217–45.
Green, T. H. *Lectures on the Principles of Political Obligation and Other Writings*. Edited by Paul Harris and John Morrow. New York: Cambridge University Press, 1986.
Grey, Alexander. *The Socialist Tradition, Moses to Lenin*. London: Longmans, Green, 1946.
Gromyko, Anatoly, ed. *African Countries' Foreign Policy*. Moscow: Progress Publishers, 1981.
Grovogui, Siba N. "The Secret Lives of the 'Sovereign': Rethinking Sovereignty as International Morality." In *The State of Sovereignty: Territories, Laws, Populations*, edited by Douglas Howland and Luise White, 261–75. Bloomington: Indiana University Press, 2009.
Guha, Ranajit. *Elementary Aspects of Peasant Insurgency in Colonial India*. Delhi: Oxford University Press, 1983.
Gulliver, P. H. *Neighbours and Networks: The Idiom of Kinship in Social Action among the Ndendeuli of Tanzania*. Berkeley: University of California Press, 1971.
———. *Social Control in an African Society: A Study of the Arusha: Agricultural Masai of Northern Tanganyika*. Boston: Boston University Press, 1963.

Hamilton, Carolyn, ed. *Refiguring the Archive*. Cape Town: New Africa Books, 2002.
———. *Terrific Majesty: The Powers of Shaka Zulu and the Limits of Historical Invention.* Cambridge, MA: Harvard University Press, 1998.
Hansard. *Tanganyika Parliamentary Debates, National Assembly Official Report.* Dar es Salaam: Government Printer, 1964.
Hanson, Holly Elisabeth. *Landed Obligation: The Practice of Political Power in Buganda.* Portsmouth, NH: Heinemann, 2003.
Hargreaves, John D. *Decolonization in Africa.* New York: Longman, 1996.
Haste, Helen. "Constructing the Citizen." *Political Psychology* 25, no. 3 (2004): 413–39.
Heald, Suzette. *Manhood and Morality: Sex, Violence and Ritual in Gisu Society.* New York: Routledge, 1999.
Heckel, Bunno. "The Yao Tribe: Their Culture and Education." In *Reports Presented to the Department of Colonial Education in the Institute for Education.* London: Oxford University Press, 1935.
Herbst, Jeffrey. *States and Power in Africa: Comparative Lessons in Authority and Control.* Princeton, NJ: Princeton University Press, 2000.
Hillman, Eugene, with G. Kohler. "An Inculturated Life." *One Heart, One Spirit: Congregation of the Holy Spirit* 36, no. 3 (2008): 1–5.
Hoare, Mike. *Congo Mercenary.* Boulder, CO: Paladin Press, 2008.
Hoffman, John. *Gender and Sovereignty: Feminism, the State, and International Relations.* New York: Palgrave, 2001.
Holland, Heidi. *Dinner with Mugabe: The Untold Story of a Freedom Fighter Who Became a Tyrant.* New York: Penguin Global, 2008.
Hopkins, Raymond. *Political Roles in a New State: Tanzania's First Decade.* New Haven, CT: Yale University Press, 1971.
Horne, Gerald. *From the Barrel of a Gun: The United States and the War against Zimbabwe, 1965–1980.* Chapel Hill: University of North Carolina Press, 2001.
Houngnikpo, Mathurin C. *Determinants of Democratization in Africa: A Comparative Study of Benin and Togo.* Lanham, MD: University Press of America, 2001.
Howell, John. "An Analysis of Kenyan Foreign Policy." *Journal of Modern African Studies* 6, no. 1 (1968): 29–48.
Hughes, Matthew. "Fighting for White Rule in Africa: The Central African Federation, Katanga, and the Congo Crisis, 1958–1965." *International History Review* 25, no. 3 (2003): 592–615.
Hughes, Richard. *Capricorn: David Stirling's Second African Campaign.* London: Radcliffe Press, 2003.
Hunter, Emma. "In Pursuit of the 'Higher Medievalism': Local History and Politics in Kilimanjaro." In Peterson and Macola, *Recasting the Past*, 156–58.
Hunter, Helen-Louise. *Sukarno and the Indonesian Coup: The Untold Story.* Westport, CT: Praeger Security International, 2007.
———. *Zanzibar: The Hundred Days Revolution.* Santa Barbara, CA: Praeger Security International, 2010.
Hyden, Goran. *Beyond Ujamaa in Tanzania: Underdevelopment and an Uncaptured Peasantry.* Berkeley: University of California Press, 1980.
———. *Tanu Yajenga Nchi: Political Development in Rural Tanzania.* Lund, Sweden: Scandinavian University Books, 1968.

Ibingira, Grace Stuart. *African Upheavals since Independence.* Boulder, CO: Westview Press, 1980.
Iliffe, John. "Breaking the Chain at Its Weakest Link: TANU and the Colonial Office." In Maddox and Giblin, *In Search of a Nation,* 168–97.
———. *A Modern History of Tanganyika.* New York: Cambridge University Press, 1979.
Ingle, Clyde R. *From Village to State in Tanzania: The Politics of Rural Development.* Ithaca, NY: Cornell University Press, 1972.
Ivaska, Andrew M. *Cultured States: Youth, Gender, and Modern Style in 1960s Dar es Salaam.* Durham, NC: Duke University Press, 2011.
———. "In the 'Age of Minis': Women, Work, and Masculinity Downtown." In *Dar es Salaam: Histories from an Emerging African Metropolis,* edited by James Brennan, Andrew Burton, and Yusuf Lawi, 213–31. Dar es Salaam: Mkuki wa Nyota, 2007.
———. "Of Students, 'Nizers,' and a Struggle over Youth: Tanzania's 1966 National Service Crisis." *Africa Today* 51, no. 3 (Spring 2005): 83–107.
Jackson, Robert. *Sovereignty: The Evolution of an Idea.* Cambridge: Polity Press, 2007.
Jackson, Robert H., and Carl G. Rosberg. *Personal Rule in Black Africa: Prince, Autocrat, Prophet, Tyrant.* Berkeley: University of California Press, 1982.
James, C. L. R. *Nkrumah and the Ghana Revolution.* Westport, CT: Lawrence Hill, 1977.
Japhet, Kirilo, and Earle Seaton. *The Meru Land Case.* Nairobi: East African Publishing House, 1967.
Jhaveri, K. L. *Marching with Nyerere: Africanisation of Asians.* Delhi: B. R. Publishing Co., 1999.
Jjuuko, Frederick, and Godfrey Muriuki, eds. *Federation within Federation: The Tanzania Union Experience and the East African Integration Process.* Kampala: Kituo cha Katiba and Fountain Press, 2010.
Jones, Adrian. "Word and Deed: Why a Post-poststructural History Is Needed, and How It Might Look." *Historical Journal* 43, no. 2 (2000): 517–41.
Jones, Gareth Stedman. "The Determinist Fix: Some Obstacles to the Further Development of the Linguistic Approach to History in the 1990s." In *Practicing History: New Directions in Historical Writing after the Linguistic Turn,* edited by Gabrielle M. Spiegel, 62–75. New York: Routledge, 2005.
Jones, Garrett. "Working with the CIA." *Parameters* (Winter 2001–2): 28–39. http://strategicstudiesinstitute.army.mil/pubs/parameters/Articles/01winter/jones.htm.
Jorgensen, Jan Jelmert. *Uganda: A Modern History.* New York: St. Martin's Press, 1981.
Juma, Waziri. "The Sukuma Societies for Young Men and Women." *Tanganyika Notes and Records* 54 (1960): 27–29.
Jumbe, Aboud. *The Partner-ship: Tanganyika Zanzibar Union, 30 Turbulent Years.* Dar es Salaam: Amana Publishers, 1994.
Kapferer, Jean-Nöel. *Rumors, Uses, Interpretations, and Images.* New Brunswick, NJ: Transaction, 1990.
Karabell, Zachary. *Architects of Intervention: The United States, the Third World, and the Cold War.* Baton Rouge: Louisiana State University Press, 1999.

Kaufman, Victor S. "Trouble in the Golden Triangle: The United States, Taiwan and the 93rd Nationalist Division." *China Quarterly* 166 (2001): 440–56.

Kay, David A. "The Politics of Decolonization: The New Nations and the United Nations Political Process." *International Organization* 21, no. 4 (1967): 796–98.

Kelly, John D., and Martha Kaplan. "Legal Fictions after Empire." In *The State of Sovereignty: Territories, Laws, Populations*, edited by Douglas Howland and Luise White, 169–95. Bloomington: Indiana University Press, 2009.

———. "Nation and Decolonization: Toward a New Anthropology of Nationalism." *Anthropological Theory* 1, no. 4 (2001): 419–37.

———. *Represented Communities: Fiji and World Decolonization*. Chicago: University of Chicago Press, 2001.

Kenyatta, Jomo. *Facing Mount Kenya*. London: Secker and Warburg, 1938.

Kershaw, Greet. *Mau Mau from Below*. Athens: Ohio University Press, 1997.

Kiano, Gikonyo. "The Pan-African Freedom Movement of East and Central Africa." *Africa Today* 6, no. 4 (1959): 11–14.

Kibwana, Kivutha. "Land Tenure." In *Themes in Kenyan History*, edited by William R. Ochieng, 230–41. Nairobi: Heinemann, 1990.

Kimambo, Isaria N. *Penetration and Protest in Tanzania: The Impact of the World Economy on the Pare, 1860–1960*. Athens: Ohio University Press, 1991.

———. "Utangulizi." In Mdundo, *Utenzi*, 1–8.

Kirk-Greene, A. H. M. "His Eternity, His Eccentricity, or His Exemplarity? A Further Contribution to the Study of H. E. the African Head of State." *African Affairs* 90, no. 359 (1991): 163–87.

Kissinger, Henry. *Years of Renewal*. New York: Simon and Schuster, 1999.

Klayman, Maxwell I. *The Moshav in Israel: A Case Study of Institution-Building for Agricultural Development*. New York: Praeger, 1970.

Knapp, Robert H. "A Psychology of Rumor." *Public Opinion Quarterly* 8, no. 1 (1944): 22–37.

Knudsen, B. R. "Dance Societies: The Voluntary Work-Associations of the Sukuma." *Tanzania Notes and Records* 81–82 (1977): 66–74.

Kombo, Thabit. *Masimulizi ya Sheikh Thabit Kombo Jecha*. Edited by Minael-Hosanna O. Mdundo. Dar es Salaam: Dar es Salaam University Press, 1999.

Krapf, J. L. *A Dictionary of the Suahili Langauge*. 1882. Farnborough, UK: Gregg Press, 1964.

Kreinin, Mordechai E. *Israel and Africa: A Study in Technical Cooperation*. New York: Praeger, 1964.

Kuhenga, Makwaia wa. *CCM na Mustakabali wa Nchi Yetu*. Dar es Salaam: Je, Tutafika? Publications, 2007.

Laclau, Ernesto, and Chantal Mouffe. *Hegemony and Socialist Strategy: Towards a Radical Democratic Politics*. Translated by Winston Moore and Paul Cammack. London: Verso, 1985.

Lal, Priya. "Self-Reliance and the State: The Multiple Meanings of Development in Early Postcolonial Tanzania." *Africa* 82, no. 2 (2012): 212–34.

Lawrence, Tony, with Christopher McRae. *The Dar Mutiny of 1964, and the Armed Intervention That Ended It*. Sussex, UK: Book Guild, 2007.

Lee, Christopher J. *Making a World after Empire: The Bandung Moment and Its Political Afterlives*. Athens: Ohio University Press, 2010.

Lekgoathi, Sekibakiba Peter. "'Colonial' Experts, Local Interlocutors, Informants and the Making of an Archive on the 'Transvaal Ndebele' 1930–1989." *Journal of African History* 50, no. 1 (2009): 61–80.

Lemarchand, René. *Burundi: Ethnic Conflict and Genocide.* Cambridge: Cambridge University Press, 1996.

Levey, Zach. "Israel's Involvement in the Congo, 1958–68: Civilian and Military Dimensions." *Civil Wars* 6, no. 4 (2003): 14–36.

———. "Israel's Strategy in Africa, 1961–67." *International Journal of Middle East Studies* 36, no. 1 (2004): 71–88.

Leys, Colin. "Tanganyika: The Realities of Independence." *International Journal* 17, no. 3 (1962): 251–68.

Li, Anshan. "Asafo and Destoolment in Colonial Southern Ghana, 1900–1953." *International Journal of African Historical Studies* 28, no. 2 (1995): 327–57.

Liebenow, J. Gus. *Colonial Rule and Political Development in Tanzania: The Case of the Makonde.* Evanston, IL: Northwestern University Press, 1971.

Lindberg, Staffan. *Democracy and Elections in Africa.* Baltimore: Johns Hopkins University Press, 2006.

———. "Forms of States, Governance, and Regimes: Reconceptualizing the Prospects for Democratic Consolidation in Africa." *International Political Science Review* 22, no. 2 (2001): 173–99.

Listowel, Judith. *The Making of Tanganyika.* London: Chatto & Windus, 1965.

Lobell, Steven E., Norrin M. Ripsman, and Jeffrey W. Taliaferro, eds. *Neoclassical Realism, the State, and Foreign Policy.* Cambridge: Cambridge University Press, 2009.

Lofchie, Michael. *Zanzibar: Prelude to a Revolution.* Princeton, NJ: Princeton University Press, 1965.

Lonsdale, John. "KAU's Cultures: Imaginations of Community and Constructions of Leadership in Kenya after the Second World War." *Journal of African Cultural Studies* 13, no. 1 (2000): 107–24.

———. "The Moral Economy of Mau Mau: Wealth, Poverty and Civic Virtue in Kikuyu Political Thought." In Berman and Lonsdale, *Unhappy Valley,* 265–314.

Luanda, Nestor. "The Playout of the Mutiny 19 to January 21, 1964"; "The British Intervention: 21 to January 25, 1964"; and "The Aftermath." In *Tanganyika Rifles Mutiny January 1964,* edited by Tanzania People's Defence Forces, 75–164. Dar es Salaam: Dar es Salaam University Press, 1993.

Lupogo, Herman. "Tanzania: Civil-Military Relations and Political Stability." *African Security Review* 10, no. 1 (2001): 75–86.

Macmurray, John. *Conditions of Freedom.* London: Faber and Faber, 1950.

Macqueen, Norrie. *The Decolonization of Portuguese Africa: Metropolitan Revolution and the Dissolution of Empire.* New York: Longman, 1997.

Madan, A. C. *English-Swahili Dictionary.* Oxford: Clarendon Press, 1902.

Maddox, Gregory H., and James L. Giblin, eds. *In Search of a Nation: Histories of Authority and Dissidence in Tanzania.* Athens: Ohio University Press, 2005.

Magotti, John M. J. *Rashidi Mfaume Kawawa: Simba wa Vita katika Historia ya Tanzania.* Dar es Salaam: Matai, 2007.

Maguire, G. Andrew. *Toward "Uhuru" in Tanzania.* Cambridge: Cambridge University Press, 1969.

Maloba, Wunyabari O. *Mau Mau and Kenya: An Analysis of a Peasant Revolt.* Bloomington: Indiana University Press, 1993.
Mamdani, Mahmood. *Citizen and Subject: Contemporary Africa and the Legacy of Late Colonialism.* Princeton, NJ: Princeton University Press, 1996.
Mandela, Nelson. *Long Walk to Freedom: The Autobiography of Nelson Mandela.* London: Little, Brown, 1994.
Manners, Robert A. "Africanization, Neo-Racialism and East Africa." *Africa Today* 9, no. 9 (1962): 4–6, 15.
Marchetti, Victor, and John D. Marks. *The CIA and the Cult of Intelligence.* New York: Knopf, 1974.
Marealle, Petro Itosi. *Maisha ya Mchagga Hapa Duniani na Ahera.* Nairobi: English Press, 1947.
Markovitz, Irving. *Léopold Sédar Senghor and the Politics of Negritude.* New York: Atheneum, 1969.
Matheson, Archie. "Maridhiano: Zanzibar's Remarkable Reconciliation and Government of National Unity." *Journal of Eastern African Studies* 6, no. 4 (2012): 591–612.
Mathews, K., and S. S. Mushi, eds. *The Foreign Policy of Tanzania: A Reader.* Dar es Salaam: Tanzania Publishing House, 1983.
Mazrui, Ali A. "On Poet-Presidents and Philosopher-Kings." *Research in African Literatures* 21, no. 2 (1990): 13–19.
Mbembe, Achille. *On the Postcolony.* Berkeley: University of California Press, 2001.
———. "On the Postcolony: A Brief Response to Critics." *Qui Parle* 15, no. 2 (2005): 1–49.
McCaskie, T. C. *State and Society in Pre-colonial Asante.* Cambridge: Cambridge University Press, 1995.
McClintock, Anne. *Imperial Leather: Race, Gender, and Sexuality in the Colonial Contest.* London: Routledge, 1995.
Mdundo, Mineal O. *Utenzi wa Jeshi la Wananchi Tanzania.* Dar es Salaam: Tanzania Publishing House, 1987.
Mill, John Stuart. *The Basic Writings of John Stuart Mill.* Edited by J. B. Schneewind. New York: Random House, 2002.
Miller, Norman N. "The Political Survival of Traditional Leadership." In *African Politics and Society*, edited by Irving Leonard Markovitz, 118–36. New York: Free Press, 1970.
Mlambo, Alois S. "From the Second World War to UDI, 1940–1965." In *Becoming Zimbabwe: A History from the Pre-colonial Period to 2008*, edited by Brian Raftopoulos and Alois Mlambo, 75–114. Harare, Zimbabwe: Weaver Press, 2009.
Mnyampala, Mathias E. *The Gogo: History, Customs, and Traditions.* Edited by Gregory H. Maddox. Armonk, NY: M. E. Sharpe, 1995.
Molony, Thomas. *Nyerere: The Early Years.* London: James Currey, 2014.
Mondlane, Eduardo. *The Struggle for Mozambique.* Harmondsworth, UK: Penguin, 1969.
Monje, Scott C. *The Central Intelligence Agency: A Documentary History.* Westport, CT: Greenwood Press, 2008.
Monson, Jamie. *Africa's Freedom Railway: How a Chinese Development Project Changed Lives and Livelihoods in Tanzania.* Bloomington: Indiana University Press, 2009.

Moore, Sally Falk, and Paul Puritt. *The Chagga and Meru of Tanzania*. London: International African Institute, 1977.

Morefield, Jeanne. "States Are Not People: Harold Laski on Unsettling Sovereignty, Rediscovering Democracy." *Political Research Quarterly* 58, no. 4 (2005): 659–69.

Mouffe, Chantal, ed. *Gramcsi and Marxist Theory*. Boston: Routledge, 1979.

Mponzi, Ignatius C. T. "Continuity and Change in the Political Organization of the Hehe Villages." Unpublished Seminar Paper. Dar es Salaam: University of East Africa, 1970.

Mudimbe, V. Y. "Review: Reading and Teaching Pierre Bourdieu." *Transition* 61 (1993): 144–60.

Mugerwa, P. J. Nkambo. "Land Tenure in East Africa—Some Contrasts." *East African Law Today*. Commonwealth Law Series no. 5 (1966): 110–11.

Mulford, David C. *Zambia: The Politics of Independence, 1957–1964*. Oxford: Oxford University Press, 1967.

Muller-Dempf, Harald K. "Generation-Sets: Stability and Change, with Special Reference to Toposa and Turkana Soceities." *Bulletin of the School of Oriental and African Studies* 54, no. 3 (1991): 554–67.

Mumford, W. Bryant. "Education and the Social Adjustment of the Primitive Peoples of Africa to European Culture." *Africa: Journal of the International African Institute* 2, no. 2 (1929): 138–61.

Musambachime, Mwelwa C. "The Impact of Rumor: The Case of the Banyama (Vampire Men) Scare in Northern Rhodesia, 1930–1964." *International Journal of African Historical Studies* 21, no. 2 (1988): 201–15.

Mutesa, King of Buganda. *The Desecration of My Kingdom*. London: Constable, 1967.

Mutibwa, Phares. *Uganda since Independence: A Story of Unfulfilled Hopes*. Trenton, NJ: Africa World Press, 1992.

Mwakikagile, Godfrey. *Life under Nyerere*. Dar es Salaam: New Africa Press, 2006.

———. *Nyerere and Africa: End of an Era*. Dar es Salaam: New Africa Press, 2007.

———. *Tanzania under Mwalimu Nyerere: Reflections on the Life of an African Statesman*. Dar es Salaam: New Africa Press, 2006.

Mwijage, Ludovick S. *Julius Nyerere: Servant of God or Untarnished Tyrant?* Leeds, UK: Wisdom House, 2010.

Myers, Garth A. "Narrative Representations of Revolutionary Zanzibar." *Journal of Historical Geography* 26, no. 3 (2000): 429–48.

Namier, Lewis B. "Richard Pares." *English Historical Review* 73, no. 289 (1958): 577–82.

Namikas, Lise. *Battleground Africa: Cold War in the Congo, 1960–1965*. Stanford, CA: Stanford University Press, 2013.

Ndlovu, Sifiso Mxolisi. "The ANC in Exile, 1960–1970" and "The ANC and the World." In *The Road to Democracy in South Africa, 1960–1970*, edited by South African Democracy Education Trust, 411–78, 541–72. Cape Town: Zebra, 2004.

Newbury, Catharine. *The Cohesion of Oppression: Clientship and Ethnicity in Rwanda, 1860–1960*. New York: Columbia University Press, 1988.

Newitt, Malyn. *A History of Mozambique*. Bloomington: Indiana University Press, 1995.

Niblock, Timothy C. "Tanzanian Foreign Policy: An Analysis." In Mathews and Mushi, *Foreign Policy of Tanzania*, 24–36.
Nimtz, August H., Jr. *Islam and Politics in East Africa: The Sufi Order in Tanzania*. Minneapolis: University of Minnesota Press, 1980.
Nkomo, Joshua, and Nicholas Harman. *Nkomo: The Story of My Life*. London: Methuen, 1984.
Nnoli, Okwudiba. *Self Reliance and Foreign Policy in Tanzania: The Dynamics of the Diplomacy of a New State, 1961 to 1971*. New York: NOK, 1978.
Noer, Thomas J. *Cold War and Black Liberation: The United States and White Rule in Africa, 1948–1968*. Columbia: University of Missouri Press, 1985.
Nugent, Paul. *Africa since Independence: A Comparative History*. New York: Palgrave Macmillan, 2004.
Nye, Joseph S., Jr. *Pan-Africanism and East African Integration*. Cambridge, MA: Harvard University Press, 1965.
Nyerere. Julius K. *Africa Today and Tomorrow*. Dar es Salaam: Mwalimu Nyerere Foundation, 2000.
———. *Freedom and Unity: A Selection from Writings and Speeches, 1952–65*. Nairobi: Oxford University Press, 1966.
———. *Uhuru wa Wanawake*. Dar es Salaam: Mwalimu Nyerere Foundation, 2009.
———. *Ujamaa—Essays on Socialism*. New York: Oxford University Press, 1968.
———. *Ujamaa Vijijini*. Dar es Salaam: National Printing Company, 1967.
Nzongola-Ntalaja, Georges. *The Congo from Leopold to Kabila: A People's History*. New York: Zed Books, 2002.
Odhiambo, E. S. Atieno, and John Lonsdale, eds. *Mau Mau and Nationhood*. Athens: Ohio University Press, 2003.
Odom, Thomas P. "Dragon Operations: Hostage Rescues in the Congo, 1964–1965." *Leavenworth Papers* 14 (1988). http://usacac.army.mil/cac2/cgsc/carl/download/csipubs/odomLP14.pdf.
Okello, John. *Revolution in Zanzibar*. Nairobi: East African Publishing House, 1967.
Othman, Haroub. "Tanzania: Beyond Sectarian Interests." *Pambazuka*, no. 430, April 30, 2009, http://pambazuka.org/en/category/comment/55984.
Ottaway, Marina. "Democratization in Collapsed States." In *Collapsed States: The Disintegration and Restoration of Legitimate Authority*, edited by I. William Zartman, 235–49. Boulder, CO: Lynne Rienner, 1995.
"Pan-African Freedom Movement of East and Central Africa (PAFMECA)." *International Organization* 16, no. 2 (1962): 446–48.
Pandey, Gyanendra. *Remembering Partition: Violence, Nationalism, and History in India*. Cambridge: Cambridge University Press, 2002.
Parsons, Timothy H. *The 1964 Army Mutinies and the Making of Modern East Africa*. Santa Barbara, CA: Greenwood Publishers, 2003.
———. Review of *Youth, Nationalism, and the Guinean Revolution*, by Jay Straker. *American Historical Review* 115, no. 2 (2010): 644.
Pateman, Carole. *The Sexual Contract*. Stanford, CA: Stanford University Press, 1988.
Peterson, Derek. *Ethnic Patriotism and the East African Revival: A History of Dissent, c. 1935–1972*. Cambridge: Cambridge University Press, 2012.
Peterson, Derek, and Giacomo Macola, eds. *Recasting the Past: History Writing and Political Work in Modern Africa*. Athens: Ohio University Press, 2009.

Petterson, Donald. *Revolution in Zanzibar: An American's Cold War Tale.* New York: Basic Books, 2002.
Pfister, Roger. "Gateway to International Victory: The Diplomacy of the African National Congress in Africa, 1960–1994." *Journal of Modern African Studies* 41, no. 1 (2003): 51–73.
Phiri, Bizeck Jube. "The Capricorn Africa Society Revisited: The Impact of Liberalism in Zambia's Colonial History, 1949–1963." *International Journal of African Historical Studies* 24, no. 1 (1991): 65–83.
Piddington, Ralph. *An Introduction to Social Anthropology.* Edinburgh: Oliver and Boyd, 1950.
Pratt, R. Cranford. *The Critical Phase in Tanzania, 1945–1968: Nyerere and the Emergence of a Socialist Strategy.* New York: Cambridge University Press, 1976.
———. "Julius Nyerere: Reflections on the Legacy of His Socialism." *Canadian Journal of African Studies* 33, no. 1 (1999): 137–52.
Price, Robert M. "Pretoria's Southern African Strategy." *African Affairs* 83, no. 330 (1984): 11–32.
Prunier, Gérard. *The Rwanda Crisis: History of a Genocide.* New York: Columbia University Press, 1995.
Radcliffe-Brown, A. R. Preface to *African Political Systems*, edited by M. Fortes and E. E. Evans-Pritchard, xi–xxi. New York: Oxford University Press, 1940.
Rathbone, Richard. *Nkrumah and the Chiefs: The Politics of Chieftaincy in Ghana, 1951–60.* Athens: Ohio University Press, 2000.
Raum, O. F. *Chaga Childhood: A Description of Indigenous Education in an East African Tribe.* London: Oxford University Press, 1940.
Rawlence, Ben. "Briefing: The Zanzibar Election." *African Affairs* 104, no. 416 (2005): 515–23.
Reckwitz, Andreas. "Toward a Theory of Social Practices: A Development in Culturalist Theorizing." *European Journal of Social Theory* 5 (2002): 243–63.
Reed, David. *111 Days in Stanleyville.* New York: Harper and Row, 1965.
Rejwan, Nissim. *Nasserist Ideology: Its Proponents and Critics.* Jerusalem: Israel Universities Press, 1974.
Renda, Mary A. *Taking Haiti: Military Occupation and the Culture of U.S. Imperialism, 1915–1940.* Chapel Hill: University of North Carolina Press, 2001.
Richards, Audrey I. *East African Chiefs: A Study of Political Development in Some Uganda and Tanganyika Tribes.* London: Faber and Faber, 1960.
Roosa, John. *Pretext for Mass Murder: The September 30th Movement and Suharto's Coup d'État in Indonesia.* Madison: University of Wisconsin Press, 2006.
Roosevelt, Kermit. *Countercoup: The Struggle for the Control of Iran.* New York: McGraw-Hill, 1979.
Rosnow, Ralph L. "Inside Rumor: A Personal Journey." *American Psychologist* 46, no. 5 (1991): 484–96.
———. "Rumor as Communication: A Contextualist Approach." *Journal of Communication* 38, no. 1 (1988): 12–28.
Ross, Alistair. "The Capricorn Africa Society and European Reactions to African Nationalism in Tanganyika, 1949–60." *African Affairs* 76, no. 305 (1977): 519–35.

———. *Guide to the Tanganyikan Papers of Marion, Lady Chesham.* York, UK: University of York, Centre for Southern African Studies, 1975.
Rotter, Andrew J. "Saidism without Said: Orientalism and U.S. Diplomatic History." *American Historical Review* 105, no. 4 (2000): 1205–17.
Rousseau, Jean-Jacques. *The Social Contract, or Principles of Political Right.* Translated by G. D. H. Cole. London: J. M. Dent, 1913.
Ruiz, Leovigildo. *Diario de una Traición: Cuba 1961.* Miami: Lorie Book Stores, 1972.
Sadleir, Randal. *Tanzania, Journey to Republic.* New York: Radcliffe Press, 1999.
Sahnoun, Mohamed. "Nyerere, the Organization of African Unity and Liberation." *Pambazuka,* no. 452, October 13, 2009. http://pambazuka.org/en/category/features/59501.
Said, Edward. *Orientalism.* New York: Penguin Modern Classics, 1978.
Said, Mohamed. *The Life and Times of Abdulwahid Sykes, 1924–1968.* London: Minerva Press, 1998.
Sakara, Abeid Hassan. *Rashidi Mfaume Kawawa.* Dar es Salaam: Hazina Enterprises, 1991.
Samoff, Joel. *Tanzania: Local Politics and the Structure of Power.* Madison: University of Wisconsin Press, 1974.
Saussure, Ferdinand de. *Writings in General Linguistics.* Oxford: Oxford University Press, 2006.
Scarnecchia, Timothy. *The Urban Roots of Democracy and Political Violence in Zimbabwe: Harare and Highfield, 1940–1964.* Rochester, NY: University of Rochester Press, 2008.
Schatzberg, Michael G. *Political Legitimacy in Middle Africa: Father, Family, Food.* Bloomington: Indiana University Press, 2001.
Schlesinger, Arthur M., Jr. *A Thousand Days: John F. Kennedy in the White House.* Boston: Houghton Mifflin, 1965.
Schlesinger, Stephen C., and Stephen Kinzer. *Bitter Fruit: The Story of the American Coup in Guatemala.* New York: Doubleday, 1990.
Schmidt, Elizabeth. *Mobilizing the Masses: Gender, Ethnicity, and Class in the Nationalist Movement in Guinea, 1939–1958.* Portsmouth, NH: Heinemann, 2005.
Schmitt, Carl. *Political Theology, Four Chapters on the Concept of Sovereignty.* Translated by George Schwab. Chicago: University of Chicago Press, 2005.
Schneider, Leander. "Colonial Legacies and Postcolonial Authoritarianism in Tanzania: Connects and Disconnects." *African Studies Review* 49, no. 1 (2006): 93–118.
———. "Freedom and Unfreedom in Rural Development: Julius Nyerere, *Ujamaa Vijijini,* and Villagization." *Canadian Journal of African Studies* 38, no. 2 (2004): 344–92.
———. *Government of Development: Peasants and Politicians in Postcolonial Tanzania.* Bloomington: Indiana University Press, 2014.
Schneider, Ronald M. *Communism in Guatemala, 1944–1954.* New York: Praeger/Foreign Policy Research Institute, 1958.
Scott, James C. *Seeing Like a State: How Certain Schemes to Improve the Human Condition Have Failed.* New Haven, CT: Yale University Press, 1998.
Shapiro, Michael J., G. Matthew Bonham, and Daniel Heradstveit. "A Discursive Practices Approach to Collective Decision-Making." *International Studies Quarterly* 32, no. 4 (1988): 397–419.

Shepperson, George. *Myth and Reality in Malawi.* Evanston, IL: Northwestern University Press, 1966.
Shetler, Jan Bender. *Imagining Serengeti: A History of Landscape Memory in Tanzania from Earliest Times to the Present.* Athens: Ohio University Press, 2007.
———. "Interpreting Rupture in Oral Memory: The Regional Context for Changes in Western Serengeti Age Organization (1850–1895)." *Journal of African History* 44 (2003): 385–412.
———. *Telling Our Own Stories: Local Histories from South Mara, Tanzania.* London: Brill, 2003.
Shibutani, Tamotsu. *Improvised News: A Sociological Study of Rumor.* New York: Bobbs-Merrill, 1966.
Shivji, Issa G. "Pan-Africanism in Mwalimu Nyerere's Thought: Being Both King and Philosopher." *Pambazuka,* no. 431, May 7, 2007. http://www.pambazuka.org/en/category/comment/56108.
———. *Pan-Africanism or Pragmatism? Lessons of Tanganyika-Zanzibar Union.* Dar es Salaam: Mkuki na Nyota Publishers, 2008.
———. *Not Yet Democracy: Reforming Land Tenure in Tanzania.* Dar es Salaam: Hakiardhi, 1998.
———. "Reforming Local Government or Localizing Government Reform." In *Commemorations of Mwalimu Julius Kambarage Nyerere's 79th and 80th Birth Dates,* edited by Gaudens P. Mpangala, Bismarck U. Mwansasu, and Mohammed Omar Maundi. Dar es Salaam: Mwalimu Nyerere Foundation, 2004.
———. *Where Is Uhuru? Reflections on the Struggle for Democracy in Africa.* Cape Town: Pambazuka Press, 2009.
Shorter, Aylward. *Chiefship in Western Tanzania.* Oxford: Clarendon Press, 1972.
Sibanda, Eliakim M. *The Zimbabwe African People's Union: 1961–1987: A Political History of Insurgency in Southern Rhodesia.* Trenton, NJ: Africa World Press, 2005.
Sivalon, John C. "Roman Catholicism and the Defining of Tanzanian Socialism, 1953–1985: An Analysis of the Social Ministry of the Roman Catholic Church in Tanzania." PhD diss., St. Michael's College, University of Toronto, 1990.
Slater, Mariam K. *African Odyssey: An Anthropological Adventure.* New York: Anchor Press, 1976.
Smith, Anthony D. *Nationalism: Theory, Ideology, History.* Cambridge: Polity Press, 2001.
Smith, W. Thomas. *Encyclopedia of the Central Intelligence Agency.* New York: Facts on File, 2003.
Smith, William Edgett. *We Must Run While They Walk: A Portrait of Africa's Julius Nyerere.* New York: Random House, 1971.
Snyder, Katherine A. "Being of 'One Heart': Power and Politics among the Iraqw of Tanzania." *Africa: Journal of the International African Institute* 71, no. 1 (2001): 128–48.
Sokoloff, William W. "Between Justice and Legality: Derrida on Decision." *Political Research Quarterly* 58, no. 2 (2005): 341–52.
Spear, Thomas. *Mountain Farmers: Moral Economies of Land and Agricultural Development.* Berkeley: University of California Press, 1997.
———. "Neo-Traditionalism and the Limits of Invention in British Colonial Africa." *Journal of African History* 44, no. 1 (2003): 3–27.

Spear, Thomas T., and Richard Waller, eds. *Being Maasai: Ethnicity and Identity in East Africa.* Athens: Ohio University Press, 1993.
Speller, Ian. "An African Cuba? Britain and the Zanzibar Revolution." *Journal of Imperial and Commonwealth History* 35, no. 2 (2007): 1–35.
Spencer, Paul. "Opposing Streams and the Gerontocratic Ladder: Two Models of Age Organization in East Africa." *Man*, n.s., 11, no. 2 (1976): 153–75.
———. *Time, Space, and the Unknown: Maasai Configurations of Power and Providence.* New York: Routledge, 2003.
Steinmetz, George, ed. *State/Culture: State-Formation after the Cultural Turn.* Ithaca, NY: Cornell University Press, 1999.
Stern, Axel. *The Science of Freedom: An Essay in Applied Philosophy.* Translated by Christopher Strachan and Rosalind Strachan. London: Longmans, 1969. First published as *Morale de la Liberté* by University of Geneva, 1943.
Stirling, David. "The Capricorn Contract." *African Affairs* 56, no. 224 (1957): 191–99.
Stokes, Eric. *The English Utilitarians and India.* Oxford: Clarendon Press, 1959.
Stoler, Ann Laura. *Along the Archival Grain: Epistemic Anxieties and Colonial Common Sense.* Princeton, NJ: Princeton University Press, 2009.
Strachan, Hew. *The Politics of the British Army.* Oxford: Clarendon Press, 1997.
Straker, Jay. *Youth, Nationalism, and the Guinean Revolution.* Bloomington: Indiana University Press, 2009.
Sunseri, Thaddeus. "Statist Narratives and Maji Maji Ellipses." *International Journal of African Studies* 33, no. 3 (2000): 567–84.
———. *Vilimani: Labor Migration and Rural Change in Early Colonial Tanzania.* Portsmouth, NH: Heinemann, 2002.
Swantz, Marja-Liisa. *Blood, Milk, and Death: Body Symbols and the Power of Regeneration among the Zaramo of Tanzania.* Westport, CT: Bergin & Garvey, 1995.
Taapopi, Leonard, and T. A. Keenleyside. "The West and Southern Africa: Economic Involvement and Support for Liberation 1960–1974." *Canadian Journal of African Studies* 13, no. 3 (1980): 347–70.
Tacitus on Britain and Germany: A New Translation of the "Agricola" and the "Germania." Translated by Harold Mattingly. London: Penguin Books, 1948.
Tambo, Oliver. *Preparing for Power: Oliver Tambo Speaks.* New York: George Braziller, 1988.
Taylor, Christopher C. *Sacrifice as Terror: The Rwandan Genocide of 1994.* New York: Berg, 1999.
Taylor, James Clagett. *The Political Development of Tanganyika.* Stanford, CA: Stanford University Press, 1963.
Thomas, Anthony. "Notes on the Formal Education of Arusha 'Murran' at Circumcision." *Tanzania Notes and Records* 65 (1966): 81–90.
Thomas, Lynn M. "Imperial Concerns and 'Women's Affairs': State Efforts to Regulate Clitoridectomy and Eradicate Abortion in Meru, Kenya, c. 1910–1950." *Journal of African History* 39 (1998): 121–45.
Thompson, W. Scott. *Ghana's Foreign Policy, 1957–1966: Diplomacy, Ideology, and the New State.* Princeton, NJ: Princeton University Press, 1969.
Thomson, J. *Through Masailand.* London: Cass, 1885.
Trest, Warren, and Donald Dodd. *Wings of Denial: The Alabama Air National Guard's Covert Role at the Bay of Pigs.* Montgomery, AL: NewSouth Books, 2001.

Tsuruta, Tadasu. "African Imaginations of Moral Economy: Notes on Indigenous Economic Concepts and Practices in Tanzania." *African Studies Quarterly* 9, no. 1 (2006): 103–21.

———. "Urban-Rural Relationships in Colonial Dar es Salaam: Some Notes on Ethnic Associations and Recreations, 1930s–1950s." *Memoirs of the Faculty of Agriculture of Kinki University* (Japan) 36 (2003): 59–72.

Tumbo, Christopher S. K. "Civic Awareness and Patterns of Participation." In *Political Culture and Popular Participation in Tanzania*, edited by Research and Education for Democracy in Tanzania Project (REDET), 48–52. Dar es Salaam: REDET and University of Dar es Salaam, 1997.

Tumbo, N. S. K. "Towards NUTA: The Search for Permanent Unity in Tanganyika's Trade Union Movement." In *Labour in Tanzania*, 8–13. Dar es Salaam: Tanzania Publishing House, 1977.

Uzoigwe, G. N., ed. *Uganda: The Dilemma of Nationhood.* New York: NOK, 1982.

Vaughan, Olufemi. *Nigerian Chiefs: Traditional Power in Modern Politics, 1890s–1990s.* Rochester, NY: University of Rochester Press, 2000.

Villafana, Frank R. *Cold War in the Congo: The Confrontation of Cuban Military Forces.* New Brunswick, NJ: Transaction, 2009.

Vittachi, Tarzie. *The Fall of Sukarno.* New York: Praeger, 1967.

Wagoner, Fred E. *Dragon Rouge: The Rescue of Hostages in the Congo.* Washington, DC: National Research University, Defense Directorate, 1980.

Walker, R. B. J. *After the Globe, before the World.* London: Routledge, 2010.

———. *Inside/Outside: International Relations as Political Theory.* Cambridge: Cambridge University Press, 1993.

Wallerstein, Immanuel Maurice. *Africa: The Politics of Independence and Unity.* Lincoln: University of Nebraska Press, 2005.

Walraven, K. van. *Dreams of Power: The Role of the Organization of African Unity in the Politics of Africa, 1963–1993.* Aldershot, UK: Ashgate, 1999.

Walsh, Richard, and the Tanganyika Conference of Bishops. *Africans and the Christian Way of Life: Pastoral Letter of the Archbishops, Bishops and Prefects Apostolic to the Catholic People of Tanganyika.* Kipalapala (Tabora): Catholic Church in Tanganyika, 1953.

Weber, Cynthia. *Simulating Sovereignty: Intervention, the State, and Symbolic Exchange.* New York: Cambridge University Press, 1995.

Weber, Max. *The Theory of Social and Economic Organization.* New York: Oxford University Press, 1947.

Weingrod, Alex. *Reluctant Pioneers: Village Development in Israel.* Ithaca, NY: Cornell University Press, 1966.

Weiss, Brad. *The Making and Unmaking of the Haya Lived World: Consumption, Commoditization, and Everyday Practice.* Durham, NC: Duke University Press, 1996.

Weissman, Stephen R. *American Foreign Policy in the Congo: 1960–1964.* Ithaca, NY: Cornell University Press, 1974.

———. "CIA Covert Action in Zaire and Angola: Patterns and Consequences." *Political Science Quarterly* 94, no. 2 (1979): 263–86.

Wenner, Kate. *Shamba Letu.* Boston: Houghton Mifflin, 1970.

Westad, Odd Arne. *The Global Cold War: Third World Interventions and the Making of Our Times.* Cambridge: Cambridge University Press. 2005.

White, Luise. *The Assassination of Herbert Chitepo: Texts and Politics in Zimbabwe.* Bloomington: Indiana University Press, 2003.

———. *Speaking with Vampires: Rumor and History in Colonial Africa.* Berkeley: University of California Press, 2000.

———. "Telling More: Lies, Secrets, and History." *History and Theory* 39, no. 4 (2000): 11–22.

Wicken, Joan. "The College at the Crossing Place." *Venture; Journal of the Fabian Colonial Bureau* (December 1961): 6–7.

Willets, Peter. *The Non-aligned Movement: The Origins of a Third World Alliance.* London: Pinter, 1978.

Williams, Michael C. *The Realist Tradition and the Limits of International Relations.* Cambridge: Cambridge University Press, 2005.

Willis, R. G. "Kaswa: Oral Tradition of a Fipa Prophet." *Africa: Journal of the International African Institute* 40, no. 3 (1970): 248–56.

Willis, Roy. *A State in the Making: Myth, History, and Social Transformation in Pre-colonial Ufipa.* Bloomington: Indiana University Press, 1981.

Willner, Dorothy. *Nation-Building and Community in Israel.* Princeton, NJ: Princeton University Press, 1979.

Wilson, Amrit. *The Threat of Liberation: Imperialism and Revolution in Zanzibar.* London: Pluto Press, 2013.

———. *US Foreign Policy and Revolution: The Creation of Tanzania.* London: Pluto Press, 1989.

Wilson, Monica. "Nyakyusa Age Villages." *Journal of the Royal Anthropological Institute of Great Britain and Ireland* 79, nos. 1–2 (1949): 21–25.

Wily, Elizabeth. "The Political Economy of African Land Tenure: A Case Study from Tanzania." PhD diss., University of East Anglia, 1988.

Wimmelbücker, Ludger. *Kilimanjaro—a Regional History.* Vol. 1, *Production and Living Conditions, c. 1800–1920.* Münster, Germany: Lit Verlag, 2002.

Wise, David, and Thomas B. Ross. *The Invisible Government.* New York: Random House, 1964.

Witte, Ludo de. *The Assassination of Lumumba.* London: Verso, 2002.

Wittgenstein, Ludwig. *The Wittgenstein Reader.* Edited by Anthony Kennedy. Oxford: Basil Blackwell, 1994.

Wolf, Markus, with Anne McElvoy. *Man without a Face: The Autobiography of Communism's Greatest Spymaster.* New York: Public Affairs, 1997.

Wolfers, Michael. *Politics in the Organization of African Unity.* London: Methuen, 1976.

Wood, J. R. T. *The Welensky Papers: A History of the Federation of Rhodesia and Nyasaland.* Durban, South Africa: Graham Publishing, 1983.

World Bank. *Economic Development of Tanganyika.* London: Oxford University Press, 1961.

Worthman, Carol M. "Interactions of Physical Maturation and Cultural Practice in Ontogeny: Kikuyu Adolescents." *Cultural Anthropology* 2, no. 1 (1987): 29–38.

Wrong, Michaela. *In the Footsteps of Mr. Kurtz: Living on the Brink of Disaster in Mobutu's Congo.* New York: Harper Perennial, 2002.

Young, Crawford. "The Colonial State and Postcolonial Crisis." In *Decolonization and African Independence: The Transfers of Power, 1960–1980,* edited by Prosser

Gifford and Wm. Roger Louis, 3–30. New Haven, CT: Yale University Press, 1988.

Young, Crawford, and Thomas Turner. *The Rise and Decline of the Zairian State.* Madison: University of Wisconsin Press, 1985.

Zacarias, Agostinho. *Security and the State in Southern Africa.* London: Tauris, 1999.

Index

Abdulla, Jamshid bin (Sultan), 207, 208–9, 213, 214, 218, 251, 252, 253
Abdullah, Mohammed bin, 251
Adu, A. L., 70
"African Cuba," 2, 207, 214, 222
African National Congress of Tanganyika (ANC), 44–46, 63, 67, 71–3, 83–84, 85, 90, 94, 146
African National Congress of Northern Rhodesia (ANC), 189–90
African National Congress of South Africa (ANC), 186
Africanization, 2, 44, 61, 63, 67, 69, 71–73, 79, 81–82, 96, 106, 142, 174, 200; Africanisation Commission (1962), 79, 81; military officers, 132–35
Afro-Shirazi Party (ASP), 207, 209, 259; Youth League, 1, 208–9, 246
age sets, 101, 159–63, 174, 176, 261
agency, 13, 14, 263–64, 267; discursive, 14–16, 19, 260, 265–67, 69–70
Algeria, 150, 188, 191, 235, 236, 243, 252
All-Muslim National Union of Tanganyika (AMNUT), 44, 94, 165
America. *See* United States
Arab Association, 140
archives, 16–17
Arensen, Felix, 91
Army Night Freedom Fighters, 136
Association for Islamic Mobilisation and Propagation (*Uamsho*), 255
authoritarianism, 5, 13, 43, 54, 268; and Nyerere, 32, 70, 91, 266; preventive detention, 88–90, 151, 170, 226; and villagization, 110
Aziz, Dossa, 54

Babu, Abdulrahman, 1; later writings, 257–61; and revolution, 207–9; and union treaty, 206, 213, 220–22; Zanzibari government, 210–11, 214–19, 223, 225, 228, 232, 240, 241, 250, 252, 256
Bakari, Seif, 208
Ball, George, 220
Banda, Hastings Kazumu, 187, 241
Bantu, Joseph Kasella, 53
Bantu groups, 163
Barongo, Edward, 52, 165
beatification, 18
Bittman, Ladislav, 237
Bomani, Mark, 223
Bomani, Paul, 75, 76, 77, 147, 156
boycott; of Asian stores, 68; of 1962 election, 86, 91, 92; in Rwanda, 197; of South Africa, 185–86, 202; in Southern Rhodesia, 191; of tripartite election, 43
brain trust, 200
Britain. *See* United Kingdom
Bryceson, Derek, 45, 71, 76, 77, 78, 85, 170, 270
Buganda, 194, 196, 218, 257
buibui, 148
Builders Brigades (Ghana) 156–57
Bukoba Native Cooperative Union, 56
Burito, Nyerere, 24
Burundi, 7, 8, 36, 46, 62, 63, 196–97, 250

Capricorn Africa Society, 39
Carlucci, Frank, 211–12, 221, 228; advocating intervention, 213–20; expulsion, 246–52
Central African Federation, 30, 31, 188, 189, 190, 194, 195

Central Intelligence Agency (CIA), 212, 213, 237–38, 246, 248–49
Chagga Democratic Party, 38
Chama (etymology), 159
Chama cha Mapinduzi (CCM), 256, 49
Chesham, Lady Marion, 1, 3, 10, 135, 172, 195
chieftaincy. *See* customary authorities
China, 35, 84, 129, 130, 150, 183, 198–99, 201, 202, 208, 210, 211, 215, 216, 229, 230, 231, 232, 233, 234, 235, 254
citizenship, 29, 43, 46, 48, 53, 97, 110, 126, 127, 166, 169, 172, 177, 264
Civic United Front (CUF), 255
Cold War, 5, 8–11, 37, 46, 98, 104, 106, 144, 149, 153, 154, 174, 198, 200, 201, 203, 206, 210–16, 224–31, 246–54
Colito Barracks, Dar es Salaam (First Battalion), 133, 135–39, 147
Collins, Sidney, 30
colonialism, 4, 32
Committee of Fourteen. *See* Group of Fourteen
communist activity, 2, 84, 93, 186, 199, 201, 206, 209–13, 217, 218, 219, 222, 224, 225, 227, 232, 233, 235, 249, 250; American fears of, 250; influence on Tanzanian government, 84, 93; Zanzibari Revolution, 259
Congo, 130, 201, 203, 206, 207, 212, 219, 227, 228, 266, 270; Cold War, 237, 238, 239, 242, 243, 244, 245, 248, 250; crisis, 5, 9–11, 247; instability, 4, 31, 37, 46, 61, 63, 96, 110, 196, 197, 199, 211, 215, 233. See also *Dragon Rouge*
Congolese rebels, 229, 239
consensus, 29, 35, 50–51, 55–57, 63, 97, 260, 263–64, 267–68
constitution, 63, 69, 79, 86, 97, 259, 261, 265; British, 28; NUTA, 152; PDP, 83; TANU, 38; TYL, 164
Constitutional Conference, 44

conviviality (Achille Mbembe), 13, 15, 122, 270
Cosme, Luis Toribio, 250
Cuba, 208, 235
customary authorities, 4, 24, 26–27, 34, 42, 50–51, 54, 64–65, 87, 99–103, 117, 119–20, 125, 160, 177, 260

decolonization, 5–8, 12–17, 28, 37, 44, 55, 89, 205, 269
Deming, Olcott, 221
democracy, 5, 11, 12, 15, 31–32, 40, 88, 99, 107, 109, 112, 123, 130, 152, 162, 164, 166, 187, 258, 264–68; one-party, 52–56, 61, 94–96
despotism. *See* authoritarianism
developmentalism, 110, 114, 177
discipline, 40, 55, 115, 117, 130, 133, 145, 167, 171–72, 174, 177, 178, 263
discourse: colonial, 36, 44, 48; diplomatic, 9, 62, 183, 207; discursive agency, 13–16, 266–70; gerontocratic, 126, 157, 178, 261; land, 111, 119, 124; political, 24, 34, 50, 89, 97, 100, 108–11, 260, 262; racial, 39–43, 53, 57, 63, 75–77, 82–83; scholarly, 13, 23
Douglas, Patrick Sholto, 133, 135, 136, 144, 147, 150, 175
Douglas-Home, Alec, 211
Dourado, Wolfgang, 212, 218, 220, 223
Dragon Rouge (military operation), 242–43

East Africa Royal Commission (report), 47, 106
East African Common Services Organisation (EASCO), 197, 200, 226
East African High Commission, 195, 197, 200
East African Muslim Welfare Society (EAMWS), 44
Edinburgh University, 23, 27–33
Eisenhower, Dwight, 9, 215
ekyaro, 26, 101, 176
Elders' Committee (TANU), 39, 51

elections; 1958, 43–44, 49, 52; 1960, 44; 1962, 83–92; 1965, 266; Northern and Southern Rhodesia, 190; recent, 255, 265
Enlai, Zhou, 199, 229
ethnic organizations, 34–37, 46–51
ethnic violence, 5, 7, 8, 9, 44, 62, 135, 140–41, 196–97, 208–10
ethnicity, 4, 34–37
expulsions, 75; of US Diplomats, 209, 211, 246–53; from Zanzibar, 208

Fabian Colonial Bureau. *See* Fabian Society
Fabian Society, 31–32, 44, 56
failed state, 11–12
Federalist, The (pamphlet), 30
Field, Winston, 190
Field Force, 138, 141, 150, 232
forgeries, 146n109, 234, 238; forged letter plot, 235–46, 251
Frente de Liberação de Moçambique (FRELIMO), 177, 187–88, 234, 236, 245
Fundikira, Abdallah, 3, 4, 66, 76, 79, 86, 87, 94–95, 146

Gama, Lawrence, 157, 170, 171, 173
gender, 13, 25–26, 29, 56, 101, 122, 148–49, 172, 267
generation sets. *See* age sets
genocide. *See* ethnic violence
Germany, east (German Democratic Republic), 85, 88, 211, 214, 216–19, 233, 235
Germany, west (Federal Republic of Germany), 199, 231, 232
gerontocracy, 26, 36, 39, 50–53, 55, 101, 107, 108, 112, 120, 121–22, 124, 157–63, 167, 172, 176
Ghana, 11, 46, 53, 64, 84, 89, 170, 192–93, 229; Ghana Trades Union Congress, 70
Gordon, Robert, 248; expulsion, 246–53
Grennan, Dennis, 241
Group of Fourteen, 208n14

Guinea, 188, 219
Gwambe, Adelino, 187

Hallstein Doctrine, 232–33
Hamoud, Ahmed, 252
Handeni settlement, 125
Hanga, Kassim, 1, 206, 213, 215, 220, 221, 222, 223, 224, 240
Harriman, Averell, 227
hegemony, 49, 103, 160, 207, 253, 261–63
Hennemeyer, Robert, 136
Hillman, Eugene, 111, 196
Hoare, Mike, 236, 242

Ilogi, Francis Hingo, 136–37, 140, 147–48, 151
independence, 2–4, 9–11, 15, 23, 48, 54, 62–64; celebrations, 74; movement, 37–46, 66–67
internal exile. *See* preventive detention
International Confederation of Free Trade Unions (ICFTU), 69
intervention, 4, 5, 9, 10, 152–54; British intervention, 131, 139, 141, 145, 147–50; in Zanzibar, 212–19, 248–49
Invisible Government (book), 248, 250
inyenzi, 197
Irenge, James, 23, 24, 26–27
Israel, 94, 109, 128, 134, 136, 171, 175, 201, 231
Issa, Ali Sultan, 207–8, 210, 212, 216, 222, 223

Jamal, Amir, 76, 77, 79, 85, 244
jundo, 160
Japhet, Kirilo, 38
Jeshi la Kujenga Taifa (JKT). *See* National Service
Johansson, Barbro, 89, 172
Johnson, Lyndon Baines, 211, 213, 217, 227, 242, 245, 249, 259
Jumbe, Aboud, 18, 209, 222–23, 248, 256

Kahama, George, 62–63, 75, 76

370 Index

Kaiser, Philip, 251
Kamaliza, Michael, 70–71, 79, 84, 93
Kambona, Oscar, 23, 45, 66, 69, 75, 76, 134, 187, 191, 248, 249, 252, 256; forged letters, 236, 239–43, 244, 245; independence movement, 39, 44; liberation committee, 192, 234; minister of home affairs, 77, 81, 82, 84, 85, 87, 88, 106, 120, 128, 165, 167, 169, 178, 184; mutiny, 3, 133–35 137–38, 140, 141–43, 144, 147, 151, 152, 154; Union Treaty, 206, 207, 213, 214, 217–23, 225, 232–33
Karimjee Trusts, 56
Karimjee, A. Y. A., 82
Karume, Abeid, Zanzibari revolution, union treaty, Zanzibari president
Kashmiri, S. M. A., 133–35, 137
Katanga, 9, 37, 46, 88, 191, 195, 236, 239, 242
Kaunda, Kenneth, 189, 192, 241
Kavana, Elisha, 137, 142, 143, 150, 250
Kawawa, Rashidi, 23, 76, 177–78; foreign policy, 183, 191, 230–31, 239, 244; mutiny, 134, 135, 143, 147, 148, 150, 151, 152; National Service, 156, 165, 170, 171, 172; prime minister, 77–82, 86, 88, 92, 94, 108, 120; TFL, 41, 68–70; vice president, 106; villagization, 114, 119, 122, 116, 129–30
Kawawa, Sophia, 40
Kayibanda, Gregoire, 8, 197
Kennedy, John Fitzgerald, 202–3, 238
Kenya, 7, 16, 39, 41, 63, 68, 84, 93, 95, 113, 191, 195, 196, 197, 241, 251, 257, 270; mutiny, 131, 132, 137, 143, 144, 151; union treaty, 203, 205, 209, 210, 219, 220, 222
Kenyatta, Jomo, 7, 137, 138, 144, 145, 162, 194, 195, 203, 214, 215, 218, 219, 220, 222
Khrushchev, Nikita, 232–33
kihamba, 112, 120
Kisumo, Peter, 34, 41
Kivukoni College, 56, 105, 184
Kombo, Thabit, 221, 255

Kongwa Camp, 234–35
Kunambi, George Patrick, 38
kung'atuka, 178
Kyaruzi, Vedastus, 10, 38, 51, 70, 78, 86; United Nations, 190, 200–201

labor, 64–67. *See also* Tanganyika Federation of Labor, union (labor)
Lameck, Lucy, 105, 152, 198–99, 201
land allocation, 26, 35, 47, 86, 99, 101–5, 112, 115–26
Legislative Council (LEGCO), 10, 37, 42, 69, 71, 72, 86. *See also* National Assembly
Leonhart, William, 1, 2, 114, 230, 241, 245, 247, 249, 250; mutiny, 143, 146, 148, 150, 153; Union Treaty, 210–12, 214–15, 218–24, 227
Liang, Kao, 154
liberation committee. *See* Organisation of African Unity
localization (policy), 69, 73, 133
Louda, Vaclav, 237
Lumumba, Patrice, 9–10, 215, 231, 233
Lusinde, Job, 23, 74–75, 76, 87, 123–24, 128, 171–72, 189, 222, 223, 239, 246; mutiny, 136, 137, 138, 141, 144, 147, 150

Macharia, Rawson, 194
Macmillan, Harold, 44
Mafoudh, Ali, 252
Maji Maji (rebellion), 39, 41
Makerere University, 23–25
Makwaia, David Kidaha, 37, 57, 64, 86–88, 90, 93
Malawi (Nyasaland), 31, 130, 160, 187, 195, 241
Malecela, John, 237
mamlaka, 14
Mandela, Nelson, 186
Mans, Rowley, 133–34
Mara TANU Youth Settlement Farm, 125
Marciandi, Brian, 147
Marealle, Petro Itosi, 98–99, 105, 152, 269

Marealle, Thomas, 3, 4, 26, 57, 87, 119
Marof, Achkar, 219
Marston, Miles, 137–39
Marxism, 30, 217
Masanja, Francis, 86, 89, 90
Mau Mau (rebellion), 7, 39, 41, 42, 113, 114, 191
Mboya, Tom, 41, 69, 84, 195
Mbwambo, Wynn Jones, 137, 145, 146
mchili, 119–21
Meir, Golda, 170
Meru Citizens' Union, 35–37
mgambo, 155
Micombero, Michel, 8
Milando, Mbuta, 50, 103
Miles, Steven, 136, 137, 143, 144, 147, 185
military, Africanization in, 132–35; mutiny, 135–150; retraining, 155–56, 231–35; settlement policy, 127–30
Mill, John Stuart, 29–31, 48, 52, 54
Miners' Union, 83
Mkello, Victor, 70, 85, 146
Mkwawa, Adam Sapi, 4, 87
Mobutu, Joseph, 203, 241, 242
Mohamed, Bibi Titi, 4, 39, 40, 141, 171, 172, 198, 199, 201, 244, 258
Mondlane, Eduardo, 116, 187–88
Mondlane, Janet, 188
moshav, 127–30
Mozambique, 7, 88, 116, 127–30, 133, 165, 177, 183, 187–88, 190, 191, 192, 194, 229, 234, 239, 254, 266
Mozambique African National Union (MANU), 187
Msuguri, David, 140, 147, 162
Mtemvu, Zuberi, 43–44, 52–52, 63, 71, 84–86, 89, 91, 93–94, 133
Mueller, Siegfried, 236
Munanka, Bhoke, 43, 44, 75, 76, 86, 125–26, 141, 148, 167, 168, 222
Murumbi, Joseph, 137, 220
Mwalimu Nyerere Foundation, 16
Mwananchi Development Corporation, 93

Mwisenge (primary school), 23, 24, 26
Mzena, Emil, 88, 137, 146, 151

Nabudere, Dan, 223
Nachingwea (Third Battalion), 129, 139, 140, 142, 149, 150, 177, 234
Namibia (Southwest Africa), 188
National Agricultural Products Board, 94
National Assembly, 72, 76, 79, 82, 84, 86, 88, 170, 172, 175, 195, 223, 224. *See also* Legislative Council (LEGCO)
national ethic, 97–108, 131, 152, 175, 231
National Service, 129, 155–58, 169–179, 240
National Union of Tanganyika (NUTA), 152, 155, 157
nationalism, 3, 10, 11–13, 30, 26, 42, 46, 48, 53, 61, 62, 64, 67, 68, 89, 97, 98, 102, 108, 110, 112, 118, 126, 130, 139, 142, 155–57
Nehru, Jawaharlal, 64
Ngaiza, Christopher, 187, 200, 252
Njau, Petro, 35, 87
Nkomo, Joshua, 189–91
Nkosi Sekelele Afrika (song), 74
Nkrumah, Kwame, 64, 74, 104, 154, 186, 187, 192–93, 229–30
Nkumbula, Harry, 189
Nkupe, Hassan, 83
Noguera, Alberto, 229, 245
Northern Rhodesia. *See* Zambia
Ntare, Teresa, 92
Nyang'ombe, Mugaya, 24
nyarubanja, 102, 112
Nyerere, Joseph, 89, 93, 141, 158, 230
Nyerere, Maria, 40, 126
Nyirenda, Alex, 74, 133–34, 136, 137, 144

Obote, Milton, 3, 4, 144, 145, 195, 218
Odinga, Oginga, 154, 195, 219, 241
Okello, John, 1, 208–10, 213
Omari, Dunstan, 86

one-party state, 35, 45, 46, 51–57, 91–94, 99, 108, 124, 132, 146, 152, 157, 229, 259, 268
Organisation of African Unity (OAU), 127, 203, 230, 231, 234; liberation committee, 192–93

Pan-African Cooperative Alliance, 186
Pan-African Freedom Movement of East and Central Africa (PAFMECA), 185–86, 187, 188, 194, 202
Pan-African Freedom Movement of Eastern, Central and Southern Africa (PAFMECSA), 188–89, 192
pan-Africanism, 30, 54, 83, 184, 192, 196, 203, 205, 259, 260, 261, 265, 269
parity, racial (electoral policy), 32, 42, 43; in 1958 election, 43–44, 49, 52, 86
Parti du Mouvement de l'Emancipation Hutu (PARMEHUTU), 197
peace, 2, 12–13, 26, 62, 63, 68, 72, 90, 101, 112, 159, 175, 184, 195, 199, 202, 256, 260, 263, 265
Peace Corps (US), 139–40, 170, 243
People's Democratic Party (PDP), 46, 83–86, 90, 93, 108, 146
personalistic rule, 5, 10, 204
Petterson, Donald, 209
Picard, Frederick, 209
Plantation Workers Union, 67
police, 2, 3, 77, 82, 87, 88, 90, 117, 121, 128, 150–53, 155, 156, 161, 169, 171, 175, 177, 178, 191, 208, 210, 218, 221, 223, 224, 231, 250, 257; Africanization, 81, 87; mutiny, 2–3, 133–41, 145, 146; police state, 18; TANU Youth League, 164–67
Portugal, 7, 16, 129, 212, 237, 239–40, 245
Postal Workers' Union, 67, 73
postcolony, 13, 29, 32, 269
Preventative Detention Act (1962), 88–90, 150, 170, 226

Railway Workers' Union, 68–69, 73, 83, 84, 146

religious politics, 47, 72, 89, 94–95, 146, 165, 208, 211, 255–56, 262, 266
resignation (Nyerere), 73, 74–78
revolution. *See* Zanzibari Revolution
Rhodesia, northern. *See* Zambia
Rhodesia, southern. *See* Zimbabwe
Ruanda-Urundi. *See separate entries for* Rwanda *and* Burundi
rumor, 2–3, 141, 144, 154, 241, 243, 244, 254, 263
Rural Settlement Commission, 115, 128
Rusk, Dean, 210, 217, 250
Ruskin College, 56
rustication. *See* preventive detention
Rwagasore, Louis (prince), 8, 197
Rwanda, 7, 8, 11, 36, 44, 46, 62, 63, 98, 110, 196–97

Sadleir, Randall, 66
Sandys, Duncan, 216, 220, 249
Sapi, Adam. *See* Mkwawa, Adam Sapi
Sarakikya, Mirisho, 132, 136, 138, 140, 142, 144, 147, 150, 156, 176, 230, 231
Sauti ya TANU (newspaper), 44, 53
Serengeti (national park), 24, 111, 159, 167, 168
settlement schemes. *See* villagization
Shaidi, Elangwa, 133, 136
Shambaa Citizens' Union, 35, 103, 159n25
Shamte, Mohammed, 207, 252
Shariff, Othman, 86, 220, 222
Shepperson, George, 29, 31
Sijaona, Lawi, 148, 157, 170–71
single-party state. *See* one-party state
Sithole, Ndabaningi, 191
Songambele, Mustafa, 82, 84, 92, 152
Sonjo settlement, 111–13, 125
South Africa, 7, 72, 83, 185–86, 188, 189, 191, 192, 202–3, 212, 234, 236, 266
Southern Rhodesia. *See* Zimbabwe
sovereignty, 16, 18, 19, 25, 32, 34, 43, 57, 61, 81, 82, 83, 86, 88, 89, 91,

96, 98, 99, 101, 102, 107, 108, 109, 114, 131, 132, 139, 142, 143, 144, 147, 148, 149, 153, 154, 156, 158, 163, 165, 168, 184, 194, 200, 203, 206, 214, 221, 228, 229, 231, 235, 246, 253, 245, 255; theory, 5, 9, 12–14, 257–59, 260–61, 263–64, 265–66, 268–70
Soviet Union, 8, 35, 84, 106, 153, 187, 198, 201, 203, 210, 211, 212, 216, 219, 223, 232, 233, 234, 235, 236, 247, 250, 257, 268
Special Branch, 88, 137, 146, 150, 153, 154, 223
St. Francis (secondary school), 38, 39
St. Mary's (secondary school), 23
Stanleyville, 236, 238–39, 242–45
Stirling, David, 194
Sukumaland Council, 36–37, 90
Swahili (as official language), 74, 82, 98, 127, 141, 172, 198, 244, 265
Swai, Nsilo, 45, 66, 75, 76, 79, 127, 199, 241, 244
Sykes, Abbas, 93
Sykes, Abdulwahid, 38
Syracuse University, 114, 116, 117, 187
Syracuse University Research Corporation, 237

Tabora (Second Battalion), 136–37, 138, 139, 140, 142, 146, 147, 149, 150
Tabora Boys' (secondary school), 23
Taiwan, 201
Takadir, Sulemani, 165
Tandau, Alfred, 152
Tandon, R. K., 218, 220
Tanganyika African Association (TAA), 37–39, 51
Tanganyika African National Union (TANU), 33, 34; government, 48, 49, 51, 53, 54, 61–96, 139, 154, 156, 158, 169–70, 171, 178, 183–84, 198, 214; ideology, 56, 97–108, 142, 157, 158, 159, 169, 170, 204; independence drive, 36–46, 134; liberation, 185–87, 191, 239; military, 135–36, 140, 156, 174, 175; opposition to, 37, 40, 42–46, 52, 63, 67, 146, 195, 250; villagization, 109, 111, 117, 119, 121, 122, 124, 126, 130; Zanzibar, 213, 215, 217, 259
Tanganyika African Welfare Association, 25
Tanganyika Broadcasting Corporation (TBC), 190–91
Tanganyika Electric Supply Company (TANESCO), 155
Tanganyika Federation of Labour (TFL), 34, 41, 67–71, 73, 75, 79–80, 93, 146, 152, 157, 158
Tanganyika National Society (TNS), 39–40, 42, 43
Tanganyika Rifles, 131–35, 144, 175
Tanganyika Standard (newspaper), 9, 25, 42, 52, 67, 105
TANU Youth League (TYL), 56, 94, 109, 119, 121, 124, 125, 126, 134, 135, 136, 153, 155, 158, 163–69, 170, 172, 173, 175, 176, 178
Tanzania People's Defence Forces (TPDF), 132, 162, 183, 192, 231, 232
ten-cell system, 93, 124, 128
Tettegah, John, 70, 84
Tewa, Saidi Tewa, 76, 117, 118
three-government system, 255
Tibandebage, Andrew, 23, 25, 38, 235–36, 238, 239, 241
Tomaz, Américo, 229
tribalism. *See* ethnicity
tribe, 4, 27, 34–36, 47, 48, 49, 72, 98, 175
tripartite election. *See* parity
Trusteeship Committee (United Nations), 7, 23, 39, 104, 194, 196
Tshombe, Moïse, 189, 197, 231, 233, 235, 236, 245
Tumbo, Christopher, 67–73, 75, 79, 80, 83–91, 93, 94, 133, 146, 151, 195
Turnbull, Richard, 44–45, 74, 77, 90, 91
Tutsi. *See* Rwanda
Twining, Edward, 37, 43, 86
two-government system, 255–56
two-hats (governmental policy), 156

374 Index

Uamsho (organization). *See* Association for Islamic Mobilisation and Propagation
Uganda, 3, 16, 23, 25, 29, 36, 63, 102, 131, 132, 142, 144, 161, 194, 195, 196, 197, 210, 218, 219, 239, 270
Uhuru. *See* independence
Ujamaa, 96, 97–108, 116, 124, 125, 126, 155, 256, 266
UK. *See* United Kingdom
Umma Party, 207, 209, 210, 223
UN. *See* United Nations
União Democrátrica Nacional de Moçambique (UDENAMO), 187
Union Nationale Rwandaise (UNAR), 196–97
Union Treaty, 220–24, 232, 248, 249, 252; historical interpretations, 255–60
unions (labor), 34, 41, 46, 62, 64, 65, 67, 70–71, 73, 79, 84, 93, 152, 152, 157, 165, 185; Dockworkers' and Stevedores' Union, 67–68, 71, 145, 153; Plantation Workers' Union, 2, 67, 75, 85; Postal Workers' Union, 67, 73
United Kingdom, 7, 16, 17, 23, 26, 27, 28, 29, 30, 53, 72, 80, 89, 134, 150, 186, 189, 190, 191, 198, 202, 207, 209, 211, 212, 214, 217, 219, 223, 224, 231, 232, 245, 249, 252, 259, 269
United National Independence Party (UNIP), 190
United Nations (UN), 23, 35, 39, 40, 48, 56, 125, 148, 184, 188, 190, 198, 200–201, 202, 237, 269
United Nations High Commission for Refugees (UNHCR), 129
United States of America (US), 9, 86, 91, 114, 187–88, 196, 202–3, 208, 211–12, 214–20, 221, 224, 226–27, 229, 230, 231, 233, 237–38, 242–43, 246–54, 259. *See also* Union Treaty, expulsions
United Tanganyika Party (UTP), 42–44
Utilitarianism, 15, 23, 29–32, 42, 48, 52, 54, 56, 110, 263

Vandewalle, Frederic, 242
Vasey, Ernest, 45, 76, 77, 79, 199
village development committee (VDC), 120–24
Village Settlement Agency, 115
villagization, 29, 94, 106, 108, 109–30, 167, 169

wachili. See *mchili*
wage levels, 68, 132–33, 147
Waldron-Ramsey, Waldo E., 237
Walsh, Richard, 26, 27, 99
Walwa, Peter, 135, 139
wangwana, 168
Welensky, Roy, 189–91, 195
Whitehead, Edgar, 190
Wicken, Joan, 32–33, 56
Williams, G. Mennen, 237, 247
Wilson, Harold, 241
Wolf, Marcus, 211, 214, 217
work parties, 64–65
World Food Programme, 125, 129

X, Malcolm, 234

youth, socialization, 115, 64, 100, 108, 111, 122, 125, 128, 158–63. *See also* National Service, TANU Youth League, ASP Youth League
Yugoslavia, 129, 201

Zambia, 7, 11, 31, 189–90, 191, 192, 194, 195
Zanzibar, 9, 18, 135, 138, 150, 153, 194, 198, 205–8; recognition, 211, 215. *See also* Union Treaty
Zanzibar Liberation Army, 224, 252
Zanzibar National Party (ZNP), 207, 209, 251
Zanzibari Revolution, 1–2, 208–10; casualties, 209–10. *See also* Group of Fourteen
Zedong, Mao, 198, 211, 230, 233
Zigua Tribal Council, 49
Zimbabwe, 31, 188–91, 205, 234

In the early 1960s, nationalist politicians established in Tanzania a stable government in the face of external threats and internal turmoil. Paul Bjerk's volume chronicles this history and examines the politics and policies of the nation's first president, Julius Nyerere. One of the great leaders of modern Africa, Nyerere unified the diverse people who became citizens of the new nation and negotiated the tumultuous politics of the Cold War. In an era when many postcolonial countries succumbed to corrupt dictatorship or civil war, Nyerere sought principled government. Making difficult choices between democratic and autocratic rule, Nyerere creatively managed the destabilizing forces of decolonization.

With extensive archival research and interviews with scores of participants in this history, Bjerk reorients our understanding of the formative years of Tanzanian independence. This study provides a new paradigm for understanding the history of the postcolonial nations that became independent in a global postwar order defined by sovereignty.

Paul Bjerk is associate professor of history at Texas Tech University.

www.ingramcontent.com/pod-product-compliance
Lightning Source LLC
Chambersburg PA
CBHW071143300426
44113CB00009B/1069